# CRITICAL REFLECTIONS ON CONSTITUTIONAL DEMOCRACY IN THE EUROPEAN UNION

This book takes a wide-ranging approach to tackle the complex question of the current state of constitutional democracy in the EU. It brings together a broad set of academics and practitioners with legal and political perspectives to focus on both topical and perennial issues concerning constitutional democracy (including safeguarding the rule of law and respect for fundamental rights) in theory and practice, primarily at EU level but also with due regard to national and global developments. This approach underlines that rather than a single *problématique* to be analysed and resolved, we are presently facing a kaleidoscopic spectrum of related challenges that influence each other in elusive, multifaceted ways. *Critical Reflections on Constitutional Democracy in the European Union* offers a rich analysis of the issues as well as concrete policy recommendations, which will appeal to scholars and practitioners, students and interested citizens alike. It provides a meaningful contribution to the array of existing scholarship and debate by proposing original elements of analysis, challenging often-made assumptions, destabilising settled understandings and proposing fundamental reforms. Overall, the collection injects a set of fresh critical perspectives on this fundamental issue that is as contemporary as it is eternal.

**Volume 94 in the Series Modern Studies in European Law**

**Modern Studies in European Law**
**Recent titles in this series:**

Unity in Adversity: EU Citizenship, Social Justice and the Cautionary Tale of the UK
*Charlotte O'Brien*

The Use of Force and Article 2 of the ECHR in Light of European Conflicts
*Hannah Russell*

Environmental Crime in Europe
*Edited by Andrew Farmer, Michael Faure and Grazia Maria Vagliasindi*

Questioning EU Citizenship: Judges and the Limits of Free Movement and Solidarity in the EU
*Edited by Daniel Thym*

The European Union under Transnational Law: A Pluralist Appraisal
*Matej Avbelj*

Illegally Staying in the EU: An Analysis of Illegality in EU Migration Law
*Benedita Menezes Queiroz*

Social Legitimacy in the Internal Market: A Dialogue of Mutual Responsiveness
*Jotte Mulder*

The EU Better Regulation Agenda: A Critical Assessment
*Edited by Sacha Garben and Inge Govaere*

Administrative Regulation Beyond the Non-Delegation Doctrine: A Study on EU Agencies
*Marta Simoncini*

The Interface Between EU and International Law: Contemporary Reflections
*Edited by Inge Govaere and Sacha Garben*

The Rise and Decline of Fundamental Rights in EU Citizenship
*Adrienne Yong*

The Court of Justice and European Criminal Law: Leading Cases in a Contextual Analysis
*Edited by Valsamis Mitsilegas, Alberto di Martino and Leandro Mancano*

The EU as a Global Regulator for Environmental Protection: A Legitimacy Perspective
*Ioanna Hadjiyianni*

Citizenship, Crime and Community in the European Union
*Stephen Coutts*

**For the complete list of titles in this series, see 'Modern Studies in European Law' link at www.bloomsburyprofessional.com/uk/series/modern-studies-in-european-law**

# Critical Reflections on Constitutional Democracy in the European Union

Edited by
Sacha Garben
Inge Govaere
and
Paul Nemitz

•HART•
OXFORD • LONDON • NEW YORK • NEW DELHI • SYDNEY

HART PUBLISHING

Bloomsbury Publishing Plc

Kemp House, Chawley Park, Cumnor Hill, Oxford, OX2 9PH, UK

HART PUBLISHING, the Hart/Stag logo, BLOOMSBURY and the Diana logo are trademarks of Bloomsbury Publishing Plc

First published in Great Britain 2019



A catalogue record for this book is available from the British Library.

Library of Congress Cataloging-in-Publication data

Names: Garben, Sacha, 1982-, editor. | Govaere, Inge, editor. | Nemitz, Paul F., editor.

Title: Critical reflections on constitutional democracy in the European Union / Edited by Sacha Garben, Inge Govaere, Paul Nemitz.

Description: Chicago : Hart Publishing, an imprint of Bloomsbury Publishing, 2019. | Series: Modern studies in european law; volume 94 | Includes bibliographical references and index.

Identifiers: LCCN 2019029252 (print) | LCCN 2019029253 (ebook) | ISBN 9781509933259 (hardback) | ISBN 9781509933266 (Epub)

Subjects: LCSH: Constitutional law--European Union countries. | Rule of law—European Union countries. | Democracy--European Union countries.

Classification: LCC KJE5037 .C75 2019 (print) | LCC KJE5037 (ebook) | DDC 342.24—dc23

LC record available at https://lccn.loc.gov/2019029252

LC ebook record available at https://lccn.loc.gov/2019029253

ISBN: HB: 978-1-50993-325-9
ePDF: 978-1-50993-327-3
ePub: 978-1-50993-326-6

Typeset by Compuscript Ltd, Shannon

# FOREWORD

Do we need more literature about democracy and the European Union? To judge from this book, the answer is clearly 'yes', despite all that has already been written on the subject. The reader will benefit from a collection of chapters that are both comprehensive and thought-provoking. Despite the different backgrounds, profiles and approaches of the authors, the editors have succeeded in bringing together contributions presenting a sufficiently common thread.

The volume rightly covers not only the Union level as such, but also takes into account the national level as well as the relations between the two. This is all the more pertinent as it has become increasingly clear that the EU should be perceived as a 'federative' multi-level system rather than as a dichotomic constellation between the Union as an international organisation, on the one hand, and a group of individual Member States, on the other. Union law and national law, including Union and national constitutional law, have become interwoven to such an extent that we can speak of a common legal system even if historically, they draw upon distinct legal orders.[1]

This collection confirms that the EU (in its broad conception), and constitutional democracy in the EU, in particular, is, to put it mildly, facing a number of challenges. The authors are well aware that we are not dealing with challenges facing the Union level alone as the Member States are affected perhaps even to a greater extent. Some polls suggest that citizens have even less confidence in their national governments than in EU institutions. I would add that for those living in third countries the EU (Russia, Turkey, not to speak of Venezuela, to name but a few examples) the state of democracy in the EU, whether considered at the Union level or at national level, or viewing both levels together, may appear as a paradise.

That said, the book highlights a number of problems and challenges specific to the EU system of constitutional democracy, while avoiding getting stuck on the notion of 'democratic deficit' (which in my humble view is a misnomer). These contributions contain a number of suggestions how to improve the system; most of them would seem entirely worthwhile exploring. The warnings against what is referred to as the 'over-constitutionalisation' of rights, at the expense of the powers of legislative and other democratic (political) bodies should be heeded. What Advocate General Bobek has observed fairly recently about data protection

[1] A Rosas and L Armati, *EU Constitutional Law: An Introduction*, 3rd rev ed (Oxford, Hart Publishing, 2018) 15, 51, 63, 80.

is in my view relevant for the risk of 'over-constitutionalisation' of fundamental rights in general: 'Eventually, the overbroad application and certain "application absolutism" might end up discrediting the original idea … which was in itself very important and legitimate'.[2]

That said, whatever achievable reforms to strengthen the democratic legitimacy of the EU, they would not satisfy some of the extreme right-wing political forces now in vogue. They and their external backers are out to destroy the EU and discard the idea of European integration altogether. They see globalisation and European regional integration as obstacles to return to some pure form of nation-state and nationalism. They see themselves as the only spokesperson for the 'will of the people' in each nation. When coming to power, they will attack two pillars of constitutional 'liberal' democracy: the independence of courts and a free press. Their popular support would seem grounded in politico-cultural (ideological) outlook as much as economic grievances or actual perceived problems in the system of democratic decision-making.

At the time of writing, the European elections held on 23–26 May 2019 produced a mixed result. While the forces set out to destroy the EU gained some ground in some Member States, they encountered setbacks elsewhere. The fears that the European Parliament could be overrun by forces hostile to that very Parliament proved to be grossly overblown. There is a future for constitutional democracy in Europe but it has to be constantly adapted to new challenges and demands. This book will be an important contribution to a debate about how to improve the different components of the system, without destroying the very foundations of the system itself.

Allan Rosas

[2] Opinion of Bobek AG of 26 January 2017, para 95, in Case C-13/16 *Rīgas satiksme* EU:C:2017:336.

# TABLE OF CONTENTS

PART II
AN INSTITUTIONAL PERSPECTIVE
ON EU CONSTITUTIONAL DEMOCRACY



PART III
EU CONSTITUTIONAL DEMOCRACY:
*PISTES DE REFLECTION* FOR THE FUTURE

# NOTES ON CONTRIBUTORS

**Ana Bobić** is a postdoctoral researcher at the Leviathan Project (funded by the European Research Council) at Hertie School of Governance in Berlin

**Merijn Chamon** is a postdoctoral researcher of the Research Foundation Flanders (FWO) at the Ghent European Law Institute at Ghent University (Jean Monnet Centre of Excellence)

**Adam Cygan** is Professor of EU Law at the University of Leicester

**Frithjof Ehm** is a Legal Officer, working for the United Nations family. He has worked with the European Commission (DG REGIO), the Council of Europe (Venice Commission) in Strasbourg and at the UNDP (Democratic Governance Group) in New York

**Sacha Garben** is Permanent Professor of EU Law at the European Legal Studies Department of the College of Europe

**Michael Gordon** is Professor of Constitutional Law at the School of Law and Social Justice at the University of Liverpool

**Inge Govaere** is Professor of European Law at Ghent University and Director of the Ghent European Law Institute (GELI) as well as Director of the European Legal Studies Department at the College of Europe

**Kris Grimonprez** is Affiliated Senior Researcher at the Faculty of Law, KU Leuven

**Armin Hatje** is Professor of Public Law and European Law at the University of Hamburg

**Leo Hoffmann-Axthelm** is Research and Advocacy Coordinator at Transparency International EU and EU/NATO-Liaison for ICAN, the 2017 Nobel Peace Prize Laureate

**Christian Joerges** is Professor Emeritus of Law and Society at the Hertie School of Governance Berlin and Co-Director of the Centre for European Law and Politics in Bremen

**R Daniel Kelemen** is Professor of Political Science and Law and Jean Monnet Chair in EU Politics at Rutgers University

**Päivi Leino** is Professor of Transnational European Law at the University of Helsinki

**María José Martinez Iglesias** is the Director for Legislative Affairs in the Legal Service of the European Parliament

**Elise Muir** is Head of the Institute for European Law at the KU Leuven and Visiting Professor at the College of Europe

**Paul F Nemitz** is Principal Adviser at the European Commission, Directorate-General for Justice and Consumers. He is teaching EU Law as a visiting Professor at the College of Europe in Bruges

**Cesare Pinelli** is Professor of Constitutional Law at Sapienza University in Rome

**Allan Rosas** is Judge at the European Court of Justice and Professor of Law at the University of Turku

**Vivien A Schmidt** is Jean Monnet Professor of European Integration, Professor of International Relations and Professor of Political Science at Boston University

**Ben Smulders** is currently, inter alia, Head of Cabinet of the Vice President of the European Commission and a visiting Professor at the Free University of Brussels and the College of Europe in Bruges

**Georges Vallindas** is Référendaire at the Court of Justice of the European Union; PhD in EU Law, Aix-Marseille University

# 1

# Critical Reflections on Constitutional Democracy in the European Union and its Member States

SACHA GARBEN, INGE GOVAERE AND PAUL NEMITZ

## Constitutionalism and Democracy

There is a sense of urgency, shared by the various contributors to this book, connected to a perception of crisis in Western politics. Although the health of Western democracies has been considered, at least by some scholars, in malaise since at least the early 1990s,[1] the developments of the past decade (most notably the economic crash, surges in terrorism and the migration crisis) seem to be spurring an increasingly exclusionary, nationalist narrative capturing cross-spectrum political support and the rise of anti-establishment forces that challenge the very foundations of our political, constitutional settlement. Legal scholars tend to phrase their concerns about these developments in terms of respect for the rule of law,[2] while political scientists focus on populism,[3] but all worry, essentially, about the same thing: the system and values of constitutional democracy being under threat or 'in crisis'.[4] As Cesare Pinelli sets out in chapter two, the attacks on constitutional democracy are often disguised as a defence of democracy, against the elitist constraints of constitutionalism imposed by 'the traditional parties as an aristocratic class that has "abandoned the people"'. There may indeed be a degree

[1] See A Hakhverdian and C Koop, 'Consensus Democracy and Support for Populist Parties' (2007) 42 *Acta Politica* 401, 402, citing H Betz, *Radical Right-Wing Populism in Western Europe* (Basingstoke, Macmillan, 1994); S Pharr and R Putnam (eds), *Disaffected Democracies: What's Troubling the Trilateral Countries?* (Princeton, NJ, Princeton University Press, 2000); Y Mény and Y Surel (eds), *Democracies and the Populist Challenge* (Basingstoke, Palgrave, 2002).

[2] Editorial comments, 'The Rule of Law in the Union, the Rule of Union Law and the Rule of Law by the Union: Three Interrelated Problems' (2016) 53 *Common Market Law Review* 597.

[3] For a discussion of the definitional disputes in political science on the term and concept of populism, see ch 2 by Cesare Pinelli.

[4] See also recently, M Graber, S Levinson and M Tushnet, *Constitutional Democracy in Crisis?* (Oxford, Oxford University Press, 2018).

of inherent tension in the very concept of constitutional democracy,[5] epitomised in the theoretical discussions concerning judicial review that Elise Muir revisits in chapter five. Taming the beast of 'raw' democracy, constitutionalism circumscribes and mitigates direct majoritarian decision-making, requiring compliance with predetermined rules and procedures as well as substantive norms[6] such as fundamental rights in particular.

This book focuses on constitutional democracy. When narrowly defined, constitutional democracy constitutes but one part of a triptych of fundamental and indissociable concepts crucial to our modern societies, together with safeguarding the rule of law and respect for fundamental rights. Constitutional democracy understood in a thick sense comprises all these values. The rule of law which is currently put to the test in several Member States essentially implies that disputes will be settled by independent judges with a primary task to balance different individual and societal interests on the basis of a predetermined set of rules, in sharp contrast to any rule of power or rule of the majority. The main role of constitutional democracy in this respect is to ensure that important changes in rule-setting with a major or lasting societal impact are not subject to an 'accidental' majority at a given point in time but are rather the subject of thorough discussion and reflection, raising a sufficiently large public support for a truly constitutional law-setting which also safeguards the rights of minorities and individuals in society. Considered in that manner, the link with respect for fundamental rights of individuals ensured by independent judges thus becomes immediately apparent, especially also when faced with arguments to impose a dictate of a given majority invoking 'raw' democracy arguments.

Many will share the intuition that precisely those self-pronounced flag-bearers of democracy will seek to establish a de facto autocratic regime as soon as they can.[7] Constitutional democracy's value arguably lies in how it tackles this very democratic paradox, ie, how it prevents democracy from abolishing and delegitimising itself. Populism may come to power, but it may not come to define power and it may not wield it indefinitively, arbitrarily or at the expense of minorities. At some point sooner or later, the belief is, the scoundrels will be thrown out again.

[5] See C Mouffe, *The Democratic Paradox* (New York, Verso, 2000) on the inherent tension between the liberal values of constitutionalism and democracy.

[6] We thus follow the 'substantive school' of 'thick' theories of the rule of law and constitutional democracy. See R Peerenboom, 'Varieties of Rule of Law. An Introduction and Provisional Conclusion' in R Peerenboom (ed), *Asian Discourses of Rule of Law* (London, Routledge, 2004) 2–10. B Tamanaha, *On the Rule of Law* (Cambridge, Cambridge University Press, 2004) 92; L Pech, 'A Union Founded on the Rule of Law: Meaning and Reality of the Rule of Law as a Constitutional Principle of EU Law' (2010) 6 *European Constitutional Law Review* 359; A Arnull, 'The Rule of Law in the European Union' in A Arnull and D Wincott (eds), *Accountability and Legitimacy in the European Union* (Oxford, Oxford University Press, 2002).

[7] An intuition confirmed in empirical studies, at least in South America: S Ruth-Lovell, D Doyle and K Hawkins, 'Consequences of Populism Memo for The Guardian's The New Populism Project' *Team Populism & The Guardian* (2019): 'Over the course of their term, populist chief executives are more likely to infringe on the freedom and fairness of the electoral process than their non-populist counterparts'.

Constitutional democracy can be argued to be precisely designed for the situation where majoritarian democracy trips over itself, to help it pick itself up and carry on without irreparable damage being done. Could we therefore say that we find ourselves in a moment for constitutional democracy to shine and prove its worth? Perhaps yes, but it faces two fundamental difficulties in this regard. First, constitutional democracy itself suffers from a paradox: the political powers that it needs to contain the most, are the ones that it finds the hardest to contain. The raw forces of majoritarian nationalist politics feed on the perceived undemocratic nature of constitutionalism, and so constitutional constraints may inadvertently inflame the very fire they attempt to tame. Worryingly, empirical research seems to confirm a link between constitutionalism and populism.[8] Secondly, as Daniel Kelemen explains in chapter three, taking the sharp edges off populist autocrats and mitigating their policies through a constitutional framework into 'soft autocracies', may limit their immediate damage but can unintentionally serve to legitimise these persons, parties or regimes, facilitating their longevity. Instead of crash-and-burn autocracy, constitutional democracy may lead to a state of enduring 'autocratic equilibrium'.

Perhaps we can say that if populism can come to power in the first place (in the sense of exerting influence on the political process and outcomes thereof, not necessarily having a majority), this implies that there is a failure of the system in question to provide genuine constitutional democracy; that in a well-designed constitutional democracy such forces should not come to the fore at all. Political scientists seem to agree that populism is a 'red flag' about the health of democracy in a system.[9] It is intuitive to consider that in a society that guarantees political and social equality and freedom for all subjects through robust fundamental rights protection and through decision-making by the people, in which they feel that they meaningfully participate in deciding on questions affecting their social and economic wellbeing, anti-establishment parties will not gain more than marginal traction. Thus, as the authors in this book generally agree, a robust, functioning democracy is premised on a number of constitutional guarantees and democracy manifests itself in (and requires) many dimensions, and not just crude in-the-moment direct majoritarianism. Upon such a view, genuine democracy is not constrained by constitutionalism but instead made possible by it, making the populists' allegations misplaced. While there may not be a single perfect constitutional democracy, or society, presently existing across the globe, this does not mean that there is no ideal model to strive for – and, more practically, to provide a yardstick against which current failings can be explained to orient possible improvements. This ideal model transcends the false juxtaposition of

[8] See Hakhverdian and Koop, above n 1. Papadopoulos sees populism as a reaction to 'the excess of constitutionalism': Y Papadopoulos, 'Populism, the Democratic Question, and Contemporary Governance' in Y Mény and Y Surel (eds), *Democracies and the Populist Challenge* (Basingstoke, Palgrave, 2002) 57.

[9] Taggart sees populism as 'a gauge by which we can measure the health of representative political systems': P Taggart, *Populism* (Buckingham, Open University Press, 2000).

constitutionalism and democracy that seems both theoretically impoverished and practically counterproductive. We instead need to invest in a theory of constitutional democracy in which the dialectic relationship between its two underpinning principles is elaborated more constructively.

Sacha Garben in chapter nineteen proposes the principle of legality as the main analytical tool in this regard: interpreted in light of national constitutional law this principle seems to be the very expression of constitutional democracy, in that it requires simultaneously (i) the lawfulness of the exercise of authority (based on an authorising norm and its relevant procedures, and respecting fundamental rights); and (ii) that parliament sources this authority. Developing this approach into a legitimacy framework for the exercise of authority, it is argued that the principles of democracy and constitutionalism do not only need to be balanced against each other but that they dynamically inform each other's substantive content. On this view, constitutionalism's primary purpose is to guarantee thick democracy: to create the necessary preconditions for it, to correct any 'democratic failures' in the process and to ensure that outcomes do not undermine robust democracy in the longer term. Democracy as interpreted in light of constitutionalism, on this ideal view, means a transparent, checked-and-balanced system of decision-making that ensures that those affected by decisions take part in making those decisions through robust representation and that the institutions through which this decision-making is operated cannot abuse their powers. Ultimately, the constitutional democratic order as a whole should respect and serve the primordial values of human dignity, equality and liberty.

This approach can at least partially transcend Waldron's well-known juxtaposition of democratic decision-making on the one hand with the judicial review thereof on the basis of constitutional norms on the other:[10] democracy through and on the basis of parliamentary decision-making itself is a constitutional norm that the judiciary should uphold. Moreover, the fundamental rights that constitutionalism needs to protect are those that contribute to creating the preconditions of a healthy democracy, and to the extent that they serve to prevent cases of majoritarian injustice.[11] Of course, constitutionalism requires that democratic decision-making respects certain procedural and substantive norms, and thus may entail overturning an act of parliament on that basis. But the limits of such judicial intervention lie in that the democracy principle should equally be respected, thus precluding judgments that amount to 'judicial legislation', because such judicial activism would amount to an important exercise of public authority without parliamentary involvement.[12] Where precisely the balance between the principle

[10] J Waldron, 'The Core of the Case Against Judicial Review' (2006) 115 *Yale Law Journal* 1346. See on this point also A Young, 'A Peculiarly British Protection of Human Rights?' (2005) 68 *Modern Law Review* 858. For discussion, see Elise Muir in ch 5.

[11] One could argue that a well-functioning democracy, which ensures the appropriate preconditions as well as the correct processes of decision-making, will not lead to such injustices of, for instance, the oppression of a minority.

[12] C Gearty, *Principles of Human Rights Adjudication* (Oxford, Oxford University Press, 2004) 88.

of democracy and the principle of constitutionalism should be struck in individual cases will always be open to debate. Constitutional democracy does not necessarily provide conclusive answers in itself, but provides the terms of the arguments to be made in reasonable disagreement where it occurs, which should serve to accommodate such disagreement in a constructive way. As Cesare Pinelli also notes in chapter two, the flexibility of constitutional democracy to accommodate legitimate disagreement through, and resulting in, a continuous adjustment of the dialectic principles of democracy and constitutionalism is how this form of government 'absorbed de-structuring tensions'. Constitutional democracy is thus not a static model but a dynamic process.

# Constitutional Democracy and the European Union

## Constitutional Democracy, Federalism and the EU

If the relationship between constitutionalism and democracy is already exceedingly intricate, federalism adds further complexity to the analysis. On the one hand, standard federal theory tells us that one of the main advantages of multiplicity of government is that it protects against autocrats.[13] The fragmentation of power in a federal system as compared with a single overarching central authority, is considered to imply a spreading of risk, 'hedging our bets' against tyrants.[14] Furthermore, to the extent that a successful federation promotes subsidiarity through allowing intra-jurisdictional decision-making by the local level where possible, and multidimensional decision-making at the central level where necessary for solving inter-jurisdictional problems, the federal constitution benefits inclusive democracy in ways that constitutional democratic theory strives for. On the other hand, by contrast, Daniel Kelemen shows in chapter three that federal systems may actually be particularly prone to autocratic equilibriums, due to the incentives at federal level to tolerate autocracy on the local level; 'democratic leaders at the federal level may come to rely on authoritarian leaders at the state level to deliver votes to their federal level coalition'. Furthermore, while federalism may be aiming to do justice to democracy, involving those most concerned by decisions in the process (which in some cases may imply local decision-making and in other cases at the federal or global level), it is notoriously difficult to get this 'subsidiarity-calculus' right both in theory and practice. Moreover, federalism's complex organisation and inherently higher degrees of indirect representation (compared with centralised models) and distance to the citizen (compared with

[13] D Halberstam, 'Of Power and Responsibility: The Political Morality of Federal Systems' (2004) 90 *Virginia Law Review* 731, 753.

[14] D Halberstam, 'Federalism: A Critical Guide' (2011) University of Michigan Public Law Working Paper No 251, 16.

small single jurisdictions), presents obvious democratic challenges. This may explain the empirical finding that federal systems are more prone to populism.[15]

Adding the EU to this puzzle of federal constitutional democracy is a daunting task. At the existential level, debates are still raging on whether the EU has a constitution,[16] whether it can be considered a federation,[17] and the question whether it is a (sufficient) democracy continues to fill academic libraries as well as newspapers.[18] Nevertheless, constitutional democracy is not only a form of government but also a normative approach to the legitimate exercise of public authority, and therefore the EU's authority can – and should – be assessed against the standards of constitutional democratic theory. Of course, as many of our contributors point out, the EU should not be condemned for failing to live up to idealised national standards (which, incidentally, are not met by national states either). However, as these contributors also accept, provided that the requirements of constitutional democracy are (re-)interpreted to accommodate transnational democratic and cosmopolitan justice concerns, there is no reason why the EU could not and should not be analysed in light of the features and values of constitutional democracy. After all, 'the Union is founded on the indivisible, universal values of human dignity, freedom, equality and solidarity; it is based on the principles of democracy and the rule of law'.[19] Furthermore, the EU is increasingly facing a populist challenge to its authority, underlining the practical need to assess the EU in constitutional democratic terms. Such an assessment requires attention to the EU's democratic credentials, the quality of its constitutionalism, and to the question of how in the EU the principles of democracy and constitutionalism interact. These analytical yardsticks can be used to consider the performance of the EU in the exercise of its authority as such, but will often also include the national dimension, in considering how the EU impacts on national systems. As such, the questions of the EU's own constitutional democracy and that of its Member States should be discussed in an integrated manner.

[15] See Hakhverdian and Koop, above n 1.

[16] Although as Armin Hatje discusses in ch 6, most EU legal scholars agree that at least in a functional sense, we can speak of the founding Treaties as the constitution of the European Union. See P Craig, 'Constitutions, Constitutionalism and the European Union' (2001) 7 *European Law Journal* 125; see also on the subject matter JHH Weiler and JP Trachtman, 'European Constitutionalism and its Discontents' (1996–97) 17 *Northwestern Journal of International Law & Business* 345, 357; C Henkel, 'Constitutionalism of the European Union and Political Decision-Making by the European Court of Justice' (2000) 19 *Wisconsin International Law Journal* 153; MA Wilkinson, 'Political Constitutionalism and the European Union' (2013) 76 *Modern Law Review* 191.

[17] For discussion, and the argument that the EU should be considered a federation: R Schütze, 'Federal Tradition(s) and the European Union' in R Schütze, *From Dual to Cooperative Federalism: The Changing Structure of European Law* (Oxford, Oxford University Press, 2009).

[18] See A Follesdal and S Hix, 'Why There is a Democratic Deficit in the EU: A Reply to Moravcsik' (2006) 44 *Journal of Common Market Studies* 533, C Grombez, 'The Democratic Deficit in the European Union: Much Ado about Nothing?' (2003) 4 *European Union Politics* 101; P Kratochvíl and Z Sychra, 'The End of Democracy in the EU? The Eurozone Crisis and the EU's Democratic Deficit' (2019) 41 *Journal of European Integration* 169.

[19] Preamble of the EU Charter of Fundamental Rights.

## EU Democracy

In chapter fifteen, Adam Cygan considers the EU's democracy from the viewpoint of national parliaments, which have traditionally seen their participation in decision-making diminish due to European integration, and which are therefore at the heart of the standard 'democratic deficit' critique of the EU. Cygan notes that the EU increasingly involves national parliaments in EU legislation, especially since the Early Warning System (EWS) introduced by the Lisbon Treaty. A 'multilevel framework of parliamentary governance' seems to be emerging. This aligns with the view of several other contributors that the EU has significantly improved its democratic credentials over the years, culminating in the Lisbon Treaty, with its various democratic innovations and improvements in addition to the EWS, such as the European Citizens' Initiative, analysed by Päivi Leino in chapter sixteen and the *Spitzenkandidaten* process discussed by Daniel Kelemen, Paul Nemitz and Frithjof Ehm, Ben Smulders and María José Martínez Iglesias and in chapters three, eighteen, ten and eleven respectively. The EU legislative process can be considered the world's most accomplished feat of transnational constitutional democracy, with its dual democratic legitimacy derived from both national parliaments on whose support the Council depends and who participate directly through the EWS, and the European Parliament which compensates not only for a loss of democratic control at the national level but also national parliaments' inherent inadequacy to govern a globalised world. The Commission for its part benefits from a 'double legitimacy (and multiple accountability)' of its own, deriving from the European Parliament and the Council, as Ben Smulders argues in chapter ten. This unique institution plays a profoundly constitutional role in guaranteeing inclusive, transnational democracy: 'bridging differences between big and small, north and south, east and west'. The EU constitutes the only possible political space for an effective democracy, as María José Martínez Iglesias argues in chapter eleven. Following this argument, national parliaments cannot alone adequately provide democratic rule in the modern interconnected world, meaning that the EU's dual legitimacy through European and national parliamentary participation is, in reality, the most democratic option available. However, these foregoing observations notwithstanding, the various contributions to this book reveal that (at least) three central democratic challenges remain.

### *First Democratic Challenge: Low Turnout for European Elections*

The first challenge concerns the low, and consistently decreasing, turnout to the European Parliament elections. As Paul Nemitz and Frithjof Ehm point out in chapter eighteen, since the first direct elections in 1979, the turnout in European elections has fallen steadily from 61,99 per cent to 42,61 per cent in 2014. They note the strikingly dire levels in some of the newer Member States, and as Ana Bobić adds in chapter eight, in all Member States (except Estonia), the turnout for European Parliament elections is consistently lower than the turnout for national parliamentary elections. This suggests a (deepening) gap between the EU and its citizens. As Kris Grimonprez discusses in chapter seventeen, for a non-negligible group of nationals, paradoxically, the EU dimension of voting in European Parliament elections needs to be explained. European elections are 'popularity tests of national politicians or parties'. They are not the 'centre of democracy'[20] at European level that they should be, as Armin Hatje argues in chapter six. European Parliament elections thus appear to remain 'second-order elections'.[21] Päivi Leino in chapter sixteen agrees, stating that:

> [w]ith little proper political formation at the European level and scarce interest in EU matters in the mainstream media, its elections are almost entirely dominated by national themes and actors, leaving the voter with little chance of forming an informed picture of how different electoral options would affect Union policies.

As is well known, this decreasing interest in the European Parliament has, paradoxically, coincided with an increase in its formal powers.[22] But perhaps the citizen disconnect is still partially driven by the European Parliament's lack of several key democratic powers that 'real' parliaments are considered to have. It does not have the right to legislative initiative, nor can it change the government of Europe. As Armin Hatje points out in chapter six:

> [I]n terms of governance, the Parliament can only exercise influence over the Commission, which is the seemingly weaker part of the European leadership. Political change – the replacement of the government in the sense of Karl Popper – is therefore beyond the reach of EU citizens and their voting rights at national and European level. Herein lays the actual democratic deficit of the European Union.

Meanwhile, the European political parties and the political foundations on the EU level are severely underfunded, as Paul Nemitz and Frithjof Ehm discuss in chapter eighteen. By way of example, while the two foundations of the Socialists (Foundation of European Progressive Studies – FEPS) and Conservatives (Martens Center) on the EU level receive less than 10 million euro annually from the EU budget,[23]

[20] As Armin Hatje sets out in ch 6: 'In terms of procedural law, legitimacy and control of the government through elections are at the centre of democracy. It is fair to discuss whether democracy is about legitimising future politics or sanctioning the government's previous political activity; whether it is about the individuals or about programme. In any case, in elections, as the philosopher Karl Popper has pointedly summarised, the decisive element of democracy manifests: the possibility of a peaceful change of government; or in the more drastic words of Joseph Schumpeter the expulsion of "idiots and windbags" from office'.

[21] K Reif and H Schmitt, 'Nine Second-order National Elections – A Conceptual Framework for the Analysis of European Election Results' (1980) 8 *European Journal of Political Research* 3.

[22] In the words of Joseph Weiler: 'What is striking about these figures is that the decline coincides with a continuous shift in powers to the European Parliament, which today is a veritable co-legislator with the Council. The more powers the European Parliament, supposedly the vox populi, has gained, the greater popular indifference to it seems'. See JHH Weiler, 'The Political and Legal Culture of European Integration: An Exploratory Essay' (2011) 9 *International Journal of Constitutional Law* 678, 681.

[23] See the report card of the European Parliament on the funding of political foundations, available at: www.europarl.europa.eu/pdf/grants/Grant_amounts_foundations%2001-2018.pdf.

the similar foundations in Germany alone (Friedrich Ebert Stiftung and Konrad Adenauer Stiftung) have a budget of over 360 million euro annually.[24]

All this not only undermines one strand of the Union's dual democratic legitimation (making the effective involvement of national parliaments all the more crucial, as Adam Cygan states in chapter fifteen), it can also have consequences for the quality of constitutional democracy on the national level. Daniel Kelemen explains in chapter three that

> the Europarties who are allied with national level authoritarians and who have protected them against EU sanction have paid no political price for doing so. Because few voters even realise that Europarties exist, these parties (and their other national member parties) have not feared paying any political price for their association with autocrats.

As a major positive development, the 2019 elections saw more than 50% of EU citizens eligible to vote take part, presenting the highest turnout in 20 years and the first time since the first direct elections in 1979 that turnout has increased. Challenges remain, but the situation is not as dire as predicted – and presumably hoped for by some 'populists'.

## *Second Democratic Challenge: Transparency*

The second democratic challenge that our authors identify relates to transparency. This is an important aspect of what Vivien Schmidt calls 'throughput legitimacy' – an indispensable component of democratic legitimacy as she explains in chapter seven. A lack of transparency (and throughput legitimacy more generally) is 'likely to undermine public perceptions of the legitimacy of EU governance, and it can even skew the politics and taint the policies'. In chapter twelve, Leo Hoffmann-Axthelm considers in this respect that 'while the European Commission has increased transparency, and while the European Parliament has strengthened its link to European citizens while expanding its ability to hold EU institutions to account, the Council is glaringly absent from improvements to the EU's democratic legitimacy'. Merijn Chamon considers the transparency and accountability of EU decentralised agencies in chapter fourteen, identifying a number of remaining challenges not tackled by the 2012 Common Approach. At the same time, he warns against an approach that blindly imposes additional accountability and transparency requirements, as this may be counterproductive and lead to transparency overload – a risk that the EU faces more generally as Schmidt points out in chapter seven. A more fundamental consideration about the place of agencies in the EU's constitutional democracy is in order, argues Chamon, and this seems to be a valid point for the position of transparency in the EU legal and political order as a whole.

[24] See annual report 2017 of Konrad Adenauer Stiftung, with a total budget of 182 million euro in 2017, p 39 of the report, available at: www.kas.de/c/document_library/get_file?uuid=a5ee2563-5295-af5c-fdb4-2c07f56e5240&groupId=252038; and the annual report of the Friedrich Ebert Stiftung, with a total budget of 176 million euro in 2017, p 71 of the report, available at: library.fes.de/pdf-files/fes/03208/jb-2017.pdf.

Päivi Leino in chapter sixteen concurs that there is a problem concerning transparency in the EU, regardless of the Lisbon constitutional reforms. She attributes this to the 'fundamental mindset of Union institutions' which seems to be little affected by the Treaty's new approach to openness and direct democracy, testified by 'the refusal of the institutions to update secondary legislation (Regulation No 1049/2001) to reflect the Lisbon provisions, and second, when the Court of Justice of the European Union (CJEU) has taken the lead, in their reluctance to apply its jurisprudence'. As to the CJEU's positive role in developing a 'doctrine of legislative transparency', Georges Vallindas' contribution in chapter thirteen confirms 'the Court's push for transparency before it was cool'. In its more recent case law, the CJEU has explicitly bridged transparency and the rule of law, thereby improving the accountability of the Coreper.[25] Vallindas considers that 'one could foresee that the intensification of the rule of law's invocability will drive the transparency principle case law further by limiting even more the exceptions to what can be judicially controlled, be it at the EU or even national levels'. Furthermore, the Court's case law may 'increase the healthy peer-pressure between Member States that have no historic tradition of transparency to renew their administrative and legislative practices in order to ensure effective separation of powers and functioning checks and balances'. This means that while it is important to recognise, as many of our authors do, that the EU is still considered at odds with the principle of democracy as regards its transparency in some regards, its positive contribution as a driver of 'good governance' and transparency on the Member State level also needs to be recognised.

## *Third Democratic Challenge: Economic Governance*

The third democratic challenge that clearly emerges from the various contributions is European economic governance. The old concern for 'de-parliamentarisation' of the exercise of authority in the context of EU legitimacy may have been mitigated as regards the EU legislative process, but it once again rears its head in the context of the European Semester and Euro-crisis governance. Cygan observes that

> the economic crisis would appear to have challenged the democratic model of representative and parliamentary governance within the EU and created a tension between national budgetary sovereignty and legislative autonomy to deliver the socio-economic policies demanded by the voters on the one hand, and the EU's objective of securing economic stability and deeper economic integration on the other. In particular, it has been the EU's governance response to the economic crisis and the tension between the use of executive and legislative powers that has caused most concerns for national parliaments.

[25] Case C-626/15 and Case C-659/16 *Commission/Council (AMP Antarctique)* EU:C:2018:925, para 61.

Pointing at the same democratic sore spot from the perspective of the European Parliament, Paul Nemitz and Frithjof Ehm (chapter eighteen) consider that:

> Some of the European decisions of biggest impact on people in Member States, namely those relating to the economic and financial crisis, are not taken in the form of legislation, with co-decision by the EP. They are taken by the Council alone, or even, in an intergovernmental format, among Member States. The never-ending discussion on the role of the Troika exemplifies the challenge to democracy – both on EU level and on Member State level – of these decisions.

In an alternative approach to democracy, inspired by Ostrom's theory of polycentricity which places the individual at the centre of the legitimate governance framework,[26] Ana Bobić in chapter eight argues that the current institutional set-up of EU economic governance suffers from two main malaises which, as its result, has political inequality between EU citizens: it favours the principle of equality of Member States to the detriment of the principle of solidarity between Member States, which creates asymmetries in influence on the political realm and access to accountability mechanisms among EU citizens and secondly, 'the current architecture of EU economic governance limits the number of those able to contest political decisions, the number of routes available for such contestation, and the ultimate answerability of decision-makers'. Bobić considers that accountability needs to be separated from democratic representation rooted in the tradition of nation states and focus instead on achieving political equality of citizens as the crucial tenet of democracy.

There is yet another aspect of democracy that is offended by EU economic governance: its 'throughput legitimacy'. Vivien Schmidt in chapter seven applies her theory of legitimacy to the Eurozone crisis, arguing that:

> The initial actions taken, involving reinforcing rules-based, numbers-targeting governance, raised legitimacy problems not only in throughput terms – regarding its efficacy, accountability, transparency, inclusiveness and openness – but also in terms of how these negatively affected output performance and input responsiveness. The subsequent response to the deterioration of output policy performance and the increase in the volatility of national input politics, which involved the reinterpretation of the rules 'by stealth', added additional problems of throughput legitimacy.

It would therefore seem that our contributors share a wide and deeply held concern about the legitimacy of EU euro-crisis and economic governance, from a variety of democratic perspectives. Even if it is hard to clearly establish causal links, it would seem that this democratic deficit in input, output and throughput terms is linked to the rise in populism and Euroscepticism on the national level.[27] Christian Joerges asks the hard questions in chapter nine: 'Do we have to live with

[26] See J van Zeben and A Bobić (eds), *Polycentricity in the European Union* (Cambridge, Cambridge University Press, 2019).

[27] A Pirro et al, 'The Populist Politics of Euroscepticism in Times of Crisis: Comparative Conclusions' (2018) 38 *Politics* 378.

the replacement of political ownership of democratically legitimated governments by austerity-driven "structural reforms"? It is important to remain aware of the tragic choices at stake'.

## EU Constitutionalism

Despite the important achievements over the course of various Treaty revisions, the EU thus continues to face a challenge of under-democratisation. At the same time, it is facing criticism as regards its perceived over-constitutionalisation.[28] As Armin Hatje discusses in chapter six, at the heart of this critique is the fact that the EU has insulated a number of norms, particularly economic freedoms, from the national and European democratic process. The Treaty's internal market provisions on the free movement of goods, services, persons and capital are primary law norms that the CJEU, together with the national courts, applies directly in the context of national rules and practices. Hatje considers that the 'attempts of Member States to obstruct cross-border trade for economic policy reasons are well known' and that 'the fundamental freedoms therefore had to be "constitutionalized" in order to prevent the single market from failing at the outset'. In this context, the Court has given a very wide interpretation of what is considered, prima facie, to be a restriction of these constitutional norms, which seems to theoretically capture any rules that potentially make economic activity less attractive. Of course, as Hatje points out, 'the exceptions to the fundamental freedoms and the mandatory requirements protect non-economic interests, including social matters'. But while such prima facie restrictions can be justified in principle, they have to comply with a strict proportionality assessment, showing that they are the least restrictive option available to pursue an interest considered legitimate by the Court and that they do not excessively limit the economic freedom in question (which is treated as the rule, not the exception).[29] This can lead to the disapplication of national norms, adopted through the national democratic process, on the basis of the EU constitutionalised market provisions as interpreted by the EU's Constitutional Court. It thus amounts to far-reaching judicial review of national legislation, not on the basis of traditional fundamental human rights but on the basis of the EU's 'economic constitution'. Certainly not always, but definitively sometimes, this may go at the cost of traditional fundamental human rights such as the freedom of assembly.[30]

[28] F Scharpf, 'After the Crash: A Perspective on Multilevel European Democracy' (2015) 21 *European Law Journal* 384; D Grimm, 'Defending Sovereign Statehood against Transforming the European Union into a State' (2009) 5 *European Constitutional Law Review* 353; S Schmidt, *The European Court of Justice and the Policy Process* (Oxford, Oxford University Press, 2018).

[29] C Barnard, 'Restricting Restrictions: Lessons for the EU from the US' (2009) 68 *Cambridge Law Journal* 575.

[30] See further Sacha Garben in ch 19.

This is potentially problematic from a perspective of constitutional democracy, as it can lead to an over-constitutionalisation and under-democratisation of the question what place the economy has in society vis-a-vis all other public interests. It disempowers national parliaments and governments, as well as private organisations such as trade unions, in areas that are of fundamental concern to them. Elise Muir in chapter five warns against the dangers of detaching such sensitive decisions from the domestic sphere, for such decision-making may become 'perceived as so exogenous' that it is 'ultimately rejected altogether', thus – we may extrapolate – potentially breeding populist Euroscepticism. She states that

> the danger of enhanced supranationalisation of fundamental rights questions – if the institutional design is not carefully thought through – means to trigger or feed a feeling among national constituencies that their political preferences are being disregarded. Such a process may not rely on channels that allow for genuine participation of all the stakeholders because of the disjuncture between domestic and the EU legal order. This disjuncture is related to specific criticisms of the EU institutional framework, as aforementioned, as much as to the general dynamics of supranational human rights governance. Sociologists have shown that while the supranational level offers multiple opportunities for fundamental rights actors to support and shape progressive agendas despite reticence at the domestic level, the same 'circumvention logic' explains why the outcome reached at the supranational level may trigger the supranational domestic resistance. By couching their policy and fundamental rights arguments at level in cosmopolitan terms or in terms of a broader European identity, civil society actors may create a source of resistance within domestic spheres related to the 'perceived threat to national identities and allegiances'.[31]

Muir makes this argument in the context of EU fundamental rights legislation, where one could at least argue that the displacement of national democracy has been compensated for (to an extent) by the European legislative process. Furthermore, as Muir herself points out in line with arguments made by Walker,[32] 'a greater focus on fundamental rights protection may actually attract greater political attention and thus act as a trigger for greater democratic activity at the European level' provided that it is entrusted to EU political institutions (such as by Article 16 TFEU on data protection or Article 19 TFEU on non-discrimination) so as to pay tribute to the 'sensitive and deliberative context for assessing the force and deciding the practical import for various compensatory arguments within the extended chain of rights'.[33] When the European-level decision-making that displaces the national democratic process emanates instead from the European

[31] Elise Muir here refers to C Ruzza, 'Civil Society Actors and EU Fundamental Rights Policy: Opportunities and Challenges' (2014) 15 *Human Rights Review*, 65, 70. For a contrasting view specific to the feminist movement see C Hoskyns, *Integrating Gender: Women, Law and Politics in the European Union* (London, Verso, 1996) 17.

[32] N Walker, 'Human Rights in a Post-National Order: Reconciling Political and Constitutional Pluralism' in T Campbell, KD Ewing and A Tomkins (eds), *Sceptical Essays on Human Rights* (Oxford, Oxford University Press, 2001) 127.

[33] Walker, above n 32, 141.

judiciary, either through a non-deferential interpretation of EU secondary legislation (giving expression to fundamental rights as Muir discusses, or otherwise) or of EU primary law (or both in combination), this poses a more profound legitimacy challenge. The European legislator is obliged to respect EU primary law, which includes the CJEU's doctrines and case law on economic rights and their relationship to other public interests, including fundamental political and social rights. While it is true that, as Armin Hatje points out in chapter six, that 'the free movement of persons, services and capital would not work without political decisions by the legislator' and that 'the internal market in its concrete form is the result of political decisions', these decisions, when taken with the European Parliament, have to abide by the interpretations given by the CJEU. The only way to fundamentally strike a different balance between the various competing interests at stake is through either the Court's reinterpretation of its own case law or a Treaty revision; thus not within the direct reach of either the national or European parliaments.

The insulation of certain norms from the political process is a key feature of constitutional democracy. A simplistic rejection of all judicial review of democratically enacted norms should in this context be avoided. However, a constitutional democracy does not give carte blanche to the judiciary either. As Sacha Garben argues in chapter nineteen, the principle of legality (as the core legal expression of constitutional democracy) itself indicates the appropriate purposes and intensity of judicial review, at least in theory. As regards fundamental rights, the extent of judicial deference or active review should depend on the importance of the fundamental right in question for a healthy democracy or for the correction of grave majoritarian injustice. The further removed from these two functions that a fundamental right is in the particular case before the judge, the more hesitant the judge should be to enforce that right against the democratic exercise of authority that is challenged. This of course in itself does not provide clear and uncontested results, and in every case an element of interpretation will play into the decision on the right (re)calibration of the principles of democracy and constitutionalism in the specific instance. But it does provide for the normative framework within which this assessment is made; for the terms of the argument. As the analysis in chapter nineteen reveals, the Court does not however seem to use these terms for its arguments. As regards outcomes, some judgments could be considered to be in line with these constitutional democratic stipulations, others less so. Particularly problematic is the extensive protection (and thus active judicial application) of the 'economic freedoms' (ie, the internal market provisions laid down in the Treaty and the freedom to conduct a business of Article 16 EU Charter) on the one hand, and the relatively weak protection given to the freedom of assembly, including the right to strike and bargain collectively, on the other. But most importantly, it does not seem that the Court's approach is guided by an overarching theory of constitutional democracy and the position of the judiciary within it, instead interpreting fundamental rights (and their interrelation) in a more ad hoc fashion, with the *effet utile* of EU law as a guiding principle. This risks feeding into a deeper constitutional imbalance between 'the economic' and 'the social' in the EU.[34] That imbalance, which can be expected to find some traction in certain populist narratives, is present not only in the Court's interpretation of the internal market and economic and social rights more generally, but perhaps even more so in the area of European economic governance. It was discussed in the previous section that this area raises concerns about democratic legitimacy with many of the contributors to this volume, but in addition, the decision-making in this area does not seem to comply with the requirements of constitutionalism either – as discussed in more detail in chapter nineteen.

## Constitutional Democracy in the Member States

It is difficult to establish the relationship between the imperfections in the EU's own constitutional democratic legitimacy and the perceived crisis of constitutional democracy on the national level. On the one hand, the malaise in constitutional democracy seems to transcend the EU, affecting the Americas too. On the other hand, as Cesare Pinelli states in chapter two, EU membership 'has given populists their best opportunity for exploiting popular discontent towards national governments and traditional party politics'. He points to the dominant role of the Council especially since the economic and/or financial crisis and the lack of transparency fuelled by the EU's 'governance turn' [which] 'goes to the point of acting as an "anti-politic machine" in which accountability becomes progressively blurred, decision-making increasingly remote and obtuse, and the citizens of Europe – in whose name the EU claims to speak – ever-more voiceless', a view echoed in various other contributions to this book. If at least one of the reasons for the current challenge to constitutional democracy in European countries is that a part of the people feels somehow disempowered, politically, socially and/or economically, then the EU's various features as outlined above can reasonably be assumed to play some part in that. This means that at least to some extent the crisis in national constitutional democracy is also one of EU constitutional democracy.

However, the specificities of national dynamics and circumstances also need to be given due consideration. Nowhere is this clearer than in the case of Brexit, discussed by Michael Gordon in chapter four, which has created a range of domestic difficulties 'which have challenged the constitution, democracy, and the very idea of constitutional democracy in the UK'. In some ways, it seems, the EU and secession from it have merely been an external trigger to a domestic ticking time bomb. Taking the EU out the equation, apparently, does not resolve a crisis of constitutional democracy on the domestic level, but it fuels it. Gordon notes:

> The constitutional overload generated by Brexit has … revealed flaws in the structures of the UK's democratic constitution. But if even if this does amount to a significant

[34] S Garben, 'The Constitutional (Im)Balance between "the Market" and "the Social" in the European Union' (2017) 13 *European Constitutional Law Review* 23.

> 'constitutional moment', it is far from clear that a shift to a more traditional conception of constitutional democracy would provide a solution. While in the dominant liberal account of constitutional democracy we might expect to see the constitutional operating to temper democratic politics, in the UK democratic politics is driving the constitutional. In such circumstances, attempts to more deeply constrain institutional power arguably represent a diversion. The democratic tensions evident in this context are deeply embedded, and were not simply created by the 2016 referendum. The UK's struggle with Brexit may tell us something about the modern limitations of the nation state, and the extent to which democratic decision-making within it is confined by external factors. This is not to suggest that the nation state is now unviable as the basic unit of governance, but that Brexit may be a lesson in the difficulty – or perhaps futility – of pursuing a strategy of constitutional isolation. If this is the case, Brexit may demonstrate the increased fragility of national authority in the face of globalised power networks. This suggests the priority should be to strengthen the democratic state to better respond to these developments and agendas, rather than to use constitutionalism to restrain democracy so that the status quo become impossible to challenge.

In a profoundly interconnected global society, with high levels of economic interdependence through international trade networks and increasing socio-cultural integration through digital media, the EU may very well be argued to be, on balance, a source of empowerment rather than disempowerment for the European people(s) (even if independent statehood is not wholly unviable). That does not mean one has to accept the EU's constitutional democratic failings as discussed above, but it does mean that it is probably more effective to try to improve the system from within rather than to exit it. Actually, despite what populists would lead us to believe, the majority of European citizens seem to agree with this: Eurobarometer data suggests majority levels of support not only for EU membership but for a leading role for Europe on a range of 'sensitive' policy issues, and the EU institutions on balance enjoy more trust from the European citizens than they trust their national parliaments and governments.[35]

Apart from the question to what extent the EU's own constitutional democratic imperfections feed populism and Euroscepticism on the Member State level, the EU's powers and actions as regards respect for the values of constitutional democracy on the national level are an important remaining part of our puzzle. In this regard, the schism between the EU's pre-accession conditions and EU membership obligations remains striking.[36] EU fundamental values have a broader legal force in the enlargement context than internally vis-a-vis the Member States, as respect for fundamental rights is both an eligibility condition for membership, as expressed by the first Copenhagen criterion and Article 49(1) of the Treaty on

[35] See European Commission, Standard Eurobarometer 87, May 2017, available at: ec.europa.eu/commfrontoce/publicopinion/index.cfm/Survey/getSurveyDetail/instruments/STANDARD/surveyKy/2142.

[36] See C Hillion and V Delhomme, 'EU Enlargement, Extra-Territorial Application of EU Law and the International Dimension' in I Govaere and S Garben, *The Interface Between EU and International Law* (Oxford, Hart Publishing, 2019).

European Union (TEU), as well as an integral part of the EU *acquis*, contained in a specific chapter on 'judiciary and fundamental rights' which the candidate country must embrace, as a matter of priority.[37] The EU Charter is used to assess whether candidates respect the values of Article 2 TEU, meaning that it receives a wider application in the enlargement context than inside the EU.[38] While we have, of course, Article 7 TEU, this is not a general competence for the EU to take measures to enforce and promote constitutional democratic values in the Member States. As to Article 7 TEU itself, Cesare Pinelli in chapter two laments 'the European Council's inertia vis-a-vis what has been called "the purposeful destruction of the rule of law"'[39] [in] Hungary and Poland, reflects partisan tactics that vanishes both the maintenance and the credibility of the 'common values'. Admittedly, the EU institutions are increasingly making use of the opportunities under EU law to counter this situation. In September 2017, the European Commission triggered the procedure provided by Article 7(1) TEU against Poland. In September 2018, the European Parliament voted in favour of launching Article 7 TEU proceedings against the Hungarian government on the basis of the Sargentini Report. In October 2018, the CJEU ordered Poland to suspend the application of the provisions of national legislation relating to the lowering of the retirement age for Supreme Court judges.[40] However, the lack of a fully-fledged competence for the EU in this regard, coupled with the ultimately political nature of the Article 7 mechanism, mean that any EU actions will inevitably come as 'too little too late'.[41] This is not only connected to the EU's imperfect democracy as explained by Daniel Kelemen in chapter three, but it also suggests a lack of constitutionalism at EU level.

## The Future of Constitutional Democracy in the EU: Proposals for Reform

Where do we go from here? Kris Grimonprez makes a strong case in chapter seventeen for an increased EU investment in Education for Democratic Citizenship (EDC). She argues:

> When applying EDC standards as to constitutional democracy in the European Union, EDC must be provided in a way consistent with the Treaties and EU Charter. They show

[37] ibid.

[38] ibid.

[39] J-W Müller, 'Reflections on Europe's "Rule of Law Crises"' in PF Kjaer and N Olson (eds), *Critical Theories of Crisis in Europe. From Weimar to the Euro* (London, Rowman & Littlefield, 2016) 162.

[40] Order in C-619/18 R *Commission v Poland* EU:C:2018:1021 (English not available at time of writing).

[41] S Carrera and P Bárd, 'The European Parliament Vote on Article 7 TEU against the Hungarian Government – Too Late, Too Little, Too Political?' CEPS Commentary, 14 September 2018, available at: aei.pitt.edu/94390/1/EP_vote_on_Article7.pdf.

how EU citizenship is evolving. The 1992 Maastricht Treaty inserted EU citizenship in the Treaty and connected it with a limited list of citizenship rights. The 2009 Lisbon Treaty connected EU citizenship with the provisions on democratic principles in Title II TEU. Ten years later, time has come to connect EU citizenship and democratic principles with EDC standards in mainstream education. Recent challenges, such as populism and radicalisation, build momentum. In view of a Union based on the values of Article 2 TEU going beyond a market rationale, the European public space needs an educational substratum. EDC aims to empower citizens 'to exercise and defend their democratic rights and responsibilities in society'. To move beyond rhetoric, rights and obligations under EU law should contribute to the core content of the EU dimension in EDC. Integrating an EU dimension in EDC furthermore empowers citizens to value diversity and to participate in democratic life in their double role of national citizens and EU citizens, strengthening the dual democratic legitimacy of the Union and enhancing its social legitimacy.

While recognising national responsibility for the content of teaching and the organisation of education systems, 'the EU should offer more concrete guidance for the EU dimension of EDC'. Grimonprez provides a number of concrete proposals: (i) Council of Europe materials can be adapted to the specific EU context and made available in all EU languages; (ii) a common EDC reference framework should be set up; (iii) the EU level could propose specific objectives and learning outcomes for the EU dimension in line with the Treaties and CFR; (iv) the EU dimension in teacher training should be promoted by funding or EU labels of excellency; (v) a school friendly version of selected provisions of the Treaties and CFR should be made available as a basis for EDC; and (vi) an EU Agency for Education for Democratic Citizenship could support Member States, inter alia, by providing information and educational materials for EDC and its EU dimension.

Paul Nemitz and Frithjof Ehm propose a European Democracy Charter in chapter eighteen. Such a Charter would aim to help address the many challenges to democracy on the EU level, within the Member States, and, third, in the relation between the EU and the Member States. Building on a wide range of existing documents and proposals, they propose for the Democracy Charter's possible content: (i) a definition of the core elements and the common denominator of European democracy, building on Article 2 TEU, with reference to 'majority rule' as had been included in the first Draft Preamble of the European Constitution, as well as human rights, free and fair elections, the rule of law, a multiparty system, separation of powers, and an independent judiciary; (ii) the Europeanisation of European elections through electoral reform; (iii) the increase of co-decision; (iv) the codification of best practices such as those relating to *Spitzenkandidaten*; (v) enhancing EU competences as regards the respect for constitutional democracy on the Member State level (eg, the setting up of a 'Copenhagen Commission' which should continuously assesses democracy and the rule of law within Member States, or allowing national courts in a situation when human rights are systemically violated to invite the CJEU to consider the legality of national actions in the light of Article 2 TEU); and (vi) creating new mechanism related to the enforcement of democracy in the EU. The Charter should be adopted using the tried and tested methodology which led to the adoption of the Charter of Fundamental Rights, to produce a major document, that contains a clear and visible commitment of the EU to democratic values and that addresses the challenges to democracy in the EU, in the Member States and between them, and potentially complements the European legal framework in the long run. They also propose that the Commission make democracy and opening up EU secondary law for citizen's engagement a top priority in secondary law-making. They suggest a democracy mainstreaming for all legislative proposals and an active quest to use secondary legislation for protecting and strengthening vital elements of democratic process and societal engagement, taking the Whistle Blower Directive and the Data Protection Regulation as examples.

In chapter twelve, Leo Hoffmann-Axthelm proposes three ways to improve transparency in the Council. First, the Council should systematically record the positions of individual governments on legislative files, and publish them – even if this were to happen with a delay (eg, for particularly sensitive files). This transparency, 'mediated by journalists, national parliaments and civil society, [will] ensure that politicians are accountable for the positions they take in the Council'. Secondly, national accountability of the Council should be complemented by an additional, European level accountability mechanism in the case of executive Council decisions. This 'will increase the visibility of political debate, sharpen arguments in favour and against this or that decision, and improve the democratic legitimacy of any outcome by providing a public space for political deliberation, beyond the *in camera* debate within the Council'. Thirdly, Hoffmann-Axthelm argues that further improvements can be made in the field of recording (legislative) documents, agendas and outcomes systematically, and making them available where possible. This is a problem in particular for the Council working parties, Committees of Permanent Representatives and preparatory committees. He states: 'in a democratic, political system taking decisions on behalf of 500 million citizens spanning the entire continent, voters should be able to follow policy processes at the click of a button on the Council website'.

Sacha Garben in chapter nineteen develops a research agenda focusing on the question of how constitutional democratic theory can be developed into an analytical framework for the EU's legitimate exercise of public authority. The principle of legality is proposed as the anchor point in this approach, since it is uniquely able to capture the dialectic relationship between constitutionalism and democracy through its traditional emphasis on both lawfulness and parliamentary sovereignty. It can serve to operationalise constitutional democracy in a legal sense, for both scholars and practitioners. Garben considers that the principle of democracy as part of the principle of legality should require that the people should take part in the exercise of power through the intermediary of a representative assembly at least as regards decisions that are salient to the polity.[42]

[42] Salience, Garben argues, should be determined in particular in reference to factors such as the potential scale (eg, number of people affected); intensity (eg, deeply affecting the position of at least one person); or irreversibility/consequentiality of the exercise of authority in question. See ch 19 for the elaboration of this argument.

The more salient the decision, the more demanding the principle of democracy becomes: requiring higher degrees of representativeness of the respective assembly and more extensive and direct participation in actual decision-making beyond consultation, information and delegation. In turn, concretely, the principle of constitutionalism as part of the principle of legality requires authority to be exercised (i) on the basis of the correct authorising norm and in compliance with the accompanying procedures; (ii) in respect of the principle of democracy; and (iii) respecting fundamental human rights, in particular to the extent that these fundamental rights contribute to creating the preconditions of a healthy democracy, and to the extent that they serve to prevent cases of majoritarian injustice. The rights of equality, liberty and dignity are primordial in this respect, and fundamental are the traditional democratic civil liberties such freedom of thought and expression, assembly and association. The position of (other) social and economic rights is more ambiguous: constitutional protection of these rights is primarily necessary to the degree that they create the socio-economic conditions for a well-functioning democracy (allowing social mobility, emancipation and corrections of societal power asymmetries),[43] and their application should not displace democratic decision-making on substantive socio-economic issues.

The application of this theoretical framework to the EU in chapter nineteen confirms a number of well-known democratic and constitutional problems, partially also addressed in the other contributions to this book. Moreover, it allows a more refined and integrated analysis thereof, capturing their interconnectedness in a holistic, comprehensive understanding. This is not a purely academic exercise to create 'a theory of everything', as precise and concrete reforms can be distilled from the assessment. Most fundamentally, the CJEU could adopt, implicitly or explicitly, the principle of legality or, generally, a theory of constitutional democracy, as an overarching normative system to situate itself in relation to other European and national institutions and to guide its case law. As argued in chapter nineteen, that framework suggests first that a more active judicial role is warranted in relation to the choice of legal basis, in cases where there is an option to choose between procedures that differ in terms of parliamentary involvement. The CJEU should develop a doctrine that (at least) in the case of salient decisions, the more democratic legal basis needs to be used. Secondly, in its balancing of fundamental rights, especially where there is a clash between economic and social rights, the CJEU should consider the relative importance of the fundamental right in question for the proper functioning of a robust democracy or for the correction of grave majoritarian injustice. The further removed from these two functions a fundamental right is in the particular case before the Court, the more hesitant it should be to enforce that right against the democratic exercise of authority that is challenged or against a conflicting fundamental right. Finally, considering the

[43] On the importance thereof, see R Bellamy, *Political Constitutionalism. A Republican Defense of the Constitutionality of Democracy* (Cambridge, Cambridge University Press, 2007) 81.

necessarily high salience of exercise of punitive authority, expressed in the specific requirement of the legality principle of *nulla poene sine lege*, the CJEU should proceed with special care in the area of criminal law, reconsidering its application of the principle of *effet utile* of EU law to the EU's competence in this area, and instead adopting a more interventionist stance as regards undemocratic EU decision-making in this area. These wide-ranging implications show the potential of operationalising constitutional democracy in the way proposed, and these terms of argument can be used in the settlement or at least in the accommodation of many other areas of controversy in the EU legal and political order.

## Conclusion

Bringing together a wide range of contributions from academics and practitioners, legal and political perspectives, focusing on both topical and perennial issues concerning constitutional democracy in theory and practice, in the past, present and future, primarily at EU level but also with due regard to national and global developments, this book cannot be summarised in a single overarching narrative. When it comes to the question of the current state of constitutional democracy and the European Union, it is in any event doubtful that there is a single *problématique* to be analysed and resolved: we are facing a kaleidoscopic spectrum of related challenges that influence each other in elusive, multifaceted ways. Yet it is remarkable that in the rich variety of sub-topics, angles and approaches that this book contains, a number of commonalities nevertheless emerge. First and foremost, there is a widely shared concern about the EU's Euro-crisis and economic governance, which seems to be considered in need of catching up with the EU's otherwise very positive achievements in establishing a supranational constitutional democracy. Other common concerns relate to the still wanting transparency especially in the Council, the distance between the citizens and the EU and, to a certain extent, the insulation of certain important questions from the democratic process through a(n) (over)constitutionalisation of economic rights at EU level. Our authors provide meaningful contributions to the rich array of existing scholarship and debate, by proposing original elements of analysis, challenging often-made assumptions, destabilising settled understandings and proposing fundamental reforms, with and without the change of primary law. Overall, the collection thus injects a set of fresh critical perspectives on this fundamental issue that is as contemporary as it is eternal. Political resolve and wise statesman- and womanship is now required to move on from the discussions and proposals of our authors to the new constitutional settlement which secures and strengthens democracy in Europe for the future.

# PART I

# Critical Reflections on the Current State of Constitutional Democracy in the EU and Beyond

# Section 1: Autocracy, Populism and Brexit

# 2

# The Rise of Populism and the Malaise of Democracy

CESARE PINELLI

## On the Terms 'Populism' and 'Constitutional Democracy'

In the political and media language of our time, the term 'populism' designates 'an ideology that separates society into two homogeneous and antagonistic groups, "the pure people" and "the corrupt elite", and that holds that politics should be an expression of the "general will" of the people'.[1] With regard to national identity, populism 'pits a mystically unified "nation" against corrupt "elites" and external enemies, and claims for a charismatic leader the power to voice the will of the nation'.[2]

These definitions might appear simplistic vis-a-vis the disputes that the term raises among political theorists. For some, the sources of populism 'are to be found in tensions at the heart of democracy', namely 'two styles of modern politics', the 'redemptive' (*vox populi vox dei*) and the 'pragmatic' ('ballots not bullets') face of democracy.[3] For others, populism should be conceived 'as an internal periphery of democratic politics', consisting in 'a region where the distinction between inside and outside is a matter of dispute and cannot be thought outside a polemic'.[4] The distance between democracy and populism is further increased while stressing that the latter reflects Schmitt's view of 'the substantial homogeneity of the identity

[1] C Mudde, 'Europe's Populist Surge. A Long Time in the Making' (2016) (November/December) *Foreign Affairs* 19, 25.

[2] N Shenkkan, *Nations in Transit 2017. The False Promise of Populism* (Washington DC, Freedom House, 2017) 2, available at: www.freedhomhouse.org.

[3] M Canovan, 'Trust the People! Populism and the Two Faces of Democracy' (1999) 47(3) *Political Studies* 2 ff.

[4] B Arditi, *Politics on the Edges of Liberalism* (Edinburgh, Edinburgh University Press, 2007) 2 ff. See also P-A Taguieff, *L'illusion populiste* (Paris, Flammarion, 2007); and E Laclau, *On Populist Reason* (London, Verso, 2005).

and the will of the people', and that 'populism, by its nature, should be seen as a dangerous threat to democracy'.[5]

These approaches rely on styles of politics, collective perceptions of democracy and political thought with the sometimes explicit aim of purporting an 'ideal-typical analysis' of the issue,[6] thus neglecting Isaiah Berlin's warning against the utility of searching 'the idea of Platonic populism'.[7] They deserve attention instead for being centred on the supposed proximity of 'populism' to 'democracy', with the former covering a spectrum that goes from being an inner tension of democracy to an external threat to it. This shifting needs to be taken into account in this contribution, where the populist claim that the people's will is the sole source of legitimacy is confronted with constitutional democracy conceived as a form of government, rather than as a normative ideal or a theoretical concept. Although concerning other democratic countries as well, the issue will be treated solely with regard to the European countries due to the specific features that it has there acquired.

My point of departure consists in considering constitutional democracy as capable of combining principles and institutions that correspond to different, and theoretically opposed, modes of legitimacy, namely the popular one, through election of political representatives or referendum, and the rule of law. It is a form of government, I contend, that results from continuous adjustments among these potentially conflicting principles and institutions, which are themselves open to different interpretations: it is due to such flexibility that constitutional democracy for decades even absorbed de-structuring tensions within a certain number of European countries, and put the premises for their mutual integration through the EU.[8]

However, this form of government is going through an increasing malaise. I will first concentrate on the 'disaffection', or 'disappointment', towards political representation,[9] with a view to giving an account of the factors that are likely to provoke it, including the failures of European integration. The subsequent electoral rise of populism should be appreciated against such a background. While regularly participating in the elections and accepting at least the basic rules of the representative system, populist parties exploit its crisis by depicting the traditional parties as an aristocratic class that has 'abandoned the people'. The same occurs with the referendum. Although usually aimed at contributing to the good functioning of democracy, these appear a symptom of its crisis while perceived as

[5] K Abts and S Rummens, 'Populism versus Democracy' (2007) 55(6) *Political Studies* 406, 407 ff.

[6] ibid 420.

[7] I Berlin, 'To Define Populism' (Conference, London School of Economics, 20–21 May 1967) The Isaiah Berlin Virtual Library, 6.

[8] C Pinelli, 'The Formation of a Constitutional Tradition in Continental Europe since World War II' (2016) 22 *European Public Law* 257, 266.

[9] See, eg, M Van Wessel, 'Political Disaffection: What We Can Learn from Asking the People' (2010) 63 *Parliamentary Affairs* 504; and B Seyd, 'Exploring Political Disappointment' (2015) 69 *Parliamentary Affairs* 327.

an opportunity for the people of expressing its ultimate sovereignty at the expense of parliamentary powers.

With the advent of populist governments, neither the representative system nor the referendum have been questioned as such, while the independence of the judiciary, of constitutional courts, and more generally of non-majoritarian authorities, is jeopardised with the claim that these institutions lack democratic legitimacy. The populist attitude towards the institutions of constitutional democracy appears thus differentiated according to the respective modes of legitimacy.

Hungary and Poland have been particularly prone to these developments, having acquired only recently the features of a constitutional democracy. Hence the fact that

> [d]espite their apparent maturation, the media, the judiciary, and institutions of democratic representation in Poland and Hungary have turned out to be quite vulnerable, lacking both elite consensus on their inviolability and the necessary public support to turn back partisan attacks.[10]

But even where constitutional democracy is more consolidated, populists not only gain a growing electoral consent, but succeed in imposing their political agenda, and once in office may easily overturn the institutional assessments that characterise constitutional democracies.

Given these elements, I will finally focus on the structural ambiguity of populists towards constitutional democracy. Is their observance of the legal order sufficient to exclude dangers to the credibility of democratic values? Should their appearance of genuine interpreters of the people's will be taken for granted, vis-a-vis the alleged distance of traditional parties from the electorate? Finally, how are constitutional democracies reacting, and how should they react, to populism?

Once again, rather than with constitutional theory, these questions have to do with how democracy is currently perceived and practised. Both because, as I will attempt to demonstrate, contemporary populism does not follow a single constitutional theory, but a pragmatic approach varying from country to country, and because the challenges it poses should be viewed as dependent from a malaise that affects the practice of democracy within European countries not less than the EU.

## Establishment and Consolidation of Constitutional Democracies in Continental Europe

In continental Europe, the premises of constitutional democracy were laid down in the aftermath of the totalitarian demise. The old Rechtsstaat was then

[10] Shenkkan, above n 2, 11.

discredited, and substituted by a far more complex institutional system where any given subject is prevented from determining the community's ultimate ends of liberty, dignity, equality and democracy as embodied in substantive principles enshrined in the constitution.

Although remaining at the centre of democratic life, Parliament was no more perceived as its unique source, nor as being capable of guaranteeing fundamental rights. In addition, constitutions frequently made provision for holding a referendum in order to complement democracy, even when it was likely to counteract the parliamentary majority's will. The establishment of a federal or regional state structure was considered an important tool for both enhancing popular participation in public affairs and dividing public power along vertical lines, whereas the principle of separation of powers was intended to divide it at the horizontal level. At the same time, a sophisticated version of the rule of law was introduced through the establishment of constitutional courts aimed at checking the conformity of ordinary legislation with the constitution, with the implication of ensuring an effective protection of fundamental rights. Politics was thus conceived as limited both internally through the diffusion of a pluralistic version of democracy, and externally through the interventions of the judiciary and of the newly established constitutional courts in particular.

A further limitation of politics concerned political representation itself, through the recognition of the venerable rule that a member of parliament is not subject to repeal in the course of his mandate. In spite of its seemingly aristocratic origin, being theorised by Edmund Burke and James Madison for the aim of defending the people against their own temporary errors and delusions, such a rule resisted the advent of universal suffrage and the organisation of political parties. While acquiring the function of preventing parties from repealing MPs that may counter their decisions, the open mandate served then as a limitation to partisan politics. In addition, it was designed to enhance political accountability, giving voters the opportunity of evaluating how their representatives exert their power for an entire legislature.

Finally, the European constitutions abandoned the absolute, and therefore monist, conception of the state with regard to external sovereignty. After the Second World War, the idea appeared untenable that international law is founded on the mere coexistence of sovereign states, putting at risk peace and international security. From this standpoint, post-totalitarian constitutions explicitly admitted 'limitations of sovereignty', for the purpose of accepting the obligations deriving from membership of international or supranational organisations aimed at promoting peace and justice among nations. These provisions paved the way for the acceptance of EU law, including its 'direct effect' in the domestic legal orders. Constitutional pluralism is not alien to these legal orders and it does not stand as a matter of fact with which they have to deal; instead it is built in their constitutions.[11]

[11] C Pinelli, 'Constitutional Pluralism' in L Motoc et al (eds), *New Developments in Constitutional Law. Essays in Honour of Andras Sajo* (The Hague, Eleven International Publishing, 2018) 315 ff.

Overall, post-totalitarian constitutions might primarily be viewed as attempts to demonstrate how a new beginning can be conceived without forgetting the past and, vice versa, how awareness of the past can temper an excess of faith in the future. The achievements of these constitutions in fact go far beyond their formal endurance. The premises were thus put for the civilisation of political conflict, and the formation of a tradition capable of reshaping the conventional antinomy between the 'evolutionary' British constitutionalism and the 'artificial' one of the continent, corresponding to what has been called 'the pervasive post-Enlightenment antinomy between tradition and change'.[12]

## How the Crisis of Political Representation is Leading to the Question of Why We should be Represented

Notwithstanding these achievements, constitutional democracies appear affected by an increasing malaise. Its first symptoms preceded the emergence of populist parties, and should be taken into account for an understanding of the latter. A 2008 report on the state of democracy in the UK, admitted a 'prevalence, and inadvertent nurturing of, an anti-political culture', where people 'combine a substantial level of cynicism about politics with occasional outbursts of moral indignation as to its failings and frustrations'.[13] Never before in the history of post-war Europe, it was added, were political leaders held in such low regard, due to a growing distance between each party and the voters it purported to represent, and at the same time to an ever closer association with its political competitors.[14]

New communicative systems have in the meanwhile structured the public debate in terms of singular events rather than of policies or principles.[15] Far from favouring awareness of a common future, and a reflexive attitude with respect to external events, these systems have tended to obscure the previous perception of time. From a reasoned confrontation between programmes concerning the future of the country and policies needing time to take shape and then to be evaluated by the voters, politics has thus been transformed into a competition between personalities. Relieved from the burden of being evaluated according to their policies, and obsessed by daily opinion polls, representatives and political parties tend to concentrate on the construction of a successful image before their electors and to mirror their current preferences.[16]

[12] M Krygier, 'Law as Tradition' (1986) 5 *Law & Philosophy* 237.
[13] C Hay, G Stoker and A Williamson, *Revitalising Politics: Have We Lost the Plot?* (London, Hansard Society, 2008).
[14] P Mair, *Polity-Scepticism, Party Failings, and the Challenge to European Democracy* (Wassenaar, Netherlands Institute for Advanced Studies, 2006) 23 ff.
[15] See J M Guéhenno, *La fin de la démocratie* (Paris, Flammarion, 1993).
[16] Y Mény and Y Surel, *Par le peuple, pour le peuple* (Paris, Fayard, 2000) 75 ff.

The good reasons for a long-sighted perspective of politics are denied,[17] and political representation is reduced to the resemblance of the representative to the elector. It is in this sense that the current crisis differs radically from those that periodically characterised its bicentennial life. As it has been noted,

> [t]he question has always been posed in terms not of *why*, but of who and how? Whom shall we entrust to represent us? How do we ensure that they remain true to their mission? How do we protect ourselves from those who lead or govern? This has for two hundred years or so been the stock in trade of thinking about politics … But what is becoming clearer is that the growing alienation from representative practices and processes is moving us beyond the 'who' and 'how' questions towards the 'why'.[18]

The emergence of the 'why question' presupposes the above-mentioned malaise, and it goes beyond it. It challenges definitively the twofold idea that political representation requires a distance between the representative and the represented, and that it consists in a partial, and therefore political, interpretation of the will of the people, that needs to be confronted in parliament with further political interpretations. Significantly, the rise of populism corresponds to the emergence of the 'why question' among the electors. While traditional parties have adapted themselves to the media-driven scenario of politics for maintaining their power, populists have naturally tended to mirror the people's will, as if they were, per se, alien to give an interpretation of it. Accordingly, their regular participation in the elections is detached from their acceptance of the traditional meaning of political representation. What populists deny is 'any kind of pluralism or social division: in the populist imagination there is *only* the people on the one hand and, on the other hand, the illegitimate intruders into our politics'.[19]

## The Ambivalent Role of National Governments in the EU Institutional System

Why is the populist imagination meeting growing favour both for what it denies, and for the idea of the people's will that it encapsulates? In answering this question, attention needs to be paid to events affecting democracies from the outside, particularly those that are prone to be presented as external threats. It is here that populists are at ease in fuelling a politics of fear that implies per se the idea of a threatened people, irrespective of inner political cleavages. Issues such as globalisation of markets and the flow of immigrants are frequently presented in

[17] G Hermet, Les populismes dans le monde. Une histoire sociologique. XIXe-XXe siècle (Paris, Fayard, 2001) 50.

[18] S Tormey, *The End of Representative Politics* (Cambridge, Polity, 2015) 58.

[19] J-W Müller, '"The People Must be Extracted from Within the People": Reflections on Populism' (2014), available at: www.princeton.edu/~jmueller/Constellations-Populism-JWMueller-March2014-pdf.pdf *Constellations* 11, 13.

such a way. However, it is the European Union's membership that has given populists their best opportunity for exploiting popular discontent towards national governments and traditional party politics.

Thirty years ago, it had been noted that '[i]n the absence of an European government with a popular political base of its own, all possibilities of institutional transformation are entirely determined by the self-interests of national governments'.[20] Such prognosis has so far remained unchallenged. It is true that, under the Lisbon Treaty, legislative decisions no longer depend on the Council acting unanimously, but on the European Parliament (EP) acting jointly with the Council, that decides on the basis of qualified majority unless the Treaties provide otherwise (Article 16 TEU). But the unanimity rule of Member States is still requested (with limited exceptions) both for the approval and for the ratification of the European treaties (Article 48 TEU).

The rule that the Commission's President is appointed by the European Council 'taking into account the elections of the European Parliament', and then elected by the EP (Article 17, para 7, TEU), was indeed complemented in 2014 with the 'Spitzenkandidat system', a conventional device according to which the top candidate of the most popular party after the EU vote is nominated for the post. However, the emergence of a true parliamentary form of government was practically impeded by the dominant role that the European Council acquired due to the fallout of the global financial crisis. Such role has not been without costs for national governments, pushing them to the centre of the EU institutional stage. For a long time, they had preferred to remain behind it. Given the dispersal of power affecting the EU institutional arrangement, national governments were able to leave to the EU the burden of hard choices, starting with those concerning the national budget, without paying electoral costs. Rulers dislike being held accountable. It was arguably in their own interest both to maintain the EU system as it was, with no chance of identifying accountable rulers behind the blue sky and the stars, and to let people believe the media tale of 'Brussels' as a seat of inaccessible technocracy.

Although clearly artificial, the divide between national politics and supranational technocratic governance permeated the popular imagination, hiding the dilemma between the adoption of long-term policies that require time to be understood by citizens and are not without risks in terms of electoral approval, and the mere administration of the present, with the related dismissal of politics. While regularly preferring the latter, the national governments' condition is to lay the blame of the European malaise on the 'obscure and unelected' officials of Brussels.

While influencing the self-representation of the EU institutions, a further distance from popular imagination was put by the mainstream scholarly emphasis

[20] FW Scharpf, 'The Joint-Decision Trap: Lessons from German Federalism and European Integration' (1988) 3 *Public Administration* 239, 265.

on a 'European post-national governance' founded on a discursive process and on contestation between interests.[21]

The 2000 Lisbon Strategy was supported by an ambitious design of governance, the 'Open Method of Coordination', relying on coordination, peer review, networks and heterarchy, rather than on centralised hierarchical tools of compliance. The bulk of the whole design nonetheless depended on the national governments' discretionary power in engaging in internal structural reforms of the welfare sectors.[22] Governments soon realised that a shift of financial resources from traditional social policies to investments in technology would endanger their own electoral consent. The Commission's 2001 White Paper on European Governance echoed to an even greater extent post-national concepts, with the intention of melting together the old communitarian method and a pluralist political arrangement in which the decision-making powers of national governments are decentralised and displaced to a plethora of multilevel organisations, NGOs, civil society institutions, and public and private interests.[23]

However, it was objected, the 'governance turn' goes to the point of acting 'as an "anti-politic machine" in which accountability becomes progressively blurred, decision-making increasingly remote and obtuse, and the citizens of Europe – in whose name the EU claims to speak – ever-more voiceless'.[24] An oversimplified opposition 'pushing a "governance" approach at the expense of one honed towards a traditional notion of "government", or deliberative democracy at the expense of representative democracy',[25] was presupposed by the 2001 White Paper, as well as by the claim of the Commission's Green Paper that globalisation heralds the end of representative democracy as we know it.[26] Paradoxically, such approach relied on the elitist paradigms of post-modernism with a view to get closer to citizens, in the awareness of the increasing sense of remoteness of European policies.[27]

Legal texts reveal that very anxiety, although treated with an opposite rhetoric. Think of the heroic declaration that 'while remaining proud of their own national identities and history, the peoples of Europe are determined to transcend their former divisions and, united ever more closely, to forge a common destiny' (Preamble to the Constitutional Treaty). Furthermore, in an attempt to respond to popular discontent with 'Europe' that emerged from the 2005 French and Dutch

[21] See eg J Shaw, 'Postnational Constitutionalism in the European Union' (1999) 6 *Journal of European Public Policy* 579, 580.

[22] R Colliat, 'A Critical Genealogy of European Macroeconomic Governance' (2012) 18 *European Law Journal* 6, 16.

[23] European Commission, 'European Governance: A White Paper' COM (2001)428.

[24] C Shore, 'European Governance or Govermentality? The European Commission and the Future of Democratic Government' (2011) 17 *European Law Journal* 287, 299, 303.

[25] D Curtin, 'Tailoring Legitimacy to the Shape of the EU' (2005) 3 *European Constitutional Law Review* 421, 426.

[26] T Burns, C Jaeger, A Liberatore, Y Mény and P Nanz, *The Future of Parliamentary Democracy: Transition and Challenge in European Governance* (European Commission, 2000), available at: ec.europa.eu/governance/docs/docs_en.pdf.

[27] European Commission, 'European Governance: A White Paper', above n 23, 35.

referendums, the Lisbon Treaty solemnly states that 'The functioning of the Union shall be founded on representative democracy' (Article 10, para 1, TEU), and then adds:

> Citizens are directly represented at Union level in the European Parliament. Member States are represented in the European Council by their heads of State or Government and in the Council by their governments, themselves democratically accountable either to their national Parliaments, or their citizens (para 2).

Such text presupposes that European citizens should content themselves with that version of representative democracy. The aim behind this rather thin rationale appears to be to dismiss the whole debate on the democratic deficit.

At the time of the Lisbon Treaty's enactment, national governments were still attempting to hide behind the EU flag for fuelling popular distrust at home against 'Europe'. And yet, they were sawing off the branch they were sitting on. It was the Eurozone crisis that increased the dominance of intergovernmentalism,[28] to the point of pushing national governments to the centre stage. The old game was over. The European Council's crucial role in the adoption of financial measures aimed at reducing national expenditures for the citizens' welfare could no longer be denied. It complemented for the people an image of the EU that already consisted of the fictions and the vacuity of its official language, as well as the tricks of national governments.

Being presented as a defensive move against external threats, the populist attacks on the EU have thus appeared genuine to huge sectors of the electorate, particularly to those exacerbated by the scarce governmental response to their basic needs, and forged the idea of a concrete popular will.

In addition, in many countries an institutional device was available to that end: the referendum. Unlike the election, where the populist claim of expressing the sole legitimate will of the people has at least to be confronted with a plurality of choices, the 'yes/no' alternative on which the referendum is founded provides populists with the opportunity to mobilise the electorate against a single target.

## The Referendum in a Constitutional Democracy

Debates over the referendum's function in a liberal democracy go back to the nineteenth century, and leading scholars such as Dicey, Carré de Malberg and Friedrich, credited the referendum with the beneficial effect of correcting the absolutism of representative democracy or of partisan politics. According to Albert Venn Dicey (1835–1922), the referendum was 'the only check on the predominance of party which is at the same time democratic and conservative', since it would make 'democracy a check on party tyranny', without undermining the system of

[28] O Cramme, 'The Worrying Inevitability of EU Intergovernmentalism' *Policy Network* (May 2012).

representative government which 'appears to be an essential characteristic of a civilized and progressive state'.[29] Such assumptions presupposed that the referendum was to have a purely negative effect, notwithstanding the French tradition of plebiscites, in which both Napoleon Bonaparte and Napoleon III used referendums 'from above' to acquire popular legitimacy: 'Dicey was at pains to show that the intention as well the consequence of the referendum was purely conservative'.[30] This was even more true for the French Raymond Carré de Malberg (1861–1935), who was however deeply involved in the question of how to limit the 'absolute parliamentarism' of the Third Republic which he considered a 'degenerescence' of national sovereignty. The referendum appeared to him as a way of giving the people a chance of representing the nation, with a view to counterweighting the parliamentary assembly's dominance.[31] In a different context, Carl J Friedrich (1901–84) conceived the referendum as 'a genuine adjustment for modern constitutionalism', provided it was used only 'from time to time' and 'circumscribed by constitutional provisions guaranteeing a free choice to the electorate'.[32]

Post-totalitarian constitutional assemblies oriented their choice according to the perception of the recent past of the country. While most constitutions make provision for holding a referendum within the limits recommended by Friedrich, the German Basic Law does not allow for it at the federal level due to the fear of manipulation of the people that this might engender. The French Fifth Republic's Constitution gives the President the power to call for a referendum in case of emergency or regarding adhesion to international treaties, while in most countries the referendum can be initiated not only by public authorities but also by a certain portion of the electorate.

For a long while, in spite of the extreme variety of forms that it can take,[33] the referendum was not believed to contradict the basic assumption that, under post-totalitarian constitutions, no organ, including the people, has an existence distinct from or prior to the constitution: it is the latter that constitutes whichever entity as an organ. No organ could therefore be called to exercise constituent powers, and could thus be considered as the ultimate possessor of sovereignty. Under these constitutions, a referendum is usually provided for only with the negative effect of repealing a law, or as part of a constitutional amendment procedure. Therefore, 'the people' could not exert sovereign powers through the referendum, not only because it acts as a regularly constituted electorate, but also because it is not

[29] Quoted in M Qvortrup, *A Comparative Study of Referendums: Government by the People*, 2nd edn (Manchester, Manchester University Press, 2005) 47.

[30] Qvortrup, above n 29, 50.

[31] R Carré de Malberg, 'Considérations théoriques sur la question de la combinaison du référendum avec le parlementarisme' [1931] *Annuaire de l'Institut International de Droit Public* 268, 272.

[32] CJ Friedrich, *Constitutional Government and Democracy* (Boston, MA, Ginn, 1950) 571.

[33] L Morel, 'Referendum' in M Rosenfeld and A Sajo (eds), *The Oxford Handbook of Comparative Constitutional Law* (Oxford, Oxford University Press, 2012) 508.

allowed to take a decision in positive terms, namely to exercise a power lying at the core of the sovereignty concept.

Notwithstanding this conventional opinion, the referendum maintains a structural ambivalence. Someone, according to the legal provisions and/or to the circumstances, might succeed in calling a referendum on a single given issue with the intention of giving the people the opportunity to exercise a constituent power, or at least leaving room for controversy as to the extent to which popular sovereignty might prevail over parliamentary power. National referendums on the EU frequently fall under such category, irrespective of whether they are inserted within a treaty-ratification procedure. Legal issues affecting the popular sovereignty versus parliamentary sovereignty dilemma may follow from time to time in the countries concerned, without questioning however the constitutional order as such. Which kind of challenge, then, are these referendums likely to pose to constitutional democracy? And is such a challenge somewhat connected with the populist rise?

## Why National Referendums on EU Issues Concurred in Structuring the Populist Version of 'the People'

The referendums for the ratification of the 1992 Maastricht Treaty and of the 2001 Nice Treaty already demonstrated the remoteness of the EU from huge sectors of the electorate, if not their hostility to it, and, conversely, that national governments were 'not fully equipped to "sell" integration treaties in referendums'.[34] Nonetheless, the construction of 'a people' against the 'external threat' of the EU was not mature yet. In France it became so in 2005, when President Jacques Chirac announced a referendum for the ratification of the EU Constitutional Treaty in the typical plebiscitarian attitude that characterised De Gaulle towards referendums.[35] The resulting 'no' majority was largely composed of those who had lost confidence in traditional political parties, were pessimistic as to their future,[36] and could in the meanwhile identify themselves as a concrete 'people' through the referendum. Paradoxically, it was therefore the presidential use of the referendum, not a populist design, that put the premises for such identification. The same occurred with the 2016 referendum on 'Brexit'. It was the Prime Minister David Cameron who

[34] M Shu, 'Referendums and the Political Constitutionalisation of the EU' (2008) 14 *European Law Journal* 423, 441. See also S Binzer Hobolt, *Europe in Question. Referendums on European Integration* (Oxford, Oxford University Press, 2009) 161 ff; and S Tierney, *Constitutional Referendums. The Theory and Practice of Republican Deliberation* (Oxford, Oxford University Press, 2012).

[35] C Mazzucelli, 'The French Rejection of the European Constitutional Treaty: Two-level Games Perspective' in F Laursen (ed), *The Rise and Fall of the EU's Constitutional Treaty* (Leiden, Nijhoff, 2008) 174, 177.

[36] R Dehousse, 'The Unmaking of a Constitution: Lessons from the European Referenda' (2006) 13 *Constellations* 151, 156.

decided to announce it with a view to neutralise UKIP's pressure in favour of withdrawal from the EU, notwithstanding the fact that the UK was already believed as one of the most important locations of the populist *Zeitgeist* against European integration.[37] In this sense, the 'return to the national State' was perceived as definitive. The construction of a concrete 'people' in the public's imagination was indeed the unintended consequence of a referendum's announcement that was conceived from above. But it was also fuelled by the management of the campaign from both sides.

These contradictions were already discernible in the French referendum on the 2004 EU Constitutional Treaty. It was composed of more than 400 articles, most of which reproduced the EC Treaty's rules on the European market in force since 1957. But when the French government sent every citizen a copy of the Treaty, without giving an explanation of its content, the 'No' campaign depicted that text as representing the triumph of Anglo-Saxon economic liberalism over a French-inspired 'social Europe'. Similarly, in the 2016 UK referendum 'The Remain campaign was marked by the low key and selective presentation of the case for UK membership; the Leave campaign included an assortment of lies, half-truths and misinformation'.[38]

These attitudes characterise each camp wherever a debate is open on the issue. Advocates of EU integration propose reasonable arguments in a defensive tone, whereas opponents boldly claim their conviction without proving it, if not denying well-ascertained facts. These tones reveal the strength of the populist discourse on 'Europe' in the public sphere. Vis-a-vis the rarefied atmosphere of the EU locations, and the growing awareness of the national governments' involvement in the EU political decision-making, populists appear genuine, even if they are not, and supporters of the EU integration appear to the contrary compromised by these elements, even when their arguments are well founded.

The referendums on EU issues have thus given populists a good opportunity for 'creating a people'; both because, contrary to the elections, referendums are structured on a yes/no alternative, and because the EU can easily be presented as an external threat against which the 'people' need to react.

## What Kind of 'People' are thus Created?

As is correctly observed, although populists do not seek to actualise totalitarian practices as we know them from twentieth-century history, their claim to be the sole legitimate representative of the authentic people contains an affinity with the

[37] B Wellings and E Vines, 'Populism and Sovereignty: The EU Act and the In-Out Referendum, 2010–2015' (2015) 69 *Parliamentary Affairs* 309.

[38] AW Bradley, 'Pressures on a Historical Constitution: The Brexit Decision in the UK Supreme Court' (2017) 1 *Diritto pubblico* 3, 8.

totalitarian image of a pre-procedural people, as represented by a party or a single leader seeking to occupy democracy's empty space of power.[39]

Totalitarianism succeeded in constructing a concrete and fixed image of people vis-a-vis the abstractedness that in the nineteenth century characterised the concept of nation in the tradition républicaine or the Rechtsstaat. The point is that, unlike the absolutist or the authoritarian regimes of the past, which confined themselves to the repression of dissent, totalitarian regimes needed active consent from the people, not least because universal suffrage had brought large sectors of the population into the public sphere, *qua* electorate. Such consent was obtained not only through a system of police-controlled terror, and the creation of a single mass party, hierarchically organised and closely interwoven with the state bureaucracy. It was also reached through massive propaganda, whose novel technological devices were for the first time in history put at the disposal of political power. Schmitt's emphasis on 'a turn towards the concrete'[40] went in the same direction. While attacking the 'abstractedness', or 'formalism', of the Rechtsstaat's legacy, he assumed that concepts such as political representation or separation of powers amounted to empty formulae wherever the state resulted from 'the self-organisation of society', and political parties carved up the state through their representatives in Parliament.[41] Accordingly, he denounced the failure of liberal democracy on the presumption that 'the modern mass democracy attempts to realise an identity of governed and governing, and thus it confronts parliament as an inconceivable and outmoded institution'.[42]

Although populists of our time do not tend to renew totalitarian practices, their idea of 'people' echoes the totalitarian one in its reference to a fixed and concrete image, consisting of ideals and interests that can be simply mirrored, rather than politically interpreted. Democratic politics, on the contrary, depend on the invocation of a bounded 'We': its boundaries 'are not drawn once and for all, its identity is never fixed, the self of self-legislation remains to be formed by and in the legislation it gives itself. The legal institutionalisation of sensitivity to this dialectic can be found in constitutional democracy's insistence on both majority rule and rights of minorities'. The latter, in particular, provides minorities with 'the opportunity to defer any fixation of the identity of the people'.[43]

It is worth adding that constitutional democracies were founded and flourished on the understanding that free elections tie in with the rule of law and the safeguard of fundamental rights. Outside the perimeter of what has traditionally been labelled a 'violation of civil liberties' lie further threats to constitutional

[39] Müller, '"The People Must be Extracted from Within the People": Reflections on Populism', above n 19.

[40] C Schmitt, *On the Three Types of Juristic Thought* (1934) (Westport, CT, Praeger, 2004) 25.

[41] C Schmitt, 'The Way to the Total State (1931)' in C Schmitt, *Four Essays* (Washington DC, Plutarch Press, 1999) 37.

[42] C Schmitt, *The Crisis of Parliamentary Democracy* (1923) (Cambridge, MA, MIT Press, 1988) 15.

[43] L Corrias, 'Populism in a Constitutional Key: Constituent Power, Popular Sovereignty and Constitutional Identity' (2016) 12 *European Constitutional Law Review* 6, 24.

democracy. Phenomena such as the virtual monopoly of the media by governing parties through patronage deals or proxy arrangements, or the disparity of resources between incumbents and the opposition created by state/party/business ties, are likely not to be framed as civil liberties violations (as the closure of newspapers would be for example). And yet such uses of political power constitute an infringement of citizens' political rights, the exercise of which is necessary for free elections.[44]

The concept of democracy emerging from the practice and theory of constitutional democracy is thus more demanding than the sole electoral competition, both because it is referred to a people whose identity is dynamic and political, and because it is intrinsically connected with the rule of law and the safeguard of fundamental rights, and such connection is believed to guarantee and further pursue equality among citizens through time. Therefore, the fact that in constitutional democracies no organ, including the people, could be called to exercise a constituent power, needs to be distinguished from the purposes which such organization is believed to attain *ex parte populi*, including equality among citizens through time.

## Populism as 'Democratic Illiberalism': A Critique

It is sometimes assumed that '[t]o be classified as populist, a party must display two antithetical characteristics. It must harbor an allegiance to democracy, and it also must endorse illiberal tactics': it must 'take part in competitive elections and ... offer allegiance to representative pluralist democracy', and, at the same time, it must be 'prone to intolerance of minorities, impatient with institutional legalities, and inclined toward raw majoritarianism'.[45] But how long could a party preserve such contradictory elements? And could populists be credited with the attitude of offering 'allegiance to representative pluralist democracy'? Respect for the representative system, which they undoubtedly exhibit, is something different from harbouring an allegiance to pluralist democracy, that runs counter to the main populist claim of expressing the people's will.

These objections might partially be extended to the fortunate formula of 'illiberal democracy', that was tentatively proposed to designate regimes which could be said to stand at some point between constitutional democracy and totalitarianism. In 1997 it had been noted that many countries 'are settling into a form of government that mixes a substantial degree of democracy with a substantial degree

[44] S Levitsky and LA Way, *Competitive Authoritarianism: Hybrid Regimes after the Cold War* (Cambridge, Cambridge University Press, 2010) 6.

[45] TS Pappas, 'Distinguishing Liberal Democracy's Challengers' (2016) 27(4) *Journal of Democracy* 22, 29 ff.

of illiberalism', with the implication that 'Illiberal democracies gain legitimacy, and thus strength, from the fact that they are reasonably democratic'.[46]

What the formula implies is that the holding of elections is sufficient to qualify a certain system as democratic. Fundamentally, it rests on the assumption that the Schumpeterian view of democracy as an electoral competition aimed at selecting governmental authorities also applies to constitutional democracies. However, as we have seen, there is much more to the structure of a democracy in the constitutional system than mere electoral competition.

In light of the above, it may be argued that the 'illiberal democracy' formula is a misnomer, suggesting that the regimes it designates are substantially democratic, although illiberal. They should rather be regarded as a type of illiberal regime that differs in certain respects from the totalitarian. European countries led by populist governments should fall under that category.[47]

## Is there a Populist Constitutional Theory?

A further thesis is that the populist emphasis on the principle of popular sovereignty reflects a constitutional theory, recalling continental Europe's revolutionary legacy founded on the constituent power's absolute sovereignty, with the related suspicion for the rule of law, especially in its institutional implication of preserving the independence of the judiciary, and rejection of an individualistic vision of society. Similarly, populists engage in projecting constitutional reforms aimed at asserting the primacy of the people's political will over different sources of legitimacy.[48]

It should first be objected that the categories forged by the revolutionary tradition reflect an artificial paradigm: even the idea that the collectivity comes prior to the individual lies on the presumption that the former is a social construction, not a natural element. For contemporary populism it is instead an allegedly natural community, 'the people', that takes centre stage. Rather than with the revolutionary legacy, populism reveals here a strong resemblance with the organicism that permeated the European cultural mainstream at the end of the nineteenth century and, on the other hand, with the above-mentioned Schmittian 'turn towards the concrete'. Even these similiarities however appear hardly sufficient for crediting populists with a constitutional theory.

[46] F Zakaria, 'The Rise of Illiberal Democracy' (1997) 76(6) *Foreign Affairs* 16, 22.

[47] See, eg, KL Scheppele, 'Understanding Hungary's Constitutional Revolution' in A von Bogdandy and P Sonnevend (eds), *Constitutional Crisis in the European Constitutional Area. Theory, Law and Politics in Hungary and Romania* (Oxford, Hart Publishing, 2015); and C Pinelli, 'Populism and Illiberal Democracies: The Hungarian Case' in Z Szente, F Mandak and F Mejes (eds), *Challenges and Pitfalls in the Recent Hungarian Constitutional Developments. Discussing the New Hungarian Fundamental Law* (Budapest, L'Harmattan, 2015).

[48] P Blokker, 'Populist Constitutionalism' (*Verfassungsblog.de*, May 2017); and Corrias, above n 43, 16 ff.

Nor does such a theory emerge from the populists' engagement in constitutional reform. Unlike the constitutional texts reflecting the revolutionary tradition, whose declared purpose was to build an entirely new world, those approved by populist majorities tend to insert some reference to the country's national, or ethnic, or religious identity in the frame of the previous constitutions. Their approach to the liberal pillar of constitutional democracy is pragmatic as well. The authors of these texts do not need to abolish the constitutional courts, or alter the provisions regarding the rule of law and fundamental rights; they prefer to undermine by other means (eg, court-packing plans, ad hoc changes of the judges' age of retirement) the counter-majoritarian function of constitutional courts and the independence of the judiciary. This is typically the case in Hungary, while the Polish government's attitude appears far less sophisticated, experienced in a series of direct violations of the Constitution without bothering to change its provisions according to the new regime's spirit.

In Italy, where a populist government has been in charge since 2018, constitutional change might take a different direction. The parliamentary majority is composed of two parties, the Lega and the Five Star Movement, expressing different versions of populism. While the former is explicitly inspired by the Hungarian or the Russian model, the Five Star Movement's version is founded on the claim of the parliamentary open mandate's obsolescence vis-a-vis the new possibilities of direct democracy afforded by the web, where the Movement acquired massive success before standing for election. MPs are in this view merely spokespersons of citizens participating in politics through the web. According to the parliamentary group's internal regulations, MPs expelled or withdrawing from the Movement have to pay a penalty of 100,000 euro to the party. However, it is the party, not the citizens, that decides to expel an MP in cases of political dissent. These regulations thus contrast strikingly with the assumption that MPs are mere spokespersons of citizens and, on the other hand, with Article 67 of the Italian Constitution, that prohibits the MPs' binding mandate. The Five Star Movement has even proposed the abolition of this rule, although for the moment only informally. Its ideology might then consist in a sort of 'post-modern populism',[49] a subtle, and particularly dangerous, way of collecting popular discontent with political representation.

Overall, these elements may suffice to demonstrate that contemporary populism is unlikely to afford a constitutional theory of its own. Its attack on constitutional democracy does not result in restoring the people to the constituent power's exertion, in the sense of the revolutionary tradition. The different parties or movements that exhibit a populist inspiration tend rather to an oversimplification of the democratic process, and follow a pragmatic approach in adapting their conduct to the national contexts, which is one key of their respective electoral success.

[49] ME Lanzone, 'The "Post-Modern" Populism in Italy: The Case of the Five Star Movement' in D Woods and B Wejnert (eds), *The Many Faces of Populism: Current Perspectives* (Bingley, Emerald Publishing, 2014).

On the other hand, the populist challenge consists in denouncing 'the failure of constitutional democracies to be consistent with its promises of guaranteeing that all citizens enjoy an equal political power and public equality is the norm leading institutions, politicians, and citizens'.[50]

## Reactions to the Populist Challenge

Populist parties, we have seen, regularly take part in elections and respect formally the representative system, without harbouring an allegiance to pluralist democracy. In particular, they despise political debate, and deny the public the possibility of checking the credibility of their own proposals. Even while ruling a country populists feel relieved of the burden of answering questions such as whether their immigration policy really meets security needs, or why, in spite of their attacks on the EU, they refrain from calling a national referendum for withdrawal from the EU. The fact that, particularly in Hungary and Poland, economic growth has been strongly driven by the European cohesion funds may shed light on such a contradiction.

The point is that these questions are not even posed in the public debate. The parliamentary opposition, usually led by parties that are virtually attached to the values of constitutional democracy as well as to those of the EU, appears mute in this respect, and at any rate unable to force populists in giving account of their policies before the electorate. The issue is crucial for an understanding of how constitutional democracies are reacting, and of how they should react, to the populist challenge.

Can populism be contrasted by legal means? Even in Germany, whose Basic Law allows the Federal Constitutional Court to declare the dissolution of any political party that seeks to undermine or abolish the free and democratic order or to endanger its existence (Article 21 BL), the Court has recently refrained from adopting such a measure against an ultranationalist party like the NPD,[51] thus declining 'to provide further fodder for the populists' familiar narrative that the establishment systematically suppresses the voice of "the people"'.[52] As has been significantly affirmed, reactions to the populist challenge should derive primarily from the political process itself.[53]

[50] R Bellamy and W Merkel et al, 'Challenges of Inequality to Democracy' in IPSP (ed), *Rethinking Society for the 21st Century* (Cambridge, Cambridge University Press, 2018) 68.

[51] Federal Constitutional Court, 17 January 2017, *Neue Juristische Wochenschrift* 611, on which see L Schuldt, 'Mixed Signals of Europeanization: Revisiting the NPD Decision in Light of the European Court of Human Rights' Jurisprudence' (2018) 19 *German Law Journal* 817.

[52] A Pirang, 'Renaissance of Militant Democracy?', available at: www.lawfareblog.com, 27 March 2017.

[53] A Voßkuhle, 'Demokratie und Populism' (2018) 57 *Der Staat*, 119, 120, 134.

A different kind of response to populism might be caught in EU law. Article 7 TEU entrusts the European Council, composed of the Heads of State or Government of the EU Member States, with the powers of ascertaining the existence of systemic violations by a Member State of the 'common values' enumerated in Article 2 TEU, including 'the rule of law and respect for human rights', and of adopting a series of related measures that can go to the point of suspending the voting rights of the representative of that Member State.[54] These measures are not meant to outlaw populist governments as such. Rather, they aim at sanctioning systemic breaches of the EU 'common values' that might recur within a Member State, irrespective of the contingent political colour of its government. Their nature is thus legal, not political, although the enforcement of Article 7 TEU's mechanisms rests entirely in the hands of national governments. Against such a background, the European Council's inertia vis-a-vis what has been called 'the purposeful destruction of the rule of law inside EU member states',[55] departing from Hungary and Poland, reflects partisan tactics that wipes out both the maintenance and the credibility of the 'common values'.

The extreme weakness of traditional parties in dealing with the issue is confirmed at the domestic scale. These parties differ from the populist ones because of their historical connection with constitutional democracy, not because of their current capacity to give reasons for their policies to the electorate or to shape a common future. Both camps pay more attention to opinion polls and media-driven perceptions than to policies. The crisis of political representation is thus leading to the question of 'Why should we be represented?' irrespective of each camp's legacy.

The difference between these camps lies rather in the fact that it is traditional parties, as well as national governments, that appear responsible for the inadequate responses to the basic needs of their electors due, inter alia, to EU failures, together with the holes and the fictions affecting the narrative of the European crisis. Voters feel betrayed by traditional parties, and correspondingly tend to credit populists with a genuine expression of protest: the latter do not have to bother with matching their discourse to factual elements, nor to account for the consequences of their proposals. Populists are then, in turn, authorised to lie.

## In a World of Fictions?

To speak the truth is a fundamental duty of democratic politics, being required for ensuring mutual trust between representatives and citizens.[56] When it is

[54] For further references see C Pinelli, 'Protecting the Fundamentals. Article 7 of the Treaty on European Union and Beyond', FEPS Jurists Network, 25 September 2012.

[55] J-W Müller, 'Reflections on Europe's "Rule of Law Crises"' in PF Kjaer and N Olson (eds), *Critical Theories of Crisis in Europe. From Weimar to the Euro* (London, Rowman & Littlefield, 2016) 162.

[56] P Rosanvallon, *Le bon gouvernement* (Paris, Seuil, 2015) 327 ff.

ostensibly neglected by the former, and the public even loses sight of its value, democracy is deeply eroded from within. There is ground for assuming that this is the case in contemporary democracies.

It is against such a background that we should evaluate the fact that populist parties confine themselves to respect for the formal rules of the representative system. These are indeed poor democratic credentials, and yet appear a symptom of a broader malaise of constitutional democracy. A malaise that might transform it into a world of fictions, where power can be acquired and preserved in the people's name without giving account of how it is effectively exerted. My intention, however, was not to predict events. It was to afford an insight into how the populist rise, together with the elements that have contributed to it such as popular discontent with politics and with the EU, may transform the scenario of what can still be called constitutional democracy in most parts of Europe.

# 3

# The 'Democratic Deficits' of the US and the EU Compared

R DANIEL KELEMEN

## Introduction

Democracy – 'government of the people, for the people, by the people' as Abraham Lincoln put it – is an ideal to which all democracies may aspire, but which none can fully achieve in practice. All real existing democracies are imperfect, but they are imperfect in different ways and some are more imperfect than others. An extensive literature has critiqued the EU's democratic shortcomings – its so-called 'democratic deficit'. However, most debates about the EU's supposed 'democratic deficit' have suffered from a lack of comparative perspective. Too often critics have compared the EU to an abstract ideal of democracy, rather than to the flawed democracies of the real world. The parochialism of these debates has led many EU scholars to make major mistakes in assessing democracy in the EU, overestimating some democratic deficits and underestimating others. First, they have tended to overstate the democratic shortcomings of EU-level institutions. When compared with real world democracies, rather than to the ideal of a perfect democracy, the supposed democratic deficits of EU institutions in Brussels, Strasbourg and Luxembourg seem grossly exaggerated. Second, scholars and policy-makers have tended to underestimate the threats posed by democratic deficits at the national level in EU Member State governments. Comparative analysis suggests that in large, diverse, federal and quasi-federal polities like the EU, some of the greatest threats to democracy are likely to come not from the federal centre but from the emergence of autocratic regimes at the Member State level.

This chapter aims to address these shortcomings in the literature through a comparison of democratic deficits in the US and the EU. The US and the EU are suitable for comparison because of their many institutional similarities as political systems.[1] But the real proof of the utility of the comparison comes in the insights it

[1] The US and EU are two of the three instances (the other being Switzerland) of 'coming-together federalism' in modern history, and the only two that have sought to construct democratic governance

reveals. First, comparative analysis of the EU and the US demonstrates that while EU-level democracy has flaws, they are hardly any worse than those of the US. Second, the comparison sheds light on why democratic polities like the US and EU often tolerate autocratic member states and how efforts to 'democratise' politics at the federal level may, ironically, increase incentives for federal politicians to tolerate state autocracies.

The remainder of this chapter is divided into four sections. The first section clarifies the central concepts used in the analysis. The second section compares democratic deficits in the US and the EU, highlighting the fact that while EU-level democracy certainly has shortcomings, they do not appear much worse than those found in the US. The third section explores the dynamics of subnational authoritarianism, explaining how partisan politics leads broadly democratic federations like the US and EU to tolerate authoritarian governments in some member states of their unions. The fourth section concludes.

## Democracy, Democratic Deficits and Hybrid Regimes

Before we can compare the democratic deficits of the US and EU, some clarification of concepts is necessary – above all the concepts of democracy, competitive authoritarianism and regime juxtaposition. Though there are of course many definitions of democracy, most scholars have built on Schumpeter and Dahl's work to converge around a 'procedural minimum' definition, which – as Levitsky and Way[2] explain, requires,

> (1) free, fair, and competitive elections; (2) full adult suffrage; (3) broad protection of civil liberties, including freedom of speech, press, and association; and (4) the absence of nonelected 'tutelary' authorities (eg, militaries, monarchies, or religious bodies) that limit elected officials' power to govern.[3]

To put it even more succinctly, at minimum, democracy is a political system in which leaders are chosen through regular, free and fair elections based on near universal adult suffrage. Crucially, to satisfy the criteria of 'free and fair elections,' a democracy must guarantee those fundamental rights – such as freedoms of

at a continental scale out of previously autonomous jurisdictions. For other EU–US comparisons concerning the democratic deficit see T Zweifel, 'Who is Without Sin Cast the First Stone: The EU's Democratic Deficit in Comparison' (2002) 9 *Journal of European Public Policy* 812; and C Crombez, 'The Democratic Deficit in the European Union: Much Ado about Nothing?' (2003) 4 *European Union Politics* 101.

[2] S Levitsky and L Way, *Competitive Authoritarianism* (New York, Cambridge University Press, 2010) 5–6.

[3] Also see RA Dahl, *Polyarchy: Participation and Opposition* (New Haven, CT, Yale University Press, 1971); P Schmitter and T Karl, 'What Democracy Is … and Is Not' (1991) 2(3) *Journal of Democracy* 75; and L Diamond, *Developing Democracy* (Baltimore, MD, Johns Hopkins University Press, 1999) 7–1[illegible]

speech, assembly and the press, and minority rights – that are necessary for fair elections. And to guarantee those rights, a democracy must have institutions – such as an independent judiciary – that safeguard the rule of law. In other words, only a liberal democracy can be a real democracy.

Throughout history, actual democracies have fallen short of this ideal in various ways. In some cases, electoral rules or small-scale electoral fraud have meant that elections were 'free' but not entirely fair. In other cases – and this was particularly true until recent decades – restrictions on the franchise (ie, on the basis of race, gender or wealth) violated the universal suffrage criteria. Thus arguably no country was a democracy until it gave women the right to vote (which in Switzerland was not until as late as 1971). Likewise, given the historic restrictions on the voting rights of African Americans, 'liberal democracy – with full adult suffrage and broad protection of civil and political liberties – is a relatively recent development in the US. By contemporary standards, the country became fully democratic only in the 1970s'.[4]

While recognising that all democracies are imperfect and fall short of democratic ideals in various ways, it is still crucial to distinguish flawed democracies from authoritarian regimes. A challenge in distinguishing democracies from non-democracies is that many contemporary authoritarian regimes seek to cloak themselves in some of the garb of democratic institutions to conceal their true character. Most of today's authoritarian regimes are not totalitarian dictatorships that prohibit elections, and rule with an iron fist. Much more commonly, we find systems of 'competitive authoritarianism'. As Levitsky and Way explain:

> In competitive authoritarian regimes, formal democratic institutions are widely viewed as the principal means of obtaining and exercising political authority. Incumbents violate those rules so often and to such an extent, however, that the regime fails to meet conventional minimum standards for democracy … Although elections are regularly held and are generally free of massive fraud, incumbents routinely abuse state resources, deny the opposition adequate media coverage, harass opposition candidates and their supporters, and in some cases manipulate electoral results. Journalists, opposition politicians, and other government critics may be spied on, threatened, harassed, or arrested.[5]

Crucially, while such regimes hold generally free elections, these are so unfair that the regimes should not be categorised as democratic.

The distinctions between democracy and non-democracy are further muddled by the growing popularity of the term 'illiberal democracy'. Fareed Zakaria coined the term 20 years ago to describe polities that, as he understood it, held free and fair elections, but did not guarantee the rule of law and the protection of

[4] R Mickey, S Levitsky and L Way, 'Is America Still Safe for Democracy?' (2017) 96(3) *Foreign Affairs* 22.

[5] S Levitsky and L Way, 'The Rise of Competitive Authoritarianism' (2002) 13(2) *Journal of Democracy* 52.

'basic liberties of speech, assembly, religion, and property'.[6] However, 'illiberal democracy' is a misnomer and a category error.[7] The concept is inherently flawed, because if fundamental rights to speech, assembly and association – rights that are crucial to the democratic process – are not guaranteed, then elections by definition cannot be fair. 'Illiberal democracy' is thus a contradiction in terms, and it inappropriately attaches (a qualified version of) the appellation democracy to what political scientists more accurately conceptualise as competitive authoritarianism.[8] It is no coincidence that the current crop of autocrats have seized on the term 'illiberalism' – for instance with Orbán in 2014 proudly declaring his intention to build an illiberal state with Russia and China as models.[9] The term 'illiberal democracy' serves these leaders well, as it disguises the true nature of their autocratic regimes and enables them to claim that they are democrats, simply ones who reject certain 'liberal' values.

Finally, when studying democracy and its deficits in federal-type polities such as the US or EU, one must take into account the concept of 'regime juxtaposition' or 'subnational authoritarianism'.[10] Federal polities may be subject to a particular form of democratic deficit in which they may be broadly democratic at the federal level of governance, while containing state-level regimes that are authoritarian.[11] Indeed, as discussed below, scholars of comparative politics show that such 'regime juxtaposition' is very common. The literature on regime juxtaposition also sheds light on what type of authoritarian state governments are likely to emerge in the context of democratic federations: because the democratic federation places some outer limits on the acceptable level of repression by state-level autocrats, these state governments are much more likely to be competitive authoritarian regimes or other forms of soft autocracy than to be fully authoritarian, dictatorial regimes. These soft-authoritarian regimes will typically not arrest political opponents or journalists and will not resort to force (or only very sparingly) to perpetuate their rule. Rather, they will, as political scientist Carlos Gervasoni puts it,

> resort to subtle means to restrict democracy. Elections are held and ballots are counted fairly, but incumbents massively outspend challengers; the local media are formally

[6] F Zakaria, 'The Rise of Illiberal Democracy' (1997) 76(6) *Foreign Affairs* 22.

[7] JW Müller, 'The Problem with Illiberal Democracy' (2016) *Project Syndicate*, 21 January, available at: www.project-syndicate.org/commentary/the-problem-with-illiberal-democracy-by-jan-werner-mueller-2016-01?barrier=accessreg.

[8] Levitsky and Way, *Competitive Authoritarianism*, above n 2; and Levitsky and Way, 'The Rise of Competitive Authoritarianism', above n 5.

[9] Z Simon, 'Orban Says he Seeks to End Liberal Democracy in Hungary' *Bloomberg* (28 July 2014), available at: www.bloomberg.com/news/articles/2014-07-28/orban-says-he-seeks-to-end-liberal-democracy-in-hungary.

[10] E Gibson, 'Boundary Control: Subnational Authoritarianism in Democratic Countries' (2005) 58 *World Politics* 101.

[11] ibid 107. In principle the inverse is also true: namely that a federation could be authoritarian at the federal level while some state governments were democracies. In practice, however, it is unlikely that a consolidated autocratic regime at the federal level would tolerate real democracy at the state level. Likewise, as discussed below, a leader trying to roll back democracy at the federal level in a federal polity might be thwarted by powerful democratic actors at the state level.

> independent but are bought off to bias coverage in favor of the ruling party; dissidents are not jailed, just excluded from coveted public jobs.[12]

Often, to minimise conflict with the federal legal system, such state-level regimes may deploy the techniques of 'autocratic legalism' – abusing ostensibly legal mechanisms to disempower opponents and critics and to wield autocratic power.[13] With these central concepts set out clearly, we can now turn to an assessment of democratic deficits at the federal and state level in the EU and US.

## Democratic Deficits at the Federal Level

A voluminous literature argues that the EU suffers from a grave democratic deficit. In short, the bill of indictment of EU democracy emerging from this literature can be summarised as follows. First, the EU lacks the common public sphere and a 'demos' (people) characteristic of national democracies.[14] Lacking a demos, the EU cannot be a democracy. Second, too much policy-making authority in the EU lies in the hands of unaccountable executive actors – either unelected Commission officials or national government ministers acting in the Council behind closed doors and beyond the scrutiny of their national parliaments. Third, the EU's main representative institution, the European Parliament, is too distant from its citizens. As a result, citizens feel disengaged and turnout in European Parliament elections is low and has declined steadily over the past four decades. Finally, and most importantly, taking the overall structure of the EU into consideration, European citizens do not have the sense that they can change the direction of EU policy and hold EU policy-makers accountable at the ballot box through a truly 'European' election.[15]

Without question, such critiques point to real shortcomings of EU democracy. That being said, critiques of the EU's democratic deficit have always been

[12] C Gervasoni, 'A Rentier Theory of Subnational Regimes' (2010) 62 *World Politics* 302.

[13] J Corrales, 'Autocratic Legalism in Venezuela' (2015) 26(2) *Journal of Democracy* 37; KL Scheppele, 'Autocratic Legalism' (2018) 85 *University of Chicago Law Review* 545.

[14] For a classic debate on this theme, see D Grimm, 'Does Europe Need a Constitution?' (1995) 1 *European Law Journal* 282; J Habermas, 'Remarks on Dieter Grimm's "Does Europe Need a Constitution?"' (1995) 1 *European Law Journal* 303; and JHH Weiler, 'European Democracy and its Critique' (1996) 18 *West European Politics* 4. Also, see Kalypso Nicolaides who emphasises that the EU has a plurality of demoi, rather than a single demos; K Nicolaides, 'European Democracy and its Crisis' (2013) 51 *Journal of Common Market Studies* 351.

[15] The literature on the democratic deficit in the EU is too vast to summarise here. For exemplary works providing overviews of core arguments concerning the EU's democratic deficit see for instance A Føllesdal and S Hix, 'Why There is a Democratic Deficit in the EU: A Response to Majone and Moravcsik' (2006) 44 *Journal of Common Market Studies* 533; S Hix, *What's Wrong with the European Union and How to Fix it* (Cambridge, Polity Press, 2008); C Lord, *A Democratic Audit of the European Union* (Basingstoke, Palgrave MacMillan, 2004); VA Schmidt, *Democracy in Europe* (Oxford, Oxford University Press, 2006); A Warleigh, *Democracy and the European Union* (London, Sage Publications, 2003); Weiler, above n 14.

exaggerated, in part because the EU has been held up for comparison against unrealistic ideals of democracy rather than real existing democracies and in part because many critics have misconstrued the nature of EU democracy. As Zweifel noted, the EU compares favourably to leading models of federal democracy (the US and Switzerland) on many major measures of democracy.[16] Before assessing the EU's alleged democratic deficits in detail, therefore, it is instructive, for comparative purposes, to consider some of the shortcomings of American democracy.[17] First, due to gerrymandering of congressional districts (along with the tendency of Democratic voters to concentrate in urban centres) and the structure of the Electoral College system, the outcome of American congressional and presidential elections does not necessarily reflect the expressed will of voting majorities (or pluralities for that matter). For instance, in the 2012 congressional election, Democratic candidates won a total of more than 1.4 million (1.4 per cent) more votes than Republicans, yet Republicans won a 33-seat majority in the House of Representatives. Similarly, in the 2016 presidential election, Hillary Clinton won more than 2.1 million more votes than Donald Trump, yet he won decisively in the Electoral College and became President.

Second, the US Senate is a profoundly undemocratic institution. The 39 million citizens who live in California are represented by two senators, while the 39 million citizens who live in America's 22 smallest states are represented by 44 senators. Though many legislatures in democracies have some degree of malapportionment that violates a strict reading of the one-person, one-vote principle, the degree of malapportionment in the US is shocking: for instance, today the ratio of representation of Wyoming residents to California residents is 66:1.[18] Given the distribution of Republican and Democratic voters, these discrepancies give a huge advantage to the Republican Party in national politics. Given the decisive role of the Senate in US legislative politics and given the Senate's supermajority requirements, small minorities can block policy change in the US. As it takes 61 votes to override a filibuster in the US Senate, 40 senators representing 20 states can block legislation. Taken together

[16] Zweifel, above n 1. Similarly see Crombez, above n 1, arguing that EU institutions are not necessarily less democratic than those in the US.

[17] For more detailed analyses of the democratic shortcomings of American institutions, see R Dahl, *How Democratic is the American Constitution?* (New Haven, CT, Yale University Press, 2003); S Levinson, *Our Undemocratic Constitution: Where the Constitution Goes Wrong* (New York, Oxford University Press, 2006); M Gilens and BI Page, 'Testing Theories of American Politics: Elites, Interest Groups and Average Americans' (2014) 12 *Perspectives on Politics* 564. On the risk of democracy giving way to autocracy in the US and the role of American institutions in that process, see S Levitsky and D Ziblatt, *How Democracies Die* (New York, Crown Publishers, 2018); and A Huq and T Ginsburg, 'How to Lose a Constitutional Democracy' (2018) 65 *UCLA Law Review* 78.

[18] The democratic deficit with respect to unrepresented territories of the US such as Puerto Rico and Washington DC is even more egregious. Puerto Rico has a population larger than 20 US states, and yet it has no representation in the US Congress – a fact that surely helps explain the lacklustre federal response as American citizens in Puerto Rico languished without access to electricity and running water in recent months.

the 40 senators representing the 20 least populous states, from Iowa down to Wyoming, have a total population that constitutes just over 11 per cent of the US population, but they can block policies that the other 89 per cent favour. Though that particular constellation is of course rare, it is very common for senators representing a minority of voters to block legislation favoured by a large majority. The problem appears likely to get worse over time with demographic shifts: a recent estimate suggested that by 2040 two-thirds of Americans will be represented by 30 per cent of the Senate.[19]

Taken together, such anti-democratic features of the US Constitution help explain why federal policies do not reflect the preferences of the majority of Americans on so many issues, and why citizens are so dissatisfied with their government's performance. As Yascha Mounk notes in an article provocatively titled 'America is not a Democracy':

> If [policy did reflect majority preferences], the country would look radically different: Marijuana would be legal and campaign contributions more tightly regulated; paid parental leave would be the law of the land and public colleges free; the minimum wage would be higher and gun control much stricter; abortions would be more accessible in the early stages of pregnancy and illegal in the third trimester.[20]

Likewise, these anti-democratic features of the American constitutional order help explain Gilens' and Page's finding that the views of ordinary citizens have 'virtually no independent effect at all' on policy outcomes.[21] This situation clearly frustrates voters, helping to explain why over the past decade only roughly 20 per cent or less of voters have approved of Congress' performance while roughly 80 per cent have disapproved,[22] and more generally why public confidence in American political institutions is so low.[23]

How undemocratic do the EU's institutions look in comparison? The EU's most powerful body, the Council, is hardly undemocratic as it is composed of elected governments. While critics may be right to complain that governments in the Council conduct their business in too much secrecy, this is less an indictment of the EU than it is an indictment of national parliamentary democracies, and the inability of most national parliaments to control the governments who are supposedly their agents. The European Parliament is composed of directly elected MEPs. Critics complain that citizens feel little sense of connection with the European Parliament and that voter turnout (at just over 42 per cent in the 2014 election) is low. That may be true, but again, this hardly distinguishes the EU from other established democratic polities such as, for instance, the US where turnout

[19] P Bump, 'By 2040, two-thirds of Americans will be represented by 30 percent of the Senate' *Washington Post* (28 November 2017).
[20] Y Mounk, 'America Is Not a Democracy' *The Atlantic* (March 2018).
[21] Gilens and Page, above n 17.
[22] See: news.gallup.com/poll/1600/congress-public.aspx.
[23] See for instance Gallup poll results indicating low levels of public confidence in Congress and the presidency, available at: news.gallup.com/poll/1597/confidence-institutions.aspx.

at the 2014 mid-term congressional elections was just over 36 per cent[24] – a full six points lower than in the European Parliament election. Likewise, many critics of EU democracy point to survey results finding (supposedly) little support for EU democracy. But such claims do not stand up to comparative scrutiny. For instance, 33 per cent of Europeans have a positive image of the European Parliament, while only 21 per cent have a negative image (with 42 per cent having a neutral image). Certainly, these are not great numbers, but the European Parliament clearly enjoys more support than the US Congress – of which between 75 and 80 per cent of Americans have disapproved in recent years.[25] Notably, EU institutions also enjoy – on average – greater trust than national institutions within the EU. According to the European Commission Standard Eurobarometer 87, 45 per cent of citizens tend to trust the European Parliament and 41 per cent trust the European Commission, while only 36 per cent trust their national parliaments and only 37 per cent trust their national governments.[26]

Until recently, it could fairly be pointed out that the EU's executive – the European Commission – lacked a clear democratic mandate in that it was composed not of elected officials but of bureaucrats appointed by (elected) national leaders. However, over the past decade the European Parliament has asserted greater and greater control over the selection of the Commission President – culminating in the 2014 *Spitzenkandidat* process and the (at least quasi) 'election' of Jean-Claude Juncker as Commission President.[27] Whatever one thinks of this new process,[28] it seems clear that the Parliament has succeeded in injecting a greater dose of democratic participation into the selection of the Commission presidency. The half-baked 'campaigns' and barely viewed presidential candidate debates of 2014

[24] The Editorial Board, 'The Worst Voter Turnout in 72 Years' *New York Times* (11 November 2014), available at: www.nytimes.com/2014/11/12/opinion/the-worst-voter-turnout-in-72-years.html.

[25] For recent Gallup polls on Americans' approval and disapproval of Congress see: news.gallup.com/poll/1600/congress-public.aspx.

[26] See European Commission, Standard Eurobarometer 87, May 2017, available at: ec.europa.eu/commfrontoce/publicopinion/index.cfm/Survey/getSurveyDetail/instruments/STANDARD/surveyKy/2142.

[27] For a review of the EP's efforts to gradually increase its control over the selection of the Commission President, see RD Kelemen, 'A President for the People' *Foreign Affairs* (30 June 2014), available at: www.foreignaffairs.com/articles/western-europe/2014-06-30/president-people.

[28] In the run up to the 2014 EP election, each major party group in the European Parliament named a candidate – a so-called *Spitzenkandidat* (top candidate) – for the presidency in advance of the election. The parties made it clear to the heads of state and government in the European Council that the only candidate they would endorse was the winning *Spitzenkandidat*. In effect, the Parliament sought to leverage its power (under Treaty of Lisbon, Art 17(7)) to approve the candidate for President in order to transform the Commission President into a kind of prime minister selected by the Parliament and serving with the backing of a parliamentary majority. As the Parliament tried to assert this new power, a battle ensued between it and reluctant Member States in the European Council – above all the UK. The Parliament argued that the *Spitzenkandidat* process would make the EU more democratic, critics argued the process was an illegitimate power grab by the Parliament. Ultimately, the European Parliament prevailed and a majority of heads of state and government voted to appoint Jean-Claude Juncker, the *Spitzenkandidat* of the winning European People's Party (EPP) as Commission President. For more detailed discussion of this battle, see Kelemen, 'A President for the People', above n 27.

may have been less than inspiring, but the process is likely to attract far greater attention in 2019 if member governments allow it to be repeated – as the European Parliament is insisting it will be.

The controversy surrounding the process of selecting – or electing – the Commission President brings us back to another misconception about EU democracy that has long distorted the democratic deficit debate. Many of the critiques of the inadequacy of electoral accountability in the EU misunderstand the character of EU democracy. Critics of past European Parliament elections have complained that the electoral outcomes have not changed the direction of EU politics in a way that voters could observe, and that therefore it appeared that little if anything was really at stake in the elections[29] – which depressed voter interest and turnout. Some such critics view the new *Spitzenkandidat* process as an opportunity for voters to elect a leader who will shift the partisan orientation of the EU's executive branch and thus change the direction of policy (which will in turn enhance voter engagement in EU politics and reduce the democratic deficit). However, this view seems to be based on a majoritarian, Westminster view of democracy, where a party that wins the most seats in the lower chamber of the legislature takes power and governs (typically in a single party government).

But the EU is not and will never be a Westminster system. Even more than the US (which combines elements of majoritarian and consensus democracy), the EU is a consensus democracy[30] that is based on dividing power between multiple institutions, encouraging a wide representation of diverse interests and building broad, multiparty coalitions to govern. Regardless of the partisan affiliation of the Commission President, as long as individual Member States (which will inevitably have governments representing a variety of party families) appoint the other members of the Commission, the EU's executive will remain a body with members representing multiple parties' views. As a result, it is unlikely to resemble a partisan government that pursues the clear partisan agenda of a parliamentary majority on the left or right, but instead will seek to develop policies based on a broad cross-party consensus.[31] Likewise, the Council of Ministers, which remains the most powerful legislative actor in the EU, represents a wide swathe of partisan views. Any sober assessment of EU democracy must get away from majoritarian, Westminster thinking and recognise that however democratic EU politics becomes, no single pan-European election will dramatically alter the direction of EU policies. Rather, the EU is and will remain a consensus democracy – based on compromise between a broad range of democratically elected representatives from national governments and the European Parliament.

[29] See Føllesdal and Hix, above n 15.

[30] A Lijphart, *Patterns of Democracy* (New Haven, CT, Yale University Press, 1999).

[31] If any national analogue for the Commission is appropriate, it would most likely be something akin to the multiparty Swiss collective executive (the Federal Council).

## Democratic Deficits at the State Level

Analysing EU democracy from a comparative perspective and considering the US experience suggests that EU scholars have been focusing their attention on the wrong democratic deficit. While most EU scholars have focused on the democratic deficit at the EU level, in fact the most profound threats to democracy in the EU stem from the democratic deficits of its Member States – as was long the case in the US. Indeed, US experience, along with that of many other federal systems, suggests that authoritarian regimes at the state level may persist for decades within otherwise broadly democratic federations. Moreover, political science literature on the US and other federal systems provides an explanation for the persistence of state-level authoritarian enclaves that can also explain the EU's failure to address recent episodes of democratic backsliding in EU Member States.

Scholars of American political development and comparative politics have explained how, in the context of multilevel, federal-type systems, partisan politics can help sustain autocratic regimes at the state level within otherwise democratic federations.[32] In such contexts, democratic leaders at the federal level may come to rely on authoritarian leaders at the state level to deliver votes to their federal level coalition. As Gibson explains, 'Authoritarian provincial political elites, with their abundant supplies of voters and legislators, can be important members of national [*aka federal level*] governing coalitions'.[33] So long as the local autocrat delivers needed votes in the federal legislature, federal leaders of their party or coalition will be inclined to overlook their authoritarian practices and to defend them against any federal interventions in the name of democracy that might threaten to dislodge them. For this reason, perversely, increasing democratisation at the federal level may help to entrench authoritarian rule at the state level.[34] Efforts to enhance partisan, democratic politics at the federal level may strengthen incentives for national political leaders to protect state-level autocrats who contribute needed votes to their national coalitions.

These dynamics played a pivotal role in sustaining authoritarian government in southern states after the Civil War. In short, the national Democratic Party shielded southern Democrats against federal intervention as they constructed authoritarian enclaves in southern states because they needed their votes to secure majorities in Congress and to elect presidents. As Mickey, Levitsky and Way put it:

> Beginning in the 1890s, after the Civil War and the failure of Reconstruction, Democratic politicians in each of the 11 states of the old Confederacy built single-party,

[32] As these scholars examine this phenomenon in states within national federations, they refer to it as 'subnational authoritarianism'. In the EU's supranational context, the equivalent is 'national authoritarianism' within a supranational polity.

[33] Gibson, 'Boundary Control: Subnational Authoritarianism in Democratic Countries', above n 10, 107.

[34] ibid; RD Kelemen, 'Europe's Other Democratic Deficit: National Authoritarianism in Europe's Democratic Union' (2017) 52 *Government and Opposition* 211.

> authoritarian enclaves. Having wrested some room to maneuver from the Supreme Court, the executive branch, and their national party, conservative Democrats disenfranchised blacks and many poorer white voters, repressed opposition parties, and imposed racially separate – and significantly unfree – civic spheres. Their goal was to ensure cheap agricultural labor and white supremacy, and they used state-sponsored violence to achieve it. For half a century, southern states capitalised on their influence in Congress and the national Democratic Party to shield themselves from outside reform efforts.[35]

The crucial lesson here is that so long as a powerful national political party is willing to shield local autocrats from federal intervention, those local authoritarian enclaves may persist within a democratic union.

Similar dynamics are at work in the EU today and help explain the EU's reactions – or rather non-reactions – to democratic backsliding in Eastern Europe. As I have detailed elsewhere,[36] these incentives help explain why leaders of the European People's Party (EPP) have long defended Hungary's autocratic leader Viktor Orbán – an EPP member – against EU intervention. Orbán's Fidesz party delivers 12 seats to the EPP in the European Parliament (where EPP holds a total of 217 seats), helping it sustain its narrow lead over the second largest party, the social democratic S&D group (which holds 189 seats), enabling it to take a leading role in legislative processes within the European Parliament. In short, the EPP has sold out its professed commitment to liberal democracy in order to keep Fidesz' MEPs in its coalition and to benefit (usually though not always) from Orbán's support in the Council.

These dynamics also help explain why the EU has been somewhat more vigorous in its response to democratic backsliding and attacks on the rule of law in Poland since 2015. As I note in my earlier paper,[37] Poland's governing PiS party is a member of the nationalist, Eurosceptic European Conservatives and Reformists (ECR) Party in the European Parliament, which is much weaker than the EPP and hence less able to protect it against EU action. This helps explain why the Commission was willing to launch the rule of law framework against Poland and to trigger Article 7(1) in reaction to the ongoing attacks on the rule of law and democracy in Poland,[38]

[35] Mickey, Levitsky and Way, above n 4, 23. More generally see R Mickey, *Paths Out of Dixie. The Democratization of Authoritarian Enclaves in America's Deep South*, 1944–1972 (Princeton, NJ, Princeton University Press, 2015); and E Gibson, *Boundary Control* (New York, Cambridge University Press, 2012).

[36] Kelemen, 'Europe's Other Democratic Deficit', above n 34.

[37] ibid; also see RD Kelemen and O Mitchell, 'Europe's Autocracy Problem' *ForeignAffairs.com* (7 January 2016); RD Kelemen, 'Poland's Constitutional Crisis' *ForeignAffairs.com* (25 August 2016), available at: www.foreignaffairs.com/articles/poland/2016-08-25/polands-constitutional-crisis/; RD Kelemen, 'Europe's Authoritarian Equilibrium' ( *ForeignAffairs.com*, 22 December 2017).

[38] For overviews of developments in Poland see L Pech and KL Scheppele, 'Illiberalism Within: Rule of Law Backsliding in the EU' (2017) 19 *Cambridge Yearbook of European Legal Studies* 3; and W Sadurski, 'How Democracy Dies (in Poland): A Case Study of Anti-Constitutional Populist Backsliding' (2018) Sydney Law School Research Paper No 18/01, available at: papers.ssrn.com/sol3/papers.cfm?abstract_id=3103491.

and why many EPP MEPs who long opposed EU action against Hungary's government were so quick to support action against Poland's.[39]

The literature on subnational authoritarianism also identifies two sets of dynamics through which partisan politics may eventually work to depose local authoritarians. First, if federal parties who are not part of the local authoritarian's coalition are able to intervene to support local opposition parties, they may bring them the resources they need to break the local authoritarian's grip on power and dislodge him. Second, if the local autocrat's behaviour becomes so egregious that it imposes significant political and reputational costs on the federal-level party with which it is allied, those party leaders may withdraw their support or even press for the ouster of the autocrat.[40]

Synthesising these arguments suggests why in recent years the EU has been trapped in what I term an 'authoritarian equilibrium,' while also suggesting why it now may be on the verge of breaking out of this equilibrium On the one hand, EU politics has become sufficiently politicised that there are great incentives for Europarties to protect national autocrats who belong to their party groups and deliver needed seats in the European Parliament. The incentives for Europarties to protect local autocrats have increased along with efforts to democratise the EU, for instance by linking the selection of the Commission President to winning a plurality of seats in the European Parliament. Thus, ironically, efforts to democratise the EU may have made the survival of Member State autocracies more likely by making their votes more valuable to the EU-level co-partisans who can protect them. On the other hand, the EU's half-baked partisan politics have not developed to the point where they can trigger either of the two dynamics (mentioned above) through which they might help to dislodge local authoritarians. The Europarties allied with the local opposition in an autocratic Member State are prohibited from providing them the material support that might help them mobilise more effectively, as it is illegal for EU-level political parties or their party foundations to fund national parties.[41] And even if it were not illegal, such direct intervention would likely be perceived as illegitimate meddling in domestic political affairs. Meanwhile, the Europarties who are allied with national level authoritarians and who have protected them against EU sanction have paid no political price for doing so. Because few voters even realise that Europarties exist, these parties (and their other national member parties) have not feared paying any political price for their association with autocrats. However, in the run-up to the 2019 European Parliament elections, there are some indications that public awareness of these

[39] However, the fact that the EPP leadership so long shielded Orbán from EU sanctions for its own partisan reasons has put him in the position to veto sanctions against Poland's PiS government under Art 7(2) (in a showing of the cross-party solidarity of autocrats).

[40] A Giraudy, 'The Politics of Subnational Undemocratic Regime Reproduction in Argentina and Mexico' (2010) 2(2) *Journal of Politics in Latin America* 53; Gibson, 'Boundary Control: Subnational Authoritarianism in Democratic Countries', above n 10.

[41] See Art 7 of Regulation (EC) No 2004/2003 of the European Parliament and of the Council of 4 November 2003.

linkages – and hence 'guilt by association' – may be increasing in a way that could finally break the 'authoritarian equilibrium'.

The partisan dynamics identified by scholars of subnational authoritarianism explain why leaders of the EPP protected the Orbán regime from EU censure for years even as it attacked the independent judiciary, the free press, and civil society organisations and – ultimately – consolidated one party, semi-authoritarian rule.[42] When EU leaders in the Council or Parliament affiliated with other political parties called for EU action in reaction to attacks on the rule of law and democratic norms in Hungary, EPP leaders such as EPP President Joseph Daul, leader of the EPP faction in the European Parliament, Manfred Weber, routinely blocked them.[43] Weber repeatedly dismissed critiques of Orbán as politically motivated attacks by leftists and praised him. And yet, because few voters are even aware of the existence of Europarties, the EPP and the national parties that belong to it for years paid no political price for supporting Orbán's autocratic regime.

In polities with more fully developed party systems, federal parties may pay a political price for supporting a brazen autocrat, as his actions may tarnish their party's 'brand'. However, in the EU's half-baked party system where there has been so little public awareness of EU-level parties, the EPP and leaders such as Manfred Weber, Donald Tusk, Jean-Claude Juncker and Antonio Tajani, along with leaders of EPP member parties such as Angela Merkel, seemed, at least until very recently, to pay no political price for supporting and protecting Orbán. However, there are some recent indications that this may be changing.

In 2017 and 2018, the European Parliament's Civil Liberties Committee (LIBE) prepared a report assessing whether the Parliament should trigger Article 7(1) against Hungary, due to the Hungarian regime's serious and persistent breaches of the EU's fundamental democratic values. Though the EPP leadership had opposed the drafting of such a report, when it was finally presented to the plenary in September 2018 for a vote, the EPP leadership's position changed. After having defended Orbán for years, the EPP's leader in the European Parliament, Manfred Weber, announced on the eve of the vote that he would be endorsing the report

[42] For overviews of the dismantlement of pluralist democracy in Hungary, see KL Scheppele, 'Understanding Hungary's Constitutional Revolution' in A Von Bogdandy and P Sonnevend (eds), *Constitutional Crisis in the European Constitutional Area. Theory, Law and Politics in Hungary and Romania* (Oxford, Hart Publishing, 2015); Pech and Scheppele, above n 38; FIDH (International Federation for Human Rights), 'Hungary: Democracy Under Threat. Six Years of Attacks against the Rule of Law' (November 2016), available at: www.fidh.org/IMG/pdf/hungary_democracy_under_threat.pdf; European Parliament, 'Resolution On the Situation of Fundamental Rights: Standards and Practices in Hungary (Pursuant to the European Parliament Resolution of 16 February 2012) P7_TA(2013)0315' 3 July 2013 (Tavares Report); and European Parliament, 'Draft Report On a Proposal Calling on the Council to Determine, Pursuant to Article 7(1) of the Treaty on European Union, the Existence of a Clear Risk of a Serious Breach by Hungary of the Values on which the Union Is Founded' 4 April 2018 (Sargentini Report), available at: www.europarl.europa.eu/resources/library/media/20180411RES01553/20180411RES01553.pdf.

[43] RD Kelemen, 'EPP ♥ Orbán' *Politico Europe* (18 June 2015), available at: www.politico.eu/article/epp-defends-hungary-orban-against-criticism/.

and its call for triggering Article 7(1).[44] Ultimately the Party remained divided, but with Weber's endorsement nearly 60 per cent of EPP MEPs voted to endorse the report and trigger Article 7(1) against Hungary. These EPP votes proved crucial to the report's passage.[45]

What explained this volte face by the EPP leadership and a majority of its MEPs? It seems that the launching of the *Spitzenkandidat* process in the run-up to the 2019 European Parliament elections played a crucial role: in short, it seems likely that the democratic process at the EU level may finally be developing to a point where politicians are concerned that they may pay a political price if they continue to support and be associated with local autocrats. The vote on the Sargentini Report coincided with the start of the *Spitzenkandidat* process. Just a week before the vote, Manfred Weber announced his desire to be *Spitzenkandidat* for the EPP, competing for the position of European Commission President. Immediately, many press reports noted his long-standing support for Orbán, and EPP MEPs with stronger commitments to democratic principles made it clear that they were no longer comfortable with Fidesz' membership in the EPP and with Weber's support for Orbán.[46] It seems likely that Weber's sudden volte face and decision to endorse the report critiquing Orbán's government was designed to assuage critics of his association with Orbán and thereby to aid his campaign to become the EPP's *Spitzenkandidat*.

While the vote on the Sargentini Report represented a shift on the part of the EPP, partisanship seemed to take priority over principle again just a week after the vote. At its Party Congress a week after the vote on the report, the EPP announced that it would not be ejecting Fidesz from the Party despite the findings of the report.[47] At the time of writing, it seems likely that the EPP will keep Fidesz in its party group through the 2019 European parliamentary elections in the hope that his Fidesz MEPs will help the EPP secure a plurality of seats and with it the presidency of the Commission. Though the controversy surrounding the Sargentini Report suggests that the cost to Europarties of supporting autocratic member parties may be increasing, those costs are still outweighed by the political benefits of keeping them within the fold. In other words, it seems that for the time being, the EU remains mired in an authoritarian equilibrium.

[44] P Kingsley, 'EU's Leadership Seeks to Contain Hungary's Orban' *New York Times* (11 September 2018), available at: www.nytimes.com/2018/09/11/world/europe/viktor-orban-european-peoples-party.html.

[45] P Krekó, *The Vote on the Sargentini Report: Good News for Europe, Bad News for Orbán, no News for Hungary* (Brussels, Heinrich Böll Foundation, 2018), available at: eu.boell.org/en/2018/09/21/vote-sargentini-report-good-news-europe-bad-news-orban-no-news-hungary.

[46] Kingsley, above n 44; M Peel, M Khanand and V Hopkins, 'Orbán Heads into EU Showdown after Centre-Right Allies Desert Him' *Financial Times* (13 September 2018), available at: www.ft.com/content/d05646fa-b6b5-11e8-bbc3-ccd7de085ffe.

[47] M de la Baume, D Herzenhorn and L Bayer, 'Europe's Center Right won't Expel Orbán, leader says' *Politico Europe* (19 September 2018), available at: www.politico.eu/article/europes-center-right-wont-expel-hungarian-prime-minister-viktor-orban-leader-says-joseph-daul-epp/.

## Conclusion

Existing literature on the EU's democratic deficit highlights some real shortcomings of EU democracy, above all the fact that the EU's executive (the European Commission) was not – at least until the advent of the *Spitzenkandidat* process – elected. However, comparing the EU with the US suggests that many of the supposed democratic deficits of EU institutions have been exaggerated, while the more significant threat of democratic deficits at the Member State level has been underestimated. History shows that even as the US steadily democratised at the federal level, it allowed authoritarian enclaves at the state level to persist for a century after the Civil War. Thus, even if we are appalled by the EU's failure to intervene as democracy and the rule of law are dismantled in Hungary and Poland, the experience of the US and many other federal systems suggests we should not be surprised.[48] Sadly, US experience suggests we should not be shocked if the EU remains mired in an 'authoritarian equilibrium', with a democratic federal union tolerating autocratic Member State governments, for many years to come.

Those who despair at this assessment of the prospects for an authoritarian equilibrium to persist in the contemporary EU can perhaps take solace in two observations. First, as Martin Luther King Jr put it, 'Let us realize the arc of the moral universe is long, but it bends toward justice'. If one takes that cautiously optimistic view, one may anticipate that the local authoritarian enclaves in Europe's democratic union are likely, eventually, to give way to democracy and the rule of law. Second, the autocratic regimes that are emerging in EU Member States such as Hungary and Poland are milder than the dictatorships that existed in many European states at previous points in their history, or than those that exist today just outside the EU's borders in states such as Belarus, Russia or Turkey. One important lesson of the literature on subnational authoritarianism is that membership in an overarching democratic federation tends to soften the form of authoritarianism practised at the state level – such that the local autocrat can avoid provoking a federal intervention. Thus, while the EU may gravely disappoint supporters of liberty by not ensuring that its members remain democracies, it may at least prevent softer, competitive authoritarian regimes from turning into more hard-core dictatorships. Given the ugly history of governance in some European states such as Hungary over the past century, one might consider this modest progress.

[48] Gibson, 'Boundary Control: Subnational Authoritarianism in Democratic Countries', above n 10; and Gibson, *Boundary Control*, above n 35.

# 4

# Constitutional Overload in a Constitutional Democracy: The UK and the Brexit Process

MICHAEL GORDON*

## Introduction

Brexit presents an immense challenge to the UK constitution. The delivery of the UK's exit from the EU is an undertaking of near unprecedented scale and extent. The initial withdrawal was also to be delivered in an almost unbelievably brief two-year period of time.[1] This has tested and will continue to test the institutions of the UK constitution to (and perhaps well beyond) their limits – Brexit requires governmental activity at a number of levels simultaneously, with decisions reached (or not reached) at each level having the potential to impact significantly on other strands of activity. We see negotiations at the European level shaping legislative and policy activity at the UK level, with decisions also subject to internal negotiations between the UK government and the devolved institutions in Scotland, Wales and (when constituted) Northern Ireland, between the government and opposition parties, within the governing parties, and indeed within the Cabinet. Judicial actors intervened early in the process in the high-profile case of *Miller*,[2] and may yet have a further impact at the end of the process, through the possibility created by the *Wightman* reference.[3] The electorate took the decision to exit the EU, and, while it remains a remote possibility, they could yet be asked to confirm or reconsider it directly.

* I'm grateful to the organisers and all those present at the College of Europe conference on the 'Future of Constitutional Democracy in Europe' in Bruges in February 2018 for their comments, along with my colleagues in the EU Law@Liverpool research unit, and in particular Harriet Gray, at our 2018 research away day.

[1] Art 50(3) Treaty on European Union. The two-year withdrawal negotiation period has now been extended twice, initially by two weeks to 12 April 2019, and then by seven months to 31 October 2019. It could be extended again by the agreement of the EU 27 and the UK.

[2] *R (Miller) v Secretary of State for Exiting the European Union* [2017] UKSC 5, [2018] AC 61.

[3] C-621/18 *Wightman and others v Secretary of State for Exiting the European Union* CSIH 62 EU:C:2018:999.

Yet Brexit is not just a critical (ongoing) constitutional case study because of the scale and complexity of separating the UK's legal system from that of the EU, and preparing for the reacquisition of competences which previously have been pooled with the remaining 27 Member States. It raises questions about constitutional capacity, but also about constitutional principles. The decision to exit the EU was also ostensibly driven (at least in part) by constitutional concerns. The 'Leave' campaign's rhetoric that Brexit meant 'taking back control' was rolled up with claims about the UK's loss of law-making authority and the diminution of sovereignty. This confused constitutional narrative, fuelled by fundamental misunderstandings and conflations of different kinds of sovereignty and power, coupled with unrealistic expectations about the influence of a single nation state on the European and international stage, still shapes the UK government's response to Brexit.[4] The caricature of unfettered authority at home and abroad which underpins such a vision of the UK constitution quite clearly deviates from constitutional reality. However, there was also a sense at the highest levels of Theresa May's government that this did not really matter – the meaning of Brexit was defined in circular terms, and it has become an end in itself.[5]

These challenges of constitutional capacity and principle raise important questions about the state of constitutional democracy in the UK. The way Brexit is delivered and the way in which it is understood will have a major impact on the UK's constitution, but also on the ways in which key elements of the UK constitution correspond to ideas of democracy. There is no straightforward way to assess this, however, because the UK's democratic constitution is structurally atypical, and based on a relationship between democracy and the constitution which is fluid rather than fixed. The UK's democratic system is not based on a legally fundamental set of constitutional norms, established in an overarching text and enforced by a supreme court. Instead, the UK's democratic arrangements are the product of an uncodified constitution, based on a range of interacting legal and political norms, competing sources of institutional power, and ultimately subject to definition and redefinition through the legislation of a sovereign Parliament.[6] In the UK, the development of democracy legitimised pre-existing constitutional arrangements,[7] and those constitutional structures, including Parliament and the Crown, have not just been adapted to accommodate democracy, but – at least as a matter of principle – now exist subject to the ordinary democratic will of

[4] See further M Gordon, 'The UK's Sovereignty Situation: Brexit, Bewilderment and Beyond' (2016) 27 *King's Law Journal* 333, 333–35.

[5] The Prime Minister repeatedly claimed that 'Brexit means Brexit', which became a defining phrase of this process; see, eg, 'Theresa May's Conservative conference speech: Key quotes' *BBC News* (2 October 2016), available at: www.bbc.co.uk/news/uk-politics-37535527.

[6] See, eg, M Gordon, *Parliamentary Sovereignty in the UK Constitution: Process, Politics and Democracy* (Oxford, Hart Publishing, 2015) esp ch 2.

[7] See, eg, P Foot, *The Vote: How It Was Won, and How It Was Undermined* (London, Bookmarks, 2012).

the electorate. In that sense, the UK's contemporary constitution is both the product of and contingent on democratic politics, rather than a normative vessel which constrains the political system.

The UK's approach to constitutional democracy therefore produces a high flexible polity, albeit one which nevertheless has, in practice, some deeply embedded fundamental ideas and institutions. Yet when the constitution is not hierarchically superior to democracy, questions of process are not preordained, but resolved (or at least confronted) in response to democratic events. In such circumstances, and especially when faced with an extraordinary political challenge like Brexit, even core ideas become susceptible to revision and displacement. And it is from this perspective – aware of the complex relationship between the UK's constitution, its politics and its approach to democracy – that we must explore the particular challenge which Brexit poses, and the broader potential consequences of this dramatic reorganisation of the UK political system.

This chapter will review a range of the domestic difficulties which have been encountered in delivering Brexit, and which have challenged the constitution, democracy, and the very idea of constitutional democracy in the UK. The chapter will explore challenges relating to, first, the activities of the UK Parliament and government; second, the position of the devolved institutions in Scotland, Wales and Northern Ireland; and, third, the role of the courts. It will argue that the combined effect of these overlapping, interacting and proliferating challenges has been to place the UK in a period of constitutional overload. One significant consequence of the UK's constitutional overload is that it raises potential democratic difficulties, both in terms of ensuring the adequate functioning of democracy in the present, as well as with respect to the possibilities for reform of the democratic political system in the future. In the present, constitutional overload means that contemporary democratic tensions are more challenging to resolve. And for the future, constitutional overload means that ways of enhancing democratic practice are even more difficult to identify and implement. In that sense, constitutional overload is one of the biggest challenges to democracy faced by the UK.

## The Challenges of Brexit

Brexit has tested the UK's constitutional democracy in a range of ways. There have been (ongoing) debates about the status and implications of the 2016 referendum decision, the legislative role of Parliament in commencing, implementing and concluding the UK's withdrawal, the extent to which the government has been subject to adequate accountability during the exit negotiations, the input and consent of the devolved institutions, and the role of the courts in determining questions of process. A crucial common theme of these debates has been clashing ideas of democracy, and how the constitution should respond to or manage these democratic tensions. This section will consider some of the key events of the Brexit process to this point, and explore the competing ideas of democracy which underpin the controversies associated with these events. First, we consider the activities of the UK Parliament and government, second, the role of the devolved institutions, and third, the involvement of the courts.

## Parliament and the Government

The UK Parliament and government have been the domestic institutions at the centre of the Brexit process. The government has conducted the exit negotiations with the EU Commission's negotiating Task Force, while Parliament has been faced with the challenge of legislating for EU withdrawal. If a deal is agreed and a withdrawal treaty is ratified, Parliament will have enacted a trilogy of withdrawal legislation by the time the UK exits the EU. First, the European Union (Notification of Withdrawal) Act 2017 was the formal (and sparse) legislative act which authorised the Prime Minister to 'trigger' the official exit process set out under Article 50 TEU. Second, the European Union (Withdrawal) Act 2018 was a far more elaborate legislative exercise, establishing powers and structures to prepare the UK's legal system for the widespread consequences of removing the domestic authority of norms derived from EU law. Third, the government has committed to introduce a European Union (Withdrawal Agreement) Bill in order to implement the provisions of an exit treaty in UK law.[8]

The negotiations and the legislative withdrawal trilogy have monopolised the domestic political agenda, and raised an extraordinary range and volume of constitutional questions. Yet what is perhaps most notable is that all this energy has been expended in pursuit of an outcome which does not have majority support in Parliament, and to which the Prime Minister in office during this process was originally opposed. Instead, the institutions of representative democracy have been dominated by their attempts to deliver a decision taken (at least initially) by a different entity: the electorate in the June 2016 referendum. Of course, the decision to pass direct responsibility for the UK's choice on EU membership was made by the government led by the then Prime Minister David Cameron, and was given effect by Parliament's legislation in the form of the European Union Referendum Act 2015. But uncertainty as to the status of the 2016 referendum result, in formal constitutional terms, has loomed over the entire Brexit process, and the difficulty experienced by the UK's regular representative institutions in responding to the sudden, irregular authority of the direct democratic vote has been evident in this context, and elsewhere.

The referendum has played a crucial role in shaping the interactions between Parliament and the government throughout the Brexit process. The government of

[8] Joint Report from the Negotiators of the European Union and the United Kingdom Government on Progress During Phase 1 of Negotiations under Article 50 TEU on the United Kingdom's Orderly Withdrawal from the European Union, TF50 (2017) 19 (8 December 2017) 36.

Theresa May has tried to adopt the mandate of the referendum and absorb legitimacy for its decision-making from the fact it is focused on delivering the outcome of that popular vote. This became essential because the Prime Minister lost her majority at the snap general election she called in June 2017, which produced a hung Parliament and a weak minority government.[9] That this minority Conservative government is bolstered in power through a 'confidence and supply' agreement with the Democratic Unionist Party (DUP) from Northern Ireland has had implications for the Brexit process more broadly.[10] It has arguably compelled the UK government to give greater priority to the views of one (particularly Eurosceptic) party within Northern Ireland, at a time when there is no devolved government in place in that nation, than it has to the views of other constitutional actors with stronger claims of democratic representativeness. For example, the other devolved institutions in Scotland and Wales have consistently complained about being left on the outside of the Brexit process by the UK government,[11] and the official Opposition can claim to represent a far greater section of the population than the DUP. Of course, in a parliamentary system a government will inevitably do whatever it deems necessary to obtain and sustain the confidence of the House of Commons – but this demonstrates even further the precarious position of Theresa May's government following the 2017 election failure, and the consequent need to lean heavily on the referendum result as a source of democratic authority.

The referendum decision is a further democratic input complicating a relationship between Parliament and the government which is already structured by different democratic characteristics. The government exists to deliver on the manifesto commitments it has made to the electorate to obtain office, whereas within Parliament, the House of Commons operates to represent a much wider spectrum of public opinions, while holding ministers and officials to account as they pursue policy goals.[12] The relationship between Parliament and the government is therefore inherently interactive, with the nature of those interactions and the boundaries between different areas of institutional activity subject to ongoing negotiation.[13] The Brexit process has proved an especially acute test of this process of constitutional interaction and negotiation, with a number of key pressure points.

[9] See 'General Election 2017: results and analysis' *House of Commons Library*, CBP 7979 (updated 8 April 2018).

[10] See *Confidence and Supply Agreement between the Conservative and Unionist Party and the Democratic Unionist Party* (26 June 2017), available at: www.gov.uk/government/publications/conservative-and-dup-agreement-and-uk-government-financial-support-for-northern-ireland#history.

[11] See, eg, the joint letter by the First Ministers of Scotland and Wales sent to the Prime Minister on 19 September 2017; 'Scottish and Welsh leaders seek to ward off Westminster "hijack" of powers' *The Guardian* (19 September 2017), available at: www.theguardian.com/politics/2017/sep/19/scottish-and-welsh-leaders-seek-to-ward-off-westminster-hijack-of-powers.

[12] The House of Lords also holds the government to account and can give voice to particular perspectives, yet it is not a democratically representative institution.

[13] See generally, M Gordon, 'Brexit: The Relationship between the UK Parliament and the UK Government' in M Dougan (ed), *The UK After Brexit: Legal and Policy Challenges* (London, Intersentia, 2017).

First, after the Supreme Court had decided that a new Act of Parliament was required to give the Prime Minister authority to give notice of the UK's withdrawal in accordance with Article 50 TEU, there was extensive debate over whether this power ought to be made subject to specific statutory conditions or qualifications. After the Bill passed the Commons, two particular amendments were made in the House of Lords, defeating the government in both cases. The first sought to protect the rights of EU citizens living in the UK, requiring the government to develop plans to ensure unilateral continuity of EU-derived rights;[14] the second sought to make the UK's final exit from the EU (whether with or without a deal) subject to the approval of both Houses of Parliament.[15] Both were rejected as seeking to tie the hands of the government and frustrate the result of the referendum,[16] and overturned when the Bill returned to the Commons. The Act was ultimately passed without amendment, and in its sole substantive section, conferred an unqualified power on the Prime Minister to notify the UK's intention to withdraw from the EU.[17] But the controversy over the terms of notification also gave a clear indication of what was to follow in future legislative contests, with Parliament trying to establish statutory guarantees of legal continuity, the protection of specific values and, perhaps most significantly in constitutional terms, seeking to use legislation to expand and formalise its own role in the Brexit process. The approach of the government, in contrast, was to try to resist parliamentary attempts to alter the terms of withdrawal legislation, and instead offer ministerial commitments made in the legislature (indeed often during the course of the legislative process) as to, for example, the preservation of the rights of EU citizens, and the role of Parliament in approving a Brexit deal.

A second major controversy concerned the extent to which legislative power could be delegated to the executive to carry out the detailed changes to domestic legal regulation necessary to produce a functioning statute book after exiting the EU. Following the UK's notification under Article 50 on 29 March 2017 (just 13 days after the EU (Notification of Withdrawal) Act 2017 became law upon receiving royal assent), the challenge of preparing the UK legal system for the domestic legal consequences of the withdrawal of EU norms became the main focus of legislative activity. The ludicrous rhetoric of the Prime Minister's promised 'Great Repeal Bill' did not survive contact with legislative reality,[18] and instead the European Union (Withdrawal) Bill was introduced to Parliament. While one

[14] HL Deb 1 March 2017, vol 779 cols 814–16.

[15] HL Deb 7 March 2017, vol 779, cols 1251–52.

[16] See, eg, the objections of the then Secretary of State for Exiting the European Union, David Davis MP: HC Deb 13 March 2017, vol 623, cols 38–44.

[17] European Union (Notification of Withdrawal) Act 2017, s 1.

[18] The language of the 'Great Repeal Bill' is found throughout the government's White Paper *Legislating for the United Kingdom's Withdrawal from the European Union* (Cm 9446, 30 March 2017). Yet it is curiously now absent from the title of the relevant government website, where the language has been downgraded to that of 'the Repeal Bill'; see: www.gov.uk/government/publications/the-repeal-bill-white-paper.

of the principal purposes of this legislation was to repeal the European Communities Act 1972, it also sought to establish a system based on the retention of EU legal rules. In pursuit of legal continuity and certainty on exit day, existing norms would be retained in the UK legal system, subject to modifications made by secondary legislation to address any 'deficiencies' affecting the operation of retained EU law.[19]

The scope of the legislative powers to rewrite the law so far as ministers deem it 'appropriate' to remedy deficiencies, which may (for example) arise as reciprocal arrangements are undone, EU functions are removed, or legal rules become redundant, have been hotly contested. While these very extensive delegated legislative powers have been criticised as going beyond what is necessary,[20] the scale of the legislative change required in a short space of time made it inevitable that the government, rather than Parliament, would carry out the core of the detailed work in drafting an estimated 800–1,000 statutory instruments.[21] And while there were some concessions made by the government in terms of the scope of the powers – for example, shifting from an indicative list of potential deficiencies to an exhaustive (although amendable) list of the circumstances in which these powers could be exercised[22] – the major change was to accept a reinforced scrutiny process relating to the use of these still very broadly framed powers.[23] This saw a European Statutory Instruments Committee established in the House of Commons (working alongside an equivalent committee in the Lords),[24] with powers to make recommendations (but not binding decisions) about whether it was appropriate for draft delegated legislation to come into force via a negative procedure, subject only to annulment by Parliament, or whether a measure was of a legal or political significance such that the positive affirmation of Parliament was necessary for it to become law. These new processes should allow the legislature more effectively to flag up controversial uses of power for further attention, although they remain limited in so far as the Committee cannot impose its decision on the government, and the vast amount of delegated legislation to be enacted

[19] European Union (Withdrawal) Act 2018, s 8.

[20] See, eg, House of Lords Select Committee on the Constitution, *European Union (Withdrawal) Bill: interim report*, HL Paper 19 (7 September 2017) 35–65. See also the full report of the Constitution Committee on the Withdrawal Bill, HL Paper 69 (29 January 2018) 157–206.

[21] See the estimate of the government reported in Procedure Committee of the House of Commons, *Scrutiny of delegated legislation under the European Union (Withdrawal) Bill: interim report*, HC 386 (6 November 2017) 29.

[22] European Union (Withdrawal) Act 2018, s 8(3).

[23] See Procedure Committee of the House of Commons, *Scrutiny of delegated legislation under the European Union (Withdrawal) Act 2018*, HC 1395 (9 July 2018).

[24] See the European Statutory Instruments Committee website at: www.parliament.uk/business/committees/committees-a-z/commons-select/european-statutory-instruments/. In the House of Lords, this sifting function has been added to the work of the pre-existing Secondary Legislation Scrutiny Committee;see:www.parliament.uk/business/committees/committees-a-z/lords-select/secondary-legislation-scrutiny-committee/; and *Sifting 'proposed negative instruments' laid under the European Union (Withdrawal) Act 2018: criteria and working arrangements*, HL Paper 174 (20 July 2018).

within a short period of time may itself represent a barrier to detailed scrutiny, whether Parliament is required to approve it affirmatively or not.[25] The scrutiny processes have also themselves been the subject of controversy: the government attempted to retreat from a commitment to make a written ministerial statement to explain and publicly justify any decision to reject a scrutiny recommendation, and only reverted to that original position after public criticism from the Procedure Committee of the House of Commons.[26]

Third, there has been considerable debate about the role of Parliament in approving any final Brexit deal. As discussed above, arguments about how to ensure Parliament has a 'meaningful vote' on the terms of EU withdrawal began in relation to the EU (Notification of Withdrawal) Act 2017. This continued in relation to the EU (Withdrawal) Bill, and ultimately this legislation was amended in two ways which incorporated government commitments about the role of Parliament in the Brexit process into statute, while also fleshing out the terms and timing of parliamentary involvement. First, the government was defeated on a Commons amendment which made the use by ministers of legislative powers to implement a withdrawal agreement 'subject to the prior enactment of a statute by Parliament approving the final terms of withdrawal of the United Kingdom from the EU'.[27] Second, a specific section was inserted formalising Parliament's role in relation to the outcome of negotiations with the EU, preventing ratification of a withdrawal treaty by the government unless the legislature has approved it (and also a statement on a future UK–EU relationship), and also designating specific dates by which the government must report to Parliament on progress if no deal had yet been reached.[28]

These provisions provided a clear structure for parliamentary input, and underpinned a guaranteed opportunity for Parliament – and in particular the House of Commons, which must positively approve a deal before ratification is triggered[29] – to influence government decision-making concerning the terms of withdrawal from the EU. Yet they did not give Parliament the final say over Brexit: if the Commons rejected a withdrawal agreement which was presented to it, without some further intervening act or an extension of the negotiations, the UK would have proceeded to exit on a 'no deal' basis on 29 March 2019.

[25] See, eg, A Tucker, 'Parliamentary Scrutiny of Delegated Legislation' in A Horne and G Drewry (eds), *Parliament and the Law*, 2nd edn (Oxford, Hart Publishing, 2018).

[26] See the exchange of letters between the Chairman of the Procedure Committee and the Parliamentary Under Secretary of State in the Department for Exiting the European Union on 13 September 2018 and 8 October 2018 respectively: www.parliament.uk/business/committees/committees-a-z/commons-select/procedure-committee/news-parliament-2017/government-undertaking-scrutiny-statutory-instruments-17-19/.

[27] European Union (Withdrawal) Act 2018, s 9(1). See generally 'Tory Brexit rebels inflict major defeat on Theresa May' *The Guardian* (14 December 2017), available at: www.theguardian.com/politics/2017/dec/13/tory-brexit-rebels-inflict-major-defeat-on-theresa-may.

[28] European Union (Withdrawal) Act 2018, s 13.

[29] The House of Lords only needs to have considered a motion on the withdrawal agreement; European Union (Withdrawal) Act 2018, s 13(1)(c).

and the referendum locks established (but never triggered) in the European Union Act 2011.[41] Yet such a comparison is surely inappropriate in this context, at least if it represents anything more than a hasty example to show the provenance and therefore the possibility of such statutory changes to the future legislative manner and form. Exactly what form the promised procedural protection might take therefore remains to be seen, but to privilege the rights of a particular group in this way might be challenged if this legislation makes it to Parliament. Whether such objections instrumentalise traditional constitutional arguments about the impossibility of binding successors or not, the government's attempt to foster good faith in the negotiations and reassure a vulnerable group of citizens in a time of major upheaval could yet prove controversial. And even if enacted, the possibility that future governments might seek to subvert any new procedural limits and undo aspects of the exit deal is just one example which demonstrates that the complex constitutional legacy of Brexit could linger well into the future.

There are many further examples which might also be considered, and which test the constitutional relationship between Parliament and the government in the context of Brexit. Among others, there have been debates about the way in which significant political values can be protected in law after Brexit, with Parliament legislating to impose specific obligations on the government in relation to environmental principles[42] and equality issues.[43] Moreover, the central examples of major constitutional legislation which have been discussed here are just part of a broader legislative picture in relation to the UK's preparations for EU withdrawal, with legislation on Trade, Immigration, Customs and in many other areas also required, often raising further questions about the respective roles of Parliament and the government in these contexts.[44] And ultimately, the intractability of these many issues, along with the power held by Parliament over a minority administration, has already led to the collapse of one government, with Prime Minister Theresa May announcing her resignation on 24 May 2019, due to her continuing failure to obtain the support of the House of Commons for the draft Brexit agreement she had negotiated with the European Union.

Fundamentally, however, the issues considered above provide the most important examples of the ways in which the relationship between Parliament and the government is being challenged by Brexit. This is a challenge underpinned by the

[41] See, eg, Gordon, *Parliamentary Sovereignty in the UK Constitution*, above n 6, esp ch 6.

[42] European Union (Withdrawal) Act 2018, s 16 creates an obligation for the Secretary of State to introduce a draft Bill maintaining environmental principles within six months after the passing of the 2018 Act.

[43] European Union (Withdrawal) Act 2018, Schedule 7 para 28(5) requires ministers to make statements that equality issues have been considered and the impact minimised when draft statutory instruments are produced by the government.

[44] See, eg, B Fowler, 'Trade Bill highlights Parliament's weak international treaty role' *Hansard Society* (9 January 2018), available at: www.hansardsociety.org.uk/blog/trade-bill-highlights-parliaments-weak-international-treaty-role; B Fowler, 'Parliamentary consent to treaty ratifications: another procedure strained by Brexit?' *Hansard Society* (20 November 2018), available at: www.hansardsociety.org.uk/blog/parliamentary-consent-to-treaty-ratifications-another-procedure-strained-by.

limitations of the constitutional capacity of these institutions whether acting separately or in conjunction to respond to a major reorganisation of the UK's legal and political system. But it is also a challenge underpinned by alternative constitutional principles, and democratic functions. This is not simply a battle for power between the legislature and the executive, but also rooted in tensions between democratic accountability and democratic action. This tension is shaped by the irregular authority of the referendum result, which in some ways stands apart from the authority of the regular political institutions, yet also requires interpretation and implementation by these core constitutional actors. Yet these democratic tensions have not just played out in this specific context – instead, the constitutional complexities generated by Brexit also have clear parallels when we consider the position of the devolved institutions in Scotland, Wales and Northern Ireland.

## Devolution

The relationship between the UK institutions and the devolved governments and legislatures in Scotland, Wales and Northern Ireland has also been strained by Brexit. These devolved institutions were created by the UK Parliament,[45] but have a deep constitutional status, such that their permanence has now been recognised in statutes in relation to Scotland[46] and Wales.[47] The authority of these institutions is reinforced by the fact that each of the devolved regimes was created following the positive approval of the respective electorates of Scotland, Wales and Northern Ireland at national referendums. Yet the competence of each of these institutions is both determined and also limited by Act of Parliament, and as a matter of legal form the devolution scheme is subject to the ultimate sovereignty of the UK Parliament.[48]

Against this backdrop, the process of UK withdrawal from the EU has produced constitutional tensions in a number of areas. First, just as the initial 2016 referendum has complicated the relationship between the UK government and Parliament, so has it complicated the relationship between the UK and the devolved institutions. In particular, we see the clear emergence of different sites of democratic activity which are attempting to pull in entirely different directions. This was evident in the result of the referendum itself, with the electorates of England and Wales voting to leave the EU, and those of Scotland and Northern Ireland voting to remain. However, there was no statutory requirement that majority support was required within each of the four nations for Brexit to proceed, and

[45] Scotland Act 1998 (amended by the Scotland Acts 2012 and 2016); Government of Wales Act 1998 (replaced by the Government of Wales Act 2006, which has been further amended by the Wales Act 2017); Northern Ireland Act 1998 (amended and suspended by a number of further Acts).

[46] Scotland Act 1998, s 63A (as amended by the Scotland Act 2016).

[47] Government of Wales Act 2006, Part A1 (as amended by the Wales Act 2017).

[48] Scotland Act 1998 s 28(7); Northern Ireland Act 1998 s 5(6); Government of Wales Act 2006 s 107(5).

instead a simple majority across the entire UK electorate was taken to be decisive. The split between the UK's four nations has nevertheless been significant in terms of the interpretation and delivery of the referendum result.

The Scottish government has offered the most effective opposition to the UK government, arguing for a close relationship with the EU based on continued membership of the single market and customs union on the basis that the people of Scotland voted to support the status quo.[49] This has been in marked contrast to the absence of an institutional voice for Northern Ireland, which for domestic political reasons has been without a government since January 2017.[50] The power-sharing arrangements according to which government is formed in Northern Ireland might have made it difficult for a common position to be adopted in any event. Yet the lack of an established forum in which such debates could occur and key issues could be raised has been especially regrettable given the border with the Republic of Ireland is the only land border between the UK and the EU, and avoiding the creation of new barriers there has been a crucial (and highly disputed) political objective of the withdrawal negotiations.[51] The position in Wales has been complicated by the fact that the electorate voted to leave but the Welsh government supported remain, with this the only place where Labour, the main UK opposition party, has been in power during this period. It has been notable that we have seen considerable coordinated work between the devolved administrations in Scotland and Wales, especially given the former is nationalist and aims to achieve Scottish independence, whereas the latter is unionist. Perhaps as a consequence of that commitment to the union, the Welsh government has also been responsible for some of the more detailed proposals for reinforcing intergovernmental decision-making processes after Brexit, including suggesting the creation of a new UK Council of Ministers.[52]

A second related area of tension concerns not just the interplay between different democratic actors with varying mandates and alternative visions for Brexit, but the extent to which the consent of the devolved institutions is formally required for the plans the UK government is intent on delivering. Under the terms of the UK's devolution arrangements, the consent of the devolved institutions is dealt with as a matter of constitutional convention, rather than as a matter of law.

[49] See the Scottish Government, *Scotland's Place in Europe* (20 December 2016), available at: www.gov.scot/publications/scotlands-place-europe/.

[50] See, eg, 'Northern Ireland latest: how did power sharing collapse at Stormont and why is there no government?' *The Independent* (6 September 2018), available at: www.independent.co.uk/news/uk/politics/northern-ireland-talks-latest-updates-stormont-power-sharing-deal-what-deal-look-sinn-fein-dup-deal-a8207916.html. In the absence of a functioning executive and Assembly, the UK Parliament has enacted legislation extending the decision-making powers of civil servants, and (again) extending the deadline for a power-sharing deal to be reached between the political parties; see Northern Ireland (Executive Formation and Exercise of Functions) Act 2018.

[51] See, eg, S de Mars, C Murray, A O'Donoghue and B Warwick, *Bordering Two Unions: Northern Ireland and Brexit* (Bristol, Policy Press, 2018) esp ch 2.

[52] See the Welsh Government, *Brexit and Devolution: Securing Wales' Future* (17 June 2017), available at: beta.gov.wales/sites/default/files/publications/2018-10/brexit-and-devolution.pdf.

The so-called Sewel convention requires devolved consent for any UK legislation which falls within an area of devolved competence,[53] or where legislation would alter the powers of a devolved institution.[54] The question of devolved consent to Brexit has emerged in two contexts: first, in relation to the UK's notification of its intention to withdraw from the EU under Article 50; and second, in relation to the domestic legislative plans to prepare the UK legal system for Brexit. In relation to notification of withdrawal, the UK government argued that it was responsible for decisions concerning EU membership, and devolved consent was not required. This position was challenged as one aspect of the *Miller* litigation, which ultimately reached the UK Supreme Court. The Supreme Court unanimously held that there was no consent requirement which it could enforce: 'Judges … are neither the parents nor the guardians of political conventions; they are merely observers. As such … they cannot give legal rulings on its operation or scope, because those matters are determined within the political world'.[55]

There is a clear contrast, however, between the position with respect to consent to notification and consent to the domestic legal preparations for Brexit. The EU (Withdrawal) Bill obviously engaged consent requirements as a matter of constitutional convention because (among other things) it would inevitably need to remove the explicit statutory limitation preventing the devolved legislatures from legislating in contravention of EU law. Yet ultimately, for the UK government, compliance with this constitutional convention was taken to be a dispensable aspiration, rather than a democratic fundamental. Agreement on the terms of the legislation could not be reached with the Scottish government, which viewed the UK government as undermining devolved competence by seeking initially to allocate control over all policy areas previously dealt with under EU law to the UK Parliament, even where such powers would otherwise relate to devolved matters. Consequently, a legislative consent motion was not passed in the Scottish Parliament.[56] The Welsh government, in contrast, did accept the concessions made by the UK government, and the National Assembly for Wales gave consent to what was enacted as the EU (Withdrawal) Act 2018.[57]

While obtaining consent from Wales provides some political cover for the UK government, to proceed without the agreement of Scotland in such significant, delicate and contested constitutional circumstances is without precedent, and presents a challenge to the democratic principles underpinning the devolution

[53] *Devolution: Memorandum of Understanding and Supplementary Agreements* (October 2013) 14.

[54] Department for Constitutional Affairs, *Devolution Guidance Note 10 – Post-Devolution Primary Legislation Affecting the Scottish Parliament* (November 2005) 4.3.

[55] Miller, above n 2, 146.

[56] See 'Holyrood refuses consent for Westminster Brexit bill' *BBC News* (15 May 2018), available at: www.bbc.co.uk/news/uk-scotland-scotland-politics-44113864.

[57] See 'Welsh Assembly backs controversial Brexit bill' *BBC News* (15 May 2018), available at: www.bbc.co.uk/news/uk-wales-politics-44109489. For general analysis, see 'Brexit and the Sewel (legislative consent) Convention' *Institute for Government* (17 May 2018), available at: www.instituteforgovernment.org.uk/explainers/brexit-sewel-legislative-consent-convention.

system at exactly the moment that Brexit will require greater collaboration between the four nations. Indeed, the approach of the UK government to the development of the UK-wide regulatory frameworks which will need to be constructed to replace the overarching norms of EU law will now be crucial. The UK government refused to accede to the Scottish request to establish legal vetoes in the EU (Withdrawal) Act 2018 to prevent common frameworks being imposed on the devolved nations, on subject matters including the environment, agriculture, food labelling, chemicals regulation, public procurement, public health and aspects of cross-border justice.[58] Instead, these common frameworks will be subject to a parallel presumption to the Sewel convention: that they will not normally be established without the consent of the devolved institutions.[59] In that sense, the failure to receive consent for the overall approach to establishing common frameworks means it is absolutely essential that the UK government respects this commitment at a more granular level, and ensures that no specific UK-wide regulatory arrangements are imposed without devolved consent, at least if this scheme is to respect the democratic character of devolution.

These competing democratic claims and mandates, and the different interpretations of ideas of consent and power distribution which they generate, are likely to continue to shape the direction of devolution in the UK after Brexit. It is important to note the genuinely constitutional character of these challenges, and the way in which these objections transcend the purely political. The status of the devolved institutions and their democratic credentials give additional authority to them as objectors to central government decision-making, and added weight to their substantive objections. Even if in a number of instances the views of the devolved institutions have not prevailed, they have played a key role in shaping national debates, in contrast to less constitutionally conspicuous constituencies, such as the northern English regions. In this sense, Brexit has shown us the potential of devolution not just as a constitutional scheme for exercising power, but as a scheme of constitutional opposition.

If one of the jobs of the UK constitution is to manage, or even resolve, these internal differences with as few ruptures as possible, it has been found lacking.

[58] See the list of 153 policy areas covered by EU law in which UK and devolved competences overlap in the UK government's *Frameworks Analysis: Breakdown of Areas of EU Law that Intersect with Devolved Competence in Scotland, Wales and Northern Ireland* (9 March 2018), available at: assets.publishing.service.gov.uk/government/uploads/system/uploads/attachment_data/file/686991/20180307_FINAL__Frameworks_analysis_for_publication_on_9_March_2018.pdf.

[59] See *Intergovernmental Agreement on the European Union (Withdrawal) Bill and the Establishment of Common Frameworks* (24 April 2018), available at: assets.publishing.service.gov.uk/government/uploads/system/uploads/attachment_data/file/702623/2018-04-24_UKG-DA_IGA_and_Memorandum.pdf. This agreement between the UK and Welsh governments covers the areas currently governed by EU law in which UK frameworks will be required. In these areas, limitations on devolved competence will therefore be in place for a time-limited period, with relevant regulations established at the UK level subject (with some exceptions) to the consent of the devolved legislatures. There is currently no Northern Irish Executive in office to opt-in to this agreement, though it is open to one to do so in future.

Yet the present mixed record might conceal ever greater challenges ahead. The mishandling of the input of the devolved institutions into the Brexit process has the potential to reintensify debates about the future of the union itself. There are no immediate plans for a second Scottish independence referendum, or a border poll on the reunification of Northern Ireland and the Republic of Ireland. However, the prospect of any such reassessment of popular consent to the UK as a national project only grows more likely if the varying democratic components of the constitution are not better accommodated in the post-Brexit domestic union. What form such accommodation might take is difficult to predict, although for some a federalisation of the UK constitution seems the inevitable trajectory.[60] Yet this would also raise democratic questions, particularly as regards the further empowerment of the judiciary it might precipitate. The inflated constitutional prominence of the judiciary has already been a key feature of the domestic response to Brexit, and highlights the extent to which litigation has been used, with varying results, as a tool to structure, and potentially also to disrupt, this political process.

## The Judiciary

In a system which is classically regarded as a 'political constitution',[61] the judiciary can generally be understood to have a subsidiary constitutional role in the UK. The fundamental constitutional principle of parliamentary sovereignty establishes a legislative power for the UK Parliament which is not subject to legal limits, and therefore confirms the basic priority of the processes of political accountability over those of legal accountability.[62] This standard position has been subject to change in the modern period. The powers flowing to the courts as a consequence of the UK's membership of the EU, and in particular the need to 'disapply' even domestic primary legislation which violates EU law, has been a key element of this process.[63] Yet this has not been the only context in which the domestic courts have been empowered: the Human Rights Act 1998 creates a scheme in which all primary legislation is subject to substantive judicial review to assess its compatibility with the European Convention on Human Rights;[64] the devolution system

[60] See, eg, M Loughlin, 'The End of Avoidance' *London Review of Books*, vol 38(15) (28 July 2016) 13. On the tensions raised in this context more generally, see House of Commons Public Administration and Constitutional Affairs Committee, *Devolution and Exiting the EU: reconciling differences and building strong relationships*, HC 1485 (31 July 2018).

[61] See JAG Griffith, 'The Political Constitution' (1979) 42 *Modern Law Review* 1; G Gee and G Webber, 'What is a Political Constitution?' (2010) 30 *Oxford Journal of Legal Studies* 273.

[62] See Gordon, *Parliamentary Sovereignty in the UK Constitution*, above n 6, ch 2.

[63] *R v Secretary of State for Transport, ex p Factortame (No 2)* [1991] 1 AC 603; *Benkharbouche v Secretary of State for Foreign and Commonwealth Affairs* [2017] UKSC 62.

[64] Although the Human Rights Act 1998 does not create a power for the courts to strike down legislation, but instead imposes a strong interpretative duty to achieve compatibility with the ECHR (by s 3) and, where this is not possible, the discretion to issue declarations of incompatibility which do not have the effect of undermining the legal validity of a statute (by s 4).

gives the courts the task of ensuring that devolved primary legislation is within competence, and the responsibility for invalidating anything which exceeds that; and the Constitutional Reform Act 2005 created a new UK Supreme Court providing an infrastructure for growing institutional self-confidence. The UK Parliament has obviously been the key actor empowering the courts through its legislative activity, but the Brexit process has demonstrated that this extension of judicial authority is altering the constitutional position of the courts, in uncertain ways.

First, we have seen the courts drawn into debates concerning the consequences of democratic decision-making and the authority of democratic institutions at the UK level. This is particularly challenging territory for the judges, given the obviously non-democratic character of the UK's judicial institutions in general, but especially when combined more specifically with the intensely contested political environment which has developed around the 2016 referendum. In this context, determination of the domestic constitutional requirements to even begin the process of negotiating withdrawal under Article 50 TEU became a major public debate, with the courts at its centre. It was ultimately resolved by the Supreme Court returning the issue to Parliament in *Miller*, the majority judgment having concluded that there was a legal necessity for fresh legislative authorisation to give notification of EU withdrawal. This decision had a limited substantive impact, given the quick response from Parliament to fill the gap in authority discerned by the Supreme Court,[65] but *Miller* nevertheless raises important questions about the constitutional position of the courts. Following hysterical criticism of the initial judgment of the High Court in *Miller*, with the judges described in some parts of the media as 'enemies of the people' supporting an attempt to frustrate the will of the electorate, the Supreme Court relied on a sharp distinction between law and politics to justify its jurisdiction:

> [T]his case has nothing to do with issues such as the wisdom of the decision to withdraw from the European Union … Those are all political issues which are matters for ministers and Parliament to resolve. They are not issues which are appropriate for resolution by judges, whose duty is to decide issues of law which are brought before them … in a democratic society.[66]

The Supreme Court in *Miller* therefore positioned itself as the arbiter of matters of pure law, and the majority paid little attention to the result or authority of the referendum, attempting to frame this instead as a narrow question about the legal powers of the government. Yet this was problematic in two ways. First, the judgment of the majority in the Supreme Court *was* explicitly based on an analysis of the constitutional context, concerning the significance of the removal of EU law as a source of the UK's legal system. Indeed, perhaps the central justification for the majority's decision was that 'it would be inconsistent with long-standing

[65] European Union (Notification of Withdrawal) Act 2017; see above n 17.
[66] *Miller*, above n 2, 3.

and fundamental principle for such a far-reaching change to the UK constitutional arrangements to be brought about by ministerial decision or ministerial action alone'.[67] These 'long-standing and fundamental' principles were not identified or articulated, making the judgment seem more like an assessment of constitutional morality than an exercise in objective legal reasoning. The second problem was that this consequentialist constitutional approach of the majority was selective. To insist on legislative authorisation at the start of the Brexit process overlooked the deep and complex set of interactions that would necessarily occur between Parliament and the government throughout the process of EU withdrawal, and as noted by Lord Carnwath in dissent, failed to take proper account of another 'fundamental' principle, that of 'Parliamentary accountability'.[68] The decision in *Miller* might therefore be criticised as taking a very broad view of the legal constitutional context, and the monumental consequences of removing EU rules as a source of domestic law, but showing little interest in the political constitutional context, and in particular the interactive relationship between Parliament and the government which would necessarily underpin the Brexit process.

In a sense, *Miller* might therefore be seen to represent a judicialisation of the domestic constitutional process of withdrawal, with law ultimately conceived as a constraint on political actors, rather than a tool through which political ends (whether good or bad) are achieved. This is not to say a simplistic distinction can be drawn between law as a limit or as an enabler, or that the government should be able to act unbound by legal rules. Instead, it is to highlight the fact that the Supreme Court has played a significant role in definitively establishing the terms of what is a political process, in a political constitution, and that very little attention has been given to the appropriateness of such crucial decisions being made by the judiciary. That we should have respect for the idea of the rule of law does not provide an adequate answer to this problem, for the very dilemma here is why such matters should be characterised as questions of law, rather than questions requiring political resolution. This confidence that there can be legal solutions to political problems has had broader consequences – we have seen a flurry of other litigation relating to Brexit, much of it futile, but still serving to propagate the notion that legal challenge is a means not just to clarify but also to obstruct the political process.[69] At a time of considerable constitutional uncertainty, this means we also have additional uncertainty about the position of the courts, and questions to ask about the scope of their role in a democratic political system.

Second, the courts have also been drawn into a dispute settlement role between the UK and the devolved institutions in the context of Brexit. Again, this puts the judiciary in a delicate position, in having to navigate a legal framework which sometimes struggles to neatly accommodate the competing democratic claims of

[67] ibid 81.
[68] ibid 249.
[69] See, eg, *R (Webster) v Secretary of State for Exiting the European Union* [2018] EWHC 1543 (Admin); *R (Wilson) v Prime Minister* [2019] EWCA Civ 304.

actors in different constitutional layers. The difficulty of this role was also made evident in *Miller*, with the Supreme Court unanimously deciding that it would not enforce the Sewel convention, which could have established a legally actionable right for the devolved institutions to consent to – or more importantly, to veto – the UK's withdrawal from the EU. This has attracted criticism on the ground that the Supreme Court failed to give legal effect to the Sewel convention despite the fact that this norm is now captured in statute, and is potentially thereby given legal force.[70] The Supreme Court was surely right, however, to decide that through this provision the UK Parliament was simply 'recognising' the convention in statute,[71] and 'not seeking to convert the Sewel Convention into a rule which can be interpreted, let alone enforced, by the courts'.[72] More problematic is that the formalistic approach taken by the Court to this issue stands in stark contrast to the far more elaborate constitutional reasoning justifying the need for the approval of the UK Parliament. The *Miller* decision is therefore left open to objections of selective engagement with principle, and an approach to consequentialist analysis that favoured the UK, but not the devolved, institutions. Indeed, this could be seen as evidence of a strategic approach by the Supreme Court – the risk of the UK Parliament halting a process it had started by passing the EU Referendum Act 2015 was very low, and to require its approval to begin the Article 50 negotiations was therefore a safe outcome. Whereas the risk of the devolved institutions in Scotland and Northern Ireland refusing consent to a Brexit which failed to attract majority support in these nations was much higher, and therefore a controversial outcome which the courts would be keen to avoid.

Whether the UK Supreme Court is seen as a fair dealer by the devolved institutions into the future may also be shaped by its decision in a second case, which was entirely premised on a disagreement between the Scottish and the UK legislatures. Following the UK government's controversial decision to seek initially to centralise powers returning from the EU which would otherwise naturally fall within areas of devolved competence, and the Scottish Parliament's refusal to consent to the EU (Withdrawal) Bill as a result, competing EU Continuity legislation was passed in Scotland.[73] This Bill was modelled on the UK Withdrawal legislation, but with some significant differences, in terms of substance (such as the retention of the Charter of Fundamental Rights in Scotland) and in terms of process (crucially giving the Scottish government co-decision-making powers in relation to subject matters returning from the EU and falling within existing areas of devolved competence).[74] Once passed, but before legal enactment, the Scottish Bill was referred to the UK Supreme Court to determine whether it was a

[70] See, eg, KD Ewing, 'Brexit and Parliamentary Sovereignty' (2017) 80 *Modern Law Review* 711.

[71] Scotland Act 1998, s 28(8) (as amended by the Scotland Act 2016, s 2).

[72] *Miller*, above n 2, 148.

[73] The UK Withdrawal from the European Union (Legal Continuity) (Scotland) Bill.

[74] Similar legislation was enacted in Wales, in the form of the Law Derived from the European Union (Wales) Act 2018. Following agreement between the UK and Welsh governments over the UK Withdrawal Act, this legislation was repealed by Regulations entering into force on 22 November 2018.

lawful exercise of devolved competence.[75] This clash of legislation left the Supreme Court in a precarious position. If it ruled against the Scottish Bill, the extent to which it is the UK's Supreme Court would never have been more apparent. Yet if the Court decided that the devolved Continuity legislation was legally valid, this would have produced the incredible complexity of related but distinct regimes governing EU withdrawal in different nations of the UK, underpinned by different values, and potentially competing attitudes to the question of regulatory change or alignment. The Supreme Court ultimately held that the Scottish Bill was, in large part, outside the legislative competence of the Scottish Parliament because the EU (Withdrawal) Act 2018, once finally enacted, had through its own terms been self-designated as a 'protected provision' in the terms of the devolution settlement.[76] The Scottish Parliament was therefore not permitted to modify the effects of the UK Withdrawal Act, or indeed other protected provisions, including section 28(7) of the Scotland Act 1998, which preserves the power of the UK Parliament to legislate for Scotland. As a result, the Continuity Bill was eventually abandoned by the Scottish Government.[77] The Supreme Court's rather surprising decision to emphasise the continuing sovereignty of the UK Parliament explicitly throughout the judgment suggests that the flexibility which the judges are increasingly attempting to develop around that constitutional principle is unlikely to be used to enhance the standing of the devolved institutions.[78] In that sense, the Supreme Court does not appear to be a forum in which more ambitious arguments based on the constitutional values underpinning devolution will be capable of transcending the legal architecture of those arrangements.

A final complexity in the context of devolution is that, the UK Supreme Court in *Miller* having avoided any attempts to make a reference to the Court of Justice of the European Union (CJEU) as to the possibility of an Article 50 notification being lawfully revoked, the Scottish courts have made such a reference to the European court. This case was brought by a group of politicians, including Members of the Scottish, UK and European Parliaments. They argued that having a clear answer as a matter of EU law as to the legality of the UK government unilaterally withdrawing its exit notice would be essential to their ability to discharge their duties as parliamentarians, by understanding the full range of possibilities when asked to vote to approve any deal which might be agreed between the EU and UK government.

[75] *The UK Withdrawal from the European Union (Legal Continuity) (Scotland) Bill – A Reference by the Attorney General and the Advocate General for Scotland (Scotland)* [2018] UKSC 64.

[76] European Union (Withdrawal) Act 2018, Schedule 3, Part 1, para 21.

[77] For analysis, see C McCorkindale and A McHarg, 'Continuity and Confusion: Towards Clarity? – The Supreme Court and the Scottish Continuity Bill' (*UK Constitutional Law Association Blog*, 20 December 2018), available at: ukconstitutionallaw.org/2018/12/20/chris-mccorkindale-and-aileen-mcharg-continuity-and-confusion-towards-clarity-the-supreme-court-and-the-scottish-continuity-bill/; M Elliott, 'The Supreme Court's judgment in the Scottish Continuity Bill case' (*Public Law for Everyone*, 14 December 2018), available at: publiclawforeveryone.com/2018/12/14/the-supreme-courts-judgment-in-the-scottish-continuity-bill-case/.

[78] For references to parliamentary sovereignty in this case, see eg *(Legal Continuity) (Scotland) Bill*, above n 75, 12, 41, 43, 53, 61, 63, 64.

This petition was rejected by the Outer House of the Court of Session, but accepted on appeal to the Inner House. Whereas Lord Boyd in the Outer House thought this case related to a hypothetical issue, rather than any concrete legal dispute, and to make such a reference amounted to an attempt to influence the parliamentary process,[79] the Inner House held there would be no interference with parliamentary privilege in making a reference, because to obtain legal clarity would not compel members of the legislature to reach any particular decision.[80] A UK government appeal to the Supreme Court was rejected on technical grounds,[81] and so the CJEU decided the matter, concluding that the unilateral revocation of the Article 50 notice would be lawful, if it was 'unequivocal', 'unconditional', and 'brings the withdrawal procedure to an end'.[82] Whether this will be material is unclear, given Theresa May's government consistently indicated it would not consider withdrawing the notice in any event. Whether this is likely to be advantageous for the litigants is also unclear – given the legal conditions now attached to revocation of notice, there may be less room for manoeuvre in extreme circumstances than had the matter been left open to resolution through the supranational political process. But from the perspective of the domestic courts, making this reference is to accept that it is legitimate for the legal process to be used to shape parliamentary decision-making. Indeed, this is the very aim of the petitioners, who are political actors. And in that sense, the decision to make a reference to the CJEU can, at the very least, be seen as an indirect interference with Parliament's democratic privilege to make decisions without the range of possibilities having been pre-emptively established in the courts.

The Brexit process therefore shows the courts drawn into a complex democratic arena, resolving disputes linked to competing democratic actors, barely concealed beneath a veneer of legality. We can see the acute difficulty in principle, and the implausibility in practice, of the judiciary purporting to take an objective legal approach in this context. That is not to say the courts are making decisions based on the first order political preferences of judges, but that they are arguably insensitive to the varying democratic ideas in play and in competition. In this sense, the idea that the rule of law stands above and apart from democratic decision-making is exposed as simply another conception of democratic government, one in which democratic activity is characterised as occurring in specific areas tightly constrained by a framework of law, rather than viewing democracy as a value which pervades and structures the entire political system. Such a formalistic

[79] *Wightman and others v Secretary of State for Exiting the European Union* [2018] CSOH 61, esp 58–60.

[80] *Wightman and others v Secretary of State for Exiting the European Union* [2018] CSIH 62 EU:C:2018:999, esp 27–28.

[81] Appeal was only available from the Inner House in relation to a final judgment, and since making a reference to the CJEU was a part, and not the end, of the legal proceedings, no appeal could be made; UKSC 2018/0209.

[82] Case C-621/18 *Wightman and Others* ECLI:EU:C:2018:999, 74.

approach to the relationship between law and democracy might be justifiable if it had been deployed consistently, yet in fact the courts have occupied a prominent position in the Brexit process, often establishing a more active constitutional role for themselves through their reasoning (especially in *Miller*) and their decisions (especially in *Wightman*). This new role sits uneasily with the UK's tradition of constitutional democracy, with the courts using constitutional ideas to establish and impose procedural requirements, rather than leaving the constitution to be shaped by democratic contestation through democratic processes. It is far from clear that the courts are institutionally or democratically suited for a role as constitutional author. And at the very least, there needs to be much better articulation of those norms which operate to constrain the engagement of the courts with sensitive political questions, as much as those principles which permit such judicial activity.

## Constitutional Overload and Constitutional Democracy

How do we begin to analyse the overall effects of this (still ongoing) series of constitutional episodes? In terms of constitutional capacity, the UK's constitution is obviously straining under the weight of delivering change of this complexity, in this volume. And from the perspective of constitutional principle, the extent of the complexity stems not merely from the regular (and necessary) democratic competition between proponents of alternative outcomes, but from clashes generated by competing institutional conceptions of constitutional democracy itself. It may be a source of some irony that in a constitution especially associated (rightly or wrongly) with the facilitation of power, perhaps the overarching and continuing deficiencies of the UK's institutions of government have been chronic indecision and a failure (or inability) to plot a clear future trajectory. As a result, the UK's political constitution risks being overwhelmed by its politics.[83]

However, when attempting to assess the impact of the Brexit process, our analysis must be more sophisticated than simply blaming all problems on the failings of the UK constitution, perhaps because of its unorthodox structure, or its emphasis, through the doctrine of parliamentary sovereignty, on the constitutional supremacy of political processes rather than legal principles. This is far from an easy story of democratic disintegration or constitutional collapse. Instead, we need to try to draw out the precise nature of the difficulties faced in this period and to better understand their effects. From this perspective, the real challenge of the Brexit process is that it is the product of a combination of factors, based on

[83] M Gordon, 'Brexit: a Challenge *for* the UK Constitution, *of* the UK Constitution?' (2016) 12 *European Constitutional Law Review* 409, 435.

competing interpretations of institutional power, of democratic will, and of constitutional authority. In essence, during the Brexit process, the UK is in a period of political turmoil, legal uncertainty, and constitutional overload.

What are the key characteristics of this period of constitutional overload? The sheer scale of the challenge of Brexit is the initial starting point, with implications across the whole spectrum of constitutional activity. Yet this constitutional overload is also about more than just the fact that Brexit means there is a vast amount of work to do in a short period of time. Instead, what crucially defines this period of overload is the way in which the various constitutional challenges are interacting, and as a result, intensifying, magnifying and proliferating. We have seen a general tendency towards escalation, with difficulties in one area cutting across into other areas, producing a levelling-up effect in terms of constitutional controversy, with each specific challenge latent with the potential to prompt further difficulties.

For example, we have seen controversial legislative decisions taken by Parliament and the government in the UK create problems in the devolution context, with the Scottish refusal to accept the terms of the EU (Withdrawal) Act 2018, which itself has created difficult problems for courts, in the litigation over the Scottish Continuity Bill. Further, we have seen the actions of devolved actors create dilemmas for the UK's political institutions, with the Scottish and Welsh legislatures reaching different decisions on consent to the EU (Withdrawal) Act 2018, and the inability to form an executive in Northern Ireland giving a lack of institutional voice to that nation and disproportionate influence to the DUP. We have also seen the Scottish government arguing for equivalent treatment if Northern Ireland obtains a special status remaining in alignment with aspects of the single market, complicating debates over the avoidance of a hard border on the island of Ireland. We have seen the actions of the judiciary creating a no-win situation for the UK Parliament after *Miller*, with the legislature then required explicitly to authorise notification of withdrawal to respect the referendum result, and therefore becoming constitutionally complicit in the decision, providing the UK government with a basis to repel subsequent parliamentary criticism and scrutiny. Similarly, the courts have profoundly weakened the position of the devolved institutions in *Miller*, formally confirming the absence of a legal consent requirement, while there is potential for the outcome of the *Wightman* litigation to place the UK government in a challenging position as regards the possibility of revoking the Article 50 notice. And, indeed, decisions taken by the UK's electorates have created challenges for all established constitutional actors, not least the result of the 2017 general election which, in creating a hung Parliament, created the perfect political storm of a weak minority government and no obvious majority for any particular outcome to the Brexit negotiations.

The constitutional overload resulting from these interacting and intensifying challenges is also exacerbated because it is framed around clashing ideas of constitutional principle. As we have seen, a defining theme of the Brexit process has been different institutional engagement with different ideas of democracy. We see competition between direct and representative democracy, between rule-bound and transformative conceptions of democracy, and between the wills of different national and subnational democratic peoples. And we see these competing democratic claims propagated and even appropriated by different institutional actors. Constitutional overload is not therefore merely the product of a build-up of different events, problems and activities which intensify in their complexity as they go unsolved, or in relation to which any potential solution seems to generate a new round of problems (with the debate about the 'backstop' designed to prevent a hard border emerging between Northern Ireland and the Republic of Ireland being perhaps the most obvious example of such a spiralling solution). Rather, constitutional overload is also a consequence of the apparent irreconcilability of competing democratic claims, and the near irresolvable institutional conflicts erupting to vindicate these claims.[84]

Constitutional overload therefore has a dual character. We see clashes of constitutional principle underpinning problems of constitutional capacity in the domestic attempts to respond to Brexit. But as a result, the constitution is not just overloaded in the sense that too much activity is required in a range of distinct areas, but with cross-cutting implications, in a short period of time. The UK constitution is also overloaded in that in this contested democratic environment it cannot establish a singular process for the UK's withdrawal from the EU. There are a range of values, priorities and functions which are all constitutional in their character, and yet pushed, pulled and strained by Brexit to the point that what the norms of UK constitutional democracy require has become impossible to define with certainty. The 2016 referendum has a clear constitutional authority, but Parliament has the right to decide how to implement the result. The government has the power to make decisions concerning the future direction of public policy and the shape of the relationship with the EU, but opposition parties have a duty to scrutinise and challenge. The devolved institutions must protect their competences and represent their electorates, yet the UK institutions have the authority to make decisions for the nation as a whole. The courts have the right to hear cases concerning legal questions associated with the process of withdrawal, but the political institutions are justified in expecting significant deference, and not interference, from non-democratic judicial actors.

In this context, the constitution is overloaded almost to the point where both everything and nothing is simultaneously constitutional.[85] And as a result, everything and nothing seems like it might be possible. This is perhaps most apparent in relation to the consequences of the failure by the House of Commons to approve the draft Withdrawal Agreement negotiated by Theresa May. It might

[84] On the idea of the intractability of competing demands as a key component of political overload in a previous era, see A King, 'Overload: Problems of Governing in the 1970s' (1975) (2–3) *Political Studies* 162.

[85] See Griffith, above n 61, 19.

have led to a general election, a change of government, a change of Prime Minister, an attempt to renegotiate with the EU, an extension of the Article 50 negotiating period, a further vote on the draft deal, a second referendum on Brexit, negotiated withdrawal of the exit notice, unilateral withdrawal of the exit notice, or simply a no-deal Brexit. And in the continued absence of parliamentary approval for any single way forward, all of these options will remain on the table. Even if a degree of unpredictability is inevitable in such unprecedented circumstances, this level of constitutional uncertainty is extreme. Constitutional overload has therefore paradoxically produced both turbulence and stasis in the UK's legal and political system, and as a result, the challenge of shaping the domestic response to Brexit only grows.

What are the implications of the UK's current constitutional overload? The tensions emerging between different conceptions of democracy, different democratic claims, different democratic actors and different democratic functions reveal democratic problems for the constitution, both practical and conceptual in nature. Yet these problems will not be easily solved, because of the constitutional overload by which they have been exposed. A lack of constitutional time and capacity presently exists to deal with intensely difficult questions concerning the appropriate future shape and character of the UK's constitutional democracy, along with a lack of imagination regarding the ways in which that constitution might be redesigned. In a period where there is too much activity, there is a regular flow of distractions from major underlying problems. Everything instantly becomes a constitutional crisis,[86] and so nothing is. The energy and institutional capacity for reform has been diminished at the exact moment the need for reform is being most acutely demonstrated. And in this sense, constitutional overload itself is one of the biggest challenges to democracy faced by the UK.

Does this mean we are destined for democratic torpor in the post-Brexit UK? What awaits the UK's constitutional system after Brexit very much remains to be seen, but a significant gap might quickly emerge between the reform that could be desirable and the reform that could be possible. In terms of what is desirable, a new internal architecture may become necessary to structure decision-making between the UK and the devolved institutions of government, to organise the use of regained competences and to establish and maintain common frameworks in legal areas where they are agreed (while ensuring they are not centrally imposed). We may need to reassess existing norms regarding how and when referendums are used, while considering additional mechanisms which might allow citizen deliberation and participation to be enhanced. The voting system should be revisited to consider how to reinforce representative institutions at a time when the system

[86] See, eg, 'Brexit: May facing constitutional crisis as Bercow says "arguable case" government guilty of contempt of Parliament over legal advice' *The Independent* (3 December 2018), available at: www.independent.co.uk/news/uk/politics/brexit-deal-latest-theresa-may-crisis-contempt-labour-conservative-parliament-government-a8665576.html.

is failing to provide either proportionate or stable outcomes. We might attempt to find a better use for the House of Lords when the necessity of breaking the hold of elites over politics has acquired new urgency. Yet a programme of constitutional rethinking incorporating these examples already has an idealistic tenor, and would be liable to disruption by further events extending the period of overload: a further independence referendum will be a high priority for pro-EU forces in Scotland, and a poll on the status of Northern Ireland cannot be ruled out as the impact of any changes to the border with the Republic of Ireland become clearer. And even if the current constitutional overload eventually subsides, this is likely to be followed by a period of constitutional fatigue and avoidance.

The constitutional overload generated by Brexit has therefore revealed flaws in the structures of the UK's democratic constitution. But even if this does amount to a significant 'constitutional moment',[87] it is far from clear that a shift to a more traditional conception of constitutional democracy would provide a solution. While in the dominant liberal account of constitutional democracy we might expect to see the constitutional operating to temper democratic politics, in the UK democratic politics is driving the constitutional. In such circumstances, attempts to more deeply constrain institutional power arguably represent a diversion.[88] The democratic tensions evident in this context are deeply embedded, and were not simply created by the 2016 referendum. The UK's struggle with Brexit may tell us something about the modern limitations of the nation state, and the extent to which democratic decision-making within it is confined by external factors. This is not to suggest that the nation state is now unviable as the basic unit of governance, but that Brexit may be a lesson in the difficulty – or perhaps futility – of pursuing a strategy of constitutional isolation. If this is the case, Brexit may demonstrate the increased fragility of national authority in the face of globalised power networks. This suggests that the priority should be to strengthen the democratic state to better respond to these developments and agendas, rather than to use constitutionalism to restrain democracy so that the status quo become impossible to challenge.

At this moment, however, Brexit-induced constitutional overload presents a major barrier to more elaborate domestic constitutional reform, at precisely the moment the constitutional events explored in this chapter are making need for systematic change so readily apparent. We clearly need a greater sense of the possibilities if we are to avoid becoming resigned to a democratically inchoate existence, and to have any chance of shaping the UK's constitutional future. However, it would be complacent to assume the contemporary prominence of constitutional issues provides a steady platform for far-reaching reform; it is perhaps more likely that when constitutional overload subsides, a return to relative normality will be mistaken for a solution to deeper-lying problems. Yet absent some more detailed

[87] See, eg, M Loughlin, 'The British Constitution: Thoughts on the Cause of the Present Discontents' (2018) 16 *New Zealand Journal of Public and International Law* 1.

[88] For the alternative argument in favour of a 'protected', codified UK constitution after Brexit see, eg, V Bogdanor, *Brexit and Our Unprotected Constitution* (London, The Constitution Society, 2018) 40.

reflection on the UK's institutional order, its distribution of power, and its democratic model, it may take a future re-emergence of constitutional overload for us to realise these problems were not solved, but simply submerged.

## Conclusion

Brexit has dominated the UK's politics, unsettled its democracy, and overloaded its constitution. Ultimately, the impact of Brexit on the state of the UK's democratic constitutional model will not be uniform or easy to predict. While constraints of some variety will inevitably remain, the UK seems set to deviate from the European model of coordination through supranational systems of law. The flow of power away from Westminster within the UK may well accelerate, and the competition between different democratic claims and actors may become even more complex. The brutal practical challenge of Brexit is already highlighting the inadequacy of some aspects of our domestic constitutional arrangements, yet paradoxically it is also sapping energy for deeper reform. The UK's current period of constitutional overload is distracting us from underlying problems, including the disempowerment of certain regions and the disenchantment of citizens, which the referendum has arguably served to exacerbate. But there are no easy answers, because Brexit demonstrates that the UK is experiencing clashes between what is 'constitutional' and what is 'democratic'. The UK's model of constitutional democracy may be premised on the idea that there is fluidity in the way that democratic decisions (re)shape the constitution, and the constitution provides space for a range of competing democratic inputs. Yet the interconnected challenges of constitutional capacity and constitutional principle which have been generated by Brexit have pushed the UK into a period of spiralling constitutional overload, and there is no clear resolution in view. The path to an enhanced democratic constitution will require us to emerge from this period of overload and, rather than succumb to fatigue or accept a resumption of the old ways, to reconsider the ideas of democracy which underpin the UK's legal and political system. At present, however, precisely because this period of constitutional overload is self-sustaining and intensifying, that path seems some way into the distance.

# Section 2: Constitutionalism in the EU

# 5

# EU Fundamental Rights Legislation: The Constitutional Imbroglio

ELISE MUIR*

## Introduction

An important shift has taken place over the past decades in EU fundamental rights law.[1] In a process that started with the Treaty of Maastricht and culminated with the Treaty of Lisbon, the mandate of the various European Union (EU) institutions on matters of fundamental rights protection has profoundly changed.

The analysis of the protection of fundamental rights in the EU is nowadays usually shaped around two main axes. A first and common question relates to the possibility to check EU acts, legislative acts in particular, or acts of the Member States falling within the scope of EU law for compliance with EU fundamental rights. This approach seeks to ensure 'the rule of law for the Union itself'.[2] A second and uniquely pressing question in recent years, is concerned with the empowerment of populist parties progressively eroding fundamental rights at domestic level across the EU. This line of research deals with 'the Rule of Law within the Union'[3] and asks how and to what extent the EU may help modifying this worrying trend.[4]

Departing from these usual approaches to the protection of fundamental rights in EU law, this contribution invites reflection on a less explored dimension of the challenges raised by the protection of fundamental rights in the EU: the increased emphasis placed on the role of the EU legislator in shaping European fundamental

* Comments welcome at elise.muir@kuleuven.be. This chapter builds on part of a broader project as agreed with the publisher: E Muir, *EU Equality Law: The First Fundamental Rights Policy of the EU* (Oxford University Press, 2018). The author is grateful to the participants – in particular Marco Dani and Sacha Garben – of the 2017 edition of the Czech Mountains Seminar organised by Jan Komárek and Marco Dani for useful feedback on an earlier draft.

[1] The expressions 'fundamental rights' and 'human rights' are used interchangeably in this chapter.

[2] Editorial comments, 'The Rule of Law in the Union, the Rule of Union Law and the Rule of Law by the Union: Three interrelated problems' (2016) 53 *Common Market Law Review* 597.

[3] ibid.

[4] eg, L Pech and KL Scheppele, 'Illiberalism Within: Rule of Law Backsliding in the EU' (2017) 19 *Cambridge Yearbook of European Legal Studies* 3 ff; D Kochenov, 'Busting the Myths Nuclear: A Commentary on Article 7 TEU' (2017) 10 EUI Working Paper.

rights law – as illustrated by EU anti-discrimination as well as data protection legislation over the past two decades.[5] Here, the focus is not so much on whether EU secondary law conflicts with primary law as in 'the rule of law for the Union itself'; nor is the focus on the calling into question of European values at domestic level as in 'the Rule of Law within the Union'. Instead, the process under scrutiny is one by which European values are being fleshed out through the democratic process at EU level. In other words, the law that governs EU approaches to the various dimensions of the rule of law identified above is substantiated by Union political institutions.

What are the constitutional implications of such a transfer of decision-making powers on fundamental right matters to the legislator in a supranational order such as the EU? Unlike in the process that led to the drafting of the Charter of Fundamental Rights of the EU (the Charter) in which much attention was devoted to ensuring democratic input in shaping primary law on fundamental rights,[6] it is now the legislator that gives expression to selected fundamental rights when empowered to do so by the EU Treaties. As is well known, the EU (still) does not have competence to 'protect against human rights violations *per se*'.[7] Yet, two important novelties impact the way one ought to understand decision-making on fundamental rights at EU level.

On the one hand, the mandate of the Court of Justice of the European Union (the Court) on matters of fundamental rights protection in the post-Lisbon era is much stronger than it used to be. The Charter now has the same legal value as the Treaties.[8] The Treaties are dotted with references to fundamental rights that enhance the legislators duty to take them into account.[9] The EU has also gained and exercised competences that touch upon fundamental rights much more directly than used to be the case, as in the fields of migration and criminal law, so that the Court acts as a more important fundamental right watchdog.[10]

[5] See, for instance, Council Directive (EC) 2000/43 of 29 June 2000 implementing the principle of equal treatment between persons irrespective of racial or ethnic origin [2000] OJ L180/22; Council Directive (EC) 2000/78 of 27 November 2000 establishing a general framework for equal treatment in employment and occupation [2000] OJ L303/16; Directive (EC) 2006/54 of 5 July 2006 on the implementation of the principle of equal opportunities and equal treatment of men and women in matters of employment and occupation (recast) [2006] OJ L204/23; Council Directive (EC) 2004/113 of 13 December 2004 implementing the principle of equal treatment between men and women in the access to and supply of goods and services [2004] OJ L373/37; Regulation (EU) 2016/679 of 27 April 2016 on the protection of natural persons with regard to the processing of personal data and on the free movement of such data, and repealing Directive 95/46/EC [2016] OJ L119/1 (General Data Protection Regulation).

[6] See, for instance, R Bellamy and J Schönlau, 'The Normality of Constitutional Politics: An Analysis of the Drafting of the EU Charter of Fundamental Rights' (2004) 11 *Constellations* 412; G de Búrca, 'The Drafting of the European Union Charter of Fundamental Rights' (2001) 26 *European Law Review* 126.

[7] AG Toth, 'The European Union and Human Rights: The Way Forward' (1997) 34 *Common Market Law Review* 491, 497.

[8] Art 6(1) TEU.

[9] eg, Arts 10 and 67(1) TFEU.

[10] G de Búrca, 'After the EU Charter of Fundamental Rights: The Court of Justice as a Human Rights Adjudicator?' (2013) 20 *Maastricht Journal of European and Comparative Law* 168, 174 ff.

On the other hand, the mandate of the EU legislator on matters of fundamental rights has also changed profoundly. The EU legislator has gained clear and explicit competences to express its understanding of selected fundamental rights such as the fundamental right to equal treatment (the main legal basis is Article 19 TFEU)[11] and the fundamental right to data protection (the legal basis is Article 16 TFEU). The same institutions have also gained competences in areas that are directly and intimately connected to fundamental rights so that the legislator may be called upon to flesh out its understanding of a specific fundamental right in this context too, for instance, the circumstances in which a person involved in a criminal trial must be deemed to have waived, voluntarily and unambiguously, his right to be present at his trial in the context of the European Arrest Warrant.[12] Furthermore, EU institutions have adjusted their legislative practices to assess the fundamental rights implications of the legal acts that they design and negotiate.[13]

These mutations in the constitutional landscape for the design of EU law-making on fundamental rights require understanding the function that the EU legislator performs in giving shape to EU fundamental rights, when compared with that of the Court, through a new lens: the Court, on the one side, is entrusted with the task of protecting fundamental rights enshrined in EU primary law (Article 19(1) TEU); the EU legislator, on the other, is intended by the Treaties to confer democratic legitimacy to decision-making on fundamental rights at EU level (Article 10(2) TEU).[14] The present chapter contextualises these changes and spells out the main conceptual as well as constitutional parameters for understanding the new mandate of the EU legislator on fundamental rights questions.

The analysis therefore proceeds in three stages. The phenomenon by which EU institutions can and do legislate specifically and explicitly in order to enhance the protection of a fundamental right is fairly new: this opens up a new era after a period in which the focus had been on elevating fundamental rights beyond the realm of ordinary politics (i). The institutional implications of this new setting are twofold: they emerge from the tension thereby created between political institutions and constitutional law-making (ii); and they are particularly intense in the context of the EU legal order where the interplay between two legal orders – domestic and European – adds to the complexity of the matter (iii).

Specific emphasis will be placed throughout the chapter on the important role that political institutions play in shaping EU intervention on fundamental rights.

[11] See also Art 157 TFEU.

[12] Art 4a(1) of Council Framework Decision 2002/584/JHA on the European arrest warrant and the surrender procedures between Member States [2002] OJ L190/1 as amended by Council Framework Decision 2009/299/JHA of 26 February 2009.

[13] See M Dawson, *The Governance of EU Fundamental Rights* (Cambridge, Cambridge University Press, 2017).

[14] I do not enter here the perfectly legitimate discussion on whether the Council and European Parliament indeed deliver the appropriate democratic input in EU decision-making processes.

These institutions enhance democratic debate on European values and allow for the plurality of approaches that may exist within the EU legal order to be exposed. The chapter therefore calls for maintaining a clear distinction between fundamental rights legislation, that marks political agreement at a given point in time and may be reopen for discussion, and related constitutional rights that lack the said flexibility, with a view to acknowledging the sensitive nature of EU intervention on such matters.

## A New Mode of Fundamental Rights Law-Making at Supranational Level

Before delving into the constitutional challenges raised by the new form of fundamental rights law-making that EU legislation constitutes at EU level, we ought to briefly reflect on how this trend relates to mechanisms of individual rights' protection at domestic and European level.

### The Dynamics of the Protection of Fundamental Rights in Europe

In contemporary history, three generations of tools for the protection of the rights of individuals may be distinguished. First, political and social rights were treated as ordinary rights, the protection of which was entrusted to the state through ordinary laws. Hoffmann recalls that in the period between the eighteenth-century revolutions and the twentieth-century world wars, it is the struggle for political and social rights that took centre stage in constitutions and politics.[15] In this context the state was seen as a guarantor of rights, rights which were regulated through ordinary laws.[16]

Secondly, selected rights were constitutionalised and internationalised: 'uploaded' to higher legal spheres for protection from the dangers of ordinary politics. In the mid-twentieth century, the mass violations that occurred during the Second World War triggered a call to entrench the protection of fundamental values in legal norms beyond the reach of 'ordinary' politics.[17] This resulted in simultaneous processes of constitutionalisation and internationalisation of selected rights as usefully accounted for by Garbaum for instance.[18]

[15] S-L Hoffmann, 'Genealogies of Human Rights' in S-L Hoffmann (ed), *Human Rights in the Twentieth Century* (Cambridge, Cambridge University Press, 2010) 7.

[16] ibid 9.

[17] A Somek, *The Cosmopolitan Constitution* (Oxford, Oxford University Press, 2014) 73–74.

[18] S Gardbaum, 'Human Rights as International Constitutional Rights' (2008) 19 *European Journal of International Law* 749, 759.

Thirdly and more recently, legislation is being adopted in order to give expression to some of the so-called fundamental rights protected at constitutional level, thus 'downloading' them and bringing them back into the political sphere. The adoption of such legislation is closely related to the uploading process just described in so far as legislation is adopted *in order to* flesh out rights that have been uploaded in a process of internationalisation and constitutionalisation.

In that sense, the process of legislating on select fundamental rights could be described as a complementary 'downloading' process bringing a protected right *back* into the political arena. The interplay between the two processes is important in so far as political institutions act in full awareness of the link between the legislation and the fundamental right protected through constitutional law. The relationship between the two layers of the same right is likely to be particularly ambiguous. The setting is thus different from where rights enshrined in legislation simply overlap with rights or principles protected at constitutional level, as is often the case.

## Locating Fundamental Rights Legislation in the EU Legal Order

The last two trends, ie, the uploading and downloading of fundamental right protection, have been uniquely reflected in the development of the EU. On the one hand, the EU could be said to constitute a 'paradigm of a constitutionalised regime of international law'.[19] Although the EU has not been designed as an organisation with human rights as its core policy, the European integration process has resulted in the 'uploading' of human rights protection beyond domestic legal spheres. This uploading of fundamental rights protection has for a long time primarily resulted from the increasingly broad ability of the EU judiciary to ensure compliance with fundamental rights, protected at constitutional level in EU law by Member States when they act within the scope of EU law.

On the other hand, the 'downloading' process that is now complementing constitutional forms of protection is only *partial* when encapsulated in EU legislation. The process indeed remains contained within the upper layer of EU norms: a right enshrined in EU constitutional law becomes the object of EU secondary law taking primacy over domestic law in its entirety and thus remaining largely removed from the ambit of ordinary domestic policy- and law-making. From the perspective of each of the Member States, it is therefore fair to state that a significant chunk of fundamental rights protection is removed from the ambit of ordinary domestic policy- and law-making owing to the powerful process of European integration.[20]

[19] ibid.

[20] This is not to say that Member State interests are inevitably neglected. It is well established that the fundamental rights protection provided in the general principles of EU law and the Charter of

This new type of EU fundamental rights legislation, that is juxtaposed to the pre-existing set of constitutional rights, performs three functions in the EU legal order. To start with, in clarifying the scope of a given right, legislation defines the scope of political intervention. In the context of the EU, this political intervention further defines the contours of supranational intervention.

Legislation further defines the content of rights and may provide for procedures to give them effect. Greater visibility is thereby given to selected rights so as to enhance their political relevance and justiciability. Meanwhile, EU political institutions may engage in a deeper reflection on how to actually improve the protection of such rights through the creation of negative or positive obligations on a plurality of actors as well as the introduction of institutional structures designed to catalyse societal change.

Finally, legislation can affect the circumstances in which a selected fundamental right may be used in a given legal order. Legislation may indeed embody the mutation of the right from an instrument protecting individuals against state arbitrariness, ie, in vertical disputes, to a tool regulating interpersonal relationships, ie, in horizontal disputes.

### Conclusion

The adoption of EU fundamental rights legislation is therefore closely related to the development of a constitutional set of rights for the protection of individuals in the EU; yet legislation performs a function that differs from that of constitutional rights. Furthermore, the said legislation results from broad political processes at European level while in many ways also depriving or at least constraining the ability of domestic spheres to further debate the matter. EU fundamental rights legislation therefore has profound implications on both the relationship between EU institutions, and between the different legal orders as we will see in the next two sections.

## Debating Systems of Fundamental Rights Protection within a Single Legal Order: Inter-Institutional Tensions

The partial downloading of fundamental rights protection described in the last section warrants an enquiry into the constitutional system of checks and balances designed for the elaboration of fundamental rights norms within a complex multilayered legal order such as that of the EU. This section investigates the inter-institutional tensions that may arise in this context within a single legal order: either domestic, or EU.

## The Interplay between Constitution and Legislation Giving Expression to Fundamental Rights in Domestic Legal Orders

### *Testing Legislation Against Constitutional Norms*

The tension between constitutional and legislative law-making is traditionally examined in the context of the debate on judicial review of legislation for compliance with constitutional norms. Here, the two layers of norms – constitutional and legislative – are clearly distinguished and the academic debate revolves around which layer is the most appropriate to regulate fundamental rights protection.

In the context of a critique of judicial review of legislation giving preference to reliance on constitutional norms, a powerful argument is made by Waldron in favour of the definition of fundamental rights protection through legislation – which is to be contrasted here with constitutional forms of protection. He explains that the gain of constitutional protection, 'in terms of an immunity against wrongful legislative abrogation, is more than offset by the loss of our ability to evolve a free and flexible discourse of politics'.[21] This is in particular because,

> [t]he circumstances under which people make judgments about issues like affirmative action, … the proper extent of welfare provision, and the role of personal desert in economic justice are exactly those circumstances in which we would expect … that reasonable people would differ.[22]

It must therefore be accepted that people disagree (in good faith) about the common good and in particular about issues of rights. As a consequence, Waldron insists that this prospect of disagreement must be put 'in the core, not at the periphery' of one's understanding of the important role of legislation in shaping fundamental rights.[23]

The counter argument to Waldron's claim is that, as Kumm puts it, 'democracy without judicial review is deficient'.[24] The central point made in response to Waldron's call to centre fundamental rights law on ordinary political processes is that judicial review is necessary to ensure that the interests of those excluded from the majority-based decision-making process are protected.[25] Constitutional justice in that sense is not expected to *know about* theories of justice or policy but

Fundamental Rights is strongly inspired by domestic constitutional traditions. Furthermore, the adoption of EU legislation having fundamental rights implications is the outcome of decision-making processes ensuring representation of Member State interests.

[21] J Waldron, *Law and Disagreement* (Oxford, Oxford University Press, 1999) 221.

[22] ibid 112.

[23] ibid 93.

[24] M Kumm, 'Rights, Balancing and Proportionality' (2010) 4 *Law & Ethics Human Rights* 142, 143.

[25] J Hart Ely, *Democracy and Distrust: A Theory of Judicial Review* (Cambridge, MA, Harvard University Press, 1980) 8.

to *know the questions to ask others*.[26] Another way of understanding the purpose of judicial review is therefore to understand it as institutionalising 'a right to justification'.[27]

Reflecting on the EU context and reconciling the two lines of arguments above, Dawson stresses that procedural criteria can act as '*normative* benchmarks' to adjust the degree of judicial review.[28] He suggests that when judicial systems as well as the democratic process are functioning normally, judicial deference is justified; in the alternative though, the judiciary shall step in. This approach allows the political process to be placed in a central position in the reflection on fundamental rights law-making.

## *The 'Loose Coupling' of Constitutional and Legislative Tools for the Protection of Fundamental Rights*

Next to these reflections on the relationship between legislation and constitutional norms in the context of judicial review, there is also a broader reflection on the changing role of constitutions and fundamental rights protected therein.[29] Political institutions are increasingly often expected to set the conditions for the realisation of fundamental rights set out in constitutions. This approach also presupposes the coexistence of two layers of norms – constitutional and legislative – but it acknowledges the existence of a particularly complex if not confused relationship between them. Constitutions are no longer understood as creating the circumstances for the exercise of public powers only; this is deemed necessary but insufficient. Instead, constitutions are increasingly perceived as calling for positive intervention by the state to ensure the realisation of fundamental rights, for instance, through legislation.

This transformation of the role of constitutional law is particularly well captured by Somek's analysis of what he calls 'Constitutionalism 2.0'.[30] In his view, constitutions shall now be understood as calling for public authorities to redress private asymmetries of power or violations of rights by private actors. Such a call results in the adoption of legislation specifically designed to give flesh to a fundamental right. This mutation is also connected to the debate on positive duties for the protection of fundamental rights as well as on their horizontal effects.[31] Both mechanisms complement the negative, defensive and vertical use of constitutional

[26] Paraphrasing, Kumm, 'Rights, Balancing and Proportionality', above n 24, 153.

[27] Kumm, 'Rights, Balancing and Proportionality', above n 24.

[28] Dawson, *The Governance of EU Fundamental Rights*, above n 13, 35.

[29] The author is particularly grateful to Bruno de Witte and Marco Dani for most helpful suggestions on this point and what follows. The usual disclaimer applies.

[30] Somek, above n 17, ch 2.

[31] ibid 103 and 109; K Möller, *The Global Model of Constitutional Rights* (Oxford, Oxford University Press, 2012) 36 and 40.

norms by allowing them to radiate further in society. Duties are thereby created for public and private authorities to give effect to the fundamental right.[32]

Such an approach is more comprehensive than the debate on judicial review as it explains the emergence of special forms of legislation. It also offers a less polarised vision of the role of fundamental rights as either framing political life in the form of constitutional norms or constituting the outcome of political processes as explored in the last subsection.[33] If constitutional norms themselves include both a negative and a positive dimension then constitutional rights ought to coexist with political activity in an intimate and complex way.[34]

As Somek puts it, the central question in terms of the relationship between constitution and legislation in this context is

> how the elaboration of fundamental rights by the ordinary legislature – ie 'sovereign power' determining the significance of rights – could ever be controlled by a court that does not seem to avail itself of a fixed basis in order to determine and enforce the controlling standards.[35]

When a fundamental right is given effect through positive intervention, the legislature must be afforded some discretion in delimiting individual spheres of freedom, structuring the legal system and relevant parts of social life.[36] Indeed, the positive dimension of fundamental rights is multifaceted: there are many ways of contributing to the realisation of a fundamental right through positive intervention. The constitutional principle of equal treatment, for instance, includes alongside its negative dimension (such as the prohibition to prevent X from doing something because X is a woman) a positive prong (such as a duty to grant the same benefit to X and Y)[37] and there are several practical avenues to remedy a breach of the abstract right to equality. One could decide to extend the granting of a given benefit to all those entitled to equal treatment; but one could also decide to end the benefit or to alter its content.

Constitutional adjudication related to the positive dimension of constitutional norms ought therefore to acknowledge the greater discretion that political institutions have in shaping such positive dimensions of fundamental rights in contrast to their negative dimension. To that effect Somek calls for a 'loose coupling' of constitutional and legislative tools. This account, as he himself warns, must not be mistaken for an 'awfully conservative' argument simply because it amounts to a call for greater leeway to the legislature.[38] Instead, it represents a sophisticated form of

[32] M Kumm, 'Constitutional Rights as Principles: On the Structure and Domain of Constitutional Justice. A Review Essay on A Theory of Constitutional Rights' (2004) 2 *International Journal of Constitutional Law* 574, 584.

[33] Kumm, 'Constitutional Rights as Principles', above n 32, 574.

[34] ibid 574, 587.

[35] Somek, above n 17, 84.

[36] R Alexy, *A Theory of Constitutional Rights* (Oxford, Oxford University Press, 2002) 304.

[37] ibid 287.

[38] Somek, above n 17, 121.

reasoning calling for a cautious approach to the use of constitutional norms when the legislator has chosen to facilitate and give effect to a fundamental right. How are these debates reflected at EU level?

## Constitutional versus Legislative Guidance on Fundamental Rights in the EU

### *A Fundamental Rights Policy for the EU?*

There has been much debate in the past decades over the need and desirability of developing a fundamental rights *policy* at the EU level – and thus for the EU to develop a political discourse on fundamental rights. One of the triggers for this has been the call for deeper European integration in the 1990s. This related to the feeling that perhaps the EU should place fundamental rights at the core of its activities to complement and counterbalance its economic focus and enhance its legitimacy.[39] Furthermore, there remains a vivid awareness that the more plural the legal order, the more important the need to debate the shape of fundamental rights protection in political terms as well as at the political level, instead of leaving this process to constitutional law-making and adjudication.[40]

However, lukewarm responses have emerged out of fear that this would prevent the use of ordinary law to address classic societal imbalances, as well as lead to a blurring of the distinction between legislative and constitutional norms. Von Bogdandy in particular argues that although it is true that the protection against fundamental right violations in the context of EU intervention should be accompanied by 'corrective regulative and distributive mechanisms',[41] this should 'not be cast in human right terms, let alone in terms of human rights policy'.[42]

This is for two reasons. First, one should be cautious before giving a constitutional anchorage to rights. Casting corrective regulative and distributive mechanisms in human rights terms may ignore the careful balancing process between liberal freedoms, political rights and social entitlements that political institutions ought to perform.[43] This point is well illustrated by the comments

[39] P Alston and JHH Weiler, 'An "Ever Closer Union" in Need of a Human Rights Policy: The European Union and Human Rights' (1999) Harvard Jean Monnet Working Paper No 1/1999, 15.

[40] R Bellamy, 'Constitutive Citizenship versus Constitutional Rights: Republican Reflections on the EU Charter and the Human Rights Act' in T Campbell, KD Ewing and A Tomkins (eds), *Sceptical Essays on Human Rights* (Oxford, Oxford University Press, 2001) 16.

[41] A von Bogdandy, 'The European Union as a Human Rights Organization? Human Rights and the Core of the European Union' (2000) 37 *Common Market Law Review* 1307, 1315. See also D Kennedy, 'The International Human Rights Movement: Part of the Problem?' (2002) 14 *Harvard Human Rights Journal* 101, 109.

[42] von Bogdandy, above n 41.

[43] ibid.

expressed by Davies on the *Test-Achats* case of the Court.[44] The Court had been asked to rule on the validity of Article 5(2) of the Directive implementing the principle of equal treatment between men and women in the access to and supply of goods and services.[45] This provision allowed Member States to decide, before 21 December 2007, whether to permit differences in insurance premiums and benefits based on one's sex, under the condition that such differences indeed reflect situations where sex is a determining factor in the assessment of risk. No temporal limitation was placed on the use of this provision. The Court found the derogation of unlimited duration to a fundamental principle of EU law to violate the said principle.[46] A remarkable feature of the case is that the Court corrected the legislator in a context in which the latter had been specifically entrusted by the TFEU to give shape to the same fundamental right against which the legislation was tested. Davies has suggested that the legislature may have been granted a greater margin of manoeuvre by the Court if it had more explicitly addressed the policy considerations at hand.[47] In doing so, as Davies suggests, the legislator would have argued on the basis of its own expertise and avoided the more abstract and principled realm of fundamental rights which the Court considers to be its domain.

Secondly, political debate on fundamental rights in the context of daily decision-making procedures will inevitably remain intertwined with a strong 'constitutional' framing. This would create pressure on the Court to increasingly engage in a human rights discourse and place it – as well as itself – in a position of greater centrality in the European political process.[48] Von Bogdandy warns that the Court may not have the necessary legitimacy to depart to such a great extent from its primary function, which is to ensure that the result of the political process should be enforced.[49]

## *Risks of Interference between Constitutional and Legislative Layers of Norms on Fundamental Rights in the EU*

The important point made by von Bogdandy is therefore that the adoption of legislation elaborating on fundamental rights cannot easily be disconnected from constitutionalisation processes, thus creating risks of interference between

[44] *Association Belge des Consommateurs Test-Achats ASBL and Others v Conseil des ministres* [2011] EU:C:2011:100.

[45] Council Directive (EC) 2004/113 implementing the principle of equal treatment between men and women in the access to and supply of goods and services [2004] OJ L373/37.

[46] *Association Belge des Consommateurs Test-Achats ASBL and Others v Conseil des ministres*, above n 44, para 34.

[47] G Davies, 'Legislative Control of the European Court of Justice' (2014) 51 *Common Market Law Review* 1579, 1597.

[48] von Bogdandy, above n 41, 1307, 1329. See also B de Witte, 'The Legal Status of the Charter: Vital Question or Non-Issue?' (2001) 8 *Maastricht Journal* 81, 84.

[49] von Bogdandy, above n 41, 1307, 1325.

two layers of norms. Such interference is unique *in* and *to* the EU legal order for two reasons.

On the one hand, EU law is characterised by a particularly high level of constitutionalisation – namely, of norms being enshrined in EU primary law (when it comes to economic law in particular) – because of the particular process by which EU integration has been engineered. The interplay between legislative law-making and constitutional interpretation on matters of fundamental rights creates a particularly strong case for 'uploading' the rights at hand.[50] Greater emphasis on fundamental rights discourses would therefore only enhance the appeal to intensify the constitutionalisation process due to the inherent 'fundamental' nature of such a discourse. The case law on the horizontal effects of the prohibition of discrimination on the grounds covered by the Directive establishing a general framework for equal treatment in employment and occupation[51] from *Mangold*[52] to the recent *Egenberger*[53] case aptly illustrates this point. The Directive indeed brought within the scope of EU law the prohibition of discrimination on grounds of age and religion or belief in employment and the Court has since then been using the general principle of non-discrimination as well as – in the latest case law – the Charter (ie, two sets of constitutional norms) to enhance the legal effects of the prohibition of discrimination in horizontal disputes.

On the other hand, and most importantly, the emphasis placed on either legislative intervention or constitutional guidance imply inter-institutional tensions which differ in a supranational legal order from those present in a domestic legal order as identified above. The debates on judicial review and the positive dimension of fundamental rights outlined above provide valuable tools to reflect on the legitimacy implications of the various sources of fundamental rights protection in the EU legal order. Nevertheless, both debates are largely shaped in the context of domestic legal orders.[54] The important role given to the legislator by the relevant theories developed in the US, UK or German contexts is to be related to the existence of large democratically accountable assemblies which have no EU equivalent. Similarly, the role of the Court as a constitutional adjudicator differs from that of domestic constitutional courts. Adding complexity, as the EU has no general fundamental rights competence and as the precise circumstances in which legislation-making takes place depends on the exact wording of the provision enabling the EU legislature to intervene, or on the 'legal basis', the practical

[50] M Dawson, 'The Political Face of Judicial Activism: Europe's Law-Politics Imbalance' in M Dawson, E Muir and B de Witte (eds), *Judicial Activism at the European Court of Justice* (Cheltenham, Edward Elgar, 2013) 11 ff; Davies, 'Legislative Control of the European Court of Justice', above n 47, 1579, 1582.

[51] Council Directive (EC) 2000/78 of 27 November 2000 establishing a general framework for equal treatment in employment and occupation [2000] OJ L303/16.

[52] *Werner Mangold v Rüdiger Helm* EU:C:2005:709.

[53] *Vera Egenberger v Evangelisches Werk für Diakonie und Entwicklung eV* EU:C:2018:257.

[54] N Walker, 'Human Rights in a Post-National Order: Reconciling Political and Constitutional Pluralism' in T Campbell, KD Ewing and A Tomkins (eds), *Sceptical Essays on Human Rights* (Oxford, Oxford University Press, 2001) 127.

implications of the theoretical debates highlighted above can only be measured by reference to a specific domain of legislative intervention.

## Conclusion

In the context thereby described, identifying institutional safeguards for the development of a fundamental rights narrative, reaching a healthy balance between democratic accountability and constitutional adjudication at EU level is a uniquely complex task. The work of both Waldron and Somek suggests that the adoption of legislation fleshing out fundamental rights provides a useful and welcome opportunity to debate European values through ordinary political processes. Yet, the contested democratic credentials of the EU legislative process as well as the Court's case law tending towards an ever broader range of constitutional rights make it difficult for the EU to firmly assert a new approach on the protection of fundamental rights through legislation. The implications of the debate are all the more important given that the EU is a multilayered legal order as we shall now see.

# Tensions between Domestic and EU Legal Orders in the Process of Europeanisation of the Fundamental Rights Discourse

The particularly authoritative nature of EU over domestic law makes it important to fully spell out the constitutional implications of fundamental rights' law-making at EU level. The EU legal order indeed is a remarkably powerful supranational legal system. Using this infrastructure to enhance fundamental rights presents both advantages and disadvantages. Important advantages have been explored elsewhere: the EU enforcement machinery can be placed at the service of fundamental rights protection[55] and the process of EU law-making can be used to mainstream fundamental rights concerns across a broad range of policy areas.[56] Yet, the risks associated with the novel competences of the EU in the field of fundamental rights shall also be spelt out as will now be done.

## Constitutive versus Divisive Effects of Supranationalisation of Fundamental Rights Discourse

If disagreement is as central to the fundamental rights discourse as suggested by Waldron, and thus potentially so divisive, why develop it in the form of a 'policy'

[55] M Dawson, E Muir and M Claes, 'Enforcing the EU's Rights Revolution: The Case of Equality' (2012) 3 *European Human Rights Law Review* 276.

[56] Dawson, *The Governance of EU Fundamental Rights*, above n 13, ch 3.

at European level? This question was already partly answered in the debate from the late 1990s on the need and desirability to develop a fundamental rights policy at the EU level. At that time there was a strong feeling that deeper European integration and a more central role for fundamental rights protection in EU politics would enhance the legitimacy of the EU legal order.[57] Walker in particular calls for an argument to be made beyond the democratic critique of the EU fundamental rights regime.[58] His reasoning is twofold. On the one hand, the protection of fundamental rights may be perceived precisely as a way of consolidating democratic scrutiny and control in the EU. On the other hand, this would compensate for the initial economic bias of the common market.[59]

The first prong of Walker's argument is useful for the purpose of a discussion of the democratic challenge of human rights in the EU. In his view, a greater focus on fundamental rights protection may actually attract greater political attention and thus act as a trigger for greater democratic activity at the European level.[60] In that sense, Walker stresses that the strength of the fundamental rights argument in such a legitimising function is that the definition of fundamental rights would be entrusted to EU political institutions – such as by Article 16 TFEU on data protection or Article 19 TFEU on non-discrimination – however imperfect these institutions may be from the perspective of democratic accountability. What is desirable then is a 'human rights *policy*'[61] with specific emphasis on the role of ordinary politics, so as to pay tribute to the 'sensitive and deliberative context for assessing the force and deciding the practical import for various compensatory arguments within the extended chain of rights'.[62] Understood through that lens, policy-making on fundamental rights matters at the EU level ought to be protected from 'constitutionalisation' or 'ossification'[63] to avoid reintroducing the democratic objection.[64]

Besides this argument that seeks to enhance the legitimacy of the very structure – the EU – that it pledges to consolidate, the most powerful and valuable external argument in favour of supranational protection of fundamental rights relates to the need for review. The existence of an exogenous set of actors monitoring fundamental rights compliance in national legal orders may indeed

[57] Alston and Weiler, above n 39. See also for instance, M Bell, *Anti-Discrimination Law and the European Union* (Oxford, Oxford University Press, 2002) 13.

[58] Walker, above n 54, 135. For another attempt at addressing the issue of legitimacy in the face of a possible deficit of the democratic juridification of governance beyond the nation state, see further J Habermas, *The Crisis of the European Union: A Response* (Polity Press, 2012) 41; this analysis however mostly focuses on constitutional law-making in the EU rather than policy-making.

[59] Walker, above n 54, 135.

[60] See also Dawson, *The Governance of EU Fundamental Rights*, above n 13, 20.

[61] (emphasis original) Walker, above n 54, 141.

[62] Walker, above n 54, 141.

[63] Opinion of AG Trstenjak, *Maribel Dominguez v Centre informatique du Centre Ouest Atlantique and Préfet de la région Centre* EU:C:2011:559, para 157.

[64] Walker, above n 54, 137. See also von Bogdandy, above n 41, 1307.

permit the calling into question of the bias deeply enshrined in domestic and/or local systems.[65] Leaving the question aside of whether this role should be fulfilled in Europe by the EU or the Council of Europe,[66] one of the implications of this approach is that the supranational level is indeed used as a tool to review, or 'a check', on domestic policy-makers.

In this context, the danger of enhanced supranationalisation of fundamental rights questions – if the institutional design is not carefully thought through – would mean triggering, or feeding, a feeling among national constituencies that their political preferences are being disregarded. Enhanced supranationalisation of fundamental rights may not rely on channels that allow for genuine participation of all the stakeholders because of the disjuncture between the domestic and the EU legal order.[67] This disjuncture is related to specific criticisms of the EU institutional framework as much as to the general dynamics of supranational human rights governance. Sociologists have shown that while the supranational level offers multiple opportunities for fundamental rights actors to support and shape progressive agendas despite reticence at the domestic level, the same 'circumvention logic' explains why the outcome reached at the supranational level may trigger domestic resistance. By couching their policy and fundamental rights arguments at the supranational level in cosmopolitan terms or in terms of a broader European identity, civil society actors may create a source of resistance within domestic spheres related to the 'perceived threat to national identities and allegiances'.[68]

The risk here is therefore that an EU fundamental rights discourse becomes detached from the domestic sphere or perceived as so exogenous that it is ultimately rejected altogether. In order to achieve the objective of acting as a source for cohesion, EU intervention elaborating on the positive dimension of fundamental rights thus ought to be mediated through political discourse as well as to be able to accommodate claims for divergent national sensitivities. Both concerns point at the importance of political debate and legislative guidance on fundamental rights. The features of EU law however do not make it easy to fully address the said concerns within the process leading to the adoption of legislation as we shall now see.

[65] JHH Weiler, 'Fundamental Rights and Fundamental Boundaries: On Standards and Values in the Protection of Human Rights' in N Neuwahl and A Rosas (eds), *The European Union and Human Rights* (The Hague, Martinus Nijhoff Publishers, 1995) 52, 74.

[66] To the extent that this book investigates policy-making on fundamental rights matters, the focus is on the EU legal order where political debates on the content of fundamental rights may lead to the adoption of related legislation.

[67] See for instance Bell, above n 57, 202.

[68] C Ruzza, 'Civil Society Actors and EU Fundamental Rights Policy: Opportunities and Challenges' (2014) 15 *Human Rights Review*, 65, 70. For a contrasting view specific to the feminist movement see C Hoskyns, *Integrating Gender: Women, Law and Politics in the European Union* (London, Verso, 1996) 17.

## The EU Principle of Subsidiarity is Ill-Suited to Regulate EU Legislative Intervention in Fundamental Rights Matters

An attempt at reconciling the call for supranational intervention in fundamental rights matters with that of respect for domestic peculiarities leads us to turn to the principle of subsidiarity. The principle is indeed often alluded to in order to articulate the relationship – or alleviate tensions – between domestic legal orders and European legal orders by ensuring that decisions be made as closely as possible to citizens.[69] Although useful, as argued elsewhere,[70] the EU version of this principle is imperfect to fully grasp the sophisticated interplays between EU and national law in the field of fundamental rights protection.[71]

As it is defined in EU law, the principle of subsidiarity only provides limited guidance to justify EU intervention on fundamental rights matters. According to Article 5(3) TEU and as it is commonly understood, the principle relies on a two-tier comparative efficiency test. The EU may intervene only if the Member States cannot sufficiently achieve the desired objective and if the EU can actually do better on the matter. This comparative efficiency test may not be appropriate to guide fundamental rights standards-setting by political institutions. Indeed, it does not allow tensions between values that are central to controversies on the EU fundamental rights discourse to be addressed.[72] The reasons have been explored by several authors,[73] and are twofold.

The first explanation is that the *function* of fundamental rights protection in EU law differs from that of competences that have a cross-border component. That makes the EU principle of subsidiarity inappropriate to provide useful guidance. The definition of the principle of subsidiarity provided for in Article 5(3) TEU relies on the assumption that the principle articulates the relationship between the EU and the Member States in a transnational context.[74] However, certain EU fundamental rights competences – especially in the case of legislation designed to 'give specific expression' to a fundamental right such as EU equality law – are

[69] eg, Recital 1 of the Protocol (No 2) on the Application of the principles of subsidiarity and proportionality [2008] OJ C 115/206.

[70] E Muir, 'The Fundamental Rights Implications of EU Legislation: Some Constitutional Challenges' (2014) 51 *Common Market Law Review* 219.

[71] See further the distinction between functional and normative subsidiarity in LR Helfer, 'Redesigning the European Court of Human Rights: Embeddedness as a Deep Structural Principle of the European Human Rights Regime' (2008) 19 *European Journal of International Law* 125, 128.

[72] See by analogy, FW Scharpf, 'The Double Asymmetry of European Integration; or: Why the EU cannot be a Social Market Economy' (2009) MPIfG Working Paper No 09/2012, available at: www.mpifg.de/pu/workpap/wp09-12.pdf 21–22.

[73] eg, G Davies, 'Subsidiarity: The Wrong Idea, in the Wrong Place, at the Wrong Time' (2006) 43 *Common Market Law Review* 63; P Craig, 'Subsidiarity: A Political and Legal Analysis' (2012) 50 *Journal of Common Market Studies* 72.

[74] T Horsley, 'Subsidiarity and the European Court of Justice: Missing Pieces in the Subsidiarity Jigsaw' (2012) 50 *Journal of Common Market Studies* 267, 275.

concerned with regulating relationships *within* states;[75] they go further in deepening European integration rather than merely regulating relationships *among* states.

There is thus a mismatch between the function of the principle of subsidiarity as defined in EU law and the function of fundamental rights standard-setting in the EU. With EU fundamental rights law-making, the EU's main aim is 'to bring into being a European public sphere based on a shared understanding of rights and so motivate agreement on a federal structure for Europe that in various ways goes beyond national allegiances and political cultures'.[76] A subsidiarity test concerned with the appropriate (national versus EU) level for the regulation of fundamental rights standards is thus foreign to the dynamics of fundamental rights standard-setting through EU legislation. This is especially so when such legislation is specifically designed to give expression to a fundamental right.[77]

The second – and closely related – element explaining the difficulty of applying the traditional EU subsidiarity test to legislation involving fundamental rights relates to the *nature* of fundamental rights standard-setting. As pointed out by Davies, genuine dilemmas and controversies on matters of fundamental rights protection primarily originate in shocks between objectives or values.[78] In contrast, the subsidiarity test as it is defined by EU law is based on an assessment of the effectiveness of the law to pursue a pre-established objective. Key conflicts on the definition of fundamental rights standards thus cannot be solved by comparative efficiency tests: they are instead concerned with prioritising and balancing values.[79] As Davies stressed, 'the value-violence [which is being done to] some states, or the autonomy cost which [is imposed by EU legislation on fundamental rights], is considerable … Subsidiarity, however, will not be involved'.[80]

The principle of subsidiarity thereby defined is ill-suited to regulate EU legislative intervention in fundamental rights matters. The principle therefore cannot easily be used for the domestic sphere to challenge the decision by the EU to set fundamental right standards through legislation. Instead, the outcome of the political negotiations leading to the adoption of fundamental rights legislation must be understood as encapsulating a subtle and sensitive balance between various values as well as levels of authority at stake.

[75] A von Staden, 'The Democratic Legitimacy of Judicial Review Beyond the State: Normative Subsidiarity and Judicial Standards of Review' (2011) Jean Monnet Working Paper No 10/2011, 9.

[76] R Bellamy, 'Still in Deficit: Rights, Regulations, and Democracy in the EU' (2006) 12 *European Law Journal* 725, 733.

[77] See also Horsley, above n 74, 275.

[78] Davies, 'Subsidiarity: The Wrong Idea, in the Wrong Place, at the Wrong Time', above n 73, 63, 67–72.

[79] Acknowledging that it is more difficult to apply precepts of comparative efficiency that underpin subsidiarity to heads of competence that are other than economic: Craig, above n 73, 72, 75.

[80] G Davies, 'Subsidiarity as a Method of Policy Centralisation' (2006) Hebrew University International Law Research Paper No 11/2006, para 5.

## The EU is Not a Subsidiary Organ

The difficulty for the EU in addressing concerns raised by domestic sensitivities on fundamental rights matters is affected by another feature of the EU legal order: namely, the EU is anything but a subsidiary organ.

### *The Supranational Features of EU Law Apply to EU Fundamental Rights Law*

Somek argues that the success of a system of fundamental rights protection such as that of the European Convention on Human Rights (ECHR) lies in the fact that it leaves participants sufficient leeway on the intensity of their involvement, allowing for a degree of self-determination.[81] The 'weak supranational character of the system', as well as techniques such as that of the 'margin of appreciation doctrine' help states to balance the costs of the narrowing of their sovereignty over the matter.[82] The ECHR thus relies on an element of subsidiarity, understood in the broad sense (not in the EU sense as discussed in the last section), that acknowledges national representative institutions as the central political bodies in the process of realisation of fundamental rights protection.[83] This allows for a combination of external monitoring and supervision of fundamental rights with internally driven mechanisms of change.

In contrast, the EU – when it intervenes on fundamental right matters – is not designed to be ancillary to national mechanisms of human rights protection.[84] This places the EU in a distinct position from that of the ECHR, the function of which is primarily to provide minimum standards, after exhaustion of domestic remedies, for all rights identified as human rights in the Convention.[85] The EU is an entity with a broad range of legislative powers that may lead to unification of selected fundamental rights. The system of allocation – and exercise – of EU competences results in circumstances in which EU law, since it takes primacy over national law,[86] may deprive Member States of any discretion in setting fundamental rights standards.

[81] Somek, above n 17, 180; see also Dawson, *The Governance of EU Fundamental Rights*, above n 13, 5–7.

[82] Somek, above n 17, 181–83.

[83] ibid 188.

[84] On the ECHR, see further Helfer, above n 71, 125, 128–30. Helfer stresses that even in the context of the ECHR, the evolution of the type of problems brought before the ECHR weakens the persuasiveness of treating the mechanism as subsidiary.

[85] See further Lord Hoffmann, 'The Universality of Human Rights' (Judicial Studies Board Annual Lecture, 19 March 2009), available at: www.judiciary.gov.uk/wp-content/uploads/2014/12/Hoffmann_2009_JSB_Annual_Lecture_Universality_of_Human_Rights.pdf, 12; and R Spano, 'Universality or Diversity of Human Rights? Strasbourg in the Age of Subsidiarity' (2014) 14 *Human Rights Law Review* 487, 493. Nuancing the distinction between the EU and the ECHR, see G Martinico, 'Is the European Convention Going to Be "Supreme"? A Comparative-Constitutional Overview of ECHR and EU Law before National Courts' (2012) 23 *European Journal of International Law* 401.

[86] LFM Besselink, 'Entrapped by the Maximum Standard: On Fundamental Rights, Pluralism and Subsidiarity in the European Union' (1998) 35 *Common Market Law Review* 629, 664.

The Court's *Melloni* case illustrates this point.[87] The European Framework Decision 2002/584[88] was so detailed about the application of the European Arrest Warrant mechanism to the situation of trials *in absentia* that Member States were left with no discretion and 'human rights protection [was] fully supranationalised'.[89] In other examples, Member States may be granted greater discretion, and thus, the EU may well be acting as a more ancillary organ. This is illustrated aptly by the *Fransson* case in which, although the Court asserted its jurisdiction over the matter, the actual implementation of the effect of the fundamental right at hand was left to the domestic court.[90] Yet, as Daniel Thym puts it, in both *Melloni* and *Fransson*, the Court determined the freedom of action of the Member States, unlike the European Court of Human Rights where greater leeway is usually left to constitutional courts or domestic authorities.[91]

Furthermore, whenever the EU exercises a fundamental rights competence, it may provide minimum as well as high levels of protection – thus clearly departing from an ancillary role.[92] EU legislation that gives expression to a fundamental right largely harmonises the way a fundamental right has to be conceptualised and implemented. The interpretation of that legislative framework equally bears the harmonising power of the said piece of legislation, and may therefore dictate a detailed and uniform understanding of a fundamental right which will be applied across the EU in both horizontal and vertical relationships.

The harmonising power of EU legislation giving expression to a fundamental right is epitomised by the controversies triggered by the Court's rulings in *Achbita*[93] and *Bougnaoui*[94] in which the Court placed a cap on employees' ability to wear headscarves by asserting the fundamental right of employers to conduct a business.[95] Irrespective of the normative choices made by the Court in this context, it shall be noted that the institutional setting of the dispute placed the Court in a remarkably delicate situation. The criticisms against these rulings become all the more intense that their outcome severely constrains the domestic sphere in the way it will be able to articulate its vision of the relevant fundamental rights.

[87] *Stefano Melloni v Ministerio Fiscal* EU:C:2013:107.

[88] Council Framework Decision 2002/584/JHA on the European arrest warrant and the surrender procedures between Member States [2002] OJ L190/1.

[89] D Thym, 'Separation Versus Fusion – or: How to Accommodate National Autonomy and the Charter? Diverging Visions of the German Constitutional Court and the European Court of Justice' (2013) 9 *European Constitutional Law Review* 391, 402.

[90] *Åklagaren v Hans ÅkerbergFransson* EU:C:2013:280; Thym, above n 89, 391, 403.

[91] Thym, above n 89, 405–06. See also N Krisch, 'The Open Architecture of European Human Rights Law' (2010) 71 *Modern Law Review* 183, 214.

[92] See, eg, AG Poiares Maduro in *S Coleman v Attridge Law and Steve Law* EU:C:2008:61, para 24. See also A Stone Sweet and K Stranz, 'Rights Adjudication and Constitutional Pluralism in Germany and Europe' (2012) 19 *Journal of European Public Policy* 92, 105.

[93] *Samira Achbita and Centrum voor Gelijkheid van Kansen en voor Racismebestrijding v G4S Secure Solutions NV* EU:C:2017:203.

[94] *Asma Bougnaoui and Association de Défense des Droits de l'Homme (ADDH) v Micropole SA* EU:C:2017:204.

[95] E Cloots, 'Safe Harbour or Open Sea for Corporate Headscarf Bans? Achbita and Bougnaoui' (2018) 55 *Common Market Law Review* 589, 621 ff.

### *Inviting Judicial Deference*

Which EU law concepts could be used to address such concerns? Cloots has suggested that the Court could be more deferential towards domestic courts and enable each Member State to have discretion when interpreting legislation regulating fundamental rights at a domestic level.[96] This approach can be supported with reference to Article 4(2) TEU, according to which the EU shall respect the national identities 'inherent in their fundamental structures, political and constitutional'. The concept of national identity is thus a tool that could be used to support self-restraint in judicial interpretation of legislative texts[97] and that could be particularly useful to acknowledge the particular nature of EU fundamental rights legislation.

A counter-argument to these claims is that, in the EU legal order, the role of the Court is to provide clear guidance on the interpretation of EU law. An integrationist vision of the EU legal order, as well as arguments drawn from legal certainty, therefore call for a uniform interpretation of EU legislation across participating Member States. The tension between the two lines of reasoning – one asking for deference and the other for uniformity and clarity – is particularly salient in relation to the interpretation of legislation giving expression to a fundamental right. Such an exercise indeed crystallises the structural difference between subsidiary forms of fundamental rights protection (such as the European Convention and Court of Human Rights) and the harmonising powers of EU legislative intervention.[98]

## Conclusion

The challenge for the EU is to find a middle ground between, on the one hand, promoting and enhancing the protection of fundamental rights at supranational level when empowered to do so by the Treaties, and on the other hand, ensuring that this form of intervention does not result in the entire edifice of the EU legal order being perceived as unduly threatening domestic systems of values. The advantage of EU competences empowering the legislator to develop specific fundamental rights policies may precisely lie in setting the scene for a political debate on these European values.

Yet, the infrastructure of the EU legal order is (still) ill-equipped to deal with these types of competences. The principle of subsidiarity does not help in addressing calls for domestic control and, conversely, once EU law exists, it constitutes a uniquely powerful fundamental rights instrument at supranational level. One should therefore be cautious to carefully respect the political nature of the

[96] E Cloots, 'The CJEU's headscarf decisions: Melloni behind the veil?' (*VerfBlog*, 2017), available at: verfassungsblog.de/the-cjeus-headscarf-decisions-melloni-behind-the-veil/.

[97] E Cloots, *National Identity in EU Law* (Oxford, Oxford University Press, 2015) 323–26 and 327–29.

[98] Arguing along similar lines see Cloots, 'Safe Harbour or Open Sea for Corporate Headscarf Bans?', above n 95.

delicate balances and compromises enshrined in that legislation and avoid confusion with constitutional and rigid forms of protection of related rights.

## Epilogue

The 'downloading' of fundamental rights protection, as identified above, is a process called for by constituent powers to allow the political sphere to reflect on the function performed by a fundamental right in a given legal order, on the scope of political intervention needed as well as on the means of action. In creating opportunities to download, constituent powers purportedly transfer authority to political institutions to substantiate a fundamental right. In the context of the EU, this invitation to download fundamental rights protection is all the more important as it has implications for the vertical allocation of powers between the EU and its Member States. Given that the rationale for EU intervention on such matters is inherently political and intended to contribute to the legitimacy of the Europeanisation process as a whole, the delineation of supranational intervention in the field is particularly sensitive.

Whether we look at fundamental rights law-making as entering a new stage in terms of its historical evolution, as a subject of inter-institutional competition within a legal order or as a controversial domain of supranational intervention, as has been done in the main three sections of this chapter, much emphasis is being placed on the political tensions underlying the process. It would be expected that a healthy EU fundamental rights policy such as that called for by Article 19 TFEU on equal treatment or that called for by Article 16 TFEU on data protection be built on two pillars. First, the constitutional value of the rights protected ought to be maintained in order to ensure compliance with the initial and legitimate objective of uploading fundamental rights protection. Secondly, the political dimension of decision-making on the matter ought to be acknowledged and respected. This is requested by the relevant constitutional framework but is also necessary to address disagreement on policy-making in the field through appropriate dialogue and to ensure the legitimacy-building function of the relevant policy. As pointed out above, this is not to say that EU legislation giving expression to fundamental rights shall be subject to no judicial review or no constitutional interpretation. The point is more nuanced: where the EU decision-making process is functioning normally, with a clear legal base and full legislative process, judicial deference may be justified.[99]

Yet, as we have seen political processes may not easily be disconnected from their constitutional framework, especially in a highly constitutionalised legal order such as that of the EU. This creates a genuine risk that the dynamics inherent to the

[99] Dawson, *The Governance of EU Fundamental Rights*, above n 13, 35 and 80.

EU legal order and to the powerful dynamics of uploading of fundamental rights protection pre-empt, hinder or hijack attempts at addressing important questions on the function, scope and tools for fundamental rights protection through political dialogue. In that sense, it may be useful also for the EU legislator and constituent powers in the future to recall the invitation issued by von Bogdandy to exercise restraint in casting corrective regulative and distributive mechanisms in fundamental rights terms. Fundamental rights narratives are so delicate for institutions and for policy-makers to articulate that they should be handled with great caution, especially as the outcome of the decision-making process carries the unique strength of the EU legal order.

# 6

# The Value of Constitutionalism in the European Union

ARMIN HATJE*

## Constitutionalism and Democracy in the European Union

What is the value of constitutionalism in the European Union? At national level constitutionalism was an essential precondition for democracy. However, analysing the relationship between constitution and democracy within the European Union poses much greater difficulties. While the founding Treaties of the European Union are often described as a constitution, they do not serve as the legal foundation for a state.[1] Furthermore, the EU Treaties are lacking an autonomous decision of a European constituent power. Nevertheless, they serve as a legal framework for governance. The Treaties define the objectives of the Union, equip them with far-reaching powers, organise the decision-making processes of the institutions, ensure the legitimacy of their actions and limit supranational powers through fundamental rights protected by independent courts. In a functional sense, one can therefore speak of the founding Treaties as the constitution of the European Union.[2]

But what is the added value of this terminology? From the constitutional nature of the founding Treaties, immediate legal consequences cannot be deduced. However, by thinking in constitutional categories the basic structures, procedures and principles of the European Union can be better described and

* Many thanks to Edward Martin for his valuable assistance.

[1] Regarding the legal nature of the EU: R Schütze, *European Constitutional Law* (Cambridge, Cambridge University Press, 2012) 47, 66.

[2] Explaining the different conceptions P Craig, 'Constitutions, Constitutionalism and the European Union' (2001) 7 *European Law Journal* 125; see also on the subject matter JHH Weiler and JP Trachtman, 'European Constitutionalism and its Discontents' (1996–97) *Northwestern Journal of International Law & Business* 345, 357; C Henkel, 'Constitutionalism of the European Union and Political Decision-Making by the European Court of Justice' (2000) 19 *Wisconsin International Law Journal* 153; MA Wilkinson, 'Political Constitutionalism and the European Union' (2013) 76 *Modern Law Review* 191.

critically appreciated.[3] The analytical capacity of a constitutional understanding of the founding Treaties becomes particularly evident in the example of the democratic principle. The democratic legitimacy of the European Union is one, if not *the* question of the further integration process. The European Communities have already been labelled as possessing a democratic deficit. The European Union must also defend itself against the accusation that its actions are not sufficiently democratically legitimised.[4]

In response, the Treaty of Lisbon has particularly strengthened the rights of the European Parliament. However, it has been the founding Treaties themselves, which have recently been criticised for being responsible for the lack of democratic legitimation within the European Union. According to the critique, the constitutional character of the Treaties and the detailed definition of European economic policy in particular made the Court of Justice the main actor, while the political institutions could merely act upon what was decided in Luxembourg.[5] As a consequence, some demand the reduction of legal requirements in the founding Treaties, which could be described as a sort of 'deconstitutionalisation' of the Union. Namely the fundamental freedoms and the competition rules should be 'downsized' to secondary law. This in turn should create the necessary space for free political discourse, the main precondition of a living democracy.[6] Since this point of view in a special way connects the constitutionalisation of the European Union with its democratic status, I will focus on the question of the connection between the constitutional character of the Treaties and the democratic legitimacy of the European Union, and whether this relationship results in a democratic deficit.

## Constitution and Governance in the European Union

A constitution establishes and limits political powers. Originally, the European Treaties were meant to be the basis of an international organisation. The citizens did not play any significant role, neither as bearers of rights, nor as subjects of

[3] See the methodological explanations of the research project 'Global Constitutionalism and Global Governance' of the Max Planck Institute for Comparative Public Law and International. Law international, available at: www.mpil.de/de/pub/forschung/nach-rechtsgebieten/voelkerrecht/global-constitutionalism.cfm; on the recent discussion, see I Cengiz, 'European Constitutionalism and its Future after BREXIT' (2017) 8 *Inonu Law Review* 551.

[4] See PD Marquardt, 'Deficit Reduction: Democracy, Technocracy, and Constitutionalism in the European Union' (1994) 4 *Duke Journal of Comparative & International Law* 265, with further references; R Bellamy, 'Still in Deficit: Rights, Regulation, and Democracy in the EU' (2006) 12 *European Law Journal* 725; SC Sieberson, 'The Treaty of Lisbon and its Impact on the European Union's Democratic Deficit' (2008) 14 *Columbia Journal of European Law* 446; JP Bonde, 'The European Union's Democratic Deficit: How to Fix It' (2011) 17 *Brown Journal of World Affairs* 147; BMJ Szewczyk, 'European Citizenship and National Democracy: Contemporary Sources of Legitimacy of the European Union' (2011) 17 *Columbia Journal of European Law* 151, 184.

[5] See D Grimm, *Europa ja – aber welches? Zur Verfassung der europäischen Demokratie*, 3rd edn (München, CH Beck, 2016); see also Henkel, above n 2.

[6] Grimm, above n 5.

European law. The judgments in *Van Gend & Loos* and *Costa/ENEL* have fundamentally changed the situation. The autonomy of Community law, its direct effect and primacy of application established the general primacy of European decisions.[7] Within its scope, the Member States have become politically subordinate to the Community and European Union. The legal hierarchy between the European Union and the Member States continues at the individual level. Here again, the Union, as it confers rights, can also unilaterally establish obligations. These obligations are enforceable against everybody, even if only with assistance of the Member States. The European Union thus exercises power over the Member States and their inhabitants. It is therefore understandable when, looking back on the 1960s, we are talking about the beginning of a 'constitutionalisation'. At this point, the democratic principle comes into play.

## Governance and Democracy at the European Level

Democracy should legitimise sovereign powers. For more than 50 years it has been disputed whether the Union has sufficient democratic legitimacy. A look at the EU Treaty may raise hopes, but only helps to a limited extent.

### Democracy in European Constitutional Law

According to Article 2 TEU, democracy is one of the fundamental values of the Union. It shapes the Union's social structure, it is a precondition for accession and violations are subject to sanctions under Article 7 TEU. Furthermore, the principle of democracy has its own title in the Treaty on European Union. Within this title, we find expressions of commitment to representative democracy, participatory forms of decision-making, participation of national parliaments in European decision-making and the introduction of a pan-European referendum.[8] Normatively, European democracy could hardly fare better. Yet, as indicated in the introduction, complaints about a democratic deficit of the Union have not stopped. The reasons therefore must lie deeper. They become clearer when one considers the core elements of the principle of democracy.

### Democracy as Collective Self-Determination

Democracy is based on the idea of individual self-determination and equality of the people. In the context of collective rule these principles can only be preserved,

[7] See JHH Weiler, 'The Transformation of Europe' (1991) 100 *Yale Law Journal* 2403, 2413; I Pernice, 'Multilevel Constitutionalism and the Crisis of Democracy in Europe' (2015) 11 *European Constitutional Law Review* 541.

[8] See Arts 10 and 11 TFEU.

if the individual can participate in the exercise of political power autonomously and on an equal basis. This means, as Abraham Lincoln has put it in his famous Gettysburg Address from 1863: 'Government of the people, by the people, and for the people' – wording which, by the way, can be found in Article 2 of the French Constitution.[9] Lincoln's description of the very essence of democracy points to the subject of legitimation: governance in the sense of leadership in a community. In terms of procedural law, legitimacy and control of the government through elections are at the centre of democracy. It is fair to discuss whether democracy is about legitimising future politics or sanctioning the government's previous political activity; whether it is about the individuals or about programme. In any case, in elections, as the philosopher Karl Popper has pointedly summarised, the decisive element of democracy manifests: the possibility of a peaceful change of government;[10] or in the more drastic words of Joseph Schumpeter, the expulsion of 'the moron or the windbag' from office.[11]

## Control of Government as a Goal of Constitutional Law

It is at this point where democracy and constitutionalism meet. For the central task of a constitution is to ensure effective control of government. That is why the main currents of criticism regarding the democratic deficit in the European Union have the same point of departure. They pose the question: who governs the European Union and who controls the government? Is it the political institutions at European and national level or is it the European Constitution itself from which the political direction, substantiated by the Commission and the Court of Justice, can be derived? The answer depends on how far-reaching the political freedom or, in legal terms, the discretionary powers in the European Constitution are and who has to fill them out.

# Democracy and European Governance

The view that the founding Treaties' provisions are too detailed and therefore give too much power to the Court is not new.

## Gouvernement des Juges?

The accusation of a 'Gouvernement des Juges' was already raised in the 1960s and 1970s. The true element of this view is that the Court has made decisions that were

[9] 'Son principe est: gouvernement du peuple, par le peuple e pour le peuple'.
[10] K Popper, *The Open Society and its Enemies* (London, Routledge, 2002) ch 7, II.
[11] J Schumpeter, *Capitalism, Socialism and Democracy* (New York, Harper & Brothers, 1942).

groundbreaking for the integration process.[12] I have already mentioned the judgments of *Van Gend & Loos* and *Costa/ENEL*. Moreover, the Court's decisions on fundamental freedoms have prevented the internal market in Europe from being destroyed from the outset by the recurrent protectionism of the Member States. However, the founding Treaties have now become a framework that can only function in line with its objectives if the political institutions act accordingly.

## Constitutional Change

While the Treaty on the Coal and Steel Community – because of the limited discretion of the institutions – was still commonly referred to as 'Traité loi', the EEC Treaty was already characterised as 'Traité cadre'. Its goals were no longer achievable through mere law enforcement, but had to be realised by decisions of the legislature. Whether it was the refusal to move to majority voting, or the lack of will to harmonise legislation which would have allowed more cross-border competition, the major crises of the integration process were – and are – crises of the European legislator.

Nonetheless, the idea that European integration is based first and foremost on the enforcement of legal provisions remains up to this day, and therefore sets the view that it is above all the Court in cooperation with the Commission, which sets the political direction of the European Union. The realisation of the internal market and the related policy of liberalising various sectors of the economy have been particularly criticised. This criticism fails to recognise the political scope of the Treaties and the role of the European legislature. It is therefore locating the democratic deficit in the wrong place.

## Internal Market as Law Enforcement?

However, the fact that the criticism ignites around the project of the internal market is not surprising. The single market is more than just an economic project. It is the economic foundation of the liberal society.[13] For this very reason, the key economic policy decisions and their functional guarantees are constitutionally enshrined. The rules result in a system of graded legal obligations. At the centre lies the broad discretion of the political decision-making bodies at Union level and the corresponding democratic responsibility.

[12] See JP Colin, *Le gouvernement des juges dans les Communautés européennes* (Paris, Pichon & Durand-Auzias, 1966).

[13] See A Hatje, 'The Economic Constitution within the Internal Market' in A von Bogdandy and J Bast (eds), *Principles of European Constitutional Law*, rev 2nd edn (Oxford, Hart Publishing, 2010) 591.

## *The Systemic Decision*

Fundamental to the European Economic Constitution is the systemic decision of Articles 3 TEU and 119 TFEU for a social and open market economy with free competition. The individual – entrepreneur and consumer – becomes the planning actor, private law becomes the medium for transactions, and the competition of providers and consumers becomes the regulator for the distribution of goods. While in centrally administered economic systems it is the government that controls distribution through political guidelines, the model of the Union is guided by control through market prices. Individual liberty thus takes the place of state power. This illustrates that the question of economic order is connected to the question of the relationship between market and state, competition and politics or, more generally, freedom and state constraints. This basic decision goes far beyond the sphere of economics. There is, as Walter Eucken stipulated, an 'Interdependence of Orders', a connection between economic and political freedom, between the economic and the social order.[14]

## *Fundamental Freedoms*

The systemic decision for an open market economy is substantiated by the fundamental freedoms. It is through their recognition as individual rights that the Court has been able to secure the foundations of the internal market. Attempts of Member States to obstruct cross-border trade for economic policy reasons are well known.[15] The fundamental freedoms therefore had to be 'constitutionalised' in order to prevent the single market from failing at the outset. However, liberalising markets should not be undertaken at any price. The exceptions to the fundamental freedoms and the mandatory requirements protect non-economic interests, including social matters. Harmonisation at European level requires a political decision. This limit of the judiciary has always been respected by the Court.

Therefore, the fundamental freedoms need to be concretised through secondary law. This becomes clear looking at Article 26(1) TFEU on the internal market. It states that 'The Union shall adopt measures with the aim of establishing or ensuring the functioning of the internal market, in accordance with the relevant provisions of the Treaties'. In other words: the internal market in its concrete form is the result of political decisions. The famous 1985 White Paper on the completion of the internal market was essentially an extensive legislative programme.[16] At the latest with the entry into force of the Single European Act, which was intended to ensure the completion of the internal market, the European Community and its successor, the European Union, became supranational legislative communities.

[14] ibid.

[15] A very prominent example is Case 26/62 *Van Gend & Loos* [1963] ECR 1 (Special English Edition) EU:C:1963:1.

[16] 'White Paper on the completion of the internal Market (14 June 1985)'.

In particular, the free movement of persons, services and capital would not work without political decisions by the legislator.

### *Protection of Undistorted Competition*

The rules on undistorted competition are a peculiarity. Their constitutionalisation has in fact narrowed the political discretion of the institutions. Elaborating upon the historical reasons would go beyond the scope of this presentation. It should however be remembered that in 1958, when the EEC Treaty entered into force, not every Member State of the Community had antitrust laws. Irrespective of this fact, the exemptions give rise to wide political discretion. In addition, merger control is based on a regulation of the European legislator. Also, procurement law, which systematically belongs to this context, was regulated through secondary legislation, which was the outcome of political discussions, not judicial determination.[17]

### *Services of General Interest*

Finally, there is a long-standing dispute over the legal status of businesses providing services of general interest. This is the area in which the market principle and social considerations collide. However, Article 106 TFEU merely stipulates a general principle. It permits public services of general interest, but requires justification if market freedoms are be restricted. In addition, Member States are given wide discretion in terms of implementation. This is the reason why the major liberalisation projects – particularly in the fields of telecommunication, transport and energy – are not the result of a direct application of the provision by the Court, but are based on decisions of the political bodies of the European Union.[18]

## Other Sectors of Discretion and Governance

In other policy areas, such as the Area of Freedom, Security and Justice or the Common Foreign and Security Policy, the Union's political institutions enjoy broad discretion. The European Constitution has evolved from an integration programme into an actual framework. It allows for a wide range of policy options, which the institutions may decide at their own discretion, the only limitations being the division of powers and the fundamental rights and freedoms. As a result,

[17] For the details see J Drexl, 'Competition Law as Part of the European Constitution' in A von Bogdandy and J Bast (eds), *Principles of European Constitutional Law*, rev 2nd edn (Oxford, Hart Publishing, 2010).

[18] R Geiger, DE Khan and M Kotzur (eds), *European Union Treaties: A Commentary* (München, CH Beck, 2015); Art 106 TFEU.

the political power of the Court is in fact rather limited. There is no danger of an 'overconstitutionalisation' of the Treaties,[19] which would hamper the political process at European level. I therefore do not share the criticism regarding European constitutional law mentioned at the beginning of this presentation. Nevertheless, I also see deficits in the democratic legitimacy of the European Union. But where are they to be located?

## European Government and Change of Power

A constitutional understanding of the founding Treaties has the advantage of highlighting the fundamental failings of the Member States. They arise from the procedural requirements of the democratic principle.

### The Structural Asymmetry of the European Constitution

The Member States have so far refused to embed the expanding EU competences into an institutional design that would allow for effective democratic control of the European government. In other words, the democratic deficit is the result of a structural asymmetry between the competence order on the one hand, and the institutional order on the other. While the Union now has a set of powers moving it closer to the realm of statehood, it is still governed by institutions that are unmistakably tailored to an international organisation. This precludes the possibility of a change of government at European level from the outset. In fact, it is difficult to even imagine such a change at all.[20]

### The Government of the European Union

The notion of government in the sense of allocating functions to certain organs – as known in several constitutions – does not exist in the founding Treaties. If we understand government as the political leadership of a community, at the European level the European Council, the Council and the European Commission are the points of reference. Article 15(1) TEU states that the European Council 'shall provide the Union with the necessary impetus for its development and shall define the general political directions and priorities thereof'. According to Article 16 TEU the Council, besides its legislative functions, shall 'carry out

[19] See Grimm, above n 5, 112.

[20] The following ideas have already been published by the author, A Hatje, 'Demokratie in der Europäischen Union – Plädoyer für eine parlamentarisch verantwortliche Regierung der EU' in A Hatje (ed), *Verfassungszustand und Verfassungsentwicklung in der Europäischen Union* (Baden-Baden, Nomos, Europarecht Beiheft, 2/2015).

policy-making and coordinating functions as laid down in the Treaties'. The Commission shall, according to Article 17(1) TEU 'promote the general interest of the Union and take appropriate initiatives to that end'. And nowadays the European Parliament is also participating in the formulating of the Union's policies. But how can they be held accountable?

## The Model of Dual Legitimacy

Artcile 10 TEU states that the Union's government is democratically accountable to its citizens via two means. First, heads of state and ministers are 'democratically accountable either to their national Parliaments, or to their citizens'. Furthermore, the national parliaments, according to Article 12 TEU, take part in the legislative process of the Union and possess information as well as suspensive veto rights. In addition, they may also bring a possible breach of the principle of subsidiarity before the Court. In the opinion of the Federal Constitutional Court, this strand of legitimacy secures both the sovereign statehood of Germany and democracy under the German Basic Law – in the way that the decision-making process at the European level is woven into a feedback-loop with the national parliament.[21] Secondly, the citizens of Member States in their role as Union citizens are represented in the European Parliament, whose tasks include the election and control of the Commission.[22]

## The Impossibility of Changing the Government

However, neither of the two lines of legitimation give EU citizens the possibility of bringing about a political change at European level. The weak democratic accountability of the European Council and the Council is particularly obvious. Although national parliaments through EU law are now participating in European decision-making processes, possibilities of exercising actual influence generally remain rather weak. In particular, the consequences of a national parliamentary complaint are confined to one member of the Councils. Also, in many policy areas national reservations can easily be overridden by the majority. Above all, national elections cannot bring about a change of European government.

The effectiveness of the other strand of legitimacy through the European Parliament – even though the increase in competences over the last 40 years has been remarkable – is also limited. This is the case, because in terms of governance, the Parliament can only exercise influence over the Commission, which is the seemingly weaker part of the European leadership. Political change – the

[21] BVerfGE 89, 155 (Maastricht).
[22] Art 10 para 2 TEU.

replacement of the government in the sense of Karl Popper – is therefore beyond the reach of EU citizens and their voting rights at national and European level.[23] Herein lies the actual democratic deficit of the European Union.

## Consequences

What are the consequences? Regarding my question concerning the value of constitutionalism for the European Union, it can be said that it provides an appropriate analytical framework within which to judge the efficiency and coherence of primary EU law. In particular with regard to the European Union's democratic deficit, thinking in constitutional categories helps to point out the existing imbalance between the broad political discretion of the institutions and the lack of effective control by EU citizens. How can this imbalance be eradicated? Time constraints do not permit me to make detailed proposals. However, the consequences are rather clear: either the powers of the Union are reduced, or an institutional design needs to be developed that corresponds to its political power and the Union's own democratic principles. I would argue for the latter.[24] I do not want to conceal the fact that this would move us closer towards becoming a United States of Europe. Because a real European government based, for example, on the European Commission and controlled by the European Parliament, might be perceived as the nucleus of a European statehood. However, we should not so much discuss the form, but rather the content and way of governing within the European Union, supported by thinking in constitutional terms and principles. This is the main value of constitutionalism.

[23] See Hatje, 'Demokratie in der Europäischen Union – Plädoyer für eine parlamentarisch verantwortliche Regierung der EU', above n 20, 45.

[24] ibid 46–51.

# 7

# Is There a Deficit of Throughput Legitimacy in the EU?

VIVIEN A SCHMIDT

## Introduction

Theoretical questions regarding how to legitimate the European Union's supranational governance have turned the spotlight on procedural legitimacy and its relationship to political and performance legitimacy. In EU studies, such questions translate into a focus on 'throughput' legitimacy and its relationship to 'input' and 'output' legitimacy. This chapter defines the terms, discusses their interrelationships, then elaborates on the five criteria encompassed by throughput – efficacy, accountability, transparency, inclusiveness and openness. It illustrates with examples from EU governance, ending with the throughput legitimacy problems of EU institutional actors during the Eurozone crisis. The chapter argues that whereas input politics and output performance may involve trade-offs where more of the one may make up for less of the other, there is no such trade-off for throughput processes. Good throughput cannot make up for flaws in input or output, but bad throughput can throw input and output into question. That said, throughput is an indispensable component of legitimacy, and the interrelationships of its different components as well as with output and input legitimacy are at the centre of the dilemmas of EU governance today.

Concerns about the legitimacy of the European Union have increased over the years, as deepening integration moved responsibility for decision-making from the national level to the supranational in policy area after policy area, including areas at the very heart of national sovereignty, such as money, borders and security.[1] In light of this increasing authority, questions about the EU's legitimacy have been debated ever since the 1990s.[2] But such questions have become more

[1] R Keohane and S Hoffmann, *The New European Community* (Boulder, CO, Westview Press, 1991); C Bickerton, *European Integration: From Nation States to Member States* (Oxford, Oxford University Press, 2012).

[2] eg, S Williams, 'Sovereignty and Accountability in the European Community' in R Keohane and S Hoffmann, *The New European Community* (Boulder, CO, Westview Press, 1991); D Beetham and C Lord, *Legitimacy and the European Union* (London, Longman, 1998).

pressing since the cascading series of crises that have hit the European Union in recent years, including the sovereign debt crisis, the refugee crisis, British exit from the European Union (Brexit), and the security crisis, along with the rise of populism.

For a long time, scholars remained divided among those who thought the EU legitimate[3] and those who instead argued that the EU suffered from an increasing democratic deficit.[4] Since the inception of the Eurozone crisis, however, most analysts have found the EU wanting in legitimacy in terms of the policies, politics, and/or processes.[5] In the language of EU democratic systems theorists, these translate into concerns about the EU's 'output' legitimacy, focused on policy effectiveness and performance; the EU's 'input' legitimacy, centred on citizens' political participation and governing elites' responsiveness;[6] and the EU's 'throughput' legitimacy, involving the quality of the governance processes, including their efficacy, accountability, transparency, inclusiveness and openness to interest consultation.[7]

All three mechanisms are important for legitimacy, but they are not created equal. Notably, whereas political input and policy output may be seen to involve trade-offs in terms of legitimacy – with good policy performance making up for little citizen participation or vice-versa – there is no such positive trade-off for procedural throughput. High quality governance processes cannot make up for flaws in political input or policy output, while poor quality governance can throw input and output into question.[8] The danger, therefore, is when supranational actors assume that simply following the rules of good procedures makes up for a lack of citizen participation in the decisions or even for bad results.

But although throughput legitimacy cannot stand alone, it remains an indispensable component of legitimacy. This is particularly the case for bureaucratic organisations where political input may be far removed from the administrative process, or diffuse, and where policy output is indeterminate, in particular in the short term. What is more, within the rubric of throughput legitimacy, different criteria can come into conflict with each another as well as with input or output legitimacy.

[3] G Majone, 'Europe's "Democratic Deficit": The Question of Standards' (1998) 4 *European Law Journal* 5; A Moravcsik, 'Reassessing Legitimacy in the European Union' (2002) 40 *Journal of Common Market Studies* 603.

[4] eg, FW Scharpf, *Governing in Europe: Effective and Democratic?* (Oxford, Oxford University Press, 1999); A Follesdal, 'The Legitimacy Deficits of the European Union' (2006) 14 *Journal of Political Philosophy* 441; VA Schmidt, *Democracy in Europe* (Oxford, Oxford University Press, 2006); S Hix, *What's Wrong with the European Union and How to Fix It* (Cambridge, Polity Press, 2008).

[5] FW Scharpf, 'Political Legitimacy in a Non-optimal Currency Area' in O Cramme and SB Hobolt (eds), *Democratic Politics in a European Union Under Stress* (Oxford, Oxford University Press, 2014); B Crum and D Curtin, 'The Challenge of Making European Union Executive Power Accountable' in S Piattoni (ed), *The European Union: Democratic Principles and Institutional Architectures in Times of Crisis* (Oxford, Oxford University Press, 2015).

[6] Scharpf, *Governing in Europe Effective and Democratic?*, above n 4.

[7] VA Schmidt, 'Democracy and Legitimacy in the European Union Revisited: Input, Output *and* "Throughput"' (2013) 61 *Political Studies* 2.

[8] ibid.

Under certain circumstances, for example, transparency, inclusiveness, or openness can serve to undermine procedural accountability and could thereby even negatively affect output performance. Under other circumstances, input, output and the various criteria of throughput legitimacy may all be mutually reinforcing. So the question is: which circumstances make for potential conflicts in legitimation strategies, which for mutual reinforcement?

This chapter focuses on throughput legitimacy, and asks whether the EU suffers from a particular deficit in this area. It begins by conceptualising the legitimacy of the EU's governing activities in terms of output, input and throughput mechanisms. It then focuses on throughput legitimacy in order to demonstrate its uses as an umbrella concept that covers a range of criteria, including efficacy, accountability, transparency, and inclusiveness and openness. Each of these criteria is defined on its own terms and its distinctiveness delineated also in relationship to other throughput criteria as well as to input and output legitimacy, with illustrations from many different areas of EU governance. The chapter ends with a discussion of the challenges to EU institutional actors' throughput legitimacy in the Eurozone crisis.

The contribution of this elaboration of the nature and scope of 'throughput' legitimacy is threefold. It provides further clarification of the ways in which procedural legitimacy can be theorised and applied in EU studies. It shows the value-added of using throughput as a concept that covers disparate but interconnected criteria related to procedural legitimacy, to explore both how its various criteria may complement or counter one another and how throughput legitimacy itself may complement or counter the legitimacy tied to (output) performance and (input) politics. Finally, this contribution provides a cautionary note to scholars of EU governance who have increasingly focused on procedural standards of efficacy, accountability, transparency, inclusiveness and openness as ways of improving democratic legitimacy. The 'democratic' in legitimacy refers mainly to the political. Although effective performance and accountable and accessible procedures are necessary, they are not sufficient.

## Conceptualising Legitimacy in Terms of Output, Input and Throughput

There are many different theoretical approaches to legitimacy. These generally run the gamut from normative theories that define the expected criteria a democratic political system would need to fulfill to be considered legitimate to empirical theories that evaluate the extent to which a given democratic political system is considered legitimate. The normative approaches tend to be deductive and often derived from philosophical principles concerned with the public good, political equality, justice, fairness, identity, public discourse and deliberation.[9]

[9] eg, Beetham and Lord, above n 2.

Such approaches normally set up a range of criteria or standards of evaluation by which to assess public action. The empirical approaches tend to be more inductive and derived from pragmatic questions about such things as elite and mass perceptions of economic performance, political responsiveness and administrative accountability, as evidenced in opinion polls, voting and public discourse.[10] Empirical investigation focuses on citizens' beliefs about legitimacy and on community-based evaluations of public action as well as on the ways in which institutional authorities' actions are legitimated and contested in ways that shape such beliefs.[11]

This chapter focuses mainly on a set of concepts that are normative in their criteria for legitimacy but serve at the same time as useful categories for empirical investigation – as will be demonstrated throughout the chapter via empirical illustrations of the EU in terms of its actual policy performance, citizens' political perceptions and procedural quality. It is useful to note here as an aside that this chapter is therefore concerned mainly with legitimacy as defined in terms of a governing body's activities, as opposed to the more foundational Weberian understanding of legitimacy, which refers to public acceptance of a governing body's authority. Here, we focus on the legitimacy of the EU's governing activities on the assumption that the EU has over time slowly acquired legitimacy as a governing authority in policy area after policy area. That said, the two definitions are naturally interconnected, in particular since legitimacy is a matter of discursive construction and contestation, such that public perceptions of a governing body's activities can negatively or positively affect perceptions of its authority.[12]

We turn for normative definitions of legitimacy (in terms of governing activities) to the language and concepts most often used in the EU studies literature. This is found in the political systems theory that builds on the terms of David Easton,[13] as updated and elaborated in particular by Fritz W Scharpf[14] and upon which Vivien A Schmidt subsequently expanded.[15] This approach began by focusing on two legitimising mechanisms: 'output', concerned with policy effectiveness and performance; and 'input', centred on political participation and representation, but more recently has added 'throughput', focused on the quality of governance processes.

[10] eg, H Schmitt and J Thomassen, *Political Representation and Legitimacy in the European Union* (Oxford, Oxford University Press, 1999); W Van der Brug and CH de Vreese (eds), *(Un)intended Consequences of European Parliamentary Elections* (Oxford, Oxford University Press, 2016) 277–87.

[11] J Tallberg and M Zürn, 'The Legitimacy and Legitimation of International Organisations: Introduction and Framework' manuscript (2017); S Kneip and W Merkel, 'The Idea of Democratic Legitimacy' unpublished manuscript (2017).

[12] For more detail see VA Schmidt, *Europe's Crisis of Legitimacy: Governing by Rules and Ruling by Numbers in the Eurozone* (Oxford, Oxford University Press, forthcoming); and Schmidt, 'Democracy and Legitimacy', above n 7.

[13] D Easton, *A Systems Analysis of Political Life* (New York, Wiley, 1965).

[14] Scharpf, *Governing in Europe*, above n 4.

[15] Schmidt, *Europe's Crisis of Legitimacy*, above n 12.

## Output and Input Legitimacy

Output legitimacy describes acceptance of the coercive powers of government so long as their exercise is seen to serve the common good of the polity and is constrained by the norms of the community.[16] This legitimising mechanism has a long pedigree, taking us back not just to Lincoln's famous phrase about the need to 'govern for the people' but to ancient (eg, Plato and Aristotle) and modern philosophers (eg, Hobbes and Locke) whose focus long before modern democracy was on the duties and obligations of rulers to govern wisely and well for the good of their people. But even once democracy as a political system was firmly ensconced, with citizens' political representation (input) the added criterion for legitimacy, output legitimacy retained its importance. This is because citizens' sense of legitimacy, even if now dependent upon expressing their voice (input), remains equally contingent on having their needs and desires fulfilled by governing authorities whose policies solve problems and produce good results that serve not just their individual interests but those of the polity as a whole (output).[17] The good of the people, meaning the 'big' goals of output legitimacy, have always been linked to such things as ensuring peace and security, promoting economic prosperity and social wellbeing, guaranteeing political stability and social rights, and building common identity and greater democracy.

Input legitimacy represents the exercise of collective self-government so as to ensure government responsiveness to peoples' preferences, as shaped through political debate in a common public space and political competition in institutions that ensure political officials' accountability via general elections.[18] This legitimising mechanism has an equally long pedigree, taking us back to Athenian democracy or to the Roman republic, although it has its greatest elaboration in the work of John Locke and John Stuart Mill or, in another tradition, Jean-Jacques Rousseau. Hannah Pitkin's classical definition of political representation puts it as: 'acting in the interest of the represented in a manner responsive to them'.[19] Input legitimacy is at the very basis of democratic systems of representation, and contains expectations related to the principles and practices of political participation and representation, such as free elections, citizens' right to vote, freedom of expression and the press, majority rule with respect for minority rights, and much more. But representation can be understood in two mutually reinforcing ways, in keeping with Abraham Lincoln's conceptualisations of 'government *of* the people' and 'government *by* the people'. Government *of* the people assumes that citizens are represented by people like themselves. Government *by* the people presupposes instead that citizens elect public officials who govern in their name while expressing their will.

[16] Scharpf, *Governing in Europe*, above 4.
[17] ibid.
[18] ibid; Scharpf, 'Political Legitimacy in a Non-optimal Currency Area', above n 5.
[19] H Pitkin, *The Concept of Representation* (Berkeley, CA, University of California Press, 1967) 209.

What expressing the will of the people exactly means, however, has been subject to long-standing debate, in particular in light of the dual nature of the role of representatives. Do elected officials represent 'the people' by following their expressed preferences (one way of interpreting government *by* the people) or by doing what they think is right under the circumstances (a way of interpreting government *of* the people). This is another way of stating the tension, theorised by Peter Mair,[20] between political representatives' desire to be responsive to the citizens at the same time that they also need to govern responsibly.

The first interpretation links representation to the expression of political will, generally through elections. This runs the risk, as Nadia Urbinati points out, of too closely relating political legitimacy to the correspondence between what was promised and what gets decided, and thus eliminates the judgement component of democratic representation.[21] The second interpretation points instead to how closely tied output legitimacy is to input legitimacy. We can see this not only with regard to the political representative's choice between being responsive (input) or responsible (output) but also citizens' ability to sanction governments that they deem to have failed to perform responsibly (output) and/or in ways that meet their needs, fit with their values and respond to their wishes, as expressed in the previous election cycle (input).

## Throughput Legitimacy

To this mix of legitimising mechanisms, Schmidt has added a third mechanism, 'throughput', focused on the quality of the governance processes.[22] This expands on Easton's original use of the concept, which was limited to bureaucratic practices in the neglected 'black box' of governance, between the input and the output.[23] Throughput legitimacy covers all the governance processes that go on in that black box, including policy formulation and implementation, policy coordination and evaluation, interest intermediation and consultation, rulemaking and rule adjudication, standard-setting and harmonisation, legal assessment and judicial review, and so on. As such, this mechanism encompasses all five criteria generally used to assess procedural quality: the efficacy of the policy-making, the accountability of those engaged in decision-making, the transparency of the information, and the inclusiveness and openness to interest consultation. Such legitimating

[20] P Mair, *Ruling the Void* (London, Verso, 2013).

[21] N Urbinati, *Representative Democracy. Principles and Genealogy* (Chicago, IL, University of Chicago Press, 2006).

[22] Schmidt, 'Democracy and Legitimacy', above n 7; see also, eg, M Zürn, 'Democratic Governance Beyond the Nation-State' (2000) 6 *European Journal of International Relations* 183; A Benz and Y Papadopoulos, *Governance and Democracy* (London, Routledge, 2006); T Risse and M Kleine, 'Assessing the Legitimacy of the EU's Treaty Revision Methods' (2007) 45 *Journal of Common Market Studies* 69.

[23] Easton, above n 13.

criteria, grouped under throughput, also have a long history, with efficacy and accountability in particular traceable all the way back to Confucius and forward through Hegel's *Philosophy of Right* and Max Weber's legal-rational authority on to the vast public administration literature focused on these issues. In contrast, inclusiveness and openness are often considered in the context of pluralist theories of interest intermediation, and find greatest support from American democratic theorists such as David Truman and Robert Dahl, and more recently from theorists of 'associative democracy'.[24] This is where a fourth preposition can be added to Abraham Lincoln's original three, such that governing *with* the people is seen to make up for the limits of government '*by*, *of*, and *for* the people'.[25]

Underpinning these five evaluative criteria of throughput legitimacy are other requirements, including the 'hard' criterion of legality and the 'soft' criterion of trust. Relevant actors generally need to be perceived to act legally within the rules and to inspire trust in those with whom they engage, such that they are believed to act with integrity and without bias so as to ensure equal and open access in governance while meeting expected ethical and moral standards as well as legal ones. Fairness, meaning enforcing the rules in such a way as to apply equally and appropriately to all, is also a key component, and another defining attribute of legitimacy.[26] As a result, central to throughput legitimacy are expectations about the qualities necessary to policy-makers, which can be summarised by such buzzwords as trustworthiness, integrity, fairness, impartiality and credibility. Competence, of course, is also a requirement, linked to efficacy, as is respecting citizens' democratic prerogatives, for example, by not being oppressive or biased in applying the rules or closed to citizen involvement in the decision-making process.

But however important throughput legitimacy is for governance processes, it is never enough to guarantee any overall sense of legitimacy in citizens, for whom good policy output and/or sufficient political input are essential. Whereas input politics and output policy can be seen to involve trade-offs, in which more of the one may be seen to make up for less of the other (if it is indeed possible to separate the two),[27] throughput does not interact with output and input in the same way. While weak citizen input may be seen to be offset by good policy output, and a lot of citizen input may legitimate a policy even if it is ineffective, even the highest quality throughput cannot compensate for either bad policy output or minimal input participation, however efficacious the rules, accountable the actors, or transparent, open and accessible the process. In contrast, bad throughput – consisting of oppressive, incompetent, corrupt, or biased governance practices – is likely to undermine public perceptions of the legitimacy of EU governance, and it can even

[24] J Cohen and J Rogers, 'Secondary Associations and Democratic Governance' (1992) 20 *Politics and Society* 391.

[25] Schmidt, *Democracy in Europe*, above n 4, 35; Schmidt, 'Democracy and Legitimacy', above n 7.

[26] T Franck, *Fairness in International Law and Institutions* (New York, Oxford University Press, 1995).

[27] See CS Sternberg, 'Political Legitimacy Between Democracy and Effectiveness' (2015) 7 *European Political Science Review* 615.

skew the politics and taint the policies.[28] Finally, within throughput legitimacy, the constituting criteria can also work at cross-purposes. Greater efficacy can endanger accountability or inclusiveness; transparency can reduce accountability or efficacy; and openness and inclusiveness may jeopardise efficacy or accountability.

Throughput legitimacy, in short, should not be considered to be on a par with input and output legitimacy. It is nonetheless a key component of legitimacy, in particular in contexts of supranational governance such as the EU, where input politics is at many stages removed from policy-making, and thus diffuse, while the output policy results may be uncertain for some time, and in any case subject to interpretation.

In the multilevel EU, throughput legitimacy has long been one of the central ways in which EU institutional players have sought to counter claims about the poverty of the EU's input legitimacy and to reinforce claims to its output legitimacy.[29] In so doing, such actors have operated under the assumption that good throughput may act as a kind of 'cordon sanitaire' for the EU, ensuring the trustworthiness of the processes and serving, thereby, as a kind of reinforcement or, better, reassurance, of the legitimacy of EU-level output and attention to input.[30] While this focus on throughput has been no doubt beneficial, it has been no substitute for input or output legitimacy. Moreover, when problems with regard to throughput legitimacy have occurred, they have had major negative spillover effects with regard to input and output legitimacy. The most emblematic case of this is the scandal involving the Santer Commission, when charges of nepotism and abusive contracting led to its resignation in 1999. This was not just a major blow to perceptions of the EU Commission's underlying trustworthiness, accountability, or transparency (throughput). It served to obscure the Santer Commission's notable achievements (output), such as Enlargement, while giving Eurosceptics ammunition for their claims about the EU's democratic deficit (input).[31]

Whatever the problems with throughput legitimacy, however, it has been one of the main ways in which supranational actors have sought to improve legitimacy, even if it is no cure for the problems of input or output legitimacy. In what follows, we therefore look more closely at the different criteria by which it is constituted.

## Assessing the EU's Deficits in Throughput Legitimacy

Of the five criteria that make up throughput legitimacy, the first, efficacy, is primarily a technical standard, focused on the efficiency of policy-making. The remaining

[28] Schmidt, 'Democracy and Legitimacy', above n 7.

[29] A Héritier, *Policy-making and Diversity in Europe: Escape from Deadlock* (Cambridge, Cambridge University Press, 1999).

[30] Schmidt, 'Democracy and Legitimacy', above n 7.

[31] ibid.

four constitute normative criteria of evaluation, including standards by which to assess the accountability of the policy-makers and the transparency, inclusiveness and openness of the processes. But whether technical or normative, all five criteria are significant for EU throughput legitimacy not only with regard to how they are applied to governance processes, but also in terms of how they may complement or contradict one another so as to enhance or reduce overall legitimacy.

## Efficacy

Efficacy refers mainly to engaging in decision-making and proceeding with policy implementation in an efficient manner. Buzzwords include such phrases as 'streamlining operations' or 'modernising practices'. As such, efficacy is more of a technical criterion than a normative one – unlike accountability or transparency – since there are all sorts of administrative guidelines and management studies about what constitutes, say, efficient governance or competent management. But although not a normative standard like the other criteria, efficacy is nonetheless a necessary component of throughput legitimacy, since it has long been linked to considerations of the legitimacy of rulers, as a function of rulers' competence to rule, with incompetence contributing to de-legitimisation. And although it could be said that the presence of efficacy does not necessarily legitimate a ruling authority, failures of efficacy are often linked to processes of de-legitimisation – as, for example, in Max Weber's third definition of authority as legal-rational.[32]

Throughput efficacy has in consequence most often been conflated with output effectiveness. But there is a difference between processes that are carried out with efficacy, ie, in an efficient and competent manner, and policies that are effective, ie, that work. Although it is generally likely that efficacy in creating and administering policies will have a positive impact on their effectiveness, even inefficacious because long-drawn out decision-making or poorly administered implementation can nonetheless produce good policy outcomes, if the policies themselves prove effective. The inverse is also true: that however efficient the administrative processes, the resulting policies can prove ineffective, with bad results. Efficacy, then, is mainly about processing the job well, meaning proceeding in an efficient manner, whatever the outcomes.

Efficacy has been one of the principal concerns of EU institutional actors, as they have sought to enhance the governance processes through which input politics is transformed into output policies. This has involved seeking to improve the operating efficiency of the EU's many different modes of governance. For example, the co-decision mode (which includes the European Commission, the Council and the European Parliament) has been made to function more efficiently through

[32] M Weber, 'Politics as a Vocation' in HH Gerth and C Wright Mills (translated and edited), *From Max Weber: Essays in Sociology* (New York, Oxford University Press, 1946).

fast-track legislation via early agreements through inter-institutional meetings (called 'trilogues', which went from 28 per cent between 1999 and 2004, to 80 per cent between 2004 and 2009). But this comes at the expense of transparency and accountability as well as to the detriment of input legitimacy, due to the short-circuiting of parliamentary debate and the exclusion of the views of smaller party groupings.[33]

In supranational governance as well, the EU has focused on improvements in efficacy. Periodic proclamations by the Commission that it will seek to cut red tape and streamline operations are instances of this, along with promises to simplify the procedures of the European Semester. Impact assessments have since 2003 been another way of evaluating efficacy while trying to reinforce it by tying it to principles of accountability, transparency, inclusiveness and openness – even if the Commission has often been more internally inclusive, through coordination across administrative units, than externally so, by bringing in external experts or being open to stakeholders and civil society.[34] Moreover, EU Commission failures of oversight with regard to Member State transposition and implementation of EU directives, by allowing inconsistent compliance with the rules by the Member States, also raise problems of throughput efficacy, in particular with regard to whether and when the Commission engages in the different stages of infraction proceedings against the Member States.[35]

Intergovernmental governance by the Council has also frequently been criticised for its lack of efficacy. The unanimity rule for treaties, which allows any Member State to veto any agreement, can lead to delays, dilution or deadlock, along with sub-optimal outcomes. Although there are certainly good reasons related to input legitimacy to keep the unanimity rule (because it ensures that Member States can safeguard national preferences and autonomy), unanimity often frustrates goals and values related to output legitimacy – plus it is highly inefficient in terms of throughput efficacy. The serious problems with unanimity became apparent from the mid-2000s, once the Council doubled in size. This was exemplified by the myriad delays on the Lisbon Treaty (following the failure of the Constitutional Treaty subsequent to the French and Dutch referendums), and subsequently the increasing recourse to international agreements outside the treaties, in particular during the Eurozone crisis. These are clear indications that the EU needs to find other ways of reaching binding agreements among the Member States, such as through super-majorities with opt-outs. Such problems with the EU's efficacy naturally also affect its accountability.

[33] A Héritier and C Reh, 'Codecision and its Discontents' (2012) 35 *West European Politics* 1134.

[34] E Bozzini and S Smismans, 'More Inclusive European Governance through Impact Assessments' (2016) 14 *Comparative European Politics* 89.

[35] T Börzel, 'Non-Compliance in the European Union. Pathology or Statistical Artefact?' (2001) 8 *Journal of European Public Policy* 803; A Batory, 'Defying the Commission: Creative Compliance and Respect for the Rule of Law' (2016) 94 *Public Administration* 685.

## Accountability

Accountability is arguably the most important aspect of throughput legitimacy, at least judging by the attention paid to it. It has been defined in myriad ways, often depending upon the disciplinary angle as well as the actor in focus. But stripped down to its core conceptualisation, accountability can be defined as public officials giving account of and being held to account for their actions in public forums that have the authority to judge their behaviour such that the actors can face consequences for their actions. This means that actors are expected to explain the reasons for their actions and be judged accordingly by a relevant authority, with the (potential) imposition of rewards or sanctions in cases of eventual misconduct.[36] Both of these entail that public officials have the autonomy and discretion to carry out their duties, which can be used or misused.[37]

Accountability is most often discussed in terms of the administrative activities of technical actors in non-majoritarian institutions, delegated agencies and governmental administrations, but it also applies to political actors engaged in the processes of governance. In all cases, it means that actors can be held to account – by technical and/or political oversight bodies – for what they do as they engage in processes of governance. But it also means that actors must give account of their actions in those self-same forums as well as to the public, and be judged accordingly. As such, accountability also requires relevant actors to provide information about their activities, to be open to discussion and deliberation about that information, and to be subject to (potential) rewards or sanctions.[38]

Such procedural accountability needs to be differentiated from what is often termed 'democratic' or political accountability, which refers to politicians being held accountable by their constituents for their levels of responsiveness to citizens' demands (input legitimacy). With the concept of accountability for elected officials, for example, we need to be careful to differentiate between political actors being 'held accountable' by citizens through elections (input legitimacy) and by their reason giving in public forums (throughput legitimacy).[39] Representation and accountability are different things. Accountability in public forums, as Ben Crum and Dierdre Curtin explain, is 'the *ex post* complement to the *ex ante* mechanisms of democratic election or authorization through which executive actors are initially appointed'. In other words, accountability in the throughput sense comes

[36] M Bovens, RE Goodin and T Schillemans (eds), *The Oxford Handbook of Public Accountability* (Oxford, Oxford University Press, 2014).

[37] J March and J Olsen, *Democratic Governance* (New York, Free Press, 1995) 152.

[38] M Bovens, T Schillemans and P 't Hart, 'Does Public Accountability Work? An Assessment Tool' (2008) 86 *Public Administration* 225.

[39] eg, B Cashore, 'Legitimacy and the Privatization of Environmental Governance' (2002) 15 *Governance: An International Journal of Policy, Administration, and Institutions* 503; C Borowiak, *Accountability and Democracy* (New York, Oxford University Press, 2011); C Borowiak, 'Making European Union Executive Power Accountable'; M Wood, 'Beyond Accountability: Political Legitimacy and Delegated Water Governance in Australia' (2015) 93 *Public Administration* 1012.

after input-legitimate elections, and applies to the ways in which elected officials in office are expected to justify their exercise of power in public forums, most often parliamentary, with the understanding that they will be judged on the basis of whether that exercise serves the popular constituency.[40]

Technical actors, in contrast, are generated limited to procedural accountability, in which they are expected to give account to private forums of experts or to public representative forums of how they processed executive decisions and are judged on the integrity and legality of how they executed their duties. As Giandomenico Majone specifies, because 'majoritarian standards' of (input) legitimacy are not appropriate for independent regulators, they require 'accountability'.[41] Although Majone himself places such procedural accountability under the rubric of output legitimacy, in our approach it is a part of throughput legitimacy.

EU accountability is also about actors 'giving account' of their actions, which means being subject to scrutiny by a specific forum, whether constituted by technical actors with special expertise in public administration or by political actors acting in a representative capacity for the citizenry at large.[42] Technical actors are generally assumed to give account to specialised accountability forums, consisting of networks of experts who can provide 'objective' – meaning (social) scientific – assessments of the quality of their (throughput) activities and of the effective (output) performance of the resulting policies.[43] But accountability may equally be established by forums made up of political actors, such as parliamentary bodies that 'take account' not only of the quality of technical actors' (throughput) activities and the effectiveness of their resulting (output) policies but also how such policies resonate with citizen values and the common interest. Accountability is not just about rendering accounts to specialised forums, however. It is also about making them public.

The ECB's accountability, for example, is generally seen to depend on passing scrutiny by the epistemic community of economists, banking experts and other central bankers. But the ECB also sees itself as accountable to the EP, as the forum in which it is charged to explain its actions and to hear concerns raised by MEPs.[44] That said, by mandate the ECB does not have to listen, and a more cynical view might suggest that the ECB uses the EP more as platform from which to explain and legitimate its actions to a wider audience. The Commission, in comparison, has become much more accountable to the EP over time, in particular ever since

[40] Crum and Curtin, above n 5, 64–66; M Bovens, 'Analysing and Assessing Accountability: A Conceptual Framework' (2007) 13 *European Law Journal* 447, 450.

[41] Majone, above n 3.

[42] M Bovens, D Curtin and P 't Hart (eds), *The Real World of EU Accountability: What Deficit?* (Oxford, Oxford University Press, 2010) 38.

[43] L Seabrooke, 'Epistemic Arbitrage: Transnational Professional Knowledge in Action' (2014) 1 *Journal of Professions and Organization* 49.

[44] B Braun, 'Two Sides of the Same Coin? Independence and Accountability of the European Central Bank'. Report for Transparency International EU (Brussels, 2017).

the Commission President has come to represent the majority in the EP – although its various administrative units (directorates general) are also subject to technical accountability forums.

The EP itself, as a result, has slowly grown in importance as an accountability forum, although it remains relatively weak. The EP's enhanced throughput legitimacy with regard to oversight, it is important to note, only partially serves to counterbalance its long-term lack of influence, whether as a co-decision maker or accountability forum, when it comes to the Council's intergovernmental decision-making and the Commission's supranational policy-making, along with comitology.[45] The EP continues to have little influence over initiation of legislation, no connection to comitology and little (albeit growing) connection to national parliaments.[46] Moreover, trade-offs among throughput legitimacy criteria are also in play. While any increase in the EP's oversight role over other EU actors would certainly in principle make decision-making more accountable, it could at the same time undermine efficacy by inserting (input) politics into the process, in particular were there to be more conflicts with the Council. In the end, it could even undermine accountability, given the tension between the European parliamentary groupings and national parties resulting from EP party aggregation.[47]

Finally, public accountability also demands that EU actors render accounts to the general public. This serves to build public understanding and trust in their work, to reinforce their authority, to achieve 'credible commitments', and to ensure that the public would accept the policy as appropriate and justified.[48] In consequence, EU actors have recognised the need to develop communicative strategies on a daily basis in this 'mediatised' age.[49] As a result of this, the media can also be seen to function as a kind of public 'accountability forum', with agencies giving account to the media even as the media gives account of those agencies' regulatory activities to the public.[50] This arguably works best for technical agencies speaking on specialised issues – such as when Margot Wallstrom announces a state aid ruling that sanctions Ireland's special tax regime for Apple. But it may not work as well for the EU Commission on general questions because there is no EU-wide media to which to give public account, while national media may take nationally coloured views. But this is also where transparency comes in.

[45] C Lord, *A Democratic Audit of the European Union* (Basingstoke, Palgrave Macmillan, 2004); Bovens et al, *The Real World of EU Accountability*, above n 42.

[46] A Héritier, C Moury, M Schoeller, K Meissner and I Mota, 'The European Parliament as a Driving Force of Constitutionalisation' (2016) Report for the Constitutional Affairs Committee of the European Parliament, PE 536.467.

[47] R Rose and G Borz, 'Aggregation and Representation in European Parliament Party Groupings' (2013) 36 *West European Politics* 474.

[48] Cashore, above n 39, T Schillemans, 'Does Horizontal Accountability Work?' (2011) 43 *Administration & Society* 387; Wood, above n 39.

[49] M Hajer, 'A Media Storm in the World Risk Society' (2012) 6 *Critical Policy Studies* 452.

[50] Bovens, above n 40; M Maggetti, 'The Media Accountability of Independent Regulatory Agencies' (2012) 4 *European Political Science Review* 385.

## Transparency

Transparency has long been seen as an accompaniment not only to (throughput) accountability but also to political (input) legitimacy, as a key component of any free society, related to citizens' rights to know and governments' obligation to share information about all aspects of public life. It sits at the very heart of how citizens hold their public officials accountable, and thus is closely linked to accountability. In transnational democracy, moreover, transparency can equally be seen as a component of citizen empowerment,[51] with the goal of improving public services or reducing corruption and clientelism. But transparency can also have a regulatory function, by serving to tame undue private power, with public officials mandating public disclosures about private companies' products and practices such that citizens have the requisite information to press for corporate social responsibility and performance.[52] In the EU, both senses of transparency are operative, since EU officials seek to make their own actions and publications more transparent while demanding the same of all entities that do business in the EU.

In the EU, transparency generally refers to the availability of provisions ensuring that citizens and political representatives have access to information about governance processes and that decisions as well as decision-making processes in formal institutions are public.[53] This is to enable the public to monitor the processes, with wide access to documents by any feasible and accessible means, with few exceptions.[54] In practice, this means checking on how well the public can examine the integrity and accountability of the EU actor itself as well as the functioning of inter-institutional oversight relations.[55]

The Commission has attempted to ensure general transparency by providing increasing access to the mountains of EU documents and materials for the media and interest groups as well as to the general public through the internet and the development of e-government – although the massive volume of EU-generated information has also led to information overload and thus, perversely, less transparency.[56] Access to information, however much, does not ensure that citizens will automatically gain insight and knowledge about the proceedings. And more information is not always better, since it is easier to lose any sense of what is important and what is not.

[51] M Smith, 'Developing Administrative Principles in the EU: A Foundational Model of Legitimacy?' (2012) 18 *European Law Journal* 269.

[52] S Kosack and A Fung, 'Does Transparency Improve Governance?' (2014) 17 *Annual Review of Political Science* 65.

[53] A Héritier, 'Composite Democracy in Europe. The Role of Transparency and Access to Information' (2003) 10 *Journal of European Public Policy* 814.

[54] MZ Hillebrandt, D Curtin and A Meijer, 'Transparency in the EU Council of Ministers' (2014) 20 *European Law Journal* 1.

[55] eg, B Braun, above n 44; C Ban and L Seabrooke, 'From Crisis to Stability: How to Make the European Stability Mechanism Transparent and Accountable'. Report for Transparency International EU (Brussels, 2017).

[56] Héritier, 'Composite Democracy in Europe', above n 53.

Even though transparency has been an increasing focus of EU actors more generally, there are many instances of a lack of transparency. For example, the European Stability Mechanism (ESM), which acts as a lender of last resort in conjunction with the ECB, argues that if it made the reasons for its investment decisions public, the markets would be the greatest beneficiaries, to the disadvantage of the Member State receiving ESM support.[57] In this case, considerations of output legitimacy – meaning good performance – appear to win out over the search for throughput legitimacy via transparency.

Transparency can also clash with efficacy, in particular in negotiation settings.[58] In Council meetings, for example, secrecy – meaning the lack of transparency – has been linked to greater efficacy, since it helps Member State officials clinch agreements that would not be possible if national publics knew about their officials' specific compromises, and enables fruitful side-deals.[59] Conversely, where more public debate is mandated in the co-decision process, negotiations often end up taking place over lunch or in the corridors, to the detriment of accountability as well as transparency, whether in the Council or the EP.[60]

For legitimation, then, much depends upon the reasons for the secrecy, and whether it is necessary in order to ensure against worse consequences, or instead to hide problematic decisions. In the Eurozone crisis, as Christian Kreuder-Sonnen argues, there is a difference between secrecy as crisis management in a 'reactive/defensive mode' and secrecy as crisis exploitation in an 'active/offensive mode', where those in authority benefit from opacity to gain executive discretion and adopt policies that would have otherwise not been possible.[61] An example of defensive crisis management could be seen in the ECB's moving closer to acting as a lender of last resort, to 'save the euro'.[62] An example of crisis exploitation is best illustrated by the Eurogroup in the various Greek bail-out negotiations, where the ability of Eurogroup finance ministers to act in secrecy enabled 'creditor' country ministers to wrest much more out of Greece than they would have been able had they had to make their positions public.[63] As an added factor, the opaqueness of the Eurogroup's decision-making on Greece, when they act in their capacity as the board of governors of the ESM, also reduces their accountability, since as an informal body they give accounts of their actions to no one.[64]

[57] Ban and Seabrooke, above n 55.

[58] eg, D Stasavage, 'Open-door or Closed-door? Transparency in Domestic and International Bargaining' (2004) 58 *International Organization* 667.

[59] D Naurin, *Deliberation Behind Closed Doors. Transparency and Lobbying in the European Union* (Colchester, ECPR Press, 2007).

[60] S Novak, 'The Silence of Ministers: Consensus and Blame Avoidance in the Council of the European Union' (2013) 51 *Journal of Common Market Studies* 1091.

[61] C Kreuder-Sonnen, 'Political Secrecy in Europe: Crisis Management and Crisis exploitation' (2017) *West European Politics*, available at: doi.org/10.1080/01402382.2017.1404813.

[62] Braun, above n 44.

[63] Kreuder-Sonnen, above n 61.

[64] Ban and Seabrooke, above n 55.

## Inclusiveness and Openness

Transparency as well as accountability can also be linked to the final criterion of throughput legitimacy, concerning governance processes' openness and inclusiveness. Openness means that the political and technical actors involved in creating and/or implementing policies are willing to engage with any and all of those members of the public – mainly organised in groups of citizens – desirous of having a say with regard to the policies in which they are most interested. Inclusiveness means that they are open to all such groups, and bring them in in such a way as to ensure balance in their representation.

Admittedly, it may sometimes be difficult to distinguish between citizen activities that serve the function of political representation (input) versus those that serve a function of procedural inclusiveness and openness (throughput). The former is related to the expression of political preferences and judged on the basis of whether interest groups adequately and appropriately represent the interests of the citizens for whom they claim to speak. The latter is related to accessibility, and judged on the basis of whether interest groups are adequately and fairly represented in policy-making, with every effort made to provide for a diversity of opinion. There is little question that input representation is involved when interest groups organise grass-roots letter-writing campaigns, bring busloads of farmers to national capitals or Brussels to protest a new bill, organise demonstrations of mothers for peace, and represent 'civil society', meaning citizens, in public interest-related activities meant to influence elected officials. In contrast, throughput inclusiveness and openness is instead operative when interest groups become part of an elaborate interest intermediation process focused on policy-making, in which they lobby political and technical officials, testify in committee meetings and parliamentary hearings, provide informational evidence to administrative functionaries, and serve as counterweights to one another as they seek to influence policy formulation and implementation. It is easier to distinguish throughput-related activities from input-related activities where experts or members of interest groups are involved in standard-setting committees and comitology, or invited to be part of evaluative administrative processes or accountability forums. In these venues, participants are clearly brought in for their expertise and technical knowledge, to help refine policies or to provide balance in views, as opposed to serving to represent any possible political interests.

Problems with regard to inclusiveness and openness come from the nature of intermediation, whether understood in terms of political or procedural representation. These include unequal access, differentials in power and influence, corruption related to the trading of favours, client politics, lack of accountability and the dangers of agency 'capture' by special interests – as famously elaborated for US pluralist processes of intermediation by James Q Wilson.[65]

[65] JQ Wilson, *The Politics of Regulation* (New York, Basic Books, 1980); see also A Bianculli, X Fernández-i-Marín and J Jordana (eds), *Accountability and Regulatory Governance: Audiences, Controls and Responsibilities in the Politics of Regulation* (Basingstoke, Palgrave Macmillan, 2014).

The EU has its own version of pluralism.[66] In the EU, governance *with* the people through pluralist-type consultation comes mainly through co-decision-making, and was initially focused primarily on the technical agents of the Commission. This has changed with the increasing powers of the EP in co-decision, as lobbying MEPs has been a veritable growth industry.[67] Moreover, rather than competition among interests, following the norm of the US, the Commission has fostered cooperation, with the rules of the game demanding that participants gain and maintain credibility as trusted actors providing accurate technical information.[68]

The EU has deliberately encouraged such pluralism as a way of counterbalancing the paucity of governance *by* or *of* the people through political participation and citizen representation. The Commission in particular has done much to attempt to right the balance in access and influence among organised interests representing business versus those representing unions or public interest organisations,[69] sometimes even being instrumental in bringing in under-represented interest groups (eg, women and consumers) at the EU level. But be this as it may, access and inclusiveness remain debatable,[70] in particular given the difficulties of transnational mobilisation.[71] Much has yet to be done to strengthen and redesign the existing elements of participatory democracy, as anchored in the constitutional framework of the Union.[72]

Ensuring inclusiveness and openness also has spillover effects on other aspects of throughput legitimacy. For one, ensuring greater openness to interest participation serves to improve transparency mainly through the provision of more information on rules and procedures as well as through procedural requirements for active participation by a broad range of stakeholders in regulatory decision-making.[73] Inclusiveness and openness also improve accountability, by promoting deliberative procedures that are designed to ensure that citizens' community power is adequately channelled in societal and administrative decision-making.[74]

Eurozone economic governance during the crisis has posed special problems with regard to openness and inclusiveness, in particular for organised labour in light of the European Semester, which empowered the European Commission

[66] Schmidt, *Democracy in Europe*, above n 4, ch 3.

[67] eg, D Coen and J Richardson, *Lobbying in the European Union* (Oxford, Oxford University Press, 2009).

[68] D Coen, *EU Lobbying* (London, Routledge, 2008); Coen and Richardson, above n 67.

[69] J Greenwood, 'Organized Civil Society and Democratic Legitimacy in the European Union' (2007) 37 *British Journal of Political Science* 333; M Pianta, 'Democracy Lost: The Financial Crisis in Europe and the Role of Civil Society' (2013) 9 *Journal of Civil Society* 148.

[70] S Kröger, 'Nothing but Consultation: The Place of Organized Civil Society in EU Policy-making across Policies' (2008) European Governance Papers (EUROGOV) No C-08-03.

[71] D Della Porta (ed), *Democracy in Social Movements* (Basingstoke, Palgrave Macmillan, 2009).

[72] JH Kamlage and P Nanz, 'Crisis and Participation in the European Union' (2017) 31 *Global Society* 65.

[73] C Sabel and J Zeitlin, *Experimentalist Governance in the European Union: Towards a New Architecture* (Oxford, Oxford University Press, 2010) 18–20.

[74] V Bekkers and A Edwards, 'Legitimacy and Democracy' in V Bekkers, G Dijkstra, A Edwards and M Fener (eds), *Governance and the Democratic Deficit* (Aldershot, Ashgate Publishing, 2007) 53.

to prescribe labour market policies and sanction non-complying governments. This resulted in a situation in which the EU, rather than dealing with the conflicts between business and labour at the supranational level through inclusive negotiation, 'nationalises social conflicts' through country-specific recommendations, corrective action plans and sanctions that push wage deflation and labour market deregulation.[75] In other words, in the Euro regime, national 'authoritarian' imposition in cases of countries in conditionality programmes replaced EU-level inclusiveness with regard to labour. But this is only one of the many problems for throughput legitimacy in the context of the Eurozone crisis.

## Challenges to EU Institutional Actors' Throughput Legitimacy in the Eurozone Crisis

Throughput legitimacy has become particularly salient during the sovereign debt crisis because of the focus by European leaders on Eurozone 'governing by rules and ruling by numbers'.[76] The initial actions taken, involving reinforcing rules-based, numbers-targeting governance, raised legitimacy problems not only in throughput terms – regarding its efficacy, accountability, transparency, inclusiveness and openness – but also in terms of how these negatively affected output performance and input responsiveness. The subsequent response to the deterioration of output policy performance and the increase in the volatility of national input politics, which involved the reinterpretation of the rules 'by stealth', added additional problems of throughput legitimacy.[77]

The Council has come in for criticism as a result of its intergovernmental monopoly on decision-making, dominated by Germany and other 'creditor' countries. That criticism focuses on the inefficacy of EU governance, largely because of the Council's incompetence in crisis management along with its lack of transparency as well as its perceived bias against 'debtor' countries.[78] The Commission has also been under attack, whether for its inflexibility in the European Semester between 2010 and 2012, especially by southern European countries, and subsequently for its failure to enforce the rules more rigorously, in particular by northern European countries.[79] Arguably most in question have been the institutions

[75] R Erne, 'A Supranational Regime that Nationalizes Social Conflict: Explaining European Trade Unions' Difficulties in Politicizing European Economic Governance' (2015) 56 *Labor History* 345.

[76] For a more detailed discussion, see VA Schmidt, 'Reinterpreting the Rules "by Stealth" in Times of Crisis: The European Central Bank and the European Commission' (2016) 39 *West European Politics* 1032.

[77] ibid.

[78] eg, S Fabbrini, 'Intergovernmentalism and its Limits' (2013) 46 *Comparative Political Studies* 1003; M Blyth and M Matthijs (eds), *The Future of the Euro* (New York, Oxford University Press, 2015).

[79] VA Schmidt, 'Forgotten Democratic Legitimacy: 'Governing by the Rules' and 'Ruling by the Numbers'' in M Blyth and M Matthijs (eds), *The Future of the Euro* (New York, Oxford University Press, 2015); Schmidt, 'Reinterpreting the Rules', above n 76.

constituting the Troika (IMF, ECB, Commission and the ESM), which have been faulted for their lack of accountability and transparency.[80] As Christian Joerges has argued, at the height of the crisis, such institutions were about as far from representative democracy as one can go, and more like authoritarian imposition when it came to decisions about the deficit reductions and structural reforms required for countries in trouble in exchange for bail-out funds.[81]

When EU institutional actors slowly and incrementally began reinterpreting the rules 'by stealth', that is, passing over in silence or even denying publicly that they were in fact adjusting the rules, they certainly improved output policy performance. But they at the same time split the input politics, in particular between North and South, while they raised major questions for the throughput processes. Transparency was undermined by key actors hiding the fact that they were reinterpreting the rules and with it accountability to the 'principals', ie, the Council, even if efficacy may have benefited from the increasing discretion of EU actors in applying the rules flexibly. The lack of clear guidelines for administrative discretion and flexibility, moreover, raise questions of both accountability as well as transparency, while the absence of political actors 'taking account' of technical actors' decisions raised questions for its input legitimacy. Finally, all of this jeopardised the values of trust and legality that underpin the throughput governance processes, without which EU actors have great difficulty moving forward.

In the process of reinterpreting the rules of Eurozone governance, EU actors could be seen as having created a new 'governance framework',[82] by supplementing, if not supplanting, the formal rules by informal rules. This however should not be seen as the same as 'informal governance', in which making exceptions to the rules is part of a process of negotiated agreement that actually reinforces the legitimacy of the formal governance processes (throughput), the impact of the rules (output), along with their responsiveness to citizens (input). Informal governance in the case of single market regulations, for example, is when individual Member States are occasionally given exemptions after Council-led investigation and agreement that the political fallout from domestic groups' objections could jeopardise consensual EU-level politics or national political stability.[83] In the Eurozone crisis, by contrast, governance has been not so much about making exceptions to the rules as creating exceptional rules, while denying it.[84]

[80] Ban and Seabrooke, above n 55.

[81] C Joerges, 'Three Transformations of Europe and the Search for a Way Out of Its Crisis' in C Joerges and C Glinski (eds), *The European Crisis and the Transformation of Transnational Governance. Authoritarian Managerialism Versus Democratic Governance* (Oxford, Hart Publishing, 2014).

[82] CA Alcidi, A Giovannini and S Piedrafita, 'Enhancing the Legitimacy of EMU Governance' (2014) *CEPS Special Report* No 98.

[83] See M Kleine, *Informal Governance in the European Union* (Ithaca, NY, Cornell University Press, 2013).

[84] Another way of thinking about such reinterpretation comes from Italian constitutional theory, where the 'costituzione materiale', or the constitution in practice, is accepted as malleable and legitimately reinterpreted through practice because the veto points and players make it impossible to revise the constitution. See C Mortati, *La costituzione in senso materiale* (Milano, Giuffré, 1940).

The problem for EU actors in the Eurozone crisis has been that the complexity of decision-making processes, the formal rigidity of the rules, and the divisions among key players have ensured that admitting that they were actually reinterpreting the rules has been difficult if not impossible where they have feared legal challenges or worried that political deals may unravel. Both technical and political actors have in fact had very good reasons for not admitting publicly their reinterpretation of the rules by stealth. In addition to the political splits among Member States for or against austerity policies was the volatility of the markets as well as their schizophrenia between 2010 and 2012, as they seemed to expect austerity and growth at the same time;[85] the uncertain reactions from different segments of the public within as well as between countries; and the threat of potential legal challenges (the referral of the ECB's Outright Monetary Transactions (OMT) programme to the German Constitutional Court being a case in point).

The problems with throughput legitimacy regarding the reinterpretation of the rules can also cast suspicion on output policy performance and throw input responsiveness into question. Reinterpretation by stealth could make EU technical agents appear incompetent – or ideologically bullheaded – because they appear to be sticking to rules that don't work, thereby tainting public perceptions of the output policy performance. Moreover, by obfuscating on the reinterpretations, EU political agents tend to skew the politics, making them appear less responsive than they actually are. Worse, it leaves their actions open to critique by the political extremes – who claim to 'tell the truth' while politicians lie, don't care, or care only about their own clientelism and/or class interests.[86] But even without the populist take on this, the general public can get the wrong impression, given the disingenuous discourse of political and technical elites. Legitimacy, after all, is about perceptions of policy effects as much as it is about actual effects.

Finally, in a system in which the focus on 'governing by rules and ruling by numbers' has created an increasingly rigid system of packs, pacts and compacts, any exercise in political or administrative discretion demands rules for stretching or breaking the rules – or at the very least agreement on who has the authority to make or break those rules.[87]

This raises two questions. First, how does one legitimate such reinterpretations 'by stealth', that is, by not admitting – or even denying – to the public what one is doing behind closed doors? Second, how does one go about legitimating the reinterpretation of the legally binding rules if there are no rules for bending or breaking those rules? Put another way, who judges the scientific validity or normative appropriateness of the reinterpretations?

[85] See Olivier Blanchard on this, available at: blog-imfdirect.imf.org/2011/12/21/2011-in-review-four-hard-truths/.

[86] C Mudde (ed), *The Populist Radical Right: A Reader* (London, Routledge, 2017).

[87] Thanks to André Sapir for this comment, made in the wrap-up session of the Conference on 'Europe in a Post Crisis World', Center for European Studies, Harvard University (31 October–1 November 2013).

The answer to the first question – how to legitimate such reinterpretations to the public – remains elusive so long as EU institutional actors do not admit what they have been doing, that is, reinterpreting the rules 'by stealth'. This was particularly problematic in the time period from 2010 to 2015, during the Barroso Commission. Subsequently, the Juncker Commission began admitting to its flexibility, even setting out rules for flexibility, which improved perceptions of throughput legitimacy. Moreover, as time has progressed, and as such reinterpretations have become increasingly contested, EU actors have more and more had to 'give accounts' publicly of their actions – such as the ECB with regard to quantitative easing and the Commission involving its derogations for France and Italy. This is one route to greater legitimacy, even if such public accounting has involved EU actors trying to hide the truth of what they are doing. Telling the truth – although more optimal in terms of accountability and transparency – remains problematic for output and input legitimacy, given Member States' divergence interests and assessments of what needs or ought to be done.

The answer to the second question, how to go about legitimating rules reinterpretation, is embedded in EU institutional actors' own definitions of legitimacy as well as in the institutional settings in which they operate. Conceptualisations not just of efficacy but even more importantly of accountability (political as much as bureaucratic) need to be embedded in institutional understandings of what constitutes 'democratic' norms and standards for evaluation, in particular in an 'unsettled polity' like the EU, where principal-agent theories of compliance and control cannot account for the complexity of organisational relations.[88] To understand how EU institutional actors build legitimacy for their reinterpretations therefore requires looking at those actors' own very different institutional configurations and frameworks for legitimation. And it entails recognising that different sets of EU actors build their authority to change the rules on different bases following different pathways to legitimacy.

## Conclusion

This chapter set out to show that the concept of throughput legitimacy is a useful and necessary accompaniment to output and input legitimacy, but not a substitute. It focuses on the quality of policy-making, in order to reinforce peoples' trust that the rules are being following fairly, in the spirit as much as the letter of the law, in ways that are responsive to citizens' input demands while ensuring the best possible policy outputs. Perceptions of illegality or unfairness, which lead to a loss of trust, serve to endanger the EU's throughput legitimacy and, in turn, its input and/or output legitimacy. But good governance (throughput) cannot make up for failures to respond to citizens' expressed demands (input) or to produce effective

[88] J Olsen, 'Democratic Order, Autonomy, and Accountability' (2015) 28 *Governance* 425.

outcomes (output). The overall question with regard to the EU's throughput legitimacy, in the end, is whether it ensures the seamless flow of input to output as part of a governing system that acts both responsively (input) and responsibly in ways that produce good outcomes (output) efficaciously via accountable and transparent processes that are also inclusive and open (throughput). In short, the answer to the question whether the EU has a throughput deficit is inextricably tied to the question of whether it has an input and/or output deficit. Since the Eurozone crisis, we probably have to answer 'yes' to all three deficits. This raises the question of whether the EU is itself democratically legitimate – but the answer to that requires another much longer chapter.

# 8

# Accountability Through Self-Governance in EU Economic Governance

ANA BOBIĆ*

## Introduction

The introduction of the Economic and Monetary Union (EMU) in the Maastricht Treaty,[1] a step of yet unprecedented integration, was followed by a sharp decline in public support present in previous Treaty revisions.[2] The development was followed by the vast literature on the democratic deficit of the EU, most prominently advocated by Fritz Scharpf.[3] In addition, the literature argued that European integration expanded into areas traditionally considered core state powers,[4] resulting in a retreat to new intergovernmental modes of governance,[5] such as differentiation through opt-outs and the establishment of regulatory agencies.[6]

These concerns were particularly exacerbated during the euro crisis, which has been much maligned in terms of its lack of democratic accountability.[7] The EU's

* I am grateful to Adina Maricut-Akbik, Josephine van Zeben, Petra Weingerl and Mark Dawson for their useful feedback and comments.

[1] Treaty Establishing the European Community (TEC) [1992] OJ C 224/1.

[2] JHH Weiler, *The Constitution of Europe. 'Do the New Clothes have an Emperor?' and Other Essays on European Integration* (Cambridge, Cambridge University Press, 1999) 4; N MacCormick, *Questioning Sovereignty* (Oxford University Press, 1999) 98–99.

[3] F Scharpf, *Governing in Europe: Effective and Democratic?* (Oxford, Oxford University Press, 1999). For an overview of the argument and the relevant supporting literature, see A Moravscik, 'In Defense of the "Democratic Deficit": Reassessing Legitimacy in the European Union' (2002) 40 *Journal of Common Market Studies* 603; VA Schmidt, 'Democracy and Legitimacy in the European Union Revisited: Input, Output *and* "Throughput"' (2013) 61 *Political Studies* 2.

[4] P Genschel and M Jachtenfuchs, 'More Integration, Less Federation: The European Integration of Core State Powers' (2016) 23 *Journal of European Public Policy* 42.

[5] CJ Bickerton et al, 'The New Intergovernmentalism: European Integration in the Post-Maastricht Era' (2015) 53 *Journal of Common Market Studies* 703.

[6] Genschel and Jachtenfuchs, above n 4, 46–48. For an overview of the literature, see A Maricut-Akbik, 'EU Politicization beyond the Euro Crisis: Immigration Crises and the Politicization of Free Movement of People' (2018) 1 *Comparative European Politics* 1, 3–4.

[7] C Fasone, 'European Economic Governance and Parliamentary Representation: What Place for the European Parliament?' (2014) 20 *European Law Journal* 164; M Dawson, 'The Legal and Political Accountability Structure of "Post-crisis" EU Economic Governance' (2015) 53 *Journal of Common*

strong reliance on output legitimacy strengthens this claim: the emphasis on authority derived from regulatory effectiveness and market integration prosperity[8] over process-centred democratic controls has been particularly visible in the ad hoc creation of the EU's economic governance mechanisms.[9] This result-oriented approach demonstrated the weaknesses of established accountability systems, such as judicial review and parliamentary scrutiny at both the national and EU level.

In this contribution I argue that the current institutional set-up of EU economic governance, specifically post-crisis, suffers from two main malaises which as its result has political inequality between EU citizens. First, it is designed so as to favour the principle of equality of Member States to the detriment of the principle of solidarity between Member States, which creates asymmetries in influence on the political realm and access to accountability mechanisms among EU citizens. Second, it relies on nation-state inspired models of democratic legitimation which are not appropriate for its specific transnational context, which is increasingly regulated through ad hoc and non-typical instruments. Majoritarian representation is, as will be shown, unable to ensure legitimation and accountability equally for citizens of all Member States. Ultimately, the current architecture of EU economic governance limits the number of those able to contest political decisions, the number of routes available for such contestation, and the ultimate answerability of decision-makers. Rather, accountability needs to be separated from democratic representation rooted in the tradition of nation states,[10] and to focus on achieving political equality of citizens as the crucial tenet of democracy.

While the present work does not offer a detailed proposal for institutional reform, it provides a starting point for further research, outlining its main theoretical features. In what follows, I argue that legal accountability in economic governance is currently suffering from two main deficiencies: first, the individual has been taken out of the equation in the design of economic governance mechanisms; and, second, the imitated nation-state accountability mechanisms have proved inadequate in ensuring the individual's ability to hold decision-makers in economic governance to account. Subsequently, I set out a proposal for accountability through self-governance and its normative underpinnings. The final part offers a broad-brush attempt at applying the model to economic governance mechanisms, and concludes with some open questions for further research.

*Market Studies* 976, 983; J Pisani-Ferry, 'Rebalancing the Governance of the Euro Area' in M Dawson, H Enderlein and C Joerges (eds), *Beyond the Crisis. The Governance of Europe's Economic, Political, and Legal Transformation* (Oxford, Oxford University Press, 2015) 72; A Maatsch, *Parliaments and the Economic Governance of the European Union: Talking Shops or Deliberative Bodies?* (London, Routledge, 2016).

[8] T Isiksel, *Europe's Functional Constitution* (Oxford, Oxford University Press, 2016) 6, 13.

[9] ibid 224 onwards. See also, J Habermas, 'Democracy, Solidarity and the European Crisis' in A-M Grozelier et al (eds), *Roadmap to a Social Europe* (Social Europe Report, 2013) available at: www.ictu.ie/download/pdf/roadmap_to_social_europe_sej_oct_2013.pdf#page=9, 4.

[10] J Teubner, '*Quod omnes tangit*: Transnational Constitutions Without Democracy?' (2018) (S1) *Journal of Law and Society* S5, S22.

# Problems of Accountability in Existing Economic Governance Mechanisms

## Deficiencies Stemming from the Design of the EU's Economic Governance Mechanisms

On an abstract level, the principle of solidarity between Member States[11] may be said to be at the heart of post-crisis instruments of economic governance.[12] Its more practical expression has, however, arguably been guided by the principle of equality of Member States as articulated in Article 4(2) TEU. The principle of equality has seen its expression, for example, in the prohibition of monetary financing envisaged in Article 123 TFEU, as well as in the no bail-out clause contained in Article 125 TFEU,[13] which presumes equality between Member States to an extent that each of them is liable for their own failures.[14] In that sense, it overlooks the economic spillovers in the area of not only a shared market, but also a shared currency, and the ensuing need for risk-sharing among Member States. Admittedly, Article 122 TFEU addresses situations in which Member States may, acting through the Council, provide help in times of severe difficulties for individual Member States, relying on the principle of solidarity between Member States. However, Article 122 TFEU inherently carries the presumption that while help may be granted, the cause and primary responsibility for resolving the difficulty lies with the Member State concerned. Otherwise, the Member State receiving the aid may be inclined not to implement a sound budgetary policy, and ultimately free ride on the assistance granted.[15]

Moreover, the European Stability Mechanism (ESM) has been established by way of an international treaty, with a set-up designed so as to ensure that the voting rights in the ESM reflect the respective contributions of Member States.[16] Using economic criteria in order to determine political rights is problematic: inequalities between creditor and debtor Member States are necessarily prolonged, as the latter are inevitably in the position of accepting the conditions attached to financial assistance measures,[17] as the case of Greek bail-outs during the Syriza's

[11] Found in Art 3(3) TEU.

[12] E Küçük, 'Solidarity in EU Law. An Elusive Political Statement or a Legal Principle with Substance?' (2016) 23 *Maastricht Journal of European and Comparative Law* 965, 981.

[13] A McDonnell, 'Solidarity, Flexibility and the Euro-crisis. Where Do Principles Fit In?' in LS Rossi and F Casolari (eds), *The EU after Lisbon Amending or Coping with the Existing Treaties?* (Heidelberg, Springer, 2014) 78.

[14] Opinion of AG Kokott in Case C-370/12 *Pringle* EU:C:2012:675, 128–30; Case C-62/14 *Gauweiler* EU:C:2015:400, 100.

[15] In that sense, see Case C-370/12 *Pringle* EU:C:2012:756136, 100.

[16] Art 4(7) of the ESM Treaty.

[17] F Fabbrini, *Economic Governance in Europe: Comparative Paradoxes and Constitutional Challenges* (Oxford, Oxford University Press, 2016) 15.

first year in government shows.[18] Taking into account that voting rights in the ESM do not represent all citizens of the EU equally, the composition of the ESM results in political inequality between citizens depending on the economic strength of their Member State. This leads to domination of creditor states, and their superiority over citizens of debtor states, undermining their political autonomy[19] in devising, applying and contesting the conditions stemming from bail-out arrangements sourced in the ESM.

The preliminary reference submitted by German Bundesverfassungsgericht in *Gauweiler* sought confirmation from the Court of Justice that the Outright Monetary Transactions (OMT) Programme, announced by the European Central Bank (ECB) in the wake of the euro crisis by way of a press release, will not undermine the conditionality of financial assistance mechanisms such as the EFSF and the ESM.[20] Unless strict conditionality is followed, the argument of the Bundesverfassungsgericht goes, budgetary autonomy of Member States would be virtually inexistent, as financial assistance could be granted without the Bundestag's approval. Rather, the reasoning proceeds, conditionality is an expression of equality of sovereign Member States who are 'Masters of the Treaties'. In addition, the Bundesverfassungsgericht sought to determine whether the OMT mechanism goes against the prohibition of monetary financing set out in Article 123 TFEU and the no bail-out clause in Article 125 TFEU. The Court of Justice provided a reasoning defending the OMT mechanism as containing in-built safeguards that would not go against these Treaty prohibitions,[21] therefore not undermining the equality of Member States. It confined its analysis to ensuring the principles of conferral and proportionality are respected. As in the assessment of the ESM, the Court of Justice made no reference to the principle of solidarity between Member States.

The current Italian political and financial crisis demonstrates a rhetoric of EU leaders remarkably resembling the one used in the height of the Greek bail-out negotiations and aggravates the problems connected to the insistence on formal equality of Member States.[22] Examples of this include Juncker calling upon Italians to 'work harder and be less corrupt';[23] the German MEP Ferber announcing it

[18] *BBC News*, 'Greece's Varoufakis: "No debt talks with EU-IMF troika"' (30 January 2015), available at: www.bbc.com/news/world-europe-31055069.

[19] EO Eriksen, 'Structural Injustice: the Eurozone Crisis and the Duty of Solidarity' ARENA Working Paper 4/2017, 13.

[20] German *Bundesverfassungsgericht* Case 2 BvR 2728/13 *Gauweiler*, Order of 14 January 2014, available at: www.bundesverfassungsgericht.de/SharedDocs/Entscheidungen/EN/2014/01/rs20140114 2bvr272813en.html, 100.

[21] Case C-62/14 *Gauweiler*, above n 14, 103–07.

[22] For an analysis of developments from 2010 to 2012 which underline the same approach of creditor toward debtor states, see CR Henning, 'The ECB as a Strategic Actor. Central Banking in a Politically Fragmented Monetary Union' in JA Caporaso and M Rhodes (eds), *The Political and Economic Dynamics of the Eurozone Crisis* (Oxford, Oxford University Press, 2016) 189.

[23] *The Guardian*, 'Juncker: Italians need to work harder and be less corrupt' 31 May 2018, available at: www.theguardian.com/world/2018/may/31/italy-cancelled-league-rallies-signal-political-impasse-may-soon-end?CMP=share_btn_tw.

might be necessary for the Troika to 'march into Rome';[24] and German Chancellor Merkel calling for more governmental oversight over the reformed ESM, that is to be heavily rooted in conditionality.[25] Regrettably all these views presuppose a separation of peoples of Europe, who can only be joined politically through their Member State representatives at the EU level, or through their nationally elected representatives in the European Parliament. Equally, the euro crisis is regarded neither as one with a joint origin, nor as one with a joint comprehensive solution.[26] Each (equal) Member State for itself, regardless of the consequences this has for its citizens.

## The Inadequacy of Nation-State Imitated Legitimation and Accountability Mechanisms

A further specificity of EU economic governance is its reliance on ad hoc and non-typical instruments that are unable to ensure political equality of EU citizens by way of majoritarian representation on the national level, and judicial review on both the national and EU level. The examples of the ESM and the OMT will again serve to portray these deficiencies.

Establishing the ESM through an international law treaty includes solely national governments in the process of its creation and design, whereas the doctrines of primacy and direct effect do not apply. The role of the citizen is reduced to national elections, leaving them without any influence as regards creating, designing and ultimately implementing the obligations stemming from the ESM. As the already mentioned Greek bail-out case aptly showed, the Greek voter ultimately had no influence on the implementation of austerity measures imposed by the Troika, regardless of the anti-Troika campaign that led Syriza to win national elections.[27] Because the ESM does not have an established accountability structure, nor is it accountable within the system of EU law, the Greek citizen lost all ability to influence or change the austerity requirements imposed by the Troika. The German citizen, on the other hand, is represented in the ESM with a decisive influence in its voting structure, and her government is the one creating conditions for financial assistance. Pernice argues that the insistence of Member States on remaining the masters of the Treaties,[28] meaning public international law applies as is also the case with the ESM, rely on national procedures as the only possible source of EU's legitimation, ultimately enabling the bypassing of citizens in decision-making.[29]

[24] *Twitter*, available at: twitter.com/StefanLeifert/status/1001825130912370688.

[25] *Reuters*, 'Highlights of Merkel interview on Europe' (3 June 2018), available at www.reuters.com/article/us-europe-merkel-highlights/highlights-of-merkel-interview-on-europe-idUSKCN1IZ0KN.

[26] McDonnell, above n 13, 74–75.

[27] See above, n 18. For an analysis on how the ESM decreased the importance of national parliaments' budgetary autonomy and the limited role of the European Parliament, see Fasone, above n 7.

[28] German Bundesverfassungsgericht Case 2 BvR 2728/13 *Gauweiler*, above n 20, 26.

[29] I Pernice, 'Multilevel Constitutionalism and the Crisis of Democracy in Europe' (2015) 11 *European Constitutional Law Review* 541, 543. See also, Pisani-Ferry, above n 7, 79.

Academic discourse,[30] however, focuses predominantly on improvement in parliamentary control of the ESM, mimicking the default legitimation route on the national level. For example, in its report on the ESM, Transparency International found serious problems with the accountability structure of the ESM, and called upon the European Parliament to increase its oversight.[31] While such reforms would formally increase supervision over the ESM and place more focus on the influence of the citizen rather than of Member States, it would in practice keep the citizen equally, if not further,[32] removed from any influence on the ESM's functioning. The powers of the European Parliament, although increased over time, have not provided a genuine parliamentary oversight as imagined on the nation-state level.[33]

Judicial review of the ESM at the EU level was weak[34] to non-existent,[35] stemming primarily from the fact that the ESM is an international treaty, meaning that the Court of Justice cannot review it in light of the Charter of Fundamental Rights.[36] Admittedly, the Court of Justice appears to be expanding its approach, by reviewing national measures implementing austerity requirements – however – in very limited circumstances.[37] Equally, the preponderance of national courts did not submit preliminary references to the Court of Justice when reviewing austerity measures imposed through bail-outs – the Court of Justice itself initially rejected them as inadmissible[38] – resulting in an inability of the current system of

[30] See, eg, J Tomkin, 'Contradiction, Circumvention and Conceptual Gymnastics: The Impact of the Adoption of the ESM Treaty on the State of European Democracy' (2013) 14 *German Law Journal* 169, 185; B Rittberger, 'Integration without Representation? The European Parliament and the Reform of Economic Governance in the EU' (2014) *Journal of Common Market Studies* 1174; McDonnell, above n 13, 76.

[31] Currently, the Managing Director appears before the European Parliament's Committee on Economic and Monetary Affairs (ECON) whenever invited, and answers questions. Transparency International, 'From crisis to stability. How to make the European Stability Mechanism transparent and accountable' (2017), available at: transparency.eu/wp-content/uploads/2017/03/ESM_Report_DIGITAL-version.pdf, 36.

[32] The turnout for European Parliament elections was 42.61%, the lowest since the introduction of direct elections for the representatives to the European Parliament in 1979. See: www.europarl.europa.eu/elections2014-results/en/turnout.html. This percentage is consistently lower than the turnout to national parliamentary elections in all Member States save for Estonia. See F Fislage, 'EU Elections – Where Are the Voters? Study about the low turnout in new EU Member States' (2015) *Facts and Findings* No 165 Konrad Adenauer Stiftung, available at: www.kas.de/wf/doc/kas_40621-544-2-30.pdf?150304143237, 4.

[33] Habermas, above n 9, 4.

[34] See Case C-370/12 *Pringle*, above n 15.

[35] Where the review of financial assistance measures based on Memoranda of Understanding were rejected as inadmissible. See A Hinarejos, 'The Role of Courts in the Wake of the Eurozone Crisis' in M Dawson, H Enderlein and C Joerges (eds), *Beyond the Crisis. The Governance of Europe's Economic, Political, and Legal Transformation* (Oxford, Oxford University Press, 2015) 119.

[36] Case C-370/12 *Pringle*, above n 15, 180.

[37] When deciding whether to cut judges' salaries, an austerity measure introduced to meet the requirements of the bail-out, the Court of Justice did not mention the ESM or any other financial assistance mechanism in the legal context of the judgment, and focused solely on the interpretation of the principle of judicial independence from Art 19(1) TEU, which it concluded was impaired by the measure in question. Case C-64/16 *Associação dos Juízes Portugueses* EU:C:2018:117.

[38] For an overview of cases, see Hinarejos, above n 35, 126–28.

judicial review to provide equal access to legal accountability to all EU citizens, and the differences are in particular visible between citizens of different debtor states. Finally, not all national courts have the same position in their constitutional set-up to review the ESM and measures stemming from it. For example, the German Bundesverfassungsgericht is seen as the dominant national constitutional court in the EU, being one of the most cited courts EU-wide, and the most prominent one in questioning the decisions of the Court of Justice.[39] However, it is also seen as pushing the ordoliberal agenda in the EU's economic policy,[40] therefore depriving citizens of other Member States having any say in the economic rationale behind governance mechanisms. This ultimately means that the ability to hold decision-makers to account depends on the behaviour of national courts, and their position in national legal systems.[41]

The shortcoming of transplanting nation-state rooted mechanisms of legitimation and accountability is further visible in the creation and review of the OMT mechanism. The mechanism was announced in a press release[42] of an uncertain legal nature,[43] without any ability of citizens to influence it through their national representatives. The Governing Council that issued the press release is composed of six members of the ECB's Executive Board (which would serve as a representation of national governments' given that they are appointed by the Council) and governors of national central banks of Eurozone countries. Although majoritarian representation is attempted to be ensured through the Council's appointment of the Executive Board, the ad hoc nature of a press release bypassed any influence of the Council and effectively failed in ensuring the representation of EU citizens in the decision-making of the ECB.

In the OMT preliminary reference before the Court of Justice,[44] the German Bundesverfassungsgericht placed an emphasis on the influence the programme would have on the budgetary autonomy of the Bundestag. It placed majoritarian representation at the centre of analysis, as the right to vote effectuated through budgetary autonomy is considered part of Germany's unamendable constitutional identity.[45] The Court of Justice, on the other hand, addressed Germany's concerns

[39] G Anagnostaras, 'Activation of the *ultra vires* Review: The *Slovak Pensions* Judgment of the Czech Constitutional Court' (2013) 14 *German Law Journal* 959, 959; RD Kelemen, 'On the Unsustainability of Constitutional Pluralism. European Supremacy and the Survival of the Eurozone' (2016) 23 *Maastricht Journal of European and Comparative Law* 136; FC Mayer, 'Rashomon in Karlsruhe: A Reflection on Democracy and Identity in the European Union: The German Constitutional Court's Lisbon Decision and the Changing Landscape of European Constitutionalism' (2011) 9 *ICON* 757.

[40] C Joerges, '"Brother, Can You Paradigm?"' (2014) 12 *ICON* 772, 780.

[41] See also, Transparency International, above n 31, 36.

[42] 'Technical Features of Outright Monetary Transactions', Governing Council of the European Central Bank (6 September 2012), available at; www.ecb.europa.eu/press/pr/date/2012/html/pr120906_1.en.html.

[43] The Court of Justice found it to be pertinent to the proceedings before the referring court, and thus admissible for interpretation. Case C-62/14 *Gauweiler,* above n 14) 27–28.

[44] German Bundesverfassungsgericht Case 2 BvR 2728/13 *Gauweiler*, above n 20.

[45] ibid, 28 and cross-referencing the reasoning from its *Maastricht* decision (Cases 2 BvR 2134/92 and 2159/92 *Brunner*, Judgment of 12 October 1993) at 19. Such an approach is an expression of the

through ensuring that the OMT mechanism does not provide assistance contrary to Articles 123 and 125 TFEU, nor that it undermines the conditionality of the ESM. However, as regards the finding that the mechanism falls within the scope of ECB's competence, it deferred to the discretion used by the ECB and found the OMT mechanism in line with EU law.

The dominance of the Court of Justice as the central judicial body in the EU[46] does not bode well with its ability to properly scrutinise measures of economic governance, given that its admissibility threshold is considerably higher in order to manage docket control.[47] Moreover, once the admissibility threshold is met, the Court usually defers to expertise and maintains a lax review of use of discretion by the ECB, most famously in the OMT case.[48] In conclusion, neither majoritarian representation nor judicial review as transplanted from the national to the EU level have resulted in legitimation and accountability mechanisms which would have allowed all EU citizens to equally influence policy and decision-making in economic governance, nor their review.

## Reconceptualising Accountability Through Self-Governance

### Accountability in the Literature

Accountability has been the object of legal and political science research alike, which has resulted predominantly in its conceptualisation as a procedural mechanism, relying on the principal-agent model.[49] Most famously expressed by Bovens,[50] a procedural concept of accountability leaves out any reference to its content, but rather devises an abstract framework – a procedural checklist once

principle of 'no taxation without representation'. See also PM Huber, 'The Federal Constitutional Court and European Integration' (2015) 21 *European Public Law* 83, 98.

[46] Asserting its hierarchical superiority in relation to national courts of all levels. See S Rodin, 'Back to the Square One: The Past, the Present and the Future of the Simmenthal mandate' in JM Beneyto and I Pernice (eds), *Europe's Constitutional Challenges in the Light of the Recent Case Law of National Constitutional Courts: Lisbon and Beyond* (Baden-Baden, Nomos, 2011) 315.

[47] S Rodin, 'A Metacritique of the Court of Justice of the EU' Bingham Centre talk, London (2 November 2015), available at: www.biicl.org/documents/772_rodins_paper_2015.pdf?showdocument=1.

[48] Case C-62/14 *Gauweiler*, above n 14. See also, M Goldoni, 'The Limits of Legal Accountability of the European Central Bank' (2017) 24 *George Mason Law Review* 595.

[49] GJ Brandsma and J Adriaensen, 'The Principal–Agent Model, Accountability and Democratic Legitimacy' in T Delreux and J Adriaensen (eds), *The Principal Agent Model and the European Union* (Cham, Switzerland, Springer International, 2017) 37–38, 42.

[50] M Bovens, 'Analysing and Assessing Accountability: A Conceptual Framework' (2007) 13 *European Law Journal* 447; M Bovens, D Curtin, and P 't Hart (eds), *The Real World of EU Accountability: What Deficit?* (Oxford, Oxford University Press, 2010).

met means the agent has been held accountable in one way or another. While useful in terms of their generalisability, Bovens' and similar procedural frameworks may be misused by decision-makers and reduced to a box-ticking exercise.[51] They fail to capture conceptually and structurally diverse relationships of any given polity, and consequently cannot be used as a Procrustean bed to accommodate the specificities of EU economic governance. Attempts at substantive conceptualisations of accountability focus predominantly on the nation state as the role model, where the concept of legal accountability introduced by Oliver[52] has been used as a basis for further research of accountability and legitimacy of the EU more generally.[53] Alternative models of accountability have been put forward, that can broadly be divided into those mimicking state models of accountability,[54] or grounding them in Bovens' framework.[55] As explained above, a notion of accountability inspired by the model of nation states is not appropriate for the study of diverse and uncommon mechanisms employed in the euro crisis. Equally, a mere procedural outlook on accountability may be misused.

In that respect, this chapter adds a novel concept of accountability through self-governance, freed from traditional state-centred mechanisms, and address the idiosyncrasies of EU post-crisis economic governance. While the euro crisis itself has been subject of extensive research,[56] such accounts only sporadically touch upon the question of accountability, without questioning the design of accountability mechanisms themselves.[57] I will explain accountability through self-governance in two steps: first, the conceptualisation of accountability in economic governance should be based on the equilibrium between principles of equality and solidarity in order to ensure political equality of EU citizens; and second, such a goal is best achieved through self-governance.

[51] For a useful overview of the deficiencies of Bovens' framework, see RL Heidelberg, 'Political Accountability and Spaces of Contestation' (2017) 49 *Administration & Society* 1379.

[52] D Oliver, *Government in the United Kingdom. The Search for Accountability, Effectiveness and Citizenship* (Milton Keynes, Open University Press, 1991).

[53] See, eg, C Harlow, *Accountability in the European Union* (Oxford, Oxford University Press, 2002); A Arnull and D Wincott, *Accountability and Legitimacy in the European Union* (Oxford, Oxford University Press, 2002).

[54] J Black, 'Constructing and Contesting Legitimacy and Accountability in Polycentric Regulatory Regimes' (2008) 2 *Regulation & Governance* 137, 138.

[55] ibid.

[56] See, eg, T Kaarlo and K Tuori, *The Eurozone Crisis: A Constitutional Analysis* (Cambridge, Cambridge University Press, 2014); T Beukers, B de Witte, and C Kilpatrick (eds), *Constitutional Change Through Euro-Crisis Law* (Cambridge University Press, 2017); M Dawson, H Enderlein and C Joerges (eds), *Beyond the Crisis. The Governance of Europe's Economic, Political, and Legal Transformation* (Oxford, Oxford University Press, 2015); A Estella, *Legal Foundations of EU Economic Governance* (Cambridge, Cambridge University Press, 2018).

[57] In this respect, a line of important questions for re-thinking accountability in post-crisis instruments have been posed in Dawson, 'The Legal and Political Accountability Structure of "Post-crisis" EU Economic Governance', above n 7.

## The Normative Underpinning: The Argument for Self-Governance

As explained in the examples of the ESM and the OMT, judicial review carried out by the Court of Justice in EU economic governance is problematic as it departs from its focus on the individual, so dominant and pervasive in other areas of EU law. Rather, it gives precedence to the principle of equality of Member States,[58] through ensuring that principles of conferral and proportionality are satisfied. National courts, furthermore, focused on majoritarian representation to be ensured for budgetary matters. Conversely, the argument put forward here is that any accountability mechanism of EU economic governance should place the individual at the centre. Normatively, I argue, this can be achieved through the application of an equilibrium between the principles of equality and solidarity of Member States, as was the case in previous crises that took place throughout the course of the development of European integration, in order to ensure political equality among all EU citizens – their ability to 'determine politically their destiny'.[59] This argument continues to promote democratic accountability, but in a different manner than that employed in the nation-state context, as it focuses on political equality of citizens as its defining characteristic and requirement.[60] Dahl defines the key characteristic of democracy as 'the continuing responsiveness of the government to the preferences of its citizens, considered as political equals'.[61] Political equality of citizens is thus a democratic imperative applicable to the EU more generally, as well as its economic governance.

But what precisely are requirements of the principle of solidarity in the context of EU's economic governance? Durkheim's work on solidarity provides a useful starting theoretical point, as he differentiates between mechanic and organic solidarity.[62] Mechanic solidarity is present in traditionally small and homogeneous societies, and assumes help is provided on the premise that it will also be received if and when necessary as an act of altruism. Further, organic solidarity exists in modern and heterogeneous societies with a multitude of interests and interdependence, and help is provided based on 'enlightened self-interest' that guides the smooth operation of the system as a whole.[63]

[58] For an argument that conditionality reduces the ability of citizens to decide on, for example, redistributive policies on the national level, see M Dawson and F de Witte, 'Self-Determination in the Constitutional Future of the EU' (2015) 21 *European Law Journal* 371, 373.

[59] Eriksen, above n 19, 13.

[60] See also, G de Búrca, 'Developing Democracy Beyond the State' (2008) 46 *Columbia Journal of Transnational Law* 101, 130.

[61] RA Dahl, *Polyarchy: Participation and Opposition* (New Haven, CT, Yale University Press, 1971) 1.

[62] E Durkheim, *The Division of Labour in Society* (1893; New York, New York Free Press, 1997).

[63] S Fernandes and E Rubio, 'Solidarity Within the Eurozone: How Much, What For, For How Long?' (2012) 51 Notre Europe Policy Paper 3–4.

Applying these categories to the EU legal system, where the precise legal nature of the principle of solidarity is unsettled,[64] it is possible to see both types of solidarity mechanisms. Mechanic solidarity is evident in the case law on EU citizenship, where the Court of Justice gradually expanded the solidarity obligations of the host Member State, albeit solely after a certain period of integration, or in the words of Domurath, of 'acquired sameness'.[65] Solidarity here is premised on a certain level of integration of free movers into the host Member State. Organic solidarity can be seen in the design of the Cohesion Policy, the aim of which is 'reducing disparities between the various regions and the backwardness of the least-favoured regions'.[66] Solidarity in that sense means recognising the high level of interdependence and a shared sense of advancing European integration to everyone's benefit.[67]

A focus on sovereignty of Member States influenced the division of competences between the EU and the national level in a way that decreased emphasis on solidarity.[68] This in turn increased the distance between the peoples of Europe, and allowed for the discourse of otherness, labelling some as lazy and debt-creating, and others as hard-working and generating growth.[69] For German Chancellor Merkel, '[solidarity] among euro partners should never lead to a debt union, rather it must be about helping *others* to help *themselves*' (emphasis added).[70] Merkel's definition strongly focuses on equality of sovereign Member States, and does not allow for a shared outlook on the crisis and means of its resolution.

Taking a step back into the history of previous crises and ways of their management, the Court of Justice based its reasoning on an interplay between equality of and solidarity between Member States. The early case law of the Court referred to solidarity to justify differentiated measures put in place to remedy the crises of the iron and steel sector in the 1980s,[71] and stated that the principle is the basis of the 'entire Community system'.[72] In fact, as Dawson reports, in states that resisted a joint solution to the crisis, out of them most infamously France, did not manage to

[64] A Ott, 'A Flexible Future for the European Union: The Way Forward or a Way Out?' in S Blockmans and S Prechal (eds), *Reconciling the Deepening and Widening of the European Union* (The Hague, TMC Asser Press, 2007) 153. This is particularly the case in relation to the rights stemming from EU citizenship and the consequences this has for national social welfare systems. C Barnard, 'EU Citizenship and the Principle of Solidarity' in E Spaventa and M Dougan (eds), *Social Welfare and EU Law* (Oxford, Hart Publishing, 2005) 161–65.

[65] I Domurath, 'The Three Dimensions of Solidarity in the EU Legal Order: Limits of the Judicial and Legal Approach' (2013) 35 *Journal of European Integration* 459, 463.

[66] See: ec.europa.eu/regional_policy/en/faq/#1.

[67] In that sense, see M Ross, 'Solidarity – A New Constitutional Paradigm for the EU?' in M Ross and Y Borgmann-Prebil, *Promoting Soldiarity in the European Union* (Oxford, Oxford University Press, 2010) 30–31.

[68] Domurath, above n 65, 466. See also, M Ekengren et al, 'Solidarity or sovereignty? EU Cooperation in civil protection' (2006) 28 *Journal of European Integration* 5, 457, 470.

[69] See above, nn 23–25.

[70] *Reuters*, above n 25.

[71] Case 154/78 *Valsabbia v Commission* EU:C:1980:81, 59.

[72] Joined Cases 6 and 11/69 *Commission v France* EU:C:1969:68, 16.

resolve it on their own.[73] Presently, the significance of solidarity in crisis management is undoubtedly diminished through an increased emphasis on reciprocity and conditionality.[74] If used, it is referred to instrumentally, solely for advancing a certain political argument, rather than holding intrinsic value in itself.[75] It also no longer features in the reasoning of the Court of Justice when reviewing measures of economic governance. Equally, the lack of risk-sharing and its embeddedness in anti-crisis mechanisms further reduced its importance.[76]

Taking the political equality of all EU citizens, ensured through the equilibrium between equality and solidarity as a substantive starting point, I will now move on to explain how it can and why it should be achieved through self-governance. The departing premise and an important inspiration in conceiving of the concept of accountability through self-governance in EU economic governance is the 'democracy-striving approach' proposed by Grainne de Búrca, based on 'the principle of fullest possible participation by, and representation of, all those concerned, with a commitment to ensuring the public-regarding nature of the process through continual revision and self-correction'.[77] I therefore argue that, in devising legitimation and accountability mechanisms in economic governance, we need to shift the focus from majoritarian representation to the political equality of citizens as more suitable for the EU as a transnational context.[78] Teubner heavily criticises the perseverance on identitarian consensus building (put into effect through majoritarian representation) as the necessary condition of democracy, which he considers unattainable in transnational contexts.[79] Rather, he focuses on the achievement that 'confrontation with alternative world views is at the centre of democratic communication'.[80] In the context of transnational regimes, he finds that representation should be surpassed and substituted by self-contestation – a responsiveness of a given transnational polity or regime to external frustrations as well as the institutionalisation of internal dissent.[81] He also rightly adds that any such institutional imagination can only be context-specific.[82]

[73] M Dawson, *New Governance and the Transformation of European Law. Coordinating EU Social Law and Policy* (Cambridge, Cambridge University Press, 2011) 37.

[74] McDonnell, above n 13, 78.

[75] A Grimmel, 'Solidarity in the EU: Fundamental Value or "Empty Signifier"' in A Grimmel and S My Giang (eds), *Solidarity in the European Union. A Fundamental Value in Crisis* (Cham, Switzerland, Springer International, 2017) 163–64.

[76] MP Maduro, 'A New Governance for the European Union and the Euro: Democracy and Justice' (2013) 16 *Yearbook of Polish European Studies* 111, 115.

[77] de Búrca, above n 60, 157. See also, K Nicolaïdis, 'Democratic Theory and Europe's Institutional Architecture in Times of Crisis' in S Piattoni (ed), *The European Union: Democratic Principles and Institutional Architectures in Times of Crisis* (Oxford, Oxford University Press, 2015) 153.

[78] See also, Dawson, *New Governance and the Transformation of European Law*, above n 73, 13.

[79] Teubner, above n 10, 6.

[80] ibid 7.

[81] ibid.

[82] ibid, 8. I concur with this position in relation to the design of accountability mechanisms in EU economic governance, below.

In line with de Búrca and Teubner, I propose a framework of legal accountability in EU economic governance through self-governance. In conceptualising accountability through self-governance, I concur with Pernice that the EU should be conceived also as a community of citizens, rather than one exclusively of states.[83] From the aspect of accountability, Dawson argues it does not need to be imagined in vertical terms towards a hierarchically superior sovereign, but can be imagined in horizontal terms.[84] On this basis, self-governance, as conceived and developed by Vincent Ostrom,[85] becomes the normative driver of conceiving accountability detached from majoritarian representation as the only defining quality of democracy beyond the state. Self-governance places the informed, active, aware and involved citizen, who is a member of a range of social groups, at the centre of governance mechanisms of a community.[86] As explained by Ostrom:

> The future belongs to those whose covenants are bonds of mutual trust grounded in principles of self-governance and who learn to use processes of conflict and conflict resolution to elucidate information, clarify alternative, stimulate innovation, and extend the frontiers of inquiry to open new potentials for human development.[87]

Teubner equally finds that a high learning capacity is a necessary condition for any imagination of democracy in transnational contexts which would then allow for organised dissent (contestation).[88] In addition, according to Domurath, learning is crucial for the enhancement of transnational solidarity.[89] Understood in this way, self-governance is capable of promoting the equilibrium between the principles of solidarity and equality in economic governance. A self-governed, enlightened and educated European citizen will acquire a sense of community of a transnational scope, and feel more attachment to other European citizens and their specific circumstances.[90] The sense of community among citizens beyond

[83] Pernice, above n 29, 543.

[84] Dawson, *New Governance and the Transformation of European Law*, above n 73, 95.

[85] See V Ostrom, *The Meaning of American Federalism: Constituting a Self-Governing Society* (San Francisco, ICS Press, 1994); V Ostrom, *The Political Theory of a Compound Republic: Designing the American Experiment* (Lanham, MD, Lexington Books, 2007); V Ostrom, *The Intellectual Crisis in Public Administration* (Alabama, University of Alabama Press, 1973); P Aligica and V Tarko, 'Polycentricity: From Polanyi to Ostrom, and Beyond' (2012) 25 *Governance: An International Journal of Policy, Administration, and Institutions* 237, 246.

[86] Ostrom, *The Meaning of American Federalism*, above n 85. A similar concept can be found in the idea of individual self-determination. Dawson and de Witte rightly argue that such an advanced manner of political participation is not yet achieved at the EU level. See M Dawson and F de Witte, 'Constitutional Balance in the EU after the Euro-Crisis' (2013) 76 *Modern Law Review* 817, 819–20. Floris de Witte does find some manifestation of individual self-determination through the use of free movement rules, where citizens move beyond the spaces for political self-determination of a nation state. See F De Witte, 'Transnational Solidarity and the Mediation of Conflicts of Justice in Europe' (2012) 18 *European Law Journal* 698. The proposal of self-governance takes this idea further and argues for the creation of spaces of political self-determination, to use the vocabulary of Dawson and de Witte, at the level of EU economic governance.

[87] Ostrom, *The Meaning of American Federalism*, above n 85, 272.

[88] Teubner, above n 10, 7.

[89] Domurath, above n 65, 471.

[90] P Hilpold, 'Understanding Solidarity within EU Law: An Analysis of the "Islands of Solidarity" with Particular Regard to Monetary Union' (2015) 34 *Yearbook of European Law* 257, 264.

the confines of the nation state promotes their equality, but also mutual support when needed.[91]

In consequence, I argue that if agentive European citizens viewed themselves, as oppose to Member States, as central to the integration project, they will be able to more effectively contest and demand answers from those making decisions that affect them.[92] In line with de Búrca's 'democracy-striving approach', such processes must be subject to permanent re-evaluation and self-correction.[93] In addition, moving the focus away from the Member States and to the citizens, my normative argument is that self-governance will inherently strive to achieve an equilibrium between solidarity and equality in economic governance of the EU.

## Conclusion: Applying the Model to Current Mechanisms of Economic Governance

From an empirical point of view, prevalence of either the principle of equality or solidarity would have negative consequences for economic governance. Insistence on formal equality, as was shown earlier, contributes to prolonging actual inequalities between Member States, but more importantly, between its citizens. Dominance of the principle of solidarity could lead to free-riding of debtor states in the short term, and may encourage fiscal irresponsibility. For this reason, as I have argued above, self-governance offers a route that reconciles the two principles and achieves political equality of all EU citizens. In this final section, I will offer some initial thoughts on possibilities for institutional design of economic governance mechanisms that would allow for genuine political and legal accountability through self-governance.

The starting point of this exercise is found in Article 10(3) TEU: 'Every citizen shall have the right to participate in the democratic life of the Union. Decisions shall be taken as openly and as closely as possible to the citizen'. Yet, in the area of economic governance, economic policy is reserved for Member States,[94] whereas the size of the EU's population has stood in the way of a more concrete application of Article 10(3) TEU to monetary policy.[95] However, large-scale bottom-up

[91] Domurath, above n 65, 460.

[92] For entertaining a similar approach, see Dawson, *New Governance and the Transformation of European Law* above n 73, 94. A broader idea of political self-governance would also include the ability of citizens to influence decision- and policy-making bottom-up. For a comprehensive contribution of the theory of polycentricity premised on self-governance as a political theory for the European Union, see J van Zeben and A Bobić (eds), *Polycentricity in the European Union* (Cambridge, Cambridge University Press, 2019).

[93] See above n 77.

[94] Art 5(1) TFEU.

[95] It is important to note that according to Art 5(3) TEU, the principle of subsidiarity does not apply to monetary policy for those Member States whose currency is the euro, given that it is an exclusive competence of the EU according to Art 3(1)(c) TFEU.

economic decision-making is not without precedent, as the case of participatory budgeting aptly shows. In essence, participatory budgeting allows non-elected citizens to make decisions on the allocation of public finances.[96] It entails a discussion and public deliberation on limited resources, with the involvement of the elected body of the administrative unit in question (city, region, etc), on a repeated basis, with an accountability mechanism in place.[97] Applied first in Porto Alegre, a city of 1.3 million inhabitants,[98] and having spread across Brazil and Latin America from 1989 onwards,[99] participatory budgeting provided a way for empowerment of large urban communities in learning about budgeting, and participating in its creation.[100] The initial experiments have developed into fully functioning frameworks of participatory budgeting that account for 2 to 10 per cent of the overall implemented budgets, where 9 per cent is the average.[101]

Participatory budgeting has been implemented in an increasing number of European cities as well,[102] drawing upon the model of Porto Alegre or similar variations. The benefits of the system are well documented – ranging from increased participation of minorities and their interests,[103] a significant increase in transparency and communication between the citizens and the elected bodies, and the ensuing comprehensive modernisation of the system.[104] Another reported benefit is the participation of citizens in the creation of the framework of participatory budgeting itself, with a strong presence of a social justice agenda in devising this framework.[105]

The benefits of a participatory budgeting model directly correspond to the flaws described above in the system of EU's economic governance. Most importantly, these concern the political equality of citizens in participation, as well as an increase in transparency and communication with the institutions. As far as the euro crisis is concerned, participatory budgeting lends itself as a way for EU citizens to decide on broad-brush monetary policy decisions, as well as the extent of solidarity to be applied in the creation of post-crisis mechanisms and the ultimate allocation of resources. For example, participatory budgeting as a model could be applied to the institutional design of the successor to the ESM, reforms addressing long-term budgetary discipline, as well as to the allocation of competences

[96] Y Sintomer, C Herzberg and A Röcke, 'Participatory Budgeting in Europe: Potentials and Challenges' (2008) 32 *International Journal of Urban and Regional Research* 164, 168.

[97] ibid.

[98] Other large cities that use participatory budgeting in Brazil are Recife (1.4 million), Belém (1.3 million), Belo Horizonte (2.3 million), as well as Montevideo, Uruguay (1.4 million). Y Cabannes, 'Participatory Budgeting: A Significant Contribution to Participatory Democracy' (2004) 16(1) *Environment & Urbanization* 27, 30.

[99] ibid, 30.

[100] For a broader analysis, see G Baiocchi and E Ganuza, 'Participatory Budgeting as if Emancipation Mattered' (2014) 42 *Politics & Society* 29.

[101] Cabannes, above n 98, 34.

[102] Sintomer, Herzberg and Röcke, above n 96, 169.

[103] Cabannes, above n 98, 39.

[104] Sintomer, Herzberg and Röcke, above n 96, 174.

[105] ibid, 167.

to the ECB. EU citizens can also decide under which circumstances individual Member States can receive financial aid without furthering the gap between debtor and creditor states. The experience of participatory budgeting across the EU could in this sense serve as an experimental basis for a more serious engagement with bottom-up mechanisms of participatory democracy. This would mean that political accountability of decision-makers does not depend on the success of its output, but is rather strongly legitimated by the input of self-governed citizens. Furthermore, Member States would no longer be able to bypass the individual by way of their focus on equality of sovereign Member States.

Furthermore, promoting and securing self-governance in the judicial review stage appears counterintuitive: if self-governance is secured in the political arena, the role of the courts should be negligible, given the importance of bottom-up political influence of citizens. However, Scott and Sturm see a new role for courts in forms of new governance as catalysts.[106] They give examples from the jurisprudence of the Court of Justice on how courts can contribute to new forms of governance, which aligns with Ostrom's ideals of structures of conflict resolution to 'elucidate information, clarify alternative, stimulate innovation, and extend the frontiers of inquiry to open new potentials for human development'.[107] These include a rethink of standing rules to more closely reflect the design of EU acts under review, such as the expansion of standing to those who had the right to be consulted in the decision-making process itself. Furthermore, Scott and Sturm add that courts' interpretations can have an additional epistemic role by way of focusing on the quality of the information-gathering and the peer-review process used to justify EU action and policies. Finally, they underline the reflexive role that jurisprudence can have on future design of policy- and decision-making by emphasising the importance of the inclusive, deliberative and participatory nature of new forms of governance,[108] also including polycentric self-governance.

Judicial review on both the EU and national level should therefore take both principles into account. For example, had the Court of Justice in its *Pringle* decision on the ESM placed an emphasis on the principle of solidarity as its rationale, it may have found the ESM Treaty incompatible with the EU legal system. This could have meant that less emphasis be placed on conditionality, and providing more leverage for debtor states in the negotiations of bail-out conditions.[109] On the national level, considerations of solidarity, in particular taking into account that

[106] J Scott and S Sturm, 'Courts as Catalysts: Re-thinking the Judicial Role in New Governance' (2006) 13 *Columbia Journal of European Law* 565.

[107] Ostrom, *The Meaning of American Federalism*, above n 85, 272.

[108] Scott and Sturm, above n 106, 573–74.

[109] According to the long-standing jurisprudence of the Court of Justice, treaties concluded by EU institutions and Member States must be compatible with EU law and cannot put into question the specific features of EU law and its autonomy. See, eg, Case 22/70 *Commission v Council* EU:C:1971:32, 17; Opinion 3/94 EU:C:1995:436, 17; Opinion 1/91 EU:C:1991:490, 25–29, 46; Opinion 1/09 EU:C:2011:123, 48; Opinion 2/13 EU:C:2014:2454, 146.

the euro crisis is one of a joint origin,[110] could perhaps have led to less emphasis on conditionality being placed by the Bundesverfassungsgericht in reviewing the OMT, in particular after the positive effects of the OMT's announcement to the euro area *as a whole*.

Ultimately, self-governance as a concept is under-researched and difficult to apply to a large-scale organisation such as the EU. However, it was the argument of this contribution that the current deficiencies in the accountability structure of the EU's economic governance can be remedied through self-governance, essentially a bottom-up influence of citizens on the creation and design of economic governance mechanisms. The institutions further applying these mechanisms gain an increase in legitimacy and accountability to those citizens, without separating them across Member States.

[110] Fernandes and Rubio explain the causes of the euro crisis as going well beyond Greece's falsification of statistical budgetary data on meeting the Maastricht criteria for entering the eurozone. Their claim is that the crisis could have been prevented, or better managed, had it not been for the failure of politicians to see interdependence and spillovers in the common currency area; also, policy-making lacked a more serious policing of national budgets in the EMU: Fernandes and Rubio, above n 63, 19–20.

# 9

# 'Where the Law Runs Out':[1] The Overburdening of Law and Constitutional Adjudication by the Financial Crisis and Europe's New Modes of Economic Governance

CHRISTIAN JOERGES

## Introduction

With Economic and Monetary Union (EMU), the Treaty of Maastricht has institutionalised a complex conflict constellation: the Treaty confirmed the autonomy of socio-economically and politically heterogeneous states in the spheres of fiscal, economic, labour and social policy but subjected them to a uniform monetary regime administered by a Central Bank (European Central Bank, ECB) of unmatched autonomy. As even Friedrich A von Hayek has underlined, a stable currency is a precondition of a market economy which the market cannot generate autonomously, a task hence within the genuine responsibility of a state.[2] The paradox then is that the ECB has to administer the monetary policy of a state, which does not exist.[3] Conceptually speaking the Maastricht Treaty has produced a

[1] A google search of 'Where the law Ends' leads to many references but not to the one to which my comment alludes, namely Gerhard Anschütz's '*Das Staatsrecht hört hier auf*. Anschütz was a renowned *Staatsrechtslehrer* (1867–1948). His pronouncement: law and jurisprudence must not step in to cure lacunae in constitutionally essential issues such as budgetary powers; see G Meyer and G Anschütz, *Lehrbuch des deutschen Staatsrechts*, 7th edn (München und Lepzig, Duncker & Humblot, 1919) 906. Anschütz' position was at the time as controversial as the issues we will address here; see M Stolleis, *Geschichte des öffentlichen Rechts in Deutschland, Dritter Band (1914–1945)* (München, CH Beck, 1999) 171 ff.

[2] FA von Hayek, *The Constitution of Liberty* (Chicago, IL, University of Chicago Press, 2011) 452: money is 'a kind of loose joint in the otherwise self-steering mechanism of the market'.

[3] H Enderlein, 'The Euro as a Showcase for Exploratory Governance. Why There Are no Simple Answers' in Hertie School of Governance (ed), *The Governance Report 2015. The Eurozone Crisis: Lessons Learned for Europe's Future* (Oxford, Oxford University Press, 2015) 29.

hybrid, an odd compromise of German and French preferences with Germany defending its stability philosophy in substantive principles and statutory norms and ceding to French preferences in the procedural norms of the General ECB Council. For nearly a decade, EMU operated reasonably well and was widely perceived as a success story. Tensions made themselves felt but seemed manageable. This changed dramatically after the economic crisis began to unfold in 2008. Since then, we have witnessed a turbo-speed establishment of new modes of transnational economic governance and a resort to unheard of regulatory techniques. Detailed descriptions are available[4] but cannot, and need not, be reproduced here. Our focus is on the judicial responses to the conflict constellation inherent in the construction of EMU, which can best be characterised as 'diagonal' as I have submitted repeatedly.[5]

This notion requires an explanatory remark. Monetary policy has become an exclusive competence of the Union (Article 3(1)c TFEU). With this provision, the Union claims supremacy in the policy area conferred to it, a conferral which did not include economic and fiscal policies. The exercise of these reserved powers can generate external effects and lead to 'horizontal' conflicts. As experienced immediately after the establishment of the EMU, monetary policy and the national policies could indeed come into conflict. This, however, is not a vertical conflict for which supremacy would provide a response. Both the Union and the Member States are certainly interested in the functioning of their economies. But the powers needed to accomplish this objective are attributed to two distinct levels of governance. The type of conflict resolution foreseen in Article 119 TFEU is 'the adoption of an economic policy which is based on the close coordination of member states' economic policies' as substantiated in Article 121 TFEU. As is plainly visible from the legal texts, this instrument was a *lex imperfecta*, an order devoid of meaningful sanctions. The 'stability community' of the EMU existed only on paper. Neither did the Treaty of Maastricht provide for mechanisms to enforce its ideational basis nor did the successive Stability and Growth Pact of 1997 complement the Treaty accordingly. The functioning of the new regime was dependent on good economic luck and constant political bargaining. Is it nevertheless possible to call this muddling through arrangement a legal framework of constitutional quality? This query leads to the crux of the matter alluded to in the title. Discrepancies between the premises and expectations on which the design of legal and constitutional provisions relied and later real world developments, are anything but unusual. The *problématique* of EMU, however, is unusual. No authority has been entrusted with powers, which would ensure that the policies pursued at the European and national levels of governance would be coordinated effectively in compliance with

[4] Most comprehensively perhaps T Beukers, B de Witte, C Kilpatrick (eds), *Constitutional Change through Euro-Crisis Law* (Cambridge, Cambridge University Press, 2017).

[5] Eg C Joerges, 'Integration Through Law and the Crisis of Law in Europe's Emergency' in D Chalmers, M Jachtenfuchs and C Joerges (eds), *The End of the Eurocrats' Dream. Adjusting to European Diversity* (Cambridge, Cambridge University Press, 2016) 312 ff.

legally valid criteria. Again, the failure to provide such a framework is neither wilful nor accidental. The economic and fiscal policies of Member States reflect the specifics of their economies and societal conditions. Their markets, to take up Karl Polanyi's famous insight, will always be 'socially embedded'.[6] This multifaceted heterogeneity with its multiple causes could not and did not dissolve under the impact of the common currency. The uniformity of European monetary policy was instead to become ever more dysfunctional.[7] What we have observed, instead, namely, the resort to intergovernmental bargaining, soft supervision and tentative coordination is hence unsurprising – and simultaneously an irritating aberration from the commitment of the integration project to the rule of law.[8]

It took its time but it was bound to happen: the conflicts inherent in the construction of EMU were reframed as legal problems and adjudicated, most famously in the controversy over the ECB's Outright Monetary Transaction (OMT) programme. The legal controversy had of course a not yet legalised background. Mario Draghi's 'Whatever it takes' announcement,[9]

> has come to be seen as the turning point of the eurozone crisis. In the aftermath, markets immediately calmed. Yields for the most vulnerable borrowers came down. There was no more talk of a eurozone breakup. It is an explanation with deep appeal. The ECB had held the key to stability all along. Draghi, finally, was the one to turn it.[10]

Thus far, the story, which the historian Adam Tooze tells us is also common knowledge in the community of European lawyers. His further reporting is not so well known. At the time of the announcement, the ECB and Draghi had no ready-made script and strategy. And the elaboration of the programme did by no means occur with the ECB acting in full autonomy:

> As usual, the inflation hawks at the Bundesbank were aghast at the idea of ECB bond buying. But for Merkel it was the better of two bad options … With backing from both

[6] K Polanyi, *The Great Transformation. The Political and Economic Origins of Our Time* [1944], First Beacon Paperback edn (Boston, MA, 1957) most famously at 57.

[7] Outside legal discourses the awareness of the broad 'varieties of capitalism' is widespread. Only a handful of lawyers have taken this issue seriously enough, among them Gunther Teubner whose seminal 'Legal Irritants: Good Faith in British Law Or How Unifying Law Ends Up in New Differences' [(1998) 61 *Modern Law Review*, 11] was republished in the classic of P Hall and D Soskice (eds), *Varieties of Capitalism: The Institutional Foundations of Comparative Advantage* (Oxford, Oxford University Press, 2001). For a recent exemplary analysis see J Hien and C Joerges (eds), *Responses of European Economic Cultures to Europe's Crisis Politics: The Example of German–Italian Discrepancies* (Florence, European University Institute, 2018), e-book available at: hdl.handle.net/1814/59884.

[8] Somewhat paradoxically, according to a widespread rumour and complaint EMU has established some ordoliberal iron cage (suffice it here to cite the non-academic yet prestigious example of *The Economist* of 9 May 2015); for an extensive discussion see J Hien and C Joerges, 'Dead Man Walking? Current European Interest in the Ordoliberal Tradition' (2018) 24 *European Law Journal* 142.

[9] 'Within our mandate, the ECB is ready to do whatever it takes to preserve the euro. And believe me, it will be enough'. *Verbatim* at: www.ecb.europa.eu/press/key/date/2012/html/sp120726.en.html, 484 and 467 ff.

[10] A Tooze, *Crashed: How a Decade of Financial Crises Changed the World* (New York, Viking, 2018) 484.

> Merkel and Schäuble the die was cast. The ECB formalised its new role as a conditional lender of last resort, under the title of Outright Monetary Transactions (OMT). But this was a strictly conditional promise. The ECB would go into action only if the country in question had agreed on an austerity and aid program approved by the ESM.[11]

Can we expect the German Constitutional Court to move from barking to biting under these conditions to falsify Joseph Weiler's irony?[12] It seems after all not so surprising that Karlsruhe submitted 'its first reference ever' to the Court of Justice (CJEU).[13] In due course Advocate General Cruz Villalòn made his views known.[14] The CJEU handed down its judgment on 16 June 2015.[15] Karlsruhe responded on 21 June 2016.[16] Both Courts are repeat players. *Gauweiler* has been prepared by *Pringle*[17] and was complemented by *Weiss.*[18] There is also much continuity with the German plaintiffs and their legal counsel.[19] The Advocates General change, but their views remain the same.[20]

My focus will be on the OMT controversy, which attracted the highest attention, addressed the constitutional issues most directly and clearly. Most remarkably in my view, two of the justices from Karlsruhe submitted dissenting opinions in which they pleaded for inadmissibility of the *Verfassungsbeschwerde* (constitutional complaint). This alternative was a road not taken by the majority and treated with benign neglect in the heated debates on the controversy. I will in the following summarise briefly the questions submitted by Karlsruhe to Luxembourg; report more extensively on the dissenting opinion by Judge Gertrude Lübbe-Wolff; then turn to the discretionary powers claimed by the ECB and the marginalisation of judicial control; look at the responses to these developments in various branches of European studies; and conclude with further reflections on my title.

[11] ibid 487; his more general comment at 374: 'Europe entered an emergency regime defined not by a single sovereign author, but by the absence of any such authority', citing J White, 'Emergency Europe' (2015) 63 *Political Studies* 300.

[12] See JHH Weiler, 'The 'Lisbon Urteil' and the Fast Food Culture' (2009) 20 *European Journal of International Law* 505, 505.

[13] BVerfG, 2 BvR 2728/13 vom 14.1.2014, §§ 1–105, available at: www.bverfg.de/entscheidungen/rs20140114_2bvr272813en.html.

[14] Opinion in Case C-62/14 *Peter Gauweiler and others v Deutscher Bundestag*, delivered on 14 January 2015.

[15] Case C-62/14 *Peter Gauweiler and others v Deutscher Bundestag*, Judgment (Grand Chamber) of 16 June 2015, EU:C:2015:400.

[16] Judgment of 21 June 2016 – 2 BvR 2728/13, 2 BvR 2729/13, 2 BvR 2730/13, 2 BvR 2731/13, 2 BvE 13/13.

[17] Case 370/12 *Pringle v Ireland*, Judgment (Grand Chamber) of 27 November 2012, EU:C:2012:756.

[18] Case C-493/1 *Heinrich Weiss and Others*, Judgment of the Court (Grand Chamber) of 11 December 2018, EU:C:2018:1000, responding to the Order of 18 July 2017 – 2 BvR 859/15 of the FCC, BVerfG, Order of the Second Senate of 18 July 2017 – 2 BvR 859/15 paras (1–137), available at: www.bverfg.de/e/rs20170718_2bvr085915en.html: www.bundesverfassungsgericht.de/.

[19] Most persistently Peter Gauweiler, Member of the Bundestag for the Christlich Soziale Union and his attorney, Professor Dr Dietrich Murswiek, once a Member of 'The Greens'; both entertain instructive webpages, which give information about their political and advisory activities and cooperation; see: archiv.peter-gauweiler.de/esm_pressemitteilungen.html and www.dietrich-murswiek.de/praxis.html.

[20] AG Pringle; OMT, *Gauweiler*, *Weiss*.

## Ad 1: Karlsruhe's Queries

The context of the proceedings in Karlsruhe was delicate.[21] What could the judges have had in mind when submitting their 'first reference ever'? Speculations aside, the questions they submitted were straightforward: did the Governing Council of the ECB with its announcement of the OMT programme act within Europe's monetary policy mandate? Did the ECB by its explicit reference and approval of the conditions of the financial assistance programmes of the European Financial Stability Facility (EFSF) and/or the European Stability Mechanism (ESM) overstep its monetary policy competence and interfere with the powers of the Member States in the sphere of economic policy? Was the OMT programme compatible with the prohibition of monetary financing (Article 123 TFEU)? The BVerfG, furthermore, wondered how the support granted could be compatible with the budgetary autonomy and responsibility of Member States which it held to be 'constituent for the design of the monetary union' (as evidenced by Article 125 TFEU).[22] How daring are these queries? The German court's position seemed supported not only by the TFEU but also by the traditional views on the role and limits of central banks as lenders-of-last resort, commented a renowned economist from Princeton.[23]

## Ad 2: Justice Lübbe-Wolff's Dissent

The dissenters did not take sides on this controversy. They moved to another institutional level and questioned the power of the German court to adjudicate: they opted for inadmissibility of the constitutional complaint. Judge Lübbe-Wolff has submitted a host of reasons.[24] Here is a selection:

a. The order goes 'beyond the limits of judicial competence under the principles of democracy and separation of powers' (3).
b. 'The more far-reaching, the weightier, the more irreversible – legally and factually – the possible consequences of a judicial decision, the more judicial restraint is appropriate' (7).
c. 'Where for reasons of law the judges' courage must dwindle when it comes to the substance, they ought not to go into the substance at all' (27).
d. 'The democratic legitimacy which the decision of a national court may draw from the relevant standards of national law (if any) will not, or not without substantial detriment, extend beyond the national area' (28).

[21] Above nn 9–11.
[22] Para 41; see also para 71.
[23] A Mody, 'Did the German Court do Europe a Favor?', Bruegel Working Paper 2014/09, available at: aei.pitt.edu/52709/1/Did_the_German_court_do_Europe_a_favour%2D_(English).pdf, 4.
[24] The following numbers go to the paragraphs of her dissent.

This latter point is particularly interesting. What Lübbe-Wolff criticises here, has been thoroughly neglected in the judgment on the rescue package for Greece, where the Court defended the budgetary power of the German Bundestag while, by the same token, not caring at all for the rights of the Greek Parliament.[25] She furthermore emphasised that the complaint could not insist on a specific action of the German government and Parliament. 'With regard to the question of whether there exists a qualified *ultra vires* act, the Federal Government and the *Bundestag* must have a margin of appreciation and discretion, which the citizen needs to accept' (15). Note that this is not the type of discretion, which is the key concept of the *Gauweiler* judgment[26] to which I now turn.

## Ad 3: The ECB's Discretionary Powers

The legally and literally decisive argument in *Gauweiler* is about the competence of the ECB. 'The primary objective of EU monetary policy, price stability, and support for the general economic policies in the Union, form the principal criterion for defining monetary policy (Articles 127(1) TFEU and 282(2) TFEU)'.[27]

What the ECB claims here is the competence to decide what monetary policy 'is'. This kind of autonomy is at odds with what has been so far a *communis opinion* among the protagonists of independent, non-majoritarian institutions, namely that they are not the masters of their mandate. Paul Tucker has recently reconstructed the rationale of the conventional wisdom with utmost care.[28] The CJEU, however, has legalised the position of the ECB without any substantial *caveats*. The Kronberger Kreis, by now the most prominent ordoliberal forum in Germany, has questioned the validity of this move,[29] indicating, however, that we may have to live with such imperfections.[30]

[25] See C Joerges, 'Der Berg kreißte – gebar er eine Maus? Europa vor dem Bundesverfassungsgericht' (2012) 65 i*WSI-Mitteilungen* 560; M Everson, 'An Exercise in Legal Honesty: Rewriting the Court of Justice and the Bundesverfassungsgericht' (2015) 21 *European Law Journal* 474, 497.

[26] *Gauweiler* judgment, above n 15.

[27] ibid, para 127.

[28] P Tucker, *Unelected Power: The Quest for Legitimacy in Central Banking and the Regulatory State* (Princeton, NJ, Princeton University Press, 2018).

[29] Kronberger Kreis (LP Feld, C Fuest, J Haucap, H Schweitzer, V Wieland, BU Wigger), 'Dismantling the Boundaries of the ECB's Monetary Policy Mandate: The CJEU's OMT Judgment and its Consequences' (2016) Berlin: Stiftung Marktwirtschaft, available at: www.stiftung-marktwirtschaft.de/fileadmin/user_upload/KK-Studien/KK_61_OMT-Judgement_2016.pdf.

[30] On page 17 we read: 'by extending the ECB's mandate so far as to encompass any "rectification" of disruptions in the monetary policy transmission mechanism, the court's judicial review practically becomes an illusion'. On page 36 we learn: 'If the German Federal Constitutional Court is required to rule on the substance of the case, then a substantial divergence from the CJEU's OMT judgement seems inescapable. In order to respect its duty to perform the ultra vires control in a Europe-friendly manner, and in order to minimise damage to the EU as a community of law, the Federal Constitutional Court may, however, wish to contain the conflict as far as possible. An option may be to uphold the CJEU's judgement in effect, but base this finding on a different reasoning'. Reconciling the irreconcilable is part of 'operative strategies' of Ordoliberalism (see fn 68).

In view of such ambivalences it seems instructive to recall how European law used to assess discretionary powers. The '*Meroni*-doctrine' with its distinction of 'wide discretionary powers' and 'clearly defined executive powers' comes to the mind of European lawyers when they encounter our notion.[31] *Meroni* is as old as it is outdated, they would tend to add. But is it really? Joana Mendes, in her recent subtle reconstruction of the relationship between discretion, law and judicial review, has documented how the *Meroni* dichotomy survived in the distinction between 'discretionary power involving policy choices and discretion stemming from technical assessments'.[32] Is this a sound refinement? It is at least a bridge to the reasoning of the court. 'Monetary policy', so the Advocate General opined is 'a highly technical terrain in which it is necessary to have an expertise and experience which, according to the Treaties, devolves solely upon the ECB'.[33] The two points are connected here. For one: in the case of monetary policy, it is the technical side of the dichotomy, which justifies discretion and requires judicial caution. Second, and somewhat surprisingly, this expertise is declared to be uncontroversial or sacrosanct. It must not be contested, not be exposed to scrutiny by other bodies because the Treaty has assigned it to the ECB. Both points are as bold as they are unconvincing. Monetary policy is a very complex matter, but by no means a merely technical one. Here, as in so many other instances, Joana Mendes correctly notes, 'technical assessments and policy choices are inextricably intertwined'.[34]

The whole weight of this assignment of discretionary powers becomes apparent only in the light of the institutional framework of EMU. The German court had not only defended another concept of monetary policy, namely that submitted by the President of the German Bundesbank, Jens Weidmann. It had also asked, or better insinuated that the ECB, by its explicit reference and approval of the conditions of the financial assistance programmes of the EFSF and/or the ESM, overstepped its monetary policy competence and interfered with the powers of the Member States in the sphere of economic policy. It had suggested that the OMT programme was incompatible with the prohibition of monetary financing (Article 123 TFEU). The Bundesverfassungsgericht, furthermore, had wondered how the support granted could be compatible with the budgetary autonomy and responsibility of Member States, which it held to be 'constituent for the design of the monetary union', as evidenced by Article 125 TFEU.[35]

The argument of the Court of Justice on the epistemic nature of monetary policy and the supremacy of the expertise of the ECB is a response to the entire range of these queries. The whole construction is such that the conferral of de facto

[31] Case C-9/56 *Meroni v High Authority* EU:C:1958:7 (*Meroni*).

[32] J Mendes, 'Bounded Discretion in EU Law: A Limited Judicial Paradigm in a Changing EU' (2017) 8 *Modern Law Review* 443.

[33] Opinion of Advocate General Cruz Villalón in Case C-62/14 *Gauweiler*, para 111.

[34] Above n 32, 471.

[35] BVerfG, 2 BvR 2728/13 vom 14.1.2014, §§ 1–105, available at: www.bverfg.de/entscheidungen/rs20140114_2bvr272813en.html.

unlimited discretionary powers to the ECB becomes but a stringent implication of the design of the EMU.

That design, so the Court stresses, is in one respect incomplete. Economic and Fiscal policy remained a reserve of the Member States, but the substance of monetary policy, which become the exclusive competence of the EU, was not positively defined. What is nevertheless clear under Articles 127(1) TFEU and 282(2) TFEU is the objective of monetary policy, namely the defence of price stability and hence the mandate of the ECB to pursue that objective with the help of the instruments described in Chapter IV of the Protocol on the European System of Central Banks (ESCB) and the ECB.[36] In the parlance of Niklas Luhmann's sociology of law,[37] the Court moves here into realms of 'purposive' programming, a move which liberates it from the disciplining power of traditional 'conditional' legal programming. This liberating move does not do away with the importance of precedential case law. In its reference the German court had cited the passage of the *Pringle* judgment in which the Court of Justice had qualified the financial aid under the ESM Treaty as a matter of economic policy.[38] Again, through the resort to purposive programming this constraint is overcome:

> When the ESM buys up bonds on secondary markets, it is 'economic policy'. When the ECB does the same, and makes these purchases conditional on compliance with the ESM's 'macroeconomic adjustment' demands, it is 'monetary policy'.

It is hence the difference between the objectives of the respective operations, which is decisive. This is precisely the magic charm of purposive programming.[39]

The ESCB/ECB are entitled to define the objectives and to determine the means in full autonomy. This cannot be otherwise once it has been held that the conduct of monetary policy 'requires an expertise and experience which, according to the Treaties, devolves solely upon the ECB'.[40] Governance in the Eurozone, we have to realise, is a technocratic exercise. By definition, this type of praxis can be exposed neither to quests for democratic legitimacy nor to the constraints of the rule of law. What does this entail? The American law and political science scholar, Alec Stone Sweet, has characterised the foundational jurisprudence a 'juridical *coup d'état*, a fundamental transformation in the normative foundations of a legal system through the constitutional law-making of a court'.[41] *Pringle* and *Gauweiler* present another example. Stone Sweet was sure to be empirically correct about the foundational jurisprudence but refrained from a definite normative assessment. Was this

[36] *Gauweiler* judgment, above n 15 paras 42–45.

[37] See, eg, N Luhmann, *Recht und Automation in der öffentlichen Verwaltung* (Berlin, Duncker & Humblot, 1966) 36 ff.

[38] Para 64.

[39] H Schepel, 'The Bank, the Bond, and the Bail-out: On the Legal Construction of Market Discipline in the Eurozone' (2017) 44 *Journal of Law and Society* 79, 96.

[40] Opinion AG Gruz Villalón, para 111.

[41] A Stone Sweet, 'The Juridical Coup d'État and the Problem of Authority' (2007) 8 *German Law Journal* 915, 924 ff.

the type of 'constitutional moment', which Bruce Ackerman has identified in the constitutional history of the United States? Is it conceivable that the present transformation will 'deserve recognition', or is this an unconstitutional amendment of the European legal order?

I will return to this point in my final remark. For the present, I am just concerned with the disquieting theoretical poverty of this revolutionary jurisprudence. One core assumption upon which it builds is plainly wrong. Technical expertise cannot be neatly separated from, or insulated against, normative assessments and policy choices.[42] A second weakness is not so plainly visible. This is the distinction between monetary policy and fiscal policy, which the Treaty has firmly institutionalised and which the OMT litigation sought to clarify. This legal architecture has a long history, which Isabel Feichtner, when she was still an assistant professor at the House of Finance at Goethe University has reconstructed in an eye-opening essay.[43] We have learned to treat money as a commodity on which the state raises taxes. Tax revenues are sound finance; the alternative is to print money, a temptation that governments have to withstand in order to avoid inflation. This is why we need politically independent monetary authorities. In order to defend us against inflation these authorities must discipline governments and their fiscal policy. This is the narrative, which we have internalised in our nation states and on which the EMU relies. But this is also why we have established in the Eurozone a governance regime, which does not content itself with the adjustment of interest rates and the use of other conventional monetary policy instruments. An irresistible logic is at work here. The ECB cannot restrain itself to a focus on price stability and leave financial stability operations to national governments. The Bank's concerns for financial stability are unlimited in their scope. They reach out into the whole range of economic and social policies with requests for structural reforms and adjustments.[44] The fundamental error, Feichtner argues, is to treat money as an external factor and to conceal its construction by the state. Money should be understood as credit, be regarded as credit; the transfers of such credit only work if a state that guarantees their enforceability exists. She refers to sophisticated literature defending this reconceptualisation. This, however, is beyond my horizon. What I can see and what I feel is clearly visible is the destruction of the separation of fiscal and monetary policy by Europe's crisis politics and the jurisprudence of the CJEU. To repeat: 'When the ESM buys up bonds on secondary markets, it is "economic policy"'[45] – this is the Pringle judgment. 'When the ECB does the same, and makes these purchases conditional on compliance with the ESM's "macroeconomic adjustment" demands, this is "monetary policy"'[46] – it all depends, hence, on who does it for what purpose.

[42] Mendes, above n 32.

[43] I Feichtner, 'Public Law's Rationalization of the Legal Architecture of Money: What Might Legal Analysis of Money Become?' (2016) 17 *German Law Journal* 875.

[44] ibid 895.

[45] Schepel, above n 39, 96.

[46] ibid.

## Ad 4: A Juridical Coup d'Etat?

However sophisticated this reasoning may seem, the practice, which it legalises, is anything but legitimate. Our crisis politics has created a sharp asymmetry between the north and the south of Europe; it has, to cite Habermas, divided Europe because of its palpable, indeed glaring social injustice.[47] The harsh critique of the famous philosopher is widely noticed but does not impress European integration studies. What I find amazing and telling are the affinities between all of its pertinent branches, law, economics, political science: a tacit consensus not to take normative concerns about the integrity of law too seriously.

This seems most amazing in my own discipline. The *Pringle* judgment has hardly irritated anybody. The decision in *Gauweiler* is praised as a thoughtful and non-polemical examination of the somehow cheekily German reference. What is true for the jurisprudence of the ECJ is *cum grano salis* also true for the enormous body of the so-called crisis law. I cite from the introductory chapter to a pertinent volume of the EUI in Florence:

> After over half a decade of legal measures and prolific commentary on those measures, it is helpful to stand back and take stock. We will consider whether euro-crisis law … has by now mainly become simply the macro-economic law of the EU.[48]

The considerations end with a principled discharge, constrained by a few caveats.

Economists have replaced us lawyers as the prime advisers in European politics. Their views are dominated by functionalist reason. Even a statement like 'The first victim of the crisis is democracy' pronounced by my Berlin colleague Henrik Enderlein, is not meant to question that commitment.[49] One of the leading German authorities in the field of monetary policy is the Director of the Max Planck Institute for Public Goods, Martin Hellwig, who seems to believe that the law has nothing useful to contribute to the praxis of monetary policy.[50] The German Constitutional Court – and then likewise its economic experts – are ignorant. 'Economists are the ones who assess economic situations, whether there is an extraordinary crisis or not, how actors have to act to improve or protect welfare and how the economic order looks like'.[51]

[47] J Habermas, 'Democracy in Europe: Why the Development of the EU into a Transnational Democracy is Necessary and How it is Possible' (2015) 21 *European Law Journal* 546, 550 ('einer Krisenpolitik …, die infolge ihrer handgreiflichen, ja schreienden sozialen Ungerechtigkeit die europäischen Nationen gegeneinander aufgebracht hat').

[48] T Beukers, C Kilpatrick and B De Witte, 'Constitutional Change Through Euro-Crisis Law: Taking Stock, New Perspectives and Looking Ahead' in T Beukers, B De Witte and C Kilpatrick (eds), *Constitutional Change through Euro-Crisis Law* (Cambridge, Cambridge University Press, 2017).

[49] H Enderlein, 'Das erste Opfer der Krise ist die Demokratie: Wirtschaftspolitik und ihre Legitimation in der Finanzmarktkrise 2008-2013' in H Buchstein (ed), *Die Versprechen der Demokratie* (Baden-Baden, Nomos, 2013).

[50] M Hellwig, 'Finanzstabilität, Transparenz und Verantwortlichkeit: Stellungnahme für das Bundesverfassungsgericht' (2017) 50 *Credit and Capital Markets/Kredit und Kapital* 421-454.

[51] F Traut, 'Banking Crisis Interventions in Germany and Italy: The Unpleasant Case of the New European Bank Resolution Framework' in J Hien and C Joerges (eds), *Responses of European Economic*

And what about political science, a discipline brought to post-war Germany to teach us, especially us lawyers, democracy? Political scientists explain events, identify independent and dependent variables, and analyse changes within the framework of their integration theories. These attitudes did not fundamentally change after the crisis.[52] 'Business as usual' – this diagnosis of my Berlin colleague Jachtenfuchs dates from 2013.[53] Business is even improving because we are witnessing a takeover of core state function by European institutions. Not only neo-functionalist, but inter-governmentalists, too, are delighted; they observe a takeover by some new 'deliberative' intergovernmentalism – more Europe hence – and this is by definition progress.[54]

## Ad 5: TINA (There Is No Alternative)?

Is it too cheap to submit critical comments without at the same time offering a 'solution'? Is the TINA mantra of Chancellor Merkel justified? Is her 'market conforming democracy'[55] what is left of the '*soziale Rechtsstaat*' of the Basic law? Do we have to live with the replacement of political ownership of democratically legitimated governments by austerity-driven 'structural reforms'? It is important to remain aware of the tragic choices at stake. They have been explained with admirable clarity in the comments on the *Gauweiler* reference of the Federal Constitutional Court (FCC) by Ashoka Mody.[56] The economist explains:

> The legal and economic question of interest is whether the OMT tried to bypass the intent of the Treaty by creating a de-facto fiscal union (a liability or transfer union in Bundesbank terminology). If so, without their explicit authorisation, countries had become fiscally responsible for the mistakes of other member countries.

To substantiate this query, Mody continues: 'Can such a fiscal union be implicitly located in the ECB without the political willingness to transparently achieve that elusive goal?'[57] The economist as true teacher of law? Mody acknowledges the constraints under which law and politics operate. He warns us to subject fundamental constitutional principles to a functionalist logic of problem-solving strategies which operate under the highest uncertainties. Lübbe-Wolff's dissent is valuable because she refuses to cover unresolved problems by a thin veneer of

*Cultures to Europe's Crisis Politics: The Example of German–Italian Discrepancies* (European University Institute, Robert Schuman Centre for Advanced Studies, San Domenico di Fiesole 2018), available at cadmus.eui.eu/handle/1814/59884.

[52] C Kreuder-Sonnen, 'Beyond Integration Theory: The (Anti-)Constitutional Dimension of European Crisis Governance' (2016) 54 *Journal of Common Market Studies* 1350.

[53] P Genschel and M Jachtenfuchs, 'Alles ganz normal! Eine institutionelle Analyse der Euro-Krise' (2013) 20 *Zeitschrift für Internationale Beziehungen* 75, 83.

[54] U Puetter, *The European Council and the Council: New Intergovernmentalism and Institutional Change* (Oxford, Oxford University Press, 2014).

[55] See Tooze, above n 10, 438 with references.

[56] Mody, above n 23.

[57] ibid 6, 4.

legality. Could we expect more? Gerhard Anschütz has been criticised for empowering implicitly non-legitimated actors with decision-making powers.[58] Somewhat ironically, the non-existence of transnational authority with comprehensive powers can turn into an asset: Europe cannot be governed by some central command-and control regime. It is destined to operate through cooperative problem-solving. Is it conceivable that the courts would impose some conditionality upon institutional and political actors? Constitutional courts would then be courageous enough to act as instigators and supervisors of deliberative political processes.

[58] See above n 1.

# PART II

# An Institutional Perspective on EU Constitutional Democracy

# 10

# The Double Legitimacy and Multiple Accountability of the European Commission: Some Reflections on its Constitutional Democratic Role

BEN SMULDERS*

## A Powerful Institution With Numerous Tasks of a Diverse Nature

The European Commission is a powerful institution. This is obvious when reading the EU Treaties and in particular Article 17 TEU: it shall promote the general interest of the EU and take appropriate initiatives to that end. With respect to most legislative procedures, it enjoys an exclusive right of initiative.[1] It shall ensure the application of the EU Treaties and, as their guardian, it oversees the application of EU law. It executes the annual budget amounting to more than 140 billion euro in 2019, including more than 50 multi-million euro funding programmes and financial instruments. It exercises coordinating, executive and management functions, as laid down in numerous EU acts of primary and secondary law. Increasingly, it is entrusted with such tasks by treaties concluded by Member States, *inter se*, ie, outside the EU legal order but with a clear *nexus* with that order, following, for example, the banking and sovereign debt crisis at the beginning of this century.[2] Moreover, the members of the European Commission include the High Representative of the Union for Foreign Affairs and Security Policy, who is also one of its Vice Presidents. The Commission and the High Representative, in their respective

* The opinions expressed in this chapter are strictly personal and in no way bind the institutions he works for.

[1] Art 289 TFEU.

[2] See the judgment of the CJEU in Case C-370/12 *Pringle* EU:C:2012:756136.

fields of competence, have the power to negotiate agreements between the Union and third countries or international organisations.[3] The President of the Commission is at the same time a member in a personal capacity of the European Council, together with its President and the Heads of State or Government of the Member States. The High Representative/Vice President of the Commission also takes part in the work of the European Council.[4] This institution provides the EU with the necessary impetus for its development and defines the general political directions and priorities thereof. The European Commission and some of its members have together indeed far-reaching powers under the judicial control of the Court of Justice of the European Union (CJEU) that could be categorised as follows:[5]

- Fulfilling political tasks, comparable to the classic tasks of a national government, such as initiating legislative proposals, executing the budget and assuring the external representation.
- Functioning as a central administrative body in the area of economic regulatory law, including competition and trade law, while fulfilling administrative tasks in many other areas, alone or in close cooperation with Member States and EU agencies, ranging from control, adjudication, application to enforcement of legal norms, which are often of an undetermined character and leaving the Commission a wide discretion of a more or less political nature. Such tasks are at national level in general not fulfilled by the national government but rather attributed to national agencies, occasionally subject to governmental control.[6]
- Assuming the role of guardian of the Treaties, implying, in the case it sues Member States before the CJEU for breach of EU law, a role comparable to that of an Attorney General and thus exercising a quasi-judicial function. More recently, this rule has evolved in such a way that it also includes the role of guardian of the EU values set out in Article 2 TEU, which has both a legal and political dimension to it.[7]

[3] Art 218 TFEU

[4] See Art 15 TEU.

[5] See for an excellent assessment of the Commission's nature and tasks as well as the role of its administration: C Ladenburger, 'Anmerkungen zur Frage der 'Eigenlegitimation der Ministerialbürokratie' im Institutionellen System der Europäischen Union' in C Franzius, FC Mayer and J Neyer (eds), *Modelle des Parlamentarismus im 21. Jahrhundert* (Baden-Baden, Nomos, 2015); compare also P Ponzano, '60 ans de relations interinsttuionnelles' (2018) 1 *Revue du droit de l'Union européenne* 107, in particular 114–15 and 119–20; B Martenczuk, 'Art 17 [Kommission]' in E Grabitz, M Hilf and M Nettesheim (eds), *Das Recht der Europäischen Union* (München, CH Beck Verlag, 2016).

[6] Compare, eg, the right of the Federal Minister for Economic Affairs and Energy to overturn certain prohibition decisions of the Bundeskartellamt in Germany (the so-called *Ministererlaubnis* based on § 42(2) GWB).

[7] See for a recent overview of Commission actions based on Art 7 TEU or Art 258 TFEU as well as related CJEU case law regarding current threats to the rule of law and to other values in the sense of Art 7 TEU: Editorial comments '2019 Shaping Up as a Challenging Year for the Union, Not Least as a Community of Values' (2019) 56 *Common Market Law Review* 3; see also B Smulders, 'De verknochtheid tussen de rechtsstaat, de EU en haar lidstaten – *Lex Rex* ipv *Rex Lex*' in BJ Van Ettekoven, J Polak, G Roes, B Vermeulen, L Weesing-Loeber and A Weggeman (eds), *Rechtsorde en Bestuur – Liber amicorum aangeboden aan PH Donner* (Den Haag, Boom Juridisch, 2018) 445–46.

- Fulfilling tasks, implying the use of considerable political discretion, in the context of the new institutional framework for ensuring budgetary discipline, economic policy coordination and financial assistance, which from 2010 onwards, as a reaction to the banking and sovereign debt crisis in the euro area, has developed inside and outside the EU legal order.

It would therefore be wrong to claim that the Commission is merely an unpolitical, technocratic and essentially 'output legitimised' administration. This amounts to a denial of the EU Treaties, the various inter-institutional agreements it has entered into with the European Parliament and the Council as well as a set of agreements between Member States *inter se* as they stand today and are applied in practice. As explained below, while continuing to be bound by its duty *ab initio* to serve in an independent way the general interest of the EU as a whole, it has evolved, as a result of successive Treaty changes, towards a political institution with both input legitimacy and output legitimacy, which is *ex post* ensured through multiple accountability.

## Essentially an Administration at its Inception

Although in the meantime overtaken by constitutional developments, the views that the Commission is and should be merely a college of technocrats were, however, dominant during the negotiations leading to the signing and eventual ratification of the EEC Treaty in 1957. For the purposes of these negotiations, the Conference of Messina created the so-called *Comité intergouvernamental*, chaired by the then Belgian Foreign Minister Paul-Henri Spaak.[8] It discussed at some point a scheme for the EEC's institutional structure, as reflected in the following document, well preserved in the archives of the European University Institute in Florence:

As can be inferred from that scheme, the embryo of the European Commission was merely a 'Board' composed of four to six qualified high officials ('*hauts fonctionnaires qualifiés*'), of which one would be President. Like the members of the Court of Justice, they would be appointed for a period of six years by a two-thirds majority of the Council. The Board was meant to enjoy a certain degree of independence vis-a-vis the Council but it would seem that that 'independence' was limited to its action in individual technical cases ('pas de lien personnel de subordination [et] pas d'instructions techniques dans [des] cas particuliers'). The Presidents of both the Board and the Court of Justice would be accountable to a Disciplinary Court. The Board would have certain powers in the area of economy, trade, social affairs, competition, transport, energy, agriculture and what was called 'fonds de

[8] The six delegations were led by Friedrich Ophüls (Germany); Félix Gaillard (France); Jean-Charles Snoy et d'Oppuers (Belgium); Lodovico Benvenuti (Italy); Gerard Verrijn Stuart (Netherlands); and Lambert Schaus (Luxembourg).

**Figure 1** Schema de la Structure Institutionnelle

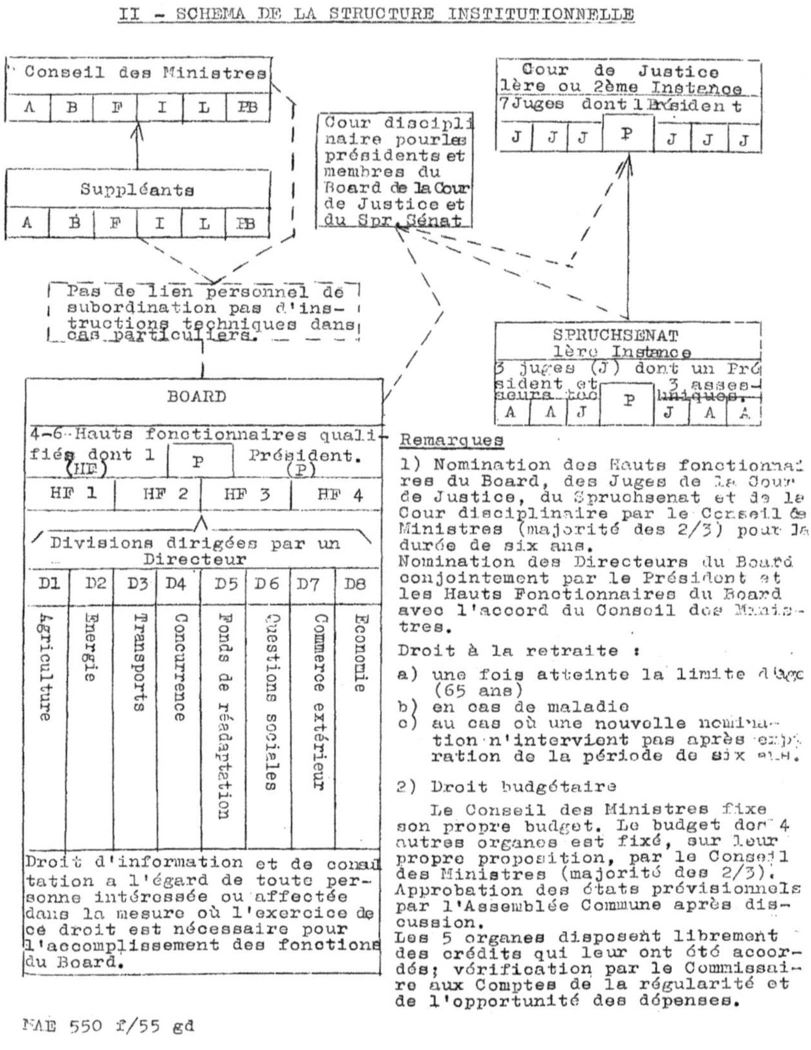


réadaptation', including a 'droit d'information et de consultation' in relation to any interested or affected person to the extent such a right was necessary for the Board in order to exercise its powers. What was eventually agreed in the context of the 1957 EEC Treaty and reflected in its Articles 158 and 161, though bearing some marks of that approach, also departs from it in that it contained a series of safeguards ensuring more independence and accountability of the Commission and refined its tasks: an executive body, consisting of nine members chosen for 'their general competence and of indisputable independence' by common consent by the Member States,[9] subject to judicial control exercised by the Court of Justice[10] and accountable to the Assembly, composed of delegates appointed by the national parliaments of the Member States.[11] Vis-a-vis the Assembly, the Commission had a duty to answer questions orally and in writing, to accept to be heard if so requested by the Assembly and had to resign if the latter adopted a motion of censure by a two-thirds majority of the votes cast, representing a majority of its members.[12] Once appointed, the members of the Commission were to perform their duties without seeking or accepting instructions from any government or other body,[13] a formula still used, mutatis mutandis, in Article 17 of the current EU Treaty. Its decisions were taken by simple majority and, as a collegiate body, it assumed collective responsibility for them. Its powers were limited though, since they were confined in essence to the following rights:

- To ensure the application of the Treaty and of the provisions enacted by the institutions of the Community in pursuance thereof.
- To formulate recommendations or opinions in matters which were the subject of the EEC Treaty.
- Under the conditions of the Treaty, to dispose of a power of decision of its own and participate in the preparation of acts of the Council and the Assembly.
- To exercise the competence conferred on it by the Council for the implementation of the rules laid down by the latter.

These powers had to be exercised in the following areas: external relations, economic and financial affairs, common market, competition, social affairs, agriculture, transport and overseas development. The Commission's prime duty was to ensure that the terms of the Treaty in these areas were enforced and that the other institutions fulfilled their respective functions. It was not given a general power to propose legislation but such power was granted to it in specific legal bases. In a limited number of very technical cases it could act independently which often were circumscribed in much detail both in terms of substance and timing, leaving limited room for policy-making, for example, the regulation of goods having entered free into Member States before the common customs tariffs were achieved,[14] the timing of the gradual removal of charges equivalent to customs duties[15] and decisions in respect of customs duties of a fiscal nature[16] or

[9] Art 158 EEC.
[10] Arts 173–75 EEC.
[11] Art 144 EEC.
[12] See H von der Groeben and H von Boeck, 'Die Kommission' in *Kommentar zum EWG-Vertrag* (Baden-Baden, August Lutzeyer Verlag, 1960); A Campell and D Thompson, *Common Market Law: Texts and Commentaries* (London, Stevens & Sons, 1962) 88–91.
[13] Art 157(2) EEC.
[14] Art 10 EEC.
[15] Art 13 EEC.
[16] Art 17 EEC.

authorising tariff quotas.[17] Furthermore, it had a duty to enforce the rules against restrictive trade practice and monopolies, enforce the rules against Member States in respect of public enterprises or state monopolies breaching the rules of competition, authorise countermeasures in the case of dumping[18] and supervise state aid.[19] Certain responsibilities of representation in the field of external economic relations[20] were also granted to the Commission, notably in connection with GATT[21] and the OECD.[22] Given the nature of these predominantly technical, strictly framed tasks of a social-economic nature, it was not surprising that the first members of the Commission were former high officials such as diplomats or academics rather than politicians, with the rare exception of a few former ministers who had held, however, a technocratic portfolio in their national governments.[23] One could argue that the then European Communities became gradually more political and less technical from the early 1970s onwards, when the Heads of State or Government announced that henceforth, together with the President of the European Commission, they would meet regularly, accompanied by their Foreign Ministers, as a formation of the Council, for the work on political cooperation. In the meantime, the European Council, originally established outside the Treaties, has become an EU institution in its own right and for nearly a quarter of century the Commission has been led by former Prime Ministers.[24] Today's College of Commissioners counts among its 28 members 22 former ministers, among whom four former Prime Ministers,[25] four former Foreign Ministers[26] and one former Finance Minister.[27]

## Double Legitimacy Stemming from EU Citizens (Via the European Parliament) and Member States (Via the European Council and the Council)

Following the successive changes resulting from the 1997 Amsterdam Treaty, 2001 Nice Treaty and in particular the 2007 Lisbon Treaty, the national parliamentary legitimisation model has increasingly influenced EU institutional law and

[17] Art 25 EEC.
[18] Art 90 EEC.
[19] Art 91 EEC.
[20] Art 111 EEC.
[21] Art 229 EEC.
[22] Art 231 EEC.
[23] eg, former Agriculture Minister Sicco Mansholt from the Netherlands.
[24] Jacques Santer (Luxembourg); Romano Prodi (Italy); José Manuel Barroso (Portugal); and Jean-Claude Juncker (Luxembourg).
[25] Jean-Claude Juncker, Jyrki Katainen (Finland); Andrus Ansip (Estonia); and Valdis Dombrovskis (Latvia).
[26] Frans Timmermans (Netherlands); Federica Mogherini (Italy); Dimitris Avramopoulos (Greece); and Tibor Navracsics (Hungary).
[27] Pierre Moscovici (France).

practice and, as a result, the Commission's composition, internal organisation, work programme and daily functioning.[28] The main reasons for that are the rules regarding the investiture of its President and, separately, of the full College of Commissioners, laid down in Article 17(7) TEU, leading, inter alia, to the directly elected Parliament electing the Commission's President. These are subsequently translated into presidential guidelines to each Commissioner individually in the form of mission letters based on the new Article 17(6) TEU. The practice of political guidelines as a precondition for the Parliament's election of the Commission President is codified in point 2 of the 2010 Framework Agreement on the relations between the Parliament and the Commission.[29] Throughout the mandate, the President and his colleagues give the highest attention to Parliament's positions. They are indeed constantly aware of their political responsibility vis-a-vis Parliament given the fact, as explained below, that Parliament has many means to hold them accountable for delivering on the political guidelines, which are the basis on which it elected the Commission President and gave its consent to the nomination of the College as a whole. Relevant in the context of the investiture of the Commission is also the lead candidate (or *Spitzenkandidat*) process, launched by the Parliament for the first time in 2014.[30] This new concept has the objective of establishing a stronger link between the parliamentary elections and the Commission, infusing more democratic legitimacy in the election of the President of the Commission while avoiding that such election is the result of an opaque backroom deal. It led to a revision of the Framework Agreement in 2018.[31] Together with the practice of public Commissioner-designate hearings since 1995, which has led to the withdrawal of various Commissioner-designates and changes of their portfolios, it reinforces the parliamentary steering oversight. A logical and inevitable consequence of the way the process of investiture is designed and the Parliament's far-reaching powers in that respect is that the President of the Commission can be elected and the Commission as a whole can be appointed *only* if they have the

[28] See Ladenburger, above n 5.

[29] [2010] OJ L304, 47–62.

[30] See, eg, European Parliament resolution of 11 November 2015 on the reform of the electoral law of the EU 2015/2035(INL). This process is in essence a procedure, whereby European political parties, ahead of the European Parliament elections, appoint lead candidates for the function of Commission President, with the purpose of ensuring that the President of the Commission will become the candidate of the political party capable of marshalling sufficient support in the European Parliament. Establishing a direct link between the European Parliament elections and the Commission President is intended to increase the legitimacy of the Commission and the EU as a whole, foster transparency in the nomination process and encourage increased turnout in European Parliament elections, the voter turnout in these elections being between only 40% and 50–51% since 1999. The success of the process in practice depends on the European Council's interpretation of its powers to propose to the European Parliament a candidate for President of the Commission under Art 17(7) TEU, in particular of the first part of the first sentence of that provision ('Taking into account the elections of the European Parliament'). On 2 July 2019, after two days and nights of negotiations, the European Council decided to propose to the Parliament, for election, a candidate for President of the Commission, which was not a lead candidate. This prompted current Commission President Juncker to state three days later that he was the first and last lead candidate.

[31] [2018] OJ L45, 46.

confidence of the required majority of Members of Parliament. In practice, this means that the support of a coalition of political groups in the Parliament is necessary. This, in turn, implies that in order to maintain the confidence of a majority of the Parliament, any Commission must establish a link between any Commission and that coalition. And for that reason (and not only because of the nature of the tasks it is called to perform under the Treaty), the Commission has become an eminently political body, legitimised by the Parliament.[32] One should bear in mind that Article 10 TEU and Article 224 TFEU expressly recognise the importance of representative democracy for the functioning of the Union and the role of political parties at European level in forming European awareness and expressing the will of citizens of the Union.

As regards the Commission's second strand of legitimacy, stemming from the Member States, it is important to stress that the European Union is not a state and that the Commission is therefore not the government of a parliamentarian state. The Commission is rather a predominantly executive body of a union of citizens and states and therefore derives its legitimacy simultaneously from the European Parliament and the two institutions representing the Member States: the European Council and the Council.[33] The latter source of legitimacy dominated the first decades but this started to change with the Nice Treaty, stipulating that the Commission and its President would be from then on nominated by the Council with qualified majority and no longer by the governments of the Member States, acting in common agreement. The double legitimacy is now firmly anchored in the Treaty through the new Article 17(7) introduced in Lisbon in 2007, from which it follows that: (i) the European Council proposes, for election, to the Parliament a candidate for President of the Commission; (ii) by common accord with the President-elect, the Council adopts the list of the other persons proposed for appointment as Members of the Commission; (iii) on the basis of Parliament's consent, the European Council nominates the full College. The Commission should consist of no more than one national of each Member State.[34] Even if is true that from the 1957 Rome Treaty onwards, the Commission was conceived as an institution independent of the Member States, this double legitimacy, arguably, allows it to even better pursue its variety of tasks in the general interest or to put it differently: through the different actions which the Treaties empower it to take, to even better serve the general interest by weighing and synthesising the interests of all Member States and their citizens.

[32] It should be noted, however, that so far in the European Parliament one cannot clearly distinguish a political majority from a political minority as is the case at the level of national parliaments in certain Member States (eg, in the UK). Arguably, this gives the Commission a certain freedom of action vis-a-vis the European Parliament it would otherwise not enjoy.

[33] Art 17(7) TEU. See also Ladenburger, above n 5.

[34] Admittedly, Art 213 EC of the Nice Treaty is more explicit in this respect than the current Art 17(5) TEU.

## Multiple Accountability Through a Series of Checks and Balances

Once nominated and given the wide powers with which it is entrusted, any Commission should account for its acts and omissions by being subject to a series of political, legal and financial checks and balances commensurate with its responsibilities. It is submitted that this is indeed the case, not only in theory but also in practice.

As regards the Commission's *political accountability*, the European Parliament has a crucial role to play. It is vested with a power of censure of the Commission.[35] So far, none of the eight motions of censure brought before Parliament has been adopted, mostly due to the very high threshold (two-thirds majority). In 1999, the Santer Commission stepped down before Parliament forced its resignation, which happened after the latter had refused to give discharge to the Commission for the way it had executed the budget in 1996. The Treaties do not provide for individual responsibility of Commissioners but consider the Commission as a collegiate body responsible to Parliament. However, according the 2010 Framework between Parliament and Commission the Parliament can ask the Commission President to withdraw confidence in an individual Member of the Commission or change his portfolio and if the President refuses to do so, he has to explain that non-decision to Parliament.[36] This provision has never been applied. According to Article 226 TFEU, the Parliament has the right to set up a temporary Committee of Inquiry to investigate alleged contraventions and maladministration in the implementation of EU law.[37] Since 2009, the Parliament has set up two committees of inquiry – on emission measurements in the automotive sector following the *dieselgate* scandal (EMIS) and on money laundering, tax avoidance and tax evasion following disclosure of the Panama papers (PANA). With respect to Commission delegated acts in the sense of Article 290 TFEU, the Treaty gives the Parliament the right to veto and revocation. However, as regards implementing acts in the sense of Article 291 TFEU it has no power to block them, the scrutiny power being left to Member States, which would be understandable given the difference in nature of these two types of act were it not that that difference has been relativised following the case of in CJEU.[38] That said, the Parliament does check in practice whether in exercising the legislators' empowerment to adopt an implementing act, the Commission has not exceeded the limits of such empowerment.[39] A revocation of a delegated

[35] Art 17(8) TFEU and Art 234 TFEU.

[36] See above n 30.

[37] Art 226 TFEU and European Parliament Decision 95/167/EC.

[38] Judgment of the CJEU of 18 March 2014 in Case C-427/12 *Commission v European Parliament and Council* EU:C:2014:170 ('biocides') and its judgment of 16 July 2015 in Case C-88/14 *Commission v European Parliament and Council* EU:C:2015:499 (listing of third country exempted from visa requirements).

[39] Judgment of the CJEU of 15 October 2014 in Case C-65/13 *European Parliament v Commission* EU:C:2014:2289 ('Eures').

act has never taken place and by June 2018 objections had been raised eight times. Article 230(2) TFEU allows the Parliament to address questions to the Commission for oral and written answers – 43,373 since the beginning of the Juncker Commission's mandate – and its rules of procedure allow for the organisation of question time with the Commission.[40] In addition, the Commission is bound by a series of reporting obligations vis-a-vis Parliament.[41] Also to be noted is the Commission's commitment to adopt its annual work programme (CWP) for the following year in October and to present it to Parliament and Council. This is preceded by the Commission President delivering the State of the Union address in the European Parliament plenary session in September.[42] Also relevant in this context are the numerous arrangements agreed between Parliament and Commission in their 2010 Framework Agreement in order to ensure a constructive dialogue between them and a flow of information from the Commission to the Parliament.[43]

The political accountability of the Commission exists solely vis-a-vis the Parliament, *not* the Council. This derives directly from the TEU's Title III where the Parliament is attributed functions of 'political control' (Article 14 TEU) while the Council exercises, in so far as relevant in this context, 'policy-making and coordinating' functions (Article 16). Consequently, Article 17(8) TFEU should be interpreted as meaning that the Commission is indeed responsible 'to the European Parliament' only.[44] Even though there is the right for the Council to request initiatives from the Commission of Article 241 TFEU and there is also the possibility for the Council to apply to the CJEU for the retirement or deprivation of rights of a Commission member guilty of misconduct (Articles 245 and 247 TFEU), none of this amounts to any political responsibility of the Commission vis-a-vis the Council.[45] The possibility to apply to the CJEU could be interpreted as a corollary of the role of the Council in the nomination of the Commission. As regards delegated acts, the obligations of the Commission stem from the fact that its power is indeed delegated but again do not amount to any political accountability of the

[40] Rule 129 of the European Parliament rules of procedure.

[41] See, eg, Arts 25, 121(5), 159, 161, 175, 207, 249 and 325(2) TFEU.

[42] See Annex IV(5) of the 2010 Framework Agreement on relations between European Parliament and the European Commission.

[43] See part II of the 2010 Framework Agreement on relations between European Parliament and the European Commission.

[44] Arguably, the obligations imposed on the Commission under Protocols No 1 and in particular No 2 to the Lisbon Treaty amount to a duty to account vis-a-vis the national parliaments of the Member States for the way it complies with the principle of subsidiarity and proportionality when exercising its right of legislative initiative. Their main task in the institutional setup of the EU, however, remains to scrutinise their governments in relation to the activities of the Union (*cf* the preamble of Protocol No 1).

[45] See the Council Decision 199/493/EC, ECSC, Euratom to refer the case of former Commissioner Bangemann to the CJEU on the basis of Art 213(2) TFEU, which was eventually settled (*cf* Council Decision 2000/44/EC, ECSC, Euratom). Unethical conduct of a former Commissioner has also given rise to court action initiated by the Commission: see the judgment of the CJEU of 11 July 2006 in Case C-432/04 *Commission v Cresson* EU:C:2006:455. Interesting in this context, is also the unsuccessful action in two instances of former Commissioner Dalli against the Commission (Order of the CJEU of 14 April 2016 in Case C-394/15P EU:C:2016:262).

Commission vis-a-vis the Council. This conclusion is not changed by the 2016 inter-institutional agreement between Commission, Council and Parliament (IIA-BLM), which makes several references to the relation between Commission and Council.[46] The IIA-BLM establishes, inter alia, that the Commission will engage in a dialogue with the Council both before and after the adoption of the CWP and take due account of its views, and also that the Commission must give prompt and detailed consideration to requests for proposals for Union acts made by the Council and present its reply, on request, in the Council.[47] There is a series of other mutual political commitments but they do not imply any political accountability and merely amount to engagements taken freely by the three institutions to improve law-making. These engagements cannot alter in any way the institutional balance defined by the Treaties.

In terms of *legal accountability*, it suffices to point at the role of supranational adjudicator and accountability forum the Treaties confer on the CJEU, acting as the independent and ultimate arbiter of the law while enjoying a formal separation of its overarching judicial powers from the other institutions, including the Commission.[48] The actions for annulment of Commission acts or for the Commission's failure to act, the action for damages, the plea of illegality as well as the possibility for the CJEU to give preliminary rulings on the validity of Commission acts at the request of national judges, taken together, provide for a refined and comprehensive system of legal protection against the Commission. This has been reinforced, since the entry into force of the Lisbon Treaty, by on the one hand, the lowering of the standing requirements in cases of actions for annulment, and on the other hand, the possibility of review for violation of the rights provided in the EU Charter of Fundamental Rights. Because of the increased politicisation of the Commission over the years, doubts have been cast as to whether it should continue to fulfil its role as guardian of the Treaties. A question that has attracted comment more particularly is whether the system of enforcement of competition law, whereby the Commission acts allegedly as 'investigator, prosecutor, judge and jury' is compatible with the principle of due process, as laid down in Article 47 of the Charter and Article 6 of the European Convention on Human Rights. However, that question has now been answered in the affirmative by the European Court of Human Rights[49] and by the CJEU[50] given the possibility of full judicial

[46] Interinstitutional Agreement of 13 April 2016 between the European Parliament, the Council of the European Union and the European Commission on Better Law-Making of 12 May 2016 [2016] OJ L123, 1–4. See for Parliament's rights in this respect: Art 225 TFEU.

[47] See point 6 of the IIA-BLM.

[48] See D Curtin and M Weimer, 'The Court of Justice of the European Union Supranational Adjudicator and Accountability Forum' in PJ Kuijper, F Amtenbrink, D Curtin, B de Witte, A McDonnell and S van den Bogaert (eds), *The Law of the European Union* (Alphen aan de Rijn, Kluwer Law International, 2018).

[49] Judgment of the European Court of Human Rights of 27 September 2011 in Case No 43509/08 *Menarini Diagnostics v Italy*.

[50] Judgment of the CJEU of 8 December 2011 in Case C-386/10 P *Chalkor v Commission* EU:C:2011:815; and of 6 November 2012 in Case C-199/11 *Europese Gemeenschap v Otis* EU:C:2012:684.

review of Commission decisions in the area of competition before the CJEU in two instances. Even where the Commission has acted outside the EU legal order, ie, merely on the basis of a mandate granted by Member States in the context of an intergovernmental agreement such as the Treaty Establishing the European Stability Mechanism, the CJEU has declared admissibility in certain circumstances in actions for damages which were brought before it by private persons claiming compensation because of such Commission action.[51]

It has been suggested that it would be better to transfer the Commission's powers of a more technical nature and in particular those related to enforcement of EU law to agencies. Such ideas, however, disregard that the most important of these powers have been conferred on the Commission by the Treaty itself (eg, in the area of competition, anti-dumping and the Stability and Growth Pact) and that implementing these ideas would therefore require a Treaty change which is not a realistic option in the short or medium term given the difficulties to ensure ratification thereof in all Member States. Moreover, one can seriously doubt whether agencies would perform these tasks more objectively, considering that most of the existing EU agencies have a governance structure giving decisive powers to representatives of Member States and some of the more recently created even providing for qualified majority voting.[52] Regard should also be given to the need to weigh different public interests and ensure coherence between different EU policies when interpreting, applying and enforcing EU rules (eg, state aid control). This is a role the Commission, assisted by a single administration which, as are the Commissioners themselves, bound by strict rules on independence and integrity, with its variety of tasks, expertise and experience, is particularly well placed to fulfil. The CJEU *Meroni* case law actually prohibits the institutions from delegating powers to agencies, the exercise of which requires political discretion.[53] In other words, the transfer of these powers to EU agencies entails the serious risk, in the best of all scenarios, of duplication, and in the worst, of inconsistencies and legal uncertainty and is at any rate not a guarantee for more objectivity. Equally questionable would be a change of the Treaties, widening the possibilities of such transfer to agencies in as far as it would contribute to a further atomisation of executive power between different institutions and agencies, creating in itself new questions of legitimacy and accountability.

[51] See, eg, the judgments of the CJEU of 20 September 2016 in Joined Cases C-8/15 P *Ledra Advertising ao v Commission and European Central Bank* EU:C:2016:701; and in Joined Cases C-105/15 P *Malli ao v Commission and European Central Bank* EU:C:2016:702.

[52] See Regulation (EU) No 1093/2010 of the European Parliament and the Council establishing the European Banking Authority; Regulation (EU) No 1095/2010 of the European Parliament and the Council establishing the European Securities and Markets Authority; and Regulation (EU) No 1094/2010 of the European Parliament and the Council establishing the European Insurance and Occupational Pensions Authority.

[53] Judgment of the Court of Justice of 13 June 1958 in Case C-9/56 *Meroni v High Authority of the ECSC* EU:C:1958:7, confirmed by the judgment of the CJEU in its judgment of 22 January 2014 in Case C-270/12 *UK v Commission* EU:C:2014:18 ('short selling').

When it comes to *maladministration* in its activities, the Commission is also accountable to the European Ombudsman, elected by the European Parliament and having the power to conduct inquiries on his own initiative or those based on complaints and culminating into a report addressed to the European Parliament.[54] In the period from 2017 to 2018, the Ombudsman opened 445 inquiries, some of which, at times, prompted the European Parliament and in particular its Committee on Budgetary Control (CONT), which is also the driving force behind the discharge procedure discussed below, to take action itself.[55]

As regards its *financial management*, the Commission is not only accountable to Parliament in the context of the discharge procedure, to be discussed below, but also to the European Court of Auditors (ECA), which has been given far-reaching powers to fulfil its Treaty mission to examine the Commission accounts of all revenue and expenditure.[56] According to Article 287 TFEU, the ECA shall provide the Parliament and the Council with an annual statement of assurance as to the reliability of the accounts and the legality and regularity of the underlying transactions. So far, such qualified positive statement of assurance has been granted only once (in 2018). The ECA shall also examine whether all revenue has been received and all expenditure incurred in a lawful and regular manner and whether the financial management has been sound. This is not limited to purely financial audits. The ECA regularly assesses performance in its special reports, most of which are based on performance audits or a combination of compliance and performance assessments. In 28 reports issued in 2017, it checked in particular whether the objectives of selected EU policies and programmes had been met, whether results had been achieved effectively and efficiently and whether EU funding had provided added value.[57] In this respect, the report it carried out with respect to the Commission's management of the current migration crisis is particularly noteworthy.[58]

Discharge, governed by Article 319 TFEU, is the final approval of how the budget for a specific year is being implemented by the Commission. The power to give discharge lies with the Parliament, acting on a recommendation of the Council. Only on two occasions, the Parliament has refused to do so. This occurred in 1984 and, as mentioned above, in 1998, leading, inter alia, to the resignation of the Santer Commission and the creation of the European Anti-Fraud Office (OLAF). OLAF is structurally a part of the Commission. However, insofar as its most important power is concerned – the investigation function – it has far-reaching

[54] Art 228(1) TFEU.

[55] See, eg, the report of the European Ombudsman of 4 September 2018 about the Commission's appointment of a new Secretary General, finding four instances of maladministration, contested by the European Commission, which has been the subject of European Parliament resolutions on 13 December 2018, 12 February 2019 and on 26 March 2019.

[56] Art 287 TFEU.

[57] See K-H Lehne, 'President's foreword' in 2017 EU audit in brief – Introducing the 2017 annual reports of the European Court of Auditors, Publication Office of the EU, Luxemburg 2018, 4.

[58] Special report of 25 April 2017 of the European Court of Auditors pursuant to Art 287(4) 2nd sub-paragragh TFEU, 'EU response to the refugees crisis: the "hotspot" approach'.

independence in the sense that its Director-General cannot seek nor take instructions from any Member State, institution (including the Commission), body, office or agency in the performance of his duties with regard to opening and carrying out external and internal investigations. Internal investigations are within the institutions. The Director-General of OLAF can bring an action against the Commission before the CJEU if his independence is at stake.[59] In November 2017, in the context of enhanced cooperation, a European Public Prosecutor's Office (EPPO) was set up with responsibilities for investigating, prosecuting and bringing to judgment the perpetrators of certain criminal offences affecting the financial interests of the EU, complementing OLAF's administrative investigations.[60]

The concluding piece of safeguards in terms of checks and balances are the requirements of *transparency* the Commission has to meet. Such transparency allows for *direct accountability to the public.* According to Article 15(1) TFEU, in order to promote good governance and ensure the participation of civil society, the Union's institutions, bodies, offices and agencies shall conduct their work as openly as possible. The second paragraph of this provision has been used by the legislator to adopt Regulation No 1049/2001 regulating public access to European Parliament, Council and Commission documents.[61] To illustrate the massive use of this instrument, reference should be made to the year 2017, when on that basis 6,255 requests for access to documents made to the Commission, of which it fully met 3,200, partially 1,043, refused 930, while the remainder could not be met because the documents either did not exist or were not in the Commission's possession. Appeals against such Commission (partial) refusals are frequently lodged with the CJEU, which tends to interpret restrictively the exceptions provided under the Regulation to refuse requests for access. In its landmark judgment in the *Turco* case, it made clear in general terms why that is the case. It held that the public interest in a document being made accessible needs to be weighted in the light of the advantages stemming, as noted in recital 2 of the preamble to Regulation No 1049/2001, from increased openness: 'in that this enables citizens to participate more closely in the decision-making process and guarantees that the administration enjoys greater legitimacy and is more effective and more accountable to the citizen in a democratic system'.[62]

Preparing the ground for a proposal for an inter-institutional agreement on a mandatory transparency register for lobbyists, the Commission, by its Decision of 25 November 2014, put in place internal rules to ensure transparency of contacts of Commissioners, their private offices and Commission Directors-General with associations or self-employed individuals.[63] As a second step, in May 2016, the

[59] Art 17(3) of Regulation (EC) No 1073/1999 of the European Parliament and the Council, [1999] OJ L136, 1.

[60] Council Regulation (EU) 2017/1939, [2017] OJ L283, 1.

[61] [2001] OJ L145, 43.

[62] See judgment of the CJEU of 1 July 2008 in Case C-39/05 P *Sweden and Turco v Council* EU:C:2008:374, paras 44–46 and 68–69.

[63] See European Commission Decisions C(2014) 9048 final and C(2014) 9051 of 25 November 2014.

Commission adopted rules reinforcing transparency of the expertise with which it is provided through expert groups in view of its policy-making. As a third step, the Commission ran a public consultation from 1 March 2016 until 1 June 2016 on the introduction of a mandatory register, the results of which helped it to table the said proposal for an inter-institutional agreement on transparency on 28 September 2018.[64] The response given to this initiative by Council and Parliament has been rather disappointing so far.

## Internal Checks and Balances

In order to meet its duties in terms of political, legal and financial accountability, the Commission has taken and updated over the years other internal governance related measures aimed at ensuring a series of internal checks and balances upstream of any decision the College of Commissioners takes. It would go beyond the scope of this chapter to analyse them in any depth but mention should be made of the important roles it has attributed to its own Legal Service, Internal Audit Service, Personal Data Protection Officer, Mediator, Chief Competition Economist, Chief Trade Economist, Hearing Officers for competition and trade procedures, Regulatory Scrutiny Board, Independent Ethical Committee and Disciplinary Board. Also the decision-making procedures of the College of Commissioners itself have been revised in this context, sometimes after CJEU judgments compelled it to do so.[65] Its Rules of Procedures provide, for example, that its Legal Service shall be consulted on all drafts or proposals for legal instruments and on all documents which may have legal implications.[66] Empowerment to take decisions on behalf of the Commission to one or more of its Members are limited to management or administrative measures and powers conferred in this way may be sub-delegated to the Directors-General and Heads of Department unless this is expressly prohibited in the empowering decision of the Commission, thus reserving political decisions to the College of Commissioners itself.[67] Moreover, in order to maximise the objectivity of decisions in the very sensitive field of coordination and surveillance of the economic and monetary policies of Member States when taken by a written procedure, Members of the College can only suspend such procedure after sending a reasoned request to the President of the Commission. That request should explicitly indicate the aspects of the draft decision to which it relates, based on an impartial and objective assessment of the timing, structure, reasoning or result of the proposed decision.[68] Finally, it is worth mentioning the Commission decision

[64] See European Commission document COM(2016) 627 final of 28 September 2016.

[65] See, eg, judgment of the CJEU of 6 April 2000 in Case C-287/95 P *Solvay v Commission* EU:C:2000:189.

[66] Arts 23(4) and 13–15 of the European Commission rules of procedure.

[67] Arts 13–15 of the European Commission rules of procedure.

[68] Art 12(5) of the European Commission rules of procedure.

on a Code of Conduct for the Members of the Commission adopted in 2018[69] and the guidelines on ethical standards for the participation of the Members of the Commission in the campaign for the European elections, issued by the President of the Commission in 2019.[70] These instruments set or clarify standards in relation to such issues as transparency, conflicts of interests, collegiality, discretion, integrity, external activities, participation in national and European politics, post-term activities and confers an advisory role and a power of recommendation to the Independent Ethical Committee, the members of which are selected for their competence, experience, independence and professional qualities.[71]

## Conclusions

Legitimacy is a virtue, which political institutions and the decisions – about laws, policies, and candidates for political office – made within them, need to have in order to justify their existence. Judging the European Commission on its legitimacy requires that one acknowledges the originality of its construct. Unique are its various sources of legitimacy, the great variety of powers conferred to it and the manifold norms and mechanisms to enforce them in order to ensure a proper level of accountability for the way the Commission exercises these powers. According to Max Weber, that a political regime is legitimate means that its participants have certain beliefs or faith ('*Legitimitätsglaube*') in regard to it: 'the basis of every system of authority, and correspondingly of every kind of willingness to obey, is a belief, a belief by virtue of which persons exercising authority are lent prestige'.[72] Considering the foregoing, it is submitted that in the unique political regime, created by the Treaties, there are, at least as regards the European Commission, sufficient checks and balances that should warrant such a belief. This doesn't mean they cannot be improved or refined, nor that a legitimate discussion can be held about the desirable degree of politicisation of the European Commission. But in pursuing that debate, one should always remain mindful of the history and *rationale* of the institutional set-up of the EU. The essence is that due to the unique constellation of big and small Member States, of converging and diverging interests, a choice has been made to create an equilibrium between first two, then three institutions. On this basis, repeated choices could be made between actions

[69] Commission Decision of 31 January 2018 on a Code of Conduct for Members of the European Commission (Document C(2018) 700 final).

[70] Communication from the President to the Commission of 6 February 2019: Elections to the European Parliament 2019 (23–26 May 2019) – Guidelines on ethical standards for participation of the Members of the European Commission in the election campaign (Document C(2019) 990 final).

[71] PJ Kuijper, 'Missteps by Commissioners: Legal or Political Sanctions?' in F Amtenbrink, G Davies, D Kochenov and J Lindeboom (eds), *The Internal Market and the Future of the European Integration: Essays in Honour of Laurence W Gormley* (Cambridge, Cambridge University Press, 2019).

[72] See M Weber, *The Theory of Social and Economic Organization*, Talcott Parsons (ed) (New York, Free Press, 1964) 382.

on a supranational, intergovernmental or national level. The political balance was originally between Council and Commission. The third political institution, which joined as an independent actor at a much later stage, is the European Parliament.[73] This development was more or less linear until the 1973 enlargement. After that, it went in fits and starts. Gradually and certainly after the 2004 enlargement, the role of the institutions have been more and more criticised and are sometimes even put into question.[74] Here particularly the Commission is in a sensitive position due to a lacking awareness of the Commission's essential role in bridging differences between big and small, north and south, east and west, an eminently political task.

[73] See J Priestley, *Six Battles that Shaped Europe's Parliament* (London, John Harper, 2008).

[74] See, eg, J-C Piris' very critical assessment of the Commission and his radical proposals to reform it under different scenarios: J-C Piris, *The Future of Europe – Towards a Two-Speed EU?* (Cambridge, Cambridge University Press, 2012) 25–31. He strongly regrets the fact that so far no use has been made of the possibility offered by Art 17(5) TEU, introduced by the Lisbon Treaty, to reduce the number of members of the Commission, claiming it affects the credibility of its action. During the 2004 IGC leading to the Lisbon Treaty many delegations argued, however, that ensuring one Commissioner per Member State allows the Commission to better fulfil its unique task of first weighing different national and other interests before deciding, by simple majority of its Members (Art 250 TFEU), how to serve the general interest in the sense of Art 17(1) TEU.

# 11

# The Accidental Democracy: A European Model

MARÍA JOSÉ MARTÍNEZ IGLESIAS*

## A Personal Introduction to Democratic Deficit

When I started working, as a young administrator, for the institutions of what was then the European Community in the mid-1980s, the concept of democratic deficit was omnipresent. Democratic deficit was the Achilles' heel of the European project's political legitimation. At that time, which now seems so distant, this concept was easy to define and undoubtedly and appropriately depicted the reality. It was, though, also related to a positive narrative, that of promoting the transformation of the Community in a democracy, similar to those of the Member States (then only 12): the progress in the construction of Europe could then only lead to the transformation of the institutional framework in the light of more or less adapted forms of constitutional and representative democracy, putting an end to this democratic deficit.

The democratic deficit was then perceived as the result of the transfer of Member States' competences to 'Brussels'. Such competences were exercised at the national level by parliaments, but once they were transferred to the European Community, they started to fall within the decision-making sphere of the governments in their role as members of the Council of Ministers, the institution that exercised the Community's legislative[1] power. The democratic deficit arose therefore, as viewed in pure national terms, due to a shift of power from the legislature (at national level) to the executive (at Community level) creating an imbalance in terms of the classical theory of separation of powers. The national governments

* The views presented in this chapter are those of the author alone and do not represent an official position of the Legal Service of the European Parliament.

[1] The terms 'legislative' or 'legislation' are used in the present chapter in a very large meaning, corresponding to 'norm' or 'rule' in general.

acquired the competences of the national Parliaments through the transfer of Member State competences to the European Community.

Later on, the regions with legislative powers, in particular the German Länder, added their particular point of view to the concept. They were also affected by this democratic deficit since, through the transfer of powers to the European Community, the central government exercised powers within the Council, which were theirs at the national level. Hence the creation of the Committee of the Regions and, above all, the possibility of the presence of regional ministers in the Council, which was introduced by the Treaty of Maastricht.

The problem of the democratic deficit, defined purely in terms of parliamentary power and therefore of representative democracy, appeared, at least in theory, easy to resolve. Enhancing the role of the European Parliament, an institution directly elected by the citizens, would suffice. If the Parliament became a real legislature capable of compensating and balancing the decision-making power of the Council, the deficit would evaporate and, thanks to that, the Community would become a fully democratically legitimised political union.

Thirty years later, the European Parliament fully co-decides with the Council on most of the Union's policies. In fact, the generalisation of co-decision, which very appropriately has now become the 'ordinary' legislative procedure, together with the qualified majority voting in the Council, have accompanied the tremendous increase in the Union's competences during the last three decades. Furthermore, the legal order of the Union has been transformed and various mechanisms of a clearly constitutional nature have been incorporated into the Treaties as basic elements of the Union's political system, such as the principles of representative democracy, the citizenship of the Union and the Charter of Fundamental Rights with binding legal force, to name but a few. Even the national parliaments have found their place in the European constitutional framework.

However, the democratic deficit still casts its shadow over the Union, even if nobody nowadays seems to know exactly what it means. There are those who use the concept as an argument for improving the Union through deeper integration and those who employ it to the exact opposite, to show that the Union will never be able to replace the Member States, which are in possession of the monopoly of democratic legitimacy. Moreover, never before has the rejection of the European Union been so widespread and voting turnout so low, as to make it seem that the process of European construction is not as irreversible as many of us thought. Additionally, the idea that 'Brussels' is a pure bureaucracy without a soul or conscience and, above all, a technocracy without democratic legitimacy, has become a widespread idea of dangerous banality. Why is that so? What has happened with the perception of the Union? Moreover, is it really true that the European Union fails the test of democratic legitimacy? All of this deserves and is, in fact, the subject of countless reflections and discussions, to which I dare to contribute with some thoughts resulting from my experience as a witness to the transformations that have taken place in the Union in recent years.

## The Representative and Parliamentary System: Large Majorities and Consensus

The Union's institutional structure is reminiscent of that of any representative democracy, particularly as regards the legitimacy of the decision-making process. The Union's legislature today consists of two chambers, the Council, which is based on the logic of indirect and territorial representation, and the European Parliament, which is the result of the direct vote of its citizens. This structure is still quite similar to those we have seen over the last two centuries in many states and, in any case, in those which are part of the Union.

As a general rule, the Council expresses its will by qualified majority. It is important to emphasise this, because in the gradual expansion of qualified majority voting we have one of the elements that radically differentiates the Union from traditional international organisations. Its generalisation as the basic rule of decision-making in the Council distances the Union from the scope of international law. Furthermore, the spread of qualified majority voting is, in my opinion, a factor of democratic legitimacy and, above all, a symptom of political maturity.

Majority voting as a form of expression of political will is not an obvious idea. It presupposes a sophisticated conceptual development of the social body to which it is related. Indeed, to move from unanimous to majority decision-making means to give recognition to the very existence of the social body, as something different from and transcending the parts that make it up. Majority decision coincides with the very birth of political society.[2] The will of one part becomes the will of the whole. In a way, majority decision-making corresponds to a political or even parliamentary logic in relation to unanimity, which in turn, corresponds to a contractual logic.

It is not surprising, therefore, that the move towards the political integration of the Union has been paralleled by the extension of the number of areas in which decisions are taken by [qualified] majority to the point of becoming the general voting rule in the Council under the Treaty of Lisbon. Such a majority in the Union has particular characteristics and the first of these is its definition. Whenever unanimity is not required by the Treaties, the majority in the Council

[2] Coming back to the origins of political science, one cannot but quote Locke for whom the mere existence of a political commonwealth was founded on the majoritarian principle. 'And thus every Man, by consenting with others to make one Body Politick under one Government, puts himself under an Obligation to every one of that Society, to submit to the determination of the majority, and to be concluded by it; or else this original Compact, whereby he with others incorporates into one Society, would signify nothing, and be no Compact, if he be left free, and under no other ties, than he was in before in the State of Nature'. J Locke, 'Two Treatises of Government. First Treaty. Ch VIII "Of the Beginning of Political Societies" in P Laslett (ed), *Cambridge Texts in the History of Political Thought* (Cambridge, Cambridge University Press, 1988). Always in the contractualist zone, see L Hobbes, 'Of the Causes, Generation, and Definition of a Common-wealth' in R Tuck (ed), *Cambridge Texts in the History of Political Thought* (Cambridge, Cambridge University Press, 1996).

is always qualified,[3] which constitutes a peculiarity from the point of view of classical constitutionalism where simple majority prevails. A peculiarity which can be understood in the context of federal systems where not only demographic but also territorial elements must be taken into account (such as in the Union). However, the breadth[4] of the majority required in the Union in relation to both criteria is the product of a great imbalance in representation. In a double majority system (of citizens and states) such as ours, which in fact is nothing but a more visible formulation of the system of weighted voting (more common in federal systems), there is a strong recognition of the state component. Each Member State has the same weight in calculating the territorial side of the majority. In our case, it means giving the same weight to Germany, with its 81 million inhabitants, as to Malta, which has 425,000 inhabitants. This dramatic disproportion, only partially compensated by the demographic side of the equation, is unparalleled in any federal system. The consequence is the very large majority required for decision-making in the Council, but also the fact that the double majority system is complemented by safety nets in terms of the composition of the minority capable of blocking a decision. The extremely varied dimension of the Member States' population constitutes in fact a major difficulty in terms of democratic representation.

Moreover, we must not forget that in such a disproportionate situation, unanimity appears to be the most undemocratic system possible, once a certain amount of competences have been transferred to the Union. Unanimity means in fact the possibility that the representation of a ridiculously small proportion of citizens can veto a decision. Unanimity is anti-democratic for the Union in terms of efficiency as well. Maintaining transferred competences under the unanimity rule usually means paralysis, which is why, as action became necessary at Union level on a certain issue, the development towards qualified majority immediately followed.[5] Given that the legitimacy of the Union is measured more in terms of results than in terms of foundational or patriotic membership, maintaining unanimity in certain areas of action is a heavy burden for the Union.

The game of majorities is simpler or, if preferred, more classic, in the European Parliament, although the disproportion in representation is still significant.[6] However, the real specificity of the European Parliament in relation to the national parliaments is its fragmentation, which results in unpredictability. The European Parliament is organised into political groups which, although they have been evolving towards greater homogeneity, still suffer from a lack of political identity and,

[3] With the further exception of three legal bases according to which the Council votes by a simple majority of Members.

[4] 55% of the members of the Council representing at least 65% of the population of the Union when acting on a proposal from the Commission; otherwise 72% of the members of the Council representing 65% of the population.

[5] Nowhere is this phenomenon so evident as in the evolution of the areas of freedom, security and justice.

[6] The proportion varies from one Member of the European Parliament for more or less 850,000 inhabitants to one MEP for 70,000 inhabitants.

above all, from a lack of the voting discipline which usually characterises political groups or parties at national level. That situation makes constant negotiation unavoidable with no result being ever guaranteed, no matter who the rapporteur or other protagonist of the decision making process are or whichever the political commitments of one or other political group.

The two phenomena, the requirement of large majorities in the Council combined with the fragmentation in the European Parliament, have historically given rise to a strong culture of negotiation and consensus. Moreover, the practice of all decision-making procedures, influenced by the co-decision procedure, lead to negotiation and consensus. In fact, the Council does not often vote.[7] Consensus is systematically sought, a consensus that would, of course, be much more difficult to achieve if unanimity were required, majority vote acting as an excellent incentive for the search for and obtainment of consensus.

There are those who consider that this culture of consensus is one of the weakest points of the Union's political system. According to some, it makes the institutions appear monolithic, distancing them from the understanding of the citizens who are accustomed to a higher level of political struggle at the national level. They see the permanent search for consensus as a symptom of the non-existence of a European political space. Moreover, they think that it would only be possible to bring Europe closer to its citizens by recreating at the Union level the national model of political confrontation.

I do not believe that the political fight resulting from the struggle between a government supported by a parliamentary majority and a minority opposition, which antagonise in every vote, is a strictly necessary element of constitutional democracy. The ultimate goal of a political system is effectiveness in decision-making through the expression of the general will. There are many examples of scrupulously democratic countries where consensus is the usual mode of political action, Switzerland being perhaps the most characteristic instance. Our outlook of political life is surprisingly too influenced by the thesis defended by Carl Schmitt which identifies politics with struggle tinged with drama. I do not think there is any objective reason to believe that legitimate political decision-making cannot be the result of dialogue, negotiation and possibly consensus, methods that we all defend with strong conviction in other areas of social life.

## Legitimacy Through Knowledge and Impartiality

Legitimacy in constitutional democracies is not limited to political representation. All states know to a greater or lesser extent, with greater or lesser powers, institutions whose legitimacy is based on factors such as knowledge,

[7] See JP Jacqué, 'Le vote majoritaire au Conseil de l'Union européenne' in F Picod (ed), *Le principe majoritaire en droit de l'Union européenne* (Brussels, Bruylant, 2016).

specialisation or impartiality. The contribution of these institutions is essential to the overall balance of the distribution of powers between the institutions of the state. The system of checks and balances and mutual scrutiny and accountability is essential to the type of constitutional democracy consolidated after the Second World War.

Within the architecture of the European Union, that type of institution plays a particularly important role, starting with the European Commission. Indeed, the first sentence of Article 17 of the Treaty of the European Union (TEU) lays down that:

> The Commission shall promote the general interest of the Union and take appropriate initiatives to that end. It shall ensure the application of the Treaties, and of measures adopted by the institutions pursuant to them. It shall oversee the application of Union law.

This is the genuine mission of the Commission as 'Guardian of the Treaties'. Furthermore, paragraph 3 of the same provision reinforces the independent character of the Commission's mission by stating that, 'The members of the Commission shall be chosen on the ground of their general competence and European commitment from persons whose independence is beyond doubt. In carrying out its responsibilities, the Commission shall be completely independent'.

According to the Treaties, the Commission is not the executive[8] of the Union and neither is it a government like those of parliamentary regimes. The Commission is first and foremost an arbiter and that is the reason why it has privileges in relation to the decision-making procedure of the Union that would be inconceivable in the government of a democratic state. Its interference with the powers of the legislature would radically run counter to the principle of separation of powers if the Union were a classical constitutional democracy.

Indeed, the Commission has the monopoly over legislative initiative. The importance of this prerogative is not only derived from being the only institution that can propose legislation and initiate the decision-making process. In fact, albeit to a very limited extent, other 'technical' institutions such as the Court of Justice or the European Central Bank or even a limited number of countries may also do so. What is exorbitant about the Commission's power of initiative is its ability to change the majority required in the Council to adopt a proposal: if a proposal is not submitted by the Commission, the super-qualified majority of Article 238(3)(b)[9] must be attained in the Council. Furthermore, any amendment to a proposal, which is not approved by the Commission, can only be adopted by unanimity in the Council, which is also the case when such an amendment has been proposed and adopted by the European Parliament. All this without forgetting that the Commission may at any time alter or suspend the Union's

[8] See Art 191 TFEU.
[9] See above n 4.

legislative procedure beyond the will of the legislator by amending or withdrawing its proposal.

This power to intervene in the legislative procedure gives the Commission a role that would be inconceivable if it were a national government in a political regime respectful of the principle of separation of powers. It derives precisely from the Commission's particular position as 'Guardian of the Treaties', as defender of the common interest, as arbiter between the particular interests of Member States or political groups, as mediator between the priorities of Member States, large or small. This power is ultimately justified by its mission as an independent, impartial and authoritative body.

This special role of the Commission is the reason why the politicisation of the European Commission through the so-called *Spitzenkandidaten* process, may be viewed with some perplexity, even if this is one of the most popular 'constitutional' initiatives of the last years in the Brussels environment. Such an initiative could modify in an unexpected way the inter-institutional balance and, for this reason, deserves a deeper reflection on its consequences for the Union architecture.

It is true, though, that politicisation cannot, for the time being, go beyond securing the consensus of Parliament in the election of the President of the Commission. The margin of manoeuvre of the President-designate and that of the European Parliament[10] in the formation of the College is in practice restrained. The candidate members, one national from each Member State, are proposed by the governments themselves and they have to secure a qualified majority in the Council which traditionally acts by consensus in this matter. This ultimately means that political parties in government in the Member States will be represented and the alleged politicisation can only be very limited.

What is certain is that this *Spitzenkandidaten* procedure for the election of the President of the Commission, which aims to improve the visibility of the electoral campaign in the European elections by stimulating the political debate in a confrontational manner, may end up jeopardising the key role of the institution, that of arbiter and guarantor of the common interest, which is based precisely on its impartiality and independence.

The Commission is not the only institution which embodies the legitimacy of impartiality and knowledge in the Union. The European constitutional system is rich with such institutions. To begin with, the Court of Justice shall ensure, according to Article 19 TEU, that the law is respected in the interpretation and application

[10] The European Parliament at the end of the day will need to give its approval to the college. Para 7 of Art 17 TEU stipulates that 'The Council, by common accord with the President-elect, shall adopt the list of the other persons whom it proposes for appointment as members of the Commission. They shall be selected, on the basis of the suggestions made by Member States, in accordance with the criteria set out in paragraph 3, second sub-paragraph, and paragraph 5, second sub-paragraph. The President, the High Representative of the Union for Foreign Affairs and Security Policy and the other members of the Commission shall be subject as a body to a vote of consent by the European Parliament. On the basis of this consent the Commission shall be appointed by the European Council, acting by a qualified majority'.

of the Treaties. Its members 'shall be chosen from persons whose independence is beyond doubt and who satisfy the conditions (which guarantee their expertise) set out in Articles 253 and 254 TFEU'. It is certainly not necessary to insist on the historical role that the Court has played as the guarantor of legal certainty. A role that significantly reinforces the effectiveness and the predictability of the Union's legal system and by that, the legitimacy of the political system.

Along with the Court of Justice, mention must be made of the Court of Auditors, the European Central Bank, the European Ombudsman, the European Data Protection Supervisor, the future European Public Prosecutor Office, the Fundamental Rights Agency, etc. All these institutions and organs contribute to the overall 'checks and balances' architecture in the Union from a position characterised by independence and technical expertise guaranteed by appointment and operating procedures that ensure impartiality. Some of them are invested with an authoritativeness that civil society sometimes places above elected political representatives.

## Elements of Constitutionalism

If anything has characterised Western constitutional democracies since the Second World War, it has been the limitation of the exercise of power. The German fundamental law of 1949, which has served as a model for many of the more recent constitutions, is characterised by the will to protect the integrity of the political system and the rights of citizens from (ephemeral) parliamentary majorities. Parliaments (the legislature) are no longer the omnipotent and omniscient repositories of popular sovereignty. The legislator, like all the powers of the state, must abide by the constitution and the fundamental principles and rights recognised therein, independent judicial bodies guaranteeing all of which. That is the very essence of the rule of law, as we understand it today.

Ultimately, this is the framework that surrounds the legal and institutional architecture of the Union. From a purely international treaty that could not but rigidly frame the common institutions in the exercise of a very limited number of transferred competences, the system has evolved towards a peculiar constitutional framework, albeit one that features the basic elements that define modern constitutionalism.

First, the institutions and, more specifically, the legislature, see their powers delimited by a fundamental law (the Treaties) which requires unanimity of the Member States in order to be amended. This fundamental or constitutional law contains the objectives and values underlying the Union's action and the fundamental principles governing the distribution of competences between the Union and the Member States, the exercise of those competences, the establishment, composition and definition of powers of the institutions through decision-making procedures, and the recognition of citizens' rights, either directly in the Treaty or through the Charter of Fundamental Rights.

Secondly, the European constitutional framework establishes a system of checks and balances in which not only the institutions and bodies of the Union participate. Indeed, the Member States are also part of the legal-institutional framework to the point of being the main depositaries of the executive power, of course, under the control of the respective parliaments and the European Commission.

Finally, the protection of Fundamental Rights, which puts the individual and not just the citizen at the centre of the Union's action, together with a judicial system, built on the interaction between the national judge and the Court of Justice of the Union and able to guarantee legal certainty, complete the constitutional framework of the European Union.

## A Complex and Evolving Institutional Structure

It is true that the Union lacks that 'foundational' or 'constituent' moment, which is the complement of the patriotic loyalty that has long characterised the political link between citizens and a territory that defines itself as a state. It is also true that the Union has not ceased to transform itself almost from the very beginning, but especially in the last three decades, which have seen the entry into force of five new treaties. All of them have brought about significant changes, the Treaties of Maastricht and Lisbon being of particular note, as they have meant real revolutions for the Union.

This permanent transformation has, in my view, negative consequences for citizens' perception of the Union. Every time a new treaty is negotiated, the structure, the functioning, the relative weight of the Member States, the policies and the very existence of the European project are put into question before public opinion.[11] This continuous change prevents, for better or worse, the citizens from looking at and evaluating the European phenomenon with a sense of stability. Perhaps that is why we always use words like 'project' or 'construction' to refer to the European Union, as something that is not finished, whose existence is not precisely defined, and which we could live without, as we did until not so long ago.

Such permanent change and perpetual debate magnify in the eyes of the citizens the complexity of the European institutional system. However, is the Union really that complex? Is complexity necessarily negative? I do not believe that the constitutional framework of the European Union, compared both with any of its Member States and with international organisations, is so terribly complex. Yet, it is true that it is peculiar, original, different from the traditional state's political structure with which we are all familiar (although ultimately national constitutions are often equally unknown for most citizens). Nor do I believe that complexity is necessarily a defect. Governance of interdependence, which is what

[11] The failed referendums prove the stress through which the Union goes because of the permanent reforms.

the Union is after all concerned with, in itself, cannot be simple. Just like the systems of government of democratic countries in general and of large federal states in particular are themselves complex structures. In any case, ignorance generates mistrust, so whether it is true or not, whether it is necessary or not, the reputation of complexity that accompanies the Union is a very important delegitimising factor that is magnified, I repeat, by the permanent debate on the structure and functioning, the objectives, the competences and the European legal framework.

## Democratic Software: Other Governance Tools

The European institutions are well aware of the detachment of the citizens and of the lack of recognition of their legitimacy. Their political horizon is the nation state. That is the model with which they compare themselves, in the hope of awakening the same kind of citizens' commitment. In my opinion, this comparison is unjustified, and yet the resulting frustration is manifested, among other things, by an unusual focus on governance instruments such as those that are part of the Better Law-Making agenda.[12]

In the first place, one should mention the institutions' endeavour to guarantee the good quality of the decisions taken by the Union from a technical point of view, using all the means at their disposal. This category includes instruments such as impact assessments, stakeholder consultations, ex-post evaluation of existing legislation, etc. They also seek to improve the democratic quality of the decision-making process and this is why close attention is given to broad public consultation, to the application of the principle of subsidiarity or to dialogue with and information to national parliaments.

In practice, Better Law-Making instruments are also used to fine-tune the balance between the institutions. A clear example of this is the importance given to both annual and multi-annual programming, which is, in my opinion, mostly an instrument to compensate for the legislator's lack of legislative initiative by influencing politically the Commission's planning. The Interinstitutional Agreement on Better Law-Making allows for the three institutions to compromise on political priorities, calendars, legal basis, impact assessments, ex-post evaluation etc in relation to the future legal acts of the Union. In this way, the Commission accepts having its power of legislative initiative framed.

Legislative planning for the EU institutions is also a palliative to deal with the political instability caused by national elections. The perspective of regular electoral appointments, which encourages the tendency for short-term vision and

[12] All the Commissions from Delors' time have had their respective better law-making or smart regulation or good governance agendas, to which we can add the two inter-institutional agreements between the European Parliament, the Council and the Commission.

solutions, conditions government action in national states. Imagine now the challenge for the Union in developing long-term strategies, considering 28 election dates (although clearly not all of them are of equal importance).

This predilection for the instruments of good governance is also the consequence of a deep concern for the resulting product of the Union's action. The Union, which, as I said before, does not automatically generate patriotic support from the citizens, is justified mainly by its results. The European Union is expected to solve problems. It is its ability to deliver which, in the eyes of the citizens, actually justifies and legitimises it. The European Union was expected to solve the financial crisis, is asked to solve the refugee crisis, in the same way that states emerging from a dictatorship expected the Union to guarantee democracy. The Union needs to produce results in order to legitimise itself and, essentially, to survive. In this respect, the Union could be seem in unfair competition with Member States whose very existence does not depend on their effectiveness. Moreover, legitimacy purely based on results can only produce an unstable adhesion.

A final thought in relation to these instruments of democratic software concerns transparency. If there is one unfair criticism of the European Union, it is that of opacity. Both the Treaties and secondary legislation together with inter-institutional agreements or codes of conduct actually make the Union a model for the majority of Member States. Transparency is, within the framework of contemporary democracy, the indispensable instrument of accountability. Representation only makes sense if it is possible to scrutinise the use made of the mandate received from the citizens. In this context, transparency makes a very important contribution to the profile of European democracy.

Ultimately, the main goal and, in my opinion, also the result of the Better Law-Making instruments, is accountability. All those instruments actually make the EU institutions accountable to citizens to a degree that few Member States have reached. Unfortunately, as in other aspects of the action of the Union it seems that here, public perception is not following.

## The Nation State as Role Model?

Throughout the previous pages, I have made numerous references or comparisons to the nation states. This is not because I believe that the reference for the Union should be the state neither that the Union should become a state nor reproduce the structure of a state. The Union is clearly not an international organisation, but neither is it, and nor should it be, a state.

The question that must really be asked is not so much whether or not the Union should become a state but rather a constitutional democracy, which is perfectly possible outside the state model.

I will begin by contradicting a widespread belief, that of the state monopoly on democracy. I will cite as an example with very serious consequences, the reiterated positions of some constitutional courts, such as the German which, when considering the position of the Union's law in relation to national law, build on the idea that democracy can only be achieved within the national framework. Many authors have argued against this idea and I join them.[13] It is true that democracy as we know it has developed in parallel and within the nation state. It is also true that it is in this sphere, of the nation state, that democracy has been betrayed with enthusiasm, on the basis, precisely, of nationalistic values.

Democracy reduced to national level is not possible any longer, mainly because of two phenomena, the effects of which globalisation has increased. To begin with, we can observe that many of the decisions taken within the constitutional order of a country have inevitable repercussions for other states without any kind of participation on the part of the latter. If that constitutes a serious limit for democratic legitimacy, even more important is the lack of real capacity to make effective decisions in a globalised world. The example of the recent financial crisis eloquently proves this. It is not the influence or existence of the 'demos' that is put into question but rather that of the 'cratos'. The classic definitions of sovereignty that, like those of Bodin or Hobbes, emphasised its character of absolute, indivisible, incontestable and independent, perpetual power,[14] have been devoid of meaning by the contemporary world. The power of any state, even the mightiest, has become relative, dependent, interrelated, questionable, temporary.

The consequence, as Habermas points out,[15] is the inevitability of shared democracy. There is no alternative to a shared management of interdependence and this is only possible through the European Union. His concept of 'constitutional patriotism' as an adherence to common values and principles, beyond patriotism as an emotional link to a territory, is a conceptual alternative that can serve as a basis for a new constitutional pact in Europe.

Habermas' conclusion is proved by the universally accepted system of Fundamental Rights. Faced with the commitment to Human Rights Declarations, either of a constitutional or international nature, there is no room for an exclusive democracy, which would privilege citizenship over the universal concept of the human being. Since the first Declaration in the eighteenth century, universalism has necessarily accompanied respect for fundamental rights.

Today, the isolated nation state is not a viable democratic alternative. In addition to the above-mentioned phenomenon of international interdependence, there is a crisis of concepts, values and, above all, of methods. The methods, the procedure, the means by which an objective is achieved are indeed essential in our conception of democracy. It is by them that the quality of the democratic system is judged. In that context, the political crisis of national democracies is also the consequence

[13] J Habermans, *La Constitution de l'Europe* (Paris, Gallimard, 2011); D Innerarity, *La democracia en Europa* (Barcelona, Galaxia Gutenberg, 2017).

[14] Jean Bodin's definition of sovereignty: 'La souveraineté est la puissance absolue et perpétuelle d'une république'.

[15] J Habermans, *Après l'État-nation, une nouvelle constellation politique* (Paris, Librarie Arthème Fayard/Pluriel, 2013).

of the technological revolution, which is radically transforming knowledge and communication. The traditional methods of political deliberation are under pressure as a result of the clash between the new ways characterised by immediacy and anonymity and the classic process based on representation and accountability. By this, I do not mean that only the methods or procedures already consolidated are legitimate, but that it is still necessary for the new forms of participation to mature.

My conclusion is that the European Union represents an opportunity to improve democracy (or even to save it). The fact is that we have only known democracy linked to the nation state, but neither democracy nor the nation state, which appear to us today as natural phenomena, have existed for more than 200 years. I recall here Tocqueville's reflection in *Democracy in America* that it was only with the greatest possible openness of spirit and without prejudice that a phenomenon then as novel and unprecedented as the American Constitution and political system could be understood. The European evolution should be contemplated with that same 'état d'esprit'.

It is undeniable that the European Union possesses its own strong elements of democratic legitimacy. Maybe the real democratic deficit lies in our narrative about democracy, which is too narrow to integrate developments as the European Union itself. Therefore, we need a theory of democracy free of those elements which are a traditional, but yet not an essential part of it (sovereignty, territoriality, homogeneity or state form, for instance). Of course, there is room for improvement; the Union should and can do better and, in particular, should communicate better. Nevertheless, I am convinced that, building on national crisis, a new model of democracy suited to the European Union can be devised, based on its own needs and peculiar history and on delimitation of power, balance between the different sources of legitimacy, representation and accountability. There is no other viable alternative in order to achieve democracy for Europeans.

# 12

# Democratic Participation and Transparency of the EU Council

LEO HOFFMANN-AXTHELM

## Introduction

The EU democratic deficit debate is an old one. As countries come together and form a new layer of governance, it is only natural that decision-making becomes further removed from the citizen, and that a larger number of citizens and at times entire countries will inevitably find themselves on the losing side of any given argument.

At the same time, this very debate has led to constant improvements in the transparency and accountability of EU institutions, with steadily expanding powers for the European Parliament which has today developed far beyond similar experiments with parliamentary assemblies, for example, in the Council of Europe or the North Atlantic Treaty Organization. Unlike those assemblies, the European Parliament has been able to expand its hard-power competences in each round of EU Treaty reform, adding a dimension of democratic legitimacy to the European level, and enabling a directly elected institution to hold the executive to account at the European level.

Between the European Commission and the Parliament, the accountability problem was fairly straightforward: a supranational bureaucracy far-removed from the citizen, which was growing ever more powerful and required a proportionate improvement in its oversight. Democratic accountability for supranational institutions and intergovernmental rules and agreements is a classic problem, and increasing transparency while raising accountability to the same governance level at which decisions are taken is the classic solution.

Nonetheless, the debate of the democratic deficit has not disappeared, and quite on the contrary, we find ourselves faced with an unprecedented backlash against multilateralism in general and European integration in particular, with Eurosceptic governments left and right, and growing anti-establishment parties everywhere else.

## Democracy, Accountability, Transparency, Participation

Democratic standards have evolved, and an election every so many years is clearly insufficient. Various political streams have attempted to take mistrust of authorities on board by advancing elements of direct democracy, at the local, regional and national levels. But using referendums to increase citizen participation is not the same as evading political responsibility by dumping difficult decisions on the electorate. The Brexit referendum was the worst of examples: trying to solve an internal party dispute by taking a gamble on British EU membership, with Brexit imagined as so atrocious an outcome that voters could not possibly fall for it. But when you spend decades blaming Brussels for every wrong under the sun, one should not be surprised if people believe you.

An exhaustive and conclusive body of research[1] also clearly warns against the tendency of both left and right to overestimate the legitimacy of transient electoral outcomes. Illiberal democracy is the dictatorship of the majority; liberal democracy on the other hand should recognise the inherent limits of electoral outcomes, with constitutions placing additional hurdles in the way of those that garner a majority, including checks and balances via the separation of powers across the branches of government (horizontal) and federal entities (vertical).

In view of the very limited impact of any individual vote, it would indeed be a disproportionate effort on the part of voters to get up to speed with the workings of the entire political system; and in the name of the division of labour, it makes sense that not all citizens have to understand the workings of regional, national and EU government. At the same time, the political system works much better when more people vote, as abstentionism risks bolstering the extremes and breeds apathy. It can also be argued that the 'political class' is entitled to receive at least a general indication as to the direction the country should be going in – again, without declaring an electoral outcome sacrosanct just because the gerrymandering of electoral districts was successful enough to garner this or that outcome. Once legislative checks and media freedom are removed, it becomes a lot harder to restore a fair electoral contest, as we can observe in Hungary and Poland, and perhaps soon in Austria too.[2]

If elections for democratic representatives and attempts with direct democracy are insufficient, participative democracy and the empowerment of professional civil society is a sure-fire way to increase scrutiny of the exercise of political power and improve policy outcomes, thereby bolstering input and output legitimacy. It is not a surprise that illiberal regimes everywhere move decisively to curtail political space and funding for non-governmental organisations (NGOs). But whether this civil society participation is (supposedly) happening in the name of the 'public

[1] B Wittes and J Rauch, 'More Professionalism, Less Populism: How Voting Makes Us Stupid, and What to do About it' (Brookings Institution, May 2017).

[2] 'Interior Minister Kickl instructs police to 'limit communication' with critical media' (*TheLocal.at*, 25 September 2018).

good' or in the (increasingly concealed)[3] pursuit of private profit interests, it is clear that participative democracy requires not just transparency (and predictability) of policy processes and access to decision-makers. It also requires transparency about that very participation.

Particular interests have a much easier time organising themselves than the general interest does. If you stand to profit greatly from a particular legislative act, investing even millions in lobbying may pay off handsomely. The balance of lobbyists varies greatly by policy field – on the environment, the European Commission meets as many civil society representatives as industry lobbyists. On the digital economy, the balance is rather 90 per cent industry and 10 per cent NGOs. We know this because the Commission has, under President Juncker, embarked on the highest level of transparency of lobby meetings of any central government authority in the world, committing to meet only lobbyists registered on the EU Transparency Register, and to disclose meetings (and topics discussed) for Directors-General, Commissioners and their Cabinets. While this excludes the (often crucial) desk officers who are the pen-holders on a given file, and Heads of Unit and Directors, it is remarkable progress. Tools such as Transparency International EU's Integrity Watch allow citizens, academics and journalists to quantify meetings by topic, company, Commission DG, issue area, and to check on topics discussed.[4]

For any healthy democracy, this kind of access is crucial – *if* the integrity of the political process is preserved by allowing journalists and watchdogs to probe, without disproportionate effort, what interests influenced any given legislation, and how, thereby preventing political capture. This is not an ideological matter, or at least shouldn't be. If Volkswagen wrote the amendments for a law on emissions, and a particular MEP copied and pasted them, and lobbied for their approval, then voters have a right to know. This is why Juncker's promise of a *compulsory* EU Transparency Register was set to exclude any meetings with unregistered lobbyists, and was set to bind not only the European Commission, but also all MEPs and, crucially, the Council of the EU. After years languishing in inter-institutional negotiations, it is clear that the Council has no intention of joining the register, increasing transparency of lobby activities, or even disclosing the positions that individual governments have on legislative files (or their position on the issue of a Transparency Register, for that matter). The Council merely offered to exclude meeting unregistered lobbyists for the Permanent Representative of the country holding the rotating Council presidency, during the presidency and the preceding six months. This would have entailed Permanent Representations applying the Transparency Register once every 14 years.

While the European Commission has increased transparency, and while the European Parliament has strengthened its link to European citizens while expanding its ability to hold EU institutions to account, the Council is glaringly absent from improvements to the EU's democratic legitimacy.

[3] *cf* 'astroturfing'.
[4] See: www.integritywatch.eu.

## The Council of the EU: A Black Box?

The Council is notoriously difficult to pin down. Accountability starts with name recognition, and even within the EU machinery, hacks routinely mash up the Council of the EU and the European Council. While this may not be entirely its fault, the Council of the EU sounds awfully similar to the Council of Europe, and is often called Council of Ministers to differentiate it from the European Council, which groups EU Heads of State and Government and has been recognised as a separate institution since the Lisbon Treaty entered into force in 2009. Both institutions share a building and a logo, but not the presidency (the European Council has had a permanent President since 2009, while the Council of the EU continues to have a six-month rotating presidency that has exposed the standing of the institution to a bouquet of national corruption scandals in recent times).

The truth is, even avid news readers have difficulty telling one from the other, and may be forgiven for lumping everything together as 'Brussels'. But that would be a mistake. The fairest way to refer to the Council is to call participants what they are: the EU's national governments. Accountability starts with identifying who's in charge, and correctly assigning blame, after all.

Accountability also requires a clear idea of the role and composition of an institution. In legislative terms, the Council forms the upper chamber of the EU's legislature, and co-decides alongside the European Parliament. This resonates with (con-)federal systems elsewhere: the US Senate is composed of full-time representatives, but it gives an equal number of seats to each state, as representatives of states rather than citizens. The German Bundesrat (Germany's upper chamber, with the Bundestag as the lower) more closely emulates the EU model: here, too, the chamber is made up of the executives of the Länder, ie, the constitutive members of the Federal Republic.

But unlike the Länder's government representatives, the powerful national ministers don't see themselves as a mere legislative body when acting within the Council. And sure enough, on areas where the EU has no competence, the Council can operate on an intergovernmental model, even without consulting the Commission or the European Parliament, and take executive decisions (via different rules of procedure), for example, under the EU's Common Foreign and Security Policy. And of course, such decisions require greater secrecy and operate under drastically reduced transparency requirements.

In legislative terms too, the Council is not merely the ministers coming together to vote on laws. The Council is a huge legislative machinery that operates similarly to a parliament, with preparatory bodies instead of committees, and over 100 working groups churning out legislation in a level of detail that would be unthinkable in regular parliamentary bodies. These are populated by the diplomats and civil servants posted to Brussels from line-ministries from all Member States, that negotiate legislation line by line on the technical, political and ministerial level, until agreement is found. However, neither diplomats, nor civil servants from national ministries, are used to the transparency requirements of such blatantly political work. But the EU legislative process and the high stakes that come with it require drastically higher levels of transparency than, say, multilateral negotiations at the United Nations. Along with the expanding remit of EU regulation, the Council's legislative activity has now penetrated all areas of domestic policy-making, often with redistributive consequences and always with direct effect, and can therefore no longer be conducted in secrecy. The times when the Council was the sole decider on EU law, when Member State representatives struck gentlemen's agreements in a diplomatic setting, are long gone.

It is true that many Council discussions, in working parties in particular, may be of a more technical nature than classic parliamentary debates, and bringing Member States' expertise to the table is certainly one of the key additions of the Council to the EU legislative process. But the positions expressed and defended by civil servants in these settings are not purely technical. They represent interests of governments which were democratically elected to represent their citizens in accordance with a given political programme they publicly defended. Positions of Member States, at the technical as much as at the political level, are a continuation of the view defended by those governments.

The political nature of even the most technical discussions is obvious when Council representatives consider it natural to try and advance the national interest, rather than the optimal outcome for the EU as a whole. The mediation of the European Commission, itself usually intent on pushing more powers to the supranational level, and the generally more Europhile positions taken by the European Parliament, compete with these tendencies. But it is no surprise that the (EU) institution representing Member States would, as a general rule, defend national rather than EU interests.

Certainly, not all Council deliberations have to be conducted in public. But first steps would be to: (i) clearly state which working parties are working on which legislative files; (ii) make agendas of these meetings public ahead of time; and (iii) publish detailed results or minutes of meetings, clearly identifying the positions of all individual Member States that have taken the floor or made written contributions or even suggested amendments, including any scientific and socio-economic evidence presented.

But when it comes to the required level of transparency, precision is required. Clearly, the Council already publishes all kinds of information, has many public and even live-streamed sessions, maintains a document register and citizens have the right to petition release of these documents under the Regulation (EC) No 1049/2001 access to document regulation.[5] However, the fifteenth annual report on the implementation of Regulation 1049/2001 states that of the 4,500 legislative documents produced by the Council, less than half (1,955 documents) were 'public' (which does not mean they were published

[5] Regulation (EC) 1049/2001 of the European Parliament and of the Council of 30 May 2001 regarding public access to European Parliament, Council and Commission documents [2001] OJ L145/43 (ATD Regulation).

proactively, but rather that the public may petition for their release), while another 2,545 documents were issued as 'LIMITE'.[6] Regulation 1049/2001 foresees only very narrow exemptions from the requirement to publish legislative documents, leading the Dutch delegation of the Conference of Parliamentary Committees for Union Affairs of Parliaments of the European Union (COSAC) to affirm that the Council regularly violates EU transparency regulations. Contrary to the intention of the EU transparency legislation, transparency seems to be the exception rather than the rule.

The Council does publish the result and positions of Member States in the final votes on legislation. But this is a cosmetic type of transparency, given that the Council very rarely votes, preferring to patch up compromises that enable every delegation to give unanimous approval, and allows no conclusions as to which government pushed for which provision and compromise to be included. Similarly, the Council publishes its joint position in negotiations vis-a-vis the European Parliament, the so-called Common Approach, on any given legislative file, ie, the version of a draft law proposed by the Commission as amended by the Council via the mediation of the rotating Council presidency, before engaging in negotiations with the Parliament and the Commission to agree the final text of a regulation or directive (often in less-than-transparent so-called trilogue negotiations which are not even foreseen in the EU's Treaties).

But there's a hitch. The Common Approach is the amalgamated position that all 28 (or 27) EU governments could agree to. It allows no conclusions to be drawn on the individual position of any government. Voters back home have no way to vote out the Council as such, and governments cannot be held to account individually if voters back home do not know what substantive positions individual governments are taking in Council negotiations. *This has to be said clearly: citizens do not know what positions their national government is advocating 'in their name'.* It is therefore impossible for citizens to hold their government to account over their role in the EU-level legislative process. We still have to rely on insider information and leaks to find out which governments are, for example, blocking legislation on tax transparency and country-by-country reporting by multinational companies in the EU.[7]

This while legislative processes require a much higher standard of transparency than executive decisions, given that legislative processes do not produce one-off outcomes, but rather create laws that citizens will have to live with for years if not decades. The fact that national governments are members of the executive back home, while they are members of the legislature in Brussels, may make this 'cultural shift' difficult for ministers and diplomats. Nonetheless, we have to insist on the propriety of the legislative process, in line with the European Parliament's

[6] Transparency International EU submission to European Ombudsman strategic inquiry, OI/2/2017/TE.

[7] Tax Justice Network, 'Why is Germany siding with the tax havens against corporate transparency?' (13 July 2018).

demand that 'the Council, as one of the two components of the European legislature, aligns its working methods with the standards of a parliamentary democracy, rather than acting like a diplomatic forum'.[8]

Transparency is a right. The Treaty on the Functioning of the European Union (TFEU) in Article 15(1) stipulates that 'to promote good governance and ensure the participation of civil society, the Union's institutions, bodies, offices and agencies shall conduct their work as openly as possible'. It goes on to specify that 'when considering and voting on a draft legislative act', the Council shall meet in public (Article 15(2) TFEU). But in the practice of the Council, this only appears to be respected for ministers adopting final acts, rather than for the preparatory bodies thrashing out the actual compromises and legislation. In contrast, committees in Parliament meet publicly, not just the plenary that adopts the final version of a law. Granted, compromises are still brokered between political groups behind closed doors. Nonetheless, the public can always know the positions of MEPs and political groups, and is not presented with a final compromise shared by all political groups without any clue as to what positions one group or the other advocated for. Even if the Council does not see itself as merely the second chamber, the powerful role it plays would seem to raise the transparency standard citizens can expect of it.

Beyond citizens, national parliaments should also play a role in holding their governments to account. The record here is patchy: some parliaments take a much stronger interest in EU affairs, while the vast majority of parliaments do not have basic access to Council documents. German and Austrian Members of Parliament have access to diplomatic cables sent to their foreign ministries from Brussels Permanent Representations, including the reports from officials seconded from line ministries. This access was not granted by the government's will, however, but was enforced at the behest of a Constitutional Court judgment. Through a similar portal, the Austrian and Dutch parliaments also have access to Council documents, even confidential ones, but may not cite the documents, nor are they allowed to share the contents with experts or even their own staff to help them sift through the legislative machinery.

## Mounting Pressure

In a time of increasing Euroscepticism, the Council is coming under unprecedented pressure to finally apply the same standards of transparency and democratic accountability as any other EU institutions. In 2018, the Court of Justice of the EU (CJEU) ruled that documents from the secret 'trilogue' negotiations between the Council, Parliament and Commission should be made public.[9] As far back

[8] European Parliament's own initiative report 2018/2096(INI), 11 September 2018.
[9] Judgment of 22 March 2018 in Case T-540/15, *De Capitani v European Parliament* EU:C:2018:167.

as 2013, the Court ruled that in access to document requests, the Council should not be allowed to withhold the identities of Member States' substantive positions on legislative files.[10] Perversely, as a reaction to this judgment, Member States in a May 2014 Coreper meeting concluded that 'there was no legal obligation to record and identify the positions of individual Member States'. Coreper decided that Member States would be identified if deemed 'appropriate',[11] paving the way for an arbitrary system of recording Member State positions only when files are deemed uncontentious. The rules of procedure of the Council even specify that documents reflecting positions by individual governments may never be made accessible proactively by the Council General Secretariat during the legislative process.[12]

Nevertheless, in 2018 the European Ombudsman concluded a strategic inquiry[13] into the transparency of the Council, stating that the 'failure to record systematically the identity of Member States taking positions in preparatory bodies' constituted 'maladministration', the harshest admonition in the Ombudsman's toolbox. Preparatory bodies are where the substantive text of legislation is negotiated, only leaving political points of disagreement for deliberation among ministers if no agreement could be reached at Coreper. The Ombudsman further noted that the practice of systematically limiting legislative documents such as 'LIMITE' also constitutes maladministration, as documents are this way marked as secret in a non-discriminatory way. It recommends that guidelines be adopted as to what justifies a 'LIMITE'-marking of legislative documents; no such guidelines currently exist, allowing differing practices across various units of the Council General Secretariat.

This practice is particularly troubling in view of the additional hurdles it places on public access to documents. The EU access to document legislation, Regulation 1049/2001, actually requires that 'legislative documents' be made accessible to the public directly, rather than being marked as confidential. As Ombudswoman Emily O'Reilly drily notes, 'this commitment [to proactive publication] means little, if Member States' positions are not even recorded appropriately in the first place'.

While the Council failed to respond to the Ombudsman inquiry by the three-month deadline of 9 May 2018, six EU Member States published a non-paper by the title of 'Increasing transparency & accountability: The key to a better functioning Union' in June 2019, reiterating the need for proactive publication of legislative documents, a uniform approach by the Council on the publication of the Common Approach going into 'trilogues', the publication of 'milestone documents' during 'trilogues', and an overhaul of transparency legislation, showing that the Council does not have unanimity when it comes

[10] Judgment of 17 October 2013 in Case C-280/11 *Council v Access Info Europe* EU:C:2013:671.
[11] European Ombudsman recommendation, para 15 in OI/2/2017/TE, 9 February 2018.
[12] Art 11(4)b, Annex II, Council rules of procedure.
[13] European Ombudsman in strategic inquiry OI/2/2017/TE.

to its current, very restrictive approach to transparency and accountability.[14] The European Parliament also took the matter up in a resolution adopted on 17 July 2019.[15] In it, the Parliament notes that Council preparatory bodies and its more than 150 working parties composed of national civil servants do not meet publicly, unlike parliamentary committees, that legislative documents are not published proactively, and that 'information is presented in a register which is incomplete and not user-friendly'. It castigates the practice of systematic 'LIMITE'-classification of documents violates CJEU case law, and

> deems it unacceptable that the positions taken in the preparatory bodies of the Council by individual Member States are neither published nor systematically recorded, making it impossible for citizens, media and stakeholders to effectively scrutinise the behaviour of their elected governments,

while noting that

> lack of information also hampers the ability of national parliaments to control the actions of national governments in the Council, which is the essential function of national parliaments in the EU's legislative procedure, and enables members of national governments to distance themselves in the national sphere from decisions made at the European level which they shaped and took themselves.

In the words of liberal MEP Yana Toom who is a co-rapporteur on the resolution:

> The Council is a European institution just as Commission and Parliament are. And the government representatives sitting there receive a mandate from the voters. However, any monitoring of how this mandate is actually implemented is reliably covered by a conspiracy of silence.[16]

Building on this work, the European Ombudsman has in May 2019 opened three further investigations into case studies of what it calls 'opaque national government EU decision-making', focusing on the Eurogroup's largely inaccessible documents, especially as regards its preparatory bodies,[17] into the setting of annual fishing quotas involving negotiations with third countries, and national authorities' positions on the risk of pesticides to bees.[18]

But it is not just the EU level – 26 EU Affairs Committees from the EU's national parliaments have co-signed a report from COSAC, which notes 'that the Council, in particular, regularly violates EU transparency regulations' and recommends that 'documents must systematically be made public without delay' and

[14] See 'Non-paper' by Estonia, Ireland, Luxembourg, the Netherlands, Slovenia and Sweden entitled 'Increasing transparency & accountability: The key to a better functioning of the Union', following a 2015 non-paper with similar proposals.

[15] Initiative report 2018/2096(INI), above n 8.

[16] From Politico Europe 'Brussels Playbook', 26 September 2018.

[17] The Economic and Financial Committee, Eurogroup Working Group, and Economic Policy Committee.

[18] European Ombudsman press release no 3/2019, 14 May 2019.

that 'the Council must adopt more specific and detailed rules regarding reporting on legislative deliberations'.

## Conclusion

National representatives in the Council should recognise that being willing to compromise, and changing one's position, is basic democratic behaviour, and not necessarily a diplomatic loss of face. If the main function of the Council is to reach compromise between all Member States, then compromising on a government's initial negotiating position is both expected and desirable.

Such insights into negotiations will expose citizens to the diverging positions of governments from various regions and political affiliations, developing appreciation for the difficulties reconciling national realities and formulate policies that are reasonable for all 500 million citizens. Denying citizens access to the deliberations that made a national position buy into the final compromise creates doubts on the democratic legitimacy of the final outcome, and contribute to the distance of citizens from decision-making in Brussels.

Beyond increasing the EU's legitimacy in this way, transparency on Member States' positions in the Council will clearly limit the incentive and ability of national politicians to proclaim one position nationally and to defend another in the Council; the classic strategy enabling politicians to blame Brussels for outcomes they should take ownership of. The need for this is becoming increasingly obvious, with an ever-strengthening Eurosceptic and xenophobic camp feeding off a general resentment of a European Union scapegoated by politicians eager to claim wins for themselves while casting blame for any undesirable outcome on 'Brussels'.

EU-level institutions and politicians have very limited options to push back against such a narrative, due largely to the nationally fragmented nature of national media discourse. The interpretative hegemony of whether the EU has added value therefore resides with national politicians and national media.

Exhortations for national politicians to take ownership of the EU have run their course. We have to offer actual, structural incentives to ensure that national politicians engage in more constructive messaging around the EU. There are three clear avenues to ensure that both diplomats and national politicians working in the Council improve their focus on the European interest.

First, for legislative files, ensuring a sufficient degree of transparency will, mediated by journalists, national parliaments and civil society, ensure that politicians are accountable for the positions they take in the Council. Today, the Council only publishes the aggregated, compromise position that all Member States were able to agree on via the mediation of the Council presidency (the so-called Common Approach). This makes it impossible to know if an individual government, speaking in the name of its citizens and voters, was in favour of this or that proposal, before supporting the Common Approach due to unknown compromises.

This effectively prevents accountability for positions taken by national governments in legislative debates of the Council.

The Council should systematically record the positions of individual governments on legislative files, and publish them – even if this were to happen with a delay, for example, for particularly sensitive files.

Secondly, as regards executive decisions taken in the Council, it is clear that decentralised accountability (i.e., accountability via national parliaments controlling their government/ministers) is not effective in all cases,[19] given that in the few national parliaments that do take an interest in decisions taken in the Council, scrutiny by EU Affairs Committees is usually limited to the implications for that country, and not for other countries or even the EU as a whole. Organising accountability at 28 national levels, rather than at the EU-level where the decision is taken, leads to an accountability gap between the decisions taken centrally and fragmented democratic control at national level.

Complementing national accountability with an additional, European level in the case of executive Council decisions, will increase the visibility of political debate, sharpen arguments in favour and against this or that decision, and improve the democratic legitimacy of any outcome by providing a public space for political deliberation, beyond the *in camera* debate within the Council, given that executive deliberations are not livestreamed.

Thirdly, further improvements have to be made in the field of recording (legislative) documents, agendas and outcomes systematically, and making them available where possible. This is a problem in particular for the 150-odd Council working parties, Committees of Permanent Representatives (Coreper I + II) and preparatory committees. It is today possible to follow the work of the Council, but this should not require employing multiple, full-time and well-connected experts from the EU bubble. In a democratic, political system taking decisions on behalf of 500 million citizens spanning the entire continent, voters should be able to follow policy processes at the click of a button on the Council website.

In conclusion, there are many reasons why the Council is less comfortable with transparency and accountability than other EU institutions. Most importantly, change at the Council requires the consent of most, if not all, EU governments de-centrally, at national level. This makes it vastly more difficult to simultaneously convince all relevant decision-makers of the need for reform, as it would require a campaign in 28 national capitals. But even for an institution as insulated from direct public pressure as the Council, pressure is now building from all directions, creating a momentum that we can reinforce and seize.

[19] This applies in particular to Council formations that take mainly executive decisions, see, eg, Transparency International EU: 'Vanishing Act: The Eurogroup's Accountability', available at: www.transparency.eu/eurogroup.

# 13

# The Role of the Court of Justice in the Legitimation of the EU's Action: The Transparency Principle Example

GEORGES VALLINDAS*

## Introduction

The Brexit referendum and the constant rise of populist Eurosceptic political parties across Europe unfortunately demonstrate that the European integration process, while approaching its seventh decade, still suffers from a legitimacy problem. In order to limit the scope of such a fundamental criticism the EU, from the 1970s, decided to give direct democratic legitimacy to the European Parliament and to progressively integrate protection of fundamental rights.

The link between transparency and legitimation of the EU's action can be traced back to 1984, when the European Parliament issued a resolution calling for greater access to documents.[1] This new drive for transparency was strongly supported in the 1990s by Sweden, the Netherlands, Denmark and Finland, Member States with long-standing traditions of public disclosure and open government with some of their constitutions explicitly guaranteeing access to government information.

During this process, which had first been initiated via the Court of Justice of the European Union's (CJEU, the Court) case law,[2] then continued via secondary legislation and, from 2009 with the EU Charter of fundamental rights consecrated at the Treaties level, some principles obtained a special status. To begin with, the CJEU holds the judicial power in the EU's constitutional order. As such, it plays a fundamental role by its power to control the executive administration powers mainly held by the European Commission and the exercise of legislative powers

* Analysis and opinions expressed herein are personal to the author. Georges@Vallindas.eu.

[1] Parliament Resolution [1984] OJ C 172, 176.

[2] See, K Lenaerts, 'In the Union We Trust: Trust-enhancing Principles of Community Law' (2004) 41 *Common Market Law Review* 317.

held by the European Parliament and the Council. In order to ensure a correct separation of powers in the EU's legal order it is necessary to understand who is supposed to do what and how, a fundamental parameter that was quickly grasped by the Court which qualified it as the principle of openness. As Habermas states it, in a democratic society governed by the rule of law, of which the principle of separation of powers is an essential component, it is the legitimate business of the legislator to decide which social norms are to be transformed into law and it is the exclusive province of the courts to say what that law is.[3]

The sudden emergence and success of the notion of transparency, initially focused on open access to information, has been transformed since the Maastricht Treaty into a 'right to access to documents' that was completed by a real transparency principle which, as the Court established it in the *Turco*[4] and *Access Info Europe*[5] cases, clearly aims to contribute to greater legitimacy and accountability of the administration in a democratic system. Nowadays, transparency and good governance[6] have become core elements of the post-Lisbon Constitutional Framework with Articles 1 and 11 TEU, Articles 15 and 298 TFEU and Articles 41 and 42 of the Charter establishing and protecting them.

Since then, the CJEU case law has got richer and always focused on the fact that EU citizens need to have the opportunity to understand the considerations underpinning EU activities in order to exercise their democratic rights. However, despite such systematic efforts, in May 2018 the European Ombudsman had to state that the 'Council's "behind-closed-doors" approach alienates citizens'.[7]

This chapter will focus on analysing the historical, contemporary role of the Court as well as its internal transparency measures, in the legitimation of the EU's action via the transparency principle. An exhaustive analysis of case law or a final definition of the principle of transparency are out of scope of the present exercise.[8] We will limit ourselves to consider that in broad terms transparency forces the legislators and government officials to conduct their business as openly as possible, allowing the press and members of the public to scrutinise their decision-making processes.

[3] J Habermas, *Between Facts and Norms: Contributions to a Discourse Theory of Law and Democracy* (Cambridge, Polity Press, 1996) 115.

[4] Case C-39/05 P and Case C-52/05 P *Sweden and Turco v Council* EU:C:2008:374.

[5] Case C-280/11 P *Council v Access Info Europe* EU:C:2013:671.

[6] On this concept see T von Danwitz, 'Good Governance in the Hands of the Judiciary: Lessons from the European Example' (2010) 13(1) *Potchefstroom Electronic Law Journal* 2–23.

[7] M de la Baume, 'EU'S Top Watchdog Slams Council Secrecy' (2018) *Politico.eu*, available at: www.politico.eu/article/eu-top-watchdog-slams-council-secrecy-ombudsman-emily-o-reilly/.

[8] On the principle of transparency see A Prechal and M De Leeuw, 'Dimensions of Transparency: The Building Blocks of a New Legal Principle?' (2007) 1 *REAL* 51; D Curtin, *Executive Power of the European Union* (Oxford, Oxford University Press, 2011) 204–13; B Vesterdorf, 'Transparency, Not Just a Vogue Word' (1999) 22 *Fordham International Law Journal* 902; K Bradley, 'La transparence de l'Union Européenne: une évidence ou un trompe l'oeil?' (1999) 35 *Cahiers de droit européen* 283.

## The Court's Push for Transparency before it was Cool

Transparency has been omnipresent in EU case law. On the Court's databases 1,935 occurrences pop up for the key word 'transparency', the first dating back to 1962 in an Opinion of Advocate General Roemer related to imposing legal duties on States to ensure the transparency of the transport market.[9] The first judgment referring to transparency can be traced back to 1965, but only concerned a technique for preparing aluminum pellets capable of being observed by transparency in infra-red rays.[10]

The first use of transparency as an economic concept comes in a judgment of 6 October 1970, *Grad/Finanzamt Traunstein*,[11] where the Court stated:

> Article 4 [of the 1965 Decision] provides for the abolition of 'specific taxes' in order to ensure a common and consistent system of taxation of turnover. By favouring in this way the transparency of the market in the field of transport this provision contributes to the approximation of the conditions of competition and must be regarded as an essential measure for the harmonisation of the tax of the Member States in the field of transport.

During this first phase, with many judgments structured on the same model, the concept of transparency is systematically related to the market and/or the prices, transparency being according to classic economic theory a means to ensure perfect 'effective' competition.[12]

The first real use of transparency – as a magic word – can be spotted in the Opinion of Advocate General Trabucchi in the *Becher/Hauptzollamt Emden* case.[13] He stated for the first time that 'Any lack of transparency can be regarded as inconsistent with general principles of good administration and with the requirement of certainty for trade'. Once again transparency is related to the functioning of the market but this time a clear connection is made to good administration: according to the Advocate General, the Commission had calculated subjectively the compensatory amount for wheat imported into Germany from third countries.

One year later, the same Advocate General opposed the same principle to a national administration in *Van der Hulst/Produktschap voor Siergewassen*.[14]

It is also very interesting to note that the first EU text to have transparency at its core, Commission Directive No 80/723/EEC of 25 June 1980 on the transparency of financial relations between Member States and public undertakings,[15]

[9] Opinion of Advocate General Roemer in Case 9/61 *Netherlands v High Authority* EU:C:1962:20.
[10] Joined Cases 19/63 and 65/63 *Prakash v Commission* EU:C:1965:68.
[11] Case 9/70 *Grad* EU:C:1970:78 specifically para 18.
[12] See J Robinson, 'What is Perfect Competition?' (1934) 49 *The Quarterly Journal of Economics* 104.
[13] Opinion of Advocate General Trabucci in Case 154/73 *Becher* EU:C:1973:161.
[14] Opinion of Advocate General Trabucci in Case 51/74 *Van der Hulst* EU:C:1974:134.
[15] [1980] OJ L195, 35.

was attacked as void in front of the CJEU by France, Italy and the UK. The Court dismissed all of the Member State's applications.[16]

In the 1980s, the Court spotted the transparency principle in Council Directive 77/62/EEC by stating that it contains a number of provisions intended to ensure that the prohibition of restrictions on the free movement of goods is observed in the field of public supply contracts. The object of the provisions of the Directive is to coordinate national procedures concerning public supply contracts, in particular by introducing equal conditions of competition for such contracts in all Member States, and to ensure a degree of transparency allowing the prohibition of obstacles to free movement of goods to be better supervised.[17]

Transparency was also referred to by Advocate General Rozès in *Kohler/Cour des comptes*,[18] via the second paragraph of Article 25 of the Staff Regulations that provided that any decision adversely affecting an official shall state the grounds on which it is based; that involves the application to the particular circumstances of Community officials of a general legal principle based on the very principle of legality. As the Advocate General concluded, its purpose is to guarantee the transparency of individual decisions. Consequently, the statement of reasons must disclose, in clear and unequivocal wording, the essential grounds on which the appointing authority has relied when adopting its decision. For the first time, after good administration, transparency is linked to the principle of legality itself.

In 1984 Advocate General Darmon underlined 'the necessity to reconcile transparency with business confidentiality bears even more heavily on the Commission' when the rights of defence of a company under a competition law investigation are at stake[19] and used it in the same way in two 1986 and 1987 Opinions.[20]

In his Opinion in the *Luxembourg/Parliament* case, Advocate General Lenz stated that 'it is therefore only logical for the Parliament to make use of the communications media in order to ensure a high degree of transparency in the legislative process and to provide citizens with information'.[21] This is the first clear connection between transparency and the legislative process as we conceive it today.

The full expression was first used by Advocate General Jacobs in 1993, stating that 'If the principle of transparency is to have any meaning at all it is surely necessary for the Commission to be informed in advance of the precise territorial scope of the proposed aid measures'.[22]

[16] Joined Cases 188/80 to 190/80 *France and Others v Commission* EU:C:1982:257.

[17] 133/80, *Commission v Italy* EU:C:1981:43 para 2.

[18] Opinion of Advocate General Rozès in Joined Cases 316/82 and 40/83 *Kohler v Court of Auditors* EU:C:1983:381.

[19] Opinion of Advocate General Darmon in Case 264/82 *Timex v Council and Commission* EU:C:1984:377.

[20] Opinion of Advocate General Darmon in Case 248/84 *Germany v Commission* EU:C:1986:487; and in Case 233/85 *Bonino v Commission* EU:C:1987:29.

[21] Joined Cases C-213/88 and C-39/89 *Luxembourg v Parliament* EU:C:1991:449, para 81.

[22] Opinion of Advocate General Jacobs in Case C-364/90 *Italy v Commission* EU:C:1993:61, para 21.

It is in 1995 that the first judgment, by the Court of First Instance (CFI), deals with transparency in its full scope:[23] in *Carvel v Council*, a case on public access to information, and not much later, in 1996, in *Commission v Belgium* as a principle of public procurement.

As the CFI established it, on 6 December 1993, within the framework of the preliminary steps towards implementing the principle of transparency, the Council and the Commission approved a Code of Conduct concerning public access to Council and Commission documents,[24] aimed at establishing the principles to govern access to Council and Commission documents. In interpreting Article 4(2) of Decision 93/731, it must first be borne in mind that Decision 93/731 is the last of the three measures adopted in December 1993 containing provisions relating to the implementation of the principle of transparency. Of those three, it is the only the legislative measure which deals with public access to documents. Decision 93/731 is, therefore, the only measure governing citizens' rights of access to documents. In key paragraph 65, the CFI stated that it is clear both from the terms of Article 4 of Decision 93/731 and from the objective pursued by that decision, namely to allow the public wide access to Council documents, that the Council must, when exercising its discretion under Article 4(2), genuinely balance the interest of citizens in gaining access to its documents against any interest of its own in maintaining the confidentiality of its deliberations and therefore annulled the decision of the Council not to grant access to the requested documents.

Advocate General Ruiz-Jarabo Colomer was the first to refer to the transparency of the decision-making process in 1995.[25] The requirement that Community legislative acts must state the reasons on which they are based is laid down in the Treaty and failure to fulfil that requirement undoubtedly constitutes a breach of essential procedural requirements for the drawing up of such acts. Article 190 of the EC Treaty provided that 'regulations, directives and decisions adopted ... by the Council or the Commission shall state the reasons on which they are based and shall refer to any proposals or opinions which were required to be obtained pursuant to this Treaty'. That requirement, *which has always existed in Community law* (author's emphasis), has acquired added significance since the entry into force of the Treaty on European Union, and Declaration No 17 on the right of access to information[26] annexed to the Final Act thereof, stating that 'the transparency of the decision-making process strengthens the democratic nature of the institutions and the public's confidence in the administration'. What is remarkable here is that the Advocate General underlines that – according to him – such a requirement always existed in EU law even before the Maastricht Treaty.

[23] Case T-194/94 *Carvel and Guardian Newspapers v Council* EU:T:1995:183.

[24] [1993] OJ L340, 41.

[25] Opinion of Advocate General Ruiz-Jarabo Colomer in Case C-267/94 *France v Commission* EU:C:1995:333, paras 17–19.

[26] [1992] OJ C 191, 101.

It is in a 1996 judgment[27] that the Court will refer by itself to Declaration 17 on the right of access to information. It stated that:

> It was in order to conform to this trend, which discloses a progressive affirmation of individuals' right of access to documents held by public authorities, that the Council deemed it necessary to amend the rules governing its internal organisation, which had hitherto been based on the principle of confidentiality. So long as the Community legislature has not adopted general rules on the right of public access to documents held by the Community institutions, the institutions must take measures as to the processing of such requests by virtue of their power of internal organisation, which authorises them to take appropriate measures in order to ensure their internal operation in conformity with the interests of good administration.

This was a clear invitation by the Court to the EU legislator to adopt much more detailed and specific rules concerning the right of public access to documents and transparency in the EU institutional setting.

In the first years of litigation under the new EU texts, the CFI adopted a strong stance in favour of the right of access by showing a willingness to interpret the exceptions narrowly and by requiring, when an exception was justified, that access be denied line-by-line, redacting if necessary, rather than excluding entire documents or sets of documents.[28] Later cases have confirmed such an approach and have ensured that broad access is awarded by the institutions.

First introduced by the case law of the Court of Justice, formally introduced by the Treaty of Amsterdam via Article 255 TCE as a general right of public access to European Parliament, Council and Commission documents, which was finally implemented by Regulation 1049/2001,[29] until 2001, the fragile nature of the legal basis of transparency required the intense intervention of the Union's judicature. This judicial involvement proved to be crucial in guaranteeing a minimum level of protection for this right. The subsequent adoption of Regulation No 1049/2001, changed the basis but still required, as for any new legal norm, case-law interpretation. The interpretation of the text along with the list of the exceptions to public access stipulated by the Regulation led both the Court of Justice and the General Court to increase the number of interventions.

From this point on, developments are characterised by the simultaneous emergence of a principle of transparency in various fields of EU law. All strands of the principle were further developed in considerable detail in subsequent case

[27] Case C-58/94 *Netherlands v Council* EU:C:1996:171, paras 36–37.

[28] Case T-309/97 *Bavarian Lager v Commission* EU:T:1999:257; Case T-194/94 *Carvel and Guardian Newspapers v Council* EU:T:1995:183; Case T-14/98 *Hautala v Council* EU:T:1999:157; Case T-124/96 *Interporc v Commission* EU:T:1998:25.

[29] For an overview of the genesis and evolution of the principle of transparency in EU law, see, eg, S Peers, 'From Maastricht to Laeken: The Political Agenda of Openness and Transparency in the European Union' in V Deckmyn (ed), *Increasing Transparency in the European Union?* (Maastricht, EIPA, 2002).

law making an important contribution to the specific content of transparency as conceived in EU law.[30] The obligations derived from the principle varied from providing the widest possible access to documents held by the institutions to a prohibition to change the terms of a tender after the contract was concluded. The transparency obligations inherent in other principles of EU law, like the duty to give reasons and the rights of defence, were also deepened.[31] Nowadays transparency is mostly invoked in cases dealing with public access to information, to public procurement, and to cases about the institutional structure of the Union, competition and state aid law. A number of more or less isolated occurrences in many EU law fields can also be spotted, which underlines the imperialist nature of the transparency principle, such as telecommunications, VAT, regulation of the energy market, equal pay, consumer law, data protection, fundamental freedoms, language rules, milk quotas, notification of a Commission decision, research grant. The numerous and rich judgments of the General Court and the Court towards more transparency are too broad to fit into the scope of the present chapter. What must be retained is that these progressive case law and legislative developments allowed the principle of transparency to reach a constitutional status in the EU.

## Transparency Today and the Rule of Law

As the activities of the EU were expanding rapidly and transfers of sovereignty were taking place, similar guarantees as those provided by the liberal democracies of the Member States to their citizens were needed at EU level.[32] In fact, transparency has counterparts in the classic constitutional law in that parliamentary debates are open, minutes are available and published, any legislative act must be published in order to come into force. It also resonates with established obligations of information provision in national administrative law, as the right to be heard or the obligation to provide motives for decisions.

In Declaration 17 to the Final Act of the Treaty of Maastricht, improvements in transparency of the decision-making process were specifically seen as a means of strengthening 'the democratic nature of the institutions and the public's confidence in the administration'. Under the heading: 'The democratic challenge facing

[30] eg, Case C-186/96 *Demand* EU:C:1998:609 on milk quota; Case C-149/96 *Portugal v Council* EU:C:1999:574 on international trade agreements; and Case T-134/94 *NMH Stahlwerke v Commission* EU:T:1999:44 on competition law.

[31] See, A Buijze, 'The Principle Of Transparency in EU Law' (PhD thesis, BOX press, 2013).

[32] On constitutional democracy principles see J Habermas, 'Constitutional Democracy: A Paradoxical Union of Contradictory Principles?' (2001) 29 *Political Theory* 766; A Héritier, 'Composite Democracy in Europe: The Role of Transparency and Access to Information' (2003) 10 *Journal of European Public Policy* 814.

Europe', the text states that the Union must be 'brought closer to its citizens'[33] and aims for 'More democracy, transparency and efficiency in the European Union'.

The White Paper on European Governance[34] mentioned 'openness' as one of the principles of good governance, in line with, among other things, participation, and effectiveness. It can fulfil a crucial role in law and policy-making processes, where the principle of legality is too theoretical to be applied concretely, law being unable to provide specific rules for all factual public decision-making circumstances. This is notably the case, in informal ways of decision-making in the EU, as is the comitology phenomenon. In other words, transparency is becoming the new counterpart of the classic principle of legality. Moreover, transparency naturally fits in with big data and the internet age, as a principle of modern governance that takes up the traditional values underlying the principle of legality and brings them into the twenty-first century. In fact, despite the legal fiction that no one is supposed to ignore the law, normal citizens cannot be expected to examine the legality of a decision-making process: what is legal is too complex to allow for citizen participation in governance. Thus, seeing transparency in this light enables us to realise the crucial role it plays in achieving real, perceptible legitimacy in the eyes of the citizen by facilitating citizen participation.

In 2010 the Court stated, following the entry into force of the Treaty of Lisbon, that the introduction of Article 15 TFEU, which replaced Article 255 EC, extended the scope of the principle of transparency in EU law.[35] As a result of this progressive emergence of the transparency principle at the EU level, openness and good administration have become core elements of the actual EU Constitutional Framework.[36] Article 10(3) TEU establishes openness as one of the foundations of democracy in the Union. Currently enshrined in Article 1 TEU ('decisions are taken as openly as possible to the citizen') and Article 15 TFEU ('EU institutions shall conduct their work as openly as possible'), this transparency principle is instrumental to the effectiveness of the right to participate in the democratic life of the Union as formulated by Article 10(3) TEU.

In Article 2 TEU, the rule of law is explicitly mentioned as a value which is common to the EU and its Member States.[37] The preamble to the Treaty of the European Union and Article 6(1) TEU underline the attachment of the signatories

[33] S Van Bijsterveld, 'Transparency in the European Union: a Crucial Link in Shaping the New Social Contract Between the Citizen and the EU' (Tilburg University).

[34] European Commission, 'European Governance: A White Paper' COM(2001)428.

[35] See, to that effect, Judgment of 21 September 2010 in Cases C-514/07 P; C-528/07 P; and C-532/07 P *Sweden and Others v API and Commission* EU:C:2010:541, para 81.

[36] See A Alemanno, 'Unpacking the Principle of Openness in EU Law: Transparency, Participation and Democracy' (2014) 39 *European Law Review* 72; see, eg, Curtin, above n 8 205; J Mendes, *Participation in EU Rulemaking* (Oxford, Oxford University Press, 2011) 113; J Lodge, 'Transparency and EU Governance: Balancing Openness with Security' (2003) 11 *Journal of Contemporary European Studies* 95.

[37] On this concept see, T von Danwitz, 'The Rule of Law in the Recent Jurisprudence of the ECJ' (2014) 37 *Fordham International Law Journal* Art 7; and K Lenaerts, 'The Principle of Democracy in the Case Law of the European Court of Justice' (2013) 62 *International & Comparative Law Quarterly* 271.

to 'the principles of liberty, democracy, and respect of human rights and fundamental freedoms and the rule of law' that are common to the Member States. The EU Treaties do not however provide a definition, nor do most national constitutions that refer to the rule of law. In the context of EU enlargement policy, where it has been used as a standard against which to measure the progress of accession States, the European Commission offered a working definition of the rule of law in 2014, which itself closely reflects the definition proposed by the Council of Europe's Venice Commission in 2011. The core meaning of the rule of law entails compliance with the following six legal principles: legality; legal certainty; prohibition of arbitrariness of the executive powers; independent and impartial courts; effective judicial review including respect for human rights; and finally, equality before the law. Next to that, the explanations relating to the Charter,[38] state that Article 41 of the Charter is based on the existence of the Union as subject to the rule of law, whose characteristics have been developed in the case law which has enshrined good administration as a general principle of law.

While transparency is not directly cited, it is a fundamental component of the rule of law in liberal democracies and can be considered as the alter ego of accountability[39] which is directly related to prohibition of arbitrariness of the executive powers, an absolute condition for the existence of the rule of law. Without transparency, the prohibition of arbitrariness, which is intrinsically connected to the concepts of accountability and good administration, is almost impossible to satisfy therefore fundamentally affecting the liberal democratic nature of any constitutional regime.

The rule of law expression can be spotted 1,910 times in the case-law database of the CJEU. But it is interesting to underline that only 619 of these results relate to the 'Etat de droit' significance of the concept. It is in most recent years that the Court has started using this expression in a way in which it can be understood as having its own substance, legal power and effects. In fact, from an average of 20 mentions from 2000 to 2010, we have reached a historic high with 60 mentions in 2016 and 2018.

In its landmark case *Les Verts v Parliament*,[40] back in 1986, the Court stated that the European Union is a community based on the rule of law, inasmuch as neither its Member States nor its institutions can avoid a review of the question whether the measures adopted by them are in conformity with its basic constitutional charter, the Treaty, or the law which derives from it. This fundamental definition was later confirmed and expanded progressively by being referred to in the key judgments of *Kadi*,[41] *Inuit*[42] and *Schrems* to state that the European Union

[38] [2007] OJ C 303, 17.

[39] See, C Harlow, *Accountability in the European Union* (Oxford, Oxford University Press, 2002) 7.

[40] Case 294/83 *Les Verts* EU:C:1986:166, para 23.

[41] Case C-402/05 P and C-415/05 P *Kadi and Al Barakaat International Foundation v Council and Commission* EU:C:2008:461, paras 281 and 316.

[42] Case C-583/11 P *Inuit Tapiriit Kanatami and Others v Parliament and Council* EU:C:2013:625, para 90.

is a union that is based on the rule of law in which all acts of its institutions are subject to review of their compatibility with, in particular, the Treaties, general principles of law and fundamental rights.[43]

Most recently, it is the Court's judgment in the case of *Associação Sindical dos Juízes Portugueses*[44] that has established the new reference concerning the principle of rule of law in the EU, by adding to *Les Verts* a new strand that is directed to create some peer pressure towards Member State actions. As such, there is a parallel to be drawn with the US Supreme Court case of *Gitlow v New York* as regards the principle of effective judicial protection. The Supreme Court previously held, in *Barron v Baltimore*[45] that the Constitution's Bill of Rights applied only to the federal government. *Gitlow* partly reversed that precedent and established that while the Bill of Rights was designed to limit the power of the federal government, the incorporation principle allows it to be applied to states. In fact, *Gitlow* led to the progressive application of the US federal Bill of Rights to all state norms even outside any federal intervention.[46]

In a February 2018 judgment the EU Court considered that in accordance with Article 19 TEU, which gives concrete expression to the value of the rule of law affirmed in Article 2 TEU, it is for the national courts and tribunals and the Court of Justice to ensure the full application of EU law in all Member States and judicial protection of the rights of individuals under that law.[47] The very existence of effective judicial review designed to ensure compliance with EU law is of the essence of the rule of law,[48] analysis which was quickly confirmed in July 2018 in the *Minister for Justice and Equality* case.[49] In order for that protection to be ensured, maintaining the independence of those bodies is essential, as confirmed by the second paragraph of Article 47 of the Charter, which refers to access to an 'independent' tribunal as one of the requirements linked to the fundamental right to an effective remedy.[50] In the EU Member States judges are entrusted with the role of upholding the rule of law. Judicial power within the framework of EU law is shared between the Court of Justice and national courts. While it is for the Court of Justice to interpret EU law, it is for national courts to apply that law to the specific cases that come before them.

[43] Case C-362/14 *Schrems* EU:C:2015:650, para 60 and the case law cited therein.

[44] Case C-64/16 *Associação Sindical dos Juízes Portugueses* EU:C:2018:117, para 31 and the case law cited therein.

[45] SCOTUS *Barron v Baltimore* 32 US 243 (1833).

[46] SCOTUS *Gitlow v New York* 268 US 652 (1925).

[47] Case C-64/16 *Associação Sindical dos Juízes Portugueses* EU:C:2018:117, para 32; Case C-248/16 *Achmea* EU:C:2018:158, para 36; Case C-583/11 P *Inuit Tapiriit Kanatami and Others v Parliament and Council* EU:C:2013:625, para 90; and Case C-456/13 P *T & L Sugars and Sidul Açúcares v Commission* EU:C:2015:284 para 45.

[48] Case C-64/16 *Associação Sindical dos Juízes Portugueses* ECLI:EU:C:2018:117, para 36.

[49] Case C-216/18 PPU *Minister for Justice and Equality (Défaillances du système judiciaire)* ECLI:EU:C:2018:586 para 51.

[50] Case C-64/16 *Associação Sindical dos Juízes Portugueses* EU:C:2018:117, para 41; and Case C-216/18 PPU *Minister for Justice and Equality (Défaillances du système judiciaire)* EU:C:2018:586, para 53.

This means that the Court of Justice and national courts are called upon to cooperate transparently, principally by means of the preliminary ruling mechanism. In that regard, national jurisdictions have always been considered, since the founding Treaties that established the Preliminary Procedure mechanism, as an independent network of judges that are able to bypass national administration resistance by asking questions to the Court and in this way effectively applying EU law and ensuring that EU derived rights are protected all over the EU territory. The recent CJEU judgments are protecting this network and are putting into practice the recognised idea that 'the first instance national judges are the first EU law judges'.

Next to the national judiciaries, the rule of law obviously still applies to the EU itself and has direct connections with the extent of judicial review and the transparency of the decision-making process of the institutions which still remains a key issue brought before the Court. In a Grand Chamber ruling of 4 September 2018, the CJEU annulled two decisions of the Commission to refuse access to documents on impact assessment reports in environmental matters. The decision is an important precedent to ensure greater transparency of the EU institutions at the early stages of legislative action.[51] Although the submission of a legislative proposal by the Commission is, at the impact assessment stage, uncertain, the disclosure of those documents is likely to increase the transparency and openness of the legislative process as a whole, in particular the preparatory steps of that process, and, thus, to enhance the democratic nature of the EU by enabling its citizens to scrutinise that information and to attempt to influence that process. The Court considered that such a disclosure, at a time when the Commission's decision-making process is still ongoing, enables citizens to understand the options envisaged and the choices made by that institution and, thus, to be aware of the considerations underlying the legislative action of the EU. In addition, that disclosure puts those citizens in a position effectively to make their views known regarding those choices before those choices have been definitively adopted, so far as both the Commission's decision to submit a legislative proposal and the content of that proposal, on which the legislative action of the EU depends, are concerned. Quoting *Turco*, the Court will underline that by increasing the legitimacy of the Commission's decision-making process, transparency ensures the credibility of that institution's action in the minds of citizens and concerned organisations and thus specifically contributes to ensuring that that institution acts in a fully independent manner and exclusively in the general interest. It is rather a lack of public information and debate which is likely to give rise to doubts as to whether that institution has fulfilled its tasks in a fully independent manner and exclusively in the general interest.[52]

Even more recently, in November 2018 the Court dealt with a separation of powers constitutional case known as *AMP Antarctique*. This judgment marked,

[51] Case C-57/16 P *ClientEarth v Commission* EU:C:2018:660.
[52] Case C-39/05 P and C-52/05 P *Sweden and Turco v Council* EU:C:2008:374, para 59.

in our view, the bridge between the rule of law and the call for more transparency. Indeed the Court explicitly stated that, while the function of preparing the work of the Council and of carrying out the tasks assigned by it does not give Coreper the power to take decisions, a power which belongs, under the Treaties, to the Council,[53] the fact remains that, *as the European Union is a union based on the rule of law* (author's emphasis), a measure adopted by Coreper must be amenable to judicial review where it is intended, as such, to produce legal effects and therefore falls outside the framework of that preparation and implementation function.[54] While the preparation and implementation functions are one of the main exceptions to the transparency of any decision-making process in the EU, the Court by explicitly referring to the rule of law and the necessity for judicial review, imposed transparency on a measure adopted by Coreper.

The rule of law being directly connected to judicial review and its efficiency, one could foresee that the intensification of the rule of law's invocability would drive the transparency principle case law further by limiting even more the exceptions to what can be judicially controlled, be it at the EU or even national levels. As Judge Von Danwitz stated, it is

> the democratic nature and all public transparency of the political process are not sufficient to ensure the rule of law. For the protection of minorities and, in particular, of individuals, a reasonably intense judicial review both of individual decisions and legislative acts appears indispensable to effectively ensure the rule of law.[55]

The Court has in our opinion established that the concept of 'rule of law' is going to be the next decade's vehicle for accompanying the deepening of the EU's political integration. Rule of law can, following these judgments, also be defined as the quality of Member States to have legal institutions that can function in a stable and independent way vis-a-vis the political changes that may intervene in its national sphere. As President Lenaerts has stated it, 'national diversity and EU legislative consensus must both comply with values which are regarded as pan-European, ie, those that are the object of a constitutional consensus at EU level'.[56] Independence of justice and transparency of the decision-making process are undoubtedly today among them.

## Judicial Transparency at the EU Level

Obviously the key role of the Court in establishing transparency as an EU law principle imposed on it a duty to progressively adopt a transparency framework concerning its own functioning as an EU institution.

[53] Case C-25/94 *Commission v Council* EU:C:1996:114, para 27.
[54] Case C-626/15 and C-659/16 *Commission/Council (AMP Antarctique)* EU:C:2018:925, para 61.
[55] von Danwitz, 'The Rule of Law in the Recent Jurisprudence of the ECJ', above n 37, Art 7.
[56] K Lenaerts, 'EU Values and Constitutional Pluralism: the EU System of Fundamental Rights Protection' (2014) 34 *Polish Yearbook of International Law* 135.

First, concerning its own composition, future Members of the CJEU are now interviewed by the panel provided for in Article 255 of the Treaty on the Functioning of the European Union.[57] Established by the Treaty signed in Lisbon, the panel composed of seven experts, mainly senior national judges that may also have a European experience proposed by the President of the Court to the Council, began its work immediately after the entry into force, on 1 March 2010, of the Decision No 2010/124/EU and Decision No 2010/125/EU of 25 February 2010 whereby the Council of the European Union established the operating rules of the panel. The panel's mission, pursuant to the provisions of Article 255 TFEU, is to 'give an opinion on candidates' suitability to perform the duties of Judge and Advocate General of the Court of Justice and the General Court before the governments of the Member States make the appointments referred to in Articles 253 and 254 of that Treaty. The panel proceeds by an analysis of candidates CVs and a live interview unless it is a reappointment procedure.

Despite the fact that the 255 panel is advisory, this process has resulted in the negative opinion given to around 10 per cent of the proposed candidates of the Member States, which goes up to 19 per cent if we only take into account first-appointments, opinion that has always been respected by the governments of the Member States. Secondly, most Member States have, as a result of this pressure, established public national procedures for the selection of future candidates, making it possible in this way to check the CVs of potential candidates. While these procedures vary a lot among Member States, and that the opinion's reasoning remains secret in order to preserve the personal data of the candidate, the undeniable result of the establishment of the 255 panel is an increase of transparency concerning the appointment of new EU judges and advocates general. Its annual reports are published on the CJEU's website.[58]

The Court of Justice has also improved its level of communication with national judges, by reinforcing the framework for a transparent dialogue, in order to ensure that the preliminary ruling procedure fulfils its potential for increasing the coherence and uniform application of EU law. For the preliminary ruling procedure to operate as an effective mechanism, it is essential that the national court's order for reference should comply with a series of requirements so that the CJEU fully understands the questions referred to it, as well the factual background and the national law applicable to the case at hand. To that end, the Court recently reviewed its 'Recommendations to national courts and tribunals in relation to the initiation of preliminary ruling proceedings' which are published on its website and provide national judges with all the practical guidance needed.

[57] For an analysis on how nominations were made before the insertion of article 255 TFEU see H de Waele, 'Not Quite the Bed that Procrustes Built. Dissecting the System for Selecting Judges at the Court of Justice of the European Union' in M Bobek, *Europe's Judges. A Critical Review of the Appointment Procedures to the European Courts* (Oxford, 2015).

[58] The most recent Panel 255 report can be accessed at: curia.europa.eu/jcms/upload/docs/application/pdf/2018-05/5eme_rapport_dactivite_du_c255_-_en_final_-_public.pdf.

By establishing such transparent requirements, it allows all national judges to include in their preliminary references the same elements, giving them some judicial certainty about the admissibility of their questions but also enabling Member States – which under Article 23 of the Statute of the Court of Justice are notified of the questions raised in their respective official languages – to submit observations. Such a transparent functioning of the preliminary ruling procedure allows the Court to proceed having heard all possible arguments and envisaged interpretations of the EU norm at stake.

Transparency in its relations with national courts is also one of the main reasons why the Court of Justice makes publicly available a significant amount of information regarding its case law on the CURIA website in all official languages of the EU, which now has an updated search engine. Better knowledge of EU law among lawyers allows for more EU law questions to be raised in front of national judges, which can then introduce a reference that is specifically referring to the CJEU's case law thus enhancing the effectiveness of the dialogue between national and EU judges. The case law produced following such questions is later published in all the official languages, at least concerning the most important cases, thereby perpetuating the cycle of transparency.

The CJEU also seeks to bring EU law closer to European citizens, most of whom are not law experts. That is why those cases in which the general public may have a particular interest are summarised in press releases which use normal simplified language so as to make it easier for the general public, and the journalists who act as intermediaries in reporting the rulings to the public, to understand what the CJEU has actually decided. In the same way, the transparency of the EU judiciary is also strengthened by facilitating the public's access to the Court's hearings. Save in exceptional circumstances, the Court's hearings have always been held in public.

The Court also physically makes an effort to be open to all. The new CJEU's buildings are characterised by the strong presence of glass on the Palais, the Anneau, the Galerie and the three towers, underlining, according to its French architect Dominique Perrault, the transparency of EU justice. In this regard, the Court welcomes thousands of visitors each year, almost 20,000 in 2017: judges, lawyers and academics as well as pupils, students, journalists and pensioners, not only for the hearings which are public but also for legal seminars on the Court's functioning or specific EU law questions. An open-doors day is organised every 9 May allowing the general public to admire the works of art that are loaned to the Court by the Member States but also to obtain many documents that explain in non-legal language the internal functioning and important case law of the CJEU. In order to make EU law more understandable the Court has also established a *YouTube* channel and communicates important judgments also via *Twitter*, the recent announcement of the C-621/18 *Wightman*, Brexit-related judgment interpreting Article 50 TEU,[59] receiving more than 7,500 retweets and

[59] *Wightman and others v Secretary of State for Exiting the European Union* EU:C:2018:999.

10,000 likes. More importantly, the Court has also now established three different annual reports, one for the general public which describes key moments of the last judicial year; one that focuses on last year's case law in the ever expanding scope of EU law; and one that is technical and focuses on the financial management of the institution.[60]

It is nowadays clear that the website of the Court is the vitrine of its judicial transparency. As a recent addition, under 'the institution' menu, last in order but not least, one can find an 'Access to documents' page. Subtitled 'Access to administrative documents', this page thoroughly explains the legal basis and the procedure to obtain access to documents related to the CJEU. Pursuant to Article 15(3) of the Treaty on the Functioning of the European Union, the Court of Justice of the European Union had adopted the Decision of 11 December 2012 concerning public access to documents held by the Court of Justice of the European Union in the exercise of its administrative functions,[61] which has been replaced by its Decision of 11 October 2016,[62] that puts in place rules concerning public access to the documents held by it in the exercise of its administrative functions. Any EU citizen and any natural or legal person residing or having its registered office in the EU has a right of access to the documents of the CJEU listed in Article 1(1) subject to the conditions laid down in that decision. This Decision applies to all documents held by the CJEU, that is to say, documents drawn up or received by it and in its possession, as part of the exercise of its administrative functions.

To make an application for access to a document held by the Court in the exercise of its administrative functions, one has to complete the form available on the Court's website.[63] The application must be written in one of the EU's official languages and can be sent to the Court by post, by fax or electronically. The application must be made in a sufficiently precise manner and must contain, in particular, sufficient elements to enable the Court to identify the document or documents requested. Note that documents can be supplied only in existing languages and formats. The Court is not required to create a new document, translate a document or gather information in order to reply to an application. As soon as the Court receives an application, an acknowledgement is sent. The Court will deal with the application within a maximum of one month, unless that period is extended on the conditions laid down in the Decision. The procedure to access a document of the CJEU is laid down in Articles 4–12 of the 2016 Decision.

The key exception concerning the principle of access to documents drawn up or received by the Court and in its possession as part of the exercise of its

[60] The three annual reports of the CJEU can be downloaded on: curia.europa.eu/jcms/jcms/Jo2_7000/en/.

[61] [2013] OJ C 38, 2.

[62] Decision of the Court of Justice of the European Union Of 11 October 2016 Concerning Public Access to Documents Held by the Court of Justice of the European Union in the Exercise of Its Administrative Functions, [2016] OJ C 445, 3, available at: eur-lex.europa.eu/legal-content/EN/TXT/HTML/?uri=CELEX:32016D1130%2801%29&from=EN.

[63] See: curia.europa.eu/jcms/jcms/P_184871/en/, 'Application for access to documents' form available at the end of the webpage, as an online document or as a pdf file to be printed.

administrative functions, is that the Decision does not apply to legal documents. 'Legal documents' mean all documents that are part of a case's file. All publicly available information and documents relating to cases can be consulted in the case-law database. While this exception may seem quite broadly formulated, one has to keep in mind that almost no national court gives access to the writings and annexed documents/proofs of the parties to natural or legal persons that did not formally intervene in the case file.

The Court may refuse access to a document, inter alia, where its disclosure would undermine the protection of public interest, as regards: public security, defence and military matters, international relations, the financial, monetary or economic policy of the EU or a Member State, but would also undermine the privacy and the integrity of the individual, in particular in accordance with EU legislation regarding the protection of personal data.

The CJEU shall also refuse access to a document where disclosure would undermine the protection of: commercial interests of a natural or legal person, including intellectual property, court proceedings and legal advice, the purpose of inspections, investigations and audits. Access to a document drawn up by the CJEU for internal use or received by it, which relates to a matter on which the decision has not been taken by it, shall be refused if disclosure of the document would seriously undermine the decision-making process of the CJEU. This exception also applies to documents containing opinions for internal use as part of deliberations and preliminary consultations carried out within the CJEU or outside thereof if the Court has participated in them even after the decision has been taken if disclosure of the document would seriously undermine the decision-making process of the CJEU. Concerning third-party documents in its possession, the CJEU shall not grant access to them until it has received the consent of the third party concerned.

If the application is refused, or if no reply is given within the period laid down, the applicant may make a confirmatory application to the Court within one month using the same form, stating that it is a confirmatory application and giving the registration number which will have been sent with the acknowledgement of the initial application.

However, the Court's decision to ensure transparency provides that the exceptions set out will not apply if there is an overriding public interest in disclosure of the document concerned. If only parts of the requested document are covered by one or more of the exceptions, the remaining parts of the document shall be disclosed. Moreover, the exceptions shall apply only for the period during which protection is justified on the basis of the content of the document and for a maximum period of 30 years.

As we can understand this Decision applies existing EU legislation as interpreted by the case law on the access to administrative documents of the CJEU itself. In principle, the public may have access to the documents of the EU institutions, bodies, offices and agencies in accordance with the EU Treaties, the aim being 'to promote good governance and ensure the participation of civil society' (Article 15(1) TFEU). However, access to the documents of the Court of Justice is limited to those that relate to the administrative aspects of its governance and operations (Article 15(3) TFEU). As is the case in many national courts, public access to documents that relate to the CJEU's judicial activities is excluded. The reason for that exclusion lies in the fact that in the interest of the sound administration of justice the Court's proceedings must be protected against any form of external pressure or interference.

It is very interesting to note that, while the CJEU recognised the right of access to the file as a part of the right of defence in the field of competition law, the judicial nature of its own tasks have led the institution to refuse the access to the file of a case.[64] But is this justification still valid if the proceedings are no longer pending, ie, when the Court has already given judgment in the case? The Court of Justice gave indications concerning that question in the *Breyer* judgment which concerned the refusal of the Commission to give Mr Breyer access to the written submissions made by Austria in the context of an already closed infringement action.[65] It should be recalled in this connection that in its judgment C-514/07 P,[66] the Court accepted the existence of a general presumption that disclosure of the written submissions lodged by an institution in court proceedings would undermine the protection of court proceedings within the meaning of the second indent of Article 4(2) of Regulation No 1049/2001, as long as those proceedings remain pending. That general presumption of confidentiality also applies to written submissions lodged by a Member State in such proceedings. However, as the Court has stated, the existence of such a presumption does not exclude the right of the person concerned to demonstrate that a document whose disclosure has been requested is not covered by that presumption. Article 4(5) of Regulation No 1049/2001 does not confer on that Member State a general and unconditional right of veto enabling it to oppose, in a discretionary manner, the disclosure of documents originating from it and held by an institution. The Court noted that the non-applicability of the system of access to documents laid down in the first sub-paragraph of Article 15(3) TFEU to the Court of Justice of the European Union when it exercises judicial functions does not preclude the application of that system to an institution to which the provisions of Article 15(3) TFEU and Regulation No 1049/2001 are fully applicable, such as the Commission, where that institution holds documents drawn up by a Member State, such as the written submissions at issue, relating to court proceedings. So, while full transparency is not possible concerning the judicial proceedings because secrecy of deliberations is a key part of an independent justice system, an important part of a closed case

[64] See, eg, H Ragnelman, 'The Community Courts and Openness within the European Union' (1999) *The Cambridge Yearbook of European Legal Studies* 2; Vesterdorf, above n 8.

[65] Case C-213/15 *Commission/Breyer* EU:C:2017:563; see specifically paras 41–43 and 49.

[66] Case C-514/07 P, C-528/07 P and C-532/07 P *Sweden and Others v API and Commission* EU:C:2010:541 paras 102–03.

file, specifically Member State briefs, can be accessed when it is in possession of an intervening EU institution like the Commission.

Nevertheless, the Court's decision on the access to administrative documents, as any new norm, is inevitably going to create some litigation when a demand for an access to a document falls under the scope of an established exception and access is, as a consequence, refused. These specific limits to transparency that are inherently existent for all judicial bodies, including national ones, should not diminish the multilevel and systematic transparency efforts of the Court over the recent years that are trying to set an example on how transparency should work for EU institutions.

## Conclusion

While pre-existing in many northern Member States, transparency at the EU level emerged in the Court's case law and is guaranteed today by the constitutional frame of the EU. The Court has undoubtedly helped introduce into EU decision-making a greater measure of transparency and has opened the possibility for the EU to make a positive contribution to national constitutional updates by the introduction of the principle of transparency into other Member States' legal orders.

The increasing case law of the Court relating to the rule of law will probably also increase the healthy peer pressure between Member States that have no historic tradition of transparency to renew their administrative and legislative practices in order to ensure effective separation of powers and functioning checks and balances. This way, transparency enhances legitimacy of the EU as a whole and can create goodwill via peer pressure. Transparency is a precondition in order to assess the outcome and exercise effective accountability towards people in power. Without transparency, the conditions for effective rule of law as conceived in liberal democracies cannot be fulfilled. The objective here is not theoretical perfection, the concept of the rule of law being fluid itself, but ensuring that all EU citizens can benefit from a functional democratic system that includes their participation and supervision not only at the EU level but also – and maybe more importantly – at the Member State level which is closer to the citizen as in all federal systems.

The CJEU's case law has actively contributed to establishing a real system of legal accountability for the EU institutions by imposing transparency as a component of liberal democracy and good administration. Still one has to keep in mind, and the author is convinced that is the case for the Court, that the balance of power should not tilt too far towards a democratically non-accountable judiciary since this may have the secondary effect of weakening the political process, a regression called by Wincott the 'perversion of democracy'.[67] As such, institutional

[67] D Wincott, 'Does the European Union Pervert Democracy? Questions of Democracy in New Constitutionalist Thought on the Future of Europe' (1999) 4 *European Law Journal* 411.

transparency and judicial transparency have key roles to play in the legitimation of the EU's action: for the EU to be successful, it must be successful in the eyes of its citizens. Maintaining and increasing citizen support for the European project is vital to it. Transparency is one of the main means to increase the legitimacy of the work of the EU institutions and the Court's case law has historically proven to be a key factor in increasing it. While transparency still has its limits in the EU sphere, one has to keep in mind the Court reasons in a given legal frame[68] and that its case law can always evolve according to the legislative and constitutional changes that may come.

[68] On the limits of Law see J Raz, 'Legal Principles and the Limits of Law' (1972) 81 *Yale Law Journal* 823.

# 14

# Transparency and Accountability of EU Decentralised Agencies and Agencification in Light of the Common Approach on EU Decentralised Agencies

MERIJN CHAMON*

## Introduction

Raising the issue of the transparency and accountability of EU agencies is raising the perennial challenge of the EU's legitimacy. After all, transparency and accountability are core elements of good governance which in turn is one of the means to instil supranational governance with a sufficient degree of legitimacy.[1] Both principles are also linked since transparency is a necessary but insufficient condition for accountability.[2] Institutions and decision-making processes should therefore be elaborated in such a way that there are no accountability or transparency deficits. At the same time, more recent contributions refer to the risks of both accountability and transparency overload,[3] hampering governmental actors in realising their

* I would like to thank Andreas Eriksen, Chara Vlachou and James Wood for their comments on an earlier version of this chapter. All errors and omissions remain mine.

[1] D Esty, 'Good Governance at the Supernational Scale: Globalizing Adminsitrative Law' (2006) 115 *Yale Law Journal* 1490 ff. The Commission's white paper on European governance and its reform agenda was also based on this assumption. See European Commission, 2001, 'European Governance: A White Paper' COM(2001) 428 final, 10 ff.

[2] J Cross and J Bølstad, 'Openness and Censorship in the European Union: An Interrupted Time Series Analysis' (2015) 16 *European Union Politics* 216, 218; M Bovens, 'Analysing and Assessing Accountability: A Conceptual Framework' (2007) 13 *European Law Journal* 447, 453.

[3] M Busuioc and M Groenleer, 'The Theory and Practice of EU Agency Autonomy and Accountability: Early Day Expectations, Today's Realities and Future Perspectives' in M Everson, C Monda and E Vos (eds), *European Agencies in between Institutions and Member States* (Alphen aan de Rijn, Kluwer Law International, 2014) 196–97; S Brown, *The European Commission and Europe's Democratic Process* (London, Palgrave Macmillan, 2016) 27.

objectives. Both EU institutions and scholars have therefore struggled with the question where the elusive right balances in (note: not between) transparency and accountability for both EU agencification and EU agencies lie.

The present chapter will not answer this question, also because the right balance will vary from agency to agency but instead argues that some preliminary groundwork is required before the much sought 'right balance' may be properly identified. Taking a constitutional perspective to the problem gives rise to three separate (but interrelated) questions, depending on the level of enquiry:

- How do individual agencies conform to these principles of good governance in their actual functioning (micro)?
- Does an individual agency's framework (governing its functioning) reflect the principles of good governance (meso)?
- Is the process of agencification itself characterised by good governance (macro)?

The three levels are interrelated since ensuring good governance at a lower level will be frustrated if it is not upheld at the higher level. Conversely, lack of good governance at a lower level will exert pressure for change at the higher level. In light of this volume's central question, it is fitting to focus on the questions at the macro and meso levels. The enquiry thus focuses on whether the EU institutions have acted in line with good governance and put in place a system that requires EU agencies to act in accordance with good governance. To keep a sufficient focus, the present chapter will trace the principles of accountability and transparency in the rationale of EU agencification and verify whether and to which extent those principles are also reflected in the institutional framework by scrutinising the Common Approach (CA) on Decentralised Agencies of 2012.

An important caveat is in place here since other legal sources (eg, the Staff Regulations, Financial Framework Regulation, Access to Documents Regulation, etc) also impose accountability and transparency requirements on the EU agencies. A complete picture of the agencies' accountability and transparency would therefore require looking into these documents. However, constraints of space do not allow such an elaborate survey. The focus on the CA is then justified because, while non-binding, it is the fruit of more than 10 years of contemplation[4] and it reflects the consensus shared between the three political institutions on the process of agencification and the role and place of EU agencies in the EU institutional framework. The CA thereby also becomes the object of critical study: this chapter develops an *immanent critique*, but not

[4] Building on the 2001 White Paper on Governance, the Commission in 2002 adopted the Communication on 'The operating framework for the European Regulatory Agencies'; see COM(2002) 718 final.

an ideology critique,[5] taking the institutions' substantive premises on 'good governance' as a yardstick to study actual institutional practice.

## The Notions of Transparency and Accountability

Since both concepts are essentially contested, it is useful to first set out how they are understood for the purposes of the present chapter. For accountability, the working definition of Bovens will be used where accountability is a relationship between an actor and a forum where there is an obligation for the actor to explain and justify its conduct in light of pre-defined objectives and where the forum may raise questions, pass judgement and rectify the actor's conduct.[6] Delving deeper in the accountability concept, this means that the present chapter looks for accountability in the broad sense at the macro level and accountability in the narrow sense at the meso level.[7] At the meso level, accountability equates with ex post control and it is therefore an element in the wider notion of control (together with ex ante and ongoing control).[8] Indeed, in line with Busuioc, accountability is not equated with control here. Whereas control implies that an actor directs, steers and influences an agent's decision-making and behaviour, accountability is more restrictive and emphasises the need for the agent to justify and explain.[9] After all, if an actor fully controls an agent, there is no need for the latter to justify and explain its conduct. Accountability only makes sense if an actor has (partially) relinquished some ex ante and ongoing control, granting the agent a degree of autonomy.

For transparency, the working definition of Grimmelikhuijsen and Welch is used who refer to 'the disclosure of information by an organization that enables external actors to monitor and assess its internal workings and performance'.[10]

[5] This chapter does not seek to challenge the substantive premise of good governance itself. See J Romero, 'Zur Aktualität immanenter Kritik in der Sozialphilosophie' in J Romero (ed), *Immanente Kritik heute – Grundlagen und Aktualität eines sozialphilosophischen Begriffs* (Bielefeld, Transcript Verlag, 2014) 17–20.

[6] Bovens, above n 2, 450.

[7] According to Bovens et al, in the broad sense '[a]ccountability … is seen as a virtue, as a positive quality of organizations or officials' while in the narrow sense, accountability 'is seen as a social "mechanism", as an institutional relation or arrangement in which an actor can be held to account by a forum'. See M Bovens, T Schillemans and P 't Hart, 'Does Public Accountability Work? An Assesment Tool' (2008) 86 *Public Administration* 225, 227. Thus, the question at the macro level is whether accountability as a virtue plays a role in agencification, while at the meso level the question is whether the necessary institutional arrangements are in place to hold actors accountable.

[8] M Scholten, M Luchtman and E Schmidt, 'The Proliferation of EU Enforcement Authorities: A New Development in Law Enforcement in the EU' in M Scholten and M Luchtman (eds), *Law Enforcement by EU Authorities: Implications for Political and Judicial Accountability* (Cheltenham, Edward Elgar, 2017) 7–8.

[9] M Busuioc, 'Accountability, Control and Independence: The Case of European Agencies' (2009) 15 *European Law Journal* 599, 605–06.

[10] S Grimmelikhuijsen and E Welch, 'Developing and Testing a Theoretical Framework for Computer-Mediated Transparency of Local Governments' (2012) 72 *Public Administration Review* 562, 563.

As will be shown below, the case of the EU agencies is a revealing illustration of the dependent relationship linking transparency with accountability.

## Good Governance and the Rationale Pushing EU Agencification

During the first boom of academic attention for the rise in EU agencies, the phenomenon was linked by some to that of the paradigm of 'new governance'.[11] At the time, new governance was not only debated among academics but also by policy-makers who therein sought recipes for the reform of the EU in line with the principles of good governance, the Commission's White Paper on European Governance being a case in point.

This raises the question whether EU decentralised agencies are an emanation of new governance.[12] Answering that question would first require a more precise definition of new governance itself, a feat that after two decades still seems to elude the academic community. Indeed, Craig and de Búrca note that the new governance debate has resulted in 'a dizzying and often confusing picture for those seeking to grasp [its] essentials … and a broad overview of what is at stake'.[13] If, for instance, new governance is conceptualised as anything that deviates from the *Idealtype* of the Community Method, as Scott and Trubek suggested,[14] new governance has actually characterised the EU since its conception in 1957.[15] Sabel and Zeitlin on the other hand refer to *experimentalist* governance and an emergent architecture of EU public rule, the function of which is to allow the definition by the EU of abstract framework goals, whereby lower levels are left the freedom to achieve those goals. A circular process then follows in which the performance of the lower-level units is peer reviewed and the goals themselves are updated

[11] S Hix, 'The Study of the European Union II: The "New Governance" Agenda and its Rival' (1998) 5 *Journal of European Public Policy* 38, 40.

[12] Curtin and Dehousse nuance, but do not outright reject, the idea that agencies constitute 'new governance', mainly because the agencies have not been turned into powerful independent regulators. See D Curtin and R Dehousse, 'European Union Agencies: Tipping the Balance?' in M Busuioc, M Groenleer and J Trondal (eds), *The Agency Phenomenon in the European Union* (Manchester, Manchester University Press, 2012) 195. For the same reason, and the fact that agencification results in centralisation (rather than decentralisation) Scott questions the 'new governance' nature of EU agencies. See C Scott, 'Governing Without Law or Governing Without Government? New-ish Governance and the Legitimacy of the EU' (2009) 15 *European Law Journal* 160, 168.

[13] P Craig and G De Búrca, *EU Law: Text, Cases and Materials* (Oxford, Oxford University Press, 2015) 163.

[14] J Scott and D Trubek, 'Mind the Gap: Law and New Approaches to Governance in the European Union' (2002) 8 *European Law Journal* 1. In the same seminal article Scott and Trubek identify the reasons driving new governance and its characteristics but few of them seem to apply to the EU decentralised agencies.

[15] The first major specimen of new governance would then perhaps be the Luxembourg compromise of 1965.

and revised where necessary.[16] For Sabel and Zeitlin the structural or institutional terms employed to perform these four functions are immaterial but despite these authors finding EU agencies to be experimentalist governance, the ratio of EU agencification (see below) does not actually align with these scholars' set of necessary functions defined for experimentalist governance: while EU agencies are multilevel bodies that may be qualified as instances of institutional experimentation and their decision-making is certainly (partially) deliberative in nature,[17] qualitative agencification is also characterised by formalisation (rather than informality), uniformisation and increasingly detailed policy goals which would be the antonyms of experimentalist governance as described by Sabel and Zeitlin. Finally, Craig and De Búrca have defined the core and unifying theme of new governance as the shift away from hierarchical governance,[18] but EU agencification is in part also characterised by hierarchisation. As will be argued below, it would seem that because the governance in which EU decentralised agencies are integrated is largely hierarchical (as to its structure) and non-voluntary (as to its process),[19] EU agencification appears to be merely *new-ish* governance.[20]

## The Rationale of EU Agencification

From the outset it should be noted that EU agencification is not as such driven by a concern for good governance, ie, the quantitative and qualitative importance of EU agencies in the EU administration has not increased to pursue principles such as transparency and accountability as ends in themselves. While deconcentrating government to the EU agencies could have been relied upon as a means to reform the Commission (the legitimacy of which was undermined at the end of 1990s as a result of several crises) and to contribute to greater transparency and accountability,[21] this has never been EU agencification's driving force as such.

The early commentators of EU *agencification* largely relied on functional arguments to explain the phenomenon's surge.[22] In doing so the same reasons relied upon to explain national agencification were recycled, disregarding the fact that *agencification* is always the result of a polity's specific constitutional and

[16] C Sabel and J Zeitlin, 'Learning from Difference: The New Architecture of Experimentalist Governance in the EU' (2008) 14 *European Law Journal* 271, 273–74.

[17] See ibid 272–73.

[18] Craig and De Búrca, above n 13, 163.

[19] See T Börzel, 'European Governance: Governing with or Without the State?' in P Dobner and M Loughlin (eds), *The Twilight of Constitutionalism?* (Oxford, Oxford University Press, 2010) 75–76.

[20] *cf* Scott who argued that a lot of new governance in the EU is actually only 'new-ish', Scott, above n 12, 161 ff.

[21] E Vos, 'Reforming the European Commission: What Role to Play for EU Agencies?' (2000) 37 *Common Market Law Review* 1113, 1119.

[22] See D Kelemen and A Tarrant, 'The Political Foundations of the Eurocracy' (2011) 34 *West European Politics* 922, 923.

inter-institutional dynamics.[23] More recently it has been argued that a new institutionalist reading of EU agencification reveals that EU agencies constitute a form of administrative integration (ie, centralisation) which became necessary in the post-Single European Act era to realise the EU's ambitious internal market agenda. Rational Choice New Institutionalism thereby explains why the EU institutions and Member States have struck a grand compromise on the hybrid structures, which EU agencies are, as the organisational means to realise this administrative integration, while Historical New Institutionalism helps in explaining how establishing agencies or further empowering existing ones has by now become entrenched as the default response to policy needs or crises.[24]

Of course, the fact that EU agencification is not as such spurred on by a desire to give teeth to the good governance principles of transparency and accountability does not mean that EU agencification cannot result in more accountable and transparent EU decision-making or in a more transparent and accountable EU administration. Whether EU agencification's potential is realised in this regard depends on how the EU institutions at a lower (meso) level define the frameworks applicable to the individual agencies. A final question concerning the macro level then is whether the process of agencification itself is sufficiently framed in respect of the principles of transparency and accountability. This question draws the attention to the EU institutions: how have they acted when establishing and empowering agencies? The key document in this respect is the 2012 Common Approach on Decentralized Agencies.

## The Common Approach: Furthering Good Governance?

Before turning to the content of the CA, a number of preliminary observations should be made. A first is that the CA dates from 2012 and that before that date no 'common approach' of the EU institutions on EU agencification existed. Agencification was characterised by ad hocery, resulting in a poor transparency of the process and reduced accountability of the institutions: the lack of a template resulted in a lack of foreseeability and meant there was no clear standard in light of which the institutions had to explain and justify their choices. A second observation deals with the CA's non-binding nature. Originally, the Commission had conceived the would-be CA as a binding instrument,[25] but this was opposed by

[23] D Halberstam, 'The Promise of Comparative Administrative Law: A Constitutional Perspective on Independent Agencies' in S Rose-Ackerman and P Lindseth (eds), *Comparative Administrative Law* (Cheltenham, Edward Elgar, 2010) 193–200.

[24] M Chamon, EU *Agencies: Legal and Political Limits to the Transformation of the EU Administration* (Oxford, Oxford University Press, 2016) 111–15.

[25] European Commission, 2002, 'The operating framework for the European Regulatory Agencies' COM(2002) 718 final 6. European Commission, 25 February 2005, 'Draft Interinstitutional Agreement on the operating framework for the European regulatory agencies' COM(2005) 59 final 3. See also L Verhey, 'Good Governance: Lessons from Constitutional Law' in DM Curtin and

the Council which did not want to pre-empt its future discretion by agreeing to binding rules.[26] While transparency may be increased by explicitly defining the non-binding principles governing agencification, the fact that these principles are non-binding still frustrates the accountability of the institutions involved: the discretion left to an actor to follow (or not) non-binding principles will largely undo that actor's obligation to explain or justify its conduct and will affect which accountability forums are available.[27]

With these important qualifications in mind we may turn to the content of the CA to determine (i) whether it contains any principles that make the process of agencification more transparent by guiding the institutions in their decision-making and (ii) whether it contains standard provisions to be included in agencies' establishing acts that improve the accountability of and transparency in those agencies' functioning. The institutions were clearly aware of both these challenges since they observed in their Joint Statement which accompanied the Common Approach that '[t]he establishment of agencies was done on a case by case basis and has not been accompanied by an overall vision of their role and place in the Union'. Further on in the statement they noted that the ad hoc working group had looked into 'the coherence, effectiveness, accountability and transparency of these agencies'.

For any horizontal instrument to instil the process of agencification with greater transparency it needed to address the following four questions: (i) which of the EU bodies, offices and agencies qualify as *decentralised* agencies to which the CA is applicable, ie what is the definition of an EU decentralised agency? (ii) When do we establish a new EU agency? (iii) How do we determine which (new) powers ought to be granted to an agency and, given that EU decentralised agencies are typically scattered around the EU? (iv) How do we determine where an agency is to be located in the EU?

Remarkably, the CA does not define the specimen of EU decentralised agency. Hence it is not clear to which bodies the CA applies and in every legislative negotiation on a new body there will be a discussion on whether the CA should apply at all to the body at issue.

On the second issue, the Common Approach only devotes a single sentence: 'The decision to create a new agency should be based on objective impact assessments of all relevant options'. This commitment was merely a reconfirmation of an obligation which had already resulted from the 2003 interinstitutional agreement on better law-making.[28] More importantly, it was not further elaborated in

RA Wessel (eds), *Good Governance and the European Union: Reflections on Concepts, Institutions and Substance* (Antwerp, Intersentia, 2005) 64.

[26] F Comte, 'Agences européennes: relance d'une réflexion interinstitutionelle européenne?' (2008) *Revue du Droit de l'Union Européenne* 463,487.

[27] *cf* Bovens' definition of accountability. See Bovens, above n 2, 450.

[28] See Interinstitutional agreement on better law-making [2013] OJ C 321/1 para 29. See also E Bernard, 'Accord sur les agences européennes: la montagne accouche d'une souris' (2012) 3 *Revue du Droit de l'Union Européenne* 399, 412.

the Common Approach, meaning that it is insufficiently precise to qualify as an element contributing to greater transparency. Legislative practice at the meso level attests to this since the quality and approach in the different impact assessments (for different agencies) has varied greatly.[29] A corollary to this is the practice of abolishing merging existing agencies. On this issue the Common Approach was more innovative and elaborate, suggesting that agencies might be merged 'where their respective tasks are overlapping, where synergies can be contemplated or when agencies would be more efficient if inserted in a bigger structure'. Similarly, agencies might be abolished when agencies are chronically under-performing. However, the first litmus test proved to be a sobering experience for those hoping for greater rationality in agencification: when the Commission in 2013 proposed merging Europol with the European Police College (CEPOL), an agency which because of its small size had faced problems in handling the 'complexities of the EU's financial and staff regulations',[30] the Council and Parliament agreed on keeping both entities as separate agencies.[31]

The third issue brings us to the elephant in the room during the institutions' negotiations on the Common Approach. Although the uncertain framework for the delegation of powers was probably regarded by practitioners and academics alike as the most pressing agencification issue, the Common Approach is completely silent thereon.[32] As a result, it failed to give any guidance on the decision when to grant which powers to agencies.

The fourth issue relates to perhaps one of the most innovative parts of the Common Approach, which dedicates an entire page to the issue of selecting the agency's seat. The decision-making on this issue before the Common Approach exemplified EU bad governance at its worst: Member States in the (European) Council put their national interest in acquiring 'their part of the cake' before the objective of having a properly functioning agency.[33] The Common Approach laying down pre-defined criteria governing the choice for a seat thus allowed for more transparent decision-making and greater accountability of the institutions when choosing the location of agencies. Unfortunately, however, by 2012

[29] See Chamon, above n 24, 168–70. Ramboll, *Evaluation of the EU Decentralised Agencies in 2009 – Final Report*, Vol I, 18 ff; Inter-institutional working group on decentralised agencies, Analytical fiche No 2, 3 ff. In addition, for one of the latest agencies, the SRB, the Commission did not conduct a specific impact assessment (IA) and referred instead to the IA for the BRRD Directive (which could not make an assessment of the decision to establish and empower an EU agency). See European Commission, COM(2013) 520 final 5.

[30] See Decision (EU) 2010/556 of the European Parliament on discharge in respect of the implementation of the budget of the European Police College for the financial year 2008 [2010] OJ L252/232.

[31] Chamon, above n 24, 98. This despite the Parliament earlier calling for a merger, see point 57 of the Resolution of the Parliament of 17 April 2013, [2013] OJ L308/374. The failed merger has not stopped the Parliament from paying lip service to the potential, in increased efficiency, of merging agencies. See point 41 of Resolution 2016/1606, [2016] OJ L246/447.

[32] For a critique, see Bernard, above n 28, 436–41.

[33] See especially the discussions on the EFSA's seat reported in E Vos, 'European Agencies and the Composite EU Executive' in M Everson, C Monda and E Vos (eds), *European Agencies in between Institutions and Member States* (Alphen aan de Rijn, Kluwer Law International, 2014) 15–16.

the fourth wave of agencification had concluded and no new agencies, apart from the atypical Single Resolution Board, were established. It thus appeared that the Common Approach's guiding principles would not be tested in practice.

## *Recent Practice in Relocating Agencies*

Yet, in December 2012, the UK government informed the EU that it could no longer host CEPOL on its territory. This meant that CEPOL had to be relocated and provided a first test for the 'rationalised' criteria for choosing an agency's seat. As noted above, the Commission had proposed solving the issue by merging CEPOL with Europol, thus locating CEPOL in The Hague. The Member States opposed such a merger and the Council presidency instead invited the Member States to submit applications for temporary hosting of CEPOL. Out of the seven applications received,[34] the Member States, following successive voting rounds, selected Budapest in common accord as the new location for the agency's seat.[35] Relying on Article 76(b) TFEU the Member States subsequently proposed an amendment to the CEPOL Decision to formalise this decision.[36] While the Common Approach indeed refers to 'the political decision on an agency's seat taken by common agreement' between the Member States, this is based on a questionable reading of Article 341 TFEU (which only refers to the seat of the institutions). Instead, this decision should (only) be subject to the applicable legislative procedure. In addition, while the Council noted that it had conducted an impact assessment, as required by the Common Approach, only the Budapest candidacy was assessed, rather than all seven original submissions.[37] Despite the Common Approach then, the decision to relocate CEPOL to Budapest cannot be said to have been taken in a significantly more transparent and accountable manner.

The UK's decision to leave the EU altogether offered a retry to the Member States, which they also partially seized. After having defined the general guidelines in April 2017, the Member States adopted a note in the margins of the June 2017 European Council, setting out a precise procedure, inspired by the one used for the CEPOL relocation, for choosing the new seats of the European Banking Authority (EBA) and European Medicines Agency (EMA) and developing the substantive criteria which candidate host cities should meet.[38] The procedure involved an organised call for public offers (resulting in eight offers for the EBA and 19 for the EMA) and a public and objective assessment of each offer by the Commission,

[34] See Council of the European Union, 2 October 2013, Doc 14312/13.

[35] See Council of the European Union, 13 November 2013, Doc 14607/13, 7.

[36] See Council of the European Union, 29 November 2013, Doc 17043/13. The Commission delivered a negative opinion on this initiative; see European Commission, COM(2014) 7 final.

[37] See Council of the European Union, 9 December 2013, Doc 17043/13 ADD 2.

[38] See Procedure leading up to a decision on the relocation of the European Medicines Agency and the European Banking Authority in the context of the United Kingdom's withdrawal from the Union (22 June 2017).

before the Member States voted on the offers by secret ballot in three successive voting rounds. While this procedure clearly made the decision on the agencies' location more transparent, important issues remain. For one, the formal decision on the agencies' seats has to be taken through the ordinary legislature which has been represented by an intergovernmental[39] fait accompli.[40] At the same time, that intergovernmental decision has also been challenged before the Court by Italy. Having lost out against the Netherlands for hosting the EMA, Italy is arguing before the Court that the Dutch bid could not have been picked by the Council since it did not conform to the substantive criteria set out by the European Council.[41] A final critical question is whether this new procedure will also be used as a template for future decisions. Although the June 2017 note itself provides that the prescribed procedure 'is specific to the current situation and does not constitute a precedent for location of agencies in the future' it would appear difficult to revert to the traditional common accord decision-making, as indeed the selection of the seat of the new European Labour Authority in June 2019 demonstrates.[42]

## Good Governance in the Common Approach on Decentralised Agencies

The central question at the meso level is whether and to which extent EU agencies, under their establishing act and further relevant legislation, are (i) under an obligation to function transparently and (ii) can be held accountable for their (in)action(s).[43] While there is a clear trend in increased accountability mechanisms for the more recent agencies and the agencies established pursuant

[39] Tovo has rightly noted that the proceduralisation and notably the increased transparency, the involvement of the Commission and the decision by majority rather than consensus amount to a 'communautarisation' but evidently the decision remains intergovernmental. See C Tovo, 'The Procedure for Relocating EU Agencies after Brexit: An Encouraging Precedent? (*EUTARN Blog*, 2 July 2017).

[40] The EMA and EBA Regulations were amended in November 2018, see Regulation 2018/1717 (EBA), [2018] OJ L291/1 and Regulation 2018/1718 (EMA), [2018] OJ L291/3. The Parliament therefore did not block this decision, but still expressed critique, see points 8–11 of the Resolution of the Parliament of 14 February 2019 (P8_TA(2019)0134).

[41] See Case C-59/18 *Italy v Council* [2018] OJ C 94/15. The admissibility of the action is doubtful however, meaning it is likely that the Court will not have to assess Italy's pleas on their merits.

[42] Yet it cannot be excluded that there will be a backlash against the new procedure since its ultimate result *in casu*, Amsterdam and Paris being picked to host the EMA and EBA, is not in line with the December 2003 Decision of the Member States to 'give priority to Acceding States, once they have joined the Union, in the distribution of the seats of other offices or agencies to be set up in the future'. See European Council, December 2003 conclusions, Doc 5381/04, 27. It may be noted here that the Luxembourg and French delegations also expressed reservations as to the procedure used for the CEPOL relocation; see Council of the European Union, 13 November 2013, Doc 14607/13, 7 and 11.

[43] This is also referred to as the *de iure* accountability and transparency, as opposed to the *de facto* accountability and transparency (at the micro level). See M Guidi, 'Modelling the Relationship Between Independence and Accountability of Regulatory Agencies' in A Bianculli, X Fernández-i-Marin and J Jordana (eds), *Accountability and Regulatory Governance: Audiences, Controls and Responsibilities in the Politics of Regulation* (Basingstoke, Palgrave Macmillan, 2015) 107.

to the ordinary legislative procedure,[44] the first port of call in this regard is again the Common Approach which was the result of the Commission's attempt to streamline agencies' establishing acts.

## EU Decentralised Agencies' Accountability

Instead of listing all the provisions of the Common Approach that (may) contribute to ensuring agencies' accountability, the following section will go back to the working definition of accountability to determine which elements of accountability are (further) operationalised by the Common Approach and which elements remain inoperative. Relying on Bovens' definition we would thus be looking for (i) a clear relationship between the agency and a forum (principal), (ii) an obligation for the agency to explain and justify its conduct in light of (iii) pre-defined objectives, (iv) the possibility for the forum to raise questions and pass judgement and finally the possibility of (v) rectification. Retracing the elements in the Common Approach will shed light on the question of which perspectives on accountability the EU institutions subscribe to in relation to the agencies: a democratic, constitutional or learning perspective?[45]

### *A Focus on the Director's Accountability*

As the Joint Statement rightly remarked, the agencification of the EU administration had 'not been accompanied by an overall vision of [the agencies'] role and place in the Union'. This had repercussions for the agencies' accountability since such a vision seems indispensable to identify the forums of accountability. In this regard the Common Approach was to be welcomed for clearly spelling out that agencies' directors are 'first and foremost, accountable to their Management Board … They are also accountable to the European Parliament and the Council for the use of the EU contribution through the annual discharge procedure'. Nonetheless, it remains problematic that the relationship with the Parliament and Council is seemingly confined to the discharge procedure.[46] In addition, by not establishing a relationship between the directors and the Commission, the Common Approach (implicitly) rejects the Commission's original idea that it is up to the Commission to ensure the unity and integrity of the executive function at EU level.[47] If this would reflect a conscious choice on the role and place of

[44] N Font, 'Designing Accountability Regimes at the European Union Level' in A Bianculli, X Fernández-i-Marin and J Jordana (eds), *Accountability and Regulatory Governance: Audiences, Controls and Responsibilities in the Politics of Regulation* (Basingstoke, Palgrave Macmillan, 2015) 136–37.

[45] See Bovens et al, above n 7, 230–32.

[46] However the Common Approach (at para 29) also makes clear that the current practice of the Directors presenting the annual work programme to the relevant parliamentary committee should continue.

[47] See European Commission (COM)2002 718 final 2.

the agencies in the Union it should be welcomed if only for its clarity. However, the Common Approach seems to lack coherence if the (fifth) element of rectification is added to the equation. While the budgetary authority may withhold discharge and the Board may fire a director, the Common Approach also provides that the procedure for dismissing the Director should mirror the appointment procedure.[48] This effectively means that agency directors are in a way accountable to the Commission, since the latter can sanction them by proposing their dismissal to the Board.

More understandable is the Common Approach's lack of elaboration of the second and fourth elements of the working definition. Since the Management Board acts as the Director's appointing and disciplining authority, it has the means to require the Director to explain and justify his or her managing of the agency and to discipline him or her.[49] Similarly, the budgetary discharge procedure was already harmonised and well established at the time of the Common Approach.[50] The blind spot here is that the Common Approach did not offer a solution to the lack of external discharge procedure for the fully self-financed agencies.[51] Combined with its focus on the discharge procedure to operationalise accountability vis-a-vis Parliament and Council, the directors of these agencies would only be accountable to their own Boards.

## *Putting Performance in the Limelight*

Turning to the third element in the working definition leads us to find a significant novelty in the Common Approach as it notes that the discharge procedure has

[48] See Common Approach, para 19.

[49] A point which may be raised here again however is that it seems difficult to hold the Management Board to account when it is felt (by Parliament, Commission, Council, stakeholders or the public at large) that the Director should be summoned or disciplined but the Management Board fails to do so.

[50] See Arts 94–95 of Regulation (EC) 2343/2002 of the Commission on the framework Financial Regulation for the bodies referred to in Art 185 of Council Regulation (EC, Euratom) No 1605/2002 on the Financial Regulation applicable to the general budget of the European Communities, [2002] OJ L357/72.

[51] The Common Approach only noted that the 'possibilities for securing democratic accountability for fully self-financed agencies (ie, financed by their clients) should be explored, as they are Union bodies in charge of implementing EU policies but not subject to a discharge within the meaning of the TFUE. A possibility could be that the agencies in question, submit to the European Parliament, to the Council and to the Commission an annual report on the execution of their budget and consider requests or recommendations issued by the Parliament and Council'. For a long time, the Parliament has been trying to extend its authority over these bodies as well. See, eg, the Legislative Resolutions of the European Parliament embodying Parliament's opinion on the proposals for Council Regulations amending the basic regulations of certain decentralised Community agencies, [1998] OJ C 104/40; Amendment 126 in the Report of 8 March 2006 on the proposal for a Council regulation amending Regulation (EC, Euratom) 1605/2002 on the Financial Regulation applicable to the general budget of the European Communities, 2006, A6-0057/2006, PE 367.649v02-00. Following the Common Approach, the Commission proposed a revision of both the EUIPO and CPVO without putting forward a revision of the budgetary procedure. See European Commission, COM(2013) 161 final; European Commission, COM(2013) 262 final. In the legislative negotiations the Parliament did not try to extend its budgetary authority over these agencies.

not sufficiently focused on the performance of the agencies: 'Agencies' Directors should therefore be more clearly accountable for performance. To this end, tailored performance indicators should be introduced allowing for effective assessment of the results achieved in terms of objectives'.[52] Yet, as Blanc and Ottomofiore point out, such indicators in themselves are not enough to ensure accountability for the performance of an agency. Proper accountability first depends on how the goals or mandate of the agency is defined (in its establishing act) and subsequently on the balance achieved between those goals/mandates and the precise indicators.[53] The risk as identified by Blanc and Ottomofiore is that the indicators focus too much (or even exclusively) on process rather than product (ie, whether the agency contributes to actually realising the policy goals for which it was established and empowered).[54] Clearly as much depends on the thoughtful wording of an agency's mandate as the definition of the indicators. The latter were not elaborated by the Common Approach itself which left this for the Commission to do. The Commission defined a number of key performance indicators (KPIs) in March 2015[55] and urged the agencies to integrate (tailored) KPIs in their annual work programmes, for which the Common Approach also prescribed a template.[56] The Commission guidelines on the KPIs make a distinction between operational and financial and budgetary KPIs. When it comes to policy output, the guidelines are rather underwhelming as only the following KPIs are identified:

- Timely submission of the draft annual work programme.
- Percentage of completion of the activities of the annual work programme.
- Timely achievement of objectives of the annual work programme.

The first of these KPIs does not enquire into output, but rather process, while the second and the third seem to (partially) overlap. More fundamentally, the KPIs refer back to the work programme for which the Director him or herself cannot be held accountable.[57] This again raises the question of how the Board translates the agency's mandate, as defined by the EU legislature, into KPIs in the work programme.

The KPIs then result in a 'handicapped' accountability because, even apart from how they are phrased (an issue to be situated at the micro level), (i) the link

[52] See Common Approach, para 15.

[53] F Blanc and G Ottimofiore, 'The Interplay of Mandates and Accountability in Enforcement within the EU' in M Scholten and M Luchtman (eds), *Law Enforcement by EU Authorities: Implications for Political and Judicial Accountability* (Cheltenham, Edward Elgar, 2017) 276.

[54] ibid 276–77.

[55] See European Commission, SWD(2015) 62 final.

[56] The template was ultimately adopted by the Commission, see European Commission, C (2014) 9641 Annex I.

[57] The Commission guidelines indeed provide: 'Point 15 of the Common Approach appears in the section dedicated to the Director … It is therefore clear that the indicators at stake should focus on the Director and limited to the areas where (s)he has effective control. In other terms, the Key Performance Indicators at stake in the present note should aim at assessing the Director's results and not those of the agency'. See ibid 2.

with the agency's mandate is not assured, (ii) the KPIs are only formulated to assess the director's functioning and, more fundamentally, (iii) the Common Approach and the Commission's guidelines amount in any case only to non-binding instructions.

### *Accountability Beyond the Director?*

Looking beyond the accountability relationships involving the Director, a further genuine blind spot of the Common Approach is that it in no way defines an accountability relationship for the Management Board, although it is the Management Board that defines the agency's policy in its work programme which the Director has to implement. The Common Approach might at first sight be said to establish an accountability relationship between the Board and the Commission, through the novel early warning system,[58] but upon closer inspection the early warning system is not an accountability mechanism. Like other novel elements in the Common Approach,[59] it is an instrument of ex ante or ongoing rather than ex post control of EU agencies. The agencies or their boards are not expected to justify their action but instead the aim simply is to preclude certain agency action.

### *The Accountability Image Resulting from the Common Approach*

To summarise, the accountability regime that results from the Common Approach is incomplete and partial. It is incomplete because part of the agency's activities (those of its Management Board) appear entirely off the accountability radar. It is only partial because the Common Approach envisages only a limited number of accountability forums: the Director's professional accountability may be ensured by the Board's scrutiny. His or her political accountability results from scrutiny performed by the Parliament (and Council) but it is narrowly construed around the budgetary procedure. Finally there is administrative accountability before the audit authorities in the budgetary procedure.

A learning perspective on accountability thus seems to be dominant in the Common Approach: the Director who manages the agency is first and foremost accountable to an apolitical body of experts which helps in keeping the agency's

[58] See Common Approach, para 59. This mechanism allows the Commission to signal its objection to an envisaged decision in the Management Board if the Commission believes that the Board is about to take a decision that may not comply with the agency's mandate, may violate EU law or is in manifest contradiction with EU policy objectives. Remarkably, the mechanism thus does not allow the Commission to disagree simply for political reasons (unless there is a manifest contradiction with policy goals). The Commission nonetheless refers to the mechanism as political in nature, mainly because its representative does not have the competence to suspend a decision of the Board. See European Commission, COM(2015) 179 final 7.

[59] For instance the requirement to have working arrangements between the relevant Commission DG and an agency on the latter's international relations in para 25 of the Common Approach.

staff 'smart and sharp'.[60] A democratic perspective on accountability can also be identified in the Common Approach given the (albeit incomplete, *cf* above) role foreseen for the European Parliament. On the other hand a constitutional perspective, where other public institutions keep a check on the agency in order to prevent abuses of power, seems largely absent from the Common Approach. At least in part this could be explained by the fact that, despite staying silent on the issue of delegation, the Common Approach is still premised on the idea that EU decentralised agencies are not genuine regulatory agencies, their powers only being relatively modest from a comparative perspective. The questions of abuse of power and the risk of power concentration, associated with a constitutional perspective on accountability,[61] are then pre-empted by limiting these risks in an ex ante manner.

## EU Decentralised Agencies' Transparency

As noted, transparency is conceptualised for the purposes of this chapter as 'the disclosure of information by an organization that enables external actors to monitor and assess its internal workings and performance'.[62] Disclosure in this regard can be proactive as well as reactive. A reading of the Common Approach from this perspective reveals that no attention is devoted at all to reactive transparency. This may be explained by the fact that this part of transparency, just like the budgetary procedure, is one of the few issues that had already been addressed in a horizontal manner before the adoption of the Common Approach. Thus every establishing act of an EU decentralised agency already referred back to the general transparency Regulation (1049/2001), providing a sound framework for access to documents held by the EU agencies.

The Common Approach's limited focus on transparency, despite referring to it throughout, then centres on elements of transparency of the decision-making process and transparency of policy content.[63] The Common Approach indeed foresees a template for both the annual report and the annual work programme.[64] The Common Approach's only explicit mentioning of transparency to the benefit of the citizen is when it prescribes that EU agencies' websites should be as multilingual as possible 'in order to facilitate their consultation by citizens of all Member States'.[65] In addition the agencies' websites are (implicitly) indicated as the primary portal through which 'information necessary to ensure transparency' is made available.[66] Strikingly, and this despite the varying degree to which this

60 Bovens et al, above n 7, 232.
61 ibid 231.
62 Grimmelikhuijsen and Welch, above n 10, 563.
63 See Cross and Bølstad, above n 2, 218.
64 See paras 27 and 46 of the Common Approach.
65 See para 64 of the Common Approach.
66 ibid.

issue is regulated in existing establishing acts,[67] the Common Approach does not provide any further guidance on which information is deemed necessary in this regard.

As regards the agencies' internal workings, the main transparency element that may be identified in the Common Approach is its significant attention to the need to prevent and manage conflicts of interest. The Common Approach reiterates this in relation to the members of the Management Board, the Directors and the members of agencies' scientific committees.[68] Following the Common Approach, the Commission assessed the agencies' practice on the matter and adopted guidelines addressed to the agencies. Although they are formally non-binding, the guidelines are worded in coercive language.[69] Recent legislative practice also shows that the Commission and EU legislator are imposing related legal requirements on the agencies when establishing acts are reviewed.[70]

## *The Limited Attention to Transparency Explained in Light of the Common Approach's View on Accountability*

The limited attention for transparency in the Common Approach may appear puzzling at first sight. However, if it is recalled that transparency is a necessary but insufficient condition for accountability this becomes less of an enigma. Indeed, the way in which accountability has been conceptualised in the Common Approach has a direct bearing on the degree to which it (could) devote(d) attention to the value of transparency.

Above it was noted that the Common Approach does not seem to reflect any consideration of social accountability and that political accountability is focused on the Parliament (and Council) in the discharge procedure. This means that the public at large (citizens, stakeholders and social organisations) were not regarded as significant accountability forums. Instead, the Common Approach identified other professionals (*in casu* the Board) as the primary accountability forum. For the forums identified by the Common Approach then, the required transparency is already present. The discharge authority has all the required information through the budgetary procedure, while the Management Board has access to the required information through the Director. For the purposes of accountability as defined in the Common Approach, the type and degree of transparency foreseen in the Common Approach is indeed sufficient.

[67] Compare for instance the provisions on proactive transparency in two very similar agencies, the EMA and EFSA. See Art 80 of Regulation 726/2004 (EMA) and Art 38 of Regulation 178/2002 (EFSA).

[68] See paras 11, 18 and 20 of the Common Approach.

[69] European Commission, 'Guidelines on the prevention and management of conflicts of interest in EU decentralised agencies' (10 December 2013).

[70] See Art 85(2)p in the Commission's proposal for a new EASA Regulation, COM(2015) 613 final; Art 61(1)j in the Commission's proposal for a new Frontext Regulation, COM(2015) 671 final. The European Parliament amended the latter proposal to also include the current Art 78 in the new Frontex Regulation 2016/1624.

This finding evidently leads back to the question whether the Common Approach deals in a satisfactory manner with the issue of the agencies' accountability. The analysis above showed that this was not the case because ultimately the Common Approach does not enshrine a genuine Common *understanding* on the place and role of EU agencies in the EU institutional set up. A truly satisfactory approach would thus require this fundamental question to be resolved first. In light thereof, the required accountability mechanisms would then be defined. This would subsequently allow the transparency regime to be worked out, prescribing the required openness in function of the selected accountability mechanisms.

Whether resolving that fundamental question is at all feasible is of course a different matter. In any case it has been argued that at EU level there is a risk that any such understanding would be the result of an unclear and ambiguous compromise between supranationalist and intergovernmentalist forces with the ensuing risks that constitutional values (such as accountability and transparency) would not be adequately safeguarded.[71]

## Institutional Practice Post-2012: Superseding the Common Approach

Following the discussion of the substance of the CA, the pertinent question becomes how the drafting of subsequent legislation establishing EU agencies has been affected by the CA. In general terms it has been noted that the provisions of the CA merely amounted to a partial codification of existing institutional practice, containing few genuinely innovative elements, and that the legislative acts adopted following the CA contain provisions that generally go beyond the 'minimal' provisions of the CA.[72]

This is no different if one focuses specifically on the issue of accountability. Indeed, recent institutional practice shows that the EU institutions have imposed additional accountability requirements (not foreseen in the CA) on EU agencies. However, in light of what has been argued above, these additional requirements do not necessarily improve the accountability of agencies. Indeed, since they do not seem to be informed by a clear view on the role and place of EU agencies in the EU's institutional set-up, these additional requirements simply result in another cost imposed on an already overburdened administration. As a result, they do not result in more or better accountability but instead may result in accountability overload. Three particular issues are worth highlighting in this respect: the Parliament's attempts to act as an accountability forum for the agencies' Directors; the novelty of Europol's Joint Parliamentary Scrutiny Group (JPSG); and the way the Parliament maximises its leverage in the discharge procedure.

[71] Verhey, above n 25, 53.
[72] Chamon, above n 24, 97–101.

## *Agencies' Directors before the Parliament*

From a simple reading of the Common Approach, one would be excused to think that the Parliament and the agencies' directors do not have any relationship beyond the discharge procedure. In reality however, we can see that the agencies' directors maintain intense relations with their ('parent') parliamentary committee. While only some establishing regulations provide that the Parliament may *summon* the agency's Director, in practice all agency directors typically appear before the relevant Parliament when invited. While a formal obligation to appear before the Parliament is thus lacking, practice shows a de facto obligation for the directors to justify and explain the agency's conduct. The horizontal resolutions adopted by the Parliament in the discharge procedure (*cf* below) show that the Parliament is keen on 'generalising' this arrangement and detaching it from the discharge procedure.[73]

A further illustration may be seen in the appointment procedure of the Director on which the CA only provides that the Board will appoint the Director based on a proposal from the Commission. However, recent legislative acts provide for an increased role of the Parliament in the procedure. While it could be argued that the appointment of the Director has more to do with ex ante control than with accountability, the latter also provides a useful lens of analysis: the appointment procedure may be worked out in such a way that a Director-designate has to justify and explain his or her plans for the agency whereby the sanctioning may consist of the refusal to nominate.

Today, only the Executive Directors of the three European Supervisory Authorities require a formal confirmation by the Parliament.[74] Some of the most recent establishing regulations adopted prior to the CA provided that the Parliament would adopt an opinion after hearing the Director-designate and that the Board would inform the Parliament of how it took the opinion into account.[75] In a way the CA frustrated the further reinforcement of the Parliament's position in the appointment procedure, since the Commission sometimes strictly adheres to the CA, which does not foresee a role for the Parliament, as a template when proposing the establishment of new agencies[76] or the revision of existing agencies. For the revision of the European Railway Agency (ERA) Regulation, the Commission went beyond the prescriptions of the CA and itself proposed that the designated candidate could be invited before the Parliament,[77] a provision which did not figure in the original ERA regulation. In contrast, in its 2015 proposal for revising the Frontex Regulation, the Commission did not foresee a special role

[73] See point 53 of the Resolution of the Parliament of 17 April 2013, [2013] OJ L308/374; point 18 of the Resolution of the Parliament of 3 April 2014, [2014] OJ L266/359; and notably point 35 of the Resolution of the Parliament of 29 April 2015, [2015] OJ L 255/431.

[74] See the identical Arts 51(2) of the three ESA Regulations (1093/2010, 1094/2010, 1095/2010).

[75] Chamon, above n 24, 78.

[76] See for instance Art 32 of the Commission proposal to establish a European Labour Authority, COM(2018) 131 final, which does not foresee any role for the Parliament.

[77] See Art 62(2) of COM(2013) 27 final.

for the Parliament.[78] At the insistence of the Parliament however, the Regulation now provides that all three candidates proposed by the Commission will appear before the Parliament.[79] If the Board nominates a candidate other than the Parliament's preferred candidate, the Regulation provides that the Board has to inform the Parliament in writing how it took Parliament's opinion into account.[80]

Summarising this state of affairs: because of a lack of a common understanding between the institutions on the role and place of EU agencies in the institutional set-up, the relationship between the Parliament and the agencies' directors is worked out in a half-hearted way in the appointment procedure (explain and justify but no possibility to sanction). The extra accountability requirements then result in an extra burden but in no way contribute to strengthened accountability.

### *The Novelty of Europol's JPSG: Accountability before National Parliaments*

Another illustration of the apparent tendency to keep adding accountability requirements without considering the more fundamental question of which accountability is actually needed may be seen in the new Europol Regulation.[81] Article 51 of the Regulation establishes the JPSG bringing together the European and national parliaments. The JPSG may invite the Management Board's chair and the Director of Europol to discuss Europol's functioning. This mechanism adds a new actor (the Board's chairperson)[82] and forum (the JPSG which includes national parliaments) but the 'explain and justify' element is not complemented by a clear sanctioning element, since the JPSG only adopts conclusions that are then forwarded to the EU institutions. Here again, an accountability mechanism is introduced in both a half-hearted (no sanctioning) and poorly considered way: involving national parliaments in an agency's accountability mechanism does not seem informed by a clear view on the agencies' role and place in the EU institutional set-up.

### *The Parliament's Horizontal Discharge Resolutions*

Since 2009 (budgetary year 2007) the European Parliament not only adopts discharge decisions and resolutions for specific agencies but it discusses

[78] See Art 68(2) of COM(2015) 671 final.

[79] That all candidates, rather than only the Director-designate, should appear before the Parliament was already foreseen in point 32 of the 2010 Framework Agreement concluded between the Parliament and the Commission (see [2010] OJ L304/47). Significantly, this requirement was not included in the CA.

[80] See Art 69(2) of Regulation 2016/1624, [2016] OJ L251/1.

[81] Regulation 2016/794, [2016] OJ L135/53.

[82] That the chair of the Management Board may be held accountable for the agency's policy is exceptional but not unique. Art 12 of the EMCDDA Regulation (1920/2006) provides that 'The European Parliament may also ask for a hearing with the Director and the Chairperson of the Management Board on any subject related to the Centre's activities'.

overarching issues relevant to all agencies in a 'horizontal' resolution. The practice of adopting such a horizontal resolution in itself shows how the Parliament is instrumentalising the discharge procedure for purposes not strictly related to the budgetary procedure.[83] While the Parliament has perfectly legitimate (political) reasons for this 'improper' use of the discharge procedure, this practice shows how channelling the accountability relationship between EU agencies and the Parliament exclusively through the discharge procedure (as the CA does) is not satisfactory.

As far as transparency goes, the Parliament through its horizontal resolutions has consistently put pressure on the agencies to develop proper policies on preventing and managing conflicts of interests[84] and on providing a multilingual online presence containing relevant information for EU citizens.[85] Recently, the Parliament added to this that agencies should also put in place specific policies on whistleblowing 'in order to foster a culture of transparency and accountability in the workplace'.[86] This shows how the Parliament's practice of adopting horizontal resolution has contributed to transparency, since it uses the instrument to put pressure on the agencies to update their governance, even if these governance issues (conflicts of interest, whistleblowing) might only be incidentally relevant for the agencies' budgets.

Focusing on the issue of accountability, the Parliament's horizontal resolutions show its wavering position on the Common Approach. On the one hand it commits the fallacy of equating 'additional accountability requirements' with 'reinforced accountability' by noting that the CA has resulted in greater accountability.[87] At the same time, the Parliament has implicitly recognised the resulting accountability overload[88] and it has hinted at the more fundamental issue of the agencies' place in the EU's institutional set-up, when it noted in relation to the Commission's follow up of the CA that 'a comprehensive assessment of the current agencies landscape' is still lacking.[89] While the Parliament seems to reproach the

[83] This is of course a practice which the Parliament also pursues vis-a-vis the Council itself. It would seem that the agencies themselves have already complained about this to the Parliament; see Letter of 19 October 2012 from Marc Sprenger, chair of the Network of Agencies, to Martin Schulz, president of the European Parliament on the handling of the 2010 discharge procedure and its possible outcome (on file with the author).

[84] See points 52–60 of the Resolution of the Parliament of 10 May 2012, [2012] OJ L286/388; points 29–46 of the 2013 Resolution; points 58–76 of the 2014 Resolution; points 36–44 of the Resolution of the Parliament of 29 April 2015, [2015] OJ L255/431; points 21–30 of the 2016 Resolution; points 41–50 of the 2017 Resolution.

[85] See point 49 of the 2012 Resolution; point 55 of the 2013 Resolution; points 45–54 of the 2015 Resolution; points 32–34 of the 2016 Resolution; and point 51 of the 2017 Resolution.

[86] See point 41 of the 2017 Resolution. See also point 24 of the 2016 Resolution.

[87] See point 5 of the Resolution of the Parliament of 28 April 2016, [2016] OJ L246/447; point 12 of Resolution 2017/1750 of the European Parliament, [2017] OJ L252/372.

[88] See point 13 of Resolution 2017/1750 of the European Parliament, [2017] OJ L252/372; point 28 of the Resolution of the Parliament of 14 February 2019 (P8_TA(2019)0134).

[89] See point 49 of the Resolution of the Parliament of 17 April 2013, [2013] OJ L308/374.

Commission for this, it should be clear that this shortcoming should be traced back to the CA itself.

Indeed, while the Parliament would like to see itself, rather than the Commission,[90] as the political principal of the agencies,[91] this ultimately depends on how we consider the EU system: should it (further) evolve into a parliamentary system? Should it adopt a unitary executive model? These fundamental issues have ramifications for the agency question but were not addressed in the CA.

## Conclusion

This chapter has focused on the macro and meso levels of accountability and transparency, ie, is the process of agencification itself characterised by these principles of good governance and do we see these principles reflected in the frameworks regulating the functioning of EU agencies? To keep a sufficient focus, these questions where addressed by studying the Common Approach on Decentralised Agencies since it reflects the state of the institutions' thinking on the role and place of EU agencies in the EU's institutional framework. The chapter has thereby also developed an immanent critique on the Common Approach: how far does the CA live up to the promise of introducing good governance in European governance?

Focusing on agencification, the CA had the potential of infusing the process with greater accountability and transparency but failed to do so. In terms of accountability this was the result of the CA's non-binding nature: since the institutions are free to ignore the CA, they cannot be held accountable if they fail to respect its prescriptions. In terms of transparency the CA failed to fulfil its potential since it does not prescribe the principles governing issues such as which bodies qualify as decentralised agencies in the first place, when recourse to an agency is justified and which powers can be conferred on agencies.

Turning to the meso level, a clear picture on how the accountability of the agencies is conceptualised may be distilled from the CA. That said, the accountability as conceptualised in the CA is also both partial and incomplete. It is partial because the CA focuses exclusively on professional accountability and a limited political accountability (solely through the budgetary procedure). It is incomplete because only the Director is identified as a relevant actor, whereas an agency's actual policy is defined by the agency's Board. The CA's lack of attention to transparency is a logical consequence of this, given the dependent relationship between the constitutional values of accountability and transparency. The CA's unfulfilled promise of securing accountability and transparency in the agencies' functioning is also evidenced by the post-CA institutional practice in which the institutions

[90] ibid point 50.

[91] See point 16 of the Resolution of the Parliament of 3 April 2014, [2014] OJ L266/359.

have advocated or imposed further accountability and transparency requirements going beyond what the CA prescribes.

This chapter's findings should not be equated with a plea for additional accountability and transparency requirements. Instead, the main point advanced here is that the EU institutions should redo their homework and properly address the fundamental question of what the role and place is of EU decentralised agencies in the EU's institutional set-up. From addressing that fundamental question the solution to the question how and by which actors the agencies should be held accountable will almost automatically result and from that the necessary transparency requirements. As a result, the proper way forward is not just to impose additional accountability and transparency requirements on the agencies, as is presently being done, but to impose well-considered requirements, which might well result in fewer requirements imposed resulting in greater accountability and transparency.

# 15

# From Deparliamentarisation to a Parliamentary Renaissance? National Parliaments in the EU Polity

ADAM CYGAN

## Introduction

European integration or 'Europeanisation' utilises a distinct multilevel governance framework which has created a shared policy and legislative agenda which Member States are bound to implement. Through successive Treaties, legislative competences have been progressively transferred to the Council and European Parliament at the expense of national institutions and actors.[1] In particular, it has been the absence of direct national parliamentary participation in decision-making, together with the limited and often ineffective domestic accountability of the executive in EU affairs that has been identified as the primary cause of the democratic deficit within the EU's legislative process.[2] This isolation of national parliaments within the integration process has been more commonly referred to as the 'de-parliamentarisation' of the EU[3] and is why national parliaments have been referred to as 'victims' of EU integration.[4]

The marginalisation of national parliaments may be more accurately defined as 'de-national parliamentarisation'. The Treaty of Lisbon acknowledged this criticism by including a revised Protocol 1 on National Parliaments and Article 12 TEU, which states that 'national parliaments contribute *actively* to the good functioning

[1] H Kassim, 'Europeanization and Member State Institutions' in S Bulmer and C Lesquene (eds), *The Member States of the European Union* (Oxford, Oxford University Press, 2005) 297–303.

[2] P Kiiver, *The National Parliaments in the European Union: A Critical View on EU Constitution Building* (Kluwer Law International, 2006) 41–42.

[3] J O'Brennan and T Raunio, 'Deparliamentarisation and European Integration' in J O'Brennan and T Raunio (eds), *National Parliaments within the Enlarged European Union: From Victims of Integration to Competitive Actors* (London, Routledge, 2007).

[4] A Maurer, 'National Parliaments in the European Union Architecture; From Latecomers Adaptation Towards Permanent Institutional Change' in A Maurer and W Wessels (eds), *National Parliaments on their Ways to Europe: Losers or Latecomers?* (Baden-Baden, Nomos, 2001).

of the Union' (emphasis added). This 'active contribution', for example through participation in subsidiarity monitoring under Protocol 2, creates an expectation that, collectively, national parliaments may inject enhanced democratic legitimacy into EU legislation. However, Protocol 2 per se has, arguably, failed to fully deliver improved oversight with the subsidiarity Early Warning Mechanism (EWM) yielding only three yellow cards since 2009. Yet, notwithstanding this, it would be inappropriate to only measure the success of the EWM by virtue of these results.

The 'active contribution' of national parliaments has also manifested itself in other 'softer' ways with national parliaments taking greater control of their political responsibilities. By changing their modus operandi for policy and legislative scrutiny, partly in response to subsidiarity monitoring, improving coordination between national parliaments through sharing information, and opening up political dialogue between national parliaments and the Commission, the Treaty of Lisbon may be more appropriately identified as having provided an impetus for national parliaments to become more proactive and self-assured institutions. National parliaments use the opportunities provided by the Treaty, not necessarily for the purpose of improving the throughput legitimacy of EU legislation, but to enhance the accountability of ministers to *their* parliaments. In short, parliaments may be said to have become more 'Europeanised', but primarily to the extent that the enhanced recognition of national parliaments within the Treaty provides a concurrent opportunity for improved oversight over ministers to their parliaments. The issue which this chapter considers is whether, overall, the procedural opportunities for national parliaments after the Treaty of Lisbon can be said to have addressed criticisms of de-parliamentarisation?

In recent years, the principles and aims of EU integration have been challenged by the economic crisis. Adopting a critical stance, the economic crisis would appear to have challenged the democratic model of representative and parliamentary governance within the EU and created a tension between national budgetary sovereignty and legislative autonomy to deliver the socio-economic policies demanded by the voters on the one hand, and the EU's objective of securing economic stability and deeper economic integration on the other.[5] In particular, it has been the EU's governance response to the economic crisis and the tension between the use of executive and legislative powers that has caused most concerns for national parliaments. Indeed, it may be argued that the EU's response to the crisis has shifted the perspective of the de-parliamentarisation and democratic deficit debate away from the ordinary legislative process to one more focused on the absence of effective parliamentary scrutiny and accountability of EU economic governance. This has proved challenging, not least because the EU's response to the management of the economic crisis has utilised a preponderance

[5] D Jančić, 'National Parliaments and EU Fiscal Integration' (2016) 22 *European Law Journal* 225; A Cygan, 'Legal Implications of Economic Governance for National Parliaments' (2017) *Parliamentary Affairs* 1.

of executive dominated governance procedures and in particular the role of the European Council.

The EU's response to the crisis has created an EU economic governance model the overriding objective of which is to centrally coordinate and control both macroeconomic policies and public finances within the Member States. This form of governance utilises both legislative and non-legislative measures, such as treaties and soft law instruments to address the problems and is distinct from the ordinary legislative procedure because of the limited role for the European Parliament. Moreover, EU economic governance does site national parliaments within the centre of this governance process, notwithstanding that these are democratically elected institutions that are most challenged by the EU's economic governance model. In the light of these developments this chapter considers whether a new form of de-parliamentarisation and democratic deficit is emerging arising from the EU's response to the economic crisis and whether national parliaments have been able to effectively respond to the regulatory realignment?

Finally, in addition to the challenges posed by the economic crisis has been the expansion of EU competence in external relations which attracts criticisms of de-parliamentarisation, for example, in the development of EU trade and investment policy and especially in the context of Mixed Agreements. In this context, the role of the European Parliament in EU foreign relations is limited and its capabilities to effectively represent the voice of EU citizens in the area of EU external trade and investment policy has been questioned.[6] Moreover, a tension exists between the European Parliament and national parliaments in delivering democratic legitimacy in this sphere, which was manifested in the conclusion of the EU–Canada Comprehensive Economic and Trade Agreement (CETA). This chapter considers whether the direct involvement of national parliaments is necessary, or even possible, in order to ensure better representation of EU citizens in EU trade and investment policy. Is a representative function for national parliaments the only way to avoid the emergence of a democratic deficit or does an enhanced role for the European Parliament provide the necessary representative democracy required when the EU concludes trade agreements?

## De-Parliamentarisation within the EU

### 'Victims' of Integration

National parliaments have been described as 'victims' of EU integration.[7] The process of EU democratisation may have led to increased legislative powers for the

[6] M Krajewski, 'External Trade Law and the Constitution Treaty: Towards a Federal and More Democratic Common Commercial Policy? (2005) 42 *Common Market Law Review* 91.

[7] Maurer, above n 4.

European Parliament and strengthened representative democracy at the EU level, but this has been accompanied by a simultaneous decrease in legislative powers for national parliaments. Furthermore, EU integration has also been identified for eroding national parliamentary control over national governments. Thus, Jans and Piedrafita[8] summarised the de-parliamentarisation thesis as being composed of three key elements; namely reduced national competences and legislative autonomy, a shift in the domestic–executive legislative balance, and information asymmetries which hampered national parliaments when they conducted their EU scrutiny activities.

The defining feature of EU integration has been the constitutionalisation of the EU and the creation of what the Court, in *Van Gend en Loos* referred to as a 'new legal order'[9] in which the primacy of EU law is paramount. Together with the Europeanisation of policy, the centre of gravity for legislative action has shifted from the national arena to the EU, but national parliaments were also slow to respond to Europeanisation and in particular to 'Europeanise' their parliamentary activities to maximise their influence. One feature of the integration has been the peripheral role which national parliaments have held throughout the integration process, particularly with regard to decision-making, but this is largely because of the constitutional sovereignty of Member States and the absence of 'harmonisation' with respect to EU scrutiny practices which remain individual and diverse across the Member States. Moreover, EU decision-making does not require formal ratification of legislative acts by national parliaments and, notwithstanding the Treaty of Lisbon, remains dominated by the institutions with the Treaty balancing the supranational (Commission), the intergovernmental (Council) and the multinational (European Parliament).

The constitutional sovereignty of the Member States has drastically limited the possibility of involving national parliaments in the EU policy-making process. This lack of participation should, however, be distinguished from the scrutiny activities of national parliaments of EU legislative and policy proposals. In this context national parliaments are defined by their domestic constitutional arrangements, which has led to national parliaments being categorised as 'strong' (or in some cases 'weak') actors in EU affairs.[10] Because of this constitutional sovereignty, national parliaments are by and large individual actors in EU affairs which the provisions of Protocol 1 reinforces by stating that the way 'national parliaments scrutinise *their governments* in relation to the activities of the Union is a matter for the particular constitutional organisation and practice of each Member State' (emphasis added). In a number of Member States, for example, Denmark, Germany and even

[8] T Jans and S Piedrafita, 'The Role of National Parliaments in European Decision-Making' (2009) EIPASCOPE Working Paper 2009/1.

[9] Case 26/62 *Van Gend en Loos* [1963] ECR 1 (EU:C:1963:1).

[10] K Goetz and JH Meyer-Sahling, 'The Europeanisation of National Political Systems: Parliaments and Executives' (2008) 3 *Living Reviews in European Governance* 2, available at: www.livingreviews.org/lreg-2008-2.

the United Kingdom, the objective of this scrutiny has traditionally focused on securing domestic accountability of ministers for decisions taken within Council and not on injecting throughput or output legitimacy to EU legislation. This also rebuts arguments that, post-Lisbon, the focus for national parliaments has changed because of Article 12 TEU or the need for some collective response under the subsidiarity monitoring arrangements of Protocol 2. For example, suggestions of the creation a post-Lisbon virtual third chamber of national parliaments or a new institutional organ[11] arising from the provisions of Article 12 TEU and Protocol 2[12] are unrealistic. Meanwhile, the formal task of national parliaments to implement directives leaves little scope for discretion by national parliaments and underlines their limited involvement in EU decision-making. In the case of implementation any failure by a national parliament of timely and proper implementation of directives constitutes a violation of EU law, the consequence of which may result in the payment of damages by the offending State.[13]

## From Legislators to Implementers

The transfer of competence and the reduction in policy and legislative autonomy for national parliaments is, undoubtedly, the main cause of de-parliamentarisation, but one for which national parliaments are, paradoxically, primarily responsible. By ratifying treaties which have extended EU competences and that have created a legislative procedure within which national parliaments have only a marginal role, national parliaments affect themselves. The major question is then *how* do national parliaments most appropriately respond to this and adapt to the dynamic institutional and procedural challenge. Within an EU of 28 Member States[14] how effectively can parliamentary actors in diverse national and socio-political settings, arising from different national traditions adapt to common challenges constraints and opportunities for which they are primarily responsible through ratification of new treaties?

As a result of EU integration legislative autonomy has been replaced with national parliaments undertaking the transposition of EU law into the national legal order. Moreover, the ordinary legislative procedure with its use of qualified majority voting has diminished executive accountability by reducing the ability of national parliaments to impose detailed ex ante commitments on national governments prior to Council meetings. It is this weakness of national parliaments in the EU decision-making process which is commonly cited by some commentators

[11] D Jančić, 'A New Organ of the European Union: "National Parliaments Jointly"', Federal Trust Policy Commentary, available at: www.fedtrust.co.uk/uploads/Parliaments_Jointly.pdf.
[12] I Cooper, 'A "Virtual Third Chamber" for the European Union? National Parliaments after the Treaty of Lisbon' (2012) 35 *West European Politics* 441.
[13] Case 6/90 *Francovich v Italian State* [1991] ECR I-5357 (EU:C:1991:428).
[14] After Brexit this will be reduced to 27 Member States.

as the reason why the EU continues to suffer with a democratic deficit,[15] though this is not a universally held view. Others, such as Moravcsik place EU integration within a supranational context and highlight that within such a constitutional and institutional framework it is inevitable that national parliaments would not occupy the role of primary legislators.[16]

In this constitutional setting, attention has been focused upon the increased legislative powers and representative functions of the European Parliament to alleviate the democratic deficit which are held out as providing the necessary legitimacy and accountability for EU decision-making, but this proposition may be challenged. The absence of a direct constituency link between MEPs and their electorates, together with EU affairs being a low priority for many citizens translates into MEPs not necessarily being held accountable for their activities to the same extent as national MPs. Thus, increasing the role of national parliaments in EU affairs, whether collectively through subsidiarity monitoring or individually by treaty recognition of scrutiny reserve resolutions, has become a component part of the EU's response to rebut criticisms, not just of the democratic deficit and de-parliamentarisation, but also that citizens progressively feel a disconnect and isolation from the EU.

## Domestic Constitutional Realignment

Despite their tangential role in EU decision-making, national parliaments remain the primary legislative chambers within the Member States and provide the principal form of political representation for EU citizens. National parliaments are an embodiment of political and constitutional sovereignty; they are directly elected and have the function of controlling the executive. Furthermore, national parliaments are an expression of cultural identity and their composition broadly reflects the socio-cultural values of each Member State. Yet, notwithstanding this view there is no doubt that EU membership and the process of integration, which at its core necessitates the transfer of legislative competences, has transformed the constitutional status of national parliaments. However, Raunio and Hix have suggested that it would be inaccurate to conclude that EU membership and Europeanisation alone are solely responsible for de-parliamentarisation.[17] Constitutional and administrative changes within the Member States have, they argued, also played a part.

[15] D Doukas, 'The Verdict of the German Federal Constitutional Court on the Lisbon Treaty: Not Guilty, but Don't do it Again' (2009) 34 *European Law Review* 866.

[16] A Moravscik, 'Introduction; The Choice for Europe' in A Moravscik (ed), *The Choice for Europe: Social Purposes and State Power from Messina to Maastricht* (Ithaca, NY, Cornell University Press, 1998).

[17] T Raunio and S Hix, 'Backbenchers Learn to Fight Back: European Integration and Parliamentary Government' (2003) 23 *West European Politics* 142.

One constitutional development that can be witnessed in many Member States is the process of the modernisation of government and public administration. The changes brought through the growth of regional parliaments, the increased use of non-governmental agencies, and privatisation have all contributed to the progressive alteration of the position of the state which includes the institutional and constitutional status of national parliaments. As part of these changes, national parliaments have been portrayed as reactive institutions casting rather modest influence on policy initiatives coming from the executive. For example, the reorganisation of government and administration in the United Kingdom, through constitutional changes such as devolution and the extended use of agencies in policy delivery and regulation, has been highlighted as one significant transformation in the relationship between the executive and Parliament. As a result, Raunio and Hix argue that these developments demonstrate that European integration is not per se responsible for the decline of influence by national parliaments. They state that, 'notwithstanding the transfer of constitutional, executive and legislature powers to the European level, the overall impact of European integration on parliamentary government in the domestic area has actually been rather modest'.[18] By contrast, proponents of the 'de-parliamentarisation' thesis suggest that treaty developments have, almost exclusively, restricted national parliaments and pursued an objective of EU democratisation rather than seeking full parliamentarisation. Consequently, the preferred reform has been to grant increased powers to the European Parliament. Though the Treaties recognise the presence of domestic legislatures, this is to monitor subsidiarity once a legislative proposal is drafted rather than to participating directly in the process of decision-making.

If the constitutional and administrative developments that have extended the powers of non-governmental agencies are considered alongside the Europeanisation of law and policy within the Member States, it may be argued that national parliaments have been fighting a rearguard action to maintain their influence both at the EU and domestic level. Yet, Europeanisation and constitutionalisation reflect a depth of integration and the extent to which domestic government policy is influenced or directed by EU objectives. To address the specific point of Raunio and Hix, while there undoubtedly does exist a domestic political, legislative and constitutional realignment which has impacted upon the ability of national parliaments to exercise effective accountability and control, this should neither be exaggerated nor considered in isolation from the pervading nature of EU competences or the general principles of EU law. Accordingly, any domestic legislative proposal may infringe either EU competences or the general principles of EU law and, under Article 4(3) TEU Member States are required to refrain from doing this. Moreover, the development of soft law and the open method of coordination has made additional inroads into domestic competences and through a process of 'creeping competences' mainstreamed additional policy areas within the scope of EU competences, for example, public health and education.

[18] ibid 146.

The open method of coordination has strengthened the leadership role of the European Council which takes the lead in policy coordination with the Commission adopting a strategic role by setting objectives and issuing guidelines and recommendations to national governments. The European Parliament remains on the periphery of this process, as do national parliaments. At the national level the open method falls predominantly within the activities of civil servants who possess expertise on the issues and in this sense shares many of the features of the comitology process. As the open method is primarily intergovernmental in character, national parliaments should be in a constitutionally strong position to influence the proceedings. However, the difficulty lies in finding the parliamentary time to conduct the necessary scrutiny. Furthermore, reviewing what may in some instances be no more that abstract guidelines or targets which are set by the Commission are not priorities for national parliaments within a busy parliamentary timetable.

## A More Proactive Response?

The new legal order, referred to in *Van Gend en Loos* is, today, contained within the comprehensive treaty framework which recognises the presence of an omnicompetent EU and where the primacy of EU law is protected by the Court. However, this process of constitutionalisation and Europeanisation has not rendered national parliaments completely irrelevant with Article 12 and Protocol 1 of the Treaty of Lisbon providing legal recognition of the democratic significance of national parliaments and their constitutional diversity. Moreover, it would be inaccurate to suggest that national parliaments are, today, the passive bystanders and victims of integration that they once considered themselves to be and that de-parliamentarisation has been, at least, partially addressed. Since the Treaty of Lisbon, national parliaments have, most importantly, benefited from improved provision of information directly from the Commission and utilised their constitutional arrangements and internal parliamentary mechanisms and practices to maximise accountability of their governments in EU affairs. Parliamentary procedural devices, for example scrutiny reserves, are acknowledged within Protocol 1 indicating that national parliaments have institutional qualities, constitutional values and procedural mechanisms that ought to be respected within EU decision-making.[19]

In its Conclusions, Working Group IV of Constitutional Convention on the Role of National Parliaments stated that national parliaments can only conduct their scrutiny activities with the timely provision of information.[20] With the rejection

[19] K Auel and A Benz, 'The Politics of Adaptation: Europeanisation of National Parliamentary Systems' (2005) 11 *Journal of Legislative Studies* 372.

[20] CONV 353/02 Working Group IV The Role of National Parliaments, Final Report of Working Group IV on the Role of National Parliaments.

of the Constitutional Treaty the introduction of political dialogue between the Commission and national parliaments in 2006, under the so-called 'Barosso Initiative'[21] was a politically astute act by Barosso, because it gave national parliaments much, if not more, than the Constitutional Treaty delivered through a Protocol. Since its inception, the process of political dialogue with the Commission has, with some significant success, addressed the information asymmetries which Jans and Piedrafita identified as one of the primary causes of de-parliamentarisation. This included, for the first time, the transmission not only of all legislative proposals but also policy consultation papers *directly* to national parliaments. By contrast, the assessment of the EWM under Protocol 2 is more negative than for the political dialogue. This procedure, which was hailed as the core component of national parliamentary involvement in EU affairs, is now largely ineffective if not redundant. In short, a procedural device aimed at restricting an excess of EU legislation by benchmarking it against compliance with the principle of subsidiarity was introduced at a time when reliance upon EU legislation as a public policy instrument has been decreasing and other modes of governance are being preferred, for example, the open method of coordination. In addition, the Commission is undoubtedly more 'subsidiarity conscious' and through the Better Regulation Agenda ensures that legislative proposals are unlikely to infringe subsidiarity.

The Barroso Initiative has since its inception been underpinned by two objectives which place the convergence of parliamentary participation in EU affairs at the centre. First, it includes a commitment to national parliaments to provide a wider selection of documents that goes beyond legislative proposals and which reinforces the argument of a reduced reliance on Protocol 2. Secondly, the Initiative encourages both a vertical and a horizontal political dialogue with the Commission and between national parliaments. Protocol 1 remains important because it provides legally binding guarantees but parliaments have, in practice, benefited more directly from the Initiative which encourages them to position themselves within the EU polity through a vertical political dialogue with the Commission. Accordingly, national parliaments have reacted positively to the Initiative and generated over 4,000 opinions which have been sent to the Commission since 2006.[22]

The Treaty of Lisbon provisions and Barroso Initiative have endeavoured to bring national parliaments from the margins of EU decision-making and situate them within the EU polity. Crucially, both developments recognise the need for improved accountability secured through a political dialogue and institutional participation and notwithstanding the limited success of the EWM, overall national parliaments are, today, more prominent and self-assured actors in EU

[21] D Jančić, 'The Barroso Initiative: Window Dressing or Democratic Boost?' (2012) 8 *Utrecht Law Review* 78.

[22] 2006–17, European Commission, *Annual Reports on the relation with national parliaments*. 2017, European Commission, available at: ec.europa.eu/dgs/secretariat_general/relations/relations_other/npo/index_en.htm and European, Commission General Secretariat.

affairs; though de-parliamentarisation is by no means addressed and criticism that the EU continues to suffer from a democratic deficit have not abated either. The next section considers the EU's multilevel parliamentary framework and whether, and to what extent, this has democratised EU decision-making.

# National Parliaments, Legitimacy and the Democratic Deficit

## EU Democratisation

Scharpf has drawn a distinction between input and output legitimacy when assessing the democratic credentials of the EU and, in particular, Scharpf identifies that democratic governance requires that when legislators and policy-makers make choices, that these reflect the priorities and preferences of the citizens. In the EU's system of multilevel governance this has witnessed a process of EU democratisation with an increase of powers for the European Parliament, which is intended to provide input legitimacy within the legislative process.[23] Weatherill and Menon have described this need to connect with citizens within the legislative process as requiring a 'chain of accountability linking those governing to those governed'[24] which implies that if the EU is criticised for de-parliamentarisation, legislative legitimacy cannot be fully achieved. Following the Treaty of Lisbon the two key links in the legitimacy chain are the directly elected European Parliament and national parliaments which through subsidiarity monitoring *may* be able to inject some element of output legitimacy into the legislative process and possibly provide some form of intermediate connection between the citizens and the EU. The search for democratisation of the EU, through the allocation of increased powers for the European Parliament should not be underestimated, but the European Parliament, though performing a representative function, has not displaced national parliaments as the foremost representative institutions that reflect the views of the citizens. To this extent it is questionable whether subsidiarity monitoring adequately addresses the criticism of de-parliamentarisation.

The paradox of EU democratisation is that it would appear to have distanced the EU from the very citizens who are the intended beneficiaries of the legislation; hence involving national parliaments more directly in EU affairs may be considered as a strategic response to criticisms of a democratic deficit. Alternatively, this may be dismissed as creating an illusion of parliamentary engagement. Either way,

[23] F Scharpf, *Governing in Europe* (London, Routledge, 1999); F Scharpf, 'Legitimacy in the Multi-Level European Polity' in P Dobner and M Loughlin (eds), *The Twilight of Constitutionalism* (Oxford, Oxford University Press, 2010).

[24] A Menon and S Weatherill, 'Legitimacy, Accountability and Delegation in the European Union' in A Arnull and D Wincott (eds), *Accountability and Legitimacy in the European Union* (Oxford, Oxford University Press, 2002) 116.

Scharpf's core assertion that the key feature of a democratic system of governance is the presumption that the exercise of all public authority and legislative actions emanates from the consent of the citizens is undoubtedly correct. But, in terms of the legitimacy as derived from the citizen this cannot be determined merely by a regulatory model of governance where the output, or results of the decision-making process, is used as the sole benchmark of legitimacy. The search for legitimacy in the EU, both in terms of the input into and output of the legislative process, requires effective institutional accountability both horizontally and vertically across all levels of the EU's multilevel governance structure. The hallmark of a democracy is that it observes the rule of law and that accountability is secured through institutions that are representative of the citizen, but caution must also be maintained whether this form of accountability can ever be realistically achieved within the EU's complex multilevel institutional architecture. In the search for democratic accountability and legitimacy the EU is therefore no different from its constituent Member States where the challenges of multilevel governance regularly bring conflicts between central government and federal or devolved governments with regard to the exercise of competences and the powers of elected institutions. The challenge is to ensure that each level of governance remains constitutionally relevant and fulfils the representative functions that it has been allocated.

## Parliamentary Democracy within the EU's Multilevel Governance Framework

The Treaty of Lisbon provided legal recognition of the democratic significance of national parliaments and Article 2 TEU provides a clear expression of the democratic foundations of the EU and that it respects the values of respect of, inter alia, democracy and the rule of law. It is assumed that this includes respect for democratically elected national institutions which form a constituent part of the EU's multilevel governance framework. Within the EU's institutional architecture it is the European Parliament which provides the institutional expression of the views of EU citizens through the process of direct parliamentary elections. Accordingly, Article 2 TEU describes democracy as being based upon the principle that 'every public authority must be directly elected or answerable to a directly elected parliament',[25] which would appear to place the European Parliament at the centre of achieving this accountability. However, the generic nature of this provision would also appear to leave scope to imply that *national* parliamentary institutions, at all levels of governance, have a role to play in promoting good governance and that this is recognised within Article 12 TEU. Moreover, Article 2 TEU further suggests

[25] OJ C 120/01. Art 17(2) of the Declaration of Fundamental Rights and Freedoms adopted by the European Parliament on 12 April 1989.

that democratic accountability and adherence to the rule of law are not the only considerations of legitimate governance, but that a democratic system of governance also requires a comprehensive system of checks and balances to prevent the concentration of power and the consequences of abuse of power which this can bring.

The provisions within Articles 9–12 TEU which annunciate the democratic principles upon which the EU is founded represent a much clearer statement, by comparison with previous treaties, of how the EU seeks to meet the standards of democracy and accountability which it places upon all its Member States.[26] While this is welcome, these treaty provisions should not be viewed either as a panacea or that their inclusion provides a remedy to all the EU's institutional defects, or that they provide a comprehensive set of provisions through which citizens will engage more readily in EU affairs. Though an improvement, it is questionable whether Articles 9–12 TEU adequately address the dual problems of accountability and disconnection which were articulated by the Laeken Declaration,[27] the Commission's White Paper on European Governance[28] and the subsequent establishment of the Convention on the Future of Europe. The Convention, whose conclusions have largely shaped the Treaty of Lisbon, highlighted the accountability challenge facing the EU and stated that the EU must 'rethink its role, improve its operation and go down new avenues of progress and democracy'.[29]

Article 10 TEU identifies that the cornerstone of EU democracy is that it engages with the citizen and so its reference to the principles of representative and participatory democracy underscore the importance of consent of the citizen to EU integration. Under the Treaty of Lisbon the EU seeks to secure this consent in two specific ways. First, under Article 10(1) TEU the Treaty states that the functioning of the Union is founded upon representative democracy and identifies that this will be provided directly by the European Parliament. Secondly, Article 10(1) TEU implies indirect representation for EU citizens and that 'Member States are represented in the European Council by their Heads of State or Government and in the Council by their governments, themselves democratically accountable to their national parliaments or to their citizens'. It is securing this accountability of individual ministers to their national parliaments for their participation in the decision-making process which has traditionally been the preoccupation of national parliaments through the operation of their national scrutiny mechanisms and which was recognised by the Amsterdam Protocol on national parliaments.

A novel aspect of Article 10(4) TEU is that it promotes a more Europeanised response to political parliamentary accountability by identifying the importance

[26] For a comprehensive review of the constitutional landscape post Lisbon and how the Treaty promotes democracy and participation see generally P Wouters, L Verhey and P Kiiver (eds), *European Constitutionalism beyond Lisbon* (Antwerp, Intersentia, 2009).

[27] Laeken Declaration on the Future of Europe, December 2001, available at: www.europa.eu.int/futurum/documents/offtext/doc151201_en.htm.

[28] European Commission, European Governance: A White Paper' COM(2001) 428.

[29] CONV 67/1/02, 8.

of political parties in decision-making which in the European Parliament are organised on lines of political affiliation rather than on national lines. This cross-national organisation of political groupings attempts to create a strong pan-EU representative institution[30] out of the European Parliament and aims to reinforce the concept of a European *demos* which Scahrpf has identified as both lacking from EU integration and essential to improving citizen participation. However, there is limited evidence that Article 10(4) TEU has created a Europeanised political system which transcends traditional national allegiances, or that EU citizens elect MEPs solely on the basis of EU issues rather than being influenced by the domestic political agenda.

The absence of an EU *demos*, which is central to Scharpf's analysis, has been contested by Weiler who considers this a problem of translation in that 'the very language of modern democracy, its grammar, syntax and vocabulary, [which] revolve around the state, the nation and the people-its *demos*' is transposed to the Union which is not a state.[31] Weiler's core assertion that it is wrong to impose the criteria of nation-state democracy on to a supranational EU is not without merit. Instead, Weiler has argued for 'the very conceptual decoupling of nationality from citizenship' and advocates that democracy beyond the nation state becomes possible if one understands the European *demos* in *civic* and political rather than ethno-cultural terms.[32] Such ideas have found some favour within the Citizenship line of case law in the European Court of Justice,[33] but politically there is far less consensus for moving away from the idea of an EU of nation states whose parliaments provide both the executive and which are the primary source of accountability. For example, judgments such as that of the German Federal Constitutional Court (FCC) in the *Lisbon Treaty* judgment, illustrate that there remain real concerns about handing over further competences to a supranational organisation that fails to have adequate constitutional safeguards.[34]

Democracy is traditionally associated with sustainable and active parliaments which play an integral role in securing the legitimacy of the legislative process. This participation manifests itself in a variety of forms, but the overriding consideration is the need to ensure direct accountability of the ultimate decision-makers

[30] Case 138/79 *Roquette Frères v Council* [1980] ECR 3333, 33–35 (EU:C:1980:249) where the Court highlighted the importance of political groupings and the representative function they perform.

[31] JHH Weiler, The Constitution of Europe: 'Do the New Clothes Have an Emperor?' and Other Essays on European Integration (Cambridge, Cambridge University Press, 1998) 268.

[32] Ibid 344.

[33] In Case C-499/06 *Halina Nerkowska v Zakład Ubezpieczeń Społecnych* [2008] ECR I-3993 (EU:C:2008:132) Advocate General Maduro argued that EU Citizenship, to have its full effect, should not be determined by reference to nationality. At para 23 of the Opinion the Advocate General Stated 'Citizenship of the Union must encourage Member States to no longer conceive of the legitimate link to integration only within the narrow bounds of the national community, nut also within the wider context of the society of the peoples of the Union'.

[34] Judgment of June 20 2009 Bundesverfassungsgericht, BVerfG, 2 BvE 2/08. See also A Steinbach, 'The Lisbon Judgment of the German Federal Constitutional Court: New Guidance on the Limits of European Integration? (2010) 11 *German Law Journal* 367, 376; D Doukas, above n 15, 887.

to a directly elected legislative body. While this traditional understanding of accountability is appropriate within the context of the nation state, it does not sit comfortably within the multilevelled and supranational integration of the EU where there is no comparable parliamentary system that may provide the necessary accountability. Though subsidiarity monitoring may offer some form of constitutional review by national parliaments, the lack of clear definition of subsidiarity, together with the limited horizontal cooperation between national parliaments within the Protocol 2 arrangements, merely reinforces the criticism that national parliaments are unable (if not unwilling) to provide proxy legitimacy for EU legislation. The absence of an EU *demos* underscores why national parliaments continue to maintain a 'nation-state' focus and pursue their individual scrutiny activities, the overriding objective of which is to secure executive accountability. Thus while national parliaments may have become more 'Europeanised' in terms of their procedures and practices and utilise the improved access to information and communication with the Commission, this has been in order to secure more effective executive accountability, rather than to (collectively) provide improved legitimacy to EU legislation. Scrutiny remains firmly focused on the level of governance that national parliaments can influence.

## Subsidiarity and the EWM

The primary effect of the institutionalisation and democratisation of the EU is that this has led to a progressive transfer of competence to supranational institutions for policies that were previously within the exclusive sovereign jurisdiction of Member States. In many cases the Treaty provides that competence is shared between the EU and the Member States leading to inevitable tensions concerning the application of these competences. This explains, in large part, why subsidiarity monitoring under Protocol 2 has been largely ineffective and led to only three yellow cards.[35] For example, in the regulation of the internal market, in circumstances when competence is shared and the principle of subsidiarity is relevant, the determinant of EU action at the EU or national level is whether EU legislation is necessary and that the desired result can be more efficiently achieved through a single legislative measure. When the Commission makes such judgements, which should be based on quantitative and qualitative factors,[36] such a decision is then benchmarked against the principle of subsidiarity in Article 5 TEU. However, though the political judgement of national parliaments may decide against the need for EU legislation the Court

[35] M Goldoni, 'The Instrumental Value of Horizontal Parliamentary Cooperation: Subsidiarity Review and the Political Dialogue' in N Lupo and C Fasone (eds), *Interparliamentary Cooperation in the Composite European Constitution* (Oxford, Hart Publishing, 2016) 167.

[36] This is part of the Commission's broader Better Regulation Agenda. See COM(2005) 97 final Communication from the Commission to the Council and European Parliament – Better Regulation for Growth and Jobs in the European Union.

has consistently held that once it is considered necessary to adopt common rules to regulate the Internal Market then this can *only* be achieved through EU action.[37] Thus it may be argued that the reason for only three yellow cards is not necessarily that EU law is subsidiarity compliant, but rather that national parliaments have concluded that there is only limited value in using Protocol 2.

The presumption underlying the Court's reasoning has been that the legislative measure will comply with the principle of subsidiarity and, from a political accountability perspective this would appear to imply that national parliaments have accepted the efficiency argument. However, this presumption is not without difficulty and while it may be procedurally correct to conclude that the legislative measure conforms to the principle of subsidiarity this does not immediately confirm that the legislation can be considered as legitimate. For example, notwithstanding the EU Better Regulation Agenda and the systematic use of Impact Assessments, concerns have been expressed that the reasons given by the Commission for EU legislative action tend to lack sufficient quantitative and qualitative justifications.[38] This raises questions of when the EU does legislate whether it does so excessively and whether the legislative content also conforms to the principle of proportionality under Article 5 TEU. It is the inability of national parliaments to sufficiently reach agreement under Protocol 2 TEU, as the three yellow cards illustrates, that leaves open the possibility of the evolution of a newly formulated democratic deficit rising at the national level as a result of national parliaments not being to apply the principle of subsidiarity with consistency and consensus.[39] This may be an unintended consequence, but Protocol 2 requires constant and coherent horizontal interparliamentary cooperation in order for it to be effective. While this cooperation may have improved, the evidence of only three yellow cards in 10 years strongly suggests that optimism about the constitutional potential of Protocol 2 were misplaced.

## De-Parliamentarisation Reborn? National Parliaments and Budgetary and Economic Coordination

### National Parliaments within the European Semester

The economic crisis had, and continues to have, a profound effect on the EU and its Member States. In addition to the socio-economic impact upon the Member

[37] Case C-49/01 *R v Secretary of State for Health ex parte British American Tobacco and Imperial Tobacco* [2002] ECR I-11453 in particular paras 177 and 185 (EU:C:2002:741).

[38] Interinstitutional Agreement between the European Parliament, the Council of the European Union and the European Commission on Better Law-Making, [2016] OJ L123, 1 available at: eur-lex.europa.eu/legalcontent/EN/TXT/?uri=CELEX%3A32016Q0512%2801%29.

[39] See further A Cygan, *Accountability, Parliamentarism and Transparency in the EU: The Role of National Parliaments* (Cheltenham, Edward Elgar, 2013) chs 5 and 6.

States, the EU's response to the crisis has also yielded constitutional and institutional changes which reignite criticisms of de-parliamentarisation and democratic deficit. In the EU's crisis management the concept of institutional balance has been altered with some institutions, especially the European Council and European Central Bank,[40] gaining importance, while others namely the European Parliament are more peripheral. In addition, new processes, especially the European Semester[41] not only reinforce the institutional realignment but have provided a structured framework for budgetary surveillance which utilises legislative as well as non-legislative soft forms of governance which impact upon the prerogatives and participation of both the European Parliament and national parliaments. However, it is the position of national parliaments that is most pertinent and especially if, and to what extent, they may be considered as 'victims' of the EU's response to the crisis with respect to the consequences crisis management has had on the budgetary sovereignty of the nation state?

The EU's institutional realignment in the wake of the crisis has seen the European Council become ever more dominant in the EU's institutional architecture.[42] The Heads of State or Government characterised as the 'Union's highest executive leaders'[43] have turned the European Council into the dominant actor within the EU's multilevel polity largely at the expense of the European Parliament. In particular, in response to the crisis the European Council has demonstrated an executive dominance and taken key political decisions which profoundly impact upon the budgetary sovereignty of the Member States and their parliaments. Institutionally, these decisions can be traced back to the development in the European Council to provide increased strategic and prescriptive political leadership which is arguably beyond that provided for in Article 15 TEU. Under this Treaty provision the European Council's role is to provide the EU with 'the necessary impetus for its development and shall define the *general* political direction and priorities thereof' (emphasis added). Though this strongly suggests that the European Council should be more concerned with long-term issues and general guidelines it has become directly involved in the decision-making process of economic governance.

Criticisms of the European Council's modus operandi illustrate the concern that by operating under rules of 'professional secrecy' decisions with long-lasting economic and political significance have been taken without adequate debate,

[40] D Jančić, 'Accountability of the Euopean Central Bank in a Deepening Economic and Monetary Union' in D Jančić (ed), *National Parliaments after the Lisbon Treaty and Euro Crisis* (Oxford, Oxford University Press, 2017) 141.

[41] C Lord, 'Parliamentary Control of the European Semester. Constraints and Opportunities' (2017) 70 *Parliamentary Affairs* 673.

[42] W Wessels, *The European Council* (Basingstoke, Palgrave Macmillan, 2014); D Fromage, 'Executive Accountability to National Parliaments in Post Crisis EU Affairs: The Persistent Shortcomings in the Council and European Council Oversight' in D Jančić (ed), *National Parliaments after the Lisbon Treaty and Euro Crisis* (Oxford, Oxford University Press, 2017) 159.

[43] ibid 43–47.

transparency or parliamentary involvement.[44] This has been described as 'post-democratic executive federalism'[45] and reinforces the critical narrative that national parliaments and their democratic practices are not mainstreamed within economic governance. In summary, these developments bring into sharp focus the polarised positions with respect to the EU's crisis management where expediency and effective accountability have, on a number of occasions, become competing values. But do these constitutional and institutional developments warrant the criticisms that national parliaments are once again 'victims' of integration or have national parliaments learned from their past experiences to adapt and overcome the challenges posed by EU economic governance and utilise the procedural mechanisms available and their constitutional prerogatives to maximise control over their executives?

The primary consequence of the European Semester is that it has added a new layer of surveillance which places constraints on national parliaments and, it has been suggested, undermines democratic legitimacy.[46] The European Semester has been described as coercive.[47] Though the Stability and Growth Pact had always included sanctions against transgressing Member States, the European Semester has significantly widened the scope of these powers. In particular these now include fines for transgressions of the rules, including for excessive debt, to a wide range of macroeconomic imbalances. Moreover, by dividing the Stability and Growth Pact into 'preventive' and 'corrective' arms, the Semester has also made Member States liable for fines for failing to follow recommendations to prevent problems, as well as for failing to correct them. Sanctioning powers are seemingly also more automatic and less discretionary. It is these developments in the enforcement of EU economic governance that has raised the question of whether 'enhanced economic coordination at the European level … indicates a renewed trend of de-parliamentarisation in EU affairs' because national parliaments are no longer the sovereign policy and legislative institutions in the context of economic governance.[48] To address this question it is necessary to consider the context and purpose of the European Semester which, given the effects of the crisis may be considered necessary. Thus rather than constraining Member States from delivering their obligations to the public, an alternative narrative could be that the legitimacy of the European Semester may be derived from how it assists each

[44] Inaugural speech by Martin Schulz following his election as President of the European Parliament, 17 January 2012, available at: www.europarl.europa.eu/former_ep_presidents/president-schulz-2012-2014/de-en/press/press_release_speeches/speeches/sp-2012/sp-2012-janua/inaugural-speech-by-mar.

[45] NV Motroshilova and J Habermas, 'The Crisis of the European Union and the Concept of Solidarity (2011–2013)' (2015) 52(4) *Russian Studies in Philosophy* 45.

[46] I Cooper and J Smith, 'Governance Without Democracy? Analysing the Role of Parliaments in European Economic Governance after the Crisis: Conclusions' (2017) 70 *Parliamentary Affairs* 728.

[47] See Lord, above n 41; and Cooper and Smith, above n 46.

[48] K Auel and O Hoing, 'National Parliaments and the Eurozone Crisis: Taking Ownership in Difficult Times?' (2015) 38 *West European Politics* 375.

Member State democracy to meet its obligations to its own electorate within a framework of fiscal and economic responsibility. However, such an understanding is not without its problems, not least because this may have implications for the input, output and throughput legitimacy that should be expected of the European Semester and which are crucial to enhancing legitimacy. Where does this leave national parliaments?

Both Member States and EU institutions have acknowledged a need for parliamentary involvement, notably in a report jointly written by the Presidents of the European Central Bank, the European Commission, the European Council, the European Parliament and the Eurozone group.[49] Yet, parliamentary participation in EU decisions can take many forms.[50] The European Semester is no exception and the underlying presumption for the participation of national parliaments in the European Semester should be that parliamentary participation should enable the effective management of externalities between member democracies in order that this ensures transparent public control, political equality and that justifications for decisions are provided to each of those democracies. Yet meeting that standard is not easy and going back to the German Federal Constitutional Court's *Maastricht Treaty* judgment[51] it was already identified how some benefits of international coordination – including, presumably, managing externalities – may presuppose 'long-term international commitments' that restrict how far voters can choose and control their own economic policies by electing their national parliaments.[52] Discussion of how far the European Semester may have made that predicament more acute is important to understanding possibilities and problems of parliamentary participation in it.

In the context of economic governance, the pre-Semester position for Member States drew together an irregular combination of monetary centralisation and almost complete decentralisation of fiscal and other socio-economic policies. This reflected the multi-democracy monetary union which was composed not of a single state, but of many states, each of them parliamentary democracies, often at different stages of the economic cycle and not all members of the Eurozone. Though Eurozone parliamentary democracies shared the currency they, by and large, continued to make their own decisions on taxation, spending and borrowing. This preserved national budgetary autonomy for key socio-economic policy choices, for example the welfare state, and of core political values that depend on

[49] European Commission, 'Completing Europe's Economic and Monetary Union' (2015) *The Five Presidents' Report* (Brussels, European Commission).

[50] C Neuhold and J Smith, 'Conclusion' in C Hefftler, C Neuhold, O Rozenberg and J Smith (eds), *The Palgrave Handbook of National Parliaments and the European Union* (Basingstoke, Palgrave Macmillan, 2015) 669–70.

[51] Case 2134/92 *Brunner v The European Union Treaty* [1994] 1 CMLR 57.

[52] R Bellamy and A Weale, 'Political Legitimacy and European Monetary Union: Contracts, Constitutionalism and the Normative Logic of Two-level Games' (2015) 22 *Journal of European Public Policy* 257, 264.

fiscal autonomy. Moreover, this arguably reinforced the notion of social solidarity within the Member States in the delivery of essential public services.[53]

By contrast, the overriding characteristic of the European Semester is that it appears to intrude deeply into the autonomy of national economic policy-making. For example, its objective of evaluating and improving any public policy that could affect the ability of a Member State to survive and thrive unaided in a monetary union, draws the Semester into the detail of national democracies. In addition to taxation, spending and borrowing, the European Semester covers a diverse range of social entitlements and public policy considerations including pensions, social benefits, labour markets, female participation in the workforce, and 'wage-setting in line with productivity growth'.[54] What is clear is that, post-Semester, neither Member States, nor their parliaments, are able to exercise complete budgetary sovereignty. According to the Commission,[55] 'before the crisis, policy planning largely "took place at the national level" in fiscal, structural and social matters'. By contrast, the European Semester has introduced a more integrated 'Europeanised' budgetary procedure, which is itself integrated into wider commitments to coordinate multiple economic and social policies. All Member States, irrespective of whether they are Eurozone members, follow the same simultaneous budgetary cycle. They submit their budgets (annual and multiannual) to EU institutions as soon as they are made public. They also have EU obligations including to accept 'peer reviews' and multilateral surveillance of how well their budgets fit pre-agreed 'adjustment paths' towards 'medium-term budgetary objectives'.

Thus, the conclusion would appear to be that the European Semester *does* encroach upon Member State democracy and reinforces the idea of de-parliamentarisation. While there may be benefits for coordinating national competences at the EU level, it remains an overriding principle of constitutional government that national governments must remain responsible to their own parliaments and courts for the exercise of their own powers. In this context the European Semester and EU economic governance more generally would appear to comply with the critique that the primary consequence of this transfer of budgetary competences and Europeanisation is a newly emerging parliamentary schism within the Member States.

## Economic Governance and Interparliamentary Cooperation

Both national parliaments and the European Parliament have been disadvantaged by the advances in European economic governance and while it may have been

[53] Cygan, 'Legal Implications of Economic Governance for National Parliaments', above n 5, 11.

[54] J Zeitlin and B Vanherke, 'Socializing the European Semester? Economic Governance and Social Policy Co-ordination in Europe 2020' (Swedish Institute for European Policy Studies, 2014).

[55] European Commission, 'The EU's Economic Governance Explained' (2015).

anticipated that, given the loss of budgetary sovereignty, national parliaments may have intensified their cooperation, this has not proved to be the case. Article 13 of the Treaty on Stability, Coordination and Governance in the Economic and Monetary Union is the only formal interparliamentary body that provides for coordinated responses by national parliaments within economic governance. The Inter-Parliamentary Conference on Stability, Economic Coordination and Governance (the SECG Conference) has met twice a year since its inception in 2013, but has generated little impact which underscores the criticism that EU economic governance suffers from a democratic deficit.[56]

The primary response by national parliaments to the economic crisis has been an internal one with attention focused on domestic reform of scrutiny procedures rather than the pursuit of collective action.[57] This reinforces the 'individual' approach by national parliaments to EU scrutiny activities generally and continues a trend witnessed in the limited application of the EWM and the greater use of direct vertical political dialogue and improved parliamentary procedures. As has been argued above, the EWM has limited scope and application within EU governance beyond the ordinary legislative process and while national parliaments have developed experience of collective action through the EWM they have also come to recognise its limitations, for example, through the outputs of the SECG conference. Thus, in the context of EU economic governance, which operates through 'soft' instruments of governance, these will not generally be subject to the EWM and thus unlikely to generate effective horizontal interparliamentary responses. In response to the loss of budgetary sovereignty national parliaments have, primarily, enhanced their own internal procedures to maximise ministerial accountability as a form of substitute sovereignty whereby enhanced parliamentary scrutiny is intended to make up for the loss of competence.[58]

Overall, interparliamentary cooperation in response to the economic crisis has been limited. For its part, the European Parliament has seen some merit in cooperation with national parliaments, but has rejected more formal cooperation to 'parliamentarise' economic governance.[59] The reason for this is that it would threaten its position as the principal parliamentary institution of the EU where the European Parliament envisages a system of centralised oversight in which the scrutiny of EU policies is conducted by the European Parliament.[60]

[56] The SECG Conference was, in part, modelled on existing interparliamentary conferences of EU affairs Committees (COSAC) and of foreign and defence committees (the CFSP-CSDP Conference). Similar to these two conferences, the SECG has no substantive powers.

[57] T Winzen, *Constitutional Preferences and Parliamentary Reform: Explaining National Parliaments' Adaptation to European Integration* (Oxford, Oxford University Press, 2017).

[58] A Cygan, 'Parliamentary Scrutiny of EU Affairs by the UK Parliament: The Primacy of Ministerial Accountability' in A Jonsson Cornell and M Goldoni (eds), *National and Regional Parliaments in the EU-Legislative Procedure Post-Lisbon* (Oxford, Hart Publishing, 2015) 278–79.

[59] European Parliament, 'Budgetary capacity for the euro area', European Parliament resolution of 16 February 2017 on budgetary capacity for the euro area, 2015/2344(INI), P8_TA-PROV(2017)0050.

[60] ibid 8–10.

The European Parliament has, historically, rejected a process of joint oversight in which the scrutiny task is shared by the European Parliament and national parliaments in a multilevel parliamentary framework. Thus, regardless of the attempts by national parliaments to become involved in EU economic governance through increased domestic oversight, there is only a limited capability for this involvement to provide legitimacy in an EU-wide context. The different motivation and capability of national parliaments to exercise effective control over their heads of government raise significant questions of whether this can provide an adequate counter-balance to the increased power of the European Council. As argued earlier, EU processes for economic governance have altered the EU's institutional balance and without some improved coordinated horizontal cooperation between national parliaments, which goes beyond the SECG, there will continue to be no effective counterweight to the exercise of executive power by the European Council.

## Supranational Trade Policy and Parliamentary Legitimacy

In the area of trade policy, an exclusive competence of the EU, national parliaments have no direct involvement. In the COSAC Report of November 2008[61] it was stated that in the context of EU trade policy 'the national parliaments' influence is limited to the scrutiny of the Government position in the Council'.[62] However, it is open to national parliaments to be involved in the context of a mixed agreement if their national constitutions enable them to do so[63] but even here national parliaments are not usually involved in the phase when the Council authorises the Commission to open trade negotiations. Rather, parliaments become involved at a later stage when mixed agreements are subjected to standard constitutional and parliamentary procedures for the ratification of international agreements. Yet this absence of direct parliamentary involvement in EU trade policy and the executive dominance in this field raises questions of legitimacy, accountability and whether a democratic deficit exists in EU trade policy.

Prior to the entry into force of the Treaty of Lisbon 2009, it has been commonly acknowledged that the level of democratic legitimacy of the EU's Common Commercial Policy (CCP) was relatively low.[64] In the past, the Member States

[61] COSAC, 'Tenth Bi-annual Report: Developments in European Union Procedures and Practices Relevant to Parliamentary Scrutiny', COSAC Secretariat (Paris, 3–4 November 2008).

[62] ibid 40.

[63] R Passos, 'Mixed Agreements from the Perspective of the European Parliament' in C Hillion and P Koutrakos (eds), *Mixed Agreements Revisited: The EU and its Member States in the World* (Oxford, Hart Publishing, 2010); I Van Der Steen, 'Mixity in Practice: A View from the Netherlands' in C Hillion and P Koutrakos (eds), *Mixed Agreements Revisited: The EU and its Member States in the World* (Oxford, Hart Publishing, 2010).

[64] M Krajewski, 'External Trade Law and the Constitution Treaty: Towards a Federal and More Democratic Common Commercial Policy?' (2005) 42 *Common Market Law Review* 91; S Woolcock, 'The Treaty of Lisbon and the European Union as an Actor in International Trade' ECIPE Working Paper 01/2010, 7.

prioritised efficiency in concluding international trade agreements over the accountability of the process. Thus, since the Treaty of Rome 1957 until the Treaty of Lisbon 2009, this area of EU competence was characterised by the executive dominance, with the Council and the Commission holding all formal powers in relation to the negotiations and conclusions of international trade agreements.[65] At that time, the Treaty did not give the European Parliament even a mere right to be consulted on matters relating to the conclusion of trade agreements. Krajewski suggested that such an institutional design reflected the classic doctrine of necessity of unlimited and unchecked foreign affairs powers, which was based on 'an archaic assumption that external trade policy is best conducted without any parliamentary input or interferences'.[66] Nonetheless, the democratic deficit in this area, at least in theory, was alleviated by the fact that as the spheres of the EU's exclusive competence were limited just to trade in goods, the vast majority of the international commercial agreements were concluded using the mixed procedure, which required the involvement of all national parliaments.[67]

The expansion of the scope of the CCP to areas, such as trade in services, commercial aspects of intellectual property rights and foreign direct investment in the Treaty of Lisbon 2009 was expected to dispense with the need to involve national parliaments in the ratification of trade agreements.[68] However, the move towards complete exclusivity in the CCP created an accountability gap, which gave rise to the functional pressure for further treaty reform. In this situation, the obvious choice of a solution was to grant the European Parliament the power to scrutinise the trade and investment treaty-making practice of the Commission.[69] Thus, with the entry into force of the Treaty of Lisbon 2009 the position of the European Parliament, rather than national parliaments, in the CCP has been significantly enhanced. Article 207 TFEU, now requires that the European Parliament is informed on the progress of negotiations conducted by the Commission.[70] Furthermore, from an institution that did not possess any formal powers to influence the direction of the EU's trade policy,[71] the European Parliament became, alongside the Council, a co-legislator in the field,[72] and its consent is required for the conclusion of any international trade agreements.[73]

The broadly defined objectives for the future of the EU in the Laeken Declaration is not the only functional pressure, which resulted in the enhanced role of the European Parliament in the CCP. In addition to improved legitimacy and

[65] Consolidated versions of the Treaty on European Union and of the Treaty Establishing European Community (Treaty of Nice) [2002] OJ C 325/1, Art 133.

[66] ibid 98.

[67] Woolcock, above n 64.

[68] ibid; A Pollet-Fort, 'Implication of the Lisbon Treaty on EU External Trade Policy' (2010) Background Brief No 2 EU Centre in Singapore, 15.

[69] Passos, above n 63.

[70] Art 207(3) TFEU.

[71] P Koutrakos, *EU International Relations Law* (Oxford, Hart Publishing, 2015) 133.

[72] Art 207(2) TFEU.

[73] ibid Art 218(6)(a)(v).

institutional balance, the more general objectives of EU trade policy can also be regarded as a force behind this reform.[74] For the past two decades the Union has tried to use its trade agreements not only to develop new commercial relations with other states, but also to promote key non-economic values such as human rights, rule of law and democracy.[75] In the neo-functionalist framework of EU integration, these ancillary aims can be considered as another endogenous factor that facilitated supranationalisation of the CCP and was a positive force that contributed to the extension of the powers of the European Parliament, but arguably at the expense of national parliaments.

As the EU enjoys considerable market power in international trade derived from the size of its economy, the deepening of the international trade agenda has been to a large extent influenced by the EU's foreign policy.[76] The new generation of the EU's comprehensive economic agreements require a degree of regulatory convergence, which means that international treaties signed by the EU increasingly affect national legislative frameworks. Perhaps unintentionally, this intrusion of matters of international trade into domestic policies has given national parliaments and NGOs a stake in international trade negotiations whereby national socio-economic values are expressed.[77] This dovetails with the European Parliament's position in which it has historically attached great importance to 'non-traditional trade-related issues' and focused on the promotion of social rights and environmentally friendly approaches.[78] However, the lack of any formal role of the European Parliament in the EU's trade policy, which increasingly affected the welfare of EU citizens, was considered to undermine its legitimacy and led to the reforms in the Treaty of Lisbon.[79]

While the EU's supranational trade policy has seen an expansion in the European Parliament's powers and the consequent maintenance of institutional balance within the EU institutional architecture, there are identifiable limits to the European Parliament's input. The main weakness in the European Parliament's position stems from the division of competences between the EU and the Member States in the area of investment. As the Court of Justice of the European Union confirmed in Opinion 2/15, the EU does not possess exclusive powers in the sphere of investment, hence conclusion of any agreements in this area will require involvement of all Member States.[80] This ruling significantly undermines the

[74] AR Young and J Peterson, 'The EU and the New Trade Politics' (2006) 13 *Journal of Public Policy* 795.

[75] ibid; M Baldwin, 'EU Trade Politics: Heaven or Hell?' (2006) 13 *Journal of European Public Policy* 926, 936; S Meunier and K Nicolaïdis, 'The European Union as a Conflicted Trade Power' (2006) 13 *Journal of European Public Policy* 906, 907.

[76] Young and Peterson, above n 74, 795, 803.

[77] ibid 795; Woolcock, above n 64, 7.

[78] M Armanoviča and R Bendini, 'In-Depth Analysis: The Role of the EP in Shaping the EU's Trade Policy after the Entry into Force of the Treaty of Lisbon' (Director-General for External Policies, Policy Department, 2014) 12.

[79] Baldwin, above n 75.

[80] Opinion 2/15 (2017) ECR 376.

European Parliament's position in the CCP because, notwithstanding Article 207 TFEU, it has to share the function of providing democratic legitimacy to the EU international investment policy with all national and regional parliaments. In this context, Majone has argued that the interests of European citizens find a more natural expression in their national parliaments, which speak in favour of their involvement in EU foreign relations.[81] Kuijpier, on the other hand, disagrees and considers that the participation of national representative bodies in conclusion of the EU investment agreements is an attack on the constitutional order of the Union and undermines the autonomy of the Union vis-a-vis the Member States.[82]

These conflicting views have been reflected in the debates that started after the signing of the EU's first post-Lisbon agreement that included an investment chapter. The initial veto of the agreement by the Belgian regional parliament of Wallonia significantly complicated the process and inspired the conclusion of two declarations: Namur and Trading Together.[83] The former calls for strengthening of the involvement of national assemblies in the process of concluding international agreements by the EU. The latter, on the other hand, advocates for complete exclusivity in EU trade relations and greater powers being granted to the European Parliament, which is regarded as the best source of democratic legitimacy in this area. The Trading Together declaration also takes the stance that the participation of national parliaments weakens the EU's position on the international scene.[84]

The saga concerning the signature of CETA demonstrates that the involvement of national parliaments complicates and prolongs the process of conclusion of the EU international investment agreement. Already prior to the emergence of the Union as an actor in the area of investment, Rosas observed that the mixed procedure may pose 'a systemic risk for an orderly conclusion of international agreements and the credibility of the EU as a negotiator'.[85] The events surrounding the conclusion of CETA, suggest that Member States, or more accurately their national parliaments, are not afraid to withhold their consent to trade agreements in order to extract last-minute concessions, even if this means jeopardising the interests of the entire Union. In this context, Bulgaria and Romania, for example, have made their ratifications conditional upon obtaining visa free travel guarantees from Canada.[86] Furthermore, the signature of the Treaty was blocked

[81] G Majone, *Dilemmas of European Integration: The Ambiguities and Pitfalls of Integration by Stealth* (Oxford University Press, 2005) 25.

[82] PJ Kuijper, 'Post-CETA: How We Got There and How to Go on' (*Blog Active EU*, 28 October 2016), available at: acelg.blogactiv.eu/2016/10/28/post-ceta-how-we-got-there-and-how-to-go-on-by-pieter-jan-kuijper/.

[83] Namur Declaration of 5 December 2016, available at: declarationdenamur.eu/en/; Trading Together Declaration of 27 January 2017, available at: www.trading-together-declaration.org/.

[84] ibid.

[85] A Rosas, 'The Future of Mixity' in C Hillion and Koutrakos (eds), *Mixed Agreements Revisited: The EU and its Member States in the World* (Oxford, Hart Publishing, 2010) 369.

[86] Council (EU), Comprehensive Economic and Trade Agreement (CETA) between Canada, of the one part, and the European Union and its Member States, of the other part – Statements of the Council minutes, 27 October 2016, 13463/1/16 REV 1, paras 34, 35.

by the Parliament of Wallonia, one of the Belgian regions, due to its concerns over the investor–state dispute resolution mechanism,[87] as well as the opening of the farming market to cheaper Canadian products and industrial imports.[88] By contrast, the European Parliament approved the agreement by 408 votes to 254 with 33 abstentions[89] suggesting some divergence of interests between the European Parliament and national parliaments.

The continued use of the mixed procedure undermines the attainment of the Lisbon objectives, one of which was to improve efficiency of the EU's external action. It is apparent from the changes that have been introduced that this goal in the context of the CCP was to be achieved through expanding the scope of the EU's exclusive competences and enhancing the role of the European Parliament to ensure adequate representation of the EU citizens. These two amendments were intended to reduce the importance of the mixed procedure. However, in the light of Opinion 2/15 and the subsequent *Achmea* judgment,[90] the involvement of the national parliaments has to be endured for the foreseeable future in the sphere of international investment.[91] While this may, ostensibly, address the legitimacy question, it may reinforce Kuijpier's concerns of efficiency and would suggest that national parliaments may be considered the problem and not necessarily the solution to improved legitimacy within the CCP.

Despite the Council's opposition, the greater role of the European Parliament in the CCP does attain the objectives of increased legitimacy and improved effectiveness. There is no doubt that the involvement of national parliaments in the conclusion of international treaties complicates and prolongs the process. In the absence of treaty rules, the currently used mixed procedure, which has developed in the EU constitutional practice gives each national parliament a veto power over not only parts of the agreements that fall within the scope Member States' powers, but also those that have been already transferred to the EU. This significantly undermines the Union's ability to establish itself as a credible actor in the field, which was demonstrated during the conclusion of CETA. Moreover, the participation of the parliaments of the Member States increases the risk of corrupting the EU's trade negotiations with often difficult to reconcile national interests and protectionist behaviour. This adds to the dialectical process of integration, another source of countervailing forces.

[87] G van der Loo, 'CETA's signature: 38 Statements, a joint interpretative instrument and uncertain future', *CEPS Commentary*, 31 October 2016, available at: www.ceps.eu/publications/ceta%E2%80%99s-signature-38-statements-joint-interpretative-instrument-and-uncertain-future.

[88] H von der Burchard, S Marks and A Mucci, 'Wallonia Sends EU Trade Policy Back to the Drawing Board' *Politico* Europe Edition, 24 October 2016, available at: www.politico.eu/pro/pm-charles-michel-tells-eu-that-belgium-cannot-sign-canada-deal/.

[89] European Parliament, Legislative Observatory, available at: www.europarl.europa.eu/oeil/popups/summary.do?id=1476916&t=e&l=en.

[90] Case C-284/16 *Slovak Republic v Achmea BV* Judgment of 20 April 2018.

[91] Opinion 2/15, above n 80.

Nonetheless, perhaps the preference of the Member States and their parliaments for mixed procedure indicates that the European Parliament is not a sufficient source of democratic legitimacy in relation to international investment agreements, which are perceived to deeply affect domestic legislative frameworks of Member States.[92] In this context, it may be argued that the paradox of EU democratisation is that the legislative process is being removed further away from the citizens through increasing powers of the European Parliament and the reduction in the involvement of national parliaments.[93] In relation to the emerging EU investment policy, a closer cooperation between these two sources of democratic legitimacy in EU foreign relations could improve the efficiency and public acceptance of the mixed procedure.

At present there is no forum for interparliamentary cooperation that can bring the multiple levels together, but it has been suggested that COSAC could undertake such a function.[94] The parliamentarisation of trade policy at the EU level could offer improved accountability especially if, as the European Parliament's Committee on International Trade acknowledged, this included the scrutiny by national parliaments of draft EU trade agreements.[95] However, for the moment the power struggle between the national parliaments and the European Parliament for the position of the source of democratic legitimacy for the common investment policy continues. The ability of the European Parliament to closely monitor the negotiations of the EU investment treaties, puts it in a more advantageous position in comparison to the national parliaments.[96] The latter have the ability to scrutinise the agreement only after parties concluded the negotiating phase and reached an agreement in principle; hence unlike their EU counterpart, national parliaments cannot shape the content of the EU investment treaties without undermining the whole deal. Thus, the European Parliament could use this advantage to prove to national parliaments that it is capable of effectively representing the interests of their citizens. While this may be presented as increasing the strength of the positive forces in the process of integration in the CCP and arguably creates the right constitutional environment for the further transfer of competences, this argument is very unlikely to be accepted by national parliaments.

## Concluding Remarks

Throughout the literature on national parliaments they have regularly been depicted as 'victims' or 'losers' of increased European integration. To some extent, this

[92] K Tienhaara, 'Regulatory Chill and the Threat of Arbitration: A View from Political Science' in C Brown and K Miles (eds), *Evolution in Investment Treaty Law and Arbitration* (Cambridge, Cambridge University Press, 2011).

[93] Cygan, *Accountability, Parliamentarism and Transparency in the EU*, above n 39.

[94] COSAC 'Biannual Report' 2014, 29.

[95] ibid.

[96] Art 207 TFEU.

chapter continues that trend. As has been argued, national parliaments' limited ability to legislate and control their executive branch properly in the areas devolved to the EU level has been a recurrent point of criticism of the EU's institutional system. However, EU integration is not just a story of increased de-parliamentarisation, but has also been characterised by a process of democratisation with increased powers conferred on the European Parliament. However, as this chapter has argued, such an empowerment of the EU's only directly elected institution has not failed to adequately compensate for national parliaments' loss of influence. The low turnout in European Parliament elections and the low visibility of EU affairs nationally suggest that national parliaments remain the main political institution voters relate to directly. Overcoming the EU's (purported) democratic deficit is therefore inextricably tied to giving national parliaments a greater voice in EU decision-making, especially in areas such as economic governance and EU trade policy.

Yet the solution to national parliaments also lies, to a great extent, in their own hands. Notwithstanding their peripheral position in the EU polity, national parliaments have not been idle bystanders to the erosion of their parliamentary powers but set up scrutiny mechanisms to hold their governments to account, and should seek to develop and expand these mechanisms to address the growth of executive dominance and soft law techniques within economic governance. Individually, national parliaments continue to pursue their EU scrutiny priorities.

The Lisbon Treaty has tried to increase the EU's legitimacy by increasing the possibility for national parliaments to, collectively, ensure that the Commission does not overstep its authority. However, these provisions have proved to be of limited value against national parliaments' loss of competences. Though the increased transmission of EU documents from the Commission to national parliaments has reduced the information asymmetry between national parliaments and their governments, national parliaments' ability to play a more active role in EU decision-making remains limited. Moreover, the limited contact between MPs and MEPs suggests that national politicians remain domestically focused, as the response to the economic crisis illustrates, and they lack the appetite to engage more actively in EU policy-making. While national parliaments have reinforced Member State sovereignty and protecting national interests, the European Parliament has not filled the institutional vacuum at the centre of EU representative governance and has been unable to significantly increase EU solidarity and provide an alternative single European voice which both citizens and national parliaments can rally around.

# 16

# Disruptive Democracy: Keeping EU Citizens in a Box

PÄIVI LEINO*

## What Place for Citizens in the EU Constitutional Democracy?

This chapter searches for the place of citizens in the EU constitutional democracy. The starting point for this search is the observation that, for an entity entrusted with so much public power, the European Union is remarkably remote to and poorly understood by its citizens. This 'democratic malaise' has been long recognised,[1] but an effective cure has proved elusive. Many of its contemporary democratic challenges the EU shares with its Member States, such as low levels of satisfaction with democracy and falling political trust and electoral participation. But these challenges are compounded by other types of democratic deficit that are more specific to the Union. The European Parliament remains painfully limited in its task of translating citizens' will into policies. With little proper political formation at the European level and scarce interest in EU matters in the mainstream media, its elections are almost entirely dominated by national themes and actors, leaving the voter with little chance of forming an informed picture of how different electoral options would affect Union policies. And with little political oversight from the Parliament, the Commission as the executive is using oversized powers, with no clear paths of accountability to the people.[2] As to direct democracy, the little contact the EU has had with it has been turbulent, taking place mainly through

* paivi.leino@helsinki.fi, earlier versions of this chapter have been presented at the University of Leuven and the University of Stockholm, and at the 2018 Annual Seminar of the Council Legal Service. I thank all participants, in particular Julio Baquero Cruz and Emanuele Rebasti, for discussions and Ida Koivisto, Liisa Leppävirta and Daniel Wyatt for comments on an earlier draft.

[1] See, eg, K Newton and B Geissel (eds), *Evaluating Democratic Innovations: Curing the Democratic Malaise?* (London, Routledge, 2011).

[2] A Follesdal and S Hix, 'Why There is a Democratic Deficit in the EU: A Response to Majone and Moravcsik' (2006) 44 *Journal of Common Market Studies* 533, 534–37.

national referenda of which it has been the object, mostly with less than flattering outcomes.[3]

The general response to democratic deficits and legitimacy crises has been to invent new ways to increase citizen involvement.[4] For the EU, this response came with the Treaty of Lisbon (2009). Not content with only (once again) increasing the powers of the European Parliament, the Lisbon Treaty also took a clear turn towards more participatory democracy in Europe. It provided new avenues for direct involvement of citizens in forming and influencing the EU agenda. Through a more democratic and participatory process, these were meant to help the Union to acquire broader legitimacy in the eyes of its citizens. In this chapter, I will discuss two key initiatives that spearheaded this push towards more citizen participation: opening up the EU legislative process through 'the widest possible' access to legislative documents, and the European Citizens' Initiative (ECI).

First, Article 10(3) TEU establishes that '[e]very citizen shall have the right to participate in the democratic life of the Union. Decisions shall be taken as openly and as closely as possible to the citizen'. Under the Treaties, openness is particularly important when the European Parliament and the Council adopt legislation. These principles have been interpreted by the Court broadly to signify how '[t]he principles of publicity and transparency are therefore inherent to the EU legislative process'.[5] The Council and the Parliament are to be considered the EU's legislative body. For this reason,

> (t)he mind-set of discretion and even secrecy, which is justified in the context of relations between sovereign players, is out of place in the context of the European Union, which, in this respect, sees itself primarily and increasingly as a community based on the principles of the rule of law and democracy.[6]

As to the second initiative, the ECI may be used by not less than one million EU citizens to invite 'the European Commission, within the framework of its powers, to submit any appropriate proposal on matters where citizens consider that a legal act of the Union is required for the purpose of implementing the Treaties' (Article 11(4) TEU). The Commissioner responsible at the time of adoption of the Lisbon Treaty stated emphatically that,

> the European Citizens' Initiative is one of the Treaty's most important innovations. It adds a whole new dimension of participatory democracy to the Union. It represents a significant step forward in the democratic life of the Union. It provides a unique

[3] F Mendez and M Mendez, 'The Promise and Perils of Direct Democracy for the European Union' (2017) 19 *Cambridge Yearbook of European Legal Studies* 48.

[4] See, eg, RJ Dalton, *Democratic Challenges, Democratic Choices: The Erosion of Political Support in Advanced Industrial Democracies* (Oxford, Oxford University Press, 2004); P Norrisk, *Democratic Deficit: Critical Citizens Revisited* (Cambridge, Cambridge University Press, 2011).

[5] Case T-540/15 *Emilio de Capitani v European Parliament* EU:T:2018:167.

[6] Opinion of AG Cruz Villalón in Case C-280/11 *Council v Access Info Europe* EU:C:2013:325, para 69.

opportunity to bring the Union closer to the citizens and to encourage greater cross-border debate about EU issues.[7]

But have these two initiatives in reality translated into improved access to and influence in the Union's legislative process by its citizens? Building on institutional argumentation in concrete EU institutional decisions, I examine how the Union's institutional attitudes have shaped the practical effects of these initiatives. I argue that the main culprit is the fundamental mindset of Union institutions, which seems to be little affected by the Lisbon constitutional reforms. Regarding legislative transparency, this attitude is visible, first, in the refusal of the institutions to update secondary legislation (Regulation No 1049/2001) to reflect the Lisbon provisions, and second, when the Court has taken the lead, in their reluctance to apply its jurisprudence. In the context of the ECI, failure can be traced back to how the Commission has applied the instrument.[8] Competences have been interpreted in a manner that severely limits the ECI's scope,[9] and the Commission has proved passive in guiding the applicants on ways to improve their chances of success.[10] As a result, only one initiative has so far resulted in legislative action. For the Commission, the ECI has constituted 'an interference in an ongoing legislative procedure'.[11] Essentially, the institutions remain in resistance mode. Their mindset continues to be geared towards protecting the internal workings of the institutions from citizen distraction.[12] Reality has fallen far short of the lofty expectations inscribed in festive declarations. There simply has been little actual progress in the citizens' ability to participate in the EU's political life.

## The CJEU's New Constitutional Doctrine on Democracy as Openness

Regulation No 1049/2001 on public access to documents was adopted nearly twenty years ago. Since then, the legal framework relating to EU public access rules has been affected by Treaty change, a growing body of jurisprudence, not only from the Court of Justice of the European Union (CJEU) but also the European Court

[7] M Šefčovič, Vice-President of the European Commission, 'The Lisbon Treaty: enhancing democracy in the EU', Meeting of the Constitutional Affairs Committee of the European Parliament, Speech/10/502, available at: europa.eu/rapid/press-release_SPEECH-10-502_en.htm.

[8] Case C-589/15 P *Alexis Anagnostakis v European Commission* EU:C:2017:663.

[9] Case T-646/13 *Bürgerausschuss für die Bürgerinitiative Minority SafePack – one million signatures for diversity in Europe v the European Commission* EU:T:59.

[10] See: www.ombudsman.europa.eu/en/decision/en/59205 *Decision of the European Ombudsman closing her on-initiative inquiry OI/9/2013/TN concerning the European Commission*, paras 20–21; Letter from Emily O'Reilly, European Ombudsman, to European Commission President José Manuel Barroso (15 July 2014), available at: www.ombudsman.europa.eu/en/correspondence/en/54609.

[11] Case T-754/14 *Michael Efler and others v European Commission* ECLI:EU:T:2017:323, para 47.

[12] See also D Curtin and P Leino, 'In Search of Transparency for EU Law-making: Trilogues on the Cusp of Dawn' (2017) 54 *Common Market Law Review* 1673.

of Human Rights, the adoption of a vast amount of new EU legislation (such as the General Data Protection Regulation), as well as international commitments.[13] None of these changes are reflected in the text of the Regulation, leaving it clearly substantively outdated in many respects.[14] In addition, new technologies relating to document creation and handling are not incorporated in the text of the Regulation.

The Regulation is particularly vague in light of the EU's new constitutional focus on democratic principles.[15] In particular, it does not provide detailed rules relating to the implementation of Article 15(2) TFEU, which provides that law-making in the European Parliament and Council should take place in open sessions. The Regulation approaches the question of legislative transparency from a temporal perspective: that access to legislative documents should be organised by the institutions at their own initiative instead of being based on requests. Beyond this provision, it gives limited guidance on exactly what, when and how, as well as on the application of the exceptions in the Regulation in respect of legislative documents. The Commission has made no legislative proposal following the entry into force of the Treaty of Lisbon that would address these provisions. Article 15 TFEU however clearly recognises the relevance that transparency and access to documents play in ensuring participation in EU democratic processes: 'openness, through its participation component, is no longer conceived exclusively as instrumental to the improvement of the quality of the decision-making process and outcome, but it appears to carry an autonomous, self-standing normative value'.[16]

These democratic principles have laid the ground for the Court's jurisprudence, where it has given Regulation No 1049/2001 particular significance in safeguarding democratic rights. This is an unorthodox solution as far as public access rules are concerned. In Member States, public access rules do not usually deal with legislative matters but rather focus on the administrative machinery. The recent jurisprudence of the CJEU takes nearly the opposite approach: it turns Regulation 1049/2001 into a quasi-constitutional document, the main function of which is to defend the EU's democratic credentials.[17] The core parameters in all

[13] International commitments include the Aarhus Convention and the Council of Europe Convention on Access to Official Documents (CETS No 205, 2009).

[14] D Curtin and P Leino, 'Openness, Transparency and the Right of Access to Documents in the EU: In-depth Analysis' (2016) Working Paper, European University Institute, available at: www.europarl.europa.eu/RegData/etudes/IDAN/2016/556973/IPOL_IDA(2016)556973_EN.pdf.

[15] Art 12(2) establishes that 'legislative documents, that is to say, documents drawn up or received in the course of procedures for the adoption of acts which are legally binding in or for the Member States, should, subject to Arts 4 and 9, be made directly accessible'. This is further elaborated in the preamble which stipulates that '[w]ider access should be granted to documents in cases where the institutions are acting in their legislative capacity, including under delegated powers, while at the same time preserving the effectiveness of the institutions' decision-making process'. This sentence in the preamble is the only part of the legal framework that mentions the word effectiveness, but it has provided the institutions ample ground for developing the idea further.

[16] A Alemanno, 'Unpacking the principle of Openness in EU Law: Transparency, Participation and Democracy' (2014) 39 *European Law Review* 72, 89–90.

[17] I thank Julio Baquero Cruz for this point.

four cases have been the same: the institutions see transparency as contributing to inappropriate outside inference and have defended the efficiency of their internal decision-making procedures. In all these cases, the institutional line of defence has built (in full or in part) on Article 4(3) of the Regulation. The applicants, supported by the Court, have defended their democratic right to gain access to institutional argumentation while the decision-making procedure has been ongoing, with the view of influencing its outcome.

The Court's new doctrine of legislative transparency relies directly on the Treaty provisions relating to democratic principles and its own previous jurisprudence, which it has developed in stages. Its reading of what democracy requires in terms of public access essentially relies on four cases relating to four key categories of legislative documents, addressed in turn to each of the three institutions involved in the EU legislative procedure:[18]

1. Legal advice given by the institutions' legal services in the context of a legislative procedure.
2. Member State positions recorded in documents relating to the early stages of Council decision-making.
3. Trilogue documents held by the European Parliament.
4. Commission impact assessments produced in the context of preparing its legislative proposal.

The first case (*Turco*, given in 2008) related to the publicity of legal advice given by the Council Legal Service in the context of legislative matters. The key question in the case was whether public access to legal advice hinders the institutions from receiving frank, objective and comprehensive advice, thereby preventing efficient decision-making. The Treaty of Lisbon had not yet entered into force, so the Court referred to the preamble of Regulation 1049/2001, which quotes the importance of transparency for Union legitimacy. The CJEU ultimately established that:

> Those considerations are clearly of particular relevance where the Council is acting in its legislative capacity … Openness in that respect contributes to strengthening democracy by allowing citizens to scrutinize *all the information which has formed the basis of a legislative act*. The possibility for citizens to find out the considerations underpinning legislative action is a precondition for the effective exercise of their democratic rights.[19]

The Court specifically rejected the fear expressed by the Council that disclosure of a legal opinion could lead to doubts as to the lawfulness of the legislative act concerned. Instead, openness would contribute to conferring greater legitimacy on the institutions in the eyes of European citizens, since it would allow divergences between various points of view to be openly debated. For the Court, it was

[18] Joined Cases C-39/05 P and C-52/05 P *Kingdom of Sweden and Maurizio Turco v Council of the European Union* EU:C:2008:374; Case C-280/11, above n 6; Case T-540/15, above n 5; Case C-57/16 P *ClientEarth v European Commission* EU:C:2018:660.

[19] Joined Cases C-39/05 P and C-52/05, above n 17, 374 para 46 (emphasis added).

rather a lack of information and debate that create doubts in the minds of citizens reaching beyond individual acts to the legitimacy of the EU decision-making process as a whole (paragraph 59). Finally, the Court considered the arguments raised by the Council and the Commission relating to the negative effect of public pressure on decision-making, and concluded that,

> even if the members of that legal service were subjected to improper pressure to that end, it would be that pressure, and not the possibility of the disclosure of legal opinions, which would compromise that institution's interest in receiving frank, objective and comprehensive advice and it would clearly be incumbent on the Council to take the necessary measures to put a stop to it.[20]

What the Court seems to be saying is this: in a constitutional structure based on allocated powers, competence considerations are a highly democratic matter. Citizens should be able to know if the EU's competence is challenged.

The second case (*Access Info Europe*, decided in 2013) involved a Council working party document relating to the negotiations on recasting Regulation No 1049/2001, which contained Member States' positions in the footnotes. To the extent that such documents had been disclosed earlier, this had been done without disclosing the identities of Member States that had proposed amendments or opposed certain formulations. The matter at hand involved a much broader and fundamental question of the institutional identity of the Council post-Lisbon: a diplomatic conference or a legislative body? As Advocate General Cruz Villalón stated in his opinion:

> Member States taking part in an EU legislative procedure as members of an institution are more like the common perception of a national legislature than they are like a sovereign body playing a role in relations governed by international law.[21]

But the Council's mindset remained that of a diplomatic conference. It proposed following its previous practice by reference to the preliminary nature of discussions. Disclosing the identities of Member States would reduce their room for manoeuvre during the negotiations. This would in turn impair the Council's ability to reach an agreement.[22]

The Court disagreed, establishing that 'public access to the entire content of Council documents constitutes the principle, or general rule, and that that principle is subject to exceptions which must be interpreted and applied strictly'.[23] For the Court,

> the various proposals for amendment or re-drafting made by the four Member State delegations which are described in the requested document are part of the normal legislative process, from which it follows that the requested documents could not be regarded as sensitive – not solely by reference to the criterion concerning the involvement of a

[20] ibid para 64.
[21] Opinion of AG Cruz Villalón in Case C-280/11, above n 6.
[22] ibid para 7.
[23] ibid para 35, confirming the previous General Court ruling.

> fundamental interest of the European Union or of the Member States, but by reference to any criterion whatsoever.[24]

The ruling initially led to great concern about the stalling of EU legislative activity.[25] If Member State positions were indeed public, would the Council lose its capacity to take decisions? Would it be better altogether to discontinue reporting from legislative negotiations, in which case there would be no reports to hand out? But also this could hinder Council efficiency, since such reporting was seen to contribute to its capacity to act. As a compromise, a decision was taken to continue much as before. It seems that the fears were largely unjustified. The Council recently concluded that 'the disclosure of documents relating to ongoing legislative files that contain individual delegations' positions following a request for access, does not seem to have had any disruptive effects on the decision making process'.[26] What remains unclear is the extent to which such reports have in fact been handed out. In practice, this would seem seldom to happen proactively as long as the Council decision-making process is pending (see below).

The third case, brought by Emilio de Capitani and decided in 2018, involved access to the four column documents used as a basis for trilogue negotiations between the European Parliament, Council and Commission. The main question in the case involved access to the fourth column, which is used to map the advancement negotiations and the proposals on the table. The four column document is the only jointly drafted document that can explain how legislative negotiations progress between the three institutions prior to their provisional conclusion; provisional however usually only in the sense that the result is subject to formal approval by the institutions and not that there would be an expectation of further amendments being made.[27] This was a rather delicious case: not only was it brought by a previous employee, but also against an institution – the European Parliament – which had professed to champion more transparency in trilogues[28] but now proved reluctant to live up to this commitment.

Trilogue transparency had also been placed on the political agenda by the new Interinstitutional Agreement (IIA) on Better Regulation, which addressed the organisation of the ordinary legislative procedure, in general, and the transparency

[24] ibid para 63.

[25] See Council of the European Union, 'Drafting of documents relating to legislative activities', 8622/1/14 REV 1 LIMITE (13 May 2014); Council of the European Union, 'Outcome of the proceedings of the 2479th meeting of the Permanent Representatives Committee held on 15 May 2014', 10078/14 LIMITE (22 May 2014).

[26] See: www.statewatch.org/news/2018/aug/eu-council-legislative-transparency-11099-18.pdf. Council of the European Union, *Legislative Transparency*, 11099/18 (13 July 2018).

[27] Curtin and Leino, 'In Search of Transparency for EU Law-making', above n 12.

[28] European Parliament Resolution on public access to documents (Rule 116(7)) for the years 2014–2015, 2015/2287(INI), para 21: 'Points out that transparent law-making is of the utmost importance to citizens; calls on the institutions to make available documents forming part of, or related to, legislative procedures; considers, in particular, that the EU institutions should make as many documents as possible accessible to the public via their websites'.

of trilogues, in particular.[29] Some national parliaments had also long drawn attention to various practices that restrict access to information during the legislative process, which for them is highly problematic from the perspective of holding their own government representatives in the Council to account. Governments are, especially at the stage of inter-institutional negotiations, generally reliant on the presidency and the direct information they may receive through MEPs. National parliaments in turn rely on information provided by their national governments. The positions of national parliaments are usually based on the initial Commission proposal, which is often significantly altered during the fast-moving trilogues, something that hinders effective scrutiny. Therefore, the question relating to the publicity of trilogues not only concerned the dimension of civil society access, but also questions relating to the prerogatives of national parliaments in the EU law-making process.

The European Parliament's line of defence in *de Capitani*, backed up by the two other institutions, built on how access during a trilogue would destroy the efficiency of the process. It would increase public pressure on the rapporteur, shadow rapporteurs and political groups.[30] 'Trilogues should be granted a minimum level of confidentiality as long as the legislative procedure is on going', the European Parliament argued.[31] Never mind its earlier high-minded proclamations on the matter, the European Parliament (represented in litigation by its legal service) now found it sufficient that access to trilogue documents be provided after the conclusion of the negotiations; this would be more than enough to enable accountability to operate.

The Court, however, disagreed. It found that in a system based on the principle of democratic legitimacy, co-legislators must be held accountable to the public for their actions. This means that if citizens are to be able to exercise their democratic rights, they must be in a position to follow in detail the decision-making process between the legislative institutions and have access to all the relevant information. For this reason,

> [t]he expression of public opinion in relation to a particular provisional legislative proposal or agreement agreed in the course of a trilogue and reflected in the fourth column of a trilogue table forms an integral part of the exercise of EU citizens' democratic rights, particularly since such agreements are generally subsequently adopted without substantial amendment by the co-legislators.[32]

In response to the public reactions and civil society debate that the institutions feared that would be caused by transparency, the Court also specifically rejected the arguments relating to pressure. Not excluding the possibility that some

[29] See: www.ec.europa.eu/smart-regulation/better_regulation/documents/iia_blm_final_en. The Interinstitutional Agreement on Better Regulation (2016) Arts 32–40.

[30] See: www.europarl.europa.eu/RegData/publications/avis/2016/0795/EP-PE_AVS(2016)0795_XL.pdf. Defence of the European Parliament in Case T-540/15, above n 5, paras 52–58.

[31] ibid para 46.

[32] Case T-540/15, above n 5, para 98.

negotiations could, exceptionally, be particularly sensitive, the Court indicated that not all trilogue negotiations could benefit from general secrecy presumption, which all three legislative institutions had been jointly insisting on. Instead, the Court established that '[t]here is nothing in the file demonstrating a reaction beyond what could be expected from the public by any member of a legislative body who proposes an amendment to draft legislation'.[33] In other words, if a politician is disturbed by her work being subject to public debate, perhaps she should reconsider her career options.

*ClientEarth*, the fourth and most recent case (2018), involved access to Commission impact assessments.[34] The General Court had accepted that, in using its right of legislative initiative, the Commission was in fact not exercising legislative functions, and that its task of proposing legislation required utmost independence and confidentiality.[35] On appeal, the CJEU disagreed and rejected the argument that the independence of the Commission requires preserving a space for deliberation when planning legislative action. For the Court, impact assessment reports contain information constituting important elements of the EU legislative process, which forms part of the basis for the EU legislative action.

In this case, the Commission had specifically referred to consultations as the specific form of participation established by Article 11(3) TEU. Impact assessments, carried out by the Commission as a part of its better regulation agenda, while finalising a legislative proposal, may also be subject to a public consultation. However, the Commission has discretion as to what it sees as initiatives that 'are expected to have significant economic, environmental or social impacts'[36] and thus require consultation. For the Court, while providing a channel of participation, consultations on a future proposal could not replace the possibility of gaining access to impact assessments. The disclosure of such documents is likely to increase the transparency and openness of the legislative procedure as a whole, in particular the preparatory steps of that process, and will therefore enable citizens to understand the options envisaged and the choices made by that institution and thus be made aware of the considerations underlying legislative action. The Court's logic here is entirely convincing: consultations build on engaging with citizens largely for the purpose of 'evaluating and developing existing policy preferences in a technocratic process … and with no expectation, certainly no obligation, of influence on the decision-making agenda'.[37]

Also in this case, the Court needed to address the timing of disclosure. The Court stressed that democratic participation does not only require information, but rather access to that information must be possible 'in good time, at a point

[33] ibid para 99.
[34] C-57/16 P, above n 17.
[35] Case T-424/14 *ClientEarth v European Commission* EU:T:2015:848.
[36] Interinstitutional Agreement of 13 April 2016 on Better Law-Making, [2016] OJ L123/1.
[37] On this, see J Organ, 'EU Citizen Participation, Openness and the European Citizens Initiative: The TTIP legacy' (2017) 54 *Common Market Law Review* 1713, 1746.

that enables them effectively to make their views known regarding those issues'.[38] Therefore, while providing information after the decision-making process has ended might sometimes be enough for the purposes of ensuring accountability; it is never enough for the purposes of enabling participation.

Finally, the Court tackled the question of the workload feared by the Commission. After all, if the Commission provided information, civil society might actually get some substance in support of the slogan 'act – react – make a real impact' used in the context of previous elections to the European Parliament.[39] As a worst case scenario, the (so far passive and thoroughly under-informed) citizens might feel a sudden urge to comment or criticise, or even reach out to the institutions with the expectation that they should get a response. This could certainly be detrimental to institutional efficiency, if civil servants needed to spend their days responding to enquiries and defending their choices, maybe even reconsider or justify them, instead of promoting the preset institutional agenda. Countering such fears, the Court established that openness does not require that the Commission needs to respond, on the merits and in each individual case, to all possible remarks received following disclosure of a document under Regulation No 1049/2001.[40] In all, the Court argued, it had not been demonstrated that openness would seriously affect, prolong or complicate the proper conduct of internal discussion or decision-making.[41]

The four rulings culminating in *ClientEarth* stress how the EU's democratic legitimacy is in the hands of its citizens who have the right to know. They are to be considered active participants in the European project, and not just passive recipients of what it may produce. Access needs to be provided in real time, without unnecessary delay. Contrary to what the institutions claim, the Court does not seem convinced that transparency would seriously undermine efficiency and, in any case, democracy matters more. Again, in the words of Advocate General Cruz Villalón:

> [I]nconvenient though transparency may be … it must be said that it has never been claimed that democracy made legislation 'easier', if easy is taken to mean 'hidden from public scrutiny', as public scrutiny places serious constraints on those involved in legislating.[42]

What the Court seems to give weight to in these cases is also the identity and background of the applicant, even though the Regulation specifically stipulates that the applicant's reasons for applying need not be stated (Article 6(1)). In the four cases the applicants have been civil society representatives in the broad sense: either individual citizens (Maurizio Turco, MEP, or Emilio de Capitani, a

[38] Case C-57/16 P, above n 17, para 84.

[39] This slogan was used in the context of EP elections, see: www.europarl.europa.eu/news/en/headlines/eu-affairs/20130905STO18724/act-react-impact.

[40] Case C-57/16 P, above n 17, para 107.

[41] ibid para 108.

[42] Opinion of AG Cruz Villalón in Case C-280/11, above n 6, para 67.

former employee of the European Parliament) or NGOs (Access Info Europe or ClientEarth). In comparison, the Court's response has been negative when similar kinds of legislative documents have been requested by companies involved in private litigation who are requesting access to preparatory documents that would assist them in challenging the validity of an EU legal act.[43]

The idea of broad legislative transparency has been met by strong institutional resistance.[44] That the citizens have the right to vote in the elections to the European Parliament is clear, as is the accountability relationship between the Council and national parliaments. If the citizens are dissatisfied with the choices made, they can certainly express this in the next elections, at least to the extent they are able to identify a link between the offending choices and the electoral programmes offered – something that tends to be far from clear in European Parliament elections. But that citizens should in fact have the right to gain information while decision making processes are ongoing with the purpose of influencing its outcome remains contested and is experienced as harmful to the EU agenda. Especially challenged is the idea that rights of participation might extend beyond those specifically mentioned in Article 11 TEU:[45] such as the duty incumbent upon the Commission to organise consultations, and the ECI. While important, consultations are about supporting the institutional agenda based on the key premises set by the institution itself. The limitations of such an approach are clear; 'when values have been named, issues identified, agendas set, and options delineated, most of what is meaningful in politics has already taken place'.[46] Consultations are also organised very early in the legislative process, at the time when the Commission is planning legislative action, and only address its initial plans. However, they seem to continue to represent the preferred form of participation by the EU institutions as institution-initiated outlets whose main purpose seems to be not to disrupt but to support existing modes of governance or its preferences.[47]

[43] See, Case T-18/15 *Philip Morris Ltd v European Commission* EU:T:2016:487; Case T-796/14 *Philip Morris Ltd v European Commission* EU:T:2016:483; Case T-800/14 *Philip Morris Ltd v European Commission* EU:T:2016:486; Case T-710/14 *Herbert Smith Freehills LLP v Council of the European Union* EU:T:2016:494; Case T-755/14 *Herbert Smith Freehills LLP v European Commission* EU:T:2016:482; Case T-520/13 *Philip Morris Benelux v European Commission*, closed with an order of the Court since the Commission disclosed the requested impact assessment after commencement of the action and there was no longer a need to adjudicate on the action.

[44] See: www.ombudsman.europa.eu/en/decision/en/69206, Summary, Decision of the European Ombudsman setting out proposals following her strategic inquiry OI/8/2015/JAS concerning the Transparency of Trilogues.

[45] These include the obligation to offer citizens and representative associations the opportunity to make known and publicly exchange their views in all areas of Union action and to maintain an open, transparent and regular dialogue with representative associations and civil society. For the Commission, Art 11(3) TEU involves a duty to carry out broad consultations with relevant parties.

[46] B Barber, *Strong Democracy. Participatory Politics for a New Age* (Berkeley, CA, University of California Press, 2003) 157.

[47] Organ, 'EU Citizen Participation, Openness and the European Citizens Initiative', above n 36.

One would think that the Court's clear jurisprudence would now have settled the key issues in legislative transparency. However, an examination of institutional practice demonstrates how resistance reaches beyond cases that are lost in court. Complying with a ruling concerning an individual document, which following several years of litigation is likely to be outdated anyway, might not be problematic as such. However, similar considerations are likely to affect hundreds or thousands of other documents that perhaps should be made available proactively, without the need to request, and litigate, each one separately. It is in particular here that resistance continues when jurisprudence should be applied in new cases through various bureaucratic practices.

It is in particular the Council that has been accused of failing to adapt to changes in its environment and effectively apply Court jurisprudence.[48] This is indeed clearly visible in its failure to update its Rules of Procedure (2009) to reflect Court jurisprudence, and its extensive use of *limité* documents in legislative matters. *Limité* documents are defined as 'documents internal to the Council'.[49] However, under the current Council policy, which was reconfirmed summer 2018, *limité* documents can be shared with just about any institution or shareholder. Yet the Council claims that 'untimely public disclosure of such documents could adversely affect the Council's decision-making processes'. Currently most legislative documents are stamped *limité* immediately as they are produced, and they continue as *limité* until a specific request is made for one of them, in which case the labelling will be reconsidered. This practice questions whether rulings like *Access Info* have had any effect on the Council's public access policy. *Limité* is just the Council's own definition of 'not public', and its broad use in legislative matters is highly suspicious.

It is more than a little ironic that, in 2018 and after the aforementioned Court rulings, a legislative institution would still produce a document entitled 'legislative transparency' and then stamp it as *limité* and thus confidential. This Council document (11099/18), which could be best described as a valiant attempt to restate the old Council policy by dressing it in pompous language, was only made public after several months and following specific requests. It presents the idea of a 'Milestone Approach' to legislative transparency, proposing that documents associated with 'milestones' would be made directly accessible. In defining such milestones, the Council makes some concessions to the Court's new jurisprudence: Council's trilogue mandates would be endorsed at Council level, through a general approach, making them public, instead of the old practice of secret mandates settled in Coreper. Trilogue documents would be made public after submission to Member States, and state of play or progress reports after consideration by Coreper.

[48] Curtin and Leino, 'In Search of Transparency for EU Law-making', above n 12; V Abazi and M Hillebrandt, 'The Legal Limits to Confidential Negotiations: Recent Case Law Developments in Council Transparency' (2015) 52 *Common Market Law Review* 825; P Leino, 'Secrecy, Efficiency, Transparency in EU Negotiations: Conflicting Paradigms?' (2017) 5(3) *Politics and Governance* 6.

[49] Council of the European Union, *Handling of documents internal to the Council* 7695/18 and 11336/11.

The problem with this approach is that Regulation No 1049/2001 is clear about making legislative documents directly accessible, and this applies without qualification to all legislative documents produced at any stage of Council decision-making. There is nothing in the legislative framework or Court jurisprudence that limits legislative transparency to the Coreper stage. On the contrary, the *Access Info* ruling involved specifically a working party document from early stages of Council decision-making, and the Court showed no hesitation in declaring it public. At the same time, the Milestone approach institutionalises the practice of *limité* documents which has no grounding in Regulation 1049/2001. While doing so, the document also conveniently ignores the need to update the Council Rules of Procedure.[50] What the Council seems to forget is that its working arrangements need to be compatible with the Treaty demands, not the other way around.

Difficulties in ensuring legislative transparency at EU level also influence how democratic accountability can be realised at Member State level. The idea of representative democracy as enshrined in the Treaties partly relies on national parliaments. Under the Treaties, national parliaments provide the second element in ensuring that the EU remains accountable by supervising the actions of their governments in Council. As Rautio notes 'the multilevel EU governance system presents serious challenges for legislatures, not least regarding informational asymmetries'.[51] National democracy not only supports but is vital for EU arrangements, since the European construction largely claims its legitimacy through the national arena.[52] The national dimension is something that the EU has been reluctant to regulate outside the avenues of subsidiary control. A proposal that was considered and subsequently rejected at the time of the Constitutional Convention was the adoption of a code of conduct obliging each Member State to give an assurance that its national parliament has been involved, in accordance with national constitutional requirements, in forming the positions that the Member State represents in the Council. However, the relationship between governments and parliaments in EU matters is considered a constitutional matter and therefore largely a national competence reserve. While some governments operate subject to strict parliamentary guidance or instructions, in other Member States EU matters remain largely an executive function with little parliamentary oversight or input. Even when parliaments do enjoy generous prerogatives in relation to EU matters, these might be difficult to realise due to EU-level constraints, either because the government may not have the information (*cf* trilogues above) or because the matter is confidential in the EU and, as is the case usually in legislative matters,

[50] For criticism of the document see, eg: www.commissie-meijers.nl/sites/all/files/cm1813_note.pdf the Meijers Committee, '*Note to the Presidency of the Council concerning the General Secretariat draft policy paper on legislative transparency*' (3 October 2018) COM1813.

[51] T Raunio, 'Control and Scrutiny: Parliaments as Agents of Administrative Law' in C Harlow, P Leino and G della Cananea (eds), *Research Handbook on EU Administrative Law* (Cheltenham, Edward Elgar, 2017) 317.

[52] FW Scharpf, 'Legitimacy Intermediation in the Multilevel European Polity and Its Collapse in the Euro Crisis' (2012) Max Planck Institute for the Study of Societies Discussion Paper 12/6, 17.

included in *limité* documents.[53] These challenges are specifically addressed by a recent initiative by the Conference of Parliamentary Committees for Union Affairs of Parliaments of the European Union (COSAC), which stresses that national parliaments can play a larger role in bringing the Union closer to its citizens.[54] Transparency is important for the execution of accountability. However,

> more transparency of political decision-making is needed within the EU. More openness facilitates better public and parliamentary debates before votes take place, and afterwards ensures that citizens know how their governments voted. Transparency could thus create more accountability for the outcomes of political decision-making, as well as making decision-making process itself more legitimate by opening it up for input from citizens, stakeholders, media and national parliaments.[55]

The difficulties experienced by national parliaments in scrutinising EU matters has been one of the core elements of the EU's democratic deficit. The standard institutional reply to national parliaments has been claiming professional secrecy and arguing that governments could, if they must, provide the information to their own parliaments based on confidentiality arrangements.[56] However, parliamentary scrutiny is by definition public scrutiny. What is public as a matter of EU policy matters for scrutiny at national level. It is problematic for national governments to claim confidentiality in legislative matters that under the Treaties and Court jurisprudence should, as a matter of principle, be public. And in requesting this, EU institutions indicate how fundamentally they continue to undermine the importance of national parliaments in defending the democratic nature of EU decision-making. There is no body at EU level that can replace this task.

## European Citizens' Initiative

ECI Regulation (EU) No 211/2011 on the citizens' initiative was adopted by the co-legislators in February 2011[57] and has been applicable since 1 April 2012.[58] The Regulation lays down the basic rules concerning who is entitled to organise or sign

[53] For criticism of this practice, see www.houseofrepresentatives.nl/news/internal-eu-council-documents-often-wrongly-undisclosed, the Dutch Parliament website, 'Internal EU Council Documents often wrongly undisclosed'.

[54] See: www.tweedekamer.nl/sites/default/files/atoms/files/letter_from_cosac_delegations_to_the_eu_institutions.pdf, Open Letter from the Staten-Generaal to the Presidents of the European Council, the Council of the European Union, the European Commission, and the Eurogroup (20 December 2017).

[55] Conference of Parliamentary Committees for Union Affairs of Parliaments of the European Union (COSAC) 2017.

[56] Disclosure of confidential documents, Council doc 14920/13.

[57] Regulation (EU) No 211/2011 of the European Parliament and of the Council of 16 February 2011 on the citizens' initiative [2011] OJ L65/1.

[58] It has been amended through Commission Delegated Regulation (EU) No 268/2012 of 25 January 2012, published in [2012] OJ L89 of 27 March 2012; Council Regulation (EU) No 517/2013 of 13 May

an ECI, how citizens' initiatives are registered, how they can be supported, how the statements of support are verified and certified, and how the initiative is submitted to and verified by the Commission. The Regulation requires the forming of a citizens' committee and acquiring the signatures of one million citizens from at least seven different Member States. Organisations can also run campaigns for initiatives, but the financing of initiatives needs to live up to a number of transparency related requirements. Under Article 4(1) of the Regulation, the Commission is to establish a point of contact that provides information and assistance to ECI organisers.

A key provision concerning the implementation of the ECI is included in Article 4(2), which places the Commission under an obligation to examine, prior to registration, whether the basic procedural rules have been satisfied, but also that a proposed ECI 'does not manifestly fall outside the Commission's power to submit a proposal for a legal act of the Union for the purpose of implementing the Treaties'; is 'not manifestly abusive, frivolous or vexatious' or 'manifestly contrary to the values of the Union'. If these conditions are not met, the Commission shall refuse the registration.

The Regulation offers the Commission a wide room for manoeuvre for assessing citizens' initiatives. First, it receives and considers the ECI and subsequently, 'within three months, set(s) out in a communication its legal and political conclusions on the citizens' initiative, the action it intends to take, if any, and its reasons for taking or not taking that action' (Article 10(1)c). It meets with the organisers, who will also have the opportunity to present the initiative at a public hearing of the European Parliament. The Commission is, however, not obliged to propose any legislation as a result of the initiative, a fact which reflects and reinforces its next-to-monopoly on legislative initiatives laid down in Article 17(2) TEU. The Court has confirmed that,

> in exercising its powers of legislative initiative, the Commission must be allowed broad discretion, in so far as, through that exercise, it is called upon, pursuant to Article 17(1) TEU, to promote the general interest of the Union by carrying out, possibly, the difficult task of reconciling divergent interests. It follows that the Commission must be allowed broad discretion in deciding whether or not to take an action following an ECI.[59]

The broad discretion of the Commission also influences possible court review: its final decision is only subject to limited review, 'aimed at verifying, in addition to the adequacy of its statement of reasons, the existence, inter alia, of manifest errors of assessment vitiating that decision'.[60] If a legislative proposal is made by the Commission, it proceeds through the normal legislative procedure and goes to the Parliament or the Council and may eventually become a legislative act.

2013, published in [2013] OJ L158 of 10 June 2013; and Commission Delegated Regulation (EU) No 887/2013 of 11 July 2013, published in [2013] OJ L247 of 18 September 2013.

[59] In Case T-561/14 *European Citizens' Initiative One of Us and Others v European Commission* EU:T:2018:210 para 169.

[60] ibid para 170.

Since coming into force in 2012, the ECI has proven to be almost a downright failure. The main source of dissatisfaction relates to the complexity and bureaucracy embedded in the initiative system, as well as the way the Commission has applied the instrument. Most of the initiatives either expire or are rejected at the stage of registration, which means that they never enter the stage of signature collection. This clearly limits the opportunities for European-wide public debate that the ECI was supposed to engender. The laborious process of making the ECI in practice presumes mobilisation by professional organisations and lobbyists.[61] So far, only four ECIs have received the required number of signatories and have been formally submitted to the Commission.[62] The Commission lists 17 initiatives as having been rejected, 26 initiatives have become obsolete due to insufficient support, and 15 have been withdrawn by the organisers. However, whether an ECI ultimately results in new legislation may not always be its only objective. Raising and debating issues and placing them on the political agenda also matters.

In terms of issues covered by the initiatives, we may look at the successful ones that have reached the million signatures. The first initiative to reach the Commission called for legislation that would implement the human right for water and sanitation, as recognised by the UN, and promote the provision of water and sanitation as essential public services for all ('Water and sanitation are a human right! Water is a public good, not a commodity!)' The Commission has committed to a series of actions to further the initiative and these actions are currently being implemented.[63] But in terms of affecting EU legislation, this ECI is the only success story so far.

The ECI relating to ending the financing of activities which presuppose the destruction of human embryos, especially in research ('*One of us*'), stresses the difficulty of applying the ECI criteria. Of key relevance here was the criterion relating to compatibility with the Union's values, which the ECI was specifically aimed to promote. At the same time, the moral condition is notoriously open-ended and subject to interpretation.[64] The Commission considered the existing legislation adequate.[65] The organisers have appealed the decision, and the General

[61] B Johnson, 'EU citizens' initiative under fire in European Parliament Report' *The Parliament Magazine* (3 August 2015), available at: www.theparliamentmagazine.eu/articles/news/eu-citizens-initiative-under-fire-european-parliament-report.

[62] The statistics are available on the Commission website at: ec.europa.eu/citizens-initiative/public/basic-facts.

[63] See Communication from the Commission on the European Citizens' Initiative 'Water and sanitation are a human right! Water is a public good, not a commodity!' COM(2014) 177 final; and the Evaluation and Fitness Check (FC) Roadmap on Evaluation of the Drinking Water Directive, available on the ECI website.

[64] For a discussion concerning the difficulty in using values as an objective criterion, see P Leino, 'European Universalism? The EU and Human Rights Conditionality' (2005) 24 *Yearbook of European Law* 329.

[65] Communication from the Commission on the European Citizen's Initiative 'One of Us', COM(2014) 355 final.

Court decision maintaining it,[66] and an appeal is pending before the CJEU.[67] The third initiative to reach the threshold of a million signatures challenges the current legislation regarding animal testing in research ('*Stop vivisection*'). In its reply, the Commission decided it would not submit legislative proposals on the matter, but indicated a number of softer alternative measures it might consider. The fourth, and final, initiative to receive the required number of signatories, 'Ban glyphosate and protect people and the environment from toxic pesticides' also received a negative reply from the Commission, which argued that there are neither scientific nor legal grounds to justify a ban of glyphosate (a conclusion with which many scientists and the World Health Organization would beg to disagree).[68] However, the Commission did commit to reconsidering the transparency of scientific evaluations in the European Food Safety Authority in the context of reforming its founding regulation.[69]

The initiative which has provoked the most discussion is a failed one, relating to an attempt to stop the Transatlantic Trade and Investment Partnership (TTIP). It is an example of an ECI that links to a matter with a clearly Europe-wide popular appeal and that has provoked institutional debates and contestation far beyond the ECI framework.[70] The Commission claimed that the objective of the initiative aiming at a withdrawal of the relevant negotiating mandate did not constitute a 'legal act' for the purposes of the ECI.[71] Evidencing how strongly geared the EU institutions still are towards representative democracy, the Commission argued that it and the Council have 'sufficient indirect democratic legitimacy' for the purposes of adopting acts which do not produce legal effects vis-a-vis third parties; something that the General Court rejected.[72]

The ECI appeals have offered the CJEU another opportunity to highlight what democracy requires from the institutions. In its ruling relating to the TTIP ECI, the Court referred to the principle of democracy as one of the EU's fundamental values, and emphasised 'the objective of participation in the democratic life of the European Union pursued by the ECI mechanism', which in its view 'manifestly includes the power to request an amendment of legal acts in force or their

[66] Case T-561/14, above n 58.

[67] Case C-418/18 P *One of Us v Commission*.

[68] See E Korkea-aho and P Leino, 'Who Owns the Information Held by EU Agencies? Weed Killers, Commercially Sensitive Information and Transparent and Participatory Governance' (2017) 54 *Common Market Law Review* 1059.

[69] Communication from the Commission on the European Citizen's Initiative 'Ban glyphosate and protect people and the environment from toxic pesticides', COM(2017) 8414 final.

[70] P Leino, 'The principle of transparency in EU External Relations Law: Does Diplomatic Secrecy Stand a Chance of Surviving the Age of Twitter?' in M Cremona (ed), *Structural Principles in EU External Relations Law* (Oxford, Hart Publishing, 2018) 218–19.

[71] Case T-754/14, above n 11. An earlier ECI opposing a free movement agreement between the EU and Switzerland had earlier been approved by the Commission despite being an international agreement; even the ECI was later withdrawn by its organisers.

[72] Case T-754/14, above n 11, para 38.

annulment, in whole or in part' (para 42). In the view of the Court, the Commission's specific argument about how 'the acts which an ECI proposal requests it to submit to the Council would lead to an inadmissible interference in an ongoing legislative procedure' was unacceptable:

> The aim pursued by the ECI is to allow European Union citizens to participate more in the democratic life of the European Union, in particular, by presenting in detail to the Commission the questions raised by the ECI, by requesting that institution to submit a proposal for a European Union legal act after having, as the case may be, presented the ECI at a public hearing organised at the Parliament … therefore, by stimulating a democratic debate without having to await the adoption of the legal act whose modification or withdrawal is ultimately sought.[73]

The Court referred to how it is still for the Commission to decide whether or not it will accept the ECI:

> Consequently, far from amounting to an interference in an ongoing legislative procedure, ECI proposals constitute an expression of the effective participation of citizens of the European Union in the democratic life thereof, without undermining the institutional balance intended by the Treaties.[74]

Several considerations point to a general assessment that the ECI is not be delivering as it should. Instead, the EU's new 'flagship instrument in driving participatory democracy at EU level' has 'failed to live up to its early promise with citizen groups struggling to cope with the system's complexity and bureaucracy'.[75] The dissatisfaction with how the Commission manages the ECI is clearly visible in not only a number of complaints to the Ombudsman, but also in the Court register of pending cases: the appeal rate is incredibly high. Seven denials have been appealed to the General Court, and four appeals on General Court rulings are pending. The applicants argue in particular the Commission's failure to indicate which parts of the ECI fell outside the Treaty,[76] failure to observe limits of competence,[77] misapplication of the legal test in Article 4(2)(b) of the ECI Regulation and general principles of good administration,[78] and failure to provide legal reasons for its refusal and instead using subjective and arbitrary reasons.[79] The Commission has traditionally had a limited understanding of positive duties in relation to citizens,[80] which

[73] ibid para 45.
[74] ibid para 47.
[75] Johnson, above n 60.
[76] Case T-646/13, above n 9.
[77] Case T-361/14 *HB and Others v European Commission* EU:T:2017:252. An appeal is pending before the CJEU (Case C-336/17 *HB and Others v European Commission*:EU:C:2018:74).
[78] Case T-44/14 *Bruno Costantini and Others v European* Commission EU:T:2016:223.
[79] Case T-561/14, above n 58, [2014] OJ C 409.
[80] P Leino, Efficiency, Citizens and Administrative Culture. The Politics of Good Administration in the EU (2014) 20 *European Public Law* 681.

is very much reflected in the way that it handles the ECI initiatives. For example, the Commission does not actively advise or assist organisers in drafting a proposal that might satisfy the admissibility test.[81]

The Court's Grand Chamber has stressed the importance of principles of good administration in handling ECIs. The Commission should examine the information provided by ECI organisers 'with care and impartiality',[82] and needs to provide assistance and advice, particularly with regard to the registration criteria.[83] The subsequent decision on the registration of a proposed ECI,

> must be taken in accordance with the principle of good administration, which entails, in particular, the obligation for the competent institution to conduct a diligent and impartial examination which, moreover, takes into account all the relevant features of the case. These requirements, that are inherent in the principle of good administration, apply generally to the actions of the European Union administration in its relations with the public and, therefore, also in the context of the right to submit an ECI as an instrument of citizen participation in the democratic life of the European Union. Moreover, in accordance with the objectives pursued by that instrument … consisting, inter alia, in encouraging citizen participation and making the Union more accessible, the registration condition … must be interpreted and applied by the Commission, when it receives a proposal for an ECI, in such a way as to ensure easy accessibility to the ECI.[84]

Also the European Ombudsman has criticised the Commission for failure to engage with the ECI organisers and offer them assistance in clarifying and defining the objective of the ECI with a view to avoiding its rejection for the reason that it reaches beyond Commission powers.[85]

The last point relates to the core position of competence in the procedure. The Commission interprets the admissibility criteria narrowly.[86] While established case law stresses the objective nature of choices relating to competence and legal basis, the question of whether the EU has competence to adopt an act or not also depends on what it would do and how this would be done. In EU law-making, these questions are considered to be a prerogative for experts of EU law who solve many of these challenges through drafting.[87] These kinds of legislative techniques are beyond most ECI organisers. For the Court, 'the very nature of the right to an ECI and the possible impact of a decision refusing to register a proposed ECI

[81] J Organ, 'Decommissioning Direct Democracy? A Critical Analysis of Commission Decision-making on the Legal Admissibility of European Citizens Initiative Proposals' (2014) 10 *European Constitutional Law Review* 422.

[82] Case C-589/15 P, above n 8, paras 34–35, confirming an earlier General Court ruling (Case T-450/12 *Alexios Anagnostakis v European Commission* EU:T:2015:739).

[83] Case C-589/15 P, above n 8, para 46.

[84] ibid paras 47–49.

[85] Letter from Emily O'Reilly, above n 10.

[86] Organ, 'Decommissioning Direct Democracy?', above n 80.

[87] P Leino, 'The Politics of Efficient Compromise in the Adoption of EU Legal Acts' in M Cremona (ed), *EU Legal Acts: Challenges and Transformations, Collected Courses of the Academy of European Law* (Oxford, Oxford University Press, 2018).

on the democratic life of the Union' requires the Commission to state its reasons for its decision refusing registration, including why it considers that a proposal falls manifestly outside its powers.[88] In the absence of proper reasoning, the ECI organisers are unable to identify which elements fell outside Commission powers and why, and are consequently unable to challenge the merits of that assessment. This also makes it difficult to develop and introduce a new improved ECI. In practice, in the view of the Court, Commission practices in this regard compromise the achievement of the objectives 'of encouraging participation by citizens in democratic life and of making the European Union more accessible'.[89]

Yet the competence criterion has offered the Commission a useful tool for rejecting unpopular initiatives when it wishes to do so. Many of the initiatives could be promoted in another context or format. The ECI 'offers organisers a platform from which they can generate a public debate about their issue thus allowing the organisers to be properly and genuinely listened to',[90] as the Ombudsman has put it, while also criticising the Commission for not always doing so. Instead, she urged the Commission 'to engage fully with the ECIs, so that citizens feel not only that they have a voice, but also that they have been listened to and taken seriously'.[91]

The Commission has responded to this criticism at least at the level of political rhetoric. In his State of the Union 2017 speech, Commission President Juncker presented his Commission's 'Democracy Package', which focused specifically on the reform of the ECI.[92] First Vice-President Frans Timmermans said: 'With these proposals, we are empowering Europeans to participate in the democratic process'.[93] In April 2017, the Commission announced its intention to revise the ECI Regulation and organised a stakeholder consultation. The ECI context provides a useful case study of the influence of consultations on the EU's legislative agenda.

Following the consultation, the Commission reported how stakeholders agreed that it is difficult for citizens to propose initiatives that do not fall, in the view of the Commission, manifestly outside its mandate, and that this interpretation results in a high number of refusals to register. Stakeholders also broadly agreed on the need to strengthen assistance to organisers (83 per cent of respondents to the public consultation) and suggested providing other types of support such as assistance in (re)drafting, translation of initiatives and financial support.[94] However, the Commission proposal aimed at revising the ECI regulation[95] seems

[88] Case C-589/15 P, above n 8, para 34.

[89] Case T-646/13, above n 9.

[90] Decision of the European Ombudsman closing her on-initiative inquiry OI/9/2013/TN concerning the European Commission paras 20–21.

[91] Letter from Emily O'Reilly, above n 10.

[92] Press release, European Commission 'State of the Union 2017 – Democracy Package: Reform of Citizens' Initiative and Political Party funding' (Brussels, 15 September 2017), available at: europa.eu/rapid/press-release_IP-17-3187_en.htm.

[93] ibid.

[94] A summary can be found at: ec.europa.eu/citizens-initiative/files/SG_2017_Synopsis_Report_en.pdf.

[95] The Commission published its proposal for a new Regulation on the ECI, COM(2017) 482 on 13 September 2017.

largely unconnected from the results of the consultation or more generally, the key problems that have caused the ECI to fail. The focus of the proposal is on technical arrangements. Even though it is of importance to arrange technical details as smoothly as possible, the main obstacle for the operation of the ECI has not been in the technicalities but in the 'legal' and bureaucratic obstacles that the Commission has laid in the way of its operation. The Commission proposed no substantive changes to the criteria or its obligation to guide and assist the applicants by reference to principles of good administration.[96] Considering the Commission's application practice so far, it is overly optimistic to anticipate that its practices in implementing the Regulation would change unless it is under a clear obligation to do so. Workload, which usually provokes institutional concern, would not seem to be a serious problem either. The numbers of ECI to this point are so limited that administering them much more carefully would not be a significant administrative burden. At the same time, in light of the political aims of the instrument, emphasised by the Court, the Commission should be prepared to invest in its active implementation.

In the end, its resistance demonstrates a sad picture of how the Commission bureaucrats see the function of citizen influence in settling the legislative agenda. On the whole, the 'formalistic, restrictive and sometimes selective approach taken, combined with the high number of proposals refused registration, leaves the Commission open to criticism in relation to its willingness to accept popular influence over the legislative agenda and a Union based on democracy'.[97] It is evident that if the ECI was in fact powerful, the Commission's institutional role would be the one most affected by the new instrument.[98] On the other hand, there are good grounds to wonder whether influencing the Commission's institutional role was not exactly its main purpose. While doing so, it might bring stronger legitimacy to the Union agenda, which would contribute also to strengthening the position of the institution largely in charge of setting it. This would not seem like a bad political bargain.

## EU Machinery Versus Citizen Involvement

The alienation of EU citizens has long been seen as a threat to the general support for the Union and a constraint to its further development. The Lisbon Treaty set out to find remedies to this malaise. A key part of the reforms was to improve avenues for citizens to be informed about and participate in the legislative work of the

[96] The proposal includes a slightly updated formulation: 'The Commission shall, upon request, provide information and assistance about the European citizens' initiative to citizens and groups of organisers'.

[97] Organ, 'Decommissioning Direct Democracy?', above n 80, 422, 443.

[98] D Szeligowska and E Mincheva, 'The European Citizens' Inititative: Empowering European Citizens within the Institutional Triangle: A Political and Legal Analysis' (2012) 13 *Perspectives on European Politics and Society* 270, 280.

Union. These reforms have sat uncomfortably in the EU institutional setting where there is no tradition of such citizen participation[99] and apparently little openness in allowing, let alone nurturing, it. Despite the (undoubtedly sincere) political proclamations and legislative documents professing the virtues of citizen participation, the Union bodies and officials in charge of regulating the practical channels for such participation remain, intentionally or instinctively, in resistance. Rather than recognising citizens as the main actors in democracy, institutional practice demonstrates how the Union machinery appears to perceive citizen participation as a nuisance, unavoidable but fundamentally undesirable, to be contained and made harmless. To be meaningful, citizen participation should have the capacity to actually frame the Union institutions' policy agendas, confront their existing preferences, and influence policy outcomes.

A key aspect of the EU's democratic deficit is the perception that decisions are taken by an insular elite within the Brussels 'bubble', with little interest in engaging with citizens. The EU institutions' attitudes towards the forms of participatory democracy do little to alleviate this perception. Certainly, there is no reason to think that the underlying motivations behind these attitudes are anything but benevolent. Rather, it is difficult to find genuine faith in the virtues of deeper citizen participation in the construction of Europe. Implementing citizen participation in the Union is largely in the hands of technocratic actors with technocratic instincts. Positions that are highly relevant for the exercise of citizens' political rights are formulated, with little political oversight, by bureaucrats in the EU institutions. Specifically, arguments presented in litigation over access to documents are primarily chosen by the institutions' legal services, which are seldom subjected to any kind of political control.[100] Judicial oversight exists, and defending democracy has been left to the Court. The Court has repeatedly rejected the institutional arguments building on efficiency, but they seem to remain deeply rooted in the EU institutional ethos. The institutions do what they think is necessary to protect the Union's legislative agenda and its ability to progress towards deeper integration from distraction by uncontrolled forms of direct democracy. The prevailing conviction seems to be that what counts are the results, not how you produce them. And if citizens' participation complicates progress towards results, it is better to do without it.

But as is the case with teleological belief systems in general, the dominant institutional mindset risks subordinating other worthy goals – such as democracy – to this single one, falling victim to what is known as 'noble cause corruption'. Ultimately, the choice is simple: either the Union accepts democracy in the proper sense, and with it the risk of citizen distraction, or it continues running its business as an elitist project and validates the concerns about democratic deficit. Looking at the political landscape in Europe, one wonders how long the latter option is sustainable.

[99] Organ, 'EU Citizen Participation, Openness and the European Citizens Initiative', above n 36.

[100] This is reflected in the interviews I have conducted with numerous members of the legal services. On file with author.

# PART III

# EU Constitutional Democracy: *Pistes de Reflection* for the Future

# 17

# Beyond Rhetoric: Education for Democratic Citizenship in the European Union

KRIS GRIMONPREZ*

## Introduction

In the current state of constitutional democracy, the need for citizenship education appears to be a matter of consensus. Yet, the *what*, *why* and *how* questions require clarification and critical reflection, especially with regard to the EU level of governance. The stakes are high. The Brexit referendum convincingly illustrates the structural consequences to which the gap with the citizens may lead, both for the Member State and for the EU as a whole. The causes of the 'Leave' vote are complex and cannot simply be attributed to the failure to learn about the EU at school. Yet, it is thought provoking that in the Eurydice study on 'citizenship education themes, as recommended in national curricula' (2012), some columns for the UK (though not for Scotland) were left empty, namely those relating to European identity and belonging, and European history, culture and literature.[1]

Taking democracy seriously means that citizens in the EU must be empowered to participate and this requires education. Citizenship education is both timeless (practised in Ancient Athens and Rome) and topical (responses to radicalisation, populism, or fake news). An often repeated aphorism is: 'We are not born as a citizen, we are educated to be a citizen'.[2] John Dewey states that 'democracy has to be born anew every generation, and education is its midwife'.[3] Robert Dahl

* This text is based on my doctoral dissertation (University of Luxembourg). *Education for Democratic Citizenship and the European Union: Legal Foundations for EU Learning at School* (Luxembourg Legal Studies, Baden-Baden, Nomos, forthcoming 2019).

[1] Eurydice, Citizenship Education in Europe (2012) 30. Eurydice, a network of 42 national units in 38 States (including all EU Member States) provides information on national education systems.

[2] eg, R Maxwell, 'Citizens Are Made, Not Born: How Teachers Can Foster Democracy' in *Citizens in the Making* (ASCD, 2017).

[3] J Dewey, Democracy and Education: An Introduction to the Philosophy of Education (New York, Macmillan, 1916) 9.

emphasises 'enlightened understanding' by citizens as one of the substantive criteria for democracy.[4] In the same vein, Václav Havel writes: 'A moral and intellectual state cannot be established through a constitution, or through law, or through directives, but only through complex, long-term, and never-ending work involving education and self-education'.[5]

Because of the sensitivity of the field, the first step in this chapter is to identify relevant normative instruments concerning citizenship education and to point out standards on Education for Democratic Citizenship (EDC). In the next step, the need to move beyond rhetoric is highlighted, elements for the integration of an EU dimension in EDC are proposed and suggestions for future action made.

Looking through the prism of EDC standards offers fresh perspectives on EU citizenship, since it is not mobile EU citizens who are centre stage, but static citizens, ie, the large majority of citizens who live at home in their country of origin and have become EU citizens due to its membership of the EU (Article 9 TEU). What is their 'enlightened understanding'?

## Normative Instruments Concerning Citizenship Education

### UN Instruments

In response to the dramatic use made of education under totalitarian regimes and its effect in two world wars, education was central to the 1945 UNESCO Constitution ('since wars begin in the minds of men, it is in the minds of men that the defences of peace must be constructed').[6] The authors of the 1948 Universal Declaration on Human rights (UDHR) repeatedly emphasised the importance of mentioning the aims of education.[7] Article 26 UDHR proclaims that everyone has the right to education and immediately specifies four aims to which education shall be directed, such as the full development of the human personality, the strengthening of respect for human rights and fundamental freedoms, and the understanding, tolerance and friendship among all nations, racial or religious groups. The aims of education were confirmed and developed in subsequent international agreements. The 1966 International Covenant on Economic, Social and Cultural Rights (ICESCR) and the 1989 Convention on the Rights of the Child (CRC) added the further aim that education shall prepare the child for effective

[4] RA Dahl, *Democracy and its Critics* (New Haven, CT, Yale University Press, 1989) 108–14.

[5] V Havel, *Summer Meditations* (P Wilson trans, New York, Vintage Books, 1992) 20.

[6] Preamble.

[7] Reports of the Commission on Human Rights in the Drafting of the Universal Declaration of Human Rights, eg, SR 67 and 68.

participation and responsible life in a free society (Articles 13(1) and 29(1)). The aims of education are an essential part of the international right to education. The child's right to education is not only a matter of access to education, but also of content.[8] The binding character of the aims follows from a textual interpretation (education 'shall be directed to', not 'should') and is confirmed by a reading in the light of the *travaux préparatoires* and by the practice of the Committee on Economic, Social and Cultural Rights and the Committee on the Rights of the Child.[9] Education is an empowerment right, to which obligations correspond.[10] Article 29(1) CRC includes the individual right to quality education, directed to the aims listed. The curriculum must be of 'direct relevance to the child's social, cultural, environmental and economic context and to his or her present and future needs'.[11] On a contemporary interpretation, the right to education includes a right to education for democracy and human rights education.[12]

## Council of Europe Instruments

The 2010 Council of Europe Charter on Education for Democratic Citizenship and Human Rights Education (hereafter the Charter on EDC/HRE), adopted by the Committee of Ministers, is a regional continuation of the work at UN level. It transposes the aims of quality education – including education for democracy and human rights education – to the European context.[13] After the fall of the Berlin Wall, EDC had become a central preoccupation in Europe. The values of democracy, the rule of law and human rights were at the basis of the commitment of the 47 Council of Europe Member States to the EDC project and of 'the standards they are setting themselves to achieve'.[14] Based on the expertise of many actors and work over decades, the Charter on EDC/HRE is a milestone within an impressive body of instruments on EDC. It contains a commonly accepted concept of citizenship education, more precisely labelled as 'Education for Democratic Citizenship'

[8] UN Committee on the Rights of the Child, General Comment No 1, Art 29(1): The Aims of Education, Doc CRC/GC/2001/1, para 3.

[9] KD Beiter, *The Protection of the Right to Education by International Law* (including a systematic analysis of Art 13 of the International Covenant on Economic, Social and Cultural Rights (International Studies in Human Rights 82, Leiden, Nijhoff, 2006) 469.

[10] Art 2 ICESCR; Arts 4 and 43 CRC; UN Committee on Economic, Social and Cultural Rights (ComESCR) General Comment No 3, paras 2, 5, 7.

[11] General Comment No 1, above n 8, para 9; see also paras 1, 2 and 22. Further UN ComESCR, General Comment No 13: The Right to Education (Art 13), Doc E/C12/1999/10, para 1.

[12] See, inter alia, UN General Assembly Resolution 71/8 Education for democracy (17 November 2016) Doc A/RES/71/8/; Office of the UN High Commissioner for Human Rights, 'The Right to Human Rights Education: A compilation of provisions of international and regional instruments dealing with human rights education'.

[13] Recommendation CM/Rec(2010)7.

[14] Explanatory memorandum to CM/Rec(2010)7, para 24.

and 'Human Rights Education'. The outcome is not simply knowledge, but the empowerment of learners.[15] Central to the Charter are EDC components c-1-2-3:

> 'Education for democratic citizenship' means education, training, awareness raising, information, practices and activities which aim, by equipping learners with knowledge, skills and understanding and developing their attitudes and behaviour, to empower them [c-1] to exercise and defend their democratic rights and responsibilities in society, [c-2] to value diversity and [c-3] to play an active part in democratic life, with a view to the promotion and protection of democracy and the rule of law.[16]

A necessary complement of EDC is Human Rights Education (HRE), as democracy based on majority opinion must at the same time respect human rights to protect minorities. HRE aims 'to empower learners to contribute to the building and defence of a universal culture of human rights in society, with a view to the promotion and protection of human rights and fundamental freedoms'.[17] Because EDC and HRE are so intensely intertwined,[18] the use in this chapter of the term 'EDC' presupposes HRE as well. The Charter on EDC/HRE expresses the European consensus on the concept, the objectives and principles of EDC and HRE (hereafter EDC standards). EDC/HRE is a lifelong learning process in which formal, non-formal and informal learning have a part to play.[19] In formal learning, EDC/HRE is provided in schools, ie, learning in a structured way leading to certification. Member States should include EDC and HRE in the curricula of primary and secondary schools, in general, as well as in vocational education and training, and ensure its relevance.[20]

The recent challenges of radicalisation, terrorism, and the influx of migrants have led to renewed commitment to EDC. In 2016, the Standing Conference of the Ministers of Education agreed on the strategic objective: 'To make the preparation for lifelong active democratic citizenship of all learners in education and training a hallmark of the quality of European education systems and an essential part of our response to the challenges Europe is facing'.[21] This corresponds to the concept of quality education as recommended by the Committee of Ministers in 2012 (and consistent with the UN approach): quality education, inter alia, 'promotes democracy, respect for human rights and social justice' and 'enables pupils and students to develop appropriate competences, self-confidence and critical thinking to help them become responsible citizens'.[22]

[15] Compare civics is 'the didactic transmission of factual information about constitutions and institutions', I Davies, 'Political Literacy' in J Arthur, I Davies and C Hahn (eds), *The SAGE Handbook of Education for Citizenship and Democracy* (London, Sage Publications, 2008) 9, 382.

[16] Para 2(a).

[17] Para 2(b).

[18] Para 3.

[19] Para 5(a)–(c).

[20] Para 6.

[21] Securing Democracy through Education, para 13, see also paras 20, 31.

[22] Recommendation CM/Rec(2012)13 of the Committee of Ministers to member States on ensuring quality education, para 6(d)–(e).

In 2016, the Charter on EDC/HRE was included in a Compendium of the most relevant Council of Europe texts in the area of democracy.[23] Support for its implementation comes from the Reference Framework of Competences for Democratic Culture, launched in 2018 as a means of responding to the call for quality education.[24]

The right to education in the European Convention on Human Right (ECHR) contains no indications as to quality education, but rather focuses on equal access to existing educational facilities (Article 2, Protocol 1).[25] Yet, the European Court of Human Rights (ECtHR) considers that the state is responsible for quality education and requires that, in fulfilling its educational functions, it takes care to convey the information or knowledge included in the curriculum in an objective, critical and pluralistic manner, with no aims of indoctrination.[26]

## EU Instruments

EDC standards square with the basic tenets of the EU legal order.

First, as to *EU primary law*, EDC standards relate to the EU's foundational values of democracy, respect for fundamental rights and the rule of law entrenched in Article 2 TEU. A combined reading of Articles 10(3) TEU and 165(2) TFEU confirms the link in EU primary law between citizenship and democracy on the one hand, and education on the other. The similarity in the wording of provisions inserted into the TEU by the Lisbon Treaty in 2009 is striking. Article 10(3) TEU provides that '[e]very citizen shall have the right to *participate in the democratic life of the Union*'. At the same time, a sentence added to Article 165(2) TFEU (which is the legal basis for EU education policy) states that in education matters, Union action shall be aimed at 'encouraging the *participation of young people in democratic life in Europe*' (last part of fifth indent).[27] Admittedly, this extra sentence figures in an indent on youth policy, thus not on formal (school) education. Yet, Article 165 has to be read as a whole. Participation of young people in democratic life in Europe is undeniably an objective of EU education policy. This corresponds to the EDC objective of empowerment 'to play an active part in democratic life' (component c-3).

The Treaties further stipulate that the EU shall cooperate with the Council of Europe in general (Article 220 TFEU) and on education in particular (Article 165(3) TFEU). In the 2007 Memorandum of Understanding between the

[23] Secretariat, CDDG(2016)Compendium, Ch E.

[24] *Reference Framework of Competences for Democratic Culture*, Vol 1 (2018) 16.

[25] *Belgian Linguistic* Cases No 1474/62 et al (ECtHR 23 July 1968) para 3; B Vermeulen, 'Right to Education (Article 2 of Protocol No 1)' in P Van Dijk et al (eds), *Theory and Practice of the European Convention on Human Rights*, 4th edn (Antwerp, Intersentia, 2006) 899. Some aims in Art 17 European Social Charter revised (1996).

[26] Case No 5095/71 *Kjeldsen* (ECtHR 7 December 1976) para 53; Case No 15472/02 *Folgerø* (ECtHR 29 June 2007) para 84(h).

[27] My emphasis.

Council of Europe and the EU, the EU recognises the Council of Europe as setting the benchmark for human rights, the rule of law and democracy, and EDC and HRE are named among the shared priorities and focal areas for cooperation.[28] In this context, logically, the EU acknowledges EDC standards and actively supports the implementation of the Charter on EDC/HRE.[29]

Just like the right to education in the ECHR, the right to education of the Charter of Fundamental Rights of the European Union (CFR) is silent on aims of education (Article 14). However, this right is to be interpreted in the light of the ICESCR and the CRC (international agreements to which all Member States are party, Article 53 CFR). A contextual argument for an interpretation of the EU right to education in the light of the UN compulsory aims of education is to be found in the UN Convention on the Rights of Persons with Disabilities, a Convention to which the EU has acceded and which is therefore part of EU law.[30] Article 24(1) of this Convention replicates the terms used with regard to the right to education in the ICESCR: education shall be directed to, inter alia, enabling persons with disabilities 'to participate effectively in a free society'. It suggests that the EU right to education cannot be narrowly interpreted as only relating to educational rights in cross-border situations.[31]

Secondly, EDC standards are expressed in *EU secondary law*. The 2018 Recommendation of the Council on key competences for lifelong learning, based on Article 165 TFEU, states that the Member States should support the right to quality and inclusive education. High quality education provides opportunities to develop eight key competences. One of them is the citizenship competence, ie, 'the ability to act as responsible citizens and to fully participate in civic and social life, based on understanding of social, economic, legal and political concepts and structures, as well as global developments and sustainability'.[32] Other EU legal acts, too, reflect various aspects of EDC standards. Despite disparities in terminology (citizenship education, citizenship competence, civic education), the EU clearly works within the EDC paradigm. The recent challenges of radicalisation leading to violent extremism have, moreover, brought citizenship education to the fore. Critical thinking skills are emphasised. In 2015, in response to terrorist attacks, the EU Ministers of Education and the Commissioner for Education adopted the Paris Declaration on Promoting citizenship and the common values of freedom, tolerance and non-discrimination through education.[33] A 2015 Council

[28] Memorandum of Understanding between the Council of Europe and the European Union (2007) paras 10, 14, 36.

[29] See interventions of the EU Commissioner for Education in the first and second review cycle of the Charter on EDC/HRE, below n 41.

[30] Council Decision of 26 November 2009 concerning the conclusion, by the European Community, of the United Nations Convention on the Rights of Persons with Disabilities, [2010] OJ L23/35.

[31] Compare G Gori, 'Article 14: Right to Education' in S Peers et al (eds), *The EU Charter of Fundamental Rights: A Commentary* (Oxford, Hart Publishing, 2014) 419.

[32] [2018] OJ C 189/1.

[33] 17 March 2015. A Working Group is active.

resolution on encouraging the political participation of young people in democratic life in Europe refers to 'citizenship education' without defining it, but it reflects the same objectives and principles as EDC.[34] In 2016, the Council and the Representatives of the Governments agreed that human rights and citizenship education represent powerful means of promoting common values and invited the Member States to promote citizenship education and to enhance social and civic competences.[35] In the 2017 European Pillar of Social Rights, the European Parliament, the Council and the Commission, devote the very first provision to education: 'Everyone has the right to quality and inclusive education, training and life-long learning in order to maintain and acquire skills that enable them to participate fully in society and manage successfully transitions in the labour market'.[36] Enabling full participation in society is consistent with the EDC aim of empowerment for participation (c-3) and echoes the aim of education in the ICESCR of 'effective participation in a free society'.

Some normative instruments relate to EU learning at school and citizenship education. In the 2013 Erasmus+ Regulation, the Parliament and the Council recognise the role of education in promoting active citizenship, participation in democratic life, and European values.[37] In the 2016 European Parliament resolution on Learning EU at school, all the components of the EDC concept are present, some of them literally.[38] The objectives of the 2018 'Council Recommendation on promoting common values, inclusive education, and the European dimension of teaching' include a stronger European identity and a better understanding of the Union and its Member States.[39]

## Beyond Rhetoric: Critical Reflections

Words have value. The power of speech may drive human behaviour. The many normative instruments attest to a broad consensus on the aims of citizenship education. Yet, what happens beyond rhetoric? Everyone is in favour of citizenship education (who would advocate having uneducated citizens?) Unfortunately, commitments often remain limited to lip service.

[34] [2015] OJ C 417/10, paras 18 and 34.

[35] Conclusions on the prevention of radicalisation leading to violent extremism, [2016] OJ C 467/3.

[36] Commission Recommendation (EU) 2017/761 of 26 April 2017 on the European Pillar of Social Rights, [2017] OJ L113/56.

[37] Regulation 1288/2013 of the European Parliament and of the Council of 11 December 2013 establishing 'Erasmus+': the Union programme for education, training, youth and sport and repealing Decisions 1719/2006, 1720/2006 and 1298/2008, [2013] OJ L347/50, Arts 4, 11(1)(a), 14(1)(a), recitals 16, 19 and 20. See also Council Regulation establishing the 'Europe for citizens' programme for the period 2014–2020 [2014] OJ L115/3, Arts 1–3, 6, recitals 1, 3, 4 and 19.

[38] [2018] OJ C 58/57, paras 10 and 15.

[39] [2018] OJ C 195/1, para 6, recital 18.

## Facts on Citizenship Education in Member States

The Charter on EDC/HRE leaves an important margin of appreciation to the Member States. The Committee of Ministers bears in mind that Member States are responsible for the organisation and content of their educational systems and lets the implementation of the Charter rely on a system of self-evaluation.[40] Every five years, a Council of Europe report and a conference assess the impact.[41] All the Member States which replied to the 2016 questionnaire on the implementation of the Charter (40 of 47) reported that concrete measures had been taken to promote EDC/HRE in accordance with the objectives and principles of the Charter and almost all governments could foresee further action to promote it. A main finding was that there is a shared working definition of EDC/HRE in 31 countries.[42] However, challenges are striking. The quality of EDC actually provided varies considerably between and within the Member States.[43] The majority of Member States have not yet developed criteria for the evaluation of the effectiveness of EDC/HRE programmes (asked in paragraph 11 Charter on EDC/HRE).[44] Member States do not always explicitly refer to EDC and HRE in their education laws, policies and strategic objectives (compare paragraph 5 Charter on EDC/HRE) and responded 'none' to 'scarcely' with regard to vocational education and training, and higher education.[45] A large majority of the respondents reported inconsistencies between policies (which include EDC/HRE in the curriculum) and practice (marginal implementation in schools).[46] While governments pointed to a lack of support among education professionals or referred to the educational autonomy of educational institutions, civil society organisations indicated that EDC was not a priority among decision-makers.[47] The 2017 report concludes that, with a view to the long term, EDC/HRE must be given greater political and pedagogical priority, potentially making the provision of EDC/HRE mandatory at least in formal education.[48]

In the same vein, the 2016 International Civic and Citizenship Education Study (based on questionnaires for pupils) highlighted considerable differences

[40] Recommendation CM/Rec(2010)7, preambular para 13, Appendix, paras 4, 11 and 14.

[41] First review cycle (2010–12), Conference 'Human Rights and Democracy in Action: Looking Ahead' (Strasbourg, 29–30 November 2012); second review cycle (2012–17), Conference, 'Learning to Live Together: A Shared Commitment to Democracy: Conference on the Future of Citizenship and Human Rights Education in Europe' (Strasbourg, 20–22 June 2017).

[42] Learning to live together: Council of Europe Report on the state of citizenship and human rights education in Europe (2017) 51–52, conclusions 77, 80.

[43] Secretary General, State of democracy, human rights and the rule of law – a security imperative for Europe (2016) 97. Further Learning to live together, above n 42, 29.

[44] Learning to live together, above n 42, 20, 53, 71.

[45] Government Replies to the 2016 CoE Questionnaire EDC/HRE, Q11, also Q 31. Learning to live together, above n 42, 67, figure 7 (trend in decline).

[46] Learning to live together, above n 42, 16–17, 64.

[47] ibid 18, 98. See also 77 on the lack of feedback from national parliaments (only half the countries). This contrasts with the priority they say they attach to EDC/HRE policies.

[48] ibid 7.

across and within countries.[49] In 2017, Eurydice studied official recommendations, national strategies or action plans on citizenship education in Europe and reported that the great majority of Member States confine themselves to short texts or general aims for citizenship education; far fewer set specific objectives or learning outcomes.[50]

In short, while a consensus exists on the aims of citizenship education, an implementation gap has to be acknowledged.[51]

## Facts on EU Learning at School

Learning about the EU in schools is fragmented. Authors report on patchy rules in curricula in mainstream education. The 2013 report on 'Learning Europe at school' concluded that Member States differ widely as to the aspects of the EU they expect to be taught in schools.[52] The European citizenship dimension, in particular, is rarely clearly defined. The 2016 International Civic and Citizenship Education Study found that pupils' opportunities to learn about Europe vary substantially across Europe. Teaching most often concerns European history, but far less European political and economic integration.[53] Eurydice reported in 2017 that '[a]s many as eight EU member states do not have an international dimension in the curriculum of secondary education' and that in most countries the curriculum for vocational training does not mention the EU at all.[54] The bEUcitizen project (barriers to EU citizenship) concludes a study of seven Member States by stating that all countries display a very similar approach with regard to the European dimension of citizenship: 'it is a highly neglected area within the national curriculum'; European citizenship education seems to be in its infancy.[55] Curriculum designers do not fully realise the implications of EU membership. While optional courses or ad hoc actions provide extra EU learning for specific groups,[56] the quality of the EU dimension in mainstream citizenship education – reaching

[49] W Schulz et al, 'Main Findings and Implications for Policy and Practice' in *Becoming Citizens in a Changing World* (Cham, Switzerland, Springer, 2018) 201, 202 (also in the European report).

[50] Eurydice, Citizenship Education at School in Europe (2017) 45–46. In several Member States, citizenship education is currently in the process of revision, 10.

[51] See, from 2005, C Bîrzéa, 'EDC policies in Europe: a synthesis' in *All-European Study on Education for Democratic Citizenship Policies* (CoE, 2005) 29.

[52] Commission, *Learning Europe at School* (ICF GHK, 2013).

[53] B Losito et al, *Young People's Perceptions of Europe in a Time of Change ICCS 2016* 2016 Education Report (Cham, Switzerland, Springer, 2017) 14–15.

[54] Eurydice 2017, above n 50, 67, also 29, 58, 65. See also European Parliament resolution Learning EU at school, above n 38, recitals J–L.

[55] See WE Bakker et al, *The Quest for a European Civic Culture: The EU and EU Citizenship in Policies and Practices of Citizenship Education in Seven EU Member States* (Utrecht University Repository, 2017) 3, 64. The Netherlands, Croatia, France, Germany, Ireland, Spain and Hungary focus on factual and institutional EU knowledge, rather than promoting EU values and training skills needed to exercise EU citizenship rights and to form active, participating EU citizens.

[56] Europe Days, European Youth Parliament, Back to School, eTwinning, EPAS, …

the large majority of citizens – appears largely unsatisfactory.[57] Not only do the teachers (trainers) themselves often lack essential knowledge about the EU, but so do the trainers of the trainers. Even scholars in the field of citizenship education sometimes fail to clearly distinguish between the EU and the Council of Europe or between EU citizens and immigrants.

The EU civic deficit, the disconnect between the EU and its citizens, has cognitive, affective and behavioural dimensions. Fragmented learning about the EU in schools is relevant to the civic deficit (at least) in its cognitive dimension. Studies invariably reveal a lack of knowledge about the EU. A 2018 Eurobarometer survey found that 59 per cent of Europeans feel that they understand how the EU works (subjective knowledge), yet only 18 per cent answered questions on the EU correctly (objective knowledge).[58] Poor understanding can easily become ambivalence, irritation about 'Brussels' or hostility. Negative referendum results and low turnout rates at the European Parliament elections are significant. Only 27 per cent of the 18–24 year-olds voted in the 2014 elections.[59]

If one of the basic challenges to be resolved by the EU is how to bridge the gap with its citizens, citizenship education must move beyond rhetoric. A huge number of pupils leave school at age 18 with impressive knowledge about science or literature, but in relative ignorance of the EU. The high impact of the EU on the daily life of citizens contrasts with the low importance attached to EU learning in many schools.

## Uncertainties on 'EU Citizenship Education'

To move beyond rhetoric, reflection is needed, in particular, on the question of what citizenship education means for citizens as EU citizens. What does the international right to education, directed at effective participation and responsible life in a free society, imply for citizens living in the EU? What is the impact of EU citizenship on compulsory educational aims, the hallmark of quality education? Quality education is 'adapted to the requirements of modern, complex societies' and ensures that pupils' 'full potential as citizens is developed'.[60] Should 'citizenship education' and 'EU citizenship' be linked at all?

[57] See also P Ferreira, C Albanesi and I Menezes, 'European Identity and Citizenship in Textbooks/ Educational Media' (2018) 17 *Journal of Social Science Education* 2; and five country reports in this special issue, uncovering gaps and differences. Earlier, H Walkenhorst, 'Problems of Political Education in a Multi-level Polity: Explaining Non-teaching of European Union Issues in German Secondary Schooling' (2006) 14 *Journal of Contemporary European Studies* 353; A Keating, 'Educating Europe's Citizens: Moving from National to Post-national models of Educating for European citizenship' (2009) 13 *Citizenship Studies* 135.

[58] eg, Standard Eurobarometer 89 (June 2018) 132.

[59] Young voters' turnout at the 2019 elections: figures not yet available. Global turnout: 42,61% (2014) and 50,62% (2019).

[60] CM/Rec(2012)13, above n 22, paras 2 and 23.

In general, 'citizenship education' is intended to educate individuals to be active, informed and responsible citizens.[61] Since the 1992 Maastricht Treaty introduced EU citizenship into the Treaties, it seems natural to extend the expression 'citizenship education' by adding 'EU', and to consider 'EU citizenship education' to be the education of individuals to become active, informed and responsible EU citizens, thus taking citizenship of the Union and the rights attached to this status since the Maastricht Treaty as the substance (Articles 20–24 TFEU). However, this approach is unsatisfactory. It is both reductive, seen from the EU perspective, and excessive, seen from the Member State perspective. This approach does not go far enough, inasmuch as the EU citizen is more than what 'citizenship of the Union' and the rights attached to that status imply.[62] At the same time, this approach goes too far, inasmuch as it may suggest that EU citizenship is a new citizenship to be forged by EU citizenship education in order to replace national citizenship. The aim of EU citizenship education should not be to create a new breed of citizens loyal to the EU while neglecting national allegiances. Using the term 'citizenship education' in relation to the EU may be confusing. For some, 'EU citizenship education' awakens high expectations of cultivating a sense of EU identity and feelings of belonging. For others, it leads to suspicion and the fear that it will only further undermine national sovereignty and the nation state. Citizenship education is traditionally associated with states and as such cannot be transposed to the EU.[63]

EU citizenship education needs to find a balance. On the one hand, the sphere of the Member States must be safeguarded, national identities and the division of competences between the EU and the Member States must be respected (Articles 4 and 5 TEU). Thus, the Convention on the Rights of the Child includes among compulsory educational aims the development of respect for the child's own cultural identity, language and values, and for the national values of the child's own country (Article 29(1)(c)). On the other hand, Member States must respect EU law. As *Herren der Verträge*, they have chosen to transfer competences to the EU in the Treaties and the EU exercises public power together with them. This inevitably has consequences for citizenship education and requires EU learning. 'EU citizenship education' should therefore not be understated, nor overstated (nor over-Stated, modelled on the State).

It is worth noting that EDC in the Charter on EDC/HRE is not defined by reference to the state. EDC is about empowering learners 'to exercise and defend their democratic rights and responsibilities *in society*, to value diversity and to play an active part *in democratic life*, with a view to the promotion and protection of democracy and the rule of law'.[64] The International Covenant on Civil and Political

[61] Eurydice 2017, above n 50, 9.
[62] See below.
[63] Some similar aspects as in N Walker, 'Postnational Constitutionalism and the Problem of Translation' in JHH Weiler and M Wind (eds), *European Constitutionalism Beyond the State* (Cambridge, Cambridge University Press, 2003).
[64] Above n 16.

Rights proclaims that every citizen shall have the right and the opportunity to take part in 'the conduct of *public affairs*' (Article 25).[65] The ICESCR asks education to 'enable all persons to participate effectively in a free *society*' (Article 13(1)). As Weiler writes: 'Democracy is not about States. Democracy is about the exercise of public power – and the Union exercises a huge amount of public power'.[66] EDC should reflect this, while respecting the specific characteristics of the Union. The German Constitutional Court has emphasised that the EU is not a state and that it should not be compared to one for its democratic legitimation. Participation of Germany in the EU does not mean that a federal state is coming into being, but is about 'an *extension* of the constitutional federal model by a supranational cooperative *dimension*'.[67] Applying this reasoning to EDC, the national EDC model needs *an extension* by a supranational *dimension*. It is in an adaptation perspective that an EU dimension should be incorporated into national EDC in order to adjust it to the EU multilevel system of governance. EU citizenship is additional to national citizenship and does not replace it (Article 9 TEU). In parallel, an EU dimension should to be added to national citizenship education, not replace it. Therefore, it is better to use the expression 'the EU dimension of EDC' instead of the expression 'EU citizenship education'.

What should be the content of this EU dimension?

## The Way Forward: Educating EU Citizens in the Spirit of their Constitutions

### *A Composite Constitutional System*

In the constitutional democracy of the European Union, the integration of an EU dimension into EDC should mirror the Treaties and the CFR, interconnected with Member State constitutions. Since constitutions lay down the basic choices for society, it is not only legitimate, but also necessary to educate citizens in the mindset of their constitutions. Thinkers throughout history have confirmed the principle that education must be linked to the constitution. Aristotle strongly encouraged the education of citizens in the spirit of their constitution: 'There is no profit in the best of laws … if the citizens themselves have not been attuned, by the force of habit and the influence of teaching, to the right constitutional temper'.[68]

[65] See also UNGA Res 71/8, above n 12, education for democracy aims at 'the empowerment of citizens and their participation in political life and policymaking at all levels'.

[66] JHH Weiler, 'United in Fear: The Loss of Heimat and the Crises of Europe' in L Papadopoulou, I Pernice and JHH Weiler (eds), *Legitimacy Issues of the European Union in the Face of Crisis: Dimitris Tsatsos in memoriam* (Baden-Baden, Nomos, 2017) 366.

[67] BVerfG, 2 BvE 2/08 *(Lissabon)* 30 June 2009, Absatz-Nr (1–421) para 277 (emphasis added).

[68] R Curren, 'A Neo-Aristotelian account of education, justice, and the human good' (2013) 11 *Theory and Research in Education* 231. Further D Heater, *A History of Education for Citizenship* (Abingdon, Routledge, 2004).

Condorcet (a philosopher at the time of the French Revolution who devoted much thought as to how to educate the newly born *citoyen*) affirmed that

> a constitution based on true freedom, where all social classes enjoy the same rights, cannot survive if the ignorance of some citizens does not enable them to understand its nature and limits, obliges them to express views on what they do not know; such a constitution would destroy itself after a few storms and degenerate into one of those forms of government which cannot preserve peace in the midst of an uneducated and corrupted people.[69]

A constitution is incomplete without corresponding citizenship education. So are the Treaties and CFR, which function as the constitution of the European Union. The fact that the Treaties and CFR have been agreed and ratified by all Member States in accordance with their constitutional requirements (Article 54 TEU) confirms their soundness as a pillar for EDC. The requirement of *objectivity* in education is thereby satisfied (ECtHR).[70] Contesting the validity of the Treaties and the CFR as an objective and stable basis for an EU dimension of EDC would be tantamount to denying the very essence of EU membership. Moreover, these sources express the specific characteristics of the Union briefly described by the ECJ in Opinion 2/13,[71] to be respected when applying EDC standards. They relate to the constitutional structure of the EU, ie, the principle of conferral of powers (Articles 4(1) and 5(1)(2) TEU) and to the institutional framework (Articles 13–19 TEU). Furthermore, specific characteristics arise from the very nature of EU law, stemming from the Treaties as an independent source of law, with primacy over the law of the Member States, and many of its provisions having direct effect. The legal structure of the EU is based on the fundamental premise of a shared set of common values (Article 2 TEU), recognised by the Member States, and justifying the mutual trust between the Member States. At the heart of the legal structure are fundamental rights (CFR). The pursuit of EU objectives is entrusted to a series of 'fundamental provisions' including those on EU citizenship, free movement, and the area of freedom, security and justice. They relate to the process of integration and the raison d'être of the EU itself.[72]

Functioning as the *Grundnorm* in the EU legal order and protecting fundamental rights, the Treaties and CFR operate as a constitution. The ECJ qualifies the Treaties as 'the basic constitutional charter'[73] and frequently uses the

[69] Condorcet, *Cinq mémoires sur l'instruction publique* (digital JM Tremblay edn, 1791), Premier Mémoire, IV. He was influential throughout the 19th and 20th centuries.

[70] Above n 26.

[71] *Opinion 2/13, EU Accession to the ECHR* EU:C:2014:2454, paras 165–76, 179 ff.

[72] Paras 170, 172.

[73] Case 294/83 *Les Verts* EU:C:1986:166, para 23; Joined Cases C-402/05 P and C-415/05 P *Kadi* EU:C:2008:461 para 281; *Opinion 2/13*, above n 71, para 163; Case C-621/18 *Wightman* EU:C:2018:999, para 44.

adjective 'constitutional', for example, constitutional principles, – significance, – status, – guarantee, – structure.[74] EU primary law expresses the 'constitutional consensus'.[75] Status as EU *primary* law, at the top of the hierarchy of norms in the EU legal order, is relevant for citizens. It gives numerous EU rights and principles entrenched status. If EU primary law sources are the basis on which the legal order of the EU is constructed, shaping the society in which EU citizens live, then, a fortiori, they must be sufficiently strong to have consequences for citizenship education.

EU primary law and Member State constitutions are interconnected in various ways and cannot be adequately understood in isolation. The Treaties and CFR refer to Member State constitutions at several points[76] and, conversely, most Member State constitutions contain provisions related to the EU Treaties.[77] Education of citizens aiming at national constitutional literacy and impregnating national constitutional values should be interwoven with education for literacy with regard to the EU Treaties and the values they enshrine. Calliess describes a paradigm shift which requires more transparency and more interest from EU citizens in EU objectives. He defines the EU as 'a federal type of multi-level constitutionalism, in which state sovereignty is reduced and the constitutional orders of the EU and its Member States are mutually interlocked'.[78] Therefore, if in the Aristotelian tradition citizens are to be educated in 'the spirit' of their constitution,[79] that should logically apply to the compound of Member State constitutions, the Treaties and the CFR. For Montesquieu, too, 'the spirit' of the law is central (*L'esprit des lois*). He argued that education must relate to the principle of government.[80] Today, this means that education must relate to the principles of multilevel government, whereby the spirit of the law is defined in Articles 1–6 TEU.[81]

[74] *Opinion 2/94* EU:C:1996:140, para 35; *Kadi*, above n 73, paras 285, 316; *Opinion 2/13*, above n 71 paras 158, 163, 165 and 177; *Wightman*, above n 73, para 45.

[75] K Lenaerts and JA Gutiérrez-Fons, 'The Place of the Charter in the EU Constitutional Edifice' in S Peers et al (eds), *The EU Charter of Fundamental Rights: A Commentary* (Oxford, Hart Publishing, 2014) 142.

[76] eg, Arts 4(2), 6, 42, 48, 49, 50, 54 and 55 TEU; Arts 25, 218(8), 223, 262, 311 and 357 TFEU; Arts 52(4) and 53 CFR.

[77] On the interdependency and reciprocal links, C Grabenwarter, 'National Constitutional Law Relating to the European Union' in A von Bogdandy and J Bast (eds), *Principles of European Constitutional Law*, rev 2nd edn (Oxford, Hart Publishing, 2010) 127; C Calliess, 'EU-Vertrag (Lissabon) Art 1' in C Calliess and M Ruffert (eds), *EUV/AEUV: das Verfassungsrecht der Europäischen Union mit Europäischer Grundrechtecharta: Kommentar*, 5th edn (München, CH Beck, 2016) eg, Rn 46.

[78] C Calliess, 'Europe as Transnational Law: The Transnationalization of Values by European Law' (2009) 10 *German Law Journal* 1367, 1375.

[79] See above, n 68.

[80] Montesquieu, *De l'esprit des lois* (digital JM Tremblay 2002 edn, Barillot, 1748), Livre quatrième: The laws of education therefore will differ for each kind of government: in monarchies they will be concerned with honour, in republics with virtue, where there is despotism, they will aim at creating fear.

[81] On the European spirit, also Schuman (Strasbourg, 16 May 1949).

## *The DNA of the EU: Foundational Values, Objectives and Principles*

Articles 1–6 TEU set out the foundational values, objectives and principles of the EU. They are the DNA of the EU and should be central to all EU learning at school. EDC in schools should – to the extent possible – relate to the 'intrinsic nature of the EU',[82] not to superficial information, such as the number of Members of the European Parliament or the date of accession of Bulgaria, to be learnt by heart and then forgotten. In order to empower EU citizens to exercise their rights and responsibilities, to value diversity and to participate in the democratic life of the Union (aims c-1-2-3), EDC should clarify and discuss the raison d'être of the EU and how each Member State participates in it (united in diversity). The self-perception of Member States and of their nationals is incomplete if it lacks the EU dimension, which forms part of their identity.

### Foundational Values

Even if national values are the same as the 'EU values' in Article 2 TEU, there are additional challenges in striving to respect these values in a single area without internal frontiers with 500 million citizens. In one space encompassing 28 (27) Member States, 24 official languages, with great diversity of regions, cultures, traditions, religions, etc, additional EU content must be incorporated into national EDC to clarify and discuss the concrete significance of these values for citizens. Moreover, some values (or principles) are specifically EU related, such as the equality of Member States, or mutual trust between Member States. If mutual trust is a specific feature of the EU, it should be prepared for. Mutual trust should not just be proclaimed by the ECJ[83] as a legal postulate, leaving realities as they are, hoping for the best. For mutual trust to be deserved, a substratum should be built, notably by educating citizens in Member States in the common values on which the EU is founded, and according to the same (minimum) standards. Mutual trust requires more than informing national civil servants about fundamental rights. It requires EDC and HRE for the entire population, including in its EU dimension.

### Foundational Objectives

As part of school curricula, the content of Article 3 TEU too should be discussed in classrooms, as a kick-off for participation in EU civil society, enhancing the growth of a European public space. Only if they are made aware of the EU objectives and the aim for added value, ie, the European 'project', can individuals guide the 'process' and the 'product' through democratic processes as responsible and

[82] On the intrinsic nature, *Opinion 2/13*, above n 71 para 193.
[83] *Opinion 2/13*, above n 71 para 168; Case C-64/16 *Juízes Portugueses* EU:C:2018:117, para 30.

active EU citizens. The EU is an objective driven polity and should be understood as such and monitored by Europeans.[84]

Foundational Principles

The Treaties define various systemic principles, which are the backbone of EU construction. They are essential to understanding the EU as a system and the place of one's own Member State in it, and are thus essential to empowering EU citizens. A central axis in the EU constitutional construction is the principle of conferral (Article 5(2) TEU). Citizens are often unaware of this principle, what may lead to excessive expectations, followed by disappointment if the EU does not (and cannot) deliver.[85] Other systemic principles relevant for EDC are contained in Article 5(3) and (4) (subsidiarity and proportionality); Article 4(2) and (3) (equality of Member States, respect for national identity, sincere cooperation); Article 6 TEU (fundamental rights, also in the CFR); Articles 9–12 TEU (democratic principles); Article 21 TFEU (free movement of citizens); and Articles 28, 45, 49, 56, 63 TFEU (internal market). A central tenet in EU learning, largely unknown, should be the principle of non-discrimination on grounds of nationality (Article 18 TFEU).

Educating citizens in the spirit of their constitutions corresponds to the EU principles of openness and transparency.[86] If these principles point by their very nature to the opposite of opaqueness,[87] EDC standards are part of the same current, but more 'upstream' by laying the foundations for a basic understanding of the EU. Prior EDC will increase the effectiveness of access to documents and strengthen accountability.

## *Education in an Objective, Critical and Pluralist Way, With No Aims of Indoctrination*

Critical thinking remains crucial. While citizens are to be educated in the spirit of their constitutions (directed to the common good), the universal caveat with regard to citizenship education must be kept in mind: citizenship education should not become a despotism over the mind.[88] Citizens must not be trained in

[84] G Palombella, 'Whose Europe? After the Constitution: A Goal-based Citizenship' (2005) 3 *International Journal of Constitutional Law* 357; G Davies, 'Social Legitimacy and Purposive Power: The End, the Means and the Consent of the People' in D Kochenov D, G de Búrca G and A Williams (eds), *Europe's Justice Deficit?* (Oxford, Hart Publishing, 2015).

[85] See, inter alia, the ECI, below n 120.

[86] Arts 1, 10, 11, 16 TEU; Art 15 TFEU; and Art 42 CFR. Joined Cases C-92/09 and C-93/09 *Schecke and Eifert* EU:C:2010:662, para 68; Case T-540/15 *De Capitani* EU:T:2018:167.

[87] S Prechal and ME de Leeuw, 'Transparency: A General Principle of EU Law?' in U Bernitz, J Nergelius and C Cardner (eds), *General Principles of EC Law in a Process of Development* (Alphen aan de Rijn, Kluwer Law International, 2008) 202.

[88] A large amount of literature: see, eg, B Crick, 'The Presuppositions of Citizenship Education' (1999) 33 *Journal of Philosophy of Education* 337; E Callan, 'Citizenship and Education' (2004) 7 *Annual*

uncritical obedience, preventing them from thinking outside the box. Constitutions are living documents and may evolve in response to the live issues in civil society. The relationship between constitutions and education is dynamic and dialectical: the constitution influences education and, in the long term, education may influence the constitution.[89] A basic understanding of constitutional norms enables informed participation by citizens at moments of constitutional change, for example, EU Treaty changes. At present, Article 2 TEU contains the constitutional core values, the '*Verfassungskern*' of the EU (Calliess), the 'overlapping consensus' (Rawls).[90] Freedom of education has to be balanced with respect for the core values, which is not an easy task.[91] Some Member States' constitutions explicitly limit freedom of education by requiring allegiance to the constitution.[92]

The requirement of the ECtHR that education should be conveyed in an *objective, critical and pluralistic* way, with no aims of indoctrination,[93] can be satisfied by taking EU primary law as a pillar of objectivity[94] while using the case method to allow critical thinking and pluralism. Stories based on well-selected cases of the European Court of Justice, SOLVIT, or the media, can trigger the interest of pupils and make EU learning attractive. Beyond rhetoric, case teaching shows how EU constitutional theory works in practice and illustrates the importance of the EU dimension for citizens. In specific cases, foundational values, objectives and principles may compete and require balancing. This allows interesting debates with pupils in classrooms, even at school level. Pupils realise that no situation is one-dimensional and that problems seldom have simple solutions. They learn to consider the positive and negative aspects of the options available. Case teaching may build a preventive shield against populism and one-liners.[95]

## Relevant Content for the EU Dimension in EDC in Mainstream Education

What are the effects of a combined reading of EDC standards and EU constitutional law? EDC standards recommend that Member States provide *every person* within

*Review of Political Science* 71; M Nussbaum, 'Teaching Patriotism: Love and Critical Freedom' (2012) 79 *University of Chicago Law Review* 213; B Schaffar, 'Changing the Definition of Education. On Kant's Educational Paradox Between Freedom and Restraint' (2014) 33 *Studies in Philosophy and Education* 5.

[89] E Reilly, 'Education and the Constitution: Shaping Each Other and the Next Century' (2000–01) 34 *Akron Law Review* 1; E Beaumont, 'Education and the Constitution: Defining the Contours of Governance, Rights, and Citizenship' in M Tushnet, MA Graber and S Levinson (eds), *The Oxford Handbook of the US Constitution* (2015) 968.

[90] Calliess, 'Europe as Transnational Law', above n 78, 1368, 1371; J Rawls, *Political Liberalism*, 2005 edn (New York, Columbia University Press, 1993) Part II (IV).

[91] See, eg, Case No 21787/93 *Valsamis v Greece* (ECtHR 18 December 1996) on a compulsory school parade on the Greek National Day.

[92] Germany Art 5(3) Basic law; Greece Art 16(1); Cyprus Art 20(1).

[93] Above n 26.

[94] Text to n 70.

[95] VL Golich, 'The ABCs of Case Teaching' (2000) 1 *International Studies Perspectives* 11, 12, 14.

their territory with the opportunity of EDC/HRE.[96] In order to give *all* learners the opportunity of adequate EDC, corresponding to the constitutional system, an EU dimension should be incorporated in compulsory levels of *mainstream* education, and in adapted levels of difficulty in primary and secondary education. The final years of secondary education are a particularly valuable time for exercising critical thinking. Mainstream education includes all curricula, not only specialised curricula and not only curricula targeted at the more gifted pupils before they attend university. It also includes vocational training.

A 2017 Eurobarometer survey reports:

> A large majority (89 per cent) agree national governments should strengthen school education about rights and responsibilities as EU citizens. More than eight in ten also agree that learning about European matters, such as the functioning of the EU and its institutions, EU history or European culture, should be part of compulsory school education (83 per cent).[97]

The rights and obligations of EU citizens can be screened as to their relevance for concrete content of the EU dimension in mainstream education according to four criteria: (i) do they provide additional content to national EDC? (ii) is this content significant, ie, relating to foundational (EU primary law) values, objectives and principles? (iii) do they invite critical thinking? and (iv) do they affect the large majority of EU citizens, including static citizens?[98] Not only must classic EU citizenship rights be considered (attached to the status by Articles 20–24 TFEU), but – importantly, and explained below – the democratic participation rights of EU citizens (Title II TEU), and in general, all rights and obligations which flow from EU law (EU rights). In a joint reading of EU law and EDC standards, these rights feed into the EU dimension in EDC components c-1-2-3 (the three empowerment aims).[99]

## Democratic Participation Rights of EU Citizens

That the Treaties see EU citizens as political actors is clear from the democratic participation rights in Articles 20–24 TFEU. Yet, the hard core for the EU dimension of EDC is Title II TEU, which connects the democratic principles governing the Union with EU citizenship. In legal terms, nationals of a Member State are 'citizens *of* the Union' (Article 9 TEU). In reality, they are human beings, people living in a country which is an EU Member State: they are simply citizens *in* the Union.[100]

[96] Charter on EDC/HRE, para 5(a).

[97] Flash Eurobarometer 455, European Youth (January 2018).

[98] See the analysis in K Grimonprez, *The European Union and Education for Democratic Citizenship* (Luxembourg Legal Studies, Baden-Baden, Nomos Verlag, forthcoming 2019).

[99] Above n 16.

[100] See also J Shaw, 'Citizenship: Contrasting Dynamics at the Interface of Integration and Constitutionalism' in P Craig and G de Búrca (eds), *The Evolution of EU law* (Oxford, Oxford University Press, 2011) text to fn 152.

The democratic participation rights attributed by EU law provide essential content for the EU dimension in components c-1 and c-3 of the EDC concept. Whatever their limitations, the citizens' rights of participation in the democratic life of the Union form part of the EU structure reflecting concerns as to 'effective political democracy' (in line with *Matthews v UK*).[101] If democracy is a chain of legitimation from those governed to those governing, EDC in schools is the first link of this chain.[102]

## *The Right to Participate in the Democratic Life of the Union*

Article 10(3) TEU is essential for mainstream EDC: '[e]very citizen shall have the right to participate in the democratic life of the Union' and '[d]ecisions shall be taken as openly and as closely as possible to the citizen'. It describes an authentic citizenship right, defined as a right conferred by virtue of the status of citizen of the Union.[103] It is noteworthy that this right is drafted in the same style as the citizenship rights listed in Articles 20–24 TFEU ('Every citizen … shall have the right to'). The link between Title II TEU and the citizenship rights in Articles 20–24 TFEU is guaranteed, moreover, by the European citizens' initiative, inserted into Article 11(4) TEU but with a legal basis in Article 24 TFEU. Since it is not included in Articles 20–24 TFEU, the right to participate in the democratic life of the union is often neglected as a citizenship right by scholars and in reports. It deserves much more attention.

The right in Article 10(3) TEU can be interpreted as an overarching right, relating to both representative and participatory democracy. Institutions and scholars use it in both contexts.[104] The right to a citizens' initiative, to petition the European Parliament or to refer to the Ombudsman are expressions of the general right in Article 10(3) TEU.[105] Article 10(3) TEU acquires further substance when read in conjunction with EU law provisions on the institutions.

## *The Right to Vote for the European Parliament*

The right to vote for the European Parliament (Articles 10(1)(2) and 14(3) TEU, 39(2) CFR, *Delvigne*)[106] constitutes obvious learning content for the EU dimension

[101] In line with Case No 24833/94 *Matthews v UK* (ECtHR 18 February 1999) para 52.

[102] HCH Hofmann, GC Rowe and AH Türk, *Administrative Law and Policy of the European Union* (Oxford, Oxford University Press, 2011) 146.

[103] Compare K Lenaerts and JA Gutierrez-Fons, 'Epilogue on EU Citizenship: Hopes and Fears' in D Kochenov (ed), *EU Citizenship and Federalism: The Role of Rights* (Cambridge, Cambridge University Press, 2017) 752.

[104] See, eg, European Parliament Resolution of 11 November 2015 on the reform of the electoral law of the European Union [2017] OJ C 366/7, recital U; S Smismans, 'Regulating Interest Group Participation in the European Union: Changing Paradigms between Transparency and Representation' (2014) 39 *European Law Review* 470, 604; M Ruffert, 'EU-Vertrag (Lissabon) Art 10' in C Calliess and M Ruffert (eds), *EUV/AEUV: das Verfassungsrecht der Europäischen Union mit Europäischer Grundrechtecharta: Kommentar*, 5th edn (München, CH Beck, 2016) Rn 11–12)

[105] Case C-589/15 P *Anagnostakis* EU:C:2017:663, para 24.

[106] Case C-650/13 *Delvigne* EU:C:2015:648, para 44.

of EDC in mainstream education. Voting in elections for the European Parliament is central to the image of active EU citizenship. The right involves more than ticking a box in elections. From the perspective of *substantive* democracy,[107] EU citizens need to be empowered to participate meaningfully in elections at EU level. For a non-negligible group of nationals, paradoxically, the *EU* dimension of voting in European Parliament elections needs to be explained. These elections should be more than popularity tests of national politicians or parties.[108]

## *The Right to Vote for the National Parliament and its EU Dimension*

The right to vote for the national parliament is based on national law and voting primarily means taking part in the democratic life of the *Member State*. However, voting in national elections is at the same time indirect participation in the democratic life of the *Union*, because Member State parliaments and governments are important actors at EU level and Member States' democracies are interdependent.[109] The Commission puts it succinctly: 'Full participation of EU citizens in the democratic life of the EU at all levels is the very essence of Union citizenship'.[110] Article 10(2) TEU is the basis for what is commonly referred to as the dual structure of democratic legitimacy in the Union: citizens are directly represented at Union level in the European Parliament (to which the Commission is accountable) and Member States are represented in the European Council by their Heads of State or Government and in the Council by their governments, who in turn are themselves democratically accountable to their national parliaments or to their citizens.[111] Undeniably, these specific features of democracy in the EU system should be explained and discussed with pupils.

The role of national parliaments in the EU underscores the EU dimension of the relationship of citizens with their own Member State. National parliaments 'contribute actively to the good functioning of the EU' in the six ways described in Article 12 TEU and in accordance with Protocols 1 and 2. Article 12 illustrates how EU democracy depends on Member State democracy. If national parliaments are empowered to act in the democratic life of the Union, citizens must be empowered to choose representatives fit for this purpose. Domestic votes have important cross-border repercussions. The whole of Europe attentively follows

[107] A Rosas and L Armati, *EU Constitutional Law: An Introduction* (Oxford, Hart Publishing, 2018) 140.

[108] See also European Parliament Resolution of 11 November 2015 on the reform of the electoral law of the European Union [2017] OJ C 366/7, para L.

[109] See also I Pernice, 'Editorial: Nationale Wahlen sind Europäische Wahlen' (2017) 12 *Europäische Zeitschrift für Wirtschaftsrecht* 441.

[110] Commission, 'EU Citizenship Report 2013: EU citizens: your rights, your future' COM(2013) 269, 5.

[111] A von Bogdandy, 'The European Lesson for International Democracy: The Significance of Articles 9 to 12 EU Treaty for International Organizations' (2012) 23 *European Journal of International Law* 315, 325; Commission Recommendation (EU) 2018/234 of 14 February 2018 on enhancing the European

(and sometimes holds its breath) when national elections take place in Germany, France, Italy, Poland, Greece, Spain, or Hungary, just to cite some examples. Elections for national parliaments and national presidential elections have a crucial EU dimension.[112] They determine whether more Eurosceptic or Europhile political parties will come to power and who will be the actors in the European Council and the Council.

Dual democratic legitimacy calls for an EU dimension to EDC in both tracks of legitimacy. On a simple view, national EDC prepares young citizens for democracy at Member State level, focusing on elections for the national parliament, and the EU dimension of EDC prepares them for democracy at EU level, focusing on elections for the European Parliament. In the EU's integrated multilevel system of governance, however, the reality is more complex. First, an EU dimension must be added to national EDC to strengthen EU democracy. To the extent that Member States are actors in the EU political process, the quality of democracy at EU level is contingent on the quality of democracy at national level,[113] which is contingent on EDC. Second, paradoxically, adding an EU dimension to EDC is also needed to strengthen national democracy. National parliaments are supposed to represent the will of the citizens. What is the credibility of representatives in national parliaments who act at EU level (or fail to act) if they have been chosen by citizens lacking understanding of EU matters? How legitimate is the mandate given directly by citizens to their parliaments, and indirectly to their governments, to act at EU level, if these citizens have no understanding of the raison d'être of the EU or of the EU issues on which the national actors must adopt a position? Legitimacy presupposes minimal insight on the part of nationals as to the involvement of their country in EU matters and on EU foundational values, objectives and principles. As economic actors in the market, citizens can only conclude a contract if they are informed about its constitutive elements and conditions. The consumer has a right to be informed. Before the consumer can be bound by a contract, the trader has an obligation to provide clear and comprehensible information.[114] As political actors, citizens do not enjoy such protection. No adequate prior information seems to be required for the social contract.[115] Even fake news and false promises can lead to valid votes. Therefore, at least, all reasonable efforts must be made to provide quality EDC in schools, including the EU dimension, to equip nationals with a basic preliminary understanding of the system in which they live and to develop their

nature and efficient conduct of the 2019 elections to the European Parliament [2018] OJ L45/40, see however (11); BVerfG (n 67) para 36.

[112] eg, after parliamentary elections in Italy: 'Italian crisis felt in Spain and wider EU', available at: euobserver.com/economic/141934.

[113] See also R Bauböck, 'Still United in Diversity? The State of the Union Address' (Florence, 5 May 2017): 'The value of EU citizenship depends on the quality of democracy in the member states'.

[114] See, inter alia, Art 5(1) Directive 2011/83/EU of the European Parliament and of the Council of 25 October 2011 on consumer rights, amending Council Directive 93/13/EEC and Directive 1999/44/EC of the European Parliament and of the Council and repealing Council Directive 85/577/EEC and Directive 97/7/EC of the European Parliament and of the Council, [2011] OJ L304/64.

[115] On the social contract see, eg, JJ Rousseau, *Du contrat social ou Principes du droit politique* (1762).

critical agency. The task of democracy is to educate citizens who can think critically in political campaigns and take responsibility for their votes.[116] On a reading of EU and national law in the light of EDC standards, this requires the incorporation of an EU dimension into EDC, reinforcing both tracks of representative democratic legitimacy.

## *Rights and Opportunities in Participatory Democracy*

In between elections, EU citizens can blog, twitter, protest, make their voices heard on the internet.[117] In addition to the participation rights in Article 24 TFEU, they can use the further tools for participation provided by Article 11 TEU as a means of participatory democracy. Participatory democracy gives citizens a voice. The EU dimension of EDC gives them an informed and more influential voice. Productive interaction with officials of EU institutions – be it through interest representation, consultations, dialogues, or other participatory opportunities – require prior EU knowledge and understanding. The social activist who understands the principle of conferral and the scope of EU competences in employment and social policy, will be better equipped to argue with EU institutions than one who describes the unfair situations in his region and makes – for the EU – unattainable claims. Future electricians, decorators, hotel managers, IT technicians, etc need to understand the EU dimension of their professional activities in order to defend the interests of their sector. Introduced to the relevant EU rules, they will be better armed to take up the challenges at EU level and to resist the temptation to withdraw to the stance of the individual in the nation state, only capable of a limited response to the issues of globalisation. They will participate more effectively if the citizenship education they have received at school is not limited to the nation state, but has introduced them to the systemic principles of the EU. In order to increase the visibility of particular interests and to play a confident role in the EU's participatory governance, citizens and their representatives need to be empowered. Otherwise, the 'dialogues' or 'consultations' risk being nothing more than camouflaged top-down communication and information sessions by EU institutions.[118]

## *The Right to a European Citizens' Initiative*

That EU citizens are supposed to have an understanding of the principle of conferral and of the Treaties, is also clear from the European citizens' initiative (ECI).

[116] J Oelkers, 'The European Crisis and Education for Democracy' (2017) 22 *The European Legacy* 832.

[117] I Krastev, 'Democracy of Rejection' in L Van Middelaar and P Van Parijs (eds), *After the Storm: How to Save Democracy in Europe* (Tielt, Belgium, Lannoo, 2015) 149.

[118] L Bouza García, 'How Could the New Article 11 TEU Contribute to Reduce the EU's Democratic Malaise?' in M Dougan, N Nic Shuibhne and E Spaventa (eds), *Empowerment and Disempowerment of the European Citizen* (Oxford, Hart Publishing, 2012) 272. See also J Mendes, 'Participation and the

The ECI concerns 'matters where citizens consider that a legal act of the Union is required for the purpose of implementing the Treaties' (Article 11 TEU). A condition for registration is that the proposed ECI 'does not manifestly fall outside the framework of the Commission's powers to submit a proposal'.[119] A huge number of citizens' initiatives fail to clear this hurdle.[120] Information and communication strategies are foreseen to remedy the unsatisfactory use of the ECI.[121] Education might be more effective. The EU dimension in EDC should include learning about the ECI, an opportunity for explaining the Treaties and the principle of conferral.

## EU Rights and Obligations

Reading EDC standards jointly with EU law, citizens should be empowered to exercise all rights and responsibilities flowing from the EU level of governance.[122] The rights which EU citizens (in various capacities) derive from EU law are not thin, pale, or uncertain. EU citizenship is broader and more significant than is often perceived. The perception still persists that EU citizenship is in essence a matter for mobile citizens, relating to the equality of treatment of citizens who move to another Member State.[123] Yet, EU citizenship should not be reduced to the legal status generating citizenship rights. All the nationals of Member States are EU citizens (Article 9 TEU). EU law impacts on their daily life. In addition to democratic participation rights, the list of rights which EU citizens – including static citizens – derive from EU law is *quasi* endless. They include all rights based on the direct effect (and primacy) of EU law, combined with the right to effective judicial protection; equality rights; fundamental rights when situations fall within the scope of EU law (also at home); rights related to free movement of goods and services in the internal market (at home); rights based on national law implementing EU directives (interpretation of national law in accordance with directives; autonomous EU concepts); rights in the area of freedom, security and justice; rights in fields of EU harmonisation (eg, with regard to health, safety, or

Role of Law after Lisbon: A Legal View on Article 11 TEU' (2011) 48 *Common Market Law Review* 1849, 1850.

[119] Regulation (EU) No 211/2011 of the European Parliament and of the Council of 16 February 2011 on the citizens' initiative, [2011] OJ L65/1, Art 4(2)(b).

[120] Opinion of the European Economic and Social Committee on The European Citizens' Initiative (review), [2016] OJ C 389/35 para 3.10.2: around 40% declared inadmissible at the registration; Commission, 'Report on the application of Regulation (EU) No 211/2011 on the citizens' initiative' COM(2018) 157 final: in 2018, 22 initiatives refused, 48 registered.

[121] Commission Staff working document Accompanying the document Proposal for a Regulation of the European Parliament and of the Council on the European citizens' initiative SWD(2017) 294 final, eg 58.

[122] All learners should, including third-country nationals living in the EU.

[123] See discussions in F de Witte, R Bauböck and J Shaw (eds), 'Freedom of movement under attack: Is it worth defending as the core of EU citizenship?' 2016 EUI Working Paper RSCAS 2016/69; kick-off contribution of M Ferrera in M Ferrera and R Bauböck (eds), 'Should EU Citizenship Be Duty-Free?' (2017) EUI Working Paper RSCAS, 2017/60.

food control); rights concerning working time; consumer rights, such as rights protecting against unfair terms in consumer contracts; privacy rights and rights in the digital single market; environmental rights, etc. EU obligations, too, flow from EU law and arise as a corollary to many rights.[124] EU law thus provides essential content for EDC, needed to empower citizens to achieve the aims c-1-2-3. Learning about EU rights, such as equality rights, creates the opportunity to discuss EDC component c-2, valuing diversity.

The question as to whether EU citizenship is sufficiently mature to call for adaptation of citizenship education can be reversed: how mature is national citizenship education without an EU dimension, when one observes the present state of EU law and its impact? EU law has become an essential part of national legal orders and has led to additional rights and obligations for EU citizens. EDC must keep pace with EU law.

## Conclusion and Suggestions

EU Member States share the consensus on EDC standards. As members of the Council of Europe, they have consistently participated in the bodies adopting normative instruments on EDC. It is legitimate to expect them not only to pay lip service to these standards. When honouring the right to quality education of their citizens, they cannot neglect EDC, either in its national aspects, or in its consequences of EU membership.

When applying EDC standards as to constitutional democracy in the European Union, EDC must be provided in a way consistent with the Treaties and CFR. They reflect the way EU citizenship is evolving.[125] The 1992 Maastricht Treaty inserted EU citizenship into the Treaty and connected it with a limited list of citizenship rights. The 2009 Lisbon Treaty connected EU citizenship with the provisions on democratic principles in Title II TEU. Ten years later, the time has come to connect EU citizenship and democratic principles with EDC standards in mainstream education. Recent challenges, such as populism and radicalisation, build momentum. To create a Union based on the values of Article 2 TEU going beyond a market rationale, the European public space needs an educational substratum.[126] EDC aims to empower citizens 'to exercise and defend their democratic rights and responsibilities in society'. To move beyond rhetoric, rights and obligations

[124] eg, Case 43/75 *Defrenne* EU:C:1976:56; Case C-281/98 *Angonese* EU:C:2000:296; Case C-101/01 *Lindqvist* EU:C:2003:596; Joined Cases C-569/16 and C-570/16 *Bauer and Willmeroth* EU:C:2018:871; Case C-337/07 *Altun* EU:C:2018:63.

[125] See S O'Leary, *The Evolving Concept of Community Citizenship: From the Free Movement of Persons to Union Citizenship* (European Monographs 13, Alphen aan de Rijn, Kluwer Law International, 1996).

[126] *cf* the central question 'Wie entstehen Öffentlichkeiten in der transnationalen Konstellation?' in C Calliess and M Hartmann, *Zur Demokratie in Europa: Unionsbürgerschaft und europäische Öffentlichkeit* (Tübingen, Mohr Siebeck, 2014) 150.

under EU law should be part of the core content of the EU dimension in EDC. Incorporating an EU dimension in EDC furthermore empowers citizens to value diversity and to participate in democratic life in their double role of national citizens and EU citizens, strengthening the dual democratic legitimacy of the Union and enhancing its social legitimacy.

To help them make the EU more democratic and EU citizenship more enlightened, the Member States themselves have an important tool in their hands: they are responsible for the content of teaching and the organisation of education systems (Article 165(1) TFEU). They are invited to take more action to provide quality education, which, in the present state of EU law, is no longer conceivable without an adequate EU dimension in EDC.

The EU has the supporting competence to encourage Member State action by providing incentives and making recommendations, thus contributing to the development of quality education, the European dimension in education and encouraging young people to participate in democratic life in Europe (Article 165 TFEU).[127] While respecting Member States' competences in education, the EU should offer more concrete guidance for the EU dimension of EDC. Council of Europe materials can be adapted to the specific EU context and made available in all EU languages. Given the close interdependence of the Member States' and the EU's democracy, a common EDC reference framework must be established.[128] It could be recommended at EU level, with proposals for specific objectives and learning outcomes for the EU dimension in keeping with the Treaties and CFR. This recommendation on EDC would be a major contribution to the realisation of the European Education Area. Because teachers are multipliers, the EU dimension in teacher training must also be promoted, as a prerequisite for the EU dimension in school education (through funding or EU labels of excellency).[129] A school-friendly version of selected provisions of the Treaties and CFR should be made available as a basis for EDC, just as the ECHR, the Convention on the Rights of the Child, and some Member State constitutions have been drafted in simplified forms for educational purposes.[130] Finally, some inspiration for EU action which respects Member State competence might be drawn from Germany, where education is *Länder* competence.[131] The *Bundeszentrale für*

[127] K Grimonprez, 'The European Dimension in Citizenship Education: Unused Potential of Article 165 TFEU' (2014) 39 *European Law Review* 3.

[128] *cf* n 24, adapted to the EU.

[129] On teacher training for EDC, see Charter on EDC/HRE paras 7 and 9. At present insufficient, see Learning to live together, above n 42, 53, 61, 69–70, 87.

[130] See: www.coe.int/en/web/compass/european-convention-on-human-rights; www.unicef.org/rightsite/files/uncrcchilldfriendlylanguage.pdf. In Germany, D Hesselberger, *Das Grundgesetz: Kommentar für die politische Bildung* 13th edn (Bonn, Bundeszentrale für politische Bildung, 2003); brochure *Das Grundgesetz Über den Staat* (einfach Politik, 2016, Bundeszentrale für politische Bildung); in Denmark, *My Constitutional Act, with Explanations* 12th edn (Folketinget, 2014).

[131] See, eg, Recommendation of the Standing Conference of the Ministers of Education and Cultural Affairs on the promotion of human rights in schools, Resolution of 4 December 1980 in the version of 14 December 2000 (to note para 4: 'textbooks must take account of the content of this

*politische Bildung* supports citizenship education in the *Länder* (in cooperation with *Landeszentralen*).[132] In a comparable way, an EU Agency for Education for Democratic Citizenship could support Member States, inter alia, by providing information and educational materials for EDC and its EU dimension.[133]

recommendation'). See also the 1978 Recommendation *Europa im Unterricht*, amended in 1990 and updated in 2008 (*Europabildung in der Schule*).

[132] See: www.bpb.de/die-bpb/138853/our-mission-and-activities.

[133] Compare EACEA (Education, Audiovisual and Culture Executive Agency) manages EU funding for education, culture, audiovisual, sport, citizenship and volunteering.

# 18

# Strengthening Democracy in Europe and its Resilience Against Autocracy: Daring More Democracy and a European Democracy Charter

PAUL NEMITZ AND FRITHJOF EHM*

## Introduction: The Crisis of Representative Democracy

Representative democracy is in crisis and this not only in Europe, considering developments in the US in particular.[1] EU Member States like Poland,[2] Hungary[3]

* The authors thank their colleagues in the European Commission Georgia Georgiadou (DG JUST) and Dimitrios Triantafyllou (Legal Service) for their valuable comments as well as Lilian Pye, legal trainee in DG JUST. This text reflects solely the personal opinion of the authors and does not necessarily present the position of their employers. Frithjof Ehm has contributed to this article the elements of international law in the second part of the text, based on his prior academic work.

[1] S Levitisky and D Ziblatt, *How Democracies Die* (New York, Crown, 2018); Y Mounk, *The People vs Democracy: Why Our Freedom Is in Danger and How to Save It* (Cambridge, MA, Harvard University Press, 2018); J Goldberg, *Suicide of the West: How the Rebirth of Tribalism, Populism, Nationalism, and Identity Politics is Destroying American Democracy* (New York, Crown, 2018); Y Mounk and RS Foa, 'The End of the Democratic Century, Autocracy's Global Ascendance' (2018) (May/June) *Foreign Affairs*, available at: www.foreignaffairs.com/articles/2018-04-16/end-democratic-century.

[2] M Hong, 'Constitutional Resilience: How Can a Democratic Constitution Survive an Autocratic Majority?: Freedom of Speech, Media and Civil Society in Hungary and Poland' (*Verfassungsblog*, 9 December 2018), available at: verfassungsblog.de/constitutional-resilience-how-can-a-democratic-constitution-survive-an-autocratic-majority-freedom-of-speech-media-and-civil-society-in-hungary-and-poland/; 'Proposal for a Council Decision on the determination of a clear risk of a serious breach by the Republic of Poland of the rule of law' COM(2017) 835 final 2017/0360 (NLE). K Kovács, M Kumm, M Steinbeis and GA Tóth, 'Introduction: Constitutional Resilience and the German Grundgesetz' (*Verfassungsblog*, 6 December 2018), available at: verfassungsblog.de/introduction-constitutional-resilience-and-the-german-grundgesetz/.

[3] ibid and European Parliament resolution of 12 September 2018 on a proposal calling on the Council to determine, pursuant to Article 7(1) of the Treaty on European Union, the existence of a clear risk of a serious breach by Hungary of the values on which the Union is founded (2017/2131(INL)).

and Austria[4] are governed by populists, some of them with autocratic tendencies.[5] France is facing a crisis of political violence with 'Gilets Jaunes' rampaging on its streets. Romania is riddled by corruption.[6] Ever lower participation in elections and declining membership in political parties on both sides of the Atlantic document the steady decline of engagement of people in representative democracy. At the same time, the US under President Trump tries to weaken the EU[7] and so does Russia, both spreading fake news, openly and covertly undermining democracy in Europe.[8] And the new electronic communication environment on the internet, controlled by a few mega corporations, undermines journalism and the free, privately financed press of the fourth estate. They provide not only fertile ground for populist slogans and the mobilisation of hate and violence but also the means to manipulate voters, effectively leading to situations like the Facebook Cambridge Analytica scandal and in fine the result of the Brexit vote in the UK.[9] They socialise people to instant consumption, cutting out the middlemen – and create the illusion that this is possible in democracy, as it is possible in markets, thus undermining elections, elected law-makers and representative democracy.

[4] WA Perger, 'Rechtspopulismus in Österreich: Ein Hauch von Machiavelli' *Die Zeit* (18 December 2017), available at: www.zeit.de/politik/ausland/2017-12/rechtspopulismus-oesterreich-europa-demokratie-zukunft.

[5] M Spittler in 'Gefährden Rechtspopulisten unsere Demokratie?' shows that government participation of right wing populists has a negative effect on the good functioning of democracy (*Verfassungsblog*, 3 August 2018), available at: democracy.blog.wzb.eu/2018/08/03/rechtspopulismus-in-europa-demokratie-in-gefahr/. M Spittler, 'Are Right-Wing Populist Parties a Threat to Democracy?' in W Merkel and S Kneip (ed), *Democracy and Crisis* (Cham, Switzerland, Springer International Publishing, 2018), available at: doi.org /10.1007/978-3-319-72559-8_5; see also GA Tóth, 'Laws, Conventions, and Fake Constitutions' (*VerfBlog*, 7 December 2018), available at: verfassungsblog.de/laws-conventions-and-fake-constitutions/, DOI: doi.org/10.17176/20181209-204519-0; P Oltermann, 'Can Europe's new xenophobes reshape the continent?' *The Guardian* (3 February 2018), available at: www.theguardian.com/world/2018/feb/03/europe-xenophobes-continent-poland-hungary-austria-nationalism-migrants.

[6] 'Report from the Commission to the European Parliament and the Council on Progress in Romania under the Cooperation and Verification Mechanism', 13 November 2018, COM(2018) 851 final.

[7] SB Glasser, 'How Trump Made War on Angela Merkel and Europe' *The New Yorker* (17 December 2018), available at: www.newyorker.com/magazine/2018/12/24/how-trump-made-war-on-angela-merkel-and-europe; see also R Bravo, G Viscusi, N Chrysoloras and J Green, 'Inside Steve Bannon's Plans for a New European Political Order' *Bloomberg* (19 September 2018), available at www.bloomberg.com/news/articles/2018-09-19/bannon-seeks-european-upset-with-appeal-to-eu-s-populist-forces.

[8] See on that: www.economist.com/briefing/2018/02/22/russian-disinformation-distorts-american-and-european-democracy; and ec.europa.eu/digital-single-market/en/fake-news-disinformation; see also Speech by Vice-President Ansip on cybersecurity at the RSA Conference 2018 (San Franciso, 18 April 2018) and Commissioner Jourova at Seimas (Lithuanian Parliament) on New Unity or Old Divisions: Europe at the crossroads (Vilnius, 22 November 2018): 'Russia has been identified as one of the main sources. Our team working on this since 2015 has identified over 4.000 cases of pro-Kremlin disinformation'.

[9] See on this Commission, 'Communication of 12 September 2018, Securing free and fair European elections', COM(2018) 637 final, which details the sources of information and the measures proposed by the European Commission in a reaction to the Facebook Analytica Scandal and the resulting Brexit vote; see also P Nemitz, 'Constitutional Democracy and Technology in the Age of Artificial Intelligence' at Royal Society Philosophical Transactions A 376: 20180089, available at: dx.doi.org/10.1098/rsta.2018.0089.

Many identify migration, economic and social policy causes which in the most dramatic accounts may lead to the demise of Europe.[10] And without intending to question the importance of economic causes and the need to address financial and employment risks as well as social inequalities, this contribution asks the question what the EU can do apart from economic,[11] financial,[12] labour market and social policy to strengthen democracy in Europe and to allow both the EU as such but also its Member States to withstand autocracy.[13]

A seminar in Berlin in December 2018 addressed the question what Germany can learn from the ascent of autocratic regimes in Poland and Hungary in order to make its own constitutional democracy more resilient.[14] And indeed, the ascent of populist far-right parties in Germany and France make the matter urgent, as the virus of autocracy may spread. But the hope that Member States on their own will resist, if around them their EU partners become autocracies, is in vain and European populists are getting organised across borders.

The purpose of this contribution is therefore to demonstrate that the EU can and must play an important role in avoiding a spread of the virus of autocratic populism. It can help to share among all EU Member States the historical learnings drawn from democracies sliding into dictatorship, such as happened to the Weimar Republic.[15] And it can help to learn together today from developments in Poland and in Hungary. Of course, democracy and democratic engagement of people in the Member States can never be imposed from the EU level. The rule of former German constitutional Judge Böckenförde,[16] that the democratic state does not command the preconditions on which its existence is predicated, thus that law cannot secure democracy if there is no culture of people engaging in and for democracy, is a fortiori true for the EU and in the relation between the EU and its Member States. This being said, and contrary to cheap and outdated claims that the EU itself is not democratic, the EU features a success story of progressive internal democratisation and a track record as the biggest donor for democracy and election observation worldwide, thus outside the EU.[17]

[10] TL Friedmann, 'The end of Europe?' *New York Times* (18 December 2018), available at: www.nytimes.com/2018/12/18/opinion/europe-france-economy.html.

[11] Five Presidents' Report, 'Completing Europe's Economic and Monetary Union' (2014), available at: ec.europa.eu/commission/sites/beta-political/files/5-presidents-report_en.pdf.

[12] T Piketty and A Vauchez, 'Manifesto for the democratization of Europe' (11 December 2018), available at: www.socialeurope.eu/manifesto-for-the-democratization-of-europe.

[13] Generally, without specific reference to the EU, see M Kumm, 'How populist authoritarian nationalism threatens constitutionalism or: Why constitutional resilience is a key issue of our time' (*VerfBlog*, 6 December 2018), available at: verfassungsblog.de/how-populist-authoritarian-nationalism-threatens-constitutionalism-or-why-constitutional-resilience-is-a-key-issue-of-our-time/.

[14] Kovács, Kumm, Steinbeis and Tóth, above n 2.

[15] B Carter Hett, *The Death of Democracy: Hitler's Rise to Power and the Downfall of the Weimar Republic* (New York, Macmillan, 2018); see also EJ Dionne Jr, 'The path to Autocracy is all too familiar' *Washington Post* (18 August 2018), available at: www.washingtonpost.com/opinions/the-path-to-autocracy-is-all-too-familiar/2018/08/08/6f3602f8-9b25-11e8-b60b-1c897f17e185_story.html?noredirect=on&utm_term=.dbc84c6a5d36.

[16] EW Böckenförde, *Staat, Gesellschaft, Freiheit* (Frankfurt, Surhkamp, 1976) S 60.

[17] It is telling that for the definition of 'democracy' in a recent opinion poll on Democracy in Europe by DG JUST of the European Commission, reference is made to the Foreign Policy Instrument (FPI), *Special Eurobarometer* 477, Democracy and Elections, November 2018, fn 1, page 2.

The EU will thus be able to give new meaning to engagement in democracy in times of globalisation.

Europe has built a tradition not only of external controls over its states, but actually of protecting citizens against their state, first in the area of human rights with the European Convention on Human Rights and the European Court of Human Rights, later with the system of directly applicable EU law in areas today going far beyond economic rules for the internal market. There is no reason why the EU should not also develop stronger tools to support domestic democracies and democratic engagement, using the tried and tested Community methods and thus spreading resilience against autocracy.[18] Supporting democracy and constitutional resilience in the EU is an existential matter for democracy in Europe, and the misguided silence of EU institutions on existential matters, such as domestic referendums on the EU Treaties and the Brexit vote, shall not be repeated in the matter of democracy in Europe.

## Time to Refocus on Democracy in Europe

Of the three pillars of constitutional democracy, this chapter will address neither the rule of law nor the protection of fundamental rights. The reason for this is that in both of these pillars, important steps forward have already been made in the EU which are still not present in relation to democracy.

As regards fundamental rights, the European Convention on Human Rights (ECHR) and the EU Charter of Fundamental Rights are legally binding, detailed texts, interpreted in extensive jurisprudence and enforced by the respective competent courts in Strasbourg, Luxembourg and in the Member States. The Commission in 2010 set out its policy on the application of the EU Charter of Fundamental rights in a strategy document.[19] Both the Commission and the independent Fundamental Rights Agency (FRA) in Vienna report annually on the application of the Charter.

As regards the rule of law, there is recent jurisprudence of the Court of Justice detailing its key elements.[20] The CEPEJ[21] of the Council of Europe is a core institution reporting on and assessing the rule of law situation in Member States. The Commission interacts well with this institution and in 2014 adopted a policy on

[18] In the same direction, 'The Other Democratic Deficit, A Toolbox for the EU to Safeguard Democracy in Member States', Expert Group of the Friedrich-Ebert Stiftung (Berlin, 2017).

[19] Communication from the Commission of 19 October 2010, 'Strategy for the effective implementation of the Charter of Fundamental Rights by the European Union', COM(2010) 573 final.

[20] Judgment of the Court (Grand Chamber) of 27 February 2018. Case C-64/16 *Associação Sindical dos Juízes Portugueses v Tribunal de Contas* EU:C:2018:117; Judgment of the Court (Grand Chamber) of 25 July 2018. Case C-216/18 PPU *LM (Ireland)* EU:C:2018:586; Order in Case C-619/18 R *Commission v Poland* EU:C:2018:1021 (English not available at time of writing).

[21] Council of Europe, 'European Commission for the Efficiency of Justice', available at: www.coe.int/en/web/cepej.

how to strengthen the rule of law in the Member States and how to proceed under Article 7 TEU in case of non-respect for the rule of law.[22] The Commission has also proposed a 'Regulation on the protection of the Union's budget in case of generalised deficiencies as regards the rule of law in the Member States'.[23]

However, as to democracy, EU primary law does not contain the necessary consolidations and concretisations as were achieved regarding fundamental rights in the Charter of Fundamental Rights of the European Union (CFR). Nor is there an external mechanism which, in an authoritative and obligatory manner, exercises an external discipline as to democracy over Member States as does the ECHR in respect of human rights, and the FRA and the Court of Justice as regards the CFR. Also, while President Juncker made 'Democracy in the EU' a priority of the Commission, the Commission has not yet presented an overarching policy strategy for the strengthening of democracy in Europe and for making both the EU and also its Member States resilient against the temptations and challenges of autocracy. It is also clear that while the Union is the biggest observer of elections and democracy programmes in third countries, no similar activities have been carried out so far within the EU, by the EU.

In the triangle of fundamental rights, the rule of law and democracy, democracy is thus presently the weakest link and needs work. There can certainly not be democracy without either the rule of law or the protection of the fundamental rights of individuals, which are constitutive of democracy. But there can be a certain rule of law and certain fundamental rights without democracy, as the history of Prussia teaches us. If we do not want Europe and its Member States to fall back into a state of Prussia, it is now time to renew the institutional and popular engagement for democracy in Europe.

With this in mind, this chapter continues with a brief description of the success story of evolution of democracy in the EU, setting out the main milestones in this process. Afterwards it broaches the range of challenges to democracy in Europe today. It will then jump to present sources for further work on democracy and provide a global overview of some important universal and regional democracy documents before describing possible elements of a future European Charter for Democracy (EUDC) as one part of an action plan to revive engagement of people in representative democracy and to equip the EU with the tools necessary to support the resilience of democracies in Europe against autocracy. We close with historical comparisons to the post-1968 democracy drive and process-related observations on the way towards an action plan for daring more democracy in the EU. This also includes the proposal that the EU should work on the creation of an EUDC.

[22] Communication from the Commission of 11 March 2014, 'A new Framework to strengthen the Rule of Law', COM(2014) 158 final; for its application see: ec.europa.eu/info/policies/justice-and-fundamental-rights/effective-justice/rule-law/rule-law-framework_en.

[23] Proposal 2018/0136 (COD) of 2 May 2018, COM(2018) 324 final.

# Evolution of Democracy in the EU

The democratisation of the European project has been a long, painstaking process. Main steps in this evolution were the introduction of direct elections to the European Parliament (EP), the subsequent strengthening of the EP, in particular through the broadening of co-decision, and of European political parties, and finally the nomination of the *Spitzenkandidaten* by the European political parties in the 2014 European election campaign. But difficult as it was and is, Europe must learn to recount its history of democratisation as a success story of step-by-step overcoming resistance and introducing new elements of democratisation.

## Direct Elections to the European Parliament

Article 10(1) TEU makes it clear that the Union works as a representative democracy. Article 10(2) TEU states that citizens are directly represented at Union level in the EP. Article 10(3) TEU states that every citizen shall have the right to participate in the democratic life of the Union and that decisions shall be taken as openly and as closely as possible to the citizen. Article 14 TEU sets out the basic rules on the Parliament as the centre of democracy on the EU level.

The founders of the EEC set the objective of a directly elected Parliament right from the outset of the European project. The Treaties provided for an Assembly consisting of 'representatives of the peoples of the States brought together in the Community' (Article 137 EEC), which would 'draw up proposals for elections by direct universal suffrage in accordance with a uniform procedure in all Member States' (Article 138(3) EEC). However, it took a few decades for this objective to materialise. In December 1974, the 'summit meeting' (predecessor of the European Council) decided to proceed with direct elections 'as soon as possible … at any time in or after 1978'.[24] Based on the EP's proposal of January 1975,[25] the Council reached an agreement in September 1976 on an Act concerning the election of the representatives of the EP by direct universal suffrage. This Act had the status of primary law and provided for a directly elected parliament with a five-year mandate, with polling to take place across the Community within the same three days. On this basis, the first direct elections to the EP took place in 1979. The first directly elected EP proposed in 1982[26] to extend proportional representation and to grant the nationals of Member States residing in another Member State for more than five years the right to vote in their Member State of residence. The idea about the right to vote in the Member State of residence

[24] Paragraph 12 of the Final communiqué of the Paris Summit (9–10 December 1974).
[25] See Patijn Report, Doc 368/74.
[26] See the so-called Seitlinger Report which passed the EP in March 1982.

materialised 10 years later in the Treaty of Maastricht – importantly, without the five-year residence qualification. Instead it was granted to mobile EU citizens 'under the same conditions as nationals' of the Member State of residence. This right, corollary to the right to free movement, contributed to stimulating transnational, EU-wide politics – with the participation of non-national candidates and voters. Based on the Anastassopoulos Report[27] a 2002 Council Decision,[28] amending the 1976 Act, codified proportional representation and fixed an *optional* threshold for seats to be allocated at 5 per cent or lower of the total votes obtained.

The most recent amendment of 2018, based on a proposal of the EP in 2015, failed to codify the *Spitzenkandidaten* practice, as proposed by the Parliament,[29] but introduced a number of technical improvements to the election procedures.[30]

## Increasing Powers of the European Parliament

The above-mentioned developments were accompanied by a remarkable evolution of the role of the EP in the legislative process from having a mere advisory role under the 1957 Treaty of Rome to having a co-decision role, as introduced by the Treaty of Maastricht in 1992 and extended by the Treaty of Amsterdam in 1999. This new powerful role was finally consolidated by the Treaty of Lisbon, which made the EP a full co-legislator alongside the Council. The EP now decides on the vast majority of EU legislation and has power over the entire EU budget on an equal footing with the Council.

Importantly, the power of the EP has also increased in relation to appointments to the European Commission, on which it previously was only consulted. Today, the President of the European Commission is elected by the European Parliament (Article 17(7) TEU), after nomination by the European Council with qualified majority, which must take into account the outcome of the European elections in its nomination. No one can become a member of the Commission without the agreement of its President. Only after individual hearings of each candidate for the Commission, can the Parliament then vote again on the full Commission. The Parliament indeed today carries out hearings of the candidate

[27] See Resolution on a draft electoral procedure incorporating common principles for the election of Members of the European Parliament (Anastassopoulos Report), adopted on 15 July 1998; [1998] OJ C 292.

[28] Council Decision of 25 June and 23 September 2002 amending the Act concerning the election of the representatives of the European Parliament by direct universal suffrage, annexed to Decision 76/787/ECSC, EEC, Euratom (2002/772/EC, Euratom).

[29] European Parliament resolution of 11 November 2015 on the reform of the electoral law of the European Union (2015/2035(INL)).

[30] Council Decision (EU, Euratom) 2018/994 of 13 July 2018 amending the Act concerning the election of the members of the European Parliament by direct universal suffrage, annexed to Council Decision 76/787/ECSC, EEC, Euratom of 20 September 1976, ST/9425/2018/INIT, 2018 OJ L178, 1–3, ELI, available at: data.europa.eu/eli/dec/2018/994/oj.

for the President of the Commission and every single candidate for the Commission, which have no parallel in terms of depth and transparency in Member States' processes of nomination of government, and only after satisfactory hearings does the Parliament vote.[31]

In parallel, the President gained more power over the College of Commissioners through the introduction of the principle of political guidance of the President under which the College operates, his/her organisational powers and the powers of the President in the appointment of individual Commissioners and their removal from office. In previous Treaties, the President was only consulted on the appointment of Commissioners. She or he must now agree to any individual appointment. The President can also, since the Treaty of Lisbon signed in 2007, ask individual Commissioners to step down, without support of a majority of Commissioners, which previously was necessary to remove individual Commissioners, a power that the President in the original text of the EEC Treaty until the changes in the Nice Treaty did not have at all. But as the Parliament gained the power to remove the College as a whole, through a vote of non-confidence (Article 234 TEU), after the experience with the Santer Commission, the power of the President to remove individual Members of the College needed to be strengthened, to allow the President to avoid a sanction of the full Commission in this way, thus ensuring a stability of the executive of the Union.[32]

## European Political Parties

Article 10(4) TEU and Article 12(2) of the Charter of Fundamental Rights of the European Union assign a key role to European political parties. The statute and funding of European political parties and European political foundations is regulated at European level.

The European political parties developed in parallel to the powers of the European Parliament, albeit not to their full potential. While the Treaty of Maastricht mentioned parties, it was only a decade later, with the Treaty of Nice in 2003, that a *legal base* was introduced for the creation of a Statute for European political parties (Article 191(2) EC).[33] On 4 November 2003 Regulation (EC) No 2004/2003 of the European Parliament and of the Council on the regulations governing political parties at European level and the rules regarding their funding was adopted. With this regulation the parties were given very limited resources from the EU budget as well as staffing and hence a small degree of operational autonomy vis-a-vis the parliamentary groups, which remain much better resourced. This regulation was

[31] See for further details, P Nemitz, 'Art 17 EUV' para 70 ff' in U Becker, A Hatje, J Schoo and J Schwarze (eds), *EU-Kommentar*, 4th edn (Baden-Baden, Nomos, 2019).

[32] On the history and *ratio legis* of the new Art 17(6) TEU, see Case T-562/12 *John Dalli v European Commission*, paras 136–42 (EU:T:2015:270); and Nemitz, 'Art 17 EUV', above n 31, para 69.

[33] See also Declaration on Art 191 of the Treaty establishing the European Community.

amended in 2007[34] which allowed the political parties, among other things, to set up political foundations with very little funding from the EU budget, compared with national political foundations. In the run-up to the 2014 EP elections, the European Commission issued a recommendation, in March 2013, to increase the visibility of European political parties as a means of better communicating the connection between political processes at national and EU level. It thus recommended that voters should be informed of the affiliation between national parties and European political parties during the whole electoral process, from the campaign to the casting of votes in elections to the EP.[35] A new regulation on political parties and political foundations, adopted in 2014,[36] provides EU-level legal status for European political parties and their political foundations, aiming to increase their visibility and EU-wide recognition.[37] This legal status is a precondition to receiving public funding from the EU budget.

In 2018, in a first move of what could be called a 'European democracy that defends itself', these rules were further detailed, in particular sanctioning the link of funding to the respect of the values of the Union set out in Article 2 TEU and to the visibility of the European party in the campaign materials of the national parties. The conditions on transnationality of the European parties were also tightened, in order to avoid abuse.[38] The Commission stated in 2018, as it had stated in 2013, that:

> European political parties play a key role in forming European political awareness, encouraging voter participation and in expressing the will of the citizens of the Union. This role could be enhanced if … European political parties would reach out to their national affiliate parties and civil society and raise awareness on choices regarding the future of Europe and the interests of the citizens they are representing.[39]

However, the European political parties[40] and the political foundations on the EU level are severely underfunded. To illustrate that, while the two foundations of the

[34] See Regulation (EC) No 1524/2007 of the European Parliament and of the Council of 18 December 2007 amending Regulation (EC) No 2004/2003 on the regulations governing political parties at European level and the rules regarding their funding.

[35] See the EC Recommendation on enhancing the democratic and efficient conduct of the elections to the European Parliament, Brussels, 12 March 2013, C(2013) 1303 final.

[36] Regulation No 1141/2014 of the European Parliament and of the Council of 22 October 2014 on the statute and funding of European political parties and European political foundations.

[37] The regulation sets the conditions for them to enjoy a legal status and qualify for funding from the EU budget, namely being represented in at least one quarter of the Member States and respecting the founding principles of the EU.

[38] Regulation (EU, Euratom) 2018/673 of the European Parliament and of the Council of 3 May 2018 amending Regulation (EU, Euratom) No 1141/2014 on the statute and funding of European political parties and European political foundations. [2018] OJ L114I, 1–6, available at: data.europa.eu/eli/reg/2018/673/oj; consolidated version, available at: eur-lex.europa.eu/legal-content/EN/TXT/PDF/?uri=CELEX:02014R1141-20180504&qid=1546444985179&from=EN.

[39] Commission Recommendation (EU) 2018/234 of 14 February 2018 on enhancing the European nature and efficient conduct of the 2019 elections to the European Parliament, C/2018/0900, [2018] OJ L45, 40–43, available at: data.europa.eu/eli/reco/2018/234/oj.

[40] For an extensive presentation see J Priestley, 'European Political Parties: The Missing Link, Les partis politiques européens: le chaînon manquant' (2010) Notre Europe Policy Paper No 41.

Socialists (Foundation of European Progressive Studies – FEPS) and Conservatives (Martens Center) on the EU level receive less than 10 million euro annually from the EU budget,[41] the similar foundations in Germany alone (Friedrich Ebert Stiftung and Konrad Adenauer Stiftung) have a budget of over 360 million euro annually.[42]

It is probably fair to say that the allocation of EU internal budgets for purposes of making democracy work – thus education about and supporting democracy, the rule of law and fundamental rights in the EU – have so far not been restructured in line with the development of the Union from a union of economic integration and without its own democratic structure. Furthermore, no determined reform steps have been taken so far towards a Union with its own important democratic processes and a role to play in supporting and strengthening democracy within Member States. Democracy in Europe will pay a high price if European political parties and European political foundations remain as underfunded as they have been so far, with neither being able to seriously invest in Europe-wide campaigns during election times nor indeed carry out the roles for which they are most needed, namely to engage citizens to participate in European policy-making and to provide political education about Europe in all parts of the EU.

## *Spitzenkandidaten* (Lead Candidates) for the Function of President of the European Commission

The most recent step in the democratisation of the European project has been the introduction of *Spitzenkandidaten* in the 2014 European election campaign. The first discussions in European political parties to present *Spitzenkandidaten* go as far back as 1998 but, until after the 2009 elections, no substantial progress had been made.[43]

[41] See the report card of the European Parliament on the funding of political foundations, available at: www.europarl.europa.eu/pdf/grants/Grant_amounts_foundations%2001-2018.pdf.

[42] See annual report 2017 of Konrad Adenauer Stiftung, with a total budget of 182 million euros in 2017 the report, available at: www.kas.de/c/document_library/get_file?uuid=a5ee2563-5295-af5c-fdb4-2c07f56e5240&groupId=252038, 39; and the annual report of the Friedrich Ebert Stiftung, with a total budget of 176 million euros in 2017, available at: library.fes.de/pdf-files/fes/03208/jb-2017.pdf, 71.

[43] 'In 1999 the EPP became the largest group at the EP but its right to see a member nominated from the EPP family was thwarted by the hasty compromise necessary to appoint a Commission president after the implosion of the Santer Commission, just before the elections. Separately, some socialist Prime Ministers from larger member states argued the case for nominating someone from their political family, namely, Wim Kok, the Dutch Prime Minister. Many in the EPP drew the conclusion that for future elections, the European party which topped the poll should have the right to the Commission presidency, but this was still a long way off from developing a lead candidate system'. N Peñalver Garcia and J Priestley, 'European Political Parties: Learning from 2014, preparing for 2019' (2015) Notre Europe – Jacques Delors Institute Policy Paper (hereafter referred to as 'Notre Europe paper on European parties') s 2.1; see also P Nemitz, 'Europwahl 1999: Für die indirekte Wahl des EU-Kommissionspräsidenten' in (1998) 6 *Internationale Politik/Europa Archiv* 45; A Volle and W Weidenfeld (eds), *Europa hat Zukunft, Der Weg ins 21. Jahrhundert* (Bonn, Verlag für Internationale

It was the Treaty of Lisbon in 2007 that established a new constitutional order for the EU, empowering the EP to elect the President of the Commission: the European Council must, according to Article 17(7) TEU, take into account the results of the European elections when proposing a candidate. Both the Parliament, in two resolutions issued in 2012 and 2013,[44] and the Commission, in its March 2013 recommendation,[45] called on European and national political parties to make known their nominations for the function of President of the Commission. This aimed at making the link between EU citizens' votes for prospective Members of the EP and their party's candidate for Commission President visible. It was also only logical to seek a higher legitimacy for a President of the Commission, namely through having campaigned for office as a *Spitzenkandidat*, once the President received so much additional power that the Commission was effectively no longer operating under a simple principle of collegiality, but – considering the cumulated powers in the appointment process, the power of political guidance and the power to remove individual Commissioners – factually under a presidential regime.[46]

This materialised in the 2014 elections: the European political families nominated candidates for President of the Commission for the first time, launched EU-wide election campaigns, and held public events across Europe to raise awareness of their candidates and their political programmes for Europe. Just to give an indication, as detailed in the Commission's report on the 2014 elections, the lead candidates visited 246 cities across the Member States. In addition to being mobilised in this way on the ground, the lead candidates took part in 10 televised debates in different Member States and different languages, sharing their vision for the future of Europe and on issues that particularly matter to voters, such as jobs

Politik, 1998); more recently, 'Building on the Spitzenkandidaten Model', European Political Strategy Center of the European Commission, 16 February 2018, available at: ec.europa.eu/epsc/publications/road-to-sibiu/building-on-the-spitzenkandidaten-model_en; on this see also A Armellini, 'Schulz approved as Socialist candidate for commission presidency' (1 March 2014), available at: euobserver.com/eu-elections/123323; and J Janning, 'Five lessons from the "Spitzenkandidaten" European Parliament campaign' European Council on Foreign Relations, 1 July 2014, available at: www.ecfr.eu/article/commentary_five_lessons_from_the_spitzenkandidaten_european_parliament_camp, which show that the then President of the European Parliament, Martin Schulz, was the key driver for effectively having *Spitzenkandidaten* in the 2014 elections and that he was nominated by the Party of European Socialists (PES) before the EPP was able to nominate Jean-Claude Juncker as *Spitzenkandidat*. After the elections, it was in particular the conservative heads of state, led by David Cameron of the UK, who objected to the nomination of Jean-Claude Juncker as President of the European Commission.

[44] See European Parliament resolution of 22 November 2012 on the elections to the European Parliament in 2014 (2012/2829(RSP)); and European Parliament resolution of 4 July 2013 on improving the practical arrangements for the holding of the European elections in 2014 (2013/2102(INI)).

[45] See again the Commission Recommendation on enhancing the democratic and efficient conduct of the elections to the European Parliament, Brussels, 12 March 2013 C(2013) 1303 final.

[46] H Kassim, S Connolly, R Dehousse, O Rozenberg and S Bendjaballah, 'Managing the House: The Presidency, Agenda Control and Policy Activism in the European Commission' (2017) 24 *Journal of European Public Policy* 653, available at: DOI:10.1080/13501763.2016.1154590; see also Nemitz, 'Art 17 EUV', above n 31.

and growth. The debates received wide coverage across the EU, were broadcast live and generated high volumes of social media traffic.[47]

Importantly, the European Council nominated Jean-Claude Juncker as the candidate of the party with the most seats in the EP[48] and he was subsequently elected as Commission President by the EP, with a coalition of the European People's Party (EPP), the Party of European Socialists (PES) and others. The result of the elections allowed for a stable parliamentary majority in a grand coalition that has enabled the EP to function effectively for the duration of the legislative period. The Commission highlighted in its report on the 2014 EP elections:

> These elections have laid the ground for future European elections and established a clear link between the results of the European Parliament elections and the choice of European Commission President. An important precedent has been set for 2019 and beyond, and a European-level forum for political debate has been established.[49]

Later on, the report states:

> Under this new system, voters could more easily make the link between a vote cast for a national party and the impact of this vote on the political direction of the European Union for the next five years. This allowed voters to make an informed choice between alternative political platforms for Europe, rather than on exclusively national political issues. It injected a greater element of information and choice into the election, reinforced the democratic legitimacy of the European Commission, and has the potential to enhance public interest and strengthen accountability in the future.[50]

Regarding the 2019 elections, the Commission stressed in its report:

> There is a need to act not only shortly before the start of the election campaign but also far in advance … Looking ahead to the 2019 elections, it is important to identify ways of further enhancing the European dimension and the democratic legitimacy of the EU decision-making process.[51]

On 14 February 2018, the Commission updated its recommendation on the European elections of 2013.[52]

It looked back both at the 2014 experience with *Spitzenkandidaten* but also repeated basic appeals:

> Reinforcing the democratic legitimacy of the EU and ensuring the participation of citizens in the political life at European level is essential. Citizens would be readier to vote in the elections to the European Parliament if they were more aware of the impact

[47] 'Report on the 2014 European Parliament elections', Brussels, 8 May 2015, COM(2015) 206 final, 7–8.

[48] See European Council Conclusions 26/27 June 2014, EUCO 79/14, CO EUR 4, CONCL 2, see page 2, sentence 1: 'The European Council agreed to propose Jean-Claude Juncker to the European Parliament as candidate for President of the European Commission'.

[49] 'Report on the 2014 European Parliament elections', above n 47, 5.

[50] ibid 17.

[51] ibid.

[52] C(2018) 900 final.

> of EU policies in their day-to-day life, and if they would trust that they can have their say on the Union's most important choices, such as the selection of the leaders of the EU institutions and the establishment of priorities for the future of the Union … The system of lead candidates for President of the Commission – '*Spitzenkandidaten*' – … has helped to reinforce the Union's efficiency and its democratic legitimacy, which rests on the dual pillars of direct representation of citizens in the European Parliament and their indirect representation by governments of the Member States in the European Council and the Council. It has also contributed to strengthening the Commission's accountability, in line with Article 17(7) of the Treaty on European Union. It should be continued and improved in view of the 2019 elections to the European Parliament … European and national political parties should announce well ahead of the start of the electoral campaign, ideally by the end of 2018, the candidate for President of the Commission they support and, ideally by early 2019, the candidate's own programme. This would make more transparent the link between the individual vote of a citizen of the Union for a particular political party in the elections to the European Parliament, the candidate for President of the Commission supported by that party and his/her vision for the future of Europe … By selecting their lead candidates in an open, inclusive and transparent way, eg through 'primary' elections, European political parties and their national member parties would further strengthen this process. This would also help to raise wider attention as well as to mobilise voters.[53]

The presentation of candidates for President of the Commission in the elections to the EP in 2014, which had been discussed for more than 15 years, has stopped the decline in participation.

The Heads of State in the European Council, while finally appointing Jean-Claude Juncker, the candidate of the EPP, as a goodwill compromise gesture to UK Prime Minister David Cameron, who opposed the appointment, did plant a seed of future challenge to this progress of European democracy in their Conclusions by announcing a review of the procedure of appointment of the President of the Commission in the run-up to the European elections of 2019.[54] This announcement reflects the oscillating attitude of Member States towards democracy in Europe.

It is however undeniable that the 'lead candidates process' was a success – one could say, against the odds, against the background of widespread scepticism in the media and in national capitals, because the steady fall in electoral participation was halted to a substantial degree. The credibility of the process may have been established but it still needs to be consolidated and recognised as usual practice.

This is where we stand now with regard to the evolution of democracy in the EU.

[53] Above n 39.

[54] See European Council Conclusions 26/27 June 2014, EUCO 79/14, CO EUR 4, CONCL 2, para 27, sentence 4: 'Once the new European Commission is effectively in place, the European Council will consider the process for the appointment of the President of the European Commission for the future, respecting the European Treaties'.

## Current Challenges to Democracy in Europe

In Europe, the challenges to representative democracy are found on three levels, namely on the level of the EU itself, within the Member States, and in the relation between the EU and the Member States.

Debates on the future of Europe have always been debates about how to make Europe more democratic and how to make democracy work better on the EU level. While Europe has made good progress in shaping the EU as a representative democracy, it needs to learn to tell, with enthusiasm, its stories of democratisation and the many cases of successful citizen engagement in the processes of representative democracy on the EU level, in order to encourage future increased engagement.

For example, without the engagement of Eduard Snowden and Max Schrems[55] and without the digital rights organisations coming together in the European Digital Rights Initiative (EDRI)[56] and the engagement of the people in these organisations interested in data protection during a legislative process of four years, the success of the adoption of the General Data Protection Regulation (GDPR)[57] would not have been possible. But the example of the GDPR also shows that politicians and their qualities make an important difference, be they Members of the Commission (or Member States executives) or Members of Parliament.[58] This is another important reason why engaging with representatives of democracy on the EU level and in the political parties which put forward the individuals to take political functions on the EU level is so important.

With rising populism, new questions arise: how resilient is the Constitution of the EU against autocracy on the EU level? And what can the EU do to strengthen the resilience of Member States against rising populism and risks of autocracy? Let us turn to this question first, focusing the attention on a new perspective on EU law, from how to move forward in democratisation to also include the question of how to secure against sliding back from those democratic rights and procedures already established.

[55] See, eg, ECJ Judgment of the Court (Grand Chamber) of 6 October 2015, Case C-362/14 *Maximillian Schrems v Data Protection Commissioner* EU:C:2015:650. Following his engagement for data protection during the legislative process for the GDPR, Schrems created the GDPR enforcement NGO NOYB: 'None of your Business' (at: noyb.eu/) together with the Parliamentary Rapporteur on the GDPR Jan Albrecht, one of the authors and others; a detailed history of the successful civil society engagement on GDPR, which brought together activists from many Member States, still remains to be written.

[56] See: edri.org/.

[57] Regulation (EU) 2016/679 of the European Parliament and of the Council of 27 April 2016 on the protection of natural persons with regard to the processing of personal data and on the free movement of such data, and repealing Directive 95/46/EC (General Data Protection Regulation), [2016] OJ L119, 1–88, ELI, available at: data.europa.eu/eli/reg/2016/679/oj.

[58] See in particular on GDPR Vice President of the European Commission, Viviane Albrecht, and Parliamentary Rapporteur, Jan Albrecht, in the impressive long-term cinema documentary 'Democracy – Im Rausch der Daten', David Bernet, 2015, available at: www.democracy-film.de/ which received the German Documentary Film prize 2017.

One difficult question among these is the question of referendums in Member States, and EU law. Closely linked to this, due to the Greek experience, but not expended by that, is the democratisation of the governance of the Eurozone. The new technologies of the internet have become the tools of dictators and populists alike. They create a new class of challenges for free and fair elections.

At the same time, the free press and pluralistic journalism, so important as the fourth estate in democracy, is challenged by the new technologies and autocrats alike.

Finally, a word also on public consultations and citizens' dialogues as intensified by the European Commission as part of President Juncker's priority of democratisation in Europe.

It is these issues we focus on here, without intending to neglect the importance of the many other issues in the debate on democracy and resilience, such as the need to defend and extend the space for civil society engagement and for free, independent sciences[59] in Member States and the EU.

## In Search of Constitutional Resilience and a New Democracy Policy for the EU

Resilience of democracy against autocracy certainly has many facets, and broad popular democratic engagement is most likely the best way to achieve resilience – but also the least likely to be achieved by an order of law, even though a differentiated body of primary and secondary law is vital to make possible, encourage and protect engagement in democracy.

Starting at the constitutional level, there is resilience against changes leading to autocracy in the high majorities which are usually required in constitutional democracies for the change of constitutions. In some Member States, such as in Germany, there are constitutional provisions which cannot even be changed by a constitutional majority and thus are protected in eternity. An example for this is Article 79(3) of the German Grundgesetz, which prescribes that the fundamental right to human dignity, the principle of democracy and the structure as federation as laid down in the Grundgesetz can never be abrogated.

In EU law, the Treaties provide as to their own content a high resilience, above that of national constitutions, but below the specific case of guarantees for eternity: although they do not contain eternity clauses, the Treaties can as a general principle only be revised by unanimity among Member States and ratification by all national parliaments. This is a much higher hurdle to change than the usual constitutional majority of two-thirds of the Members of the legislature.[60]

[59] Commission Press release of 24 April 2018, 'Hungary: Commission takes legal action on Higher Education Law and sets record straight on "Stop Brussels" consultation' MEX/17/1116, available at: europa.eu/rapid/press-release_MEX-17-1116_en.htm.

[60] See in addition R Passchier and M Stremler, 'Unconstitutional Constitutional Amendments in European Union Law: Considering the Existence of Substantive Constraints on Treaty

But what protections does EU law provide against autocracy taking over in Member States, and in fine, against constitutional change in Member States which legally or factually does away with domestic democracy in that Member State – in practice or as a constitutional principle?[61]

Here we fall back on the weak mechanism of Article 7 EU on the constitutional level, and on the infringement procedures in cases in which rights and processes of democracy are enshrined in secondary law, such as is the case on the right for EU citizens to vote in local and European elections.[62]

It is important not to underestimate that many rights and protections for individuals, but also institutional arrangements, which are created by secondary EU law, are key for the good functioning of democracy in Member States, in particular when also considering that the rule of law and fundamental rights are core elements of democracy.[63]

The Commission should therefore develop a policy to systematically include such hooks for democracy and democratic engagement in EU secondary legislation and develop a checklist and toolbox for such purposes, as it has done in its strategy for the application of the Fundamental Rights Charter. For example, where EU legislation foresees domestic bodies, such as sectoral regulators or data protection authorities, playing a role, the toolbox would require certain levels of participation and consultation rights as well as rights of appeal for citizens and also for civil society associations in relation to such a body. This would create space for engagement, thus addressing the problem of the shrinking space for civil society engagement where populists gain power.

As part of such a 'mainstreaming for democracy policy', impact assessments of the Commission in future would need to set out how the proposal has been systematically screened to include elements for democratic engagement in the process of legislation as well as in the institutions, rights and procedures set up through law. Impact assessments for this purpose would have to be enlarged to non-legislative action of the Commission where legislation could be an alternative to non-legislative action. These democracy impact assessments would also have to discuss what it means for representative democracy on the EU level and in Member States if the Commission chooses to prefer non-legislative action over a legislative proposal. In the case of non-legislative action, such as the recourse

Revision' (2016) 5 *Cambridge Journal of International and Comparative Law*, available at: ssrn.com/abstract=2561209.

[61] G Halmai, 'Internal and external limits of constitutional amendment sovereignty' (2010) EUI Paper, available at: www.eui.eu/Documents/DepartmentsCentres/Law/Professors/Halmai/Constitutional-Amendment-Power.pdf.

[62] Council Directive 93/109/EC of 6 December 1993 laying down detailed arrangements for the exercise of the right to vote and stand as a candidate in elections to the European Parliament for citizens of the Union residing in a Member State of which they are not nationals, [1993] OJ L329, 34–38, ELI, available at: data.europa.eu/eli/dir/1993/109/oj, as amended, concretizes Art 22(2) TFEU.

[63] The most recent example is the Commission proposal of 23 April 2018 on the protection of persons reporting on breaches of Union Law ('Whistleblowers'), COM(2018) 218 final.

to voluntary codes of conduct for industry, the impact assessment would have to assess the impact of cutting out parliamentary decision-making on the EU level and parliamentary consultation rights of Member States' parliaments, both individually for the act in question, but also seen cumulatively over time, considering other similar cases, before resorting to non-legislative measures where legislation is possible in principle.

A crucial question in democracy is which of the challenges on the table can safely and with good conscience be left to non-legislative action, self-regulation, voluntary codes of conduct or simply ethics, and which challenges need to be addressed by rules which are enforceable and based on democratic process, thus laws.

In answering this question, democracy impact assessments will have to consider the principle of essentiality which has guided legislation in constitutional democracies for so long. This principle prescribes that any matter which is essential because it either concerns fundamental rights of individuals or is important to the good functioning of the state, which includes democracy, must be dealt with by a parliamentary, democratically legitimised law.[64]

To close on this section, attack is often the best defence and thus creating and extending democratic rights of engagement wherever possible in a wave of new European, democratic creativity, may well be the best way to go for the next Commission, as a guiding principle for policy development to avoid democracy being undermined in Europe.

## Should We Allow Demagogues to Use Referendums Against Europe? Reviving Representative Democracy

The EU Treaties contain elements of direct democracy, such as the Citizen's Initiative, to be reinvigorated.[65] But Article 10(1) TEU also states clearly that Europe is a functioning representative democracy.

[64] Jo Eric Khushal Murkens considered the judgment of the UK High Court on decisions relating to Brexit not being left in the hands of the government alone, but giving Westminster a say, a case of application of the principle of essentiality; see The High Court's Brexit Decision, 'A Lesson in Constitutional Law for the UK Government' (*Verfassungsblog – On matters constitutional*, 3 November 2016), available at: verfassungsblog.de/the-high-courts-brexit-decision-a-lesson-in-constitutional-law-for-the-uk-government/; for the principle of essentiality in German, US and EU law, see J Saurer, 'EU Agencies 2.0: The New Constitution of Supranational Administration beyond the EU Commission' in S Rose-Ackerman, PL Lindseth and B Emerson (eds), *Comparative Administrative Law*, 2nd edn (Cheltenham, Edward Elgar, 2017); further recent examples in the jurisprudence of the CJEU are the judgments in Cases C-355/10 *European Parliament v Council* EU:C:2012:516, para 64 ff, with further precedent, available at: eur-lex.europa.eu/legal-content/EN/TXT/?qid=1534186617433&uri=CELEX:62010CJ0355 and C-293/12 and C-594/12 *Digital Rights Ireland* EU:C:2014:238, para 54 ff, available at: curia.europa.eu/juris/documents.jsf?num=C-293/12.

[65] See Commission Proposal of 13 September 2017, COM(2017) 482 final and European Citizens' Initiative: Political agreement reached on the Commission's proposal, press release of 12 December 2018, IP/18/6792.

And for good reasons, drawing on lessons of history, the core of the decision-making system and the appointment system is strictly based on representative democracy. Populists have abused calls for direct democracy to avoid deliberation and compromise. Referendums have become the dance floor of populism, and calling for referendums, while claiming to be the sole spokesperson for the one will of the people,[66] is a core method of populists.

The Brexit referendum of 23 June 2016[67] in the UK is the most flagrant example of alleged direct democracy dividing a people, providing a fertile ground for lies and manipulation to steal the vote.

The specificity of referendums in Member States regarding matters concerning the EU is that these referendums can be used to pitch national democracy against *pacta sund servanda* and democratic decisions on the EU level.

The invalid referendum against migration quotas orchestrated by the Orbán government in Hungary led President Juncker to comment that Europe cannot function if decisions taken under the rules of the Treaty are, ex post,[68] put in question by referendums organised by governments which do not agree with the decision.

The Irish referendum of 2001,[69] the French and the Dutch referendums of 2005[70] and the Greek referendum of 2015, the negative result of which could exceptionally not be followed by the government, precisely because it would have jeopardised the Greek membership of the Economic and Monetary Union (EMU),[71] are other cases of referendums to consider. In the last case the challenge of a clash between the EU and national democracy is more than obvious, even if the referendum itself could well be qualified as unconstitutional and, thus, null and void.[72]

The relationship between democracy on the level of Member States and on the level of the EU should in principle be resolved by the division of competences in the Treaty.

[66] A Voßkuhle, 'Ein Populist ist ein Gegner der Demokratie' (*FAZ*, 23 November 2017), available at: www.faz.net/aktuell/politik/inland/bundesverfassungsrichter-vosskuhle-und-sein-rezept-gegen-populismus-15304961.html.

[67] Official title: United Kingdom European Union membership referendum.

[68] 'Juncker rages against UK and Hungary' (*Euractiv with AFP*, 7 October 2016), updated 10 October, available at: www.euractiv.com/section/uk-europe/news/juncker-rages-against-the-uk-and-hungary/.

[69] On 7 June 2001 the people of the Republic of Ireland voted against the ratification of the Treaty of Nice in a referendum.

[70] On 29 May 2005 the European Constitution was rejected by the voters in France and on 1 June 2005 the Dutch voted against the European Constitution.

[71] In the so-called Greek bail-out referendum on 5 July 2015 it was the bail-out conditions, proposed jointly by the European Commission, the International Monetary Fund (IMF) and the European Central Bank (ECB), that were rejected by the voters, although fiscal matters are normally excluded from such referendums, according to Art 44 of the Greek Constitution.

[72] Not only because fiscal matters cannot be put to popular vote, above n 71, but also because the question to be answered was imprecise (about unknown terms still under negotiation), the alternative option (acceptance of the terms) was only presented as a second choice, the consequences of the rejection were unclear and the reflection period for the voters too short (1 week instead of 2 as the minimum recommended by the Council of Europe; see press reports of 1 July 2015).

For the rest, a simple principle of considering referendums a domestic matter for Member States will not be good enough if the referendum concerns EU matters, as such an answer does not take into account the common EU interest.

In a systematic review of referendums in the EU, one would have to distinguish a number of different constellations, namely those relating to changes in the Treaty, those on membership and those relating to decisions in secondary law, the management of the Eurozone being a particularly delicate case, dealt with in a separate section below.

Relating to changes within the Treaties, one would further have to distinguish between situations where national law obliges holding a referendum and where this is not the case, and a fortiori, where this not obligatory and is practically never done in relation to domestic policy issues.

As to membership, the domestic litigation on the division of powers between government and Parliament in the case of Brexit, and the stress that the Brexit process as such, including the need for litigation, puts on the whole of the EU, demonstrates the need for further reflection as regards orderly processes in the future.

As to referendums relating to secondary law, one would need to distinguish between referendums before and after decisions on secondary law on the EU level. One would also need to distinguish between Member States in which referendums are a common tool for deciding matters other than those relating to the EU, and those where this is not the case.

Beyond a reflection of a systematic nature, what both the EU and Member States urgently need, and not only just before elections, but from early school education onwards, is a strengthened teaching, learning and practice of representative democracy and a critical discourse on direct democracy, based on our historic experience.

It is striking that representative democracy is increasingly taken for granted. What people throughout history have fought so hard to achieve and still fight for in many parts of the world, is steadily losing support across European society. One example is the findings of the second European Youth Study carried out by pollster YouGov on behalf of the TUI Foundation. For this study 6,080 young people aged between 16 and 26 were polled in seven EU countries (France, Germany, Greece, Italy, Poland, Spain and the UK). The authors of the study concluded, inter alia, that young people tend to be more critical of the design of the democratic system: 39 per cent rate the political system in their country so poorly that they see a need for radical change. This view is predominantly expressed by respondents from Greece (66 per cent), Italy (51 per cent), Poland (41 per cent) and Spain (39 per cent).[73]

[73] See Young Europe 2018 – The Youth Study of TUI Foundation, available at: www.tui-stiftung.de/en/our-projects/young-europe-2018-the-youth-study-of-tui-foundation.

Since the first direct elections in 1979, the turnout in European elections has fallen steadily from 61.99 per cent to 42.61 per cent in the latest elections.[74] Also, although the new Member States freed themselves of dictatorships and enthusiastically embraced democracy at the outset, there was a very low European election turnout in 2014 in some of these countries. Slovakia had for example a turnout of 13.05 per cent, and countries like the Czech Republic (18.20 per cent) and Poland (23.83 per cent) showed record lows.[75] This has direct effect on the European institutions as a whole as it reduces their democratic legitimacy; Joseph HH Weiler has correctly determined that this development shows a 'democratic paradox'. He wrote:

> What is striking about these figures is that the decline coincides with a continuous shift in powers to the European Parliament, which today is a veritable co-legislator with the Council. The more powers the European Parliament, supposedly the vox populi, has gained, the greater popular indifference to it seems.[76]

Moreover, voter turnout in national elections is also dropping. When looking at the seven EU Member States in which the above-mentioned European Youth Study was carried out, the following voter turnout appears: France (2017: 42.64 per cent parliamentary and 74.56 per cent, presidential);[77] Germany (2017: 76.15 per cent, parliamentary); Greece (2015: 63.94 per cent, parliamentary); Italy (2018: 72.93 per cent, parliamentary); Poland (2015: 50.92 per cent parliamentary and 55.34 per cent presidential); Spain (2016: 69.84 per cent, parliamentary); and finally the UK (2017: 68.93 per cent, parliamentary).[78] These figures show that the downward trend is not restricted to Eastern Europe. Many countries with traditionally strong participation rates have seen participation gradually decrease since the early 1970s. The participation rate in Germany in 1972 was 91.11 per cent and in Italy 93.18 per cent. Since then, the voter turnout has been in steady decline.[79]

To close on this section, if referendums on EU-related matters are unavoidable, EU institutions need to speak out.[80] It is normal both within the US, where any President intervenes in election campaigns not only for Congress but also for governors, and in federal *Länder* in Germany, where members of the federal

[74] 'Report on the 2014 European Parliament elections', above n 47, 11.

[75] See: www.europarl.europa.eu/elections2014-results.

[76] JHH Weiler, 'The Political and Legal Culture of European Integration: An Exploratory Essay' (2011) 9 *International Journal of Constitutional Law* 678, 681.

[77] This turnout for the 2017 French presidential elections, which were said to determine the fate of Europe, was the lowest since 1969.

[78] For these numbers see the Voter Turnout Database of the International IDEA, available at: www.idea.int/data-tools/data/voter-turnout.

[79] ibid.

[80] The Commission spoke to set facts straight before the referendum in Hungary, Commission press release of 24 April 2018, 'Hungary: Commission takes legal action on Higher Education Law and sets record straight on "Stop Brussels" consultation', MEX/17/1116, available at: europa.eu/rapid/press-release_MEX-17-1116_en.htm.

government participate in and comment extensively on people and issues coming up in elections and in – rare – referendums in the *Länder*.

The recent Eurobarometer survey of the European Commission shows a high concern about populist movements in many Member States,[81] and people expect the EU to speak out and actively provide information on matters relating to the EU.[82]

## Democratising the Eurozone: The Five Presidents' Report

Some of the European decisions of biggest impact on people in Member States, namely those relating to the economic and financial crisis, are not taken in the form of legislation, with co-decision by the EP. They are taken by the Council alone, or even, in an intergovernmental format, among Member States. The never-ending discussion on the role of the Troika[83] exemplifies the challenge to democracy – both on EU level and on Member State level – of these decisions.

The Regulation on the European Financial Stabilisation Mechanism (EFSM)[84] makes the Council's decision on loan financing dependent on the conditions set by the Commission (on the basis of underlying recommendations by the Council), as well as on the approval of a reform programme prepared by the Member State concerned.[85] However, in the case of decisions taken directly on the basis of Article 126, paragraph 9[86] and Article 136 TFEU, the Council's decisions[87] go much further in regulating in detail matters for which the EU has not legislated (because it is bound by the unanimity requirement) or has no competence to legislate (mere coordination or support competences, see Article 6 TFEU). Taxation, social security and working conditions fall under the former category, whereas health and hospital care and education fall under the latter, as well as the restructuring of the national administration and justice, the privatisations or the reduction of military expenditure.[88] This encroachment on national competence, which may be justified by the urgency to save the Eurozone or, at least, the countries concerned,[89] raises the question of the democratic legitimation of the decisions imposed on the countries concerned, first on the EU level. The texts on economic governance[90] foresee

[81] 67% of respondents think that the rise of political parties protesting against the traditional political elites in various European countries is a matter of concern. Eurobarometer (November 2018).

[82] *Special Eurobarometer* 477 on Democracy and Elections (September 2018).

[83] With respect to the financial crisis the term 'troika' refers to the Commission, the European Central Bank (ECB), and the International Monetary Fund (IMF).

[84] Council Regulation 407/2010, [2010] OJ L118, 1 ff.

[85] See the Irish and the Portuguese cases.

[86] Mainly because of delays or negligence of the Member State concerned (see the Greek case).

[87] Approving the creditors' agreements with the Member State concerned ('memorandums').

[88] For an overview, see DN Triantafyllou, 'Nachholende Wirtschaftsregierung unter der Gewalt des Geldes' in *Grundlagen, aktuelle Entwicklungen und Perspektiven der EWU* (Baden-Baden, Nomos, 2012) 145 ff.

[89] See, for possible legal justifications, the previous footnote.

[90] See Regulations 1173–1177/2011, [2011] OJ L306, 1 ff.

only the invitation of Commission and Council representatives by the competent committee of the EP, as well as the invitation of the President of the EP to the Euro summit, whereas the European Stability Pact also provides for a common convention of representatives of the EP and of the national parliaments. These are provisions of a rather informative nature. The representatives of the people(s) are at best consulted, but they do not decide themselves. This is an obvious democratic deficit regarding the measures of economic governance taken on the European level.[91]

Transnational democracy in the EU, *pacta sunt servanda* in Europe, and national democracy have always been in a relation of dialectic tension. The situation between Europe and the Greek government elected in January 2015 was only the latest and possibly most dramatic example, which shows that the interaction between both worlds sometimes leads to a loss of either 'supranational democratic will' or 'national democratic will'. Furthermore, it exemplifies that there is sometimes not enough mutual respect between national and EU institutions as both sides perceive themselves as the true democratic custodians. Even if the bail-out programme is formally 'appropriated' by the national government that endorses it as a 'national programme', the fact remains that it is imposed by the Member State's creditors.[92] The discrepancy between form and reality in that respect is well reflected in the majority and dissenting opinions of the Greek Council of State[93] about the national law 'receiving' the memorandum 'agreed' with the creditors. The challenge to transnational democracy becomes even bigger if one considers the peak attained with the jurisprudence of the German Constitutional Court, which allows every citizen, on the basis of his fundamental right to elect deputies who have to approve any new expenditure (or exposure thereto), to challenge any laws (like those approving European mechanisms) that may increase their state's budgetary liability[94] (through *popular action*). Does this mean (surely asked in a provocative way) that there is a democratic 'surplus' of the creditors versus a democratic 'deficit' of the debtors?[95]

There are thus contradictory trends relating to democracy on the EU level: on the one hand, moves towards more democratisation, through direct election of the EP (1979), expansion of the scope of co-decision since then, and now the indirect election of the President of the Commission (2014). On the other hand, key decisions on the social and economic situation of European societies have been moved outside this democratic mechanism by governments of Member States. These governments, in the classic pattern of executives, also strengthen their role in legislative decision-making, including indirectly through increased activism

[91] See S Goulard and M Monti, *De la démocratie en Europe* (Paris, Flammarion, 2012).

[92] See the codified Council Decision 2011/734, [2011] OJ L296, 38.

[93] Judgment of the Plenary of 20 February 2012 in Case 668/2012 (about Greek law 3845/2010).

[94] Judgment of the German Federal Constitutional Court of 18 March 2014 (file reference 2BvR 1390/12 ao).

[95] On this aspect, see DN Triantafyllou, 'Die asymmetrische Demokratie' (2014) 4 *Europarecht* 458 ff.

of the Council Secretariat which, in contrast to the EP and the Commission, has no role as an organ in the TEU (see Title III, Articles 13–19, 'provisions on the institutions') and no democratic legitimacy.

President Juncker has made democracy in Europe one of his 10 priorities for the present Commission. He presented proposals, in the Five Presidents' Report, on the future democratisation of Eurozone governance, most likely the most crucial issue of tension between democracy in Member States and democracy on the EU level.

In the economic governance of the Eurozone, there is need for a common discipline on the EU level, which requires common binding decisions, which in turn require democratic legitimacy, as they touch on matters essential in the democracies of Member States and are traditionally very important in domestic democratic debates and decision-making.

Whether progress in this area is possible depends on whether a first framework consensus can be reached between Member States on these questions, which will be seen at the European Council in the future.

## Securing Free and Fair Elections to the European Parliament and in Member States

The European Commission has reacted swiftly to the new challenges, as identified in the Facebook Cambridge Analytica scandal. Its communication package of 12 September 2018 on 'Securing free and fair European Elections'[96] details a broad panoply of actions to secure the technical infrastructure for the elections, to ensure that personal data are not abused in the campaign and that propaganda and fake news are combated so as to avoid voters being intentionally misled. Many of the elements of this Communication are also relevant for elections at all levels in the Member State. The lessons which Member States will draw from protecting European elections in the application of the measures in this package will be extremely useful in protecting national elections.

While an important part of the Communication is an appeal to Member States and their authority to act, given the absence of EU competences, the Communication package also provides guidance on the relevance of EU law, for example in the area of data protection, to electoral campaigns.[97]

The Commission is also recommending greater transparency in online political advertisements and targeting. European and national political parties, foundations and campaign organisations should make available information on their expenditure on online advertising campaigns, by disclosing which party

[96] COM(2018) 637 final and the measures referred to therein.

[97] See on this the detailed guidance document of 12 September 2018, 'Free and Fair elections, Commission guidance on the application of Union data protection law in the electoral context' COM(2018) 638 final.

or political support group is behind online political advertisements as well as by publishing information on targeting criteria used to disseminate information to citizens. Where these principles are not followed, Member States should apply national sanctions.

The Commission for this purpose issued a Recommendation on election cooperation networks, online transparency, protection against cybersecurity incidents and fighting disinformation campaigns. National authorities, political parties and the media should take measures to protect their networks and information systems from cybersecurity threats, based on guidance developed by national authorities within the Network and Information Systems (NIS) cooperation group, with the EU Cybersecurity Agency and the European Commission Guidance on the application of EU data protection law.

A small change in the 2014 Regulation on party funding will make it possible to impose financial sanctions for breaching data protection rules in order to deliberately influence the outcome of the European elections. Sanctions would amount to 5 per cent of the annual budget of the European political party or foundation concerned. The sanction will be enforced by the Authority for European political parties and European political foundations. In addition, those found to be in breach would not be able to apply for funding from the general budget of the EU in the year in which the sanction is imposed. To keep up with the ever-evolving cyber threats, the Commission is proposing to create a Network of Cybersecurity Competence Centres to better target and coordinate available funding for cybersecurity cooperation, research and innovation. A new European Cybersecurity Competence Centre will manage cybersecurity-related financial support from the EU's budget and facilitate joint investment by the Union, Member States and industry to boost the EU's cybersecurity industry and make sure defence systems are state-of-the-art.[98]

While this package only addresses the latest, up-to-date challenges to free and fair elections made possible by new technologies of the internet and data processing, and thus is not a full guide to all important aspects for free and fair elections, it must be credited as the first document of the Commission which pulls together measures from different policy areas, dealt with in different Directorates-General of the Commission (DGs Connect, Home, Secretary General, Just) for the purposes of strengthening democracy within the EU.

As to other aspects of free and fair elections, the Commission has previously taken a position, for example, in the context of Citizens' Rights (Article 22 TFEU) and the related reports on European elections.

On more thorny issues, relating to activities of autocratic regimes, the Commission has officially been vocal when assessing democracy outside the EU, as in some

[98] This summary is taken from the press release of the package of proposals, IP/18/5681 of 12 September 2018.

developing countries or most recently in Turkey (Turkey Report of 2019),[99] and less so as to the situation within Member States, for example as regards the rules for TV political advertising in Hungary.[100]

In particular, the EU leaves election observation within its Member States to the Organization for Security and Co-operation in Europe,[101] while itself being the biggest donor to election observation worldwide.[102]

To conclude, while the package of the Commission on Free and Fair Elections is a good start and documents the relevance of secondary legislation in many areas to the good functioning of democracy also at the national level, it at the same time shows that a further consolidated and mainstream approach to democracy could yield important benefits for the Union.

## Freedom and Pluralism of the Press and Journalism

Traditionally, the EU emphasised media as a business, to be regulated as part of the Digital Single Market, rather than press and journalism as the vital Fourth Estate function of democracy. It is in this sense that the Commissioners and VPs responsible for DG CONNECT were in the lead on matters of the press and journalism, rather than the Commissioners dealing with freedom of speech, democracy and citizens' rights.

EU legislation affects the press and journalism in many ways, starting from the direct effects of legislation addressing media, such as the Audiovisual Services Directive, the Cable and Satellite Directive, the Copyright Directive, right through to legislation which may not mention media, but due to the convergence between internet and media may effectively influence the competitive position of media as compared with internet platforms.

This is the case, for example, in the e-Commerce Directive, which in its Article 13 privileges internet platforms by granting a limitation of liability for third-party content which is not available for third-party content on websites maintained by press and journalistic enterprises. This results in a costs advantage of 3–5 per cent for internet platforms, as internet platforms do not have to carry the costs of ex ante moderation of third-party content which is incumbent on press and journalistic websites.

There is EU legislation in many other areas which affects journalism and the press, ranging from the VAT rules for the printed and electronic press right through

[99] 2018 Turkey Report of 17 April 218, SWD (2018) 153 final, ch 2.1, 10 ff. See also: ec.europa.eu/europeaid/sectors/human-rights-and-democratic-governance/democracy_en; I Zamfir and A Dobreva, 'EU support to peace and democracy in the world' (October 2018) European Parliamentary Research Service PE 628.271.

[100] President Barroso in his speech of 2 July 2013 (Speech 13/608).

[101] See for an overview of forthcoming or recent election observation in EU Member States: www.osce.org/odihr/elections.

[102] See: eeas.europa.eu/topics/election-observation-missions-eueoms_en?page=1.

to the proposed rules on whistle-blower protection,[103] given that whistle-blowers are an important source of information for journalists.

Also, both the competition and State Aid rules of the Treaty have been applied to the press.[104]

And while the EU has not monitored or financed the monitoring of elections within its Member States, it has financed the monitoring of media pluralism and media freedom within the EU.[105]

The press obviously also has an important role to play in fighting fake news and foreign propaganda, a challenge which the Commission addressed recently in an action plan and with a voluntary code of conduct.[106]

Vital issues of press pluralism and journalistic freedom were discussed at the Annual Colloquium on Fundamental Rights of the Commission in 2016, and the Commission produced a detailed account of follow-up actions, based on the discussions.[107]

But since the Council Conclusions of 2013,[108] neither the Council nor the Commission have adopted an overarching, coherent policy on press and journalism in its Fourth Estate function in Europe in order to address the new challenges to freedom and pluralism of the press in Europe nor to put the challenges for the press into the context of the new challenges to democracy, and to draw the necessary policy consequences from this.

The mega trend of digitalisation and convergence between the internet and media has now led to a serious economic challenge to the free privately financed press and public broadcasting and this is compounded by the increasing grip on the press and broadcasting by populist governments. The Fourth Estate cannot be replaced or losses in its functionality compensated by the cacophony of the internet. For the sake of democracy in Europe, for which a vibrant Fourth Estate is vital, the Commission must invest in a new overall policy for the Fourth Estate, addressing all the new and old challenges in a new coherence with its policies for democracy, fundamental rights and the rule of law.

## Dialogue with Citizens and Public Consultations

The sense that the challenges of democracy in Europe must be addressed is omnipresent, both in society and politics. What characterises the Five Presidents'

[103] COM(2018) 218 final of 23 April 2018.

[104] See, as examples, the cases reported in the 'Annual Report on Competition' on 8 June 2018, COM(2018) 482 final, 7.

[105] See for details: ec.europa.eu/digital-single-market/en/policies/media-freedom-and-pluralism.

[106] See: ec.europa.eu/digital-single-market/en/fake-news-disinformation.

[107] See: ec.europa.eu/digital-single-market/en/news/european-commission-presents-follow-actions-fundamental-rights -colloquium-media-pluralism-and.

[108] Council conclusions and of the representatives of the Governments of the Member States, meeting within the Council, on media freedom and pluralism in the digital Environment, Education, Youth,

Report,[109] the Bratislava Declaration,[110] the Declaration of Rome,[111] and Juncker's White Paper on the future of Europe[112] is the knowledge that a continuation of the status quo will inevitably lead to disaster, and that change must be brought about as a Union. The EU is only strong enough to face internal and external pressures when it is a real *Union*. The heads of state and of the European institutions have reiterated their belief that the way forward must be determined together. Both the White Paper and the Declaration of Rome invite society to deliberate upon the future of the EU and the problems it currently faces. As the White Paper accurately points out, now is the time to remind ourselves of the values upon which the EU was founded and to reaffirm them. Redefining what democracy means, will enable us to mark out a path and a goal to strive for – an even stronger, more democratic Union.

As of December 2018, since the European Year of the Citizen in 2013, 160,000 citizens of all nationalities, ages, races, religions and from across the political spectrum have taken part in over 1,200 town hall style debates in city halls, universities, factories and other places all across the Union.[113]

Since January 2015, the current Commission has held 478 Citizens' Dialogues across all Member States, also in cooperation with institutional partners such as the European Parliament, national parliaments, the Committee of the Regions and the European Economic and Social Committee. Between February 2018 and 9 May 2019, the Commission intends to organise or support the organisation of around 500 additional Dialogues in cooperation with the Member States, regional, local authorities as well as with the European Parliament and other European institutions.

Several Member States have announced their readiness to engage in broad public discussions on the future of Europe, and such national dialogues are already taking place in a number of Member States. By engaging with citizens across Europe and holding outreach events, organised according to their respective political structures and practices, Member States could help raise awareness among citizens on the importance of their vote in determining which vision would best advance the European project. Such events should take place over the period between the Leaders' meeting of 23 February 2018 and the Summit in Sibiu on 9 May 2019, just ahead of the elections to the European Parliament, where heads

Culture and Sport Council meeting, Brussels, 25–26 November 2013, available at: www.consilium.europa.eu/uedocs/cms_data/docs/pressdata/en/educ/139725.pdf.

[109] 'Completing Europe's Economic and Monetary Union', report by Jean-Claude Juncker in close cooperation with Donald Tusk, Jeroen Dijsselbloem, Mario Draghi and Martin Schulz (22 June 2015).

[110] Bratislava (16 September 2016).

[111] Declaration of the leaders of 27 Member States and of the European Council, the European Parliament and the European Commission (25 March 2017).

[112] European Commission, 'Reflections and scenarios for the EU27 by 2025', COM (2017)2025 of 1 March 2017.

[113] Citizens' Dialogues and Citizens' Consultations, Progress report, December 2018, available at: ec.europa.eu/commission/sites/beta-political/files/eu-progress-report-consultations-111218_en.pdf.

of state or government are expected to draw conclusions on the next steps for the Union.[114]

While the Commission's efforts on consultation are important and its work has become increasingly transparent, there remain deficits on openness and transparency in the Council and also important deficits of the resourcing of Members of Parliament in terms of staff to assist them in their tasks. It is important for democracy in Europe that the Parliament becomes the centre of democratic debate and that it as an institution and its members are better equipped. The resourcing of central research and budget control services of the US Congress and the staffing of members of Congress in the US remain a good comparator.

As to the Commission, it needs to continue addressing the increasing imbalance between those interests which can afford a presence in Brussels and lobby intensely, and those which cannot. Much more must be done to go out to citizens not only in general dialogues, but to actively seek out interests concerned with specific legislation and invite citizens to enter into this dialogue and provide the assistance necessary for this purpose.

Transparency in consultation and dialogue is not enough; the Commission must get better in all policy areas in actively seeking a balanced picture of concerns and interests, and to proactively rebalance consultation outcomes where they are influenced by a difference in means of those concerned by the policies in question.

Consultations which are correct in process may be counterproductive in democracy, if people perceive that the complexity of the process or the substance simply does not allow them to participate in a meaningful manner. It is therefore important that the Commission develops a culture of reducing complexities and increasing accessibility of consultations also for those who will not take the initiative from their side to provide input, but who must be actively approached. This requires in particular a greater human effort from the Commission and meaningful engagement in dialogue at all levels, as well as a serious and regular check on whether electronic ways of public consultation actually allow for meaningful dialogue at all.

Engaging the College and all levels of staff of the Commission in an exercise of searching out meaningful dialogue and consultation with the public right from the beginning of the mandate, will in turn also increase sensitivity on all levels for public interests and thus overall broaden the skills of the Commission from technocratic charisma (Catherine Day)[115] to also include more political and technocratic wisdom which the Commission needs as an institution to succeed.

To close, all EU institutions must take care not to be captured by commercial consultancies but actively seek input from independent academia, where they exist. The question of the independence of academia is key for democracy, not only

[114] See recitals of the 2018 Commission Recommendation on the European Elections, above n 39.

[115] Catherine Day is a former Secretary-General of the European Commission. Appointed in November 2005 she served two terms with President Jose Manuel Barroso and continued with his successor, Jean-Claude Juncker, until she retired in September 2015.

independence towards the state (see Hungary) but also towards commercial interests. It is important that EU policies help to secure independence of academia and that the Commission, in all policy fields, complements general public consultations with a regular, public-interest oriented and nurturing dialogue with independent academia.

# Sources of Inspiration and Possible Content of a European Democracy Charter

## Constitutional Law and Practice of the EU and EU Member States

Before we address the question of sources for work on a European Democracy Charter, let it be clear that the work on an EUDC itself will be an important source of inspiration for practical understanding and learning on democracy. This journey of discovery and comparison will, as in the case of the Conventions on the Treaties and the Fundamental Rights Charter, be a key effect of work on an EUDC, first informally, then on the level of the EU institutions and eventually, if necessary, in a Convention preparing a text for a possible Treaty change. It will start a broad debate and reflection and serve the purpose of invigorating democracy by involving many in the common process of discovery, learning and constitutional debate. This is the primary purpose of the first stage of work on the EUDC, and whether treaty changes in the ever more democratic EU are necessary in the form of the EUCD (rather than in a more chirurgical, smaller intervention, limited for example only to the governance of the Eurozone and a few other issues, such as the effectiveness of Article 7 EU) can remain open. One also does not exclude the other over time.

Work on the EUDC will be the occasion to discuss questions like the advantage of representative democracy in an ever more complex world and on the scale of the EU (as compared to Switzerland), right through to the relevance of the development of technologies for democracy and what impact they may have on the formulation of rules for democracy and democratic practice.

Importantly, however, many of the challenges to democracy in Europe and in the Member States, as discussed above, can be addressed on the level of secondary law and do not need a treaty change. It is vital that the work on these challenges, as well as the general mainstreaming of all policies for democracy by the Commission, go ahead in parallel with the preparatory work on the EUDC. And again, the debates on the EUDC will inspire discovery of such possibilities to strengthen democracy in Europe, on the EU level and in Member States, via secondary law.

Turning now to the sources of inspiration. A first step of the work would simply be to collect the information on the varied texts and practices of democracy in the

EU and in the Member States. On the level of the EU, there are detailed texts on democracy in the area of international relations and development aid, as well as assessments of candidate countries, and the content of treaties and secondary law relevant to democracy is, in the case of the institutions, further detailed by inter-institutional agreements and rules of procedure as well as practice. There is also an important body of jurisprudence on democratic principle by the Court of Justice, such as on the limits of delegated law-making.[116]

The work on the EUDC will thus first be a work of collection, codification and consolidation on the level of the EU.

Then there are the similar texts and practices as well as judgments, much richer and much more elaborate on democracy and its principles, on the level of Member States. The schools of comparative constitution studies and comparative election law and parliamentary law will have important contributions to make, including on the common practices among Member States and on best practice.

There will certainly also be important learning in the comparative history of constitution-making and the materials documenting the preparatory work and debates for important constitutions of the Member States and third countries with great histories of democracy, like that of the United States.

And it is possible to draw on a newer body of materials, namely universal and regional democracy documents, to which we will now turn our attention.

## Examples of Universal and Regional Democracy Documents

The massive human rights violations – especially during the Second World War – led to the adoption of the Universal Declaration of Human Rights by the UN General Assembly in 1948. This was followed by the creation of many human rights conventions in the following decades. In a similar way it can be observed that, after 1990, the worldwide challenges to democracy have led to the adoption of a number of democracy documents in many regions of the world. Overall, there are more than a dozen fully-fledged democracy charters.

The existence of the manifold challenges described above warrants turning our attention to some of these landmark democracy documents, which address similar challenges. Broadly speaking, there are two types of universal and regional democracy document. First, there are those that have a comprehensive approach combining many topics that are directly relevant for democracy. The second group comprises concrete issue-related democracy texts that address very specific themes like, for example, the rights and duties of the opposition in Parliament or that set out criteria for free and fair elections. For this analysis, the first group

[116] See Case C-355/10 *European Parliament v Council* EU:C:2012:516, para 64 ff, with further precedents and Cases C-293/12 and 594/12 *Digital Rights Ireland* EU:C:2014:238, para 54 ff.

is particularly interesting.[117] To this category belongs, for instance, the 'Universal Declaration on Democracy' (1997) of the Inter-Parliamentary Union (IPU), which formulates the common aspirations of the international parliamentary community.

Apart from this, there are also very prominent regional democracy texts. On the African continent the 'African Charter on Democracy, Elections and Governance', adopted by the Assembly of the African Union (AU), in Addis Ababa (Ethiopia), on 30 January 2007, is surely the most important one. It is a formal international treaty, which entered into force on 15 February 2012 and is currently binding on 31 AU member states.[118] Definitely less well known than the AU Democracy Charter, but nevertheless of high sub-regional importance are the 'Protocol A/SP1/12/01 on Democracy and Good Governance' (2001) of the Economic Community of West African States (ECOWAS) as well as the 'International Conference on the Great Lakes Region Protocol on Democracy and Good Governance' (2006), which entered into force on 20 February 2008 and 21 June 2008 respectively. Also, these two protocols are legally binding instruments relating to democracy.[119] A dominant founding idea for the adoption of these African democracy documents was surely to stabilise the often fragile African democracies. This interpretation is also reflected in the fourth preamble consideration of the ICGLR Democracy Protocol, which blames 'the accumulated deficits in the matter of democratisation' as an 'origin of the conflicts in the Great Lakes Region'.

Further examples of regional documents can be found in the Americas. Among the binding treaty instruments, in particular four documents which specifically address the topic of democracy have to be highlighted. The first is the 'Framework Treaty on Democratic Security in Central America', adopted by the Central American Integration System (SICA) in 1995. The second important treaty is the 'Ushuaia Protocol on Democratic Commitment in the Southern Common Market, the Republic of Bolivia and the Republic of Chile' of 1998. Thirdly, the Additional Protocol to the Cartagena Agreement 'ANDEAN Community Commitment to Democracy' of 10 June 2000 must be mentioned in this context, which in fact, is very similar to the Ushuaia Protocol. Finally, the 'Additional Protocol to the Constitutive Treaty of the Union of South American Nations on Commitment to Democracy' of 2010 belongs to the 'contractual documents', which entered into force on 19 March 2014 and reiterates – like other texts mentioned above – the organisation's commitment to democracy and its condemnation of any unconstitutional means of overthrowing the government. However, although these

[117] All documents mentioned on the following pages are printed in F Ehm and C Walter (eds), *International Democracy Documents: A Compilation of Treaties and Other Instruments* (Leiden, Brill, 2015).

[118] See the list of countries which have signed, ratified/acceded to the African Charter on Democracy, Elections and Governance, on 10 May 2018, available at: au.int/sites/default/files/treaties/7790-sl-african_charter_on_democracy_elections_and_governance.pdf.

[119] See F Ehm, *Das völkerrechtliche Demokratiegebot – Eine Untersuchung zur schwindenden Wertneutralität des Völkerrechts gegenüber den staatlichen Binnenstrukturen* (Tübingen, Mohr Siebeck, 2013) 46, 48.

four documents are proper international treaties, the most popular, important and comprehensive democracy document on the American double-continent is the 'Inter-American Democratic Charter', which was adopted on 11 September 2001 by a special session of the General Assembly of the Organization of American States (OAS), held in Lima, Peru. Last but not least, one further example for a 'comprehensive democracy document' can be mentioned, which is the 'SAARC[120] Charter of Democracy' of February 2011.[121]

However, with regard to these documents it must be underlined – although seven of them are classical international treaties and three are merely soft-law approaches to democracy of a political rather than a legal nature – that there is the open question of implementation and that these documents have of to be course interpreted in different cultural contexts. Therefore, caution is needed and an over-optimistic assessment concerning their practical impact should be avoided.

Apart from this point, these 10 documents that have 'democracy' as their principal theme, address for example – mostly in separate chapters or sections – the following topics: (1) the definition of democracy/the principles of democracy; (2) democratic institutions; (3) the international dimension of democracy; (4) the triangle of democracy, rule of law and human rights; (5) the promotion of a democratic culture/education; (6) democratic elections; (7) election monitoring; (8) urgent measures and sanctions in case of threats or breakdown of democracy; (9) the role of the armed forces, the police and the security forces in a democracy; and (10) some final clauses.[122]

## Possible Content of a European Democracy Charter

The challenges to democracy in Europe described above and the mere existence of the above-mentioned democracy documents in other regions of the world, are reason enough to consider the creation of an EUDC. This question is even more self-evident, when we bear in mind that the only EU document that solely addresses democracy on the highest level is the 'Declaration on democracy', adopted by the European Council in Copenhagen on 7–8 April 1978, which comprises only six paragraphs. One obvious explanation for this rather moderate result is that the field of activity of the EU is – in comparison to all other international organisations – very broad, and that, of course, the Treaties contain numerous operational provisions of practical relevance for a functioning democracy, which are further specific in secondary law, as discussed above. The principle of democracy is thus explicit not only in Article 2 TEU and in its 'provisions on democratic

[120] SAARC stands for 'South Asian Association for Regional Cooperation' which is a political and economic international organisation comprising eight countries that was formed on 8 December 1985.

[121] For more background information about these documents, see Ehm and Walter, above n 117, 253 ff.

[122] With regard to some of these issues, see Ehm and Walter, above n 117, 12 ff.

principles' (Title II, Articles 9–12) but also in the provisions on the institutions in the Treaties, the Charter and in secondary law.

The EUDC could help to effectively address the many challenges to democracy on the EU level, within the Member States, and in relations between the EU and Member States. As to the issues arising in the third group, a key question is whether, without touching the division of competences between the EU and Member States, the EUDC could add value by setting out principles and processes on how to articulate democratic process on both levels in mutual respect and within the existing competence distribution.

Against this background, the following part will discuss some selected elements such a document could address, in addition to those already discussed.

With regard to the content of an EUDC, the starting point should be a provision that concisely defines the core elements and the common denominator of European democracy that build on Article 2 TEU. Generally speaking the concept of 'democracy' refers to the involvement of citizens in political decision-making and its core is based on consensus. A feasible *definition of democracy* is something which is often missing in many of the documents mentioned above,[123] which already shows how difficult it is to consolidate all the differing conceptions. However, a starting point for finding a European definition of democracy could be its intrinsic element, ie, the 'majority rule', which had been included in the first Draft Preamble of the European Constitution, and which, on the European level, has to rely both on some majority of Member States and some majority of the population, in order to also take account of the federal nature of the EU (presently set at 55 per cent and 65 per cent respectively – see Article 16 TEU).

Furthermore, one should take into account the international core consensus concerning this term. A comparative look at all relevant international democracy documents reveals six general principles for a democratic government: (1) human rights; (2) free and fair elections; (3) the rule of law; (4) a multi-party system; (5) the separation of powers; and (6) an independent judiciary.[124] However, the EU could never be content with such a 'skeletal structure definition' and it has to go – also due to its self-conception – beyond this. Simultaneously, it must be underlined that these principles are already extremely vague and open to different interpretations.[125] This being said, as outlined above, there is already a substantial body of concretisations through secondary law, practice and jurisprudence in these areas.

On the other hand, we also need a generally understandable definition that speaks to the people and has integrative capacity. A paradigmatic phrase for this is that democracy is safeguarded as long as it is 'a social structure open to change and

[123] See also Ehm and Walter, above n 117, 12 ff.
[124] Ehm and Walter, above n 117, 22.
[125] For a similar conclusion see N Petersen, *Demokratie als teleologisches Prinzip* (Heidelberg, Springer, 2009) 124 ff.

novelty, and yet preserving its own basic character'.[126] By defining the minimum requirements for a functioning pluralist democracy, the definition could serve as a new legal benchmark for the Court to assess possible democracy threats, and thus strengthen the capacity of the EU to ensure, through the concept of preserving the basic character, effective and equal protection of democracy in all Member States.[127] It could be the concrete expression of the EU maturing as a democratic constitutional system, based on common EU values.

The functioning of the EP could be improved by political practice based on existing rules, by ensuring stable democratic majorities through the development of a coalition agreement culture capable of hammering out compromises with the Council.

The use of the threshold for the allocation of seats at national level can serve as an important means to this effect.

Of the 28 Member States, only 12 have established an electoral threshold for the allocations of seats in the EP,[128] and in some it is being challenged before the national courts – with divergent results. On 26 February 2014, the German Federal Constitutional Court had found the country's 3 per cent minimum threshold unconstitutional[129] while, in a ruling handed down on 1 June 2015, the Czech Supreme Administrative Court upheld the applicable threshold of 5 per cent.[130] The Constitutional Court in Italy has also been called upon to decide on the legitimacy of the 4 per cent threshold in the elections to the EP. The case is still pending.

Needless to say, promoting this threshold becomes increasingly important in the light of the significant role the Parliament now plays in ensuring a stable executive through the election of the President and the Commission, but also through its power to censure and through its co-decision and budgetary powers. It is now no longer correct to state that in practice there is no need for a threshold, as the Parliament does not have the function of electing and supporting a stable executive.

The EP has been conducting its own reflection on the reform of the electoral law of the EU with a view to 'Europeanise' European elections and the aim of introducing more harmonisation of electoral systems in Member States.[131] While

[126] Z Barbu, *Democracy and Dictatorship: Their Psychology and Patterns of Life* (New York, Routledge and Kegan Paul, 1956) 4.

[127] See ideas about an analogous function of a possible 'Copenhagen Charter', cited in B Bugarič, 'Protecting Democracy and the Rule of Law in the European Union: The Hungarian Challenge' (2014) LEQS Paper No 79/2014, 30–31.

[128] The thresholds mostly vary between 3% and 5%. See U Bux, 'The European Parliament: Electoral Procedures' (2018) 2 *Fact Sheets on the European Union* 2.

[129] Judgment of the German Federal Constitutional Court of 26 February 2014 (file reference 2 BvE 2/13 u.a. – 2 BvR 2220/13).

[130] Press release (in Czech), file reference: Pl. ÚS 14/14.

[131] See the report of the extraordinary AFCO committee, Brussels, 1 October 2015 (OR. en), 12501/15.

many of these reflections were not taken up in the latest 2018 amendment of the 1976 Election Act, many remain valid for the future work on the EUDC.

To make the EP the core of a real European parliamentary democracy it will be inevitable to further increase co-decisions and make this procedure the norm.

Some claim the EP should have the right to initiate laws (as in the Member States where the legislative initiative is usually shared between Parliament and the executive). The argument is that the legislative initiative of the EP is needed to counterbalance the power of the Council and to correct its initiatives. In addition, it offers all political groups in the EP a way of emphasising their own political orientations.[132] However, reality shows that legislative initiatives of Member States in the Council are rare and even rarer is their success. The Community method of entrusting the independent European Commission, which only has a duty towards the European interest, with a monopoly of initiative has demonstrated its value. With the powers of appointment, co-decision, budget approval and control and censure, the Parliament has power over the Commission to ensure that it follows its orientation, including on important legislative initiatives.

Another change that could be envisaged in the perspective of strengthening European democracy would concern the selection process for party candidates for election to the EP. There is a perception that national politicians may exert pressure on MEPs, who can be 'the weakest links', particularly in cases where places on the list are given as 'gifts' by the party leaders.[133]

An avenue to explore would be to provide for a 'normal' political career for MEPs. They would first perform well as legislators and could then have the opportunity to move into the Commission, in the same way that national MPs learn their business in politics before they, if an opportunity arises, take on functions in the executive. The powers of the President in the selection of Members of the Commission and the organisational powers within the present statute of personnel for the institutions would allow the implementation of a clear orientation that a certain percentage of Members of the College must have experience in the European Parliament and that in every Directorate-General and/or Cabinet, there shall be at least one political civil servant, at thus director level or above, with a background in the EP, functioning along the model of Parliamentary State Secretaries in Germany. Proceeding in this way would acquire important political capital for the Commission, stabilise the relation with the Parliament and, as a trickle-down effect, most likely increase the interest in a career as an MEP, in comparison to the present situation in which being an MEP is often – although much less than in the past – the end of a political career. It would also be a certain counterbalance to the increasing presence, in the staff of the Commission, of civil servants with a

[132] European Commission for Democracy through Law (Venice Commission), comments on legislative initiative in Europe, by Sergio Bartole (Member, Italy), Strasbourg, 30 September 2008, Study No 446 / 2007, *cf* p 2.

[133] See Priestley, above n 40, 4.

strong background in the national government, thus on the executive and Member State side, rather than on the EU and parliamentary side.

Also, as regards some of the classic issues, long discussed, such as the transparency of the Council and the role of European political parties, the EUDC process could be helpful. One can very well imagine that an EUDC never becomes law, but still codifies certain best practices, such as relating to *Spitzenkandidaten* or in the areas just mentioned, and in doing so makes an important contribution to stabilising democracy in Europe. The same could be true as regards democracy in Member States, for which the EUDC could already be of help if it just were an aid to interpretation of the meaning of democracy in Article 2 TEU, and not only when it comes to Article 7 procedures.

There has been a rich discussion in academic circles about ways to further refine and strengthen the current powers of the EU to uphold the rule of law, democracy and fundamental rights, for instance, by setting up a 'Copenhagen Commission', which should continuously assesses democracy and the rule of law within Member States.[134] Another proposal would be to allow national courts in a situation when human rights are systemically violated in the respective Member State (and this will always have a severe effect on democracy), to invite the CJEU to consider the legality of national actions in the light of Article 2 TEU.[135] There are many more proposals addressing this issue, ranging from the most radical to the least far-reaching.[136]

A detailed 'EUDC democracy protection mechanism' could eventually complement Article 7 TEU and widen its applicability. Due to the fact of so-called 'anti-democratic pinprick tactics' in some EU Member States this mechanism should, inter alia, be applicable if a critical mass of single anti-democratic events has been exceeded ('Critical Mass Theory'). If the conclusion is that a critical mass has been reached, a warning could be issued and eventually sanctions could be applied.

To address these issues in an EUDC would raise awareness and create positive pressure to act on the stakeholders concerned. At the same time, it would mean to start doing the homework that in any event needs to be done, but in an integrated way, and with a view to the full picture and not by closing loopholes and acting only on emergencies.

[134] See JW Müller, 'Safeguarding Democracy inside the EU, Brussels and the Future of Liberal Order' (2013) Transatlantic Academy Paper Series.

[135] A von Bogdandy et al, 'Reverse Solange: Protecting the Essence of Fundamental Rights against EU Member States' (2012) 49 *Common Market Law Review* 489 ff.

[136] For an overview, see D Kochenov and L Pech, 'Upholding the Rule of Law in the EU: On the Commission's "Pre-Article 7 Procedure" as a Timid Step in the Right Direction' (2015) 356 Robert Schuman Foundation Policy Paper, 7 ff.

# Conclusions and Outlook: Daring More Democracy in Europe and an EU Democracy Charter

In his famous speech before the German Bundestag in 1969, Chancellor Willy Brandt said, 'we want to dare more democracy'.[137] The speech of the Chancellor came at a time, when right-wing extremism was on the rise. For the first time since the end of the Second World War, a far-right party, the National Democratic Party of Germany (NPD), only very narrowly missed entering the German Parliament with 4.3 per cent of the votes. In conjunction with the first big economic crisis in 1966/1967, the political landscape partly resembled that of today. The promise of Chancellor Brandt to dare more democracy came as a response to the German student movement of the 1960s, when students began protesting against what they perceived as the authoritarian structures of the German state and the discrepancies between the rapid growth of the German economy and wealth after the War in relation to the comparative stagnation of social values. The students demanded more individual rights and social democracy. This translated into them pressing for reform of the political structures and the education system, for more co-determination at universities, emancipation of women and a break with traditional authoritarian education measures. After the student movements reached their height in 1968, the new social-liberal coalition government managed to channel the movement, on multiple levels. The government introduced many pro-democratic reforms in different areas of life. The voting age was reduced from 21 to 18 in 1972. More universities were created, and many reforms introduced. Students were given more participation and self-determination in university structures. Workers were given more rights of co-determination with a reform of the Works Council Constitution Act in 1972.[138] Another huge leap for workers' rights was taken with the introduction of the co-determination law in 1976[139] which ensured that democracy does not end at the door of the big enterprises. While highly contested, the law was deemed as constitutional by the German Constitutional Court in the same year.[140] The Court confirmed the principle of co-determination and thereby introduced the idea of the economic neutrality of the Constitution and the equality of capital and work. In the 1970s, anti-democratic tendencies and general dissatisfaction were very successfully combated by the German government with the revival of democratic spirit across all layers of society and within many sectoral policies, from the economy right through to education. The policy was not only to create individual rights, but also organisational structures to empower people to

[137] Government Declaration of Federal Chancellor Willy Brandt before the German Bundestag in Bonn on 28 October 1969.

[138] Official German title: Betriebsverfassungsgesetz (BetrVG).

[139] Official German title: Gesetz über die Mitbestimmung der Arbeitnehmer (Mitbestimmungsgesetz – MitbestG).

[140] BVerfGE 50, 290.

jointly exercise these rights or delegate the exercise to the new bodies thus created, such as works councils or student councils. Routes of engagement for people were opened which were more than just consultation or exercise of defensive rights. These structures created a new balance of power in society and encouraged people to engage, in different ways, in democratic processes. European can learn from this history of democracy as much as it can learn from Weimar.

The question of balance of power is again on the table today, with the concentration of power in the hands of a few digital mega corporations. And so are proposals to extend co-determination in Europe, as a visible increase of democracy, and capitalising on the empiric reality that where people have co-determination rights in their work, they are less likely to vote for populists with autocratic tendencies.[141]

In this day and age, Europe needs to 'Dare more democracy' and continue on its way to be a democracy that defends itself, just like at the time of Brandt 'Mehr Demokratie wagen' and 'Wehrhafte Demokratie', while avoiding its pitfalls.[142]

As in time of Brandt, strong political will, leadership and readiness to innovate is now necessary on the side of the next Commission, to intensify the commitment of the Juncker Commission to democracy with a multitude of new actions. These actions should include a general democracy mainstreaming and a distinctive programme of actions for democracy to be implemented within the mandate.

The Commission could in this work also draw on the results of the annual colloquium of the Commission on Fundamental Rights in November 2018 which was focused on 'Democracy in the EU'. The colloquium aimed to reaffirm that democracy is a central value common to the EU and all its Member States and looked at how to renew democratic engagement within the EU and European societies.[143]

[141] Aufsichtsräte – Mehr Mitbestimmung wagen, Detlef Esslinger, SZ, 24 Mai 2018, available at: sz.de/1.3991244.

[142] A key action of 'Wehrhafte Demokratie' under Willy Brandt was the much-contested order against radicals from the left and the right in public service of 28 January 1972, available at: www.1000dokumente.de/index.html?c=dokument_de&dokument=0113_ade&object=translation&st=&l=de. On this, see Wissenschaftlicher Dienst des Deutschen Bundestages 2017, Parlamentarische und zivilgesellschaftliche Initiativen zur Aufarbeitung des sogenannten Radikalenerlasses vom 28. Januar 1972, Ausarbeitung WD 1 – 3000 – 012/17, available at: www.bundestag.de/blob/531136/a0a150d89d4db6c2bdae0dd5b300246d/wd-1-012-17-pdf-data.pdf; and more recently the translation of 'Wehrhafte Demokratie' as 'militant democracy' in the press release of the German Constitutional Court on an order rejecting constitutional complaints against prohibitions of associations. This order recounts in part the history of 'Wehrhafte Demokratie' and the lack of it in the Weimar Republic, German Constitutional Court, press release no 69/2018 of 21 August 2018 on the Order of 13 July 2018 1 BvR 1474/12, 1 BvR 57/14, 1 BvR 670/13, available at: www.bundesverfassungsgericht.de/SharedDocs/Pressemitteilungen/EN/2018/bvg18-069.html.

[143] See: ec.europa.eu/info/events/annual-colloquium-fundamental-rights/2018-annual-colloquium-fundamental-rights-2018-nov-26_en.

It could also draw on the non-legislative resolution, adopted by the European Parliament on 10 June 2015, in which the Commission is asked

> to present a proposal for the establishment of an EU mechanism on democracy, the rule of law and fundamental rights … to carry out an impartial, yearly assessment on the situation of fundamental rights, democracy and the rule of law in all Member States […] and […] in order to fill existing gaps and to allow for an automatic and gradual response to breaches of the rule of law and fundamental rights at Member State level.[144]

But the new Commission should also bring forward work towards a European Charter of Democracy, using the tried and tested methodology which led to the adoption of the Charter of Fundamental Rights, to produce a major document, that contains a clear and visible commitment of the EU to democratic values and that addresses the challenges to democracy in the EU, in the Member States and between them, and potentially complements the European legal framework in the long run.

This would not be a new start, but rather an important contribution to strengthen democracy in Europe, based on the great history of success of the progress of democracy, and in the light of President Juncker's emphasis on a Union of Democratic Change and Democracy as a priority of the European Commission.

[144] Para 12 European Parliament resolution of 10 June 2015 on the situation in Hungary (2015/2700(RSP)), P8_TA-PROV(2015)0227, Situation in Hungary; see also EP Press release, Hungary: MEPs condemn Orbán's death penalty statements and migration survey, Plenary sessions [10 June 2015 – 13:26].

# 19

# The Principle of Legality and the EU's Legitimacy as a Constitutional Democracy: A Research Agenda

SACHA GARBEN*

## Introduction: The Principle of Legality in Constitutional Democracy

The principle of legality is 'a cherished foundation'[1] of a democracy based on the rule of law, especially as understood in certain traditions of continental[2] European constitutional law, where it requires not just that authority is exercised on the basis of, and in compliance with (the relevant hierarchy of) legal norms (and, following the closely related principle of judicial protection, reviewable as such), but furthermore that such authority is exercised on the basis of parliamentary legislation, especially where it affects fundamental rights.[3] Understood as such, the principle is core to the very idea of constitutional democracy, as it serves the principle of constitutionalism and the principle of popular sovereignty in equal measure.[4] Contrary to perhaps a more colloquial understanding, and Kelsenian positivism,[5]

* The views expressed are personal and do not represent those of the European Commission.

[1] L Besselink, F Pennings and S Prechal, 'Introduction: Legality in Multiple Legal Orders' in L Besselink, F Pennings and S Prechal (eds), *The Eclipse of the Legality Principle in the European Union* (Alphen aan de Rijn, Kluwer Law International, 2011) 5.

[2] As explained by Besselink et al, this 'democratic' notion of legality is very much connected to the French Revolution and a reaction against the law-making role of the courts, an experience not as such shared by the common law. Nevertheless, they point out, 'the British courts and legal doctrine would fully assent to the principle that the liberty of citizens can only be restricted by act of parliament': Besselink, Pennings and Prechal, above n 1, 6.

[3] L Besselink, 'Conclusion: The Eclipse of Legality: An Assessment' in L Besselink, F Pennings and S Prechal, (eds), *The Eclipse of the Legality Principle in the European Union* (Alphen aan de Rijn, Kluwer Law International, 2011).

[4] See on constitutional democracy and the argument that a legitimate government is one that respects both principles equally J Tully, 'The Unfreedom of the Moderns in Comparison to their Ideals of Constitutional Democracy' (2002) 65 *Modern Law Review* 204.

[5] H Kelsen, *General Theory of Law and State* (New Jersey, The Lawbook Exchange, 2007) 117.

legality in this sense requires more than (the enforcement of) mere *lawfulness* (ie, a compliance with the applicable set of rules of a given polity), because it additionally requires democratic decision-making and is linked to a respect of human rights. As such, the principle of legality 'reinforces democracy' as it 'requires that all legal authority come only from the elected branch, in other words the legislature'.[6] By combining requirements of constitutionalism and democracy, the principle of legality could therefore provide a robust, multifaceted conception of the *legitimacy* of the exercise of public authority, and therewith a meaningful analytical yardstick for the assessment of some of the central questions that we want to know about a political organisation, both as legal scholars and political scientists.

The principle thus holds great analytical potential, which makes it remarkable that it has not been widely used as a lens of enquiry in EU legal studies.[7] This neglect may be due to the fact that the principle is not clearly and consistently defined within and between European legal systems, with differing views especially on its democratic component.[8] The legality principle may furthermore suffer some competition from its 'big brother': the rule of law. The latter is often defined as a (much) broader notion that encompasses legality (in the sense of lawfulness or indeed 'including a transparent, accountable and democratic process for enacting law'),[9] alongside other principles such as legal certainty and access to justice.[10] Perhaps increasingly in a transnational context, the rule of law is interpreted as the overarching concept comprising all elements of constitutionalism, including the respect for fundamental rights and other principles of law.[11] As such, some will consider the rule of law the more appropriate anchor point to contain and assess legitimacy claims. This would also find some textual support in EU primary law, which refers to 'legality' only in reference to judicial review by the Court of Justice of the European Union (CJEU)[12] and in the Charter of Fundamental Rights to its

[6] C Gearty, *Principles of Human Rights Adjudication* (Oxford, Oxford University Press, 2004) 88.

[7] Important exceptions are, inter alia, Besselink, Pennings and Prechal, above n 1 and N Lupo and G Piccirilli, 'The Relocation of the Legality Principle by the European Courts' Case Law: An Italian Perspective' (2015) 11 *European Constitutional Law Review* 55.

[8] Lupo and Piccirilli, above n 7, 57–60.

[9] European Commission for Democracy through Law (Venice Commission), Rule of Law Checklist, Adopted 11–12 March 2016, Council of Europe, available at: www.venice.coe.int/images/SITE%20IMAGES/Publications/Rule_of_Law_Check_List.pdf. Note however that this democratic element of the rule of law remains somewhat underdeveloped in the approach by the Venice Commission, which considers that 'Rule of Law promotes democracy by establishing accountability of those wielding public power and by safeguarding human rights, which protect minorities against arbitrary majority rules' rather than emphasizing the necessary democratic elements of the law-making (or, decision-making) procedures.

[10] L Pech, 'A Union Founded on the Rule of Law: Meaning and Reality of the Rule of Law as a Constitutional Principle of EU Law' (2010) 6 *European Constitutional Law Review* 359.

[11] The so-called 'substantive school' of 'thick' theories of the rule of law. See R Peerenboom, 'Varieties of Rule of Law. An Introduction and Provisional Conclusion' in R Peerenboom (ed), *Asian Discourses of Rule of Law* (London, Routledge, 2004) 2–10; B Tamanaha, *On the Rule of Law* (Cambridge, Cambridge University Press, 2004) 92; Pech, above n 10; A Arnull, 'The Rule of Law in the European Union' in A Arnull and D Wincott (eds), *Accountability and Legitimacy in the European Union* (Oxford, Oxford University Press, 2002) 254.

[12] Art 263 TFEU.

specific manifestation of *nulla poene sine lege*,[13] while it mentions the rule of law as a foundational principle.[14] The Court has furthermore adopted a substantive approach, holding that the EU is a 'community based on the rule of law in which its institutions are subject to judicial review of the compatibility of their acts with the Treaty and with the general principles of law which include fundamental rights'.[15] This comprehensive notion of the rule of law could thus comprise democracy as a general principle of law, as well as fundamental rights. Would this not, then, serve the same analytical purpose as the principle of legality as proposed here? While not dismissing the rule of law as a productive lens of enquiry,[16] we would argue that the principle of legality offers some distinct advantages. In particular, the dialectic relationship between constitutionalism and democracy can be better explored in the context of legality: in the rule of law, the principle of democracy would be only one of the many general principles of law to be respected, whereas the principle of legality rests on two pillars of which democracy is one and constitutionalism the other. This is not without consequence, because this equal value attached to constitutionalism and democracy as inherent in the very principle of legality itself, allows a more refined development of the interaction between constitutionalism and democracy, defining the situations in which these principles have to be enforced against each other and in what way – as we shall see further below. Furthermore, there does not seem to be any definitive reason why the legality principle, rather than the rule of law, could not be conceptualised as the single overarching notion that encompasses the rule of law as part of the principle of constitutionalism on the one hand, and the principle of democracy on the other. This would make the principle of legality not just *an* expression of constitutional democracy, but *the* expression of it. Finally, legality's traditional emphasis on parliament as the holder of democratic authority, rather than on a more general principle of democracy, places the most important democratic challenge of transnational government at the centre of attention.

It could be precisely because parliamentary sovereignty has been a sore spot in European integration,[17] that the democratic aspect of the legality principle has not been considered a productive analytical yardstick for the EU. Perhaps it would test a foregone conclusion: by entailing a transfer of national power to the European level the EU necessarily challenges national democratic legality[18] and as a polity

[13] Art 49 EU Charter.

[14] Preamble of the EU Charter and the TEU, Art 2 TEU.

[15] Case C-50/00 P *Unión de Pequeños Agricultores* EU:C:2002:462, para 38.

[16] See for instance Pech, above n 10.

[17] As Adam Cygan explores in ch 15 of this book, the EU is widely associated with a de-parliamentarisation of decision-making, which however seems not limited to the EU.

[18] See the case law of the German Constitutional Court on European integration. See also L Lindseth, 'Delegation is Dead, Long Live Delegation: Managing the Democratic Disconnect in the European Market-Polity' in C Joerges and R Dehousse (eds), *Good Governance in Europe's Integrated Market* (Oxford, Oxford University Press, 2002) 151; PL Lindseth, *Power and Legitimacy. Reconciling Europe and Nation-State* (Oxford, Oxford University Press, 2010) 234.

in its own right the EU has traditionally featured a relatively low parliamentary participation in decision-making. However, any suspicion that the EU may not easily pass the legality test is not an intellectual justification to disregard it.[19] While it is a fair point, made in various other contributions to this volume,[20] that the EU should not be condemned for failing to live up to idealised national standards, this does not mean that any legitimacy standard developed in a national context and that the EU might find hard to meet is unsuitable as an angle of examination. Provided that the requirements of the concept of legality are (re-)interpreted to accommodate transnational democratic and cosmopolitan justice concerns, there is no reason why the EU – as the world's most accomplished feat of supranational constitutional democracy – should not be expected to comply with the principle of legality comprising both its constitutional and democratic requirements. Moreover, beyond any narrow assessment of 'compatibility', this chapter argues that the principle of legality holds important potential to be developed into a guiding legitimacy framework for the EU. It can serve to operationalise constitutional democracy in a legal sense, for scholars and practitioners. It offers particular promise in how it allows a constructive definition of the interrelation between democratic decision-making and constitutionalism, yielding analytical yardsticks that can be applied to the EU's exercise of authority to assess (and guide) its legitimacy. More concretely, it will be argued that the CJEU could adopt the principle of legality as an overarching doctrine for its judicial review of both EU and national action.

## The Principle of Legality Operationalised

In this section, a tentative interpretation of the legality principle will be proposed that would allow its application as a framework for legitimacy for the EU. A point of departure is Tully's interpretation of constitutional democracy (drawing on the work of Habermas and Rawls) that requires respect for the principle of constitutionalism and the principle of popular sovereignty in equal measure.[21] Perhaps

[19] If anything, it forces us to face this conundrum and the engage with it. As Lupo and Piccirilli state, we need to rethink the linkages between supranational norm-production and democratic legitimation derived from the national level: Lupo and Piccirilli, above n 7, 60.

[20] See in particular the chapters by Daniel Kelemen (ch 3) and Paul Nemitz (ch 18).

[21] Tully, above n 4, 207, stating: 'two principles are "equiprimordial". They are equally basic. If the principle of constitutionalism gains priority over the principle of democracy, so the constitution is the foundation of democratic rights and institutions but is not itself subject to democratic deliberation, then the association is illegitimate. Politics is said to be reduced to "juridification" and to suffer a "democratic deficit", as, for example, in the European Union or in forms of liberalism that place the constitution prior to and independent of the practices of democratic dispute and amendment. If, conversely, the democratic principle gains priority, then the association is said to be illegitimate because it is "a tyranny of the majority", without rules and procedures, or the licentious experience of "empty willing"'. As the analysis below demonstrates, we partially share Tully's assertion that the EU

more explicitly than Tully, we follow the 'substantive school' that considers that the principle of constitutionalism also comprises fundamental rights. Arguing that the principle of legality encapsulates both sub-principles of democracy and constitutionalism, we develop the dialectic relationship between these two principles further, considering that legality not only requires the two principles to be balanced against each other, thus finding their limit in one another, but that they find their purpose in one another and inform each other's substantive content. Constitutionalism's primary purpose, on this view, is to guarantee thick democracy: to create the necessary preconditions for it, to correct any 'democratic failures' in the process and to ensure that outcomes do not undermine robust democracy in the longer term. Democracy as interpreted in light of constitutionalism, on this ideal view, means a clear checked-and-balanced system of decision-making that equally applies to all, that ensures that those affected by decisions take part in making those decisions (and where this is not possible, eg, because those affected are not (yet) politically represented, that their interest is structurally taken into account) and that guarantees that the institutions through which this decision-making is operated cannot abuse their powers. Ultimately, the constitutional democratic order as a whole should respect and serve the primordial values of dignity,[22] equality and liberty.

This 'constitutional democratic interpretation' of legality can at least partially transcend the well-known juxtaposition of democratic decision-making on the one hand with the judicial review thereof on the basis of constitutional norms on the other:[23] democracy through and on the basis of parliamentary decision-making itself is a constitutional norm that the judiciary should uphold. Of course, the constitutional side of legality requires that democratic decision-making respects certain procedural and substantive norms, and thus may entail overturning an act of parliament on that basis. But the limits of such judicial intervention lie in that the democracy side of legality should equally be respected, thus precluding judgments that amount to 'judicial legislation', because such judicial activism would amount to an important exercise of public authority without parliamentary involvement.[24] Of course, where precisely the balance between the principle of democracy and the principle of constitutionalism should be struck in individual cases will always be

suffers from a degree of over-constitutionalisation in the sense that certain economic rights and paradigms are excessively insulated from democratic decision-making.

[22] Although most constitutional traditions revolve around human dignity, an argument could be made that the core value of dignity could be interpreted as the 'dignity of living beings', like in the Swiss Constitution. See J Eisen, 'Animals in the Constitutional State' (2017) 15 *International Journal of Constitutional Law* 909.

[23] J Waldron, 'The Core of the Case Against Judicial Review' (2006) 115 *Yale Law Journal* 1346. See on this point also A Young, 'A Peculiarly British Protection of Human Rights?' (2005) 68 *Modern Law Review* 858. See also the discussion by Elise Muir in ch 5; and more generally: A Bickel, *The Least Dangerous Branch* (New Haven, CT, Yale University Press, 1986) 16; J Hart Ely, *Democracy and Distrust: A Theory of Judicial Review* (Cambridge, MA, Harvard University Press, 1980); and R Dworkin, *Freedom's Law* (Cambridge, MA, Harvard University Press, 1996).

[24] Gearty, above n 6.

open to debate: a central tension within constitutional democracy that some may perceive as paradoxical,[25] and others as inherent to its very purpose. The principle of legality interpreted as outlined above would not necessarily provide conclusive answers in itself but would provide the terms of the arguments to be made in reasonable disagreement where it occurs.

More concretely, this chapter proposes that the principle of democracy as part of the principle of legality requires that the people should take part in the exercise of power through the intermediary of a representative assembly at least as regards decisions that are salient to the polity. Salience should be determined in particular in reference to factors such as the potential scale (eg, number of people affected), intensity (eg, deeply affecting the position of at least one person) and/or irreversibility/consequentiality of the exercise of authority in question.[26] The more salient the decision, the more demanding the principle of democracy becomes: requiring higher degrees of representativeness of the respective assembly and more extensive and (less in)direct participation in actual decision-making of the respective assembly (thus beyond consultation, information and delegation).[27] In turn, concretely, the principle of constitutionalism as part of the principle of legality would require

[25] A related contradiction is found by theorists such as Mouffe, whose work reflects on a perceived internal conflict within modern democracy created by the union of two separate strands of political thought: the tradition of classical liberalism and the tradition of democratic theory, forming the institution of liberal democracy. Liberalism is considered to be served by the rule of law, the defence of human rights and the respect of individual liberty; whereas the democratic tradition's main ideas are those of equality, identity between governing and governed and popular sovereignty: C Mouffe, *The Democratic Paradox* (New York, Verso, 2000).

[26] It is for the reasons that in social and economic decision-making, identifying the (huge) number of affected parties and infinite repercussions that might result from the necessity of incessantly redefining the 'affected parties', that Fuller argues that these issues are beyond the limits of adjudication. See L Fuller, *The Morality of Law*, rev edn 1969 (New Haven, CT, Yale University Press, 1964) 208; and M Wilkinson, 'Three Conceptions of Law: Towards a Jurisprudence of Democratic Experimentalism' (2010) *Wisconsin Law Review* 673. My proposal presents a very different approach to salience than the one adopted by A Moravcsik, 'In Defense of the "Democratic Deficit" Reassessing Legitimacy in the European Union' (2002) 40 *Journal of Common Market Studies* 603, who although similarly linking the need for democratic legitimacy of decision-making to the salience of the issue, determines salience on the basis of an empirical approach to how much voters indicate they care about certain policy areas at a certain moment in time. He thus argued that '[o]f the five most salient issues in most west European democracies – health care provision, education, law and order, pension and social security policy, and taxation – none is primarily an EU competence' and that the issues in which the EU specialises – trade liberalisation, the removal of non-tariff barriers, technical regulation in environmental and other areas, foreign aid and general foreign policy co-ordination – tend to be of low salience in most European polities (615–16). In a way, this is a democratic approach to determining what decisions need democratic legitimation. The approach suggested here to establish what decisions need democratic validation, is instead constitutional one, operationalising salience through the mentioned criteria, for review by the judiciary.

[27] To make the principle of legality operational, at least for the purposes of our analysis, it would seem reasonable to limit the democratic and constitutional requirements of the principle to certain core minimum standards. Parliamentary sovereignty is part of a broader set of democratic principles and notions. It arguably can, to a certain extent, be traded off against other sources of legitimacy, such as output legitimacy. The minimum standards should thus, at least for an initial analysis, be set at the level below which no mitigation can be possible.

authority to be exercised (i) on the basis of a correct authorising norm and in compliance with the accompanying procedures;[28] (ii) in respect for the principle of democracy; and (iii) respecting fundamental human rights, in particular to the extent that these fundamental rights contribute to creating the preconditions of a healthy democracy,[29] and to the extent that they serve to prevent cases of majoritarian injustice. The rights of equality, liberty and dignity are primordial in this respect, and fundamental are the traditional democratic civil liberties such as freedom of thought and expression, assembly and association. The position of (other)[30] social and economic rights is more ambiguous: from the viewpoint of constitutional democracy as outlined above, constitutional protection of these rights is primarily necessary to the degree that they create the socio-economic conditions for a well-functioning democracy (allowing social mobility, emancipation and corrections of societal power asymmetries),[31] and their application should not displace democratic decision-making on substantive socio-economic issues. An overly ambitious constitutionalisation of socio-economic rights would lead to an unacceptable imbalance between the principle of constitutionalism and the principle of democracy.

The operationalisation of respect for the principle of legality takes place primarily through judicial review. The principle of legality, with its constitutional and democratic underpinnings, itself indicates the appropriate aims and intensity of that review, at least in theory. First, it requires an active review of compliance with the norms that authorise the exercise of authority in question, and with the procedures that have been prescribed in this respect. While the interpretation of authorising norms and procedures can certainly be subject to reasonable disagreement, and is not always separable from substantive political questions, the principle of legality would require that in such cases the principle of constitutionalism as

[28] Here, a range of 'rule of law' requirements could be imported, such as those developed by Fuller in *The Morality of Law*: generality of law-making, publicity, clarity, prospectiveness, congruence between the rules and their enforcement. A further development in this regard is beyond the scope of this paper. Fuller, *The Morality of Law*, above n 26; L Fuller, 'Positivism and Fidelity to Law: A Reply to Professor Hart' (1958) 71 *Harvard Law Review* 4. See also M Dawson, 'Soft Law and the Rule of Law in the European Union: Revision or Redundancy?' (2009) EUI Working Papers RSCAS 2009/24.

[29] See to a certain extent *contra*: the contribution of Paul Nemitz to this volume (ch 18), where he states that 'Of course, democracy and democratic engagement of people in the Member States can never be imposed from the EU level. The rule of former German constitutional Judge Böckenförde, that the democratic state does not command the preconditions on which its existence is predicated, thus that law cannot secure democracy if there is no culture of people engaging in and for democracy, is a fortiori true for the EU and in the relation between the EU and its Member States'.

[30] The freedom of assembly and association is an important social right, that is interpreted by the ECHR to include the right to strike and bargain collectively. The democratic dimension of this right is strong; as the UN Special Rapporteur put it: 'protecting the right to strike is not simply about States fulfilling their legal obligations. It is also about them creating democratic and equitable societies that are sustainable in the long run. The concentration of power in one sector – whether in the hands of government or business – inevitably leads to the erosion of democracy, and an increase in inequalities and marginalisation with all their attendant consequences. The right to strike is a check on this concentration of power'.

[31] On the importance thereof, see R Bellamy, *Political Constitutionalism: A Republican Defence of the Constitutionality of Democracy* (Cambridge, Cambridge University Press, 2007) 81.

applied by the judiciary has the 'last word'. In this assessment, the judiciary needs to take particular account of the principle of democracy and respect for fundamental rights, meaning that in case of a choice between various authorising norms and procedures, the judiciary may oblige the legislature or executive to opt for the most 'constitutional democratic' option. Secondly, the intensity of the review of whether the exercise of authority has respected the principle of democracy should depend on the salience of the decision in question. The more salient, the more important that the people participate in the decision-making through a representative parliament, and the more important that the judiciary scrutinises carefully whether that democratic validation has taken place. Of course, the judiciary is itself bound by the constitutional framework, and that framework may prescribe decision-making procedures that stand in tension with the principle of democracy. It could be argued, on the basis of the foregoing analysis, that as a foundational principle of primary law, the principle of legality should be used actively by the judiciary to interpret constitutional procedures and provisions – and certainly to scrutinise and invalidate procedures and provisions laid down in secondary norms – in light of the principle of democracy as much as possible.[32] Thirdly, the intensity of fundamental rights review should depend on the importance of the fundamental right in question for a healthy democracy or for the correction of grave majoritarian injustice. The further removed from these two functions that a fundamental right is in the particular case before the judge, the more hesitant the judge should be to enforce that right against the democratic exercise of authority that is challenged.[33]

## The Principle of Legality in the EU

While the principle of legality in its broader interpretation (thus requiring parliamentary decision-making in addition to 'mere' lawfulness) is still very important in national legal orders such as Germany and France,[34] it is also true that in reality, a multiplicity of legal sources has nuanced the idea that the (national) parliament is the main locus of public power and its exercise, even in these legal systems.[35] In the words of Lupo and Piccirilli,

> the results of th[e] evolution [of moving from the formalistic concepts of 'law' and 'legislation' to substantive ones] are a progressive decline of the formal categories that

[32] With the principle of legal certainty acting as a counterbalance.

[33] Where a decision is made with only poor democratic validation, it may be tempting for the judiciary to compensate for this through an increased intensity of fundamental rights review. However, this would risk turning the problem of democratic deficit in question into a problem of constitutional surplus, which destabilises the delicate balance between the principles of democracy and constitutionalism underpinning the legality principle. Instead, if a democratic deficit is detected by the judiciary, this should itself be scrutinised and possibly counteracted on the basis of the principle of legality itself, possibly reinterpreting the constitution or annulling the secondary norm to comply with the democracy principle.

[34] See contributions in Besselink, Pennings and Prechal, above n 1.

[35] ibid.

> dominated the public law literature in the past two centuries but, at the same time, carry the risk of also losing the democratic meaning of the legality principle, represented by the necessary linkage between the system of sources of law and the separation of powers.[36]

The EU is indicated as a major cause of the 'eclipse' of the legality principle in national legal orders.[37]

Furthermore, in the context of the EU legal order itself, the principle of legality seems to have been given a narrower interpretation, akin to lawfulness, with its democratic element featuring less prominently, if at all. In the Court's case law, the principle of legality is most explicitly discussed in its specific criminal law application of *nulla poene sine lege*,[38] and apart from that it is uttered mostly as a synonym for lawfulness. Still, although not usually explicitly conceptualised as such, the principle of conferral is the federal manifestation of the principle of legality, together with the ensuing doctrine of the legal basis.[39] Furthermore, even if not considered part of the principle of legality, democratic legitimacy has increasingly become part of the CJEU's judicial review of EU acts intended to produce legal effects vis-a-vis third parties. As it has recognised that such acts need to comply with the 'principle of democracy', derived from the provisions on 'democratic principles' as expressed in Articles 9–12 TEU, the Court could be argued to increasingly construct the EU law understanding of legality in the direction of our 'constitutional democratic' definition. Finally, Pech identifies the trend in the Court's case law to 'deepen' the interpretation of the rule of law into a meta-principle that contains substantive human rights alongside procedural guarantees.[40] While, as discussed also further above, the meta-principle is not the principle of legality, but the rule of law, it does illustrate EU law's openness to accommodate the interdependence between legality, democracy and fundamental rights.[41]

[36] Lupo and Piccirilli, above n 7.

[37] Besselink, above n 3.

[38] As also laid down in Art 49 of the EU Charter of Fundamental Rights which in its preamble refers to 'the indivisible, universal values of human dignity, freedom, equality and solidarity; it is based on the principles of democracy and the rule of law' but does not explicate a general principle of legality – nor do the TEU and TFEU.

[39] As Besselink notes, 'The case law also shows that the issue of competence in EU law is not primarily concerned with providing the democratically legitimate basis to the exercise of authority over citizens, but much rather with the division of powers between Union and Member States. The issue of attribution of power is about the enumeration of powers pretty much in the manner in which this happens in federal systems: it is a manner of legitimating power by dividing it, rather than by creating it in a particular formal manner (as nationally in acts of parliament)' above n 3, 298. From a national perspective, such as the one developed by the German Constitutional Court, the principle of conferral allows European integration in compliance with the principle of legality: national parliaments have transferred limited powers to the EU in compliance with the national constitution, and they retain the competence to define these EU powers.

[40] Pech, above n 10, 368.

[41] Case C-50/00 P, above n 15, paras 38–39: 'The European Community is … a community based on the rule of law in which its institutions are subject to judicial review of the compatibility of their acts with the Treaty and with the general principles of law which include fundamental rights. Individuals are therefore entitled to effective judicial protection of the rights they derive from the Community legal order'.

In any event, regardless of the current interpretation and application in existent legal systems, the principle of legality as requiring the exercise of public authority to comply with both the principles of constitutionalism and democracy provides an appropriate analytical tool to assess the legitimacy of a given polity, including the EU. As such, this chapter argues, it could constitute a research agenda for European studies, both legal and political. The present chapter can only provide initial, tentative elements of an application of the legality principle as conceptualised above to the EU legal order. Further research along these lines would surely reveal other relevant issues, different tension points, and reach some different conclusions as to the EU's relationship to the legality principle. As a tentative first step, nevertheless, the rest of this chapter will be devoted to applying the framework developed in the preceding section to the EU's exercise of authority. In this, the central questions are to what extent the EU's exercise of authority is (i) based on correct authorising norms and in compliance with the accompanying procedures; (ii) compliant with democracy in that the people take part in the exercise of power through parliament in salient decisions; and (iii) respecting the fundamental human rights that are necessary to create the preconditions of a healthy democracy and to prevent cases of majoritarian injustice but avoiding judicial legislation and second-guessing of socio-economic choices made in the legislative process.

## Is EU Action Based on Correct Authorising Norms and in Compliance with the Accompanying Procedures?[42]

### *Choice of Legal Basis*

Article 5(2) TEU provides that the Union shall act only within the limits of the competences conferred upon it by the Member States in the Treaties to attain the objectives set out therein and Article 13 TFEU states that '[e]ach institution shall act within the limits of the powers conferred on it in the Treaties, and in conformity with the procedures, conditions and objectives set out in them'. Although closely interrelated, the subtle distinction between these stipulations is relevant for our purposes. The first principle of conferred powers is primarily a federal principle, intended to protect the Member States against over-centralisation by the EU level. The second reflects the principle of legality more precisely, as it is about demanding an authorisation for the exercise of authority. Both stipulations however translate practically into the requirement of a legal basis for action. The Court of Justice has declared the choice of legal basis of 'constitutional significance',[43] but has also

[42] As mentioned further above, in this assessment, a range of rule of law requirements could be imported, such as concerning legal certainty, publicity and generality of law-making. In light of the limited scope of this chapter, we will focus mainly on the requirement of an authorising norm.

[43] Opinion 2/00 EU:C:2001:664.

noted that the attribution of powers and the differences between legal bases is 'not always based on consistent criteria'.[44] Indeed, one major complicating factor is that the various legal bases are not mutually exclusive, with various functional powers cutting across an array of sector-specific competences. Furthermore, as will be discussed below, the procedures for adoption and particularly the levels of parliamentary involvement can (still) vary greatly among legal bases, seemingly without there being an objective, consistent approach behind this.

When requested, the Court will review whether the EU institutions have respected the conditions for use of the legal basis in question and, if there are alternatives available, have made the right choice between different provisions. The Court will conduct this review on the basis of 'objective factors',[45] particularly the aim and content of the measure. When a measure pursues more than one aim, or concerns more than one policy area, an assessment will be made whether one aim is predominant (in which case the single relevant legal basis will be used), while both legal bases will have to be used when the aims are equally integral to the measure (and if there are differing procedures, these will have to be combined somehow). The exception to this 'centre of gravity' approach is in the case where one of the possible legal bases does not allow for the adoption of legislation. In such a case, if the other legal basis does allow such legislation, it does not matter whether the centre of gravity of the measure is within the more permissive legal basis or not.[46] The only test the Court will conduct then is whether the conditions for the use of the permissive legal basis have been met.[47] While this is clearly an expansionist approach, through this latter assessment, the Court still ensures that the principle of legality is complied with.

Of course, the fact that the CJEU needs to be presented with a case in order to control the legal basis means that not every ultra vires act in the EU legal order may be caught.[48] One could fear in this regard that the EU institutions have a mutual interest to maintain an overly wide reading of the scope of EU powers, meaning that many acts would go unchallenged, all the more because most acts are adopted consensually in the Council even in areas of majority voting. However, while *locus standi* for direct actions for annulment for individuals is strict, individuals may at any point contest the validity of an EU legal measure in a case before national courts which would then refer the question to the CJEU. Furthermore, the different configurations of institutional power laid down in the various legal bases make that the choice between them is of high inter-institutional salience

[44] Case 242/87 *Commission v Council* EU:C:1989:217, para 13.
[45] Case C-440/05 *Commission v Council* EU:C:2007:625, para 61.
[46] Case C-376/98 *Germany v European Parliament and Council* EU:C:2000:544.
[47] ibid.
[48] An interesting example is the provision in Directive 94/33/EC on young people at work which, much like the earlier Working Time Directive, prescribes that weekly rest is to be preferably taken on a Sunday. In the case of the Working Time Directive, the CJEU annulled the provision as beyond the scope of EU powers, making it a reasonable assumption that the same should apply to the younger workers directive.

and thus a relatively frequent cause of dispute – which ultimately can be, and not uncommonly is, brought before the CJEU. Dashwood wrote in a seminal article on competences: 'much of my time at the Council was spent in worrying whether this or that proposal by the Commission was based on the correct Treaty provision or whether it was not, perhaps, entirely beyond Community powers',[49] indicating that there is, in fact, more of a healthy culture of competence (self-)control in the EU institutions than sometimes alleged, as also testified by the substantial case law on the matter.

## *Competence Creep*

Yet, allegations about EU competence creep persist.[50] Central in this discussion is the idea that Member States and EU institutions consider it 'politically expedient to achieve certain extraneous objectives through common action but regardless of the constitutional niceties associated with the principle of attributed powers'[51] (over-)stretching the Treaties' legal bases beyond their reasonable interpretation and that the CJEU for its part has been permissive in this behaviour. Two provisions play a crucial role in this regard: Articles 114 and 352 TFEU. The former authorises the EU to adopt 'measures for the approximation of the provisions laid down by law, regulation or administrative action in Member States which have as their object the establishment and functioning of the internal market', and the latter provides the EU the power to 'adopt the appropriate measures … [i]f action by the Union should prove necessary, within the framework of the policies defined in the Treaties, to attain one of the objectives set out in the Treaties, and the Treaties have not provided the necessary powers'. These two provisions were subject to special scrutiny in the debate on a better division of competences between the EU and the Member States post-Laeken Declaration. Article 114 TFEU was left unaltered by the Lisbon Treaty, while Article 352 TFEU was simultaneously broadened and curtailed. This flexibility clause no longer refers to the common market (a phrase that was never taken too seriously), but it does lay down additional procedural requirements for its use concerning national parliaments (paragraph 2) and states that it cannot be used in cases where the Treaties exclude harmonisation (paragraph 3).

It is clear that both provisions have been used extensively, and that this has significantly furthered the process of European integration. The Court has, admittedly, only exceptionally struck down measures for not respecting the outer limits of these provisions, notably in *Tobacco Advertisement* and Opinion 2/94 on Accession to the ECHR.[52] But it is not at all clear that this extensive use is due to any

[49] A Dashwood, 'The Limits of European Community Powers' (1996) 21 *European Law Review* 113.
[50] For discussion, see S Weatherill, 'Competence Creep and Competence Control' (2004) 23 *Yearbook of European Law* 1.
[51] M Dougan, 'Legal Developments' (2010) 48 *Journal of Common Market Studies* 172.
[52] Opinion 2/49 EU:C:1996:140.

abuse of authority or overly lax judicial review, in breach of the legality principle. As regards Article 114 TFEU, the crux of the controversy seems to lie in its use for the pursuit of non-economic policies, such as public health and consumer protection. Indeed, there is a tension there, that the EU has not been granted (full) legislative powers in the sectoral legal bases directly pertaining to those areas that may be indirectly regulated on the basis of Article 114 TFEU. However, Article 114 TFEU itself authorises this. Already in its first version in the form of 100a introduced by the Single European Act, the provision stipulated that the Commission in its proposals envisaged on this basis 'concerning health, safety, environmental protection and consumer protection, will take as a base a high level of protection'. Clearly, the 'functioning of the market' was always conferred as a broad cross-cutting power. In fact, in *Tobacco Advertisement*, the Court gave a rather strict reading of the text, when it declared that it does not '[vest] in the Community legislature a general power to regulate the internal market'. Of course, Article 26 TFEU defines the internal market as 'compris[ing] an area without internal frontiers in which the free movement of goods, persons, services and capital is ensured in accordance with the provisions of the Treaties', but does this really preclude defining the power to adopt measures for the 'functioning' of that market as a general power to regulate it? Other views are available.[53]

The Court also stated in *Tobacco Advertisement* that such a general market regulation power would be contrary to 'the principle … that the powers of the Community are limited to those specifically conferred on it'. An argument could indeed be made that entirely open-ended conferral is not compliant with the very concept of conferred powers, but as it would be specifically related to the regulation of the internal market, it is not at all clear that such a broader reading of Article 114 TFEU would lead to an unacceptable hollowing-out of the conferral principle. If anything, then, the catch-all legal basis of Article 352 TFEU should be incompatible with that principle,[54] which the CJEU clearly does not consider to be the case. And here again, we may argue that the use of this provision in a wide range of areas can hardly be considered surprising or surreptitious as it has been specifically, explicitly and clearly designed and defined for that. In fact, even if the argument that the broad formulation of Articles 114 and 352 TFEU offends the principle of conferral were accepted, it would carry weight mostly as a federal

[53] G Davies, 'The Competence to Create an Internal Market: Conceptual Poverty and Unbalanced Interests' in S Garben and I Govaere (eds), *The Division of Competences between the EU and the Member States* (Oxford, Hart Publishing, 2017).

[54] The German Constitutional Court indeed has such worries about this provision, especially now that it is no longer textually tied to the common market. It has stated that Art 352 TFEU meets with constitutional objections with regard to the ban on transferring blanket empowerments or on transferring Kompetenz-Kompetenz, because the newly worded provision makes it possible substantially to amend treaty foundations of the European Union without the constitutive participation of legislative bodies in addition to the Member States' executive powers. VerfG, 2 BvE 2/08 vom 30.6.2009, Absatz-Nr (1-421) para 328, available in English at: www.bverfg.de/entscheidungen/es20090630_2bve000208en.html.

argument, in that such a transgression would 'unjustly' deprive the Member States of their authority. It would not necessarily mean that the legality principle as such would be infringed. To the extent that this principle entails that there should be a clear authorising norm, that there should be parliamentary participation in the adoption of the act, and that judicial review should take place to uphold democratic fundamental rights, there is nothing preventing EU acts adopted on Articles 114 and 352 TFEU to comply with it.[55]

## *EU Competence in Criminal Law*

The principle of legality has a special meaning in the context of criminal law. Most European legal systems attach particular value to the notion that an individual can only be subjected to criminal sanctions on the basis of clear (legislative) norms. The *nulla poene sine lege* principle is also explicitly protected by the EU Charter, and the Court has considered it a general principle of EU law.[56] However, the principle of effectiveness of EU law, central to the CJEU's jurisprudence, has given rise to some tension with the legality principle in the specific area of criminal law. As regards the requirement of a clear authorising norm for the exercise of punitive power, the case law of the CJEU as regards the EU's implicit competence in the area of criminal law needs to be considered. In *Commission v Council*,[57] the CJEU held that (now) Article 192(1) TFEU should have been the legal basis for Council Framework Decision 2003/80/JHA, which established a list of particularly serious environmental offences in respect of which the Member States must impose criminal penalties. Despite the fact that criminal law did not fall within the EU's competence, the Court opined that the EU legislature was not prevented from taking measures that relate to criminal law when necessary to ensure that the rules it lays down on environmental protection are fully effective. This use of the principle of effectiveness to 'augment the EU's competence over criminal law' can be criticised, in the words of Craig, from an ultra vires viewpoint:

> [I]n substantive terms, for example, that the sphere of criminal law is simply too important, too different etc to generate wide-ranging EU competence in such instances through effectiveness. We might argue that in procedural terms the Court's exiguous reasoning and mere incantation of effectiveness fell short of the kind of reasoned justification that one would expect if such a step were to be taken. We might frame the objection in consequentialist terms, by contending that the problematic outcomes

[55] This is leaving aside the question whether the Court, it its interpretation of the internal market provisions and the measures adopted on the basis of 114 TFEU complies with the third requirement; as we shall see further below this is not always the case.

[56] Joined Cases C-74/95 and C-129/95 *Criminal proceedings against X* EU:C:1996:491, para 25 and Joined Cases C-189/02 P, C-202/02 P, C-205/02 P to C-208/02 P and C 213/02 P *Dansk Rørindustri and Others v Commission* EU:C:2005:408, paras 215–19.

[57] Case C-176/03 *Commission v Council* EU:C:2005:542. On the significance of the judgment, see C Tobler, 'Case C-176/03 Commission v Council' (2006) 43 *Common Market Law Review* 835. Case C-440/05 *Commission v Council (Ship Source Pollution)* EU:C:2007:625.

> consequent upon arrogation of EU power over criminal law premised on effectiveness should have inclined the ECJ against taking this step.[58]

May we add the principle of legality, and specifically *nulla poena sine lege*, as an objection, in this regard? It remains striking to read the CJEU's finding in *Ship Source Pollution* that

> [a]lthough it is true that, as a general rule, neither criminal law nor the rules of criminal procedure fall within the Community's competence … the fact remains that when the application of effective, proportionate and dissuasive criminal penalties by the competent national authorities is an essential measure for combating serious environmental offences, the Community legislature may require the Member States to introduce such penalties in order to ensure that the rules which it lays down in that field are fully effective.[59]

This does seem to raise some tensions with regard to the requirement that an authority defining criminal sanctions needs to do so on the basis of a clear authorising mandate. However, while the judgment can be considered controversial from a federal perspective, it could be argued that the legality principle in fact was ultimately well served by the CJEU's approach. After all, with these rulings, the CJEU brought criminal measures in the scope of the Community Pillar, which contained higher levels of democratic decision-making and judicial review than the EU Treaty, which would have been the alternative basis for the EU's exercise of criminal law authority. To enforce EU environmental law through criminal penalties on the basis of a Framework Decision would have been more doubtful in light of the legality principle than through an EU Directive.[60]

More recently, the *Taricco* saga raised controversies in light of the *nulla poene sine lege* principle. The cases concerned Italian statutes of limitation applicable

[58] P Craig, 'The ECJ and Ultra Vires Action: A Conceptual Analysis' (2011) 48 *Common Market Law Review* 395, 401.

[59] Case C-440/05 *Commission v Council (Ship Source Pollution)* EU:C:2007:625, para 66.

[60] Directive 2005/35/EC of the European Parliament and of the Council of 7 September 2005 on ship-source pollution and on the introduction of penalties for infringements was subsequently challenged. The CJEU reviewed the Directive against the principle of legality and it considered that the Directive complied with it. In this regard, it used various compelling arguments, considering that it was not contrary to the principle of legality to oblige Member States to punish ship-source discharges of polluting substances if committed 'with intent, recklessly or by serious negligence', without defining those concepts. These various concepts indeed correspond to tests for the incurring of liability which are to apply to an indeterminate number of situations that it is impossible to envisage in advance and not to specific conduct capable of being set out in detail in a legislative measure. And, as the CJEU pointed out, those concepts are fully integrated into, and used in, the Member States' respective legal systems. However, the final argument used by the CJEU, that the Directive must be transposed by each of the Member States into national law and that therefore 'the actual definition of the infringements referred to in Art 4 of that directive and the applicable penalties are those which result from the rules laid down by the Member States', seems more doubtful. The Member States are under a legal obligation to do so, and to 'pass the buck' to the national legal system does not seem to duly allocate the responsibility for *nulla poene sine lege* with the source of the authority exercised. See Case C-308/06 *Intertanko* EU:C:2008:312.

to pending criminal proceedings regarding VAT fraud. The limitation periods in combination with the workload problems of the Italian justice system, resulted in a significant number of persons guilty of serious VAT fraud going unpunished.[61] In Case C-105/14 *Taricco I*, the CJEU obliged Italian criminal courts to disapply the statutes of limitations in VAT cases, in order to give full effect to Article 325 TFEU (protection of the financial interests of the EU).[62] Several parties had referred to Article 49 of the EU Charter laying down the principles of legality and proportionality of criminal offences and penalties. The CJEU considered that,

> subject to verification by the national court, the sole effect of the disapplication of the national provisions at issue would be to not shorten the general limitation period in the context of pending criminal proceedings, to allow the effective prosecution of the alleged crimes, and to ensure, if necessary, that penalties intended to protect the financial interests of the European Union and those intended to protect the financial interests of the Italian Republic are treated in the same way. Such a disapplication of national law would not infringe the rights of the accused, as guaranteed by Article 49 of the Charter.[63]

The Italian Constitutional Court disagreed (as well as numerous academic writings),[64] and indicated in a subsequent preliminary reference that it would disapply this ruling unless the CJEU would reconsider its interpretation.[65] The CJEU indeed reconsidered its stance, and held in *Taricco II* that the previously established obligation on national courts to disapply the national provisions on limitation, forming part of national substantive law, which prevented the application of effective and deterrent criminal penalties in a significant number of cases of serious fraud or which lay down shorter limitation periods for cases of serious fraud affecting Union interests than for those affecting national interests, did not apply where that

> disapplication entails a breach of the principle that offences and penalties must be defined by law because of the lack of precision of the applicable law or because of the retroactive application of legislation imposing conditions of criminal liability stricter than those in force at the time the infringement was committed.[66]

In this case, the national legislator was responsible for resolving the incompatibility with EU law, which could not be resolved by the national court. The CJEU thereby avoided a stand-off with the national constitutional court and guaranteed full compliance with the principle of legality. It could be argued that the principle

[61] M Krajewski, '"Conditional" Primacy of EU Law and its Deliberative Value: An Imperfect Illustration from Taricco II' (*European Law Blog*, 18 December 2017).

[62] C-105/14 *Taricco and Others* EU:C:2015:555.

[63] Para 55.

[64] M Krajewski, 'A Way Out for the ECJ in Taricco II: Constitutional Identity or a More Careful Proportionality Analysis?' (*European Law Blog*, 23 November 2017).

[65] 1/11 Order No. 24 Year 2017, see: www.cortecostituzionale.it/documenti/download/doc/recent_judgments/O_24_2017.pdf.

[66] Case C-42/17 *MAS, MB* EU:C:2017:936, para 62.

of legality does not include limitation periods and that therefore the first *Taricco* judgment of the CJEU was not in itself incompatible with it.[67] That judgment however did show the tension between the principle of effectiveness on the one hand, and the principle of legality and legal certainty on the other, and it could be said that the principle of legality was well served by the CJEU's revised stance in *Taricco II*.

## Is EU Action Compliant with Democracy in that the People Take Part in the Exercise of Power Through Parliament in Salient Decisions?

To some extent, this question invites us to revisit the discussion concerning the EU's democratic deficit. Many other contributions to this edited volume consider this question in detail, both from the perspective of national parliaments and the European Parliament. The present section will therefore only make a few summary remarks in this regard.

### *Incomplete Parliamentarisation of Union Decision-Making*

The Treaty of Lisbon has made a number of important improvements as regards the parliamentarisation of Union decision-making. Article 289(3) TFEU introduces legislative acts: legal acts adopted by legislative procedure. The ordinary legislative procedure relies on a triple-tracked democratic legitimacy: it does not only feature the European Parliament with its direct legitimacy and the Council with its indirect legitimacy connected to the national parliaments, but in addition the direct involvement of national parliaments through the Early Warning System in all areas that do not belong to the EU's exclusive competence. While it may be objected that the European Parliament suffers from low turnout and that the reality of the ordinary legislative procedure (OLP) tends to be more obscure due to opaque trilogues, on balance it would have to be concluded that the OLP constitutes a way of decision-making that fulfills the minimum requirements of the principle of democracy under the legality principle. Had, as Bast points out, the Treaty authors made the OLP the only legislative procedure and the only source of 'legislative acts', they would have created a convincing classification based on a procedural concept of legislation.[68] However, the co-decision rule has various exceptions in the 'special' legislative procedures (see Article 289(2) TFEU) defined in the relevant legal bases. Some of these procedures only require the

[67] P Faraguna, 'The Italian Constitutional Court in re Taricco: "Gauweiler in the Roman Campagna"' (*Verfassungsblog*, 31 January 2017).

[68] J Bast, 'New Categories of Acts after the Lisbon Reform: Dynamics of Parliamentarization in EU Law' (2012) 49 *Common Market Law Review* 885.

consultation of the European Parliament, meaning that the EU features 'legislative acts' without (co-)decision-making by its parliamentary body, which stands in tense relation to the legality principle, especially where it concerns potentially salient decisions. Furthermore, several legal bases allow the Council to adopt non-legislative acts. As Bast considers:

> There was hardly any debate within the European Convention about which powers of the Council should form part of the domain of European laws. The outcome is, to put it mildly, not in all cases convincing … Are there no good arguments for enhanced public scrutiny when the Council defines the legal framework for administrative co-operation in the area of freedom, security and justice, eg for cross-border data exchange among police authorities? Why should the Council meet in closed session when it establishes the limits and conditions for the ECB's power to impose sanctions on undertakings? … Council Regulation 407/2010 establishing a European financial stabilisation mechanism is a non-legislative act based on Article 122 TFEU. Is not this the very type of act that should be transmitted to the national parliaments to obtain their views on financial solidarity within the Euro-zone? All this appears, as Dougan has correctly noted, 'rather arbitrary'. Bypassing the higher level of public scrutiny and of parliamentary involvement is precisely what seems to have motivated the Treaty drafters when classifying such competences as 'non-legislative'. This holds all the more true when entire policies, namely the rules on competition and the Common Foreign and Security Policy, are without distinction excluded from the scope of European legislation – and thus from the new rules for openness that govern it.[69]

## *Soft Law and Policy Coordination*

From the perspective of the principle of legality, the real problem with EU democracy is therefore that not all salient decisions are taken through the OLP. The problem of EU soft law and policy coordination, compounds this. What soft law, economic governance and parallel integration have in common is that they mainly involve non-binding measures, or measures that are not binding by virtue of EU law, and as such that they formally leave the ultimate decision to the national level. One could therefore question whether they entail any displacement of parliaments at all. The answer is that only on the most narrow, formalistic and legalistic understanding of power and authority could one argue that this would not be the case. They all carry important normative power and constrain national action in various ways, doing so largely without the free involvement of the legislator and particularly the European and national parliaments. As such, these forms of harmonisation by stealth contribute to the de-parliamentarisation of European

[69] ibid, 896–97, referring to M Dougan, 'The Convention's Draft Constitutional Treaty: Bringing Europe Closer to its Lawyers?' (2003) 28 *European Law Review* 763, 784; K Lenaerts, 'A Unified Set of Instruments' (2005) 1 *European Constitutional Law Review* 57, 61; K Lenaerts and D Gerard, 'The Structure of the Union according to the Constitution for Europe: The Emperor is Getting Dressed' (2004) 29 *European Law Review* 289, 311 and 313.

integration, the legitimacy deficit of which has been examined at length in Cygan's chapter in this book (chapter fifteen).

The open method of coordination (OMC) has been left deliberately outside the (re)organisation of competences in the Lisbon Treaty, probably to maintain its flexibility.[70] In a way, its rationale is precisely to overcome the limits on EU legislative competence: a complementary form of governance for when 'harmonisation is unworkable but mutual recognition and the resulting regulatory competition may be too risky'[71] for instance 'to encourage the Member States to coordinate sensitive policy areas that are being eroded by the rulings of the Court'.[72] But the OMC does have the capacity to exercise a certain degree of coercive power, and at the same time its lack of transparency and failure to engage with the (more) democratic institutions of the EU such as the European Parliament and the Committee of the Regions as well as a broad participation of civil society have been noted to run counter to principles of good governance such as transparency, accountability and democratic input.[73] Precisely for those reasons, it can be deployed by national executives for their two-level games.[74] It is not clear to electorates exactly who is participating in these processes or which actors are successful in influencing the OMC agenda. Member State electorates cannot, therefore, hold the actors responsible for the content of the OMC objectives accountable. Neither the European nor national parliaments are involved in formulating the OMC objectives. The objectives therefore lack any input legitimacy. All this is problematic if national governments subsequently use the OMC in political discourses to justify existing policies by credit claiming or defend planned changes by blaming the EU.[75] The OMC might seem respectful of national autonomy; its executive-dominated nature and exclusion of transparent procedures and parliamentary involvement means it lacks democratic legitimacy.[76]

The European Semester, the EU's yearly cycle of economic policy coordination, poses similar problems. The Country Specific Recommendations (CSRs) are, technically speaking, not legally binding. Nevertheless, they are issued in the context of a structured framework, which features the ultimate possibility of financial sanctions in case of non-compliance. While sanctions are only possible under the macroeconomic imbalance procedure and excessive deficit procedure, the yearly package of CSRs is presented integrally and it is difficult to specify the legal basis of

[70] E Szyszczak, 'Experimental Governance: The Open Method of Coordination' (2006) 12 *European Law Journal* 486.

[71] D Trubeck and JS Mosher, 'New Governance, EU Employment Policy, and the European Social Model' in J Zeitlin and D Trubeck (eds), *Governing Work and Welfare in a New Economy: European and American Experiments* (Oxford, Oxford University Press, 2003).

[72] Szyszczak, above n 70.

[73] ibid.

[74] M Büchs, 'The Open Method of Coordination as a "Two-Level Game"' (2008) 36 *Policy & Politics* 21.

[75] ibid.

[76] M Dawson, *New Governance and the Transformation of European Law: Coordinating EU Social Law and Policy* (Cambridge, Cambridge University Press, 2011).

each CSR, meaning that all CSRs operate under the shadow of financial sanctions. Furthermore, soft norms construct a narrative and influence institutional actors' behaviour in subtler ways.[77] Very similar legitimacy problems plague the Euro-crisis measures. The Memorandums of Understanding allow 'circumvention' of the EU's limited competences on social policy, education and health.[78] Their coercive power is unlike anything previously seen, as a country faces bankruptcy if it does not accept and comply with the European-level decisions. As Scharpf notes, 'these conditionalities were not defined by European legislation under the Community Method or through consensus-oriented voting in the Council but through extremely asymmetric bargaining between creditor and debtor governments that resembled conditions of an unconditional surrender'. Admittedly, economic policy coordination is firmly rooted in EU primary and secondary law. However, the actual, substantive decision-making by contrast takes place in an untransparent, exclusionary and undemocratic way, mainly between the Commission and the Council. The problem is that the role of law here is to legalise the 'outsourcing' of highly sensitive, political questions that from a democratic perspective should be taken through the legislative process, to an executive, untransparent forum. The parliamentary complicity in setting up the framework is understandable because of the crisis at the time, but cannot validate the indefinite displacement of substantive decision-making on highly crucial issues, locating it outside the democratic legislative process.

## *European Arrest Warrant*

A very important improvement effected by the Lisbon Treaty is the dissolution of the Pillars, especially in relation to police and judicial cooperation where the co-decision procedure has now become standard. This clearly reduces the democratic deficit in this area, extending the European Parliament's powers. However, this does not retroactively resolve the problem of acts adopted in this highly salient area, with a particular importance for the legality principle and *nulla poene sine lege*, of previously adopted acts. One in particular continues to cause controversy: the European Arrest Warrant (EAW). Council Framework Decision 2002/584/JHA of 13 June 2002 on the European arrest warrant and the surrender procedures between Member States introduces a simplified cross-border judicial surrender procedure for the purpose of prosecuting or executing a custodial sentence or detention order. A warrant issued by one EU country's judicial authority is valid in the entire territory of the EU. For 32 offences, there is no verification on whether

[77] M Dawson, 'Integration through Soft Law: No Competence Needed? Juridical and Bio- Power in the Realm of Soft Law' in S Garben and I Govaere (eds), *The Division of Competences between the EU and the Member States Reflections on the Past, the Present and the Future* (Oxford, Hart Publishing, 2017).

[78] M Dawson and F de Witte, 'Constitutional Balance in the EU after the Euro-Crisis' (2013) 76 *Modern Law Review* 817.

the act is a criminal offence in both countries. The only requirement is that it be punishable by a maximum period of at least three years of imprisonment in the issuing country.

In a legal challenge brought against the measure, Advocaten voor de Wereld argued that this list of offences is too vague and imprecise, breaching the principle of legality in criminal matters.[79] The offences set out in that list are not accompanied by their legal definition but constitute very vaguely defined categories of undesirable conduct. It was argued that a person deprived of his liberty on foot of a European arrest warrant without verification of double criminality does not benefit from the guarantee that criminal legislation must satisfy conditions as to precision, clarity and predictability allowing each person to know, at the time when an act is committed, whether that act does or does not constitute an offence, by contrast to those who are deprived of their liberty otherwise than pursuant to a European arrest warrant. The CJEU rejected this claim, observing that even if the Member States reproduce word-for-word the list of the categories of offence set out in Article 2(2) of the Framework Decision for the purposes of its implementation, the actual definition of those offences and the penalties applicable are those which follow from the law of 'the issuing Member State'. Accordingly, while Article 2(2) of the Framework Decision dispenses with verification of double criminality for the categories of offence mentioned therein, the definition of those offences and of the penalties applicable continue to be matters determined by the law of the issuing Member State, which, as is, moreover, stated in Article 1(3) of the Framework Decision, must respect fundamental rights and fundamental legal principles as enshrined in Article 6 EU and, consequently, the principle of the legality of criminal offences and penalties.

This part of the judgment is convincing. However, Advocaten voor de Wereld submitted another argument: that the Council should have used a convention rather than a framework decision. The CJEU, after considering that the requirement of the legal basis had been fulfilled, considered that:

> While it is true that the European arrest warrant could equally have been the subject of a convention, it is within the Council's discretion to give preference to the legal instrument of the framework decision in the case where, as here, the conditions governing the adoption of such a measure are satisfied.[80]

As Geyer notes, from a position of democratic legitimacy, a third-pillar convention is preferable to a framework decision as only the former requires ratification in the Member States.[81] Adopting a convention might therefore have 'ease[d] the democratic setback originating in the powers limited to consultation assigned to

[79] Case C-303/05 *Advocaten voor de Wereld VZW v Leden van de Ministerraad* EU:C:2007:261.

[80] Para 41.

[81] F Geyer, 'European Arrest Warrant: Case Note of Judgment of 3 May 2007, Case C-303/05, Advocaten voor de Wereld VZW v Leden van de Ministerraad' (2008) 4 *European Constitutional Law Review* 149.

the European Parliament under Article 39 EU'.[82] While, as said, this specific choice is no longer available to the Council following the Lisbon Treaty, not only does the EAW maintain its force, it also shows us that the CJEU will not actively step in to enforce the principle of democracy and parliamentary decision-making – which it arguably could and should do on the basis of the legality principle. This does not mean that the Court should invalidate all acts adopted without parliamentary involvement, but it means that after assessing the conditions of the use of the legal basis, it could assess whether another legal basis would have been available that would have allowed the adoption of a measure with largely similar content and that would have provided for higher levels of parliamentary involvement at either national or European level. The Court could develop a doctrine that in the case of salient decisions, the more democratic legal basis needs to be used where there is a choice.

Had the Framework Decision been adopted with higher levels of democratic legitimacy, it could have been more confidently defended in subsequent controversies that have emerged in its respect, such as concerning the *Melloni* judgment. The CJEU in that case held that the Framework Decision had to be interpreted as precluding the executing judicial authorities from making the execution of a European arrest warrant issued for the purposes of executing a sentence conditional upon the conviction rendered *in absentia* being open to review in the issuing Member State, even where there would be an adverse effect on the right to a fair trial and the rights of the defence as guaranteed by a Member State's constitution. The judgment has been criticised for insufficiently respecting national constitutions and fundamental rights. However, while it may convincingly be argued that the EAW does not as such infringe the fundamental rights in question (although it does prevent a higher national level of protection of those rights in this specific situation), from the perspective of the legality principle as developed in this paper, the question is whether the EAW affects the fundamental rights of individuals (especially in a criminal law context) and if so, whether there has been sufficient parliamentary involvement in laying down the legislation in question. With the Framework Decision, this is not the case, and therefore it falls foul of the principle of democracy as required by the principle of legality.

## Does EU Action Respect the Fundamental Human Rights that are Necessary to Create the Preconditions of a Healthy Democracy and Prevent Cases of Majoritarian Injustice?

Before the entry into force of the EU Charter of Fundamental Rights, the CJEU had already developed a robust judicial review of EU action as well as national

[82] ibid.

action in the scope of EU law on the basis of fundamental rights. Since the Lisbon Treaty, the EU Charter is the central instrument in this regard. In 'vertical' terms, much analysis has focused on the important question to what extent the EU Charter may apply to Member State action, and thus how to establish the 'scope of EU law'. Like in the more general discussion on competence creep of which this debate is to a large extent part, the main concern here seems to be a federal one: the EU has not been granted a full competence to enforce and foster human rights across its territory, and any wide interpretation of the scope of EU law for the purposes of the application of the Charter is thus contestable from a viewpoint of attributed powers. In 'horizontal' terms, ie, enforcement of fundamental/human rights against the EU institutions, the CJEU's rejection of the draft agreement of EU accession to the ECHR has been hotly debated in academia, as well as the limitation of the CJEU's judicial review powers in the area of the Common Foreign and Security Policy[83] and the Court's case law in the area of migration and asylum.[84] While all these discussions clearly hold relevance for the legality principle, and it would be worthwhile to examine them from that perspective, the present analysis focuses on a fundamental controversy in the CJEU's case law where the principle of legality could provide a particularly meaningful contribution: the Court's approach to the balancing of social and economic fundamental rights.

### *Constitutional Social and Economic Rights Under the Principle of Legality*

The EU Charter recognises a wide range of social rights, such as the prohibition of forced labour (Article 5); freedom of association (Article 12); the right to equal treatment (Article 21); the right to information and consultation within the undertaking (Article 27); the right of collective bargaining and action (Article 28); the right to protection in the event of unjustified dismissal (Article 30); the right to fair and just working conditions (Article 31); the prohibition of child labour and protection of young people at work (Article 32); and the entitlement to social security and assistance (Article 34). On the other hand, it provides in Article 16 of the EU Charter for '[t]he freedom to conduct a business in accordance with Union law and national laws and practices'. It should furthermore not be forgotten that the Court of Justice treats the internal market provisions on services, establishment, goods and persons as fundamental rights, and applies them directly on the basis of the Treaties. As such, the 'EU Constitution' consisting of the Treaties and the Charter contains various economic and social rights, in addition to civil and political liberties.

[83] Pech, above n 10.

[84] T Tridimas, 'Competence, Human Rights, and Asylum: What Price for Mutual Recognition?' in S Garben and I Govaere (eds), *The Division of Competences between the EU and the Member States Reflections on the Past, the Present and the Future* (Oxford, Hart Publishing, 2017).

As mentioned above, from the perspective of the principle of legality, the constitutionalisation of socio-economic rights is a sensitive question, as such issues are by definition politically highly salient and the bread and butter of the democratic process, and in particular should not become subject to 'judicial legislation'.[85] Social and economic rights should be enforced against democratic legislation (adopted at national or EU level) only to the degree that they create the socio-economic conditions for a well-functioning democracy (allowing social mobility, emancipation and corrections of societal power asymmetries), and their application should not displace democratic decision-making on substantive socio-economic issues. We can, on this basis, design some principles to guide us in the question of how the judiciary should interpret the minimum standards of the economic and social rights in question to be upheld through judicial review of national and European legislation. The following points are an attempt in this regard:

- Equal treatment and the protection (of children) against forced labour (Articles 5, 21 and 32 EU Charter) are so intimately connected to the primordeal democractic values of human dignity, equality and liberty, that they deserve the utmost protection by the judiciary. Their crucial function in preconditioning and conditioning a meaningful democracy warrant a proactive approach by the judiciary, giving these rights a wide reading, and a narrow ground for limitations both by constitutional and legislative norms. For the same reasons, a case can be made that these fundamental rights should also bind individuals.
- The right to unionise, strike and bargain collectively (Articles 12 and 28 EU Charter) have an important role in creating and maintaining the conditions for a robust democracy. They are 'procedural' rights rather than rights establishing certain socio-economic outcomes. As the UN Special Rapporteur put it: 'protecting the right to strike is not simply about States fulfilling their legal obligations. It is also about them creating democratic and equitable societies that are sustainable in the long run. The concentration of power in one sector – whether in the hands of government or business – inevitably leads to the erosion of democracy, and an increase in inequalities and marginalisation with all their attendant consequences. The right to strike is a check on this concentration of power'. This right should therefore, in principle, be forcefully protected by the judiciary, arguably against other individuals. Information and consultation rights (Article 27 EU Charter) could been seen as part of this procedural infrastructure, facilitating the work of unions, but do seem to deserve less active judicial protection than the right to strike and bargain collectively.
- The internal market rights (Articles 30, 45, 49, 56 and 63 TFEU) serve the purpose, within this constitutional democratic perspective, of compensating

[85] Fuller, *The Morality of* Law, above n 26.

for the failures of national democracies to take due account of the impact and interests of and in their decisions across borders, and should thus be interpreted as focused specifically on reviewing direct and clear indirect discrimination – not general economic freedom for companies. In the case of a clash between the internal market 'trans-national equality rights' on the one hand and fundamental social rights on the other, the judiciary needs to proceed with due deference to the democratic process, either at national or EU level, and should accord precedence to the rights that are more important from a democratic perspective, such as the right to strike. Furthermore, the purpose of 'correcting the externalities of national democracies' in their decision-making with effects on third parties warrants the internal market provisions to be invoked against the collective power wielded by the state but would not seem to extend to private parties.

- The freedom to conduct a business (Article 16 EU Charter) has a certain role in ensuring a robust democracy, to the extent that it helps to empower individuals – especially those who are disadvantaged – through economic activity, to prevent concentrations of (economic) power and equalise societal asymmetries. This would suggest a reading where the right is about fostering the possibility of individual entrepreneurship, in the sense of enabling citizens to set up an economic activity or join a profession, within a broader picture of creating more socio-economic progress and equality in society. This human right would not, upon such a constitutional democratic reading, provide a 'sword' for companies in the operation of their business against workers, citizens and general public interest standards.
- Workers' rights or interests such as to be protected against job insecurity and to have good working conditions (Articles 31 and 34 EU Charter) are primarily for the democratic process to flesh out, and it would seem that here there is scope for significant counter-balancing with other rights and interests. Strong protection would need to be provided against unjust dismissal (on the basis of discrimination or without reason), as the lack of such protection would undermine the enforcement of any other right in an employment context and would entrench an unacceptable power asymmetry between the employer and the worker which cannot be justified in a democratic society (Article 30 EU Charter). But the scope for (collective) dismissal for economic reasons is not something that should a priori be determined by the judiciary or the Constitution, and instead is a main battleground for the political process.

## *The EU's Approach to Constitutional Social and Economic Rights*

The only aspect of the above indications that clearly coincides with the EU's current approach is that of the principle of equality and non-discrimination. As is well known, the Court has taken a leading role in developing this principle and applying it to the EU and the Member States. At times, it has been accused of judicial activism in this regard, such as in relation to the *Mangold* judgment on age discrimination or in its case law on EU citizenship, but the above framework suggests that such criticism is misplaced. While it needs to be recognised that these rights are also politically highly salient, and therefore raise controversy when asserted by the judiciary, we would argue that it is precisely here that judicial review shows its value and importance in a constitutional democracy: to prevent or correct unjust majoritarian outcomes and in turn to ensure the necessary preconditions for a well-functioning inclusive democracy.

On the other hand, as regards the right to unionise, strike and bargain collectively, many will recall the *Viking* and *Laval* sagas. *Laval* concerned a Latvian construction firm that won a government contract to renovate a school in Sweden, where it posted some of its Latvian workers. The Swedish construction union started negotiations with Laval's Swedish subsidiary to extend the sectoral collective agreement to the posted workers and to negotiate their wages. Laval refused to agree to some of the conditions in the agreement, and so the negotiations failed, and the union called a blockade of Laval's building sites, assisted by the electricians' union, leading to the subsidiary's bankruptcy. The CJEU held that the Posted Workers Directive did not authorise the imposition on a foreign services provider the obligation to conduct on-site negotiations with the trade unions to determine the rates of pay nor trade unions to force a foreign services provider to accept better conditions than the bare minimum standard allowed by the Directive and regulated by the State, and it considered that the freedom to provide services (now Article 56 TFEU) applied to the actions of the workers.[86] The Court of Justice cited the Charter of Fundamental Rights, at that time not yet legally binding, as well as the various international and EU documents that recognise a right to take collective action, concluding that the right to strike is a general principle of Community law. The Court, however, went on to state that the union's attempt to make Laval accept working conditions (other than pay) of a standard over and above the minimum set out in the Posted Workers Directive could not be justified with regard to the objective of protection of workers, since the Directive already served this purpose sufficiently. As regards the negotiations on pay, the Court reasoned that if a Member State wanted to protect workers, all it had to do was impose a minimum rate of pay through legislation or universal collective agreement; this objective could not be a justification for obliging employers to enter into negotiations on pay in a context

> characterised by a lack of provisions, of any kind, which are sufficiently precise and accessible that they do not render it impossible or excessively difficult in practice for such an undertaking to determine the obligations with which it is required to comply as regards minimum pay.

The strike action was thus unlawful, exposing the trade union to punitive damages.

[86] See A Hinarejos, 'Laval and Viking: The Right to Collective Action versus EU Fundamental Freedoms' (2008) 8 *Human Rights Law Review* 714.

In *Viking*, the case concerned the ferry ship Rosella, that sailed between Finland and Estonia under the Finnish flag.[87] Viking owned the Rosella, which was operating at a loss. This was ostensibly due to the fact that Viking had to pay Finnish wages while competing Estonian ferries had lower wage costs. Viking wanted to re-flag the ferry to Estonia in order to be able to pay lower wages. The Finnish Seamen's Union of which the Rosella's crew were members joined forces with the International Transport Workers' Federation, which in an action against flags of convenience issued a circular ordering all its affiliates not to negotiate with Viking, thus preventing the company to acquire an Estonian crew. In its ruling, the CJEU confirmed its position in *Laval* that the internal market provisions (this time the freedom of establishment) could be invoked directly against a private party, such as a trade union. While contrary to *Laval* it left it for the national court to decide whether the objectives pursued by the unions by means of the collective action 'concerned the protection of workers', it also indicated that such action could no longer be considered to fall within the objective of protecting workers if it could be shown that the jobs or conditions of employment at issue were not under serious threat (such as when the employer were to give a binding undertaking that the current crew would keep their jobs and terms of employment). Furthermore, the national court would have to check whether the union had other means at its disposal which were less restrictive of freedom of establishment, and whether the union had exhausted those means beforehand. As regards the International Transport Workers' Federation's policy against flags of convenience, the Court held it could not be justified, since the restriction on freedom of establishment was blanket, in that it would apply even if the ferry were to be re-flagged in a Member State that offered better employment standards to its workers.

Libraries have been filled with critical commentary on both judgments.[88] Pointing at the horizontal application of the internal market provisions to organised labour, the wide definition of restrictions to economic freedom, and the priority accorded to this freedom over the right to take collective action and to strike, many commentators agree that in these judgments the Court gave preference to the market freedoms at the cost of social objectives. This is often considered problematic in terms of outcomes: the judgments are criticised because they are anti-social, arguably contrary to international minimum social norms. In other work, I have argued that the main problem with these judgments and underlying

[87] For discussion, see Hinarejos, ibid.

[88] C Joerges and F Rodl, 'Informal Politics, Formalised Law and the "Social Deficit" of European Integration: Reflections after the Judgments of the ECJ in Viking and Laval' (2009) 15 *European Law Journal* 18; O de Schutter, 'Transborder Provision of Services and "Social dumping": Rights-Based Mutual Trust in the Establishment of the Internal Market' in I Lianos and O Odudud (eds), *Regulating Trade in Services in the EU and the WTO: Trust Distrust and Economic Integration* (Cambridge, Cambridge University Press, 2011); A Bücker and W Warnek, *Reconciling Fundamental Social Rights and Economic freedoms after Viking, Laval and Rüffert* (Baden-Baden, Nomos, 2011); A Davies, 'One Step Forward, Two Steps Back? The Viking and Laval Cases in the ECJ' (2008) 37 *Industrial Law Journal* 126.

doctrines is that they displace the national and European legislative process and instead see the European judiciary making very sensitive socio-economic decisions.[89] While this remains true, the above constitutional democratic analytical framework allows a more refined critique of *Viking* and *Laval*. It suggests that the CJEU attached too much weight to the internal market provisions, applying them to private parties, and too little weight to the right to strike, which should have received a more extensive reading and more forceful protection than internal market rights, thereby reaching a perverse outcome that interprets socio-economic fundamental rights to entrench the very power asymmetry (between workers and companies) that socio-economic fundamental rights are supposed to correct. In other words, if the CJEU was going to condition and correct the (national) democratic process at all in this context, it should have done it the other way around: obliging Member States to respect the right to strike (thus compulsorily allowing such strike action) within the scope of the internal market provisions. Alternatively, it could have refrained from intervening at all, holding that the internal market provisions cannot be relied on against individuals (and neither the state for not enforcing them against the right to strike against individuals), which would have both respected the democratic process and the right to strike.

Similarly problematic are the CJEU's judgments in *Alemo-Herron*[90] and *AGET*.[91] In *Alemo-Herron*, the CJEU was asked to interpret Article 3 of Directive 2001/23/EC on the approximation of the laws of the Member States relating to the safeguarding of employees' rights in the event of transfers of undertakings, which provides that the transferor's rights and obligations arising from an employment relationship existing on the date of a transfer shall be transferred to the transferee. The Directive is a minimum harmonisation in the sense that it does not affect the right of Member States to apply or introduce laws, regulations or administrative provisions which are more favourable to employees or to promote or permit collective agreements or agreements between social partners more favourable to employees (Article 8). The case concerned the question whether dynamic clauses referring to collective agreements negotiated and agreed after the date of transfer are enforceable against the transferee. The Court acknowledged 'that the clauses referring to collective agreements negotiated and agreed after the date of transfer of the undertaking concerned, providing dynamic contractual rights, are more favourable to employees'.[92] However, the Court considered that the Directive

> does not aim solely to safeguard the interests of employees in the event of transfer of an undertaking, but seeks to ensure a fair balance between the interests of those employees, on the one hand, and those of the transferee, on the other.[93]

[89] S Garben, 'The Constitutional (Im)balance between "the Market" and "the Social" in the European Union' (2017) 13 *European Constitutional Law Review* 23.

[90] Case C-426/11 *Mark Alemo-Herron and Others v Parkwood Leisure Ltd* EU:C:2013:521.

[91] Case C-201/15 *Anonymi Geniki Etairia Tsimenton Iraklis (AGET Iraklis) v Ypourgos Ergasias, Koinonikis Asfalisis kai Koinonikis Allilengyis* EU:C:2016:972.

[92] Para 24.

[93] Para 25.

It considered that these dynamic clauses were not such a fair balance as they 'limit considerably the room for manoeuvre necessary for a private transferee to make such adjustments and changes' after the transfer. It then turned to Article 16 EU Charter, to state that it 'covers, inter alia, freedom of contract, as is apparent from the explanations provided as guidance to the interpretation of the Charter' and that in the context of company transfers,

> it is apparent that, by reason of the freedom to conduct a business, the transferee must be able to assert its interests effectively in a contractual process to which it is party and to negotiate the aspects determining changes in the working conditions of its employees with a view to its future economic activity.[94]

The dynamic clauses precluded this as 'the transferee's contractual freedom is seriously reduced to the point that such a limitation is liable to adversely affect the very essence of its freedom to conduct a business'.[95]

In the *AGET* judgment[96] the CJEU held that Greek protections entailing that prior authorisation had to be obtained from a Greek authority before executing collective redundancies were contrary to the freedom of establishment laid down in Article 49 TFEU, interpreted in light of Article 16 of the Charter.[97] After having established a prima facie restriction, the Court considered the possibility of the objective justification of the national rules on grounds of worker protection and the protection of employment – which was in principle possible '[s]ince the European Union … has not only an economic but also a social purpose'.[98] The CJEU flagged up that it considered there to be an interference with Article 16 of the Charter:

> [T]he establishment of a regime imposing a framework for collective redundancies such as the regime at issue in the main proceedings constitutes an interference in the exercise of the freedom to conduct a business and, in particular, the freedom of contract which undertakings in principle have, inter alia in respect of the workers which they employ, since it is not in dispute that under that regime the national authority's opposition to certain plans for collective redundancies may result in the employer being prevented from putting those plans into effect.[99]

However, the Court did recognise that Article 16 could be limited, and it considered that 'the freedom to conduct a business is not absolute, but must be viewed in relation to its social function', and it even noted that the wording of Article 16 of the Charter 'differs from the wording of the other fundamental freedoms enshrined in Title II thereof, yet is similar to that of certain provisions of Title IV of the Charter' and concluded that 'the freedom to conduct a business may be

[94] Paras 31 and 32.
[95] Para 35.
[96] *AGET Iraklis*, above n 91.
[97] ibid.
[98] Para 77.
[99] Para 69.

subject to a broad range of interventions on the part of public authorities that may limit the exercise of economic activity in the public interest'.[100] It distinguished the underlying situation from *Alemo-Herron*: in the former case the essence of contractual freedom had been undermined according to the Court, while in this case collective redundancies were not made entirely impossible, thus not affecting the essence of the right. The Court then considered that Member States needed, in this sensitive area, to reconcile and to strike a fair balance between the interests connected with the protection of workers and of employment, in particular protection against unjustified dismissal and against the consequences of collective dismissals for workers, and those relating to freedom of establishment and the freedom of economic operators to conduct a business enshrined in Articles 49 TFEU and Article 16 of the Charter.[101] The Court considered that

> the establishment of … a framework governing the circumstances in which collective redundancies may be effected can therefore be a valid way of satisfying the requirements stemming from the principle of proportionality and is, therefore, capable of complying, from that perspective, with Article 49 TFEU and Article 16 of the Charter.[102]

However, it held that the details of the Greek arrangement infringed proportionality, and thus both Article 49 TFEU and Article 16 TFEU. The national authority charged with considering the planned collective redundancy had too much discretion to interpret the 'situation of the undertaking' and the 'conditions in the labour market' as reasons to oppose the redundancy.

That outcome could arguably be considered a balanced compromise between social and economic rights – but the legal basis for the application of these economic rights to this situation in the first place is contestable from the perspective of the legality principle. The rules applied without discrimination and do not in any way place an additional burden on foreign companies or disadvantage 'new' operators over established ones.[103] It is thus highly contestable that the freedom of establishment as laid down in Article 49 TFEU should apply. The Court is expanding its already over-expansive 'market-access' approach into a plain and simple 'market'-test, which goes far beyond the necessary scope of judicial protection for internal market rights, as explained above. Secondly, as regards Article 16 EU Charter, the Court may be using 'softer' language, but it is nevertheless applying a hard-core interpretation of a right that is traditionally weak. The Court considers that the freedom to conduct a business can only be limited by reference to Article 52(1) of the Charter:

> [A]any limitation on the exercise of the rights and freedoms recognised by this Charter must be provided for by law and respect the essence of those rights and freedoms.

[100] Paras 85 and 86. The Court referred to its judgment of 22 January 2013: C-283/11 *Sky Österreich* EU:C:2013:28, para 46.
[101] Para 90.
[102] Para 94.
[103] Case C-442/02 *CaixaBank France v Ministère de l'Économie, des Finances et de l'Industrie* EU:C:2004:586.

> Subject to the principle of proportionality, limitations may be made only if they are necessary and genuinely meet objectives of general interest recognised by the Union or the need to protect the rights and freedoms of others.

However, the very text of Article 16 EU Charter itself states that this freedom is conditional on compliance with Union law and national laws and practices: it is thus not a right that can be limited by Union law and national laws and practices but it is only recognised as a freedom to the extent that it is in accordance with Union law and national laws and practices. It is thus highly questionable whether it is an actionable right in the first place, and secondly it suggests a much wider scope for public interest mitigation than under the strict conditions of Article 51(1) of the Charter. As we have considered above, its main constitutional democratic value is to allow (disempowered) individuals to start a business or join a profession, in the name of social mobility and emancipation. That is clearly not how this right is conceptualised by the CJEU. While the social interest at stake in *Alemo-Herron* and *AGET* should be open to significant (economic) counter-balancing, it is the political process that should have decided on the balance in this case, because the counter-interest of 'conducting a business' should equally be a weaker right open to significant (social) counter-balancing. The EU legislator had, in the EU legislation at stake, not decided on that balance as regards the cases at hand – they fell outside the scope of the Directives. Thus, it should have been left to the national democratic process: the UK and Greek rules in question should have been upheld until the European legislator had acted to establish a different balance at EU level on these specific questions. Instead, the EU judiciary gave a too forceful interpretation to the freedom to conduct a business, thereby constitutionalising a certain view on the right socio-economic balance that was not necessary to establish for a democratic society.

## Concluding Reflections

A robust, functioning democracy is premised on a number of constitutional guarantees and democracy manifests itself in (and requires) many dimensions, and not just crude in-the-moment direct majoritarianism. Upon such a view, genuine democracy is not constrained by constitutionalism but instead made possible by it. While there may not be a single perfect constitutional democracy, or society, presently existing across the globe, this does not mean that there is no ideal model to strive for – and, more practically, to provide a yardstick against which current failings can be explained to orient possible improvements. This ideal model transcends the false juxtaposition of constitutionalism and democracy that seems both theoretically impoverished and practically counterproductive. We instead need to invest in a theory of constitutional democracy in which the dialectic relationship between its two underpinning principles is elaborated more constructively.

This chapter has proposed the principle of legality as the main analytical tool in this regard: interpreted in light of national constitutional law this principle seems to be the very expression of constitutional democracy, in that it requires simultaneously (i) the lawfulness of the exercise of authority (based on an authorising norm and its relevant procedures, and respecting fundamental rights); and (ii) that Parliament sources this authority. Developing this approach into a legitimacy framework for the exercise of authority, the chapter has argued that the principles of democracy and constitutionalism do not only need to be balanced against each other but that they dynamically inform each other's substantive content. On this view, constitutionalism's primary purpose is to guarantee thick democracy: to create the necessary preconditions for it, to correct any 'democratic failures' in the process, and to ensure that outcomes do not undermine robust democracy in the longer term. Democracy as interpreted in light of constitutionalism, on this ideal view, means a transparent, checked-and-balanced system of decision-making that ensures that those affected by decisions take part in making those decisions through robust representation and that the institutions through which this decision-making is operated cannot abuse their powers. Ultimately, the constitutional democratic order as a whole should respect and serve the primordial values of dignity, equality and liberty.

This approach can at least partially transcend the well-known juxtaposition of democratic decision-making on the one hand with the judicial review thereof on the basis of constitutional norms on the other: democracy through and on the basis of parliamentary decision-making itself is a constitutional norm that the judiciary should uphold. Moreover, the fundamental rights that constitutionalism needs to protect are those that contribute to creating the preconditions of a healthy democracy, and to the extent that they serve to prevent cases of majoritarian injustice. Of course, constitutionalism requires that democratic decision-making respects certain procedural and substantive norms, and thus may entail overturning an act of parliament on that basis. But the limits of such judicial intervention lie in that the democracy principle should equally be respected, thus precluding judgments that amount to 'judicial legislation'. Where precisely the balance between the principle of democracy and the principle of constitutionalism should be struck in individual cases will always be open to debate. Constitutional democracy does not necessarily provide conclusive answers in itself, but provides the terms of the arguments to be made in reasonable disagreement where it occurs, which should serve to accommodate such disagreement in a constructive way. As Cesare Pinelli also notes in chapter two, the flexibility of constitutional democracy to accommodate legitimate disagreement through, and resulting in, a continuous adjustment of the dialectic principles of democracy and constitutionalism is how this form of government 'absorbed de-structuring tensions'. Constitutional democracy is thus not a static model but a dynamic process.

The tentative application of this theoretical framework to the European Union in the present chapter has confirmed a number of well-known democratic and constitutional problems and, more importantly, it has allowed a more refined and integrated analysis thereof, aiming to capture their interconnectedness in a holistic, comprehensive understanding. This has not been a purely academic exercise to create 'a theory of everything', as precise and concrete reforms can be distilled from the assessment. Most fundamentally, the CJEU could adopt, implicitly or explicitly, the principle of legality or, generally, a theory of constitutional democracy, as an overarching normative system to situate itself in relation to other European and national institutions and to guide its case law. First, the analysis conducted in this chapter has tentatively revealed that this framework requires a more active judicial role by the CJEU in relation to the choice of legal basis, in cases where there is an option to choose between procedures that differ in terms of parliamentary involvement. The CJEU should develop a doctrine that (at least) in the case of salient decisions, the more democratic legal basis needs to be used. Secondly, in its balancing of fundamental rights, especially where there is a clash between economic and social rights, the CJEU should consider the relative importance of the fundamental right in question for the well functioning of a robust democracy or for the correction of grave majoritarian injustice. The further removed from these two functions that a fundamental right is in the particular case before the Court, the more hesitant it should be to enforce that right against the democratic exercise of authority that is challenged or against a conflicting fundamental right. Finally, considering the necessarily high salience of exercise of punitive authority, expressed in the specific requirement of the legality principle of *nulla poene sine lege*, the CJEU should proceed with special care in the area of criminal law, reconsidering its application of the principle of *effet utile* of EU law to the EU's competence in this area, and on the other hand adopting a more interventionist stance as regards undemocratic EU decision-making in this area. These wide-ranging implications show the potential of operationalising constitutional democracy in the way proposed, and these terms of argument can be used in the settlement, or at least accommodation of, many other areas of controversy in the EU legal and political order. As such, more than presenting firm conclusions, this chapter has tried to develop the initial elements of a future research agenda.

# INDEX

www.ingramcontent.com/pod-product-compliance
Ingram Content Group UK Ltd.
Pitfield, Milton Keynes, MK11 3LW, UK
UKHW020229290926
15470UKWH00001B/426